VISUAL
BASIC® 5
BIBLE

VISUAL BASIC® 5 BIBLE

by Douglas Hergert

IDG
BOOKS
WORLDWIDE

IDG Books Worldwide, Inc.
An International Data Group Company

Foster City, CA ◆ Chicago, IL ◆ Indianapolis, IN ◆ Southlake, TX

Visual Basic® 5 Bible

Published by
IDG Books Worldwide, Inc.
An International Data Group Company
919 E. Hillsdale Blvd.
Suite 400
Foster City, CA 94404
http://www.idgbooks.com (IDG Books Worldwide Web site)

Library of Congress Catalog Card No.: 97-70658

ISBN: 0-7645-8020-5

Printed in the United States of America

10 9 8 7 6 5 4 3 2

1E/RS/QW/ZX/IN

Distributed in the United States by IDG Books Worldwide, Inc.

Distributed by Macmillan Canada for Canada; by Transworld Publishers Limited in the United Kingdom; by IDG Norge Books for Norway; by IDG Sweden Books for Sweden; by Woodslane Pty. Ltd. for Australia; by Woodslane Enterprises Ltd. for New Zealand; by Longman Singapore Publishers Ltd. for Singapore, Malaysia, Thailand, and Indonesia; by Simron Pty. Ltd. for South Africa; by Toppan Company Ltd. for Japan; by Distribuidora Cuspide for Argentina; by Livraria Cultura for Brazil; by Ediciencia S.A. for Ecuador; by Addison-Wesley Publishing Company for Korea; by Ediciones ZETA S.C.R. Ltda. for Peru; by WS Computer Publishing Corporation, Inc., for the Philippines; by Unalis Corporation for Taiwan; by Contemporanea de Ediciones for Venezuela; by Computer Book & Magazine Store for Puerto Rico; by Express Computer Distributors for the Caribbean and West Indies. Authorized Sales Agent: Anthony Rudkin Associates for the Middle East and North Africa.

For general information on IDG Books Worldwide's books in the U.S., please call our Consumer Customer Service department at 800-762-2974. For reseller information, including discounts and premium sales, please call our Reseller Customer Service department at 800-434-3422.

For information on where to purchase IDG Books Worldwide's books outside the U.S., please contact our International Sales department at 415-655-3200 or fax 415-655-3295.

For information on foreign language translations, please contact our Foreign & Subsidiary Rights department at 415-655-3021 or fax 415-655-3281.

For sales inquiries and special prices for bulk quantities, please contact our Sales department at 415-655-3200 or write to the address above.

For information on using IDG Books Worldwide's books in the classroom or for ordering examination copies, please contact our Educational Sales department at 800-434-2086 or fax 817-251-8174.

For press review copies, author interviews, or other publicity information, please contact our Public Relations department at 415-655-3000 or fax 415-655-3299.

For authorization to photocopy items for corporate, personal, or educational use, please contact Copyright Clearance Center, 222 Rosewood Drive, Danvers, MA 01923, or fax 508-750-4470.

 is a trademark under exclusive
license to IDG Books Worldwide, Inc.,
from International Data Group, Inc.

ABOUT IDG BOOKS WORLDWIDE

Welcome to the world of IDG Books Worldwide.

IDG Books Worldwide, Inc., is a subsidiary of International Data Group, the world's largest publisher of computer-related information and the leading global provider of information services on information technology. IDG was founded more than 25 years ago and now employs more than 8,500 people worldwide. IDG publishes more than 275 computer publications in over 75 countries (see listing below). More than 60 million people read one or more IDG publications each month.

Launched in 1990, IDG Books Worldwide is today the #1 publisher of best-selling computer books in the United States. We are proud to have received eight awards from the Computer Press Association in recognition of editorial excellence and three from *Computer Currents'* First Annual Readers' Choice Awards. Our best-selling *...For Dummies®* series has more than 30 million copies in print with translations in 30 languages. IDG Books Worldwide, through a joint venture with IDG's Hi-Tech Beijing, became the first U.S. publisher to publish a computer book in the People's Republic of China. In record time, IDG Books Worldwide has become the first choice for millions of readers around the world who want to learn how to better manage their businesses.

Our mission is simple: Every one of our books is designed to bring extra value and skill-building instructions to the reader. Our books are written by experts who understand and care about our readers. The knowledge base of our editorial staff comes from years of experience in publishing, education, and journalism — experience we use to produce books for the '90s. In short, we care about books, so we attract the best people. We devote special attention to details such as audience, interior design, use of icons, and illustrations. And because we use an efficient process of authoring, editing, and desktop publishing our books electronically, we can spend more time ensuring superior content and spend less time on the technicalities of making books.

You can count on our commitment to deliver high-quality books at competitive prices on topics you want to read about. At IDG Books Worldwide, we continue in the IDG tradition of delivering quality for more than 25 years. You'll find no better book on a subject than one from IDG Books Worldwide.

IDG BOOKS WORLDWIDE

John Kilcullen
CEO
IDG Books Worldwide, Inc.

Steven Berkowitz
President and Publisher
IDG Books Worldwide, Inc.

Eighth Annual Computer Press Awards ≥1992

WINNER
Ninth Annual Computer Press Awards ≥1993

WINNER
Tenth Annual Computer Press Awards ≥1994

WINNER
Eleventh Annual Computer Press Awards ≥1995

IDG Books Worldwide, Inc., is a subsidiary of International Data Group, the world's largest publisher of computer-related information and the leading global provider of information services on information technology. International Data Group publishes over 275 computer publications in over 75 countries. Sixty million people read one or more International Data Group publications each month. International Data Group's publications include: **ARGENTINA:** Buyer's Guide, Computerworld Argentina, PC World Argentina; **AUSTRALIA:** Australian Macworld, Australian PC World, Australian Reseller News, Computerworld, IT Casebook, Network World, Publish, Webmaster; **AUSTRIA:** Computerwelt Osterreich, Networks Austria, PC Tip Austria; **BANGLADESH:** PC World Bangladesh; **BELARUS:** PC World Belarus; **BELGIUM:** Data News; **BRAZIL:** Annuario de Informática, Computerworld, Connections, Macworld, PC Player, PC World, Publish, Reseller News, Supergamepower; **BULGARIA:** Computerworld Bulgaria, Network World Bulgaria, PC & MacWorld Bulgaria; **CANADA:** CIO Canada, Client/Server World, ComputerWorld Canada, InfoWorld Canada, NetworkWorld Canada, WebWorld; **CHILE:** Computerworld Chile, PC World Chile; **COLOMBIA:** Computerworld Colombia, PC World Colombia; **COSTA RICA:** PC World Centro America; **THE CZECH AND SLOVAK REPUBLICS:** Computerworld Czechoslovakia, Macworld Czech Republic, PC World Czechoslovakia; **DENMARK:** Communications World Danmark, Computerworld Danmark, Macworld Danmark, PC World Danmark, Techworld Denmark; **DOMINICAN REPUBLIC:** PC World Republica Dominicana; **ECUADOR:** PC World Ecuador; **EGYPT:** Computerworld Middle East, PC World Middle East; **EL SALVADOR:** PC World Centro America; **FINLAND:** MikroPC, Tietoverkko, Tietoviikko; **FRANCE:** Distributique, Hebdo, Info PC, Le Monde Informatique, Macworld, Reseaux & Telecoms, WebMaster France; **GERMANY:** Computer Partner, Computerwoche, Computerwoche Extra, Computerwoche FOCUS, Global Online, Macwelt, PC Welt; **GREECE:** Amiga Computing, GamePro Greece, Multimedia World; **GUATEMALA:** PC World Centro America; **HONDURAS:** PC World Centro America. **HONG KONG:** Computerworld Hong Kong, PC World Hong Kong, Publish in Asia; **HUNGARY:** ABCD CD-ROM, Computerworld Szamitastechnika, Internetto online Magazine, PC World Hungary, PC-X Magazin Hungary; **ICELAND:** Tolvuheimur PC World Island; **INDIA:** Information Communications World, Information Systems Computerworld, PC World India, Publish in Asia; **INDONESIA:** InfoKomputer PC World, Komputek Computerworld, Publish in Asia; **IRELAND:** ComputerScope, PC Live!; **ISRAEL:** Macworld Israel, People & Computers/Computerworld; **ITALY:** Computerworld Italia, Macworld Italia, Networking Italia, PC World Italia; **JAPAN:** DTP World, Macworld Japan, Nikkei Personal Computing, OS/2 World Japan, SunWorld Japan, Windows NT World, Windows World Japan; **KENYA:** PC World East African; **KOREA:** Hi-Tech Information, Macworld Korea, PC World Korea; **MACEDONIA:** PC World Macedonia; **MALAYSIA:** Computerworld Malaysia, PC World Malaysia, Publish in Asia; **MALTA:** PC World Malta; **MEXICO:** Computerworld Mexico, PC World Mexico; **MYANMAR:** PC World Myanmar; **NETHERLANDS:** Computer! Totaal, LAN Internetworking Magazine, LAN World Buyers Guide, Macworld Netherlands, Net, WebWereld; **NEW ZEALAND:** Absolute Beginners Guide and Plain & Simple Series, Computer Buyer, Computer Industry Directory, Computerworld New Zealand, MTB, Network World, PC World New Zealand; **NICARAGUA:** PC World Centro America; **NORWAY:** Computerworld Norge, CW Rapport, Datamagasinet, Financial Rapport, Kursguide Norge, Macworld Norge, Multimediaworld Norge, PC World Ekspress Norge, PC World Nettverk, PC World Norge, PC World ProduktGuide Norge; **PAKISTAN:** Computerworld Pakistan; **PANAMA:** PC World Panama; **PEOPLE'S REPUBLIC OF CHINA:** China Computer Users, China Computerworld, China InfoWorld, China Telecom World Weekly, Computer & Communication, Electronic Design China, Electronics Today, Electronics Weekly, Game Software, PC World China, Popular Computer Week, Software Weekly, Software World, Telecom World; **PERU:** Computerworld Peru, PC World Profesional Peru, PC World SoHo Peru; **PHILIPPINES:** Click!, Computerworld Philippines, PC World Philippines, Publish in Asia; **POLAND:** Computerworld Poland, Computerworld Special Report Poland, Cyber, Macworld Poland, Networld Poland, PC World Komputer; **PORTUGAL:** Cerebro/PC World, Computerworld/Correio Informático, Dealer World Portugal, Mac*In/PC*In Portugal, Multimedia World; **PUERTO RICO:** PC World Puerto Rico; **ROMANIA:** Computerworld Romania, PC World Romania, Telecom Romania; **RUSSIA:** Computerworld Russia, Mir PK, Publish, Seti; **SINGAPORE:** Computerworld Singapore, PC World Singapore, Publish in Asia; **SLOVENIA:** Monitor; **SOUTH AFRICA:** Computing SA, Network World SA, Software World SA; **SPAIN:** Communicaciones World España, Computerworld España, Computerworld España, Dealer World España, Macworld España, PC World España; **SRI LANKA:** Infolink PC World; **SWEDEN:** CAP&Design, Computer Sweden, Corporate Computing Sweden, Internetworld Sweden, it.branschen, Macworld Sweden, MaxiData Sweden, MikroDatorn, Nätverk & Kommunikation, PC World Sweden, PCaktiv, Windows World Sweden; **SWITZERLAND:** Computerworld Schweiz, Macworld Schweiz, PCtip; **TAIWAN:** Computerworld Taiwan, Macworld Taiwan, NEW ViSiON/Publish, PC World Taiwan, Windows World Taiwan; **THAILAND:** Publish in Asia, Thai Computerworld; **TURKEY:** Computerworld Turkiye, Macworld Turkiye, Network World Turkiye, PC World Turkiye; **UKRAINE:** Computerworld Kiev, Multimedia World Ukraine, PC World Ukraine; **UNITED KINGDOM:** Acorn User UK, Amiga Action UK, Amiga Computing UK, Apple Talk UK, Computing, Macworld, Parents and Computers UK, PC Advisor, PC Home, PSX Pro, The WEB; **UNITED STATES:** Cable in the Classroom, CIO Magazine, Computerworld, DOS World, Federal Computer Week, GamePro Magazine, InfoWorld, I-Way, Macworld, Network World, PC Games, PC World, Publish, Video Event, THE WEB Magazine, and WebMaster; online webzines: JavaWorld, NetscapeWorld, and SunWorld Online; **URUGUAY:** InfoWorld Uruguay; **VENEZUELA:** Computerworld Venezuela, PC World Venezuela; and **VIETNAM:** PC World Vietnam. 3/24/97

Credits

Acquisitions Editor
John Osborn

Development Editors
John Pont
Barbra Guerra

Technical Editor
Don Hergert

Copy Editor
Carolyn Welch

Project Coordinator
Debbie Stailey

Graphics Specialists
Angela F. Hunckler
Brent Savage

Production Page Layout
Cameron Booker
Linda M. Boyer
Brett Black
Dominique DeFelice
Todd Klemme
Drew R. Moore
Mark Owens
Kate Snell
Michael Sullivan

Proofreaders
Joel K. Draper
Rachel Garvey
Nancy Price
Dwight Ramsey
Robert Springer

Indexer
Liz Cunningham

About the Author

Douglas Hergert began his current career in 1980 as an editor for a west coast computer book publisher. After helping to develop several works by other authors, he began producing his own books, initially as a staff writer. His earliest books were about Pascal and BASIC programming. When he eventually left his publishing job, he continued writing computer books from his home office. In the years since, he's published more than 40 titles with seven of the industry's major publishers. He's written extensively about spreadsheets, database management, and programming languages. He produced one of the first books on Visual Basic, when the product first came out in 1991. Several of his books have become top sellers in their categories.

For Andrew and Audrey

Preface

In the world of personal computers, anyone can become a programmer. All it takes is the imagination to devise useful new applications and the initiative to master the necessary programming tools. Programmers appear in every profession, including education, research, medicine, business, commerce, sales, accounting, consulting, law, politics, and all branches of science. Often a programmer is first an expert in a particular field, and second an occasional designer of applications to support this expertise.

You can think of this phenomenon as *personal programming*. Wherever you work, whatever you do, you can expand your computer's usefulness by writing applications to use in your own job. To count yourself as a working programmer, you combine your professional expertise with the inspiration and energy to develop the applications you need.

Personal programming is what Visual Basic is about. Using its versatile tools, you quickly translate an abstract idea into a program design you can actually see on the screen. Visual Basic encourages you to experiment, revise, correct, reconsider, and rework your design until the new project meets your requirements. It inspires your imagination and creativity.

The Visual Basic Approach

Visual Basic prescribes a three-step approach for creating programs:

1. Design the appearance of your application. This step takes place interactively on the screen as you select and arrange controls in the forms of your project.

2. Assign property settings to the objects of your program. Properties help you refine the appearance and behavior of your program.

3. Write the code to direct specific tasks at runtime. In Visual Basic's event-driven programming model, code is designed to respond to the activities you expect to occur during a performance. For example, you might write event procedures to respond to a mouse click, a keyboard entry, or a menu selection.

With its interactive approach to creating forms and its lucid, structured programming language, Visual Basic helps you produce satisfying results at each step along the way.

The Audience for This Book

The *Visual Basic 5 Bible* is for programmers everywhere — from the inexperienced to the experienced — who need to master the practical application of this popular programming environment. For users already familiar with the previous version of Visual Basic, the *Visual Basic 5 Bible* provides hands-on experience with the new features.

The Structure of This Book

This book is divided into three parts. Here's a sample of what you will find in each part.

Part I: Developing Programs in Visual Basic

Visual Basic 5 is a structured programming language and a complete application development environment, all in one package. To work with the elements of the language, you need to become familiar with Visual Basic's development tools. Part I introduces you to these features.

Chapter 1 explains tools — such as the Project Explorer, the Toolbox, the Properties window, and the Form Layout window. Chapters 2, 3, and 4 introduce you to the three steps of Visual Basic development and give you the opportunity to work through the process and practice the steps. Chapter 4 introduces Visual Basic's event-driven programming model, and shows you how to begin developing event procedures in the code editor. The final steps of your work involve testing, fine-tuning, and debugging your program, and Chapter 5 introduces the tools that Visual Basic provides to help you debug your code. Chapter 6 shows you how to create an executable program file from your finished project and how to prepare it for distribution to other users.

Part II: Programming Essentials

The first six chapters of Part II introduce Visual Basic's programming tools and techniques. Each chapter represents a sample application.

Chapter 7 explains the difference between event procedures and general procedures. In Chapter 8, design issues for a project that contains multiple forms are discussed, and Chapter 9 presents aspects of Visual Basic as a structured programming language. How to use Visual Basic's date file commands is the focus of Chapter 10, and the intricate details of input and output procedures are illustrated in Chapter 11. Finally, Chapter 12 wraps up the part by focusing on the standard controls and custom components (now known as ActiveX).

Part III: More Programming Techniques

After you've mastered the essentials of Visual Basic programming and project design, Part III takes you beyond the basics.

In Chapter 13 you review the significance of classes and objects while illustrating class models, property procedures, and collections. Chapter 14 discusses the use of multiple-document interface (MDI) forms within an application. The use of ActiveX components in a Visual Basic project is covered in Chapter 15, and Chapter 16 shows you how to use the data control and bound controls to create a connection between a Visual Basic form and an external database. Chapter 17 guides you through the initial steps of developing, testing, and compiling ActiveX components in Visual Basic, and Chapter 18 follows up by introducing the ActiveX Document project, a new tool designed to simplify programming tasks in an online environment.

Acknowledgments

Many people worked hard to produce this book. John Osborn worked tenaciously to get the project started. John Pont was the book's first reader and made important suggestions throughout; he also guided the project skillfully through the steps of the publication process. Don Hergert checked the technical content of the manuscript and spoke up whenever his advice was germane. At IDG Books, Andy Cummings and Barb Guerra directed the editorial work and Debbie Stailey managed production.

For their work on the first version of this book, *Foundations of Visual Basic 4,* the following people deserve a repeated note of thanks: Chris Williams, Amy Pedersen, Trudy Neuhaus, Denise Peters, Anne Marie Walker, Beth Roberts, Clare Mansfield, Susan Pink, and Don Hergert.

As always, Claudette Moore offered guidance, advice, and encouragement throughout the project.

My sincere thanks to all.

DH

Contents at a Glance

Table of Contents

Developing Programs in Visual Basic

Visual Basic 5 is a structured programming language and a complete application development environment, all in one package. Before you begin working with the elements of the language, you need to become familiar with the important development tools that the product supplies. Part I gives you a careful first look at these features.

The Project Explorer, the Toolbox, the Properties window, the Form Layout window, the form and code windows, the toolbars and menu commands — all of these appear on the screen while you're designing a new project. Chapter 1 explains what these tools are for and helps you explore their use in several hands-on exercises. You'll begin to see how you can combine forms, controls, and code to build a working project. You'll also learn how to find help when you need it. Finally, this chapter presents a simple program called the Travel Guide application. You'll load the project from disc, run it, and then briefly investigate its components.

In the three steps of Visual Basic development, you arrange the controls and forms of your project, set properties of selected objects, and write the code that makes your program work. Chapters 2, 3, and 4 introduce you to these steps in detail and guide you through several hands-on exercises to practice the steps. As you develop a program named the International Currency Exchange application, you'll see exactly how a project looks at each stage of its design.

Chapter 2 gives you the opportunity to work through the initial design process for a new project. You'll use the Toolbox to select controls and add them to a form. You'll learn how to adjust the sizes of controls and place them at appropriate positions within a form. And finally, you'll save the components of your project to disk.

Chapter 3 explores the significance of properties in the design of a project. Each class of controls has its own list of properties that help define an object's role in your program. You'll see how various properties can change the appearance and behavior of a control, and you'll learn to use the Properties window to select their settings. You'll also investigate the properties of a form and see how the settings affect your program.

Chapter 4 introduces Visual Basic's event-driven programming model, and shows you how to begin developing event procedures in the code editor. In your first experiments with the code window, you'll notice some of the useful features of Visual Basic's built-in text editor, including color coding, automatic syntax checking and statement completion, and pop-up lists of properties and methods for particular objects. After developing some simple event procedures, you'll run your project and see how it works.

The final steps of your work involve testing, fine-tuning, and debugging your program. Chapter 5 introduces the important tools that Visual Basic provides to help you debug your code. Breakpoints, the Immediate window, Auto Data Tips, the Watch window, the Debug toolbar — these and other features are the subjects you'll explore in two detailed debugging exercises. Then Chapter 6 shows you how to create an executable program file from your finished project, and how to prepare it for distribution to other users.

Creating Applications in Visual Basic

A programming language gives you the tools to develop computer applications of all varieties — small or large, simple or complex, single-purpose or multifaceted. Your essential job as a programmer is to plan and write the code that guides the computer through basic activities such as input and output, data storage, calculations, decisions, and repetition. Programming is always intense work, requiring a solid understanding of the language in use and unwavering attention to detail. But when you complete a well-designed computer program — whatever its size or scope — the creative accomplishment yields genuine satisfaction.

Visual Basic 5.0 is a powerful application development tool for the Microsoft Windows 95 operating system. The package includes not only a familiar and accessible programming language, but also an efficient interactive environment for designing forms and windows. With this unique combination, Visual Basic simplifies programming tasks, shortens development time, and improves the quality of the end product.

In Visual Basic you can quickly design the visual elements of any new programming project. Your program's interface may include the familiar controls that Windows users already know how to operate — such as command buttons, option lists, text boxes, and scroll bars. With just a few swift mouse actions, you can add any combination of these controls to a program. As a result, the design tasks that used to require many hours of detailed programming effort can now be completed in minutes.

In this first chapter you'll start Visual Basic and begin exploring the dynamic tools it offers. Along the way, you'll preview the three-step process of application development in Visual Basic:

1. Designing a program's visual interface

2. Defining the properties of individual objects in the interface

3. Writing code

The brief hands-on exercises in this chapter will help you understand the basic concepts surrounding these three steps. (In chapters to come you'll learn much more about each step individually.)

At the end of this chapter you'll take a look at a sample application named the Currency Exchange Travel Guide, which you'll load from the program disk included with this book. This program is a calculation tool designed to simplify one aspect of international business travel, a recurring theme in the programming projects presented throughout this book.

Starting Visual Basic

Once installed on your computer, Visual Basic is available directly from the Start menu in Windows 95. As illustrated in Figure 1-1, you begin your work as follows:

1. Click the Start button and choose Programs from the Start menu.

2. Choose the Visual Basic group from the Programs menu.

3. Click Visual Basic to start the program.

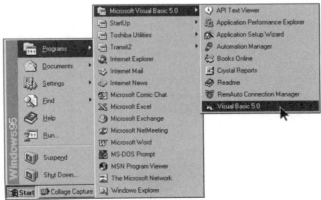

Figure 1-1: Starting Visual Basic.

Alternatively, you can easily place a shortcut to Visual Basic directly on the Windows 95 desktop. In the My Computer window or the Explorer, find and open the Visual Basic folder on your hard disk. Holding down the right mouse button, drag a copy of the Visual Basic icon from the folder to the desktop, and choose Create Shortcut(s) Here from the resulting pop-up menu.

As shown in Figure 1-2, a new shortcut icon appears on the desktop. To start Visual Basic, you can simply double-click this icon.

Figure 1-2: Creating a shortcut to Visual Basic.

Either way you choose to get started, Visual Basic opens onto the Windows desktop. Depending on how Visual Basic has been set up on your system, the first window to appear may be the New Project box. This dialog box contains three tabs of options — New, Existing, and Recent — offering you a variety of ways to begin your work:

✦ The New tab, shown in Figure 1-3, displays icons representing the various types of new projects you can start in Visual Basic 5.

✦ The Existing tab, shown in Figure 1-4, lets you browse through folders to search for a particular project that you want to open from a disk.

✦ The Recent tab, shown in Figure 1-5, lists projects that you've worked on in previous sessions, and gives you a quick way to reopen any program from the list.

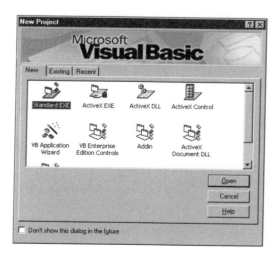

Figure 1-3: The New tab of the New Project dialog box contains icons representing the various types of projects you can start.

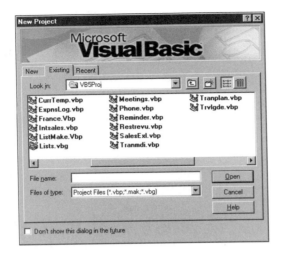

Figure 1-4: The Existing tab of the New Project dialog box allows you to browse for project files on your hard disk.

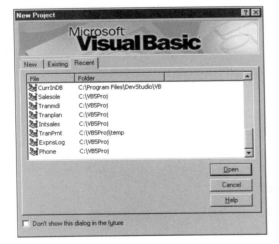

Figure 1-5: The Recent tab of the New Project dialog box lists projects you've worked on in recent sessions with Visual Basic.

To start a new "standard" project — the most familiar format for a Visual Basic application — select the Standard EXE icon on the New tab, and click Open. While you're learning Visual Basic, this is how you'll usually start your work at the beginning of each new session. In fact, if you want to make this the default action at startup time, check the box labeled "Don't show this dialog in the future," at the lower-left corner of the New Project box, and then click Open, as shown in Figure 1-6. The next time you start Visual Basic, a new standard project will be started automatically, without the appearance of the New Project dialog box.

Figure 1-6: Deactivating the New Project dialog box for future sessions with Visual Basic.

Tip If you later decide you want to reactivate the New Project dialog box so that it will again be displayed at startup time, choose the Options command from the Tools menu, click the Environment tab, and select the Prompt for project option in the frame labeled "When Visual Basic starts."

A First Look at the Development Environment

As you can see in Figure 1-7, the Visual Basic desktop provides a variety of tools to help you complete the steps of the development process. In particular, you can see four important windows arranged at each side of the desktop — the Toolbox at the left; and the Project Explorer, the Properties window, and the Form Layout window arranged in a vertical column at the right:

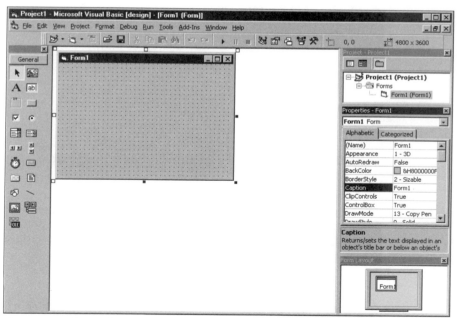

Figure 1-7: The tools you use for developing projects.

✦ The Toolbox displays a collection of icons representing the controls you can place in an application.

✦ The Project Explorer outlines the current contents of the project you're working on.

✦ The Properties window lists all the properties of a selected object, and gives you quick ways to change the property settings.

✦ The Form Layout window allows you to plan the position of windows and dialog boxes when you run the program.

You'll be learning much more about the Toolbox, the Project Explorer, the Properties window, and the Form Layout window later in this chapter. If any of these four windows are initially missing from your desktop, pull down the View menu and choose the name of an item you want to display, as shown in Figure 1-8. Otherwise, don't worry if your desktop doesn't look exactly like Figure 1-7. As you'll see shortly, Visual Basic allows you to rearrange the tools on the desktop to suit your own work patterns; your preferences are retained from one session to the next.

Figure 1-8: Using the View menu to open the project development tools.

At the top of the screen you see Visual Basic's title bar. Its caption tells you that Visual Basic is ready for you to begin designing a new program with a default name of Project1; an item named Form1 is the initial object contained in this project:

```
Project1 - Microsoft Visual Basic [design] - [Form1 (Form)]
```

During the design process, an application is known as a *project*. A project may include multiple files on disk, any of which can appear as windows on the desktop when you open the project into the Visual Basic environment. Projects may consist of several types of files; among these file types are forms, modules, and the project file itself:

✦ A *form* is a window that you design to play a specific role in your program's visual interface. To develop the contents of a form, you use the Visual Basic Toolbox to select buttons, options, lists, frames, or other controls and you arrange these objects within the form's borders. Each form is saved on disk as a separate file with an extension name of FRM. The FRM file also stores any code you write to orchestrate activities on the form. (In addition, Visual Basic creates FRX files to record special properties of forms.)

✦ A *module* is a separate code file, saved on disk with an extension name of BAS.

✦ The *project file* keeps track of all the files and objects included in a given application. Visual Basic 5 saves a project file on disk with an extension name of VBP. (Visual Basic also creates a VBW file to record information about a project.) Each application includes a project file; when you open this file, the Project Explorer window provides an outline of files that are part of the application — including forms, modules, and other objects that you'll learn about later in this book.

Given all the windows that can be open at once on the desktop, you can see the potential for ending up with a screen that's jumbled with images and information. Fortunately, Visual Basic allows you to arrange the desktop in any way that suits your own sense of clarity and efficiency.

Rearranging the Visual Basic desktop

Initially, the Toolbox, Project Explorer, Properties, and Form Layout windows are all *docked* at the sides of the desktop. In fact, the latter three windows are attached together in a single docked column, making them look like three parts of one window. This arrangement gives your screen a tidy, well-organized appearance. You always know where to find the tools you need.

But you might prefer to arrange the development tools in your own way. For example, Figure 1-9 shows a desktop in which the windows have been undocked, resized, and placed in convenient positions around Form1. Nothing has changed functionally in this arrangement — the various tools still work in the same ways — but visually and practically the desktop has a rather different presentation. In short, the Visual Basic development environment is flexible and adaptable to your own preferences.

Before you get started with the details of a first project, you might want to experiment with different arrangements on the desktop. To move and resize a docked window, follow these steps:

1. Drag the window by its title bar to a new position on the desktop.

2. Drag the borders of the window inward or outward to create a shape of new rectangular dimensions.

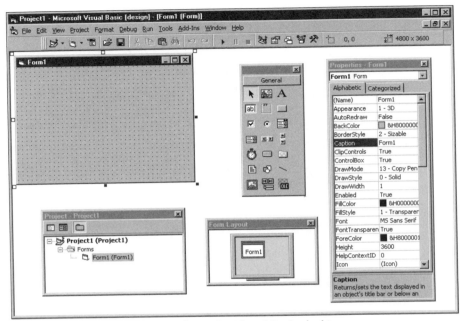

Figure 1-9: Rearranging the tools on the Visual Basic desktop.

If you later decide to return a window to its original docked position, just drag it back to the side of the desktop. With a little practice, you'll learn how to snap a window back into its place. Alternatively, double-click the title bar of the Properties window, Form Layout window, Toolbox, or Project Explorer to dock the window. When two or more windows are docked together (as they are back in Figure 1-7), you can drag their individual borders up and down to assign different sizes to each window. You can also increase or decrease the width of the docked windows by dragging the side border to the left or right.

While you're designing a project, the main focus of your attention is typically on the forms and controls you design for your program's visual interface. You'll want to leave yourself plenty of room to work with these elements. But at the same time, the Visual Basic development tools should be arranged conveniently nearby. As you continue your work, you'll find your own best ways of working with the objects on the desktop.

Using menus and toolbar buttons

Just beneath the title bar at the top of the screen, you can see the menu bar and the Standard toolbar, shown in Figure 1-10. As in any Windows application, menu commands give you ways to perform specific operations. For example, the File menu contains commands for starting new projects, opening existing projects from disk, or saving the project that you're currently working on. The Edit menu provides a variety of familiar operations, including undo, redo, cut-and-paste, copy-and-paste, find, and replace. As you've seen, the View menu lets you choose the windows that you want to see in the development environment. You'll learn more about specific menus and commands as you proceed through this book.

Figure 1-10: The menu bar and the Standard toolbar.

Tip   Like most major Windows 95 applications, Visual Basic also has shortcut menus (sometimes known as *context menus*). To view the shortcut menu for an object, click the object with the right mouse button. The resulting menu contains a list of the commands you're most likely to use for the selected object. You'll encounter a variety of shortcut menus as you continue your work in Visual Basic.

The toolbar provides shortcuts for many important menu commands. The buttons along this toolbar are arranged in groups:

✦ The first three toolbar buttons, shown in Figure 1-11, are shortcuts for opening new projects; for adding files and modules to the current project; and for opening the menu editor to develop a menu for the current form. As shown in Figure 1-12, when you click the down-arrow button next to the second of these buttons, you can see the list of forms, modules, and other files that can be added to a project.

Figure 1-11: The first group of toolbar buttons are for opening new projects, adding files to an existing project, and starting the menu editor.

Figure 1-12: Click the down-arrow button next to the second toolbar button to view the list of forms, modules, and file types that you can add to a project.

✦ The next two buttons, shown in Figure 1-13, are for opening a project from disk and for saving the current project.

Figure 1-13: These buttons are for opening and saving projects.

✦ Figure 1-14 shows the next two groups, which provide shortcuts for a variety of commands from the Edit menu, including Cut, Copy, Paste, Find, Undo, and Redo.

Figure 1-14: These buttons represent a variety of Edit menu operations.

✦ The next group, shown in Figure 1-15, contains buttons for running, pausing, and stopping a program. You'll use these buttons when you're ready to test your program's performance.

Figure 1-15: These buttons are for starting, pausing, and stopping a program run.

✦ Figure 1-16 shows the final group of buttons, which you use for opening or activating the various tools of the development environment: the Project Explorer, the Properties window, the Form Layout window, the Object Browser, and the Toolbox.

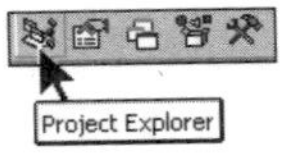

Figure 1-16. These buttons are for opening or activating the various tools of the development environment.

You'll learn much more about the buttons on the Standard toolbar as you begin creating your own Visual Basic projects. You'll also see other toolbar collections that Visual Basic displays to help you in different parts of your work. If you forget the purpose of a particular shortcut on the toolbar, you can simply rest the mouse pointer over a button; Visual Basic displays a small ToolTip box showing the name of the button, as illustrated in Figure 1-16.

Although the Standard toolbar is initially docked beneath the menu bar, you can undock it by dragging it to a new position on the desktop. For example, in Figure 1-17 the toolbar appears beneath Form1. Notice that the undocked toolbar has its own title bar, like other windows on the desktop. Double-click the title bar to return the toolbar to its docked position.

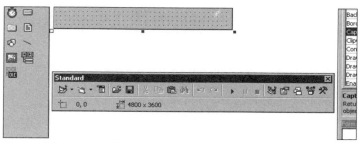

Figure 1-17: Undocking the Standard toolbar.

The Toolbox

The Toolbox displays icons representing the controls you can include in a project. This window is central to your work as you decide how to depict the options, procedures, and activities planned for a new application.

The Toolbox initially displays the set of *standard* or *intrinsic* controls — the objects most commonly found in Windows applications. Figure 1-18 shows the Toolbox of standard controls. Many other controls may be available for your use, depending on the edition of Visual Basic you've installed on your computer. Three editions are available, known as Standard, Professional, and Enterprise. Each provides additional controls designed for special purposes. As you'll learn later in the book, you use the Components command from the Project menu to add controls to the Toolbox, making them available for use in your current project.

Figure 1-18: The Toolbox of standard controls.

There's no particular need to memorize all the Toolbox buttons at this point, although you may already recognize most of the tools in the box. For example, the buttons in the top half of the Toolbox include the controls you use to organize text and graphics in a window (labels, picture boxes, and frames), controls that elicit input or instructions from the user (text boxes and command buttons), and controls that provide options (check boxes, option buttons, combo boxes, and list boxes). As shown in Figure 1-19, a ToolTip displays the name of a tool when you simply hold the mouse pointer over a button in the Toolbox.

Figure 1-19: Identifying buttons in the Toolbox.

In the next section you'll discover how easy it is to place a control on a form.

Controls, forms, and projects

Prominent in the Visual Basic development environment is the object named Form1, shown in Figure 1-20. A form is a window you design to serve as part of a program's interface. For example, a form can become a dialog box for eliciting information from the user, or a window in which your program displays specific information. You can develop any number of forms for use in a program, although a program may reasonably consist of a single form.

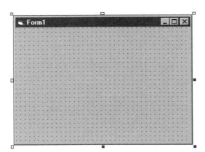

Figure 1-20: An empty form in a new Visual Basic project.

Tip   The window that displays a form may or may not be maximized in the Visual Basic development environment. To control the window in its maximized state, you can use the Minimize, Restore, and Close buttons that appear at the far right side of the Visual Basic menu bar. Click Minimize to reduce the window to a title bar on the desktop. Click Restore to produce a free-standing window that can be moved and resized. Click Close to hide the window temporarily. Closing the window does not remove the form from your project. To reopen the window, double-click the name of the form object in the Project Explorer window.

Visual Basic initially includes the Form1 file in each new standard project. You can change the form's name and caption to identify its purpose and you can begin planning the appearance of your program inside the form. In fact, the form and its contents remain at the center of your attention throughout the three major steps of program development: adding controls, setting properties, and writing code. You'll explore these steps in upcoming sections.

Step 1: Placing Controls on a Form

As a first experiment with forms and controls, the following exercise guides you through the steps of placing a variety of objects on Form1:

1. Move the mouse pointer to the command button icon in the Toolbox, and double-click the left mouse button. In response, Visual Basic places the first control — a command button — in the middle of Form1. The caption on the control is Command1, as shown in Figure 1-21. Around the perimeter of the command button are sizing handles, small solid black squares that you can use to change the dimensions of the control. The appearance of these handles indicates that this first control is the selected object in the form.

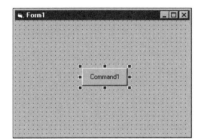

Figure 1-21: Placing a command button on Form1.

2. Position the mouse pointer over the center of the Command1 control, hold down the left mouse button, and drag the control toward the upper-left corner of Form1. As you do so, notice that the frame representing the control moves in small jumps within the dotted grid shown in the background of the form. As shown in Figure 1-22, a ToolTip box shows the current coordinates of the move. The position and size of an object are shown in *twips*, a standard unit of measurement for graphic objects on the Windows desktop.

3. Release the mouse button when you've moved the command button to its new position in the form. Take at look at the position and size indicators, located at the right side of the Standard toolbar, as in Figure 1-23. These measurements always show the current position and dimensions of a selected control or form.

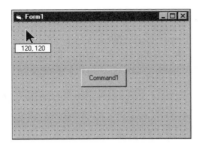

Figure 1-22: Moving a command button to a new position in Form1.

Figure 1-23: The position and size indicators, at the right side of the Standard toolbar.

4. Now try a slightly different technique for placing a control on a form. As shown in Figure 1-24, position the mouse pointer over the label tool, shown as a bold uppercase **A** in the Toolbox. Click the left mouse button once; this action selects the label control. Move the mouse pointer to a position near the top center of Form1. Hold down the left mouse button, and drag the mouse through a small rectangular area on the form. Release the mouse button, and Visual Basic places a label control in the form. The caption on this new control is Label1.

Figure 1-24: Adding a label control to the form.

5. You can resize a control by dragging any one of the small sizing handles displayed around the perimeter of the control. Try this now with Label1. Position the mouse pointer over one of the handles; the pointer becomes a two-headed arrow. Hold down the mouse button and drag the handle in any direction to change the dimensions of the control. A ToolTip box shows the current dimensions of the control; at the same time, the new size is registered in the size indicator at the right side of the Standard toolbar, as shown in Figure 1-25.

6. Now try placing several more controls on Form1. First double-click the text box control in the Toolbox, shown in Figure 1-26. A control named Text1 appears in the form. Drag this new control to a position just beneath Label1. Labels and text boxes are often paired in forms; the purpose of the label is to tell the user what kind of information to enter in the text box.

Figure 1-25: Resizing a control.

Figure 1-26: Adding a text box to the form.

7. Double-click the option button icon in the Toolbox, shown in Figure 1-27. A control named Option1 appears in the form. Repeat this step two more times to produce the controls named Option2 and Option3 in turn. Reposition these new controls to produce a column of option buttons down the left side of the form.

Figure 1-27: Adding option buttons to the form.

8. Finally, double-click the combo box button in the Toolbox (Figure 1-28). A combo box is a text box with an attached drop-down list of options.

Figure 1-28: Adding a combo box to the form.

9. Drag this new control, named Combo1, to a position near the lower-right corner of Form1. You've now placed seven controls on the form, and your work should appear approximately as shown in Figure 1-29.

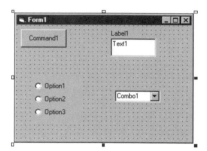

Figure 1-29: Seven controls arranged on a form: a command button, a label, a text box, three option buttons, and a combo box.

Although the steps of this exercise may have seemed a little arbitrary, you can easily imagine beginning your work on a real application by placing a similar selection of controls on a form. For example, Figure 1-30 shows an actual dialog box illustrating the controls you've been working with. This example contains a text box for entering the name of an employee, a set of option buttons and a combo box for specifying information about the employee, and a command button for requesting a search for the employee's record.

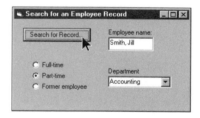

Figure 1-30: Building a real dialog box for an application.

Running a program

Now try a couple of experiments with the form you've created. You can run a program in Visual Basic before writing any code. Doing so gives you an opportunity to explore the behavior of the controls you've placed on the form. Here are three simple ways to start a program:

✦ Click the Start button on the toolbar, as shown in Figure 1-31.

✦ Choose Run⇨Start, as shown in Figure 1-32.

✦ Press F5, the shortcut key for the Start command.

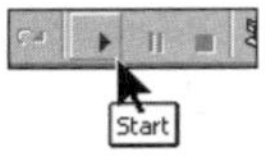

Figure 1-31: The Start button on the toolbar.

Figure 1-32: The Start command in the Run menu.

Any one of these actions switches Visual Basic from the design mode to the run mode. The Visual Basic title bar displays the bracketed word [run] to indicate that you are running your project.

But before the first program run, you might want to use the Form Layout window to plan the form's screen position at runtime. Suppose you want your form to appear approximately in the center of the screen. Take the following steps to make this happen:

1. Move the mouse pointer down to the Form Layout window and position the pointer over the small representation of a form on the screen illustration.

2. Hold down the left mouse button and drag the form to the center of the screen, as shown in Figure 1-33, and then release the mouse button. Click the Form1 title bar to select the form; notice that the position indicator — at the right side of the Standard toolbar — shows the new runtime screen position you've chosen.

Figure 1-33: Using the Form Layout window to plan the runtime position of a form.

That's all you have to do. Now click the Start button or press F5 to start the project. Then follow these steps to experiment with the controls on the form:

1. Click the Command1 button several times with the mouse. Notice the visual push-button effect that takes place on the screen with each mouse click.

2. Try entering some text in the text box. A Visual Basic text box has all the built-in editing capabilities of any Windows text box. You can insert, select, delete, cut, copy, and paste text in the box, using mouse and keyboard operations that are common to all Windows applications.

3. Click any one of the three option buttons. A bold black dot appears inside the button you've chosen. Now click a different button. The previous button is cleared and the bold black dot appears inside your most recent selection. In a group of option buttons, only one option can be selected at a time.

4. Click the down-arrow icon just to the right of the Combo1 control, as shown in Figure 1-34. Although the resulting drop-down list is empty at the moment, you can still see the behavior that's built into this particular control.

5. Now click the End button on the toolbar or choose Run⇨End, to stop the program. Visual Basic returns to the design mode, as indicated by the bracketed word [design] on the title bar.

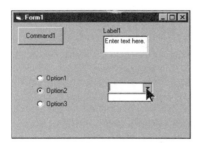

Figure 1-34: An experimental run of a Visual Basic project.

Tip When you run a project, Visual Basic normally opens the Immediate window, which appears at the bottom of the desktop. This window plays an important role in debugging a program, as you'll learn in Chapter 5. You can close this window by clicking the Close button located at the far right side of the window's title bar. (Alternatively, click inside the window with the right mouse button, and choose Hide from the resulting shortcut menu.) Open the window by choosing View⇨Immediate Window or pressing Ctrl+G at the keyboard.

Exploring the Properties window

Once you've placed one or more controls on a form, the second step in the Visual Basic development scheme is to set the properties of your forms and controls. Properties determine the appearance and behavior of individual objects in the applications you create. Each class of controls or objects has its own set of properties; for example, you'll discover properties representing the name, caption, color, style, and status of a particular control.

At design time, you can change property settings in the Properties window. You can open or activate this window at any time by taking one of these steps:

✦ Click the Properties button on the toolbar.

✦ Choose View⇨Properties Window.

✦ Press F4, the shortcut for the Properties Window command.

As shown in Figure 1-35, the Properties window is arranged as a two-column grid. The column on the left contains the names of all the properties that apply to a selected object, and the column on the right shows the setting for each property. Each property has a default setting that remains in effect unless you change it.

Figure 1-35: The Properties window, showing an alphabetic list of properties for a selected object.

One of the long-awaited innovations of Visual Basic 5 is a Properties window that offers two different views of the properties list. Notice the two tabs — labeled Alphabetic and Categorized — just above the list of properties. In the first tab, the properties are listed alphabetically, as they have always been in previous versions of Visual Basic. If you know the name of the property you're looking for, an alphabetic listing may work well for you.

But often you might find yourself looking through a long list for a property whose name you can't quite recall — even though you know the effect that the property represents for the current control. In this case, you should click the Categorized tab in the Properties window. As shown in Figure 1-36, the resulting list divides the properties of an object into functional categories. If you can't remember the name of a particular property, you can look in the most likely category grouping and find a shorter list of relevant items.

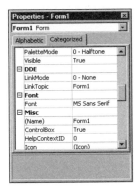

Figure 1-36: Properties listed by category.

Switch back and forth between the two Property window tabs as often as you like. Note that both lists contain exactly the same properties for a given object; they just arrange the properties differently. While you're developing a project, you're likely to spend lot of time setting properties. The new two-tabbed organization of the Properties window will streamline your work.

Step 2: Setting Properties

In the following exercise, you'll select the command button that you've placed on Form1, and quickly change three properties of this control. You'll also take the opportunity to scroll through the entire property list to see what else it contains:

1. Click the Command1 control on the form you've been creating. Sizing handles reappear around the perimeter of the command button.

2. Temporarily undock the Properties window and drag it to a position next to Form1. You can see the list of properties that apply to the command button you've selected. Click the Alphabetic tab to view the list in alphabetical order.

3. Use the scroll bar at the right side of the Properties window to scroll through the entire set of properties. You'll find about 30 properties that apply to this control. Among them are properties named Left and Top, which specify the position of the control in the containing form. You've changed these property settings already, just by dragging the command button to a new position inside the form. You'll also see properties named Height and Width, which determine the size of the control. You can change the size either by entering new settings for these properties in the Properties window, or — as you've seen — by selecting a control and dragging its size handles with the mouse.

4. Scroll back to the top of the properties list and click the Caption property. For a command button, the Caption property is the text that appears on the face of the button. As you can see, the default setting of this property is Command1 for the current control.

5. Type the new caption **Message** and then press Enter to confirm your new entry. Now look back at the command button on Form1. As shown in Figure 1-37, the button displays the new caption that you've assigned to it.

Figure 1-37: Changing the Caption property of a command button.

6. Now select the Default property in the list. A Default setting of True means that the user can select a command button by pressing Enter from the keyboard. In some applications this feature provides a convenient alternative to a mouse click. The current setting for this property is False. To change the setting, select True from the drop-down list, or simply type **T**.

7. For the final change, select the (Name) property at the top of the list. This property assigns a name by which you refer to a given control in the code of your program. As you can see, the default Name setting is Command1.

8. Enter **cmdMessage** as the new Name setting. You can assign any name you like to a control, but certain conventions will make your work easier when you begin writing code. In this example, starting the name with the letters *cmd* will help you remember later that this name refers to a command button.

9. Before you complete your work in the Properties window, notice that the window contains a list box, located just below the title bar. The box currently displays the name you've just assigned to the command button, cmdMessage. This drop-down box gives you a simple way to select a different control or form, so that you can begin changing the properties of other objects in your program. Click the down-arrow button located at the right side of the box, and you'll see a list of all the objects you've placed on Form1, as shown in Figure 1-38. To see the list of properties that apply to any one of these controls, you simply select the name of the control in the drop-down list.

Figure 1-38: The list of controls in the Properties window.

If you wish, you can now double-click the title bar at the top of the Properties window to return the window to its docked position.

So far you've examined a variety of tools that appear in the Visual Basic environment:

✦ The title bar, the menu bar, and the toolbar

✦ The Toolbox, containing icons for the controls available to you as you create your project

✦ The Form1 window, which Visual Basic includes in every new standard project

✦ The Properties window, in which you can view and change the property settings for any control or form in your program

✦ The Form Layout window, which gives you an easy way to specify the initial runtime positions of the forms in a project

One important window remains to be examined — the Project Explorer window.

The Project Explorer window

The Project Explorer window represents the contents of your current program. To view or activate the Project Explorer window, take one of these actions:

✦ Click the Project Explorer button on the Standard toolbar.

✦ Choose View⇨Project Explorer.

✦ Press Ctrl+R, the keyboard shortcut for the Project Explorer command.

The Project Explorer window lists the files contained in a project. At this point in your work, the Forms list has only one entry, Form1, as shown in Figure 1-39. But a project may contain as many forms as are necessary in the design of your program. In addition, you can add modules to a project for storing additional code in your program.

Figure 1-39: The Project Explorer window.

Without worrying too much just yet about the different roles that forms and modules play in a program, try adding some additional files to the current project:

1. Click the Add Form button, the second button on the Standard toolbar. In the resulting Add Form dialog box, accept the default Form selection, and click Open. Visual Basic adds a new form to your project, named Form2. Repeat this step to add Form3 to the project.

2. Click the down-arrow just to the right of the second icon on the toolbar, and choose Module from the resulting menu list. In the Add Module dialog box, accept the default Module selection and click Open. Visual Basic adds a module file named Module1 to your project.

3. Now press Ctrl+R to activate the Project Explorer window. Increase the window's height by dragging its lower border down toward the middle of the desktop. The window displays the list of three forms and one module that currently make up your project, as in Figure 1-40.

4. Your original Form1 is now hidden by other windows you've added to your project. The Project Explorer window gives you a quick way to return to your work on this form: Select Form1 in the list and click the View Object button, the second tool at the top of the window.

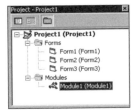

Figure 1-40: Adding new forms and modules to a project.

Notice that the Project Explorer organizes a project's files as an outline of folders. You can collapse or expand any part of the outline by clicking the minus (-) or plus (+) sign next to a category of files. You may want to do this to focus on a particular group of files in a project that contains many elements. To view any form in your project, double-click the form's name in the Project Explorer window.

Tip You can change the format of the Project Explorer window by clicking the Toggle Folders button, the third tool at the top of the window. When you do so, Visual Basic presents the contents of your project as a simple list of files rather than an outline of folders. Click Toggle Folders again to return to the original outline format.

Once you've selected and arranged the forms and controls of your project and assigned property settings as needed, the final step of your work is to begin writing code. You can store code in individual forms or in modules. In general, the code you store in a form applies to the objects in the form. The code in a module can be defined as "public" code, available anywhere in your program. You'll learn more about this distinction in upcoming chapters.

The event-driven programming model

One of Visual Basic's most important and compelling features is a design approach known as the *event-driven programming model*. When you plan a Visual Basic program, you focus on the events that you expect to take place while the program is running. Most events correspond to actions that may be performed by the person who's running your program. For example, the user clicks a button, selects an option, chooses a menu command, highlights an item in a list, or types an entry into a text box; all of these are events that are formally defined and recognized in Visual Basic applications. Much of the code in Visual Basic projects is oriented around anticipated events like these.

Accordingly, a program contains blocks of code known as *event procedures* that you design to respond to specific events. For example, suppose you're ready to write the procedure that will be performed whenever the user clicks the cmdMessage button on Form1. Visual Basic defines the name Click for the event that takes place when the user clicks a command button with the mouse. The procedure you'll write for this event is therefore named cmdMessage_Click, combining the name of the control (cmdMessage) with the name of the event (Click).

As you'll learn in the upcoming exercise, Visual Basic gives you an efficient way to open a window for developing an event procedure.

Step 3: Writing Code

The event procedures for the controls on a given form are saved as part of the FRM file. To open the code window for a form, all you need to do is double-click any control on the form. Visual Basic automatically starts an event procedure for the control you've selected.

In the following exercise you'll create a short event procedure for the cmdMessage control:

1. In the Form1 window, double-click the command button labeled Message. In response, Visual Basic opens a code window (Figure 1-41) and creates the first and last line of the cmdMessage_Click event procedure. A flashing cursor appears between these two lines of code, indicating that Visual Basic is ready for you to enter the actual code of the procedure.

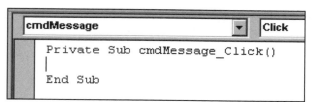

Figure 1-41: The code window, showing an event procedure named *cmdMessage_Click.*

2. Type the line **MsgBox "Hello there..."** on the line where the cursor is flashing. (After you type *MsgBox*, Visual Basic displays a help box that tells you exactly how to complete this statement. This feature is known as Auto Quick Info. You'll learn more about it in Chapter 4.) The three lines of the procedure now look like this:

```
Private Sub cmdMessage_Click()
  MsgBox "Hello there..."
End Sub
```

3. Now click the Start button on the toolbar or press F5. Visual Basic runs your project and displays the Form1 window with the various controls you've arranged in it.

4. Use the mouse to click the Message button, or simply press the Enter key from the keyboard. Doing so triggers the *cmdMessage_Click* event; accordingly, Visual Basic makes a *call* to the event procedure that you've just created. The MsgBox instruction you wrote in the procedure displays a small message box on the screen with the message "Hello there..." as shown in Figure 1-42.

Figure 1-42: The message box resulting from a click of the Message button.

5. Click OK in the message box. Then click the End button on the toolbar to end the program performance.

In short, you've just created and performed your first event procedure. You'll learn much more about the event-driven programming model as you continue in this book. The main point to keep in mind from this exercise is simple: Visual Basic recognizes certain events that may take place around the controls you place in a form; by writing event procedures, you define your program's reaction to those events.

Now you've finished your work with this first exercise. Because the forms you've created were merely experimental in this case, you can now abandon them without saving any files to disk. Here's how you do it:

1. Choose File⇨New Project.

2. A dialog box appears on the desktop asking whether you want to save the files of Project1. Click No to abandon the entire project.

3. In the New Project dialog box, keep the default Standard EXE selection, and click OK. Visual Basic creates the elements of a new Project1, including an empty Form1 window. Now the development environment looks like it did when you first started.

Getting Help

This quick tour has introduced you to the elements of the Visual Basic programming environment. The chapters ahead will fill in many more details. But before you continue, you should take a look at one more important feature — the Help window. Like all major Windows applications, Visual Basic has a useful cross-referenced help system that's never more than a few keystrokes or mouse clicks away. The Help menu provides several starting points into the system. Alternatively, you can press F1 at almost any time to get context-sensitive help about your current activity.

Try it now. Click the title bar of the Form Layout window to activate the window, and then press F1. In response, Visual Basic opens the Form Layout Window help topic, as in Figure 1-43; you can scroll through the topic to read more about this tool. You'll see other examples of context-sensitive help later in your work.

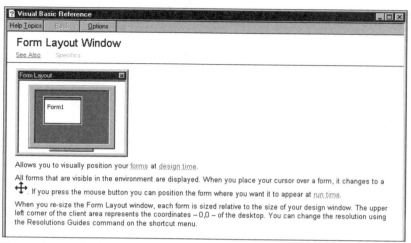

Figure 1-43: The Form Layout Window topic in the Visual Basic Reference window.

Tip

If your system is set up for connecting to the Internet, you can find online help directly from Microsoft. Choose Help⇨Microsoft on the Web⇨Online Support.

To review what you've learned so far, the final section of this chapter takes you through the steps of opening and running a sample project from the program disk included with this book. (If you haven't copied the sample programs from the program disk to your hard disk, you should do so now. See the Introduction for notes and directions.)

The Currency Exchange Travel Guide Program

In the upcoming exercises you'll examine a project named the Travel Guide program, a currency exchange calculator for international business travelers. The program is designed to read a text file named CURRENCY.TXT that contains up-to-date currency exchange rates for any number of countries. Before running the program, you need to create and store this file in the root directory of your hard disk. For example, Figure 1-44 shows a version of the file containing rates for nine countries. Notice that each line of the text file contains the name of a country, the name of the corresponding currency, and the current exchange rate in US dollars.

Figure 1-44: A sample of the CURRENCY.TXT file.

Create the file in any text editor — for example, the Windows 95 NotePad application will work just fine. On a daily basis you can download the exchange rate information from your favorite online service or copy it from a newspaper. But for now — if you simply want to try running the program with a typical data set — you can copy a test version of the CURRENCY.TXT file from the program disk to your root directory.

When you open a project from disk, the Project Explorer window provides access to all the form and module files that are part of the program. You can run the program by clicking the Start button, or you can examine the program's components in the design mode. Here are the steps for opening and running the Travel Guide project:

1. Choose File⇨Open Project, or simply click the Open Project button on the Visual Basic toolbar. In the Open Project dialog box, find and open the folder to which you've copied the files from this book's program disk. You'll see a list of the available project files with VBP extensions, as in Figure 1-45. (Visual Basic 5 also recognizes MAK files from previous versions of the language; for this reason, the Open Project dialog box also lists any MAK files that may be stored in your directory.)

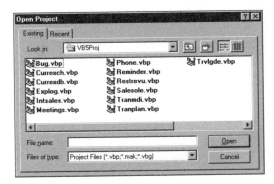

Figure 1-45: Opening a project from disk.

2. Select TrvlGde and click Open. Visual Basic loads the project into memory. In the Project Explorer window (Figure 1-46) you can see that the project consists of a form (TrvlGde.Frm) and a module (CurrExch.Bas), plus the project file itself (Trvlgde.Vbp).

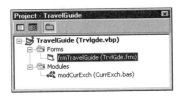

Figure 1-46: The Project window for the Travel Guide program.

3. Click the Start button on the toolbar or press F5 to run the program.

The program window, titled Currency Exchange Travel Guide, appears on the screen. At the upper-left corner of the window you see a combo box labeled Country. Click the down-arrow button at the right side of this box and select a country from the list, as shown in Figure 1-47. When you do so, the program window instantly fills with data, as you can see in Figure 1-48.

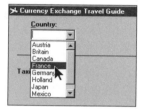

Figure 1-47: Choosing a country in the Travel Guide program.

Currency Exchange Travel Guide					
Country:		One U.S. dollar = 5.109862 franc(s)			
France		One franc = 0.1957 U.S. dollar(s)			
Taxi Ride					
francs	26	51	77	102	128
dollars	$5	$10	$15	$20	$25
Meal for Two					
francs	102	179	255	332	409
dollars	$20	$35	$50	$65	$80
Hotel per Night					
francs	383	639	894	1150	1405
dollars	$75	$125	$175	$225	$275

Print   Exit

Figure 1-48: Currency exchange data supplied by the program.

The program is designed to provide currency equivalents for a variety of expenses you might incur during an international business trip. At the top of the program window, you see the basic exchange rates for the country you've selected. Below, there are three tables of exchange data, labeled "Taxi Ride," "Meal for Two," and "Hotel per Night." These categories are merely a convenient way to organize the output data; as you can see, they display currency equivalents for dollar amounts ranging from $5 to $275.

To view data for a different country, you simply pull down the Country list again and make a new selection. The data changes completely, as shown in Figure 1-49.

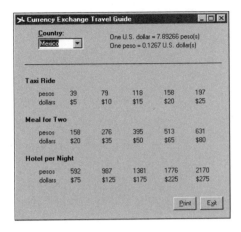

Figure 1-49: Another set of currency exchange data.

Continue experimenting with the program for a while if you want. Notice the two command buttons displayed at the lower-right corner of the program window. You can click the Print button (or press Alt+P) to print a copy of the program window and all its current data. When you're ready to stop the program, click the Exit button (or press Alt+X or simply Escape); in response, Visual Basic returns you to the design mode.

Inside the Program

As shown in Figure 1-50, the project's form contains a combo box, two command buttons, and several sets of labels. (There's also a line control that divides the top part of the window from the tables of data below.) Some of the labels have pre-defined captions that remain unchanged throughout the program run; others are blank until the program displays information in them by assigning a value to the Caption property. Like many Visual Basic properties, Caption can be set at design time in the Properties window or at runtime by your program's code.

Among the events that the program recognizes are Click events on either of the two command buttons, and a Click event for making a selection from the Country combo box. To explore a portion of the program's code, try double-clicking the combo box now in design mode. As you can see in Figure 1-51, the resulting code window shows an event procedure named cboCountry_Click. This procedure computes and displays the currency exchange information whenever the user selects a new country from the drop-down list.

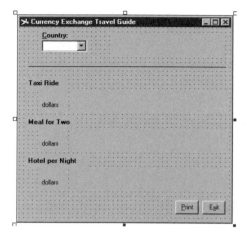

Figure 1-50: The controls in the Travel Guide project.

```
cboCountry                    ▼    Click                        ▼

  Private Sub cboCountry_Click()
   ' Read the user's country choice
   ' and display the exchange rates
   ' for the currency of the selected          I
   ' country.

  Dim i As Integer
  Dim curr As String

  For i = 0 To countryNdx
    If cboCountry.Text = CurrArray(i).country Then
      lblDollar.Caption = "One U.S. dollar = " & _
        1 / CurrArray(i).inDollars & " " & _
        CurrArray(i).currName

      If CurrArray(i).currName <> "yen" Then _
        lblDollar.Caption = lblDollar.Caption & "(s)

      lblCurrency.Caption = "One " & _
        CurrArray(i).currName & " = " & _
        CurrArray(i).inDollars & _
        " U.S. dollar(s)"
        currCountry = i
    End If
  Next i
```

Figure 1-51: Exploring the code of the Travel Guide program. This is the first part of the cboCountry_Click procedure.

In short, the Travel Guide program is a one-form project that illustrates a variety of controls, properties, and events. It gives you a first taste of Visual Basic's potential. When you're ready to close the project, choose File⇨New Project, or exit from Visual Basic altogether by choosing the Exit command.

Table 1-1 provides a summary of the project development tools you've examined in this chapter.

Table 1-1 **Visual Basic Project Development Tools**		
Tool	**Description**	**Access**
Toolbox	Displays buttons representing the classes of controls you can add to the forms of your project. Double-click a button in the Toolbox to add an instance of a control to the current form.	Click the Toolbox button on the Standard toolbar.
Project Explorer	Shows the contents of the current project. Double-click the name of any form in the list to view and activate the form.	Ctrl+R
Properties Window	Lists the properties and settings that apply to a selected object. You can view properties in alphabetic order or in categories.	F4
Form Layout Window	Provides a simple graphic tool for setting the runtime position of any form in the current project.	Click the Form Layout button on the Standard toolbar.
Standard Toolbar	Displays a collection of buttons representing common operations in the Visual Basic development environment. At the right side of the toolbar you can see the position and size indicators for the current object. By default, the Standard toolbar is docked in position just below the menu bar, but you can undock it by dragging to a new position on the desktop.	Choose View⇨ Toolbars⇨Standard.
Menus	The menu bar gives you access to standard commands for the Visual Basic environment. In addition, you can view a shortcut menu by clicking an object with the right mouse button.	

In Chapter 2 you'll begin creating a somewhat different version of the Currency Exchange program and you'll learn more about the steps of application design in Visual Basic.

Designing an Effective Interface

An *interface* includes all the visual objects and procedural
techniques that define a program's interaction with the
user, the person sitting at the computer. How does the
program get information from the user? How does the user
select among the program's options? What keyboard and
mouse techniques are available for issuing instructions to the
program? When the input data has been entered and options
chosen, how does the program present the information that
the user has requested? These are some of the questions
you'll ask yourself as you begin designing your program's
interface.

In the old days of the BASIC language — before Visual Basic
appeared on the scene — programmers spent a large percent-
age of their time solving these particular design problems.
Devising graceful ways — or practical ways, at least — to
communicate with the user typically required a greater effort
than any other single feature of a program. Long sections of
code and many hours of programming were often devoted to
the process of coordinating screen activity with the user's
input from the keyboard.

But Visual Basic has changed all that, as you've already begun
to see. In the Visual Basic environment you create your
program's interface by dragging controls into a form and
arranging them in place. The Toolbox provides an assortment
of controls that meet particular requirements in a program's
design. These controls have several important benefits. They
are intuitive; a user can learn to operate them almost without
any instruction. They are also familiar, because the same

types of controls appear in all Windows applications. And — perhaps most important from your point of view as programmer — they are ready-made; when the program is running, the keyboard and mouse techniques for using those controls are built into the objects themselves. Adding these controls to your program and making them work requires little or no programming.

The first step for creating an application in Visual Basic — the step that was most time-consuming in old versions of BASIC — is now the easiest and possibly the most fun: Decide how you want your program to interact with the user, and choose the best controls for carrying out that interaction. Place the controls on a form, and arrange them in a way that suits the program's requirements and satisfies your own sense of programming aesthetics. When you complete this step, your work already begins to take shape as a programming project. You can see what your program will look like and to a great extent how it will work.

This chapter guides you through the process of completing this first step for a real project. In Chapter 1 you examined the Travel Guide program, which is devoted to the arithmetic of international currency exchange. Now you'll design a second version of this program that allows the user to choose a currency and quickly calculate conversions between dollars and the selected currency. You'll begin your work by analyzing the program's purpose and choosing controls that best meet that purpose. To keep your work in perspective, you'll take a brief look at the finished project, which you'll load into Visual Basic from the program disk included with this book. Then you'll go back and work through the exercise of creating the program's interface. Along the way, you'll learn more about the Visual Basic development environment and the options it provides.

Planning the Program

Call this new project the International Currency Exchange application. Like its predecessor, this version will begin by reading a text file named CURRENCY.TXT. As you'll recall, this file contains a list of countries, the names of their currencies, and the value of each currency in dollars. For example, Figure 2-1 shows the sample data you'll find in the CURRENCY.TXT file provided on the program disk.

Figure 2-1: The contents of the CURRENCY.TXT file.

The program has simple expectations for this file. The information for each country should appear on one line in a specific order, and separated by commas: country name, currency name, dollar value. Otherwise, you can build the file in any way you want. The countries themselves appear in no particular order. Any number of countries can be included in the list, up to a maximum of 100. (As noted in Chapter 1, you can update this file on a regular basis by downloading the currency exchange information from an online service, or by copying it from a newspaper.)

After reading this data, the program is ready to provide exchange rates for any country in the list, and to perform conversion calculations between dollars and any selected currency.

Choosing controls for the program's features

Most of the program's activity takes place in a single window. The following paragraphs describe the various features that the program offers:

A reminder that the program must begin by reading the CURRENCY.TXT file. In the event that the user tries to run the program without first creating the currency file, the message box shown in Figure 2-2 appears on the screen, briefly suggesting the problem. When the user clicks OK, the program ends. This error message is displayed at runtime by the program's code, as you'll learn in Chapter 4; the project does not need an extra form to provide the message.

Figure 2-2: A gentle error message appears if the user tries to run the program without first creating a currency file.

A set of ToolTip messages, designed to help the user understand the program's dialog box. When the user rests the mouse pointer over selected controls in the dialog box, explanatory tips appear on the screen. For example, Figure 2-3 shows the tip that the program displays to describe the use of the Country list. Other tips appear for the Calc button and the currency text box. These tips are created by simple property settings, as you'll learn in Chapter 3.

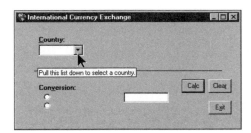

Figure 2-3: ToolTips help the user understand the controls in the dialog box.

A simple way to choose a country from the available list. The combo box control is a good way to provide this list, as shown in Figure 2-4. A label ("Country:") just above the box identifies the purpose of the control. To use the combo box, the user starts by clicking the down-arrow icon at the right side of the box. A drop-down list of countries appears below the box. When the user clicks an entry in the list, the selection is copied to the box itself and the list disappears.

Figure 2-4: A combo box presents a list of the countries that the user can choose from.

A clear display of the basic exchange rates, once the user has selected a country. A pair of label controls provide this feature, as shown in Figure 2-5. Before the user chooses a country, these two labels are blank. But as soon as a country selection has been made, the program uses the labels to display two lines of text. The dollar value of the selected currency is copied directly from the information supplied in the currency text file. By contrast, the program has to calculate the value of one dollar in the selected currency. A line control separates this basic currency information from the calculation controls displayed in the lower half of the program window.

Figure 2-5: Labels display the basic currency exchange information.

A choice between currency exchange calculations. The user can choose to compute the currency equivalent of a dollar amount, or the dollar equivalent of a specified amount in the selected currency. A pair of option buttons provides this choice, as shown in Figure 2-6. Just above the buttons, a label ("Conversion:") identifies the choice to be made. The current selection is shown as a button filled with a bold dot. To change the selection, the user simply clicks the other option. Because only one option button in a group can be selected at a time, Visual Basic automatically clears the other button when the user makes a new selection.

Figure 2-6: Option buttons offer a choice of currency calculations.

An unambiguously labeled input box for the amount that is to be converted. As you know, a text box control is Visual Basic's tool for accepting numeric or text input from the user at the keyboard. Figure 2-7 shows the text box for accepting a currency amount. A flashing cursor inside the text box indicates that the program is ready to accept an input value. Simple as it may seem as a control, the text box is actually a full-featured editing tool. It allows deletions, insertions, highlighting, and copy-and-paste operations. Notice that the program labels the text box according to the selected calculation option. If the user selects the other option, the program changes the label, as shown in Figure 2-8.

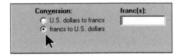

Figure 2-7: A text box for accepting a currency amount from the keyboard.

Figure 2-8: The label changes when the user selects a new calculation option.

An efficient keyboard or mouse technique to instruct the program to carry out the calculation, once a monetary amount has been entered from the keyboard. A command button is the ideal control for this operation, as shown in Figure 2-9. After entering a value in the text box, the user can click the Calc button with the mouse to complete the calculation. Alternatively, designating Calc as the *default* button allows the user simply to press the Enter key to carry out the calculation. (You'll learn more about the Default property in Chapter 3.)

Figure 2-9: A command button represents the calculation operation.

A display of the result. As soon as the user requests a new calculation, the result should appear in an obvious place in the program window. A label control located just beneath the input text box is a good solution, as in Figure 2-10. This juxtaposition gives the user a clear view of the original input value and its equivalent in the other currency.

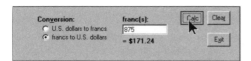

Figure 2-10: A label displays the calculated currency equivalent.

A way to clear the current data so that a new calculation can be performed. Another command button serves this purpose, as in Figure 2-11. When the user clicks the Clear button, the program clears the values from both the input text box and the label that displays the result of the calculation.

Figure 2-11: The user clicks the Clear button to start a new calculation.

An open-ended invitation to start the entire process over again. At any time, the user can pull down the country list to view a new set of currency exchange values. When this happens, the program immediately changes the basic exchange rates displayed in the labels to the right of the country list (Figure 2-12) and also the captions displayed next to the calculation option buttons. The user can then perform any number of calculations in the new currency.

Figure 2-12: Changing the country and currency selection.

An easy keyboard or mouse technique for ending the program. Another command button — typically labeled Exit — serves this purpose. To end the performance and close the program window, the user simply clicks the Exit button (see Figure 2-13). Alternatively, if Exit is designated as the form's *cancel* button, the user can simply press the Escape key on the keyboard to end the performance. (You'll learn how to define the Cancel property in Chapter 3.)

Figure 2-13: The Exit button is the user's way to stop the program.

In summary, the International Currency Exchange program will contain instances of six controls, all arranged in a single form:

+ A combo box that presents the list of countries

+ A variety of label controls, serving one of two general purposes — identifying the purpose of other controls, or displaying the results of the program's calculations

+ A pair of option button controls, offering two different calculation options

+ A text box control, where the user can enter a currency amount to be converted

+ A set of command buttons representing three operations: completing a calculation, clearing the previous calculation, and ending the program

+ A line control that divides the program window into two parts

Figure 2-14 identifies these six controls in the Visual Basic Toolbox. Once you've envisioned and planned the program's operations, the job ahead of you is clear: You need to place these controls on a form in appropriate combinations to serve the program's purposes. But before you turn to this task, take a moment now to look ahead at the program as a finished product.

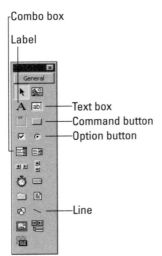

Figure 2-14: The six types of controls you'll use in the Currency Exchange project.

Previewing the finished program

The International Currency Exchange application is saved under the name CurrExch.Vbp. If you've copied the contents of the program disk to your hard disk, you can follow these steps to open the program and run it:

1. First make sure you create a currency file from today's currency exchange data — or copy the sample CURRENCY.TXT file from the program disk to the root directory of your hard disk.

2. Select Visual Basic from the Windows 95 Start menu, or double-click the Visual Basic icon on the desktop.

3. In Visual Basic's New Project dialog box, click the Existing tab. Find and open the folder where you've copied the files from this book's program disk, and select the CurrExch.Vbp file, as shown in Figure 2-15. Click the Open button.

Figure 2-15: Opening the CurrExch.Vbp project from the Existing tab of the New Project dialog box.

4. Take a look at the Project Explorer window for the application. Open the Forms folder if necessary. (To open a closed folder in the Project Explorer list, double-click the folder icon or click the + sign just to the left of the folder.) The project contains one form, as you can see in Figure 2-16.

Figure 2-16: The Project Explorer window for the CurrExch.Vbp project.

5. If the form is not already displayed on the desktop, double-click frmCurrExch in the Project Explorer list. You can then examine the controls it contains (Figure 2-17).

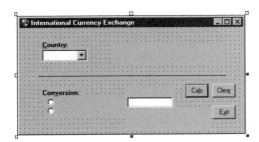

Figure 2-17: The International Currency Exchange form in design mode.

6. Press F5 to start the program. When the application window shown in Figure 2-18 appears on the screen, you'll see that many of the program's controls are blank initially. The program doesn't fill in any specific currency information until you first select an entry from the Country list.

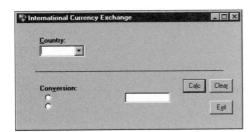

Figure 2-18: The initial appearance of the program window; most of the controls are blank until you select a country.

7. Start experimenting with the program. Pull down the Country list and select the name of a country. The program immediately displays the basic currency exchange information just to the right of the Country box. Try clicking one of the two Conversion options and notice the changes that take place in other controls in the program window. Finally, enter a currency amount in the text box and press Enter to instruct the program to carry out a conversion calculation. As shown in Figure 2-19, the result of the calculation appears just beneath the text box, in bold text. Continue making other selections until you understand exactly how the program works.

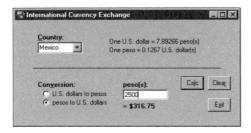

Figure 2-19: An exchange rate calculation is displayed in the program window.

8. Click the Exit button (or press the Escape key) to stop the program. Then choose File⇨New Project, to clear the CurrExch program from memory. Click No in response to the prompt asking if you want to save changes to the program files. In the New Project window, keep the Standard EXE selection and click OK. A new project appears, with an empty form named Form1.

In the upcoming exercises, you'll go through the steps for creating this program's interface on your computer. You'll use the Form1 window currently displayed on the desktop for this exercise.

Creating the Program's Dialog Box

The first steps are to resize Form1 to suit the program's design, and to plan the window's runtime position on the desktop:

1. Increase the form's width to a measurement of 6105 twips. To do so, position the mouse pointer over the black size handle displayed along the form's right border. The pointer becomes a two-headed arrow. Drag the border line to the right and release the mouse button. Refer to the size indicator at the right side of the Standard toolbar to find out the current width. Repeat these actions until you reach the desired measurement of 6105.

2. Decrease the form's height to 3300 twips. Position the mouse pointer over the black size handle displayed along the bottom border of the form, and drag the handle up toward the center of the form. Again, you may have to repeat these actions several times to achieve the desired height.

3. Use the Form Layout window to specify the form's initial position at runtime. One way to do this is simply to drag the form to the approximate center of the screen image inside the Form Layout window. Alternatively, try using commands from the window's shortcut menu: Click inside the Form Layout window with the right mouse button, and choose Startup Position⇨Center Screen from the resulting shortcut menu, as shown in Figure 2-20. In the Form Layout window, the form moves to the center of the screen image.

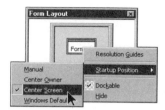

Figure 2-20: Using the Form Layout window to plan the form's position at runtime.

Figure 2-21 shows the resized Form1, alongside the Form Layout window. Notice that the form itself does not change position at design time; it always remains at the upper-left corner of its containing window. Only the Form Layout window indicates where the form will appear at runtime. At the upper-right corner of Figure 2-21 you can see the size indicator, which shows 6105 × 3300 as the current dimensions of the form.

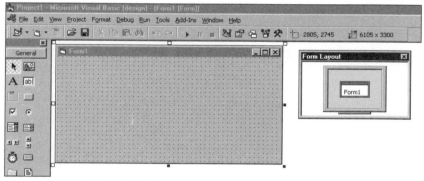

Figure 2-21: Changing the dimensions of Form1, and planning the window's runtime position on the screen.

Tip   Keep in mind that you can undock the Form Layout window and reposition it at any convenient position on the Visual Basic desktop. Likewise, you can undock and drag the Properties window, the Project Explorer, the Toolbox, and the toolbar. Look back at Chapter 1 for details and examples.

Now you're ready to begin placing controls on the form. For each new control, you'll follow the same pattern of steps:

1. Double-click the Toolbox icon that represents the control you want to add to the form. In response, Visual Basic places a new control in the middle of the form, with a default size. Sizing handles are displayed around the perimeter of the new control, indicating that the object is selected — and can be resized or moved.

2. Position the mouse pointer over the control and drag it to a new position in the form. The position measurements (*Left, Top*) for the control are shown on the position indicator at the right side of the Standard toolbar. These measurements represent the object's position in relation to the upper-left corner of the containing form.

3. Position the mouse pointer over any of the sizing handles displayed around the perimeter of the control, and drag the handle to change the size of the object. The size measurements (*Height × Width*) are shown on the size indicator at the right of the toolbar.

Adding controls to the form

You'll begin your work by placing a line control across the middle of the form. This will help you orient the remainder of your work. Then you'll add the six labels that the program uses to identify other controls and to display calculated data in the window:

1. Double-click the line control in the Toolbox. (See Figure 2-14 if you forget where this button is located.) Visual Basic places a diagonal line in the center of Form1, as shown in Figure 2-22. A sizing handle is located at each end of the line.

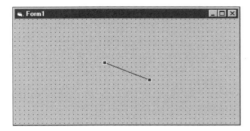

Figure 2-22: The default length and position of a new line control.

2. Drag these handles to create a horizontal line that extends across almost the entire width of the form. As you resize or move a control inside the form, Visual Basic provides a ToolTip box showing the current dimensions or position (Figure 2-23). The line's position coordinates should be 480, 1320, and its dimensions 5055 × 15. Figure 2-24 shows the form at this point in your work.

Figure 2-23: A ToolTip shows the current dimensions or position of the control.

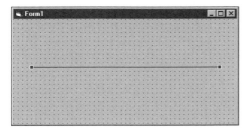

Figure 2-24: The final position and length of the line control.

3. Now double-click the label control, shown as a boldface A in the Toolbox. A new control named Label1 appears in the center of the form. Drag the label toward the upper-left corner of the form, to the position 600, 360. Then resize the label to the dimensions 735 × 255, as in Figure 2-25. Eventually this label will serve to identify the Country list.

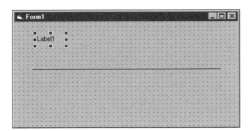

Figure 2-25: Adding the first label to the form.

4. Double-click the Label in the Toolbox two more times. In response, Visual Basic adds Label2 and Label3 to the form. (Whenever you add multiple objects of the same type to a form, the default names are numbered in this same manner — for example, Option1 and Option2, or Command1, Command2, and Command3.) These two new labels will display the basic exchange rates for a selected country. Move both labels toward the upper-right corner of the form, to positions 2520, 480 and 2520, 720, respectively. Then resize both labels to the same dimensions: 2895 × 255. Figure 2-26 shows Form1 at this stage in your work.

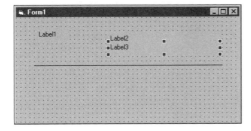

Figure 2-26: Adding labels to display currency exchange data.

5. Add the three remaining labels to the form, as shown in Figure 2-27. Label4 will eventually identify the conversion options; move it to 600, 1680 and assign it dimensions of 1095 × 255. Label5 will identify the text box; its position is 2880, 1680 and its size is 1215 × 255. Finally, Label6 will display the result of each new currency exchange calculation. Drag it to 2880, 2280 and assign it a size of 2175 × 495.

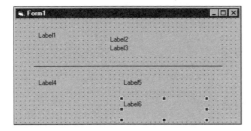

Figure 2-27: Adding the rest of the labels to the form.

6. Now your form is ready for the controls that the user can interact with in one way or another — the combo box, the option buttons, the text box, and the command buttons. Begin by double-clicking the combo box control in the Toolbox. Visual Basic places the Combo1 control in the center of the form. Drag it to its correct position (600, 600). It can retain its default dimensions of 1215 × 315, as shown in Figure 2-28.

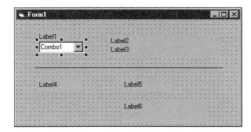

Figure 2-28: Adding a combo box to the form.

7. Double-click the option button control twice in the Toolbox. Option1 and Option2 appear in the center of the form. Resize both buttons to dimensions of 2055 × 255. Drag Option1 to 720, 1920 and Option2 to 720, 2160 (Figure 2-29).

8. Double-click the text box control once in the Toolbox. Drag the Text1 control to 2880, 1920. Then resize it to the dimensions 1215 × 285 (Figure 2-30).

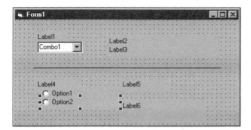

Figure 2-29: Adding two option buttons to the form.

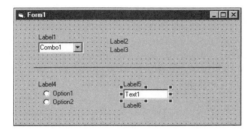

Figure 2-30: Adding a text box to the form.

9. Finally, double-click the control button in the Toolbox three times, to add Command1, Command2, and Command3 to the form. Reduce the dimensions of all three buttons to 615 × 375. Then drag Command1 to 4440, 1560, Command2 to 5160, 1560, and Command3 to 5160, 2160. Click the mouse at any blank area of Form1 to deselect all controls. Figure 2-31 shows your work.

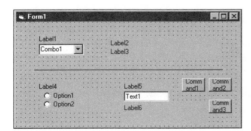

Figure 2-31: Arranging three command buttons on the form.

After all the effort of placing each control at its precise position inside the form, you'll now want to protect your work from inadvertent changes. You can do this by choosing Format⇨Lock Controls, as shown in Figure 2-32. In response, Visual Basic freezes all the controls on the current form. This command is a toggle. Choosing it once turns the lock feature on, and choosing it again turns it off. If you later want to make changes in the position or size of a control, you can simply choose Lock Controls to unfreeze the controls temporarily.

Figure 2-32: Choose the Lock Controls command to freeze the controls in their assigned sizes and positions in the form.

Saving your work

In Chapter 3 you'll continue your work on this form, focusing on a variety of properties for each control in the program. For now, the final task remaining in this exercise is to save your work to disk. You'll begin by saving Form1 as a FRM file on disk. Then you'll save the current Project1 as a VBP file:

1. Make sure Form1 is the active window on the desktop. (If it isn't, click its title bar with the mouse.) Then pull down the File menu and choose the Save Form1 As command. In the resulting dialog box, choose the folder where you want to save the file and enter **CurrTemp** in the File name box, as shown in Figure 2-33. Then click Save to save the FRM file to disk.

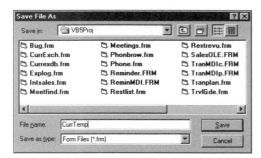

Figure 2-33: Saving the form to disk.

2. Choose File⇨Save Project As. In the resulting dialog box, choose a folder if necessary and enter **CurrTemp** in the File name box, as shown in Figure 2-34. Click Save and Visual Basic saves your project as CurrTemp.VBP. When you want to return to your work on this project, you'll open it under this name.

3. Now choose File⇨New Project. In the New Project dialog box, keep the Standard EXE selection, and click OK. Visual Basic clears your current work and opens new Project1 and Form1 windows.

Figure 2-34: Saving the project.

Adjusting the form design grid

Throughout this exercise you've arranged controls on Form1 within Visual Basic's standard form grid. This grid is represented by the rows and columns of dots that appear in the background of every form at design time. (The grid disappears when you run a program.) As you've noticed, all the changes you make in the size and position of a control are aligned to this grid by default. For most projects, the grid is a great benefit; it helps you to arrange groups of controls in relation to each other and to resize controls appropriately.

But sometimes you may prefer to work without the grid so that you'll have more freedom to move controls wherever you want them. Or, you may want to change the distance between the rows or columns of dots that make up the grid itself. Visual Basic allows you to make both of these changes. To see how, choose Tools⇨Options and then click the General tab in the resulting dialog box. In the frame labeled Form Grid Settings (Figure 2-35) you can see the options available for changing the grid:

+ To make the grid invisible, click the Show Grid check box. (The check disappears from the check box.)

+ To change the dimensions of the grid, enter new values into the Width and Height boxes. By default, the rows and columns of the grid are spaced 120 points apart.

+ To deactivate the grid, clear the check box labeled Align Controls to Grid.

After making any changes you want in the structure of the grid, click OK to confirm your choices.

Using the commands of the Format menu

The Format menu contains another set of tools that can help you adjust the sizes and positions of controls on a form. In general, you select two or more controls before selecting items from the Format menu. You can then use the menu's commands to align controls vertically and horizontally, and to adjust the dimensions of controls in relation to each other.

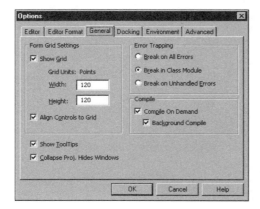

Figure 2-35: The options for changing the form design grid.

There are two easy ways to select multiple controls in a form. Use either of these techniques:

✦ Select the first control by clicking it with the mouse. Then hold down the Shift key and click one or more additional controls.

✦ Click the Pointer icon in the Toolbox. (This deselects any control icon.) Then use your mouse to draw a dotted frame around the controls you want to select. Release the mouse button to complete the selection.

Once you've made a selection of multiple controls in a form, pull down the Format menu and select a category of commands. Use the Align commands shown in Figure 2-36 to align a set of controls vertically or horizontally. Use the Make Same Size commands shown in Figure 2-37 to adjust the vertical and horizontal dimensions of the selected controls. Use the Horizontal Spacing (Figure 2-38) and Vertical Spacing (Figure 2-39) commands to equalize or change the amount of space between controls. Use the Center in Form commands (Figure 2-40) to place the selected controls in the center of the form's current dimensions. After a little experimentation with these commands, you'll find them to be an extremely useful addition to Visual Basic's form-building tools.

Figure 2-36: The Format Align commands are for aligning the positions of two or more controls.

Figure 2-37: The Format Make Same Size commands are for adjusting the dimensions of controls.

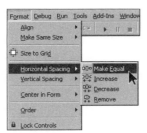

Figure 2-38: The Format Horizontal Spacing commands are for adjusting the horizontal space between controls.

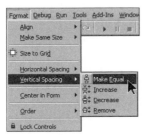

Figure 2-39: The Format Vertical Spacing commands are for adjusting the vertical space between controls.

Figure 2-40: The Format Center in Form commands are for moving controls to the center of their containing forms.

Looking Ahead

You've now completed the first step of application development — arranging controls on a form, and saving your work to disk. Comparing Figure 2-31 with the final version of the program (Figure 2-12), you can see that the project is already beginning to take shape. But there's still a lot of work left to do. For one thing, you'll need to change the captions and names of almost all the controls in the form. There are also several other property settings that will help define the behavior and performance of your program. You'll learn about these properties in Chapter 3.

Defining Properties

As you've learned, the first step of Visual Basic application development is to create and arrange the visual objects of a project — for example, to open a form and place a relevant selection of controls within its boundaries. This step takes place interactively on the desktop, almost as if Visual Basic were a special kind of Paint program in which you draw your plans for a program's visual interface.

In the second step, often just as dramatic as the first, you set the *properties* of individual objects, including forms and the controls they contain. Each class of control — command button, text box, label, option button, and so on — has its own list of properties that apply specifically to the object's design. Working with these properties, you refine your program's appearance and function, sometimes in surprisingly subtle ways. Not only can you change obvious features — such as the captions displayed on buttons, or the text fonts used in labels — but you can also modify the behavior of your program and the quality of its interaction with the user. For example, you'll find properties that define the following characteristics:

✦ The keyboard shortcuts that the user can use to perform specific operations in the program

✦ The order in which items appear in a list

✦ The status of a control at a given point in the program run — active or inactive; visible or hidden

✦ The order in which controls receive the *focus* in response to repeated pressing of the Tab key

✦ The ToolTip messages that appear when the user rests the mouse pointer over selected controls

Like the controls themselves, properties streamline the process of creating an application. Many features that require major programming effort in other languages are achieved in Visual Basic with the simple selection of a property setting. In this chapter you'll continue exploring the properties for specific controls, and you'll learn more about what they can mean for your applications.

Setting Properties at Design Time or Runtime

Many properties can be set at either design time or runtime. You've already had some experience with these two distinct operating modes in the Visual Basic environment. At *design time*, you add controls to a project, set properties, and write code. During a run, you examine your program in action, just as an end-user will eventually see it.

You follow a familiar pattern of steps to set a property at design time:

1. Select the control or object whose characteristics you want to change.

2. Activate the Properties window.

3. Scroll to the property you want to set and select its name.

4. Enter a new setting.

You'll go through these steps many times during this chapter's hands-on exercises.

During a run, property settings can be changed by specific statements in the program's code. You accomplish this by writing a special kind of assignment statement that gives a new value to a property of a selected control:

```
controlName.propertyName = value
```

At the left side of this statement, *controlName.propertyName* is a compound name identifying the control and the property that is to be reset. The *value* on the right side of the statement gives the new setting. When a program resets a property at runtime, the new setting overrides the value assigned at design time.

This is an important general point to keep in mind as you begin creating a new program. Design-time settings need not be permanent during a program run. For example, a label may display a particular design-time caption at the outset, but that caption may change many times during a program run, as your code assigns new values to the label's Caption property.

But you can postpone worrying about code for the moment. In this chapter you'll concentrate instead on the simple and direct techniques for assigning property settings at design time. Your focus will be on the Properties window and its two-column list of properties and settings. To explore this feature, you'll return to the project you began designing in Chapter 2 — a version of the International Currency Exchange program that you've stored on disk as CurrTemp.Vbp. To get started, follow these steps to open the project and display its form on the desktop:

1. Choose Visual Basic from the Windows 95 Start menu.

2. In the New Project window, click the Recent tab, as shown in Figure 3-1. Select CurrTemp among the list of recently opened projects, and click Open. Alternatively, if the New Project window doesn't appear at the beginning of your session, pull down the File menu and choose CurrTemp.Vbp from the list of recent projects at the bottom of the menu list, as shown in Figure 3-2.

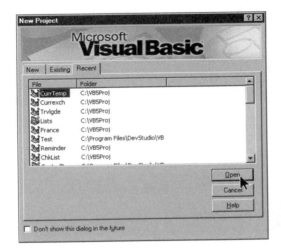

Figure 3-1: The list of recently opened projects in the Recent tab of the New Project window.

Figure 3-2: The list of recently opened projects at the bottom of the File menu.

3. If you don't see the Project Explorer window on the desktop, press Ctrl+R to display it.

4. If Form1 is not already displayed on the desktop, double-click Form1 in the Project Explorer window to view your work.

When you complete these steps, the form you created in Chapter 2 reappears on the desktop, as shown in Figure 3-3. In the exercises ahead, you'll change the properties of most controls on this form. In doing so, you'll make significant progress in completing the design of your program.

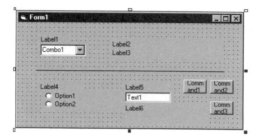

Figure 3-3: The form you began designing in Chapter 2.

Changing the Properties of Labels

This form contains six labels, currently displaying captions from Label1 to Label6. Your first job is to change these captions appropriately. As you may recall from your work with the final version of the program, shown again in Figure 3-4, several of these labels are meant to display information that may change frequently during a program run. For example, Label2 and Label3 will show the basic currency exchange rates for a selected country, and Label6 will display a calculated currency conversion. At the outset of the program, these three labels, along with Label5, should therefore have blank captions.

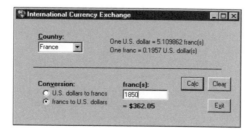

Figure 3-4: Reviewing the final version of the Currency Exchange program.

Only the captions for Label1 and Label4 remain unchanged throughout the program run. Label1 displays the word *Country*, identifying the purpose of the combo box below it; and Label4 displays the word *Conversion*, representing the choices offered in the pair of option buttons below.

But take a closer look at these two labels in Figure 3-4. Each caption contains an underlined letter — the *C* in Country, and the *v* in Conversion. This underlining identifies the *access keys* (sometimes called *keyboard shortcuts*) for the corresponding controls. During a run of the program, the user can press Alt+C to activate the Country list, or Alt+V to choose a Conversion option. This is a small but important design element for a person who prefers to use the keyboard rather than the mouse to control the action of a program.

You therefore have several tasks ahead of you in setting the captions of the program's six labels: Create blank captions for the four labels that are reserved for numeric output; supply the program's two fixed labels; and define two of the program's access keys.

Captions and access keys

The Caption property gives you simple ways to accomplish all these tasks. To create a caption, you choose Caption in the Properties window and then type a text entry as the new setting. (To create a blank caption, delete the default setting and leave it empty.) To define an access key, you place an ampersand character (&) just before the letter that you want to be underlined in the text of the caption. For example, the following setting defines Alt+V as the access key:

Con&version

In the label itself, this caption appears as

Con<u>v</u>ersion

Starting with Label1 and Label4, then, here are the steps for setting the Caption property — first for the labels and then for several other controls in your program:

1. Click Label1, near the upper-left corner of Form1. When you do so, handles appear around the perimeter of the label. Because Form1 is currently locked, the handles are represented by unfilled squares, indicating that the control is protected from inadvertent moves or resizing.

2. In the Properties window, click the Categorized tab. (You'll recall that the Alphabetic tab shows the properties all in one alphabetized group, and the Categorized tab divides them into functional groups.) As shown in Figure 3-5, the Caption property is in the Appearance category. Select this property by clicking its name in the list.

Figure 3-5: Preparing to set the Caption property.

3. Type **&Country:** and press Enter to confirm the setting. Back in Form1, notice that the label appears as <u>C</u>ountry.

4. Now click Label4 in the form.

5. Begin typing the new Caption setting, **Con&version:**. Because you've already established Caption as the current property, Visual Basic automatically activates the Properties window and accepts your new setting. Press Enter to confirm.

6. Click Label2 and press F4 to activate the Properties window. Then press F4 a second time. In the column on the right, the current Caption setting, Label2, is highlighted. Press Delete. The Caption setting is now blank.

7. Repeat Step 6 for Label3, Label5, and Label6. At this point in your work, Form1 appears as in Figure 3-6. You've successfully set the initial Caption properties for the six labels.

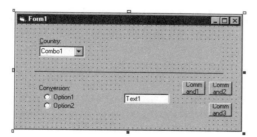

Figure 3-6: Completing the Caption settings for the six labels on the form.

Because Caption is currently selected in the Properties window, this is a convenient moment to set the captions for other controls in Form1, specifically the three command buttons and the two option buttons. Note in Figure 3-4 that each of the command button captions is to include an access key; by contrast, the option button captions are initially blank.

1. Begin by clicking Command1 and typing **Ca&lc** from the keyboard. The caption on this button is displayed as Calc.

2. Click Command2 and type **Clea&r** as the caption. Finally, select Command3 and type **E&xit**.

3. Now click Option1 in the form. Press F4 twice to activate the Properties window and highlight the current Caption setting. Press Delete to create a blank caption. Press Enter to confirm.

4. Repeat Step 3 for the Option2 control. Form1 now appears as in Figure 3-7.

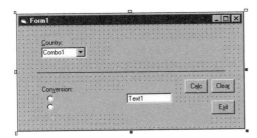

Figure 3-7: Setting the captions for command buttons and option buttons.

All the initial captions for your application are now set. But an important step remains in creating the access keys for the Country list and the Conversion options. Specifically, you need a way to link the access keys — as defined in the label captions — with the actual controls they'll activate: Alt+C for the combo box and Alt+V for the option buttons. Your tool for accomplishing this is a property called TabIndex.

TabIndex and the Focus of Controls

The Tab key is a universal shortcut for moving among the controls in a Windows dialog box. When a dialog box is open, pressing Tab moves you forward from one control to the next; pressing Shift+Tab moves you to the *previous* control. This action is sometimes called *moving the focus*.

Within a dialog box, only one control has the focus at a time. When a given control receives the focus, a small but distinctive change occurs in the control's appearance. For example, a dotted rectangle is displayed around the caption in a command button or option button; or a flashing vertical cursor appears inside a text box or a combo box. When you see this change, you know that the control is ready to record an entry or accept a selection from the keyboard.

In a Visual Basic project, you use the TabIndex property to define the *order* in which controls will receive the focus when the user presses the Tab key. By default, this property is established by the order in which you originally place controls on a form. The first control has a TabIndex setting of 0; the second, 1; the third, 2; and so on. In addition, a property called TabStop indicates whether or not a given control will receive the focus in response to tabbing.

Significantly, a label control has a TabIndex property, but no TabStop property. By definition, labels never have the focus at runtime. All the same, a label's TabIndex setting is essential for completing the definition of an access key. For example, you've used the ampersand in &Country to identify Alt+C as the access key in the Country label. Now to associate Alt+C specifically with the combo box located below the label, you have to make sure that the label and the combo box have *consecutive* TabIndex settings. If the label has a TabIndex setting of 0, the combo box must have a setting of 1.

In the following steps, you'll enter new TabIndex settings for several of the controls on Form1. You actually have two goals in this exercise: first, to make sure the access keys work the way you want them to; and second, to provide a sensible tab order for moving the focus from one control to another in the form. You'll begin your work by examining the current TabIndex setting for the Country label:

1. Click the Country label, at the upper-left corner of the form.

2. In the Properties window, scroll down to the TabIndex property in the Behavior category. Click the property name to select it. Notice that the label's current TabIndex setting is 0. (Although this label was the *second* control that you placed on the form, it is the first that has a TabIndex property. The property doesn't apply to the line control, which was the first item you placed in the form.)

3. Now select the combo box control, just beneath the Country label in the form. The current TabIndex setting for the combo box is 6.

4. Enter **1** as the new TabIndex setting for the combo box. This consecutive tab order ensures that the label's Alt+C shortcut key will activate the Country combo box list.

5. Repeat this process to change the TabIndex settings for seven more controls on the form, as shown in the following list:

Control	*TabIndex Setting*
Conversion (label)	2
Option1 (option button)	3
Option2 (option button)	4
Text1 (text box)	5
Calc (command button)	6
Clear (command button)	7
Exit (command button)	8

You've set the TabIndex property for the two label controls that define shortcut keys for other controls in the form. Other settings in the list create a convenient tab order for using the controls in the form.

At design time, the TabIndex property has no immediate visual impact on the form; its influence is evident only at runtime. For a quick demonstration, try running the project now:

1. Press F5 or click the Start button on the toolbar. A caption on the Visual Basic title bar tells you that you're now in the run mode. A flashing cursor appears in the Country combo box, indicating that this control has the focus initially.

2. Press the Tab key five times and watch as the focus moves through the other controls in the form, in the order you've defined in the TabIndex property — first the Conversion buttons, then the text box, and then the three command buttons.

3. Now try the access keys. For example, press Alt+L. The focus moves to the Calc button. (When you later write a procedure in your program's code to define the *action* of the Calc button, Alt+L will carry out that action.) Next try pressing Alt+C. The focus moves to the Country combo box.

4. When you've finished experimenting, click the End button on the toolbar to return to the Design mode.

You still have several changes to make in the appearance of your form. For example, notice back in Figure 3-4 that four of the label captions are displayed in boldface type. To achieve this effect, you use the Font property.

The Font Property

As you might guess, the Font property gives you access to a variety of typographical effects. You can use the options of this property to select any of the available fonts in your installation of Windows. You can also change the point size and you can select styles, including boldfacing. The Font property is available for many controls that display text, such as text boxes, command buttons, option buttons, combo boxes, and labels.

Unlike the properties you've worked with so far, Font provides a range of options in a special dialog box that appears on the desktop. You'll examine this dialog box in the following steps:

1. Click the Country label.

2. Scroll down the Properties list to the Font property, which is in a category of its own. Notice the small button labeled ... at the right side of the property setting box, as shown in Figure 3-8.

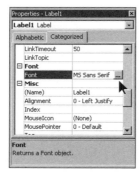

Figure 3-8: The Font property. Click the ... button to see the font options.

3. Click the **...** button once. In response, Visual Basic opens the Font dialog box, as shown in Figure 3-9. Take a moment to examine the options provided in this box. The scrollable Font list contains the names of the available fonts on your system. The Font style list contains four special typographical options (including Bold, which you'll select shortly). The Size list provides a range of point sizes for the current font selection. Additional options are available in the lower half of the dialog box.

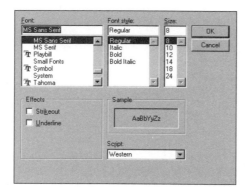

Figure 3-9: The Font dialog box.

4. In the Font style list, click the Bold option. Then click OK to confirm your selection and close the dialog box. Back in Form1, the Country caption now appears in boldface type.

5. Repeat Steps 1 to 4 for three additional labels: the Conversion label and the blank labels located just above and just below the text box.

Now Form1 appears as in Figure 3-10. You can see the boldface effect in the two nonblank label captions. Boldfacing will appear in the other labels when the program displays text in them.

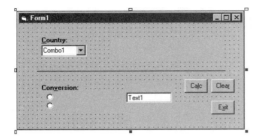

Figure 3-10: Applying the boldface style to label captions.

Next you'll turn to the Name property. As you may recall, this property defines a name by which a given control is identified in code. The default Name property for a label is the same as the caption originally displayed in the label (Label1, Label2, Label3, and so on). By supplying a more descriptive control name, you can ensure that your code will ultimately be more readable and easier to understand.

The two labels for which you've supplied nonblank captions (Country and Conversion) will never be referred to in your program's code, because their captions are fixed and they serve exclusively to identify the purpose of other controls. For this reason, you don't need to bother changing the default Name settings of these two labels. Conversely, the four labels that currently have blank captions will appear repeatedly in your code; specifically, the program will assign new Caption settings to these labels as a means of displaying the currency exchange information that the user requests. In the next exercise you'll change the Name settings for these four labels and other controls that need names in this project.

The Name Property

Here is a general suggestion regarding your choice of names for the controls in a project: Begin each name with a consistent three-letter prefix that identifies the control type. For example, begin a label name with *lbl*, a combo box with *cbo*, an option button with *opt*, a text box with *txt*, and a command button with *cmd*. As you begin writing code, this naming convention will help you keep track of the types of objects your program is working with. All the projects presented in this book follow this practice.

Here, then, are the names you'll assign to the 11 controls that will be referred to in the program's code:

Default Name	New Name Setting
Label2	lblDollar
Label3	lblCurrency
Label5	lblConvCurr

Default Name	New Name Setting
Label6	lblConvText
Combo1	cboCountry
Option1	optDollarsTo
Option2	optCurrTo
Text1	txtConvAmount
Command1	cmdCalc
Command2	cmdClear
Command3	cmdExit

Follow these steps to set the Name property for these controls, starting with Label2:

1. Click the blank label at the upper-right corner of the form; this control is currently named Label2.

2. Click the Alphabetic tab in the Properties window.

3. Scroll all the way to the top of the properties list, where the Name property is listed as (Name). Click this property to select it.

4. Type the new Name setting for the selected label, **lblDollar**, and press Enter.

5. On Form1, click the next label, currently named Label3. Then type the new Name setting, **lblCurrency**.

6. Repeat Step 5 for each of the remaining controls listed above — first the labels, then the combo box, option buttons, and text box, and finally the command buttons.

The Name setting has no visible effect on the forms or controls of your project. But the meaningful control names you've created will help clarify your program's code, as you'll see in Chapter 4.

Before you continue, this would be a good time to save your work to disk. To do so, you can simply click the Save Project button on the toolbar (or choose File⇨Save Project).

In response, Visual Basic saves any changes you've made in any file component of your current project. In this case, Form1, saved on disk as CurrTemp.Frm, is the only file you've changed.

Next you'll look at some examples of properties that affect your program's behavior. Specifically, you'll focus on the combo box and the command button controls, and you'll examine properties that make these controls more convenient to work with from the user's point of view.

Combo Box Properties

As you'll recall, the combo box in this project provides a scrollable list of countries available in the CURRENCY.TXT file. When you first run the program, the box is empty. To select a country, you click the down-arrow button at the right side of the box. A drop-down list of countries appears on the screen, as shown in Figure 3-11. Interestingly enough, the program reads these countries and first assigns them to the combo box list in the order in which they appear in the CURRENCY.TXT file, as shown in Figure 3-12. But, as you can see in Figure 3-11, the combo box displays the list in alphabetical order. Does this mean that you need to write a procedure that sorts the list before your program displays it? No, it doesn't. Visual Basic takes care of this detail automatically, in response to a simple property setting. The name of the property is Sorted.

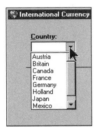

Figure 3-11: The alphabetized list of countries in the combo box list.

Figure 3-12: The countries as stored in the CURRENCY.TXT file. They are in no particular order.

To explore the Sorted property and its available settings, follow these steps:

1. Click the combo box control, near the upper-left corner of Form1.

2. Click the Categorized tab in the Properties window and scroll to the Behavior category. Click the Sorted property to select its name in the list. This property determines whether the elements of a list will appear in alphabetical order or in the original order in which they are assigned to the list. Notice that the default setting is False; this means that sorting will *not* occur.

3. Click the down-arrow button at the right side of the property setting. As you can see in Figure 3-13, there are only two settings available for the Sorted property — True and False.

4. Select the True setting.

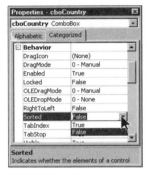

Figure 3-13: The Sorted property for a combo box.

That's all there is to it. Thanks to this simple setting, the country list will appear in alphabetical order in your program, regardless of the order of countries in the original data file. As you can see, the Sorted property is an example of a setting that enhances your program's performance without any programming effort on your part.

While you're working on the properties of the combo box, take this opportunity to scroll to the Misc category and select the Text property, which represents the current value displayed inside the combo box itself. (The setting of the Text property changes at runtime, each time the user selects a new item in the drop-down list. Your program therefore reads the user's selection by referring to this property.) At the beginning of the program run, this control should be blank:

1. Press F4 to select the property's current setting, displayed as Combo1.

2. Press Delete on your keyboard.

3. Press Enter to confirm. Notice in Form1 that the combo box is now empty.

4. While the Text property is selected in the Properties window, select the text box in Form1. As with a combo box, the Text property represents the current contents of a text box. Select and delete the current setting of this property, displayed as Text1. When you do so, the text box in Form1 is displayed as an empty box, as shown in Figure 3-14.

5. Click the Save Project button on the toolbar again to update your project on disk.

Next you'll examine two command button properties that make your program easier to use from the keyboard.

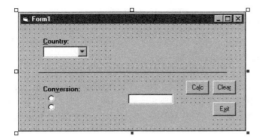

Figure 3-14: Blank Text settings for the combo box and text box.

Command Button Properties

You've already used the Caption property to supply access keys for the project's three command buttons. For example, you entered a Caption setting of **Ca&lc** for the first of the three command buttons. When the user types a numeric value into the currency text box, the purpose of clicking the Calc button is to instruct the program to perform the currency conversion — from dollars to the currently selected international currency, or vice versa. Thanks to the access key, a mouse-averse user will be able to press Alt+L from the keyboard as a substitute for clicking the Calc button.

An access key like this one is an important feature; but in many programs you may want to provide *several* ways to accomplish the same task. Redundancy in design is often the key to ease-of-use at runtime.

In this project, the most natural technique for requesting a currency calculation is perhaps to press the Enter key upon completing the input into the text box. Accordingly, you might want to add this feature to your program: Pressing Enter should be equivalent to clicking the Calc button.

Likewise, the user already has two ways of selecting the program's Exit button — click the button or press Alt+X. But because this project consists of a single dialog box, a simpler way to end the program would be to press the Escape key. Here, then, is another feature you might like to build into your program — recognizing the Escape key as a signal to terminate a run.

Visual Basic supplies two command button properties that automatically implement these two features. The properties are named Default and Cancel, and they each have two possible settings, True or False:

✦ A Default setting of True for a particular command button means that the user can press Enter from the keyboard to select the button.

✦ A Cancel setting of True for a particular command button means that the user can press Escape from the keyboard to select the button.

Each of these properties has a default setting of False for every command button you place on a form. If you decide to make use of these features, you should change the Default setting to True for only one command button and change the Cancel setting to True for a different command button.

In the Currency Exchange program, you'll designate the Calc button as the default — that is, the button that is selected when the user presses Enter. Then you'll establish Exit as the cancel button — that is, the control that's selected when the user presses Escape. Here are the steps for accomplishing this:

1. Select the Calc button in Form1.

2. In the Properties window, scroll down to the Behavior category and select Default in the properties list.

3. Change the property's setting to True by pressing T at the keyboard. (Alternatively, you can select the True setting from the drop-down list attached to the property.)

4. Select the Exit button in Form1.

5. Select Cancel in the Properties list.

6. Press T to change the setting to True.

Now activate Form1 again and take a close look at the trio of command buttons at the lower-right corner of the form. Do you notice a small change that has taken place in one of the buttons? As shown in Figure 3-15, the Calc button is now enclosed in a slightly bolder outline than the other two buttons. This visual effect indicates that Calc is now the form's default button.

Figure 3-15: Calc has become the form's default button, as indicated by the bold outline around its perimeter.

Like the Sorted property, Default and Cancel make small but important changes in your program's behavior and performance. Attention to this level of detail is what ultimately makes a program easy and inviting to use. Visual Basic encourages you to think carefully about how your user will operate the features of your program. In addition, once you've considered the best ways to design your interface, Visual Basic supplies tools and properties that make many of your design decisions very easy to implement.

A new property in Visual Basic 5 is ToolTipText in the Misc category. By entering a text setting for this property, you can provide your users with brief tips about the controls in a form. You saw examples of ToolTips in Chapter 1. Now you'll see how to create them.

The ToolTipText Property

In the following exercise, you'll enter ToolTipText settings for three of the controls on the form — the combo box, the text box, and the Calc command button. Then you'll run the program to review the effect of these settings:

1. Click the combo box control at the upper-left corner of the form.

2. In the Properties window, scroll down to the Misc category and select the ToolTipText property.

3. Enter the following text as the property's setting: **Pull this list down to select a country** (Figure 3-16).

Figure 3-16: Entering a text setting for the ToolTipText property.

4. Select the text box and type this text as the ToolTipText setting: **Enter a currency amount here.**

5. Select the Calc command button and enter this text: **Click here or press Enter to compute the exchange.**

6. Now press F5 to run the program. Rest the mouse pointer over any of the three controls to which you've just assigned ToolTipText settings. The ToolTip appears just beneath the mouse pointer, as shown in Figure 3-17.

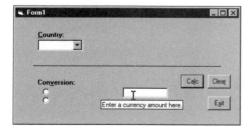

Figure 3-17: Examining ToolTips at runtime.

7. Click the Stop button on the toolbar to return to the Design mode. Then click the Save Project button to save your work.

Finally, take a quick look at three properties that apply to forms.

Form Properties

The Currency Exchange program uses Form1 to elicit input from the user and to display calculated information about currencies. From the user's point of view, this window *is* the program. Consequently, you'll want to identify this window as clearly and definitively as possible, by placing the program's name — and a representative icon — on the window's title bar. In a form, the Caption property specifies the text displayed on the title bar. Furthermore, a special form property named Icon allows you to select a predesigned icon graphic to be displayed at the far upper-left corner of the form window.

A form also has a Name property. As with other objects in a Visual Basic project, a form's Name setting provides an identifier for the form in your program's code. In this chapter's final exercise, you'll change these three properties — Caption, Icon, and Name — for the form currently named Form1:

1. Click the mouse in a blank area of Form1 — that is, at a position where no control is displayed. (Be careful not to click inside one of the blank labels.)

2. Press F4 to activate the Properties window. Notice that the notation **Form1** Form appears just beneath the window's title bar.

3. Select the Caption property in the Appearance category, and enter **International Currency Exchange** as the setting. Notice that this text now appears inside the form's title bar.

4. Select the Icon property in the Misc category, and click the **...** button displayed at the right side of the property setting. In response, Visual Basic displays a dialog box named Load Icon, as shown in Figure 3-18.

Figure 3-18: The Load Icon dialog box.

5. In the Visual Basic folder structure, open Graphics\Icons\Elements.

6. Select the Earth.ICO icon, shown in Figure 3-19.

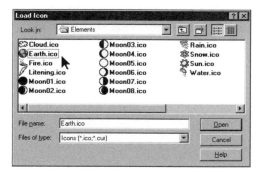

Figure 3-19: Icon files available in the Load Icon dialog box.

7. Click Open. On Form1, notice that the globe icon appears in the title bar, just to the left of the program's name, as shown in Figure 3-20. This icon represents the control menu for the form. When you click the icon at runtime, a special menu of control commands drops down onto the window.

Figure 3-20: Adding an icon to the title bar of a form.

8. Finally, click the Alphabetic tab in the Properties window and scroll up to the Name property. Select it in the list.

9. Enter **frmCurrExch** as the new name for the form. (Notice the use of *frm* as the prefix for the form name; as before, these three letters will help you identify the object type that the name represents.)

10. Now select the Project Explorer window. As shown in Figure 3-21, the new form name is recorded in this window, just next to the file name for the form.

Figure 3-21: Changing the Name setting for a form.

11. Click the Save Project button on the Visual Basic toolbar to save your work to disk. You can now exit from Visual Basic by choosing File⇨Exit.

The Next Step

You've seen the effects of several important properties in this chapter. The Caption, Font, and Text properties change your project's appearance on the screen. The TabIndex, Sorted, Default, Cancel, and ToolTipText properties define specific aspects of your program's behavior at runtime. This is only a small sampling of the many properties that apply to Visual Basic controls. You'll learn about many others as you continue in this book.

Now you're ready to develop the procedures that your program will be capable of carrying out. For that, you finally turn your attention to coding, the subject of Chapter 4.

Writing Code

After planning a project's appearance, features, and properties, your next step is to begin the essential activity of programming — writing code. Individual sections of code, known as *procedures*, define what your program will be able to do.

In this chapter you'll explore tools designed to simplify the process of developing code. Specifically you'll look at the code window and see how it's organized; you'll practice writing some short event procedures; you'll begin to discover the tips, lists, and information boxes that the editor automatically displays as you type lines of code; and you'll see how to get additional help with any element of the Visual Basic language.

Of course, program development in Visual Basic is not always a strictly linear process, flowing neatly in three distinct steps. Once you start writing code, you may often find yourself going back and revising certain elements of your basic design. For example, you may want to rearrange the controls in a form, add new objects to your program, or assign new property settings to certain controls.

Although the code itself is arguably the most challenging part of a project, Visual Basic's *event-driven* programming model gives you a clear path for organizing the work ahead of you. Once you've arranged the forms and controls that represent your program's on-screen interface, these very objects represent the procedures you'll write to complete the project.

Planning Event Procedures

Event procedures allow your program to react appropriately to the user's activities during runtime. If the user clicks a button, selects an option, changes a setting, or enters a data item, a specific event procedure determines the program's response. Knowing this, you can easily see what procedures you need to write to complete a project. Here, then, are the general steps for planning your code:

1. Identify the controls around which the main events of your program will take place — for example, the command buttons that the user can click, the text boxes where the user can enter text, and the lists from which the user selects options.

2. Determine the specific events you expect to take place around these controls.

3. Write the procedures that define your program's action when any one of these events takes place.

As you'll recall, the name of an event procedure for a particular control is a combination of two identifiers:

✦ The Name property you've assigned to the target control

✦ The name that Visual Basic defines for the event itself

In the procedure name, these two identifiers are separated by an underscore character (_), in the following format:

```
ControlName_EventName
```

For example, consider the command button named cmdClear in the Currency Exchange program you've been developing. This button represents a specific operation in the program: When the user clicks the button, you want your program to clear certain parts of the dialog box in preparation for a new calculation. Visual Basic's name for the event that takes place when the user clicks a button is — simply enough — *Click*. Accordingly, you know that the procedure you need to write for this operation is named

```
cmdClear_Click
```

This procedure will take control whenever the user clicks the Clear button.

You develop individual event procedures in a code window. You can open a separate code window for each form in a project.

The Code Window

There are two convenient ways to open a code window:

✦ Activate the Project Explorer window and select the name of the form in which you want to create a new procedure. Then click the View Code button at the upper-left corner of the Project Explorer window, as shown in Figure 4-1.

✦ Activate the form and double-click the control for which you want to create a new event procedure. (Alternatively, select a control and press F7.) In response, Visual Basic automatically writes the first and last lines of an event procedure for you.

Figure 4-1: Using the View Code button in the Project Explorer window.

The code window displays any procedures that you've already written for the selected form, and allows you to scroll from one procedure to the next. For instance, Figure 4-2 shows a code window displaying part of one procedure from the completed Currency Exchange program. In this example, the code window is maximized, and takes up all of the available space on the Visual Basic desktop. If you want to work with code in a window that can be moved and resized, click the Restore button at the right side of the Visual Basic menu bar, as shown in Figure 4-3. When you do so, the code is displayed in a separate window with its own title bar, as in Figure 4-4.

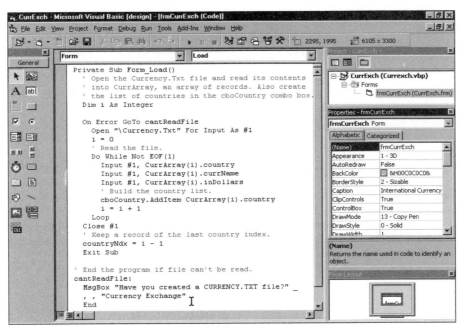

Figure 4-2: A code window displaying a procedure. This window is maximized, and takes up all of the available space in the Visual Basic environment.

Figure 4-3: By clicking the Restore button at the right side of the Visual Basic toolbar, you can change the shape and appearance of the code window.

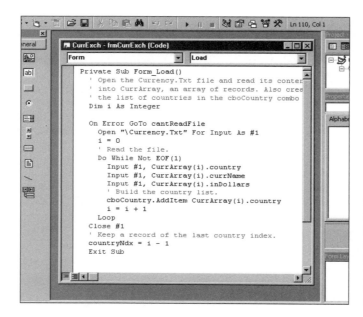

Figure 4-4: This is the code window after the Restore button has been clicked. In this format, the window can be resized and moved to new positions on the desktop.

Two ways of viewing procedures

The code window can display the procedures of your project in either of two ways:

✦ In the Procedure View, the window displays one procedure at a time. You can use the PgUp and PgDn keys to move from one procedure to the next. Figures 4-2 and 4-4 show code windows in the Procedure View.

✦ In the Full Module View, the window displays multiple procedures, separated by horizontal lines, as in Figure 4-5.

Toggle between these two views by clicking one of the two buttons at the lower-left corner of the code window, as shown in Figure 4-6. The button on the left switches the window to the Procedure View mode, and the button on the right switches to Full Module View.

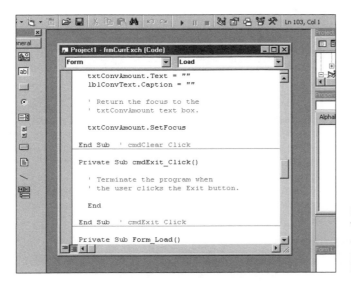

Figure 4-5: In Full Module View, the code window displays multiple procedures, separated by horizontal lines.

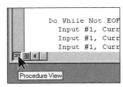

Figure 4-6: The Procedure View and Full Module View buttons are located at the lower-left corner of the code window.

As you begin writing code, you'll find different situations in which each of these code views is useful. Procedure View helps you focus on the code of one particular procedure; Full Module View can be important when you want to compare code in different procedures.

Learning the features of the code window

Of course, if you haven't yet begun writing code in a project, the code window is initially empty. To get started with this chapter's exercises, you begin by reopening your unfinished version of the Currency Exchange program and taking a first look at the code window on your own screen:

1. Pull down the File menu and choose CurrTemp.Vbp from the list of recently-opened projects at the bottom of the menu list. (Alternatively, choose File⇨Open and select the project you want to open.)

2. Press Ctrl+R if necessary to open the Project Explorer window. Open the Forms folder and select the name of the project's form, frmCurrExch, as shown in Figure 4-7.

Figure 4-7: Selecting the frmCurrExch form in the Project Explorer window.

3. Click the View Code button at the top of the Project Explorer window to open the code window for this form. Because you haven't written any code yet, the window is empty, as shown in Figure 4-8. Near the top of the window you can see two boxes, called the Object box and the Procedure box. At the outset, these boxes are designed to help you select the controls and events for which you need to write procedures. Later, they'll give you a quick way to navigate to any procedure you've written in your program.

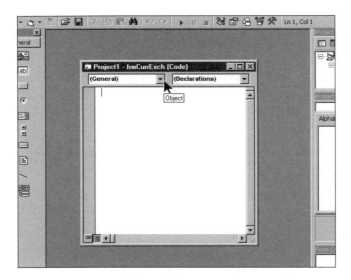

Figure 4-8: The empty code window. Just beneath the title bar you see the Object box on the left, and the Procedure box on the right.

4. Click the down-arrow button just to the right of the Object box. As shown in Figure 4-9, this scrollable list displays the names of all the controls you've placed in the active form. Any one of these controls can ultimately become the object of an event procedure. For now, click the name of one of the form's command buttons, cmdClear. When you do so, Visual Basic displays the first and last lines of the cmdClear_Click procedure in the code window. These lines serve as a kind of template for creating the procedure. A flashing cursor appears in the space between the two lines, indicating that Visual Basic is ready for you to begin entering additional lines of code.

Figure 4-9: The Object list shows the names of all the controls that the current form contains.

5. Click the down-arrow button just to the right of the Procedure box. This list displays the names of all the predefined events that can take place around the control you've selected in the Object box. As you can see in Figure 4-10, Click is only one of a list of events that may take place around a command button. Press Escape when you've finished examining the Procedure list.

Figure 4-10: The Procedure list displays the names of the event procedures that can occur around a selected object.

6. Now click the Close button at the upper-right corner of the code window. The code window disappears temporarily from the desktop.

7. In the Project window, click the View Form button to reopen the Form window. Click the window's Maximize button. The project's form appears on the screen, displaying the controls you've created to represent specific operations (Figure 4-11).

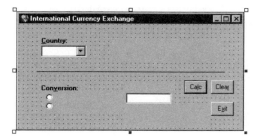

Figure 4-11: The form you've created for the Currency Exchange program.

8. Double-click the Exit button at the lower-right corner of the form. In response, Visual Basic once again opens the code window and creates the template for another event procedure, this time cmdExit_Click (Figure 4-12). You can now begin writing the code for the Click procedures you've created.

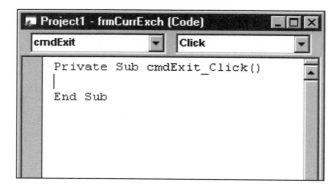

Figure 4-12: The initial code template for the cmdExit_Click event procedure.

While a code window is open, you can use the vertical scrollbar at the right side of the window to scroll through the existing code, or you can press PgUp or PgDn to scroll from one procedure to another. Alternatively, you can make selections in the Object and Procedure boxes to go directly to any procedure. First select the name of a control from the Object box, then select the name of an event from the Procedure box. In the Procedure list, Visual Basic uses boldfacing to indicate the names of any events for which you've already written procedures, as illustrated in Figure 4-13.

Figure 4-13: Boldfacing indicates event procedures that you've already written.

Again, it's up to you to decide which event procedures to write for a given project, depending on the actions you want your program to respond to. Although Visual Basic defines many different events for a given class of control, you may decide that only a small selection of these events — one or two — are relevant to your plans for a particular program.

The split bar

As you begin filling in the event procedures for a particular form, you may find that the text of your code — known as the *listing* — quickly becomes long and unwieldy. Of course, you can maximize the code window to give yourself as much viewing space as possible. But sometimes you may want to view two distant parts of your code at once. For example, you may want to compare the techniques you've implemented in two different procedures. Or you may want to perform a cut-and-paste or copy-and-paste operation to transfer a particular passage of code from one place to another. In this case, the code window has a convenient tool that allows you to divide the viewing space in two. The tool is called the *split bar*, and it's initially represented by a small horizontal rectangle located just above the scroll bar. To split the code window, follow these steps:

1. Position the mouse pointer over the split bar. As shown in Figure 4-14, the pointer becomes a two-headed arrow icon.

Figure 4-14: Use the split bar to divide the code window into two panes, for viewing two distant sections of code at once.

2. Hold down the left mouse button, and drag the split bar down the vertical scroll bar. When you do so, the code window is divided into two *panes*. Release the mouse button when the split appears where you want it.

3. Select either pane by clicking inside its code area. Then use the Object box and the Procedure box to select the event procedure that will be displayed inside the current pane. Alternatively, use the scroll bars at the right side of the code window to scroll through each pane independently.

For example, Figure 4-15 shows a code window in which the two panes display different parts of the complete Currency Exchange program. To remove the split and restore the code window to a single pane, you can drag the split bar back up to its original position near the top of the window. (Alternatively, try double-clicking the split bar.)

Using the Editor

The code window represents all the built-in capabilities of the Visual Basic editor, the environment in which you enter and revise the text of your code. This editor provides many important features designed to make programming as easy as it can be; for example:

✦ Code is displayed in multiple colors, so you can easily pick out different elements of the program.

✦ The editor automatically supplies pop-up lists and boxes of information to help you complete the individual statements of your program as efficiently as possible.

✦ You can include comments in your code to provide explanations of your program, written in your own words.

✦ The code window gives you a direct link to Visual Basic's help system whenever you need quick information about a particular element of the language itself.

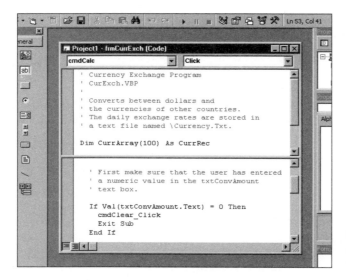

Figure 4-15: Viewing two different sections of code in the panes of a window.

You'll learn more about these topics as you begin entering procedures into the Currency Exchange program. You'll also discover another important feature of the Visual Basic development environment. You can often test the performance of a given procedure, long before you've written all the program's code. To do so, you run the program and simulate the action that triggers a specific event, resulting in a performance of the event procedure you want to test. You'll try out this process in the next exercise.

Creating Event Procedures

The goal of the steps ahead is to create two of the program's simplest event procedures: cmdClear_Click and cmdExit_Click. As you've seen, the first of these clears the text box on the form so that the user can start a new currency calcula-tion. The second terminates the program. Together, these two procedures contain only a few lines of code, so you'll be able to complete them quickly. For now, don't worry too much about the *meaning* of the code; just concentrate on the mechanical steps required for successfully entering the code into your project:

1. Activate the code window for the Currency Exchange form and click the Maximize button at the upper-right corner of the window. Scroll to the cmdClear_Click procedure, which you started creating in the previous exercise. Click the mouse on the blank line in the middle of the procedure, between the Private Sub and End Sub lines. The flashing cursor appears at the beginning of the line, indicating that the editor is ready for you to begin typing code.

2. Press Enter to create another blank line. Then press the spacebar twice to create a two-space indent for the first line of text you're about to type.

3. Type the following two lines, starting each with a single-quote character and pressing Enter at the end of each line:

```
' Clear the previous conversion
' calculation.
```

Visual Basic recognizes any line of text that begins with a single-quote character as a comment, a brief explanation that you write in plain English to help you (or others) keep track of the various parts of your code. When you run your program, Visual Basic ignores the comment lines. Comments are displayed in green to distinguish them from executable statements. Press Enter again to place a blank line between the comments and the first statement of the procedure.

4. Begin typing the following statement, which will eventually assign a new setting to the Text property of the txtConvAmount text box:

```
txtConvAmount.
```

As you'll recall, the notation for identifying a property in code is *controlName.propertyName*, where the name of the target control and the name of the property are separated by a period. When you type the period in this first statement, you may be surprised to see that a list of property names pops up in the editor, as shown in Figure 4-16. Specifically, the list contains all the properties available for a text box control. This feature is known as *Auto List Members*. To complete this statement, you can scroll down the list and select a property name.

5. Try it now. Press the down-arrow key on your keyboard repeatedly to scroll through the list of text box properties (or just hold the key down for a continuous scroll through the list). In this case, the property you want to change is Text. When Text is highlighted in the list, as shown in Figure 4-17, press the Tab key on the keyboard. The editor adds the selected property name to the statement, and leaves the flashing cursor at the end of the line so you can continue.

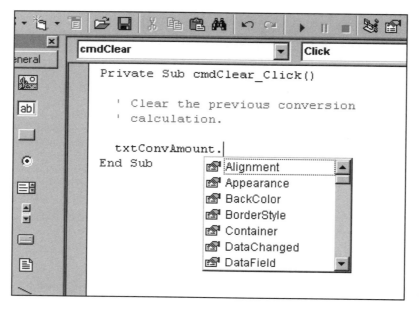

Figure 4-16: Exploring the Auto List Members feature. You can choose a property name from the list that pops up in the code window.

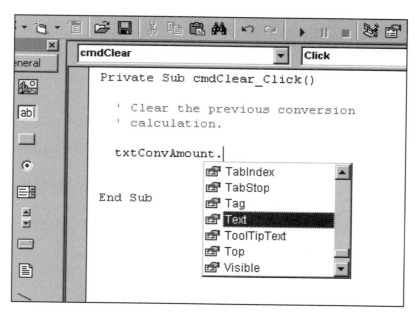

Figure 4-17: Scroll down the list of properties by pressing the down-arrow or by using the scroll bar at the right side of the list.

6. To complete the statement, type = "" (an equal sign, followed by a space and two quotation marks). Then press Enter to move to the next line of the procedure. Your work up to now appears as shown in Figure 4-18.

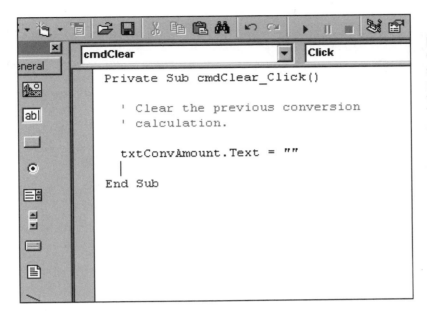

Figure 4-18: Once you've selected a property from the list, press Tab to confirm your selection. The Editor adds the property name to your current statement. You can then complete the statement by typing additional characters.

7. The next statement assigns a new setting to the Caption property of the label control named lblConvText. Try typing this line completely from the keyboard, without using the list of properties that the editor supplies. Just ignore the list when it appears; continue typing the line and then press Enter:

```
lblConvText.Caption = ""
```

As you see, you always have the option of using the pop-up list to select a property name, or simply typing the entire line manually. The list is available whenever you need help identifying a property in code. Notice the format of the two statements you've entered so far. At the left side of the equal sign, *controlName.propertyName* identifies the control and its property; at the right side you enter the new property setting. In this procedure, both the Text property of a text box and the Caption property of a label are reset to empty strings. This is the equivalent of deleting the Caption setting in the Properties window.

8. Now enter two more lines of comments:

```
' Return the focus to the
' txtConvAmount text box.
```

9. Finally, begin entering another line of code:

```
txtConvAmount.
```

When you type the period, you'll once again see the Auto List Members feature; scroll down the list to find the name SetFocus, as shown in Figure 4-19. Notice the distinct icon that is displayed for SetFocus in the pop-up list. SetFocus is a *method*, not a property. A *method* is a built-in procedure that performs an operation on a specific control or object. In this case, the control is the txtConvAmount text box; the SetFocus method returns the focus of the program to this control. (You'll learn much more about methods in later chapters.)

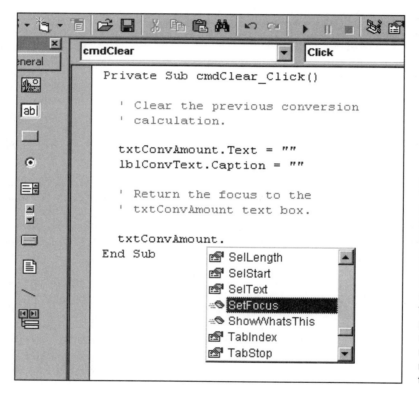

Figure 4-19: The Auto List Members feature includes both properties and methods. Notice the two different icons that identify property names and method names in the list.

10. Press the Tab key and then Enter to complete the call to the SetFocus method. When you've completed this final line, the cmdClear_Click procedure looks like Figure 4-20. On the screen you can see the color scheme that Visual Basic uses for displaying your code: comments are in green, the *keywords* of the language itself (for example, Private, Sub, and End) are displayed in blue, and other text is in black. You'll see yet another display color before you finish with this program.

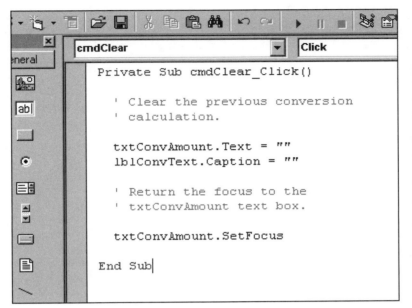

Figure 4-20: This is the complete cmdClear_Click procedure. When the user clicks the Clear button, this procedure clears information from a text box and a label, and returns the focus to the text box.

11. Scroll down to the cmdExit_Click procedure, located just below the cmdClear_Click procedure. Position the cursor on the blank line between the first and last line of the procedure, and press Enter. Type the keyword **End** and press Enter again. This procedure will terminate your program when the Exit button is clicked.

The Auto List Members feature is only one of the ways in which the editor supplies useful information about the Visual Basic language. Another feature, known as *Auto Quick Info*, displays a syntax description on the screen for any built-in *function* that you begin entering into your code. A function is a tool that calculates a value or performs some other useful operation in your program. For example, the cmdCalc_Click procedure in the Currency Exchange project uses a function named Val to confirm that the user has made a numeric entry into the conversion text box. If you were typing this procedure into the code window, you would see the small information box shown in Figure 4-21 as soon as you began entering Val. The box shows you the syntax that Visual Basic expects for correct usage of the Val function. You'll learn much more about built-in functions — and the Auto Quick Info feature — as you continue in this book.

You've now written your first two event procedures, both of them designed to respond to clicks on command buttons. You can now close the code window (by clicking the Close button at the far right side of the Visual Basic menu bar) and then click the Save Project button on Visual Basic's toolbar to save your work to disk. You're ready to try running the program to experiment with these two procedures.

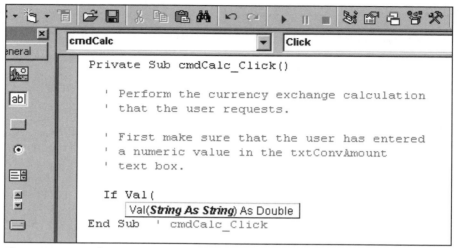

Figure 4-21: An illustration of the Auto Quick Info feature. While you're entering code into the editor, Visual Basic supplies syntax information for the use of built-in functions.

Testing Event Procedures

Even though the two procedures you've written are small parts of the whole program, they cover details that you can easily test during a program run. In the upcoming steps, you'll start the program and confirm that the cmdClear_Click and cmdExit_Click procedures are running properly:

1. Press F5 or click the Start button on the Visual Basic toolbar to start the program. The International Currency Exchange window appears on the desktop, although most of the features eventually planned for the application are not yet implemented. For example, there's no available list from which you can choose a country.

2. Press the Tab key twice to activate the text box located just to the left of the three command buttons. Type any sequence of digits into this box, as though you were planning to convert a monetary amount from one currency to another. For example, in Figure 4-22, the amount 123456789 has been entered into the box.

3. Click the Calc button, or press Alt+L — just as you might do if the program were fully operational at this point. The program gives no response, but your action does move the focus from the text box to the Calc button. (Two small details indicate that this is the case: The flashing cursor disappears from the text box and a dotted rectangular frame appears around the caption of the Calc button.)

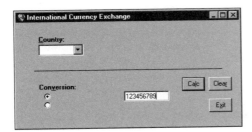

Figure 4-22: Testing the program at an early stage.

4. Now click the Clear button, or press Alt+R. As you know, this action triggers a call to the cmdClear_Click procedure that you've written in the code window for this form. The procedure performs two visible actions: First the number you've typed into the text box is erased from view; and second, the focus returns to the text box, as indicated by the reappearance of the flashing vertical cursor.

5. Finally, click the Exit button, or press Alt+X. As predicted, this action triggers a call to the cmdExit_Click procedure, resulting in a termination of the program performance.

From this sequence of events, you know that the code you've written so far is working as expected. Programmers are not always so lucky. The first time you try to run new code — even a small amount of code consisting of only a few lines — a great variety of problems can prevent a successful performance of your program. Fortunately, Visual Basic provides a number of tools that will help you write good code as early as possible in the process. You've already seen how the Auto List Members and Auto Quick Info features provide useful information while you're entering code. You'll look at some additional tools in the next section of this chapter.

Syntax Checking and Keyword Help

As you write your program's code, the Visual Basic editor automatically checks the syntax of each line you enter. *Syntax* refers to the basic grammatical rules of the programming language — the format Visual Basic expects you to follow for each particular statement in your code. If the editor finds that something is wrong with a given line, two distinct events tell you clearly that you've made a mistake:

✦ The mistyped line is displayed in red, highlighting the fact that there's some kind of syntax error in your code.

✦ An error message appears on the screen, briefly identifying the possible problem.

This sequence may take place many times while you're developing your program's code. The first few times you see the bright red highlighting accompanied by an abrupt error message, you may feel a bit disconcerted. But you'll soon learn to appreciate Visual Basic's direct technique for letting you know that something is wrong.

A good step to take immediately after an error message appears is to open the Visual Basic Help window for a review of the correct syntax. Fortunately, help is just a single keystroke away. With the cursor positioned next to a Basic keyword in the code window, you simply press F1 to get help with the syntax of that keyword.

To experiment with these features, you'll try adding another few lines of code to your program in the next exercise. Specifically, you'll go to the Declarations section of the frmCurrExch form and try entering two Dim statements to declare variables for your program. A *variable* is a name you define to represent a particular value in a program — for example, a number, a string of text, or a date. A Dim statement allows you to declare a variable name at the outset of your program. You'll learn lots more about variables and Dim statements in Chapter 7. Meanwhile, the following exercise will help you understand Visual Basic's syntax checking and help system:

1. Activate the code window again and pull down the Object list from the top of the window. Scroll to the top of the list and select the entry that reads (*General*), as shown in Figure 4-23. In response, the Visual Basic editor scrolls up to the *General Declarations section* of your code, where you can write special declarations that apply to the entire form (Figure 4-24). The Dim statement is one of the declarations that typically appears in this section.

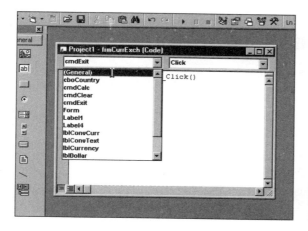

Figure 4-23: Scrolling to the General Declarations section of the program.

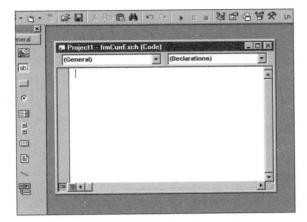

Figure 4-24: In the General Declarations section, you can write Dim statements to define variables for use in the form.

2. Type the keyword **dim**. (Enter the word in all lowercase letters for the moment.) In the correct syntax of this statement, the keyword is followed by the name of a variable you want to declare. But in this exercise, you're going to make an intentional error, omitting any further information on the Dim line.

3. Press the Enter key after typing *dim*. As you can see in Figure 4-25, Visual Basic immediately displays a small dialog box on the desktop with the error message "Expected: identifier." In essence, this message means that you pressed Enter before completing the Dim statement. In the code window, the keyword *dim* is now displayed in red, further emphasizing the fact that you've made a mistake.

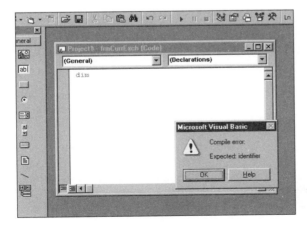

Figure 4-25: An error message appears in response to a syntax error.

   4. Click OK to close the dialog box. Back in the code window, the flashing
       cursor is located immediately after *dim*.

   5. Press F1. In response, Visual Basic opens its Help window and immediately
       displays the topic that fully describes the usage and syntax of the Dim
       statement, as shown in Figure 4-26. You can now read this information to
       figure out exactly what you did wrong in your line of code.

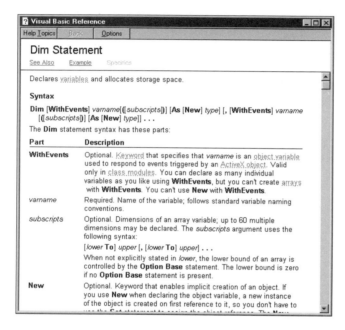

Figure 4-26: Jumping to the Visual Basic Help system.

In short, the Visual Basic editor constantly watches over your work, and is always
ready to direct your attention to an error.

Press the Escape key to close the Help window. Now you can complete your code
entry into the Declaration section. Complete the Dim statement as follows:

```
dim countryNdx as integer
```

As you do so, you'll see yet another example of the Auto Member List feature.
After you type the word **as**, a list appears in the code window to show you the
various ways you can declare a variable (Figure 4-27).

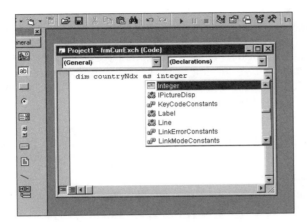

Figure 4-27: Here the Auto Member List feature supplies a list of the data types you can use for declaring a variable in a Dim statement.

Complete the statement and press Enter. If you watch closely, you'll see an additional feature that the editor uses to help you with your work — this time to confirm that you've entered the line correctly. You've entered the code mostly in lowercase letters, but the editor automatically capitalizes the first letter of each keyword when you press Enter:

```
Dim countryNdx As Integer
```

Furthermore, the Basic keywords in this statement — *Dim*, *As*, and *Integer* — appear as blue text. These small adjustments in the text of your code reassure you that you've followed the correct syntax rules for these lines. Your Declaration section now looks like Figure 4-28.

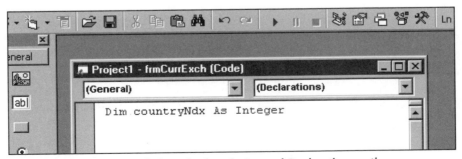

Figure 4-28: Entering code into the form's General Declaration section.

Now click the Save button on the toolbar to save your work to disk. You've seen one kind of error that can occur while you're developing a program's code. A syntax error prevents a successful run of your program; accordingly, Visual Basic encourages you to correct this type of error immediately. By contrast, a *logical* error in your code may not stop you from running your program, but may instead lead to incorrect results or unexpected behavior. Logical errors can be much more difficult to correct than syntax errors. For this reason, Visual Basic supplies a collection of techniques known as *debugging tools*, designed specifically to help you find and correct logical errors in a running program. Chapter 5 introduces some of these tools, although you may want to postpone using them until you've had more experience with writing code.

As a final exercise, you'll open the finished Currency Exchange Program from this book's program disk and take a brief look at the procedures the program contains. Along the way, you'll preview some of the major programming topics you'll be studying in the chapters ahead.

Examining the Code in a Finished Program

You'll find the complete code of the Currency Exchange program printed in Appendix A. Alternatively, you can look at the code directly on your screen. Open the program (CurrExch.Vbp) from disk and, if necessary, press Ctrl+R to open the Project window. The finished program contains one form, CurrExch.Frm, which contains all the project's code. Select this form and click the View Code button to open the code window.

Procedures

Begin with a brief overview of the listing. Each event procedure in the form begins with a *Private Sub* statement; for example, here's the first line of the cboCountry_Click procedure:

```
Private Sub cboCountry_Click
```

The *Sub* keyword identifies this block of code as a procedure, and *Private* indicates that the procedure is available for use only within the current form. As you'll recall, Visual Basic creates this line for you when you take the steps to create a new event procedure. Visual Basic also enters an *End Sub* statement as the final line of each procedure. To create an unambiguous marker for the end of each procedure, you can append a comment to each *End Sub* line, identifying the procedure by name; for example:

```
End Sub   ' cboCountry_Click
```

Although this extra comment is optional, it helps you see clearly where one procedure ends and another begins.

Long lines of code

Another important feature that you may notice in your first glance through the program listing is the convenient *line continuation* character. Visual Basic allows you to break very long statements into multiple lines of text in your listing. To indicate that two or more lines belong to the same statement, you place a space and an underscore character (_) at the end of each line except the last one. There are several appearances of the line continuation character in the cboCountry_Click procedure (Figure 4-29). For example, consider the following statement:

```
lblCurrency.Caption = "One " & _
    CurrArray(i).currName & " = " & _
    CurrArray(i).inDollars & _
    " U.S. dollar(s)"
```

```
cboCountry                          Click

Private Sub cboCountry_Click()
  ' Read the user's country choice
  ' and display the exchange rates
  ' for the currency of the selected
  ' country.

  Dim i As Integer
  For i = 0 To countryNdx
    If cboCountry.Text = CurrArray(i).country Then
      lblDollar.Caption = "One U.S. dollar = " & _
        1 / CurrArray(i).inDollars & " " & _
        CurrArray(i).currName & "(s)"
      lblCurrency.Caption = "One " & _
        CurrArray(i).currName & " = " & _
        CurrArray(i).inDollars & _
        " U.S. dollar(s)"
      currCountry = i
    End If
  Next i

  ' Display captions for the conversion
  ' option buttons.

  optDollarsTo.Caption = "U.S. dollars to " & _
    CurrArray(currCountry).currName & "s"
  optCurrTo.Caption = CurrArray(currCountry).currName
    "s to U.S. dollars"
```

Figure 4-29: The cboCountry_Click procedure contains several examples of the line continuation character. This feature allows you to separate a single statement into two or more lines of code.

These four lines make up a single statement, the purpose of which is to assign a new setting to the Caption property of the lblCurrency label. As long as you use the line continuation character correctly, Visual Basic reads these lines as a single statement. By breaking the statement into multiple lines, you avoid the printing problems that sometimes occur when a program contains very long lines of code. (In a printed listing, long lines can sometimes be broken up arbitrarily, making your code difficult to read.)

Variables and data structures

As you've seen, the General Declarations section, at the top of the code (Figure 4-30), contains declarations for the variables used in the program. The Currency Exchange program needs a convenient way to store and access the country names, currency names, and exchange rates it reads from the CURRENCY.TXT file. For this purpose, it declares an *array of records* called *CurrArray*:

```
Dim CurrArray(30) As CurrRec
```

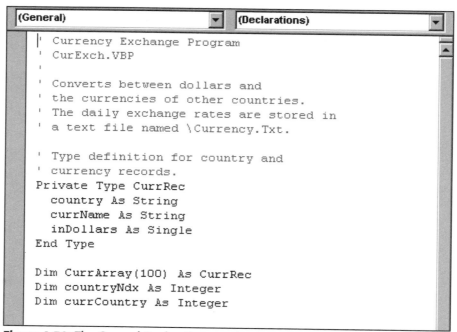

```
(General)                    ▼   (Declarations)                ▼

|' Currency Exchange Program                                    ▲
 ' CurExch.VBP
 '
 ' Converts between dollars and
 ' the currencies of other countries.
 ' The daily exchange rates are stored in
 ' a text file named \Currency.Txt.

 ' Type definition for country and
 ' currency records.
Private Type CurrRec
   country As String
   currName As String
   inDollars As Single
End Type

Dim CurrArray(100) As CurrRec
Dim countryNdx As Integer
Dim currCountry As Integer
```

Figure 4-30: The General Declarations section contains a Type declaration along with Dim statements for the program's key variables and data structures.

An array is an indexed variable that can represent many data values at once. Each element of *CurrArray* is a structure representing the data for one country — name, currency, and exchange rate. The program defines this structure as follows:

```
Private Type CurrRec
   country As String
   currName As String
   inDollars As Single
End Type
```

In addition, the program declares two numeric variables to keep track of the currency data:

```
Dim countryNdx As Integer
Dim currCountry As Integer
```

The variable named *countryNdx* represents the number of countries read from the data file; and *currCountry* identifies the country that the user has chosen most recently from the Country list.

Understanding variables, data types, and data structures is essential to your success as a programmer. You'll examine these topics in detail in Chapters 7 and 9.

The Form_Load procedure

The first event procedure performed in this program is *not* triggered by a user action such as a mouse click or a data entry. Rather, the Form_Load procedure (Figure 4-31) is performed automatically at the beginning of the run, when the program first opens the Currency Exchange form onto the desktop. In many applications, a Form_Load procedure is a good place for you to write code that initializes your program's variables and performs any other tasks that need to take place at the outset.

In the Currency Exchange program, the Form_Load procedure opens the Currency.Txt file from its storage location in the root directory of your hard disk:

```
Open "\Currency.Txt" For Input As #1
```

The procedure then reads all of the file's data into the *CurrArray* structure:

```
Do While Not EOF(1)
   Input #1, CurrArray(i).country
   Input #1, CurrArray(i).currName
   Input #1, CurrArray(i).inDollars
    ' Build the country list.
   cboCountry.AddItem CurrArray(i).country
   i = i + 1
Loop
```

After reading each record of data from the file, the procedure appends the name of the current country to the Country combo box, represented by the name cboCountry. (Another Visual Basic method, named AddItem, allows the program to build the combo box list.)

```
Form                        ▼   Load                           ▼

Private Sub Form_Load()
  ' Open the Currency.Txt file and read its contents
  ' into CurrArray, an array of records. Also create
  ' the list of countries in the cboCountry combo box.
  Dim i As Integer

  On Error GoTo cantReadFile
    Open "\Currency.Txt" For Input As #1
    i = 0
    ' Read the file.
    Do While Not EOF(1)
      Input #1, CurrArray(i).country
      Input #1, CurrArray(i).currName
      Input #1, CurrArray(i).inDollars
      ' Build the country list.
      cboCountry.AddItem CurrArray(i).country
      i = i + 1
    Loop
  Close #1
  ' Keep a record of the last country index.
  countryNdx = i - 1
  Exit Sub

' End the program if file can't be read.
cantReadFile:
  MsgBox "Have you created a CURRENCY.TXT file?" _
  , , "Currency Exchange"
  End
End Sub  ' Form_Load
```

Figure 4-31: The Form_Load procedure opens and reads the CURRENCY.TXT file at the beginning of a program performance. If the file doesn't exist, an error trap takes control and displays an error message.

Data file programming techniques are important in any programming language because they allow you to access information from files stored on disk. You'll study this topic in Chapter 10. The Form_Load procedure also illustrates a use of the On Error Goto statement to set up a structure called an *error trap*. This trap is triggered in the event that the program is unable to find and read the CURRENCY.TXT file. As you saw in Chapter 2, the program displays an error message and terminates the performance if the file can't be found. All these details are arranged in the Form_Load procedure. Chapter 10 also introduces you to error trapping.

The Click procedures

After reading the currency exchange data from disk, the program is ready to respond to the user's selections in the dialog box. Each of the user's possible actions — selecting an entry from the Country list, changing the setting of the option buttons, or clicking a command button — triggers a particular Click procedure, which defines the program's response:

✦ The cboCountry_Click procedure is called when the user pulls down the Country list and selects the name of a country. In response, this procedure calculates and displays the dollar-to-currency and currency-to-dollar exchange rates in the two labels located just to the right of the Country list. It also adjusts the option button captions appropriately.

✦ One of the two procedures in Figure 4-32 (optCurrTo_Click or optDollarsTo_Click) is called when the user clicks a Conversion option button. These short procedures take charge of supplying an appropriate label above the text box.

✦ When the user enters a numeric amount in the text box and then clicks the Calc button, the cmdCalc_Click procedure (Figure 4-33) is called. This procedure performs the conversion arithmetic, and displays the result in the label located just below the text box.

```
optCurrTo                          ▼    Click                          ▼

    Private Sub optCurrTo_Click()

        ' Change the conversion option:
        ' foreign currency to U.S. dollars.

        lblConvCurr = CurrArray(currCountry).currName & "(s):"
        cmdClear_Click

    End Sub    ' optCurrTo_Click


    Private Sub optDollarsTo_Click()

        ' Change the currency option:
        ' U.S. dollars to foreign currency.

        lblConvCurr = "U.S. dollar(s):"
        cmdClear_Click

    End Sub    ' optDollarsTo_Click
```

Figure 4-32: The Click procedures for the program's two option buttons take care of adjusting label captions when the user chooses a new conversion option.

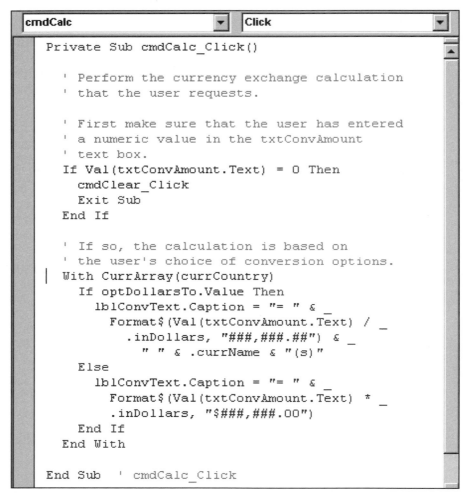

```
cmdCalc                         ▼    Click                          ▼

   Private Sub cmdCalc_Click()

     ' Perform the currency exchange calculation
     ' that the user requests.

     ' First make sure that the user has entered
     ' a numeric value in the txtConvAmount
     ' text box.
     If Val(txtConvAmount.Text) = 0 Then
       cmdClear_Click
       Exit Sub
     End If

     ' If so, the calculation is based on
     ' the user's choice of conversion options.
     With CurrArray(currCountry)
       If optDollarsTo.Value Then
         lblConvText.Caption = "= " & _
           Format$(Val(txtConvAmount.Text) / _
             .inDollars, "###,###.##") & _
               " " & .currName & "(s)"
       Else
         lblConvText.Caption = "= " & _
           Format$(Val(txtConvAmount.Text) * _
           .inDollars, "$###,###.00")
       End If
     End With

   End Sub   ' cmdCalc_Click
```

Figure 4-33: The cmdCalc_Click procedure converts a monetary amount from one currency to another.

✦ As you've seen, two additional event procedures (Figure 4-34) represent the program's response to clicks on the Clear and Exit buttons. The cmdClear_Click procedure prepares the dialog box for a new currency exchange calculation, and the cmdExit_Click procedure ends the program run.

As you examine these procedures, you'll find a variety of interesting *control structures*, designed to carry out decisions (If) and repetitions (For and Do) during the course of the program. You'll study these structures in Chapter 9.

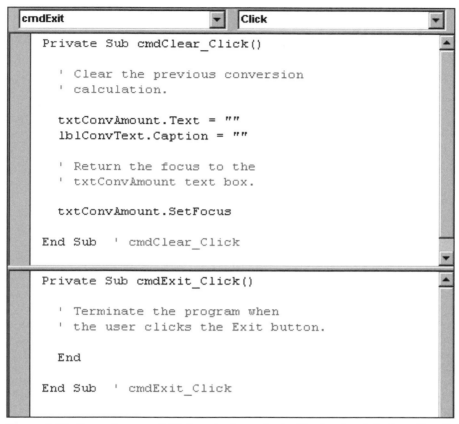

```
cmdExit ▼          Click ▼

Private Sub cmdClear_Click()

   ' Clear the previous conversion
   ' calculation.

   txtConvAmount.Text = ""
   lblConvText.Caption = ""

   ' Return the focus to the
   ' txtConvAmount text box.

   txtConvAmount.SetFocus

End Sub  ' cmdClear_Click


Private Sub cmdExit_Click()

   ' Terminate the program when
   ' the user clicks the Exit button.

   End

End Sub   ' cmdExit_Click
```

Figure 4-34: Two other small Click procedures deal with clearing data from the dialog box and terminating the program performance.

In summary, the code in the Currency Exchange program illustrates many of the language structures and programming techniques covered in Part II of this book. Now that you've looked briefly at the code, you might want to take a moment to run the program again. As you make selections from the controls in the application's dialog box, you'll now have a new perspective on the meaning of the event-driven programming model.

Debugging a Program's Code

Debugging is the process of locating and analyzing logical errors in your code — and correcting them so that your program behaves the way you want it to. Depending on the subtlety of the error, this process may demand a keen mastery of language nuances, a galling outlay of time and effort, and a generous measure of luck. The difference between a program that works and a program that fails can be a single digit or character in your code; but finding and recognizing the problem can take many hours — or days — of hard work.

Visual Basic 5 provides an accessible collection of debugging tools to help you along your way. This chapter presents two exercises designed to demonstrate many of those tools in action. Both exercises are provided as projects on this book's program disk:

   ✦ Bug1.Vbp is a version of the Currency Exchange program you developed in Chapters 2, 3, and 4. For the purposes of this exercise, the program's code has been slightly sabotaged with the introduction of a small but significant bug. You'll begin by running and testing the program to find out what's going wrong in this version. Then, as you work through the steps of debugging the code, you'll use a simple but elegant new feature known as Auto Data Tips to find the error.

   ✦ Bug2.Vbp is a more complex exercise. It's a bug-afflicted version of the International Sales application, which you'll encounter formally in Chapter 11. Fixing this program will give you the opportunity to work with several tools, all represented by icons on the Debug toolbar.

Like other elements of the development environment, Visual Basic's debugging tools are interactive, intuitive, and easy to use. But successful debugging requires a detailed understanding of the code that you're working with. For this reason, you might decide to postpone working step-by-step through this chapter's two exercises until you've learned more about the Visual Basic language. Even so, it's a good idea to read through the chapter once just to gain a general familiarity with the tools it covers. You can come back and investigate this material in greater detail at a later point in your progress through this book.

Categories of Errors

While you're developing a project, Visual Basic helps you find and correct errors in a variety of important ways. Three categories of errors typically occur during application development:

✦ *Your code contains syntactical or structural errors that prevent the program from running.* In some cases, Visual Basic displays an error message as soon as you enter a syntactically flawed statement into the editor. For example, suppose you type the keyword **If** onto a line of the code window and then press Enter. As shown in Figure 5-1, Visual Basic immediately recognizes this as an incomplete line of code, and displays an error message to let you know that you've forgotten the expression that should follow If. In other cases, an error message appears when you attempt to run the program. For example, if you enter an If statement as the beginning of a decision block in your code, but forget to place an End If statement at the end of the structure, an error message appears when you first try to run the program, as shown in Figure 5-2. These are known as *compile errors*, because they take place at the time when Visual Basic is attempting to translate your source code into executable code.

✦ *An error condition causes your program to fail at a certain point during a performance.* One example is an attempt to open a file for reading when the file doesn't exist on disk. In response to this error, Visual Basic interrupts your program run and displays the error message shown in Figure 5-3. Another common example is division by zero. Problems like these are known as *runtime errors*.

✦ *Your program runs without interruption, but it doesn't work as expected.* For example, the program might produce incorrect output, or it might respond inappropriately to an event. These are known as *logical errors,* and they can be the most difficult kinds of problems to correct.

Figure 5-1: An error message that appears when you first enter an incorrect statement into the editor.

Figure 5-2: An error message that appears when you attempt to run a program that contains an incorrect structure.

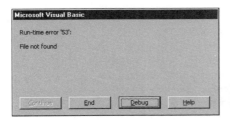

Figure 5-3: The error message that appears when your program attempts to open a file that doesn't exist.

Debugging Tools

Visual Basic's debugging tools are designed to help you find and correct logical errors and runtime errors. Most of these tools are represented by the buttons on the Debug toolbar, shown in Figure 5-4. There are two easy ways to open this toolbar onto the desktop:

✦ Click the Standard toolbar or the menu bar with the right mouse button, and choose Debug from the resulting shortcut menu (Figure 5-5).

✦ Choose View⇨Toolbars⇨Debug.

Figure 5-4: The Debug toolbar contains buttons representing Visual Basic's major debugging tools.

Figure 5-5: One way to open the Debug toolbar is to click the Standard toolbar with the right mouse button and then choose Debug from the resulting shortcut menu.

Table 5-1 provides a brief summary of the dozen buttons you see on the Debug toolbar. Notice that the first three buttons — Run, Break, and End — are also found on the Standard toolbar. The equivalent menu commands for the buttons on the Debug toolbar are located in the View, Debug, and Run menus. In the course of this chapter you'll learn much more about the tools that these icons represent.

Table 5-1 Debug Toolbar Buttons		
Debug Button	*Description*	*Shortcut Key*
Run	Begins a performance of the current project. Changes to Continue during break mode.	F5
Break	Causes a break in the performance of the current program. The Visual Basic title bar displays the notation [break]. In this mode, you can use debugging tools to investigate conditions at a particular point in the program's performance.	Ctrl+Break
End	Ends the performance of the current project. This button is available both at runtime and in the break mode.	
Toggle Breakpoint	Allows you to specify a line of code where your program's performance will break so that you can investigate the conditions at a specific point in the run.	F9
Step Into	Allows you to perform lines of code one at a time during break mode. If a statement makes a call to a procedure, you can use this button to step through the lines of the procedure itself one at a time.	F8
Step Over	Performs lines of code one at a time during break mode, but treats a procedure call as a single statement. In other words, you use this button if you don't want to step through the lines of the procedure.	Shift+F8
Step Out	Performs the remaining lines of the current procedure during break mode, and stops at the statement following the procedure call.	Ctrl+Shift+F8

Debug Button	Description	Shortcut Key
Locals Window	Opens the Locals window. During break mode, this window displays information about declared variables in the current procedure.	
Immediate Window	Opens the Immediate window. Inside this window, you can enter a line of code and press Enter to run it. For example, you might use this window to make a procedure call during break mode. (The Immediate window is open by default during break mode. To close the window, click the Close button at the far right side of the window's title bar.)	Ctrl+G
Watch Window	Opens the Watch window, which displays the current values of selected variables or expressions during a break in the program.	
Quick Watch	Gives you a way to view the current value of a variable or an expression during a break in the program.	Shift+F9
Call Stack	Displays the list of procedure calls that have led to the current procedure.	Ctrl+L

The debugging activities represented by these buttons take place during *break mode*. Break mode occurs when your program run is interrupted due to an error, or when you intentionally initiate a break yourself. As you can see in Figure 5-6, the Visual Basic title bar displays [break] when you are in this mode. One way to interrupt a program run intentionally is to click the Break button, located between the Start and End buttons on the Standard or Debug toolbar. Another way is to specify a breakpoint in your code. In the break mode, you can use Visual Basic's Immediate, Watch, and Locals windows to investigate the values of variables and to carry out other debugging activities.

Figure 5-6: In the break mode, Visual Basic's title bar displays [break].

To begin exploring some of these debugging tools, you'll work first with the project named Bug1.Vbp. Figure 5-7 shows the CURRENCY.TXT file that the program reads to produce the sequence of events outlined in the upcoming exercise. Notice that the file contains currency exchange rates for nine countries, *not* listed in alphabetical order. The first country in the list is Britain. (This is the sample CURRENCY.TXT file that's included on this book's program disk. If you use a CURRENCY.TXT file that you've developed yourself — with a different list of countries — the results of the upcoming exercise will not be precisely the same, though you will encounter an equivalent problem in the program's performance.)

Figure 5-7: The CURRENCY.TXT file that produces the sequence of events in the upcoming exercise with the Bug1.Vbp project.

Open the Bug1 project from the folder where you've copied the projects from this book's program disk. Then press F5 to start the program. The International Currency Exchange window opens onto the desktop.

A First Debugging Exercise

Up to a point, this project seems to be the same as its predecessor in Chapter 4, but you'll expose a significant bug as you begin working with this version:

1. Begin by testing the Country list: Pull down the list and select France. Repeat this action for Mexico and Germany. Each time you choose one of these countries, the program correctly displays the corresponding currency rate, as shown in Figures 5-8, 5-9, and 5-10.

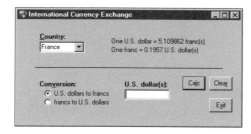

Figure 5-8: The program works correctly for some country selections. Here is the currency exchange information for France — dollars to francs and francs to dollars.

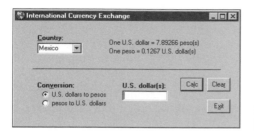

Figure 5-9: Here is the information for Mexico — exchange rates for the peso.

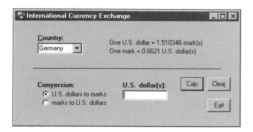

Figure 5-10: This is the correct information for Germany — exchange rates for the mark.

2. Now choose Britain. This time there's a problem (Figure 5-11). The program fails to update the currency exchange information in response to the new country selection. Incongruously, the program displays the exchange rate from the previous country selection — dollars to marks, clearly not the appropriate information for Britain. What has gone wrong? The first thing you may recall is that Britain is listed as the first country in the CURRENCY.TXT file. Will this fact turn out to be significant in the search for the bug?

Figure 5-11: The program fails when you select Britain. The exchange rates displayed here are for the mark, not the expected pound.

3. Click the Exit button to terminate this run of the program. In the Project Explorer window, select the frmCurrExch form and click the View Code button to open the code window for the form. You know that the event procedure named cboCountry_Click is responsible for displaying the currency exchange rates for a country selected from the list. To view this

procedure (Figure 5-12), select cboCountry from the Object list at the upper-left corner of the code window. By establishing a breakpoint near the end of this procedure and starting a new run of the program, you'll be able to explore the conditions that are causing the error. Click the mouse at the beginning of the second-to-last line in the procedure (a call to cmdClear_-Click). This action moves the flashing cursor to this line in the code editor.

4. Open the Debug toolbar. (Click the Visual Basic menu bar with the right mouse button and choose Debug.) The fourth icon on the toolbar is Toggle Breakpoint. Click this icon once to establish a breakpoint at the line you've selected at the end of the procedure. Figure 5-13 shows how Visual Basic marks the breakpoint in the code window. When you next run the program, the performance will be interrupted when it reaches this line.

```
cboCountry                      ▼    Click                              ▼

Private Sub cboCountry_Click()
  ' Read the user's country choice and display the
  ' exchange rates for the currency of the selected
  ' country.
  Dim i As Integer
  For i = 1 To countryNdx
    If cboCountry.Text = CurrArray(i).country Then
      lblDollar.Caption = "One U.S. dollar = " & _
        1 / CurrArray(i).inDollars & " " & _
        CurrArray(i).currName & "(s)"
      lblCurrency.Caption = "One " & _
        CurrArray(i).currName & " = " & _
        CurrArray(i).inDollars & _
        " U.S. dollar(s)"
      currCountry = i
    End If
  Next i

  ' Display captions for the conversion
  ' option buttons.
  optDollarsTo.Caption = "U.S. dollars to " & _
    CurrArray(currCountry).currName & "s"
  optCurrTo.Caption = CurrArray(currCountry).currName & _
    "s to U.S. dollars"

  lblConvCurr.Caption = "U.S. dollar(s):"
  optDollarsTo.Value = True
  cmdClear_Click
End Sub  ' cboCountry_Click
```

Figure 5-12: The cboCountry_Click procedure is the likely location of the bug. This procedure displays the basic exchange rates in response to a new selection from the Country list.

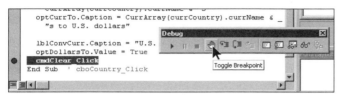

Figure 5-13: By clicking the Toggle Breakpoint icon, you can establish a breakpoint in the current procedure. When you run the program, the performance will be interrupted at the breakpoint.

5. Before you start the program, take a look at a few names that represent important information in the cboCountry_Click procedure. The cboCountry.Text property represents the country that has most recently been selected from the Country list. *CurrArray* is an array of records that the program uses to store all the information it reads from the CURRENCY.TXT file. Each record contains the name of a country, the name of the currency, and a numeric exchange rate. *CurrArray* lists the records in the same order as they appear in the CURRENCY.TXT file. The nine records read from the file are numbered from 0 to 8 in the array. Finally, the variable named *currCountry* represents the number of the most recent country selection. One of the jobs of the For loop near the top of the procedure is to search through the *CurrArray* list for the most recent selection from the country list — and to identify the country's number, *currCountry*.

6. Click Start, the first icon in the Debug toolbar. The International Currency Exchange dialog box appears on the desktop. Pull down the Country list and choose Japan. Thanks to the breakpoint you've established, the program is interrupted almost immediately and the cboCountry_Click procedure once again appears in the code window.

7. Now you have an opportunity to use the new feature known as *Auto Data Tips*. During the break mode, you can position the mouse pointer over any name in the current procedure (for example, any variable or property name) and the code editor displays the current value of that item — that is, the value at the time that the break occurred. Try it now. First move the mouse pointer over the property name *cboCountry.Text*. A small box shows you that the property's current value is "Japan," as shown in Figure 5-14. This is the Auto Data Tips feature in action.

8. Now move the mouse pointer further down the procedure, and position it over the end of the name *CurrArray(currCountry).currName*. This name represents the currency of the current country selection. The value of this expression is "yen," as you can see in Figure 5-15. Finally, try moving the mouse pointer over the name *currCountry*, the record number of the current country selection. The record number for Japan is 2 as shown in Figure 5-16. This makes sense: Japan is the third country in the CURRENCY.TXT file, as you can see back in Figure 5-7. Because the numbering of the country records begins at zero, Japan's number should be 2. All the information you've seen for this country selection seems to be correct.

```
For i = 1 To countryNdx
  If cboCountry.Text = CurrArray(i).country Then
    ┌─────────────────────────┐ = "One U.S. dollar = " & _
    │cboCountry.Text = "Japan"│
    └─────────────────────────┘
      1 / CurrArray(i).inDollars & " " & _
      CurrArray(i).currName & "(s)"
    lblCurrency.Caption = "One " & _
      CurrArray(i).currName & " = " & _
      CurrArray(i).inDollars & _
      " U.S. dollar(s)"
    currCountry = i
  End If
Next i
```

Figure 5-14: Thanks to the Auto Data Tips feature, you can examine the value of any variable in the current procedure during break mode. Here is the value of the *cboCountry.Text* property.

```
' Display captions for the conversion
' option buttons.
optDollarsTo.Caption = "U.S. dollars to " & _
  CurrArray(currCountry).currName & "s"
optCurrTo.Captio┌──────────────────────────────────┐).currName & _
              │CurrArray(currCountry).currName = "yen"│
  "s to U.S. do └──────────────────────────────────┘
```

Figure 5-15: The value of *CurrArray(currCountry).currName* indicates that the program has correctly located the currency record for Japan.

```
' Display captions for the conversion
' option buttons.
optDollarsTo.Caption = "U.S. dollars to " & _
  CurrArray(currCountry).currName & "s"
optCurrTo.Cap┌─────────────────┐rArray(currCountry).currName & _
          │currCountry = 2│
  "s to U.S. d└─────────────────┘
```

Figure 5-16: Because Japan is the third record in the *CurrArray* list, a record number of 2 is correct. (The first record in the array is numbered 0.)

9. To continue the program run, click the first icon in the Debug toolbar. (The ToolTip for this item now reads "Continue") In the International Currency Exchange dialog box, pull down the Country list and select Britain. The breakpoint causes an interruption in the program run, and you see the cboCountry_Click procedure in the code window.

10. Once again, use the Auto Data Tips feature to explore the current values of selected variables in the procedure. First, position the mouse pointer over the property name *cboCountry.Text*. The value of the current country selection is reported as "Britain." No problem here. But now examine *CurrArray(currCountry).currName* and *currCountry*. The values are the same as for the previous country selection: "yen" and "2." Clearly the procedure's For loop has been unable to find the correct record in *CurrArray* for Britain. Because you know that Britain is the first country record in the list — and should therefore have a record number of 0 — you might immediately suspect that the For loop's starting point is off by 1.

11. Look up at the top of the For loop. Sure enough, it reads as follows:

```
For i = 1 to countryNdx
```

This is probably the bug you're looking for. Inside the code window, change the 1 in this line to 0. The revised line appears as follows:

```
For i = 0 to countryNdx
```

12. Click the mouse pointer over the line that you've established as a breakpoint. Then click the Toggle Breakpoint icon on the Debug toolbar to remove the breakpoint. Your program will now run without this interruption.

13. Click the Continue icon at the beginning of the Debug toolbar. When the program's dialog box reappears, pull down the Country list and choose Britain. The program now correctly displays the currency exchange rates for pounds and dollars. Keep trying other country selections; then test the calculation of exchange amounts. Everything seems to be working as expected. You've debugged the program.

14. Click Exit to stop the program. Then choose File⇨Remove Project. Click No when you're asked if you want to save the revisions in the project. Bug1.Vbp remains in its original form on disk; you can repeat this exercise at another time if you want to.

In the next exercise you'll work with a shortened and modified version of a project called the International Sales application. (You'll examine the complete program in Chapter 11.) The program accepts numeric input into the cells of a small sales worksheet. The columns of the sheet show annual sales figures, and the rows show data by region. As you enter data into these cells, the program automatically calculates totals (by year and by region), and displays a corresponding sales chart in a small frame beneath the worksheet. To simplify testing, this version of the program has a menu command that fills the worksheet with random data entries; thanks to this command, you don't have to enter the data yourself.

As you've guessed by now, the Bug2.Vbp program contains errors that you'll have to search for and correct. In particular, you'll focus your attention on a procedure named *ColumnByYears*, shown in its entirety in Figures 5-17 and 5-18. As its name suggests, this procedure is responsible for drawing a column chart for the sales data that's entered into the worksheet.

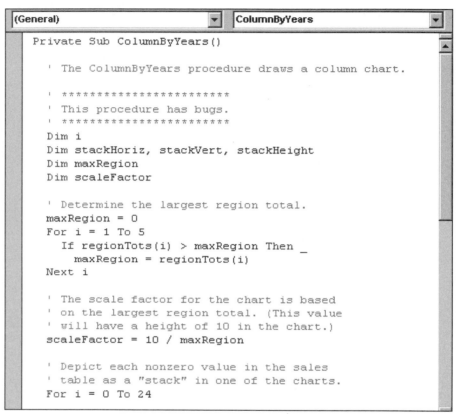

```
(General)                              ColumnByYears

 Private Sub ColumnByYears()

   ' The ColumnByYears procedure draws a column chart.

   ' ************************
   ' This procedure has bugs.
   ' ************************
   Dim i
   Dim stackHoriz, stackVert, stackHeight
   Dim maxRegion
   Dim scaleFactor

   ' Determine the largest region total.
   maxRegion = 0
   For i = 1 To 5
     If regionTots(i) > maxRegion Then _
       maxRegion = regionTots(i)
   Next i

   ' The scale factor for the chart is based
   ' on the largest region total. (This value
   ' will have a height of 10 in the chart.)
   scaleFactor = 10 / maxRegion

   ' Depict each nonzero value in the sales
   ' table as a "stack" in one of the charts.
   For i = 0 To 24
```

Figure 5-17: The top half of the *ColumnByYears* procedure.

```
(General)                                      ColumnByYears

      ' At the beginning of each row of data,
      ' reinitialize the stackHoriz and stackVert
      ' values for a new column in the chart.
    If i Mod 5 = 0 Then
      stackHoriz = 0.5 + 2 * (i / 5)
      stackVert = 0
    End If

      ' If an amount is not zero, calculate
      ' the height of the corresponding "stack."
    If amounts(i) <> 0 Then
      stackHeight = scaleFactor * amounts(i)

      ' Select a color and a fill style.
      picSalesChart.FillColor = _
        QBColor(i Mod 5 + colorOffset)
      picSalesChart.FillStyle = 0

      ' Draw the "stack."
      picSalesChart.Line (stackHoriz, stackVert) _
        -Step(1.5, stackHeight), 0, B

      ' Increment the value of stackVert by the
      ' height of the previous "stack."
      stackVert = stackHoriz + stackHeight
    End If
  Next i
End Sub  ' ColumnByYears
```

Figure 5-18: The second half of the *ColumnByYears* procedure.

A Second Debugging Exercise

Open Bug2.Vbp and take a look at the Project Explorer window (Figure 5-19). The program contains one form, which is saved on disk as Bug2.Frm. Press A5 or click the Start button on the toolbar to start a performance. When you do so, the International Sales window appears on the screen, as shown in Figure 5-20. As you can see, it contains an empty worksheet for entering a table of sales figures, and space beneath the worksheet for a chart.

Figure 5-19: The Bug2 project contains one form named *frmIntSales.*

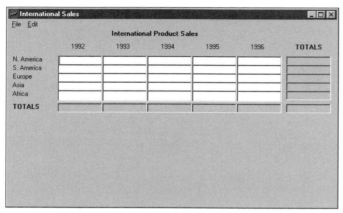

Figure 5-20: The program's dialog box displays a worksheet grid for entering sales data, and a space below where the program develops a sales chart.

In this abbreviated version of the program, only two menus appear. The File menu has an Exit command, for quitting the program. The Edit menu has two commands: Clear, for erasing the current sales data; and Random Data, for entering a set of randomly generated numbers into the sales worksheet. In response to the random data, the program is designed to build a column chart, just as if you had entered real data yourself from the keyboard. As you work with this program, you'll discover two problems: a runtime error that almost immediately interrupts the performance; and a logical error that impairs the charting procedure:

1. Choose Edit⇨Random Data, or press Ctrl+R from the keyboard. The program enters the first numeric value into the sales worksheet and attempts to begin drawing the column chart. But something goes wrong. A runtime error interrupts the program, and Visual Basic displays the message shown in Figure 5-21. The "Subscript out of range" message refers to an error in handling an array. The program has tried to access an element that is beyond the range declared for the array.

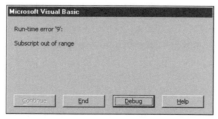

Figure 5-21: A runtime error interrupts the program.

2. Click the Debug button in the error message box. In response, Visual Basic switches into break mode, opens the code window, scrolls to the procedure in which the error occurred (the *ColumnByYears* procedure), and highlights the line that caused the error. As you can see in Figure 5-22, the offending line contains a reference to an array named *regionTots*.

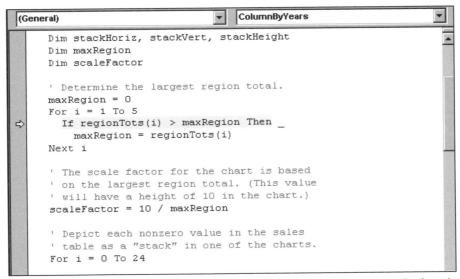

```
(General)                              ▼  │ColumnByYears                    ▼

      Dim stackHoriz, stackVert, stackHeight
      Dim maxRegion
      Dim scaleFactor

      ' Determine the largest region total.
      maxRegion = 0
      For i = 1 To 5
⇨       If regionTots(i) > maxRegion Then _
          maxRegion = regionTots(i)
      Next i

      ' The scale factor for the chart is based
      ' on the largest region total. (This value
      ' will have a height of 10 in the chart.)
      scaleFactor = 10 / maxRegion

      ' Depict each nonzero value in the sales
      ' table as a "stack" in one of the charts.
      For i = 0 To 24
```

Figure 5-22: When the interruption takes place, Visual Basic shows you the location of the error.

3. Like many runtime errors, this one is not hard to correct once Visual Basic shows you its location. If you look in the program's general declarations section, you'll see that the *regionTots* array is declared as follows:

```
Dim regionTots(4)
```

Given this declaration, the array's legal subscripts range from 0 to 4. But the For loop in the *ColumnByYears* procedure defines an index, *i*, that ranges from 1 to 5. This is the problem.

4. Sometimes Visual Basic allows you to correct a runtime error in break mode and then immediately resume the program performance, but not in this case. Click the End button on the Standard or Debug toolbar to stop the performance before you correct the code. In the code window, revise the starting and ending values of the For loop as follows:

```
For i = 0 to 4
```

5. Press F5 or click the Start button to restart the program. Once again, choose Edit⇨Random Data. This time the program successfully fills the sales table with randomly-generated numeric data and attempts to draw the corresponding chart. But as shown in Figure 5-23, there's something very wrong with the chart. Instead of drawing five solid columns to represent the varying levels of regional sales data, the program creates columns that float whimsically up the height of the chart box. This may be an interesting visual effect, but it's not the result you were hoping for.

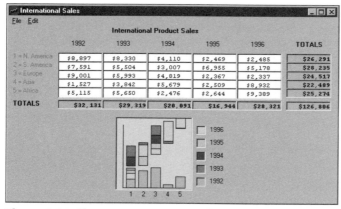

Figure 5-23: The program runs now, but doesn't draw the chart correctly.

6. Click the Break icon on the toolbar to create a pause in the program run. Examining the *ColumnByYears* procedure in the code window, you can see that the program defines the *stackVert* variable to represent the vertical starting position of each colored "stack" portion in a column, and *stackHeight* to represent the height of a stack portion. (The height is drawn in proportion to the numeric sales value that the stack portion depicts. In the scale of this chart, the tallest column has a total height of 10 units.) The *stackVert* and *stackHeight* variables are obviously the values you need to investigate.

7. Choose Debug⇨Add Watch. The resulting dialog box allows you to specify variables or expressions whose values you want to monitor. As you'll see shortly, these watch values are conveniently displayed in the Watch window.

8. Enter **stackVert** in the Expression box. Make sure the Context box displays *ColumnByYears* as the procedure in which this variable is defined, as in Figure 5-24. (If not, select *frmIntSales* from the Module list and then select *ColumnByYears* from the Procedure list.) Click OK to confirm the watch expression. When you do so, the Watch window appears at the bottom of the desktop.

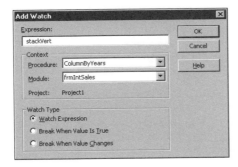

Figure 5-24: Defining a watch expression in the Add Watch window.

9. Repeat Steps 7 and 8 to define the **stackHeight** variable as a second watch expression.

10. Press F7, if necessary, to activate the code window. In the *ColumnByYears* procedure, scroll down to the statement that draws each portion of the column chart, a call to the picSalesChart.Line method. You can see that *stackVert* and *stackHeight* provide essential information for this statement. Click the mouse to move the flashing cursor to the beginning of this line and then click the Toggle Breakpoint button on the Debug toolbar (or press F9) to designate the line as a breakpoint. Visual Basic highlights the line, as shown in Figure 5-25.

```
(General)                              ColumnByYears

        stackHeight = scaleFactor * amounts(i)

        ' Select a color and a fill style.
        picSalesChart.FillColor = _
           QBColor(i Mod 5 + colorOffset)
        picSalesChart.FillStyle = 0

        ' Draw the "stack."
        picSalesChart.Line (stackHoriz, stackVert)
           -Step(1.5, stackHeight), 0, B

        ' Increment the value of stackVert by the
        ' height of the previous "stack."
        stackVert = stackHoriz + stackHeight
     End If
   Next i
End Sub  ' ColumnByYears
```

Figure 5-25: Defining a breakpoint in the procedure.

11. Now click the Watch Window icon on the Debug toolbar to activate the Watch window. The window shows the two watch expressions you've defined (Figure 5-26); they currently display no values, because the *ColumnByYears* procedure was not running at the time you interrupted the program.

12. Click the Immediate Window icon on the Debug toolbar to activate the Immediate window. Type **ColumnByYears**, as shown in Figure 5-27, and then press Enter. This is one way to make a call to a specific procedure, thereby resuming the program performance. In response, Visual Basic performs the lines of the procedure up to the breakpoint that you've designated, and then stops the program again.

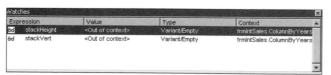

Figure 5-26: The Watch window displays the two watch expressions you've defined, but no values yet. The notation "Out of context" means that the *ColumnByYears* procedure was not running at the time the program was interrupted.

Figure 5-27: Using the Immediate window to make a call to one of the program's procedures.

13. In the Watch window you can now see the values of the two watch expressions for the first stack portion that the procedure draws (Figure 5-28). The *stackVert* variable has an initial value of zero, so that the first stack will appear at the bottom of the chart; *stackHeight* contains a calculated value representing the height of the first stack. (Because the calculation is based on randomly generated data, you'll see a different value for *stackHeight* on your computer.) To prepare for drawing the next stack, the program is supposed to add *stackHeight* to the current value of *stackVert*, ensuring that the next stack will begin where the previous one left off. Accordingly, you'd like to see the value of the expression *stackVert + stackHeight* after each stack is drawn. Enter the following statement into the Immediate window, just beneath the call to the *ColumnByYears* procedure:

```
? stackVert + stackHeight
```

Inside the Immediate window, the question mark is a command to display the value of an expression. As you can see in Figure 5-29, Visual Basic displays the sum of the two variables. According to the program's design, this sum should be the next value of the *stackVert* variable.

Figure 5-28: The Watch window now shows the values of the variables *stackHeight* and *stackVert*.

Figure 5-29: Entering an expression in the Immediate window to view the sum of two variables.

14. Press F5 to resume the program. Once again the performance stops at the breakpoint. The next values of *stackHeight* and *stackVert* appear in the Watch window. Comparing the new value of *stackVert* with the sum you generated in the Immediate window, you can see that the program is clearly not calculating the value of *stackVert* correctly (Figure 5-30).

Figure 5-30: The new value of *stackVert* in the Watch window doesn't match the sum displayed in the Immediate window.

You can continue this investigation by repeating the same pattern of steps: In the Immediate window, place the cursor after the summation expression (*stackVert* + *stackHeight*) and press Enter. In response, the Debug window displays the new sum of the two variables. Then press F5 to resume the program, and look at the Watch window when the program stops again. Each time you go through these steps, you'll confirm that the program is calculating the wrong value for *stackVert*. This is the source of the program's charting problem.

The discovery will lead you to re-examine the code of the *ColumnByYears* procedure. Just beneath the call to the Line method (where you've established the breakpoint), the following statement is supposed to increment the value of *stackVert* for each new stack of a given column:

```
stackVert = stackHoriz + stackHeight
```

Here is the error. The sum operation at the right side of the equal sign adds *stackHeight* to the wrong variable. The statement should appear as follows:

```
stackVert = stackVert + stackHeight
```

Revise the statement as shown. Then move the cursor back up to the previous statement, and click the Toggle Breakpoint button in the Debug toolbar to deactivate the breakpoint. Click the Stop button to terminate the current performance. Then click the Start button to begin again. When the International Sales window appears on the screen, choose Edit⇨Random Data. The program now works as it's supposed to (Figure 5-31). Keep experimenting with the program if you wish, then exit and close the project without saving the changes you've made. You can return to this exercise again when you've learned more about Visual Basic.

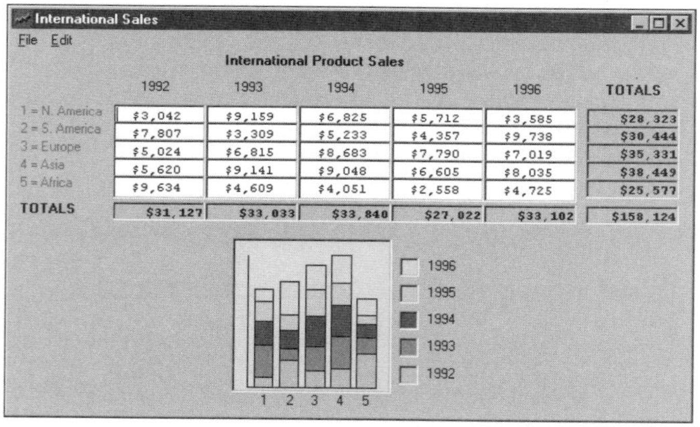

Figure 5-31: The program finally works correctly.

As you've seen in these exercises, the process of tracking down a logical error can require diligence and patience. But Visual Basic's debugging tools provide solid help along the way.

Producing an Executable Program File

♦   ♦   ♦   ♦

In This Chapter

Using the Make command

Entering information in the Properties window

Creating a Windows shortcut icon to represent the program

Creating a distribution package for installing your program on other computers

♦   ♦   ♦   ♦

After you've developed, tested, and debugged a Visual Basic application, your final task is to create an executable program file that can be run directly on the Windows 95 desktop. To do so, you use the Make command from Visual Basic's File menu. The result is an EXE file that you can run on your own computer, or on another system where Visual Basic 5 has been installed.

Using the Make Command

The steps are simple. In the following exercise, you'll create an EXE file for the Currency Exchange project that you've been working on in previous chapters:

1. Start Visual Basic and open CurrExch.vbp from disk.

2. Pull down the File menu and choose the command that's listed as Make CurrExch.exe. The Make Project dialog box appears on the screen, as shown in Figure 6-1. In the File name text box, Visual Basic suggests CurrExch.exe as the name for file; you can accept this suggestion or enter a different name of your choice. You can also use this dialog box to select the directory in which you want to store the compiled program file.

Figure 6-1: Using the Make Project dialog box to create an executable program file.

3. Click the Options button at the lower-right corner of the Make Project dialog box. The Project Properties dialog box appears on the screen (Figure 6-2). This box gives you options for identifying the version number of your program, changing the title and the icon, and entering a variety of other items to describe your program.

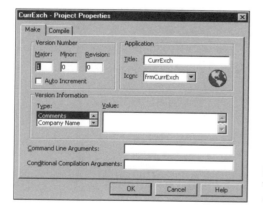

Figure 6-2: Entering information about your program in the Project Properties dialog box.

4. In the Version Information frame, select a Type item and then enter the corresponding text in the Value box. For example, you can enter copyright information, a general description of your program, and any notes you want to include with the file. (As you'll see shortly, this information will be available directly from the EXE file you're creating.)

5. Click OK on the Project Properties and Make Project dialog boxes. Visual Basic creates the EXE file and saves it in the directory you selected in the Make Project dialog box. You can now exit from the Visual Basic environment.

To view the icon for the new EXE file, use the My Computer utility on the Windows 95 desktop to open the directory in which you saved the file. By scrolling through the folder, you'll find the icon for the file. For example, Figure 6-3 shows the icon for CurrExch.exe. If you want to try running the program, simply double-click the icon.

Figure 6-3: Locating the icon for a new EXE file.

You also can examine the descriptive information that you saved with the file. To do so, click the icon with the right mouse button, and choose Properties from the resulting drop-down menu, as in Figure 6-4. A Properties dialog box appears on the screen for the program you've selected. The dialog box has two tabs named General and Version. In the General tab you can see information about the type, location, size, usage history, and attributes of the EXE file you've created.

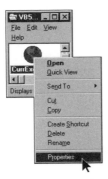

Figure 6-4: Opening the Properties window for the EXE file you've created.

Click the Version tab to view other information. As shown in Figure 6-5, the Properties window displays the information you entered into the Project Properties dialog box. At the top of the Version tab you see the version number, description, and copyright information. At the lower half of the tab, you can select entries in the Item name list and read the corresponding text in the Value box. As you can see, these items give you a useful way to document the software product you've developed.

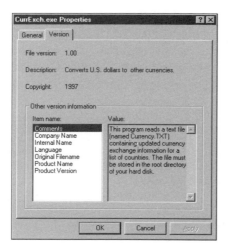

Figure 6-5: Reading the Version properties of an EXE file.

Finally, you may want to create a shortcut for your new EXE file on the Windows 95 desktop. There are two simple ways to do so. Begin by opening the folder in which the EXE file is saved. Using the right mouse button, drag the icon for the file to the desktop and choose Create Shortcut(s) Here from the resulting menu. Or, drag the icon to the desktop with the left mouse button to create a shortcut directly. The shortcut icon takes its place on the desktop along with any other icons you've already placed there, as in Figure 6-6. (If you wish, you can change the name of the shortcut. Click the icon with the right mouse button, and choose Rename from the resulting shortcut menu. Type a new name from the keyboard and press Enter to confirm.)

Figure 6-6: Creating a shortcut icon for an EXE file.

Now to run your application, simply double-click its shortcut icon on the desktop.

Tip   You can establish the Version properties of a project at any time, even if you're not planning to create an EXE file right away. To do so, choose Visual Basic's Project⇨Properties command. The resulting Project Properties dialog box contains four tabs. Click the Make tab to view a dialog box that's almost identical to Figure 6-2. Use this window to enter a variety of information about your project, including the version, description, comments, copyright information, and so on.

Using the Application Setup Wizard

The executable program file that you've created will run on any system where Visual Basic 5 has been installed. But if you want to distribute your program to users who do not have Visual Basic, you need to include some additional resources. Along with your EXE file, you must provide certain system files that your program requires.

The Application Setup Wizard is a separate program that helps you create a package of resources for installing your application on other systems. The Setup Wizard determines all the files that you need to ship with your program, and creates a Setup program that can be used to install your application.

You can use the Setup Wizard on any project that you complete in Visual Basic. To get started, follow these steps:

1. Click the Windows 95 Start button and choose Application Setup Wizard from the Visual Basic 5.0 group, as in Figure 6-7.

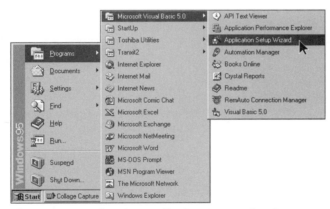

Figure 6-7: Starting the Application Setup Wizard.

2. An introductory window explains the purpose of the Setup Wizard (Figure 6-8).

3. In the next window, enter the location and name of the Visual Basic project that you want to distribute (Figure 6-9). In the Options list, choose the task that you want the Setup Wizard to perform. The first option, "Create a Setup Program," is the default. Use this option to develop a complete package of all the files you need to distribute.

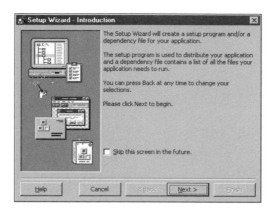

Figure 6-8: The introductory window for the Setup Wizard. Read the information it provides, and then click Next.

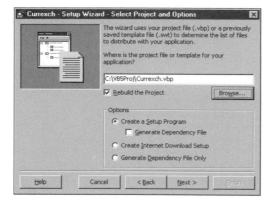

Figure 6-9: Identifying the project that you want to distribute.

4. Click Next, and follow the simple directions that the wizard provides.

When all the steps are complete, the Setup Wizard saves the distribution package on one or more floppy disks. You can then duplicate these disks for shipping to your users.

Programming Essentials

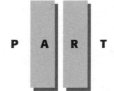

P A R T

II

The six chapters of Part II introduce the major tools and techniques of Visual Basic programming. Each chapter presents a sample application to illustrate the topics at hand. You'll run the applications to explore their features, and you'll examine each program's code in detail. Selected procedures appear as numbered figures, so you can conveniently examine specific passages of code. (Appendix A provides the complete code listings for all the applications in this book.)

Chapter 7 explains the difference between event procedures and general procedures, and shows you how to work with both. You'll learn how to create Sub and Function procedures and how to write calls to each type of routine. You'll also study variables and data types, Dim declarations, scope, assignment statements, expressions, operations, and the order of precedence. The Travel Expense Log application, a simple tool for recording and reporting travel expenses, illustrates many of these topics.

Chapter 8 addresses some important design issues for a project that contains multiple forms. You'll learn to set properties to distinguish between different roles for the forms in your project. You'll also see the significance of the startup form, and you'll use the Project Properties dialog box to choose a form for this purpose. The Show and Hide methods control the display of forms at runtime; you'll see examples of these methods in this chapter's Restaurant Review program. The application builds a personal restaurant database in which you can record information about the restaurants where you dine during business trips.

Chapter 9 discusses Visual Basic as a structured programming language. On the subject of data structures you'll learn how to work with arrays and user-defined record types. You'll also investigate a variety of control structures, including If and Select Case decisions, Do loops, and For loops. Along the way you'll learn how to use relational and logical operators in a conditional expression. Other important topics include nested loops and decisions; dynamic arrays; arrays of records; enumerated types; and the Visual Basic With structure, which you can use to abbreviate references to the elements of a user-defined type. This chapter's Meetings application illustrates these topics; you can use the program to keep records of the meetings you attend while on business trips.

Chapter 10 shows you how to use Visual Basic data file commands to manage databases, create and read text files, and store data on disk for exchange with other programs. You'll master two different sets of commands and techniques for working with random-access files and text files. The Phone Directory application will help you understand these techniques; it creates a useful database of names, phone numbers, and e-mail addresses.

Chapter 11 illustrates the intricate details of input and output procedures. In particular, you'll consider the important design issues in a program that receive extensive input from the user. You'll also see several ways in which a program can supply output, including text, numbers, and graphs. The International Sales program is a small worksheet application in which the user enters numeric sales data; in response, the program calculates rows and columns of totals and displays column charts or pie charts representing the data. This program also illustrates the use of menus in a Visual Basic project. You'll see how to use the menu editor to define the elements of a menu on a form.

Chapter 12 discusses Visual Basic standard controls and the custom components that are now known as ActiveX controls. The chapter focuses on one particular component named the common dialog control. You can use this control in a program to display Windows-style dialog boxes on the screen for opening and saving files, sending information to the printer, and a variety of other purposes. The common dialog control is illustrated in this chapter's Transportation Planner application, a tool for planning your itinerary on a multi-stop business trip.

Procedures, Variables, and Operations

◆   ◆   ◆   ◆

In This Chapter

Using the Option Explicit statement

Creating Sub and Function procedures

Writing procedure calls

Understanding arguments in procedure calls

Declaring the scope and type of a variable

Using the Variant type

◆   ◆   ◆   ◆

Devising effective ways to work with data is one of your first tasks in a new programming project. The decisions you make about handling data are basic to the success of your program. For example, as you begin planning your code, you'll think carefully about the following issues:

+ How to represent the different types of data values that your program will use

+ How to send information from one part of your program to another, given the specific data requirements of individual procedures

+ How to use operations to perform calculations and to work with multiple data values

A *variable* is a name you create to represent an item of information in a program. Depending on how you use a variable, its value might remain unchanged throughout your program or it might change frequently. If you've worked with a previous version of BASIC (QBasic, for example), you know that you can create variables to represent specific *types* of data — for example, integers, floating-point numbers, or strings of characters.

In the past, BASIC programmers have used a standard set of *type-declaration characters* at the end of variable names to indicate type. For example, under this convention the variable *city$* represents a string and *visits%* represents an integer. (The final characters in these variable names — *$* and *%* — indicate the type of data each variable represents.) But type-declaration characters are no longer used in Visual Basic 5. In their place, you can write formal *declarations* for all variables used in a program, as is the practice in other professional programming languages.

Although formal declarations have traditionally been optional in versions of Visual Basic, long programming projects become easier to manage when variables are systematically declared. Variable declarations in Visual Basic take the form of Dim statements. In one of its simplest forms, a Dim declaration appears as

```
Dim variableName As dataType
```

For example, the following statement declares a string variable named *logFileName:*

```
Dim logFileName As String
```

Using Dim — or other keywords available for declaring variables — you not only specify the names and types of the variables you intend to use in a program, but you also establish the appropriate *scope* of each variable. Scope designates the part of your program in which a given variable will be recognized and available. By carefully defining the scope of variables throughout your program, you avoid unexpected conflicts between variables in different procedures, a common problem in older versions of the BASIC language.

Using the Option Explicit statement

Because variable declarations are so important in large programming projects, Visual Basic gives you the option of *requiring* formal declarations throughout the code in a given file. To do so, you place the following statement at the top of the code in a form or module:

```
Option Explicit
```

In response, Visual Basic provides a helpful error message whenever you inadvertently omit a variable declaration.

If you want to include an Option Explicit statement in every new form or code module, you can instruct Visual Basic to insert the statement automatically. To do so, follow these steps:

1. Choose Tools⇨Options. The resulting Options dialog box is organized into six tabs of option categories. The Editor tab is selected by default.

2. In the Code Settings frame, look at the check box labeled "Require Variable Declaration," shown in Figure 7-1. If it is checked, Visual Basic already adds the Option Explicit statement to each new project. If it is unchecked, click the option once to place a check in the box.

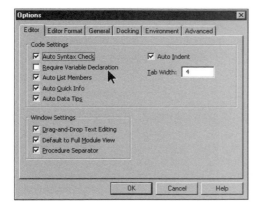

Figure 7-1: Changing the setting of the Require Variable Declaration option; when this option is checked, Visual Basic automatically inserts an Option Explicit statement at the top of the code in each new form or module.

3. Click OK to confirm this setting.

Now each new form or module you add to a project will contain an Option Explicit statement at the top of the General Declarations section, as in Figure 7-2. Thanks to this statement, the Visual Basic compiler enforces mandatory declarations for every variable you use.

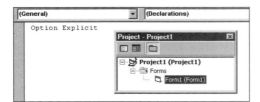

Figure 7-2: The Option Explicit statement appears at the top of the General Declarations section of a form or module.

In this chapter, you'll examine the variety of data types available in Visual Basic, and you'll learn how to declare and use variables in procedures and modules. In addition, you'll look at the convenient data type known as Variant, and you'll discover how its use can simplify data operations in a program. You'll see examples of assignments and operations using numeric and string data.

But first you'll focus on the various ways of organizing procedures in Visual Basic. You've already seen examples of event procedures designed to respond to predefined events that take place during a program run. Now you'll learn the distinction between event procedures and *general* procedures in the organization of a project. In the category of general procedures, you'll examine the practical differences between Sub and Function procedures, and you'll learn how information can be shared between one procedure and another.

To help you understand all these essential programming topics, you'll work with a sample project named the International Travel Expense Log program. As its name suggests, this program is designed to keep track of travel expenses during an international business trip. To begin your work in this chapter, you'll open the project from the program disk, run it, and see what it does.

The International Travel Expense Log Program

Start up Visual Basic if you haven't done so already, and open the Expense Log program, which is stored on disk as ExpnsLog.vbp. Then press F5 or click the Start button on the toolbar to run the program.

The program consists of one form, shown in Figure 7-3. Controls on the form are designed to elicit information about a single travel expense record: the date, the country and city where the expense was incurred, the amount spent (in local currency), a brief description, and the currency exchange rate in effect — that is, the value of one dollar in the local currency. By default, the program saves your expense data in a text file named \ExpnsLog.Txt, as indicated on the title bar; but you can specify a different file name for saving the expense records of a particular business trip if you prefer. You'll examine this feature later.

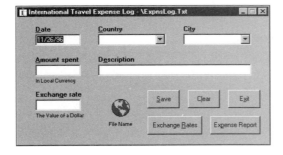

Figure 7-3: The International Travel Expense Log program gives you a simple way to record expenses during a business trip.

At the lower-right corner of the dialog box, a panel of command buttons represents the operations you can perform by clicking the mouse or by pressing a keyboard shortcut:

✦ Click the Save button — or press Alt+S — to save the current expense record. The program requires you to enter information in each of the six fields — Date, Country, City, Amount spent, Description, and Exchange rate — before saving a record. (If you leave any field blank, a reminder message appears on the desktop when you click the Save button, as shown in Figure 7-4.) Once you complete a record and click Save, the program clears the Amount spent and Description boxes, to make room for the next entry.

✦ Click the Clear button (or press Alt+L) to abandon the current record and start over again.

✦ Click the Exchange Rates button (Alt+R) for information about the exchange rates you've already recorded for a selected country. (If the expense log file doesn't exist yet, the program shows another message, as in Figure 7-5.)

✦ Click the Expense Report button (Alt+P) to produce an expense report from the current data file. The program stores this report as a text file named Expenses.Txt, which you can merge into any word-processed document or send directly to your printer. (Again, a message appears if the expense log file can't be found on disk.)

✦ Click the Exit button (Alt+X) to quit the program. Next time you run the program, you can continue recording expenses in the ExpnsLog.Txt file or in any other expense data file you've created with the program.

Figure 7-4: The program displays this message if you attempt to save an expense record without filling in all the input fields.

Figure 7-5: The program displays this message if the expense log file can't be found on disk when you click the Exchange Rates button. A similar message appears for the Expense Report button.

Suppose you're in the middle of a two-week, three-country business trip to Europe. At the end of each day, you sit down at your laptop to record the day's expenses. Using the Expense Log program, you can quickly type the information to complete each record.

At the beginning of each new record, the program automatically provides today's date as the default value in the Date box. You can accept this default or enter a different date. From there, you press Tab to move from one box to the next, as you enter the country and city, the amount, a brief description, and today's dollar-to-currency exchange rate (Figure 7-6). Finally, you click the Save button to save the current record and begin a new one.

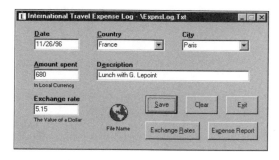

Figure 7-6: After completing an expense record you click Save to write the record to the current file.

Each time you complete a record and click Save, the program writes the information as a new line of text in the current data file — ExpnsLog.Txt, by default. You can examine this file in any text editor, such as the Windows NotePad program. For example, Figure 7-7 shows what the file might look like after several days of expense entries in three countries.

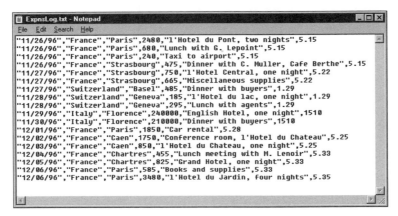

```
ExpnsLog.txt - Notepad

File  Edit  Search  Help
"11/26/96","France","Paris",2480,"l'Hotel du Pont, two nights",5.15
"11/26/96","France","Paris",680,"Lunch with G. Lepoint",5.15
"11/26/96","France","Paris",240,"Taxi to airport",5.15
"11/26/96","France","Strasbourg",475,"Dinner with C. Muller, Cafe Berthe",5.15
"11/27/96","France","Strasbourg",750,"l'Hotel Central, one night",5.22
"11/27/96","France","Strasbourg",665,"Miscellaneous supplies",5.22
"11/27/96","Switzerland","Basel",485,"Dinner with buyers",1.29
"11/28/96","Switzerland","Geneva",185,"l'Hotel du lac, one night",1.29
"11/28/96","Switzerland","Geneva",295,"Lunch with agents",1.29
"11/29/96","Italy","Florence",240000,"English Hotel, one night",1510
"11/30/96","Italy","Florence",210000,"Dinner with buyers",1510
"12/01/96","France","Paris",1850,"Car rental",5.28
"12/02/96","France","Caen",1750,"Conference room, l'Hotel du Chateau",5.25
"12/03/96","France","Caen",850,"l'Hotel du Chateau, one night",5.25
"12/04/96","France","Chartres",455,"Lunch meeting with M. Lenoir",5.33
"12/05/96","France","Chartres",825,"Grand Hotel, one night",5.33
"12/06/96","France","Paris",585,"Books and supplies",5.33
"12/06/96","France","Paris",3480,"l'Hotel du Jardin, four nights",5.35
```

Figure 7-7: An example of the ExpnsLog.Txt file. Each expense record contains six fields of information on a single line of text.

Notice that each line in this file contains six items of information, corresponding to the six boxes in the Expense Log dialog box — the date, country, city, amount, description, and exchange rate. Four of the items are stored as strings, enclosed in quotation marks; and the other two appear as digits and decimal points, not in quotes. Within a given line, each item is separated from the next by a comma. These storage characteristics make the file convenient to use for the program's other operations.

The dialog box has several features designed to simplify expense recording as you move from place to place on your business trip. For example, each time you start the program, it reads the data file and develops a list of all the countries you've recorded up to now. You can view this list — and select any country from it — by clicking the down-arrow button at the right side of the Country box, as shown in Figure 7-8. Once you've selected a country, the program searches through the data file for any cities you've already visited in the current country selection. A list of those cities appears when you click the down-arrow button at the right side of the City box, as in Figure 7-9. Thanks to these two lists, you can quickly fill in the information needed to identify the location for a given expense record.

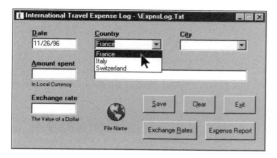

Figure 7-8: Choosing a country. The Country list shows all the countries you've recorded in your expense log up to this point.

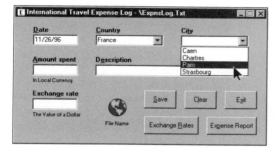

Figure 7-9: Choosing a city. Once you select a country, the City list shows all the cities you've already visited in that country.

The exchange rate in a country may change from day to day. For example, one day during a trip to France you may get a significantly better exchange than another day. Although you record your expenses in the currency of a particular country, the actual cost of any transaction depends on how much you paid for the currency. A 500-franc business lunch is more expensive to you when the exchange rate is 5 francs to the dollar rather than, say, a rate of 5.3 francs to the dollar. Keeping track of exchange rates is therefore an important part of expense accounting during international travel.

The Expense Log program provides a simple way to monitor rate fluctuations as you continue your stay in a particular country. When you've selected an entry in the Country list, you can click the Exchange Rates button for quick information about the rates you've recorded during your trip, as shown in Figure 7-10. The Exchange Rates message box shows you the lowest and highest rates found in the current data file for the country you've selected.

You may periodically want to generate an expense report that summarizes the expenses you've recorded up to a certain point. This document might serve as an intermediate review of expenses during a business trip or as a final report at the end of the trip. Either way, you can create the latest version of the report simply by clicking the Expense Report button on the dialog box. When you do so, you'll see a small message appear on the desktop, as shown in Figure 7-11.

Figure 7-10: Examining fluctuations in exchange rates. Click the Exchange Rates button to see the range of rates you've recorded for a particular country.

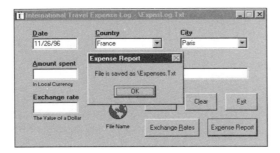

Figure 7-11: Producing an expense report. The program saves this report in the file named \Expenses.Txt. You can insert this text file into any word-processed document.

The program always saves the expense report as a text file on disk, under the name \Expenses.Txt. You can use the NotePad application to view the report, or you can send it directly to your printer as a text file. If you want to save the report, you can merge it into a word-processed document, or assign the file a new name on disk. Figure 7-12 shows an example of what the report looks like.

Unlike the original data file, the report presents expense records in columns of information. The Amount column shows each expense in dollars rather than in a variety of local currencies. (The exchange rates are omitted from the expense report altogether.) The bottom line of the report shows the total amount you spent on the business trip.

Finally, you may prefer to save your expense data under a file name that you choose, rather than the default ExpnsLog.Txt. In some cases, the default file may serve as a convenient temporary storage place for data that you ultimately plan to save elsewhere. But an alternative approach is to create a new file — under a name you supply yourself — for each business trip, and to save the original data in this file.

```
Expenses.Txt - Notepad                                              _□×
File  Edit  Search  Help
                     Travel Expense Log
                     ====== ======= ===
                     \ExpnsLog.txt

Place                Date        Amount   Description
-----                ----        ------   -----------
Paris, France        11/26/96    $481.55  l'Hotel du Pont, two nights
Paris, France        11/26/96    $132.04  Lunch with G. Lepoint
Paris, France        11/26/96     $46.60  Taxi to airport
Strasbourg, France   11/26/96     $92.23  Dinner with C. Muller, Cafe Berthe
Strasbourg, France   11/27/96    $143.68  l'Hotel Central, one night
Strasbourg, France   11/27/96    $127.39  Miscellaneous supplies
Basel, Switzerland   11/27/96    $375.97  Dinner with buyers
Geneva, Switzerland  11/28/96    $143.41  l'Hotel du lac, one night
Geneva, Switzerland  11/28/96    $228.68  Lunch with agents
Florence, Italy      11/29/96    $158.94  English Hotel, one night
Florence, Italy      11/30/96    $139.07  Dinner with buyers
Paris, France        12/01/96    $350.38  Car rental
Caen, France         12/02/96    $333.33  Conference room, l'Hotel du Chateau
Caen, France         12/03/96    $161.90  l'Hotel du Chateau, one night
Chartres, France     12/04/96     $85.37  Lunch meeting with M. Lenoir
Chartres, France     12/05/96    $154.78  Grand Hotel, one night
Paris, France        12/06/96    $109.76  Books and supplies
Paris, France        12/06/96    $650.47  l'Hotel du Jardin, Four nights

Total amount spent ...           $3,915.57
```

Figure 7-12: The Expenses report. Notice that the program has calculated the dollar equivalent of each expenditure. A total expense amount appears at the bottom of the report.

If you prefer the latter approach, the Expense Log program allows you to change the active file at any time during the program run. To do so, move the mouse pointer over the globe icon located just to the left of the panel of command buttons. The caption under the icon reads "File Name." When positioned over this icon, the mouse pointer becomes an upward-pointing hand and a ToolTip provides a brief explanation of the control, as shown in Figure 7-13. Click the globe once to view the Expense Log File Name dialog box, shown in Figure 7-14. Then enter the file name (and a path name, optionally) under which you want to save subsequent expense records. Click OK. The new file name appears on the title bar of the Expense Log program; for example:

```
International Travel Expense Log - \Africa97.Txt
```

Given this display, you always know the name of the file in which you're currently saving data.

Figure 7-13: The File Name icon. Click this control when you want to store expense records in a new file.

Figure 7-14: Working with a new expense log file. You can enter the name of an existing file in which you've already stored expense records, or you can enter the name of a new file that you want to create.

In summary, the Expense Log program is easy to use for recording expenses and generating expense reports from a business trip. This project is a good place to start your study of Visual Basic programming. It provides an introduction to the structure and organization of procedures and it illustrates a variety of techniques for working with variables and data.

Inside the Expense Log Program

The project consists of one form, which contains all the program's code. Scrolling through the code window (or examining the listing in Appendix A), you'll find the program's major event procedures, including the six Click procedures designed to carry out specific operations when buttons are clicked:

✦ The cmdSave_Click procedure (Figure 7-15) confirms that a complete expense record has been entered into the program's dialog box, and then saves the record to the current data file (ExpnsLog.Txt by default).

✦ The cmdRate_Click procedure (Figures 7-16 and 7-17) searches through the data file for records that match the current country selection (that is, the name displayed in the Country text box). By comparing the exchange rates stored in the file, the procedure determines the largest and smallest rates recorded for the current country, and displays these rates in a message box.

✦ The cmdExpReport_Click procedure (Figures 7-18 and 7-19) reads the current data file, and uses the information it contains to create an expense report that's easy to read and understand. The expense report is stored as a text file in Expenses.Txt.

✦ The cmdClear_Click procedure (Figure 7-20) assigns blank strings to the Text properties of text boxes and combo boxes.

✦ The cmdExit_Click procedure (the second routine in Figure 7-20) terminates the program run.

✦ The picFileName_Click procedure (Figure 7-21) is called when the user clicks the File Name icon. The procedure displays an input box on the desktop to elicit a new file name for storing expense records.

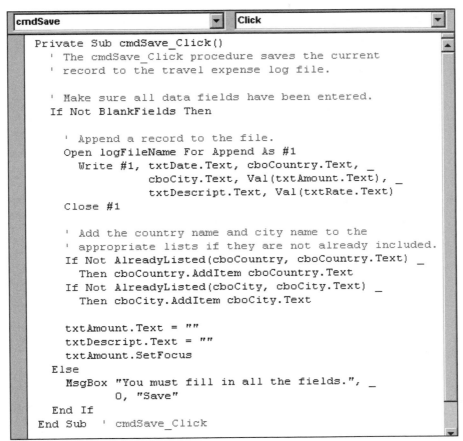

```
cmdSave                          ▼    Click                          ▼

Private Sub cmdSave_Click()
  ' The cmdSave_Click procedure saves the current
  ' record to the travel expense log file.

  ' Make sure all data fields have been entered.
  If Not BlankFields Then

    ' Append a record to the file.
    Open logFileName For Append As #1
      Write #1, txtDate.Text, cboCountry.Text, _
              cboCity.Text, Val(txtAmount.Text), _
              txtDescript.Text, Val(txtRate.Text)
    Close #1

    ' Add the country name and city name to the
    ' appropriate lists if they are not already included.
    If Not AlreadyListed(cboCountry, cboCountry.Text) _
      Then cboCountry.AddItem cboCountry.Text
    If Not AlreadyListed(cboCity, cboCity.Text) _
      Then cboCity.AddItem cboCity.Text

    txtAmount.Text = ""
    txtDescript.Text = ""
    txtAmount.SetFocus
  Else
    MsgBox "You must fill in all the fields.", _
          0, "Save"
  End If
End Sub  ' cmdSave_Click
```

Figure 7-15: The cmdSave_Click procedure writes a complete record to the expense log file.

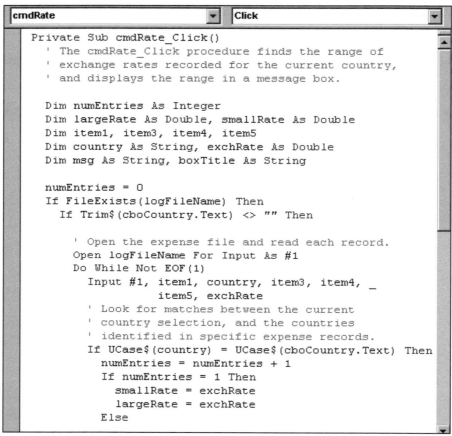

Figure 7-16: The cmdRate_Click procedure displays a message box showing the range of exchange rates recorded for the current country. This is the first half of the procedure.

```
cmdRate                          ▼    Click                              ▼
                ' Compare each exchange rate to locate
                ' the smallest and largest rates on record.
            If exchRate < smallRate Then _
               smallRate = exchRate
            If exchRate > largeRate Then _
               largeRate = exchRate
          End If
        End If
      Loop
      Close #1

      boxTitle = "Exchange Rates for " & cboCountry.Text
      If numEntries > 0 Then
        msg = "   Lowest: " & smallRate & _
              "   Highest: " & largeRate
      Else  ' If no country matches were found...
        msg = "No entries for " & cboCountry.Text & "."
      End If
    Else  ' If no country is currently selected...
      msg = "Please select or enter a country name."
      boxTitle = "Exchange Rates"
    End If
  Else  ' If logFileName doesn't exist...
    msg = logFileName & " is not available."
    boxTitle = "Exchange Rates"
  End If
  MsgBox msg, , boxTitle
End Sub  ' cmdRate_Click
```

Figure 7-17: This is the second half of the cmdRate_Click procedure.

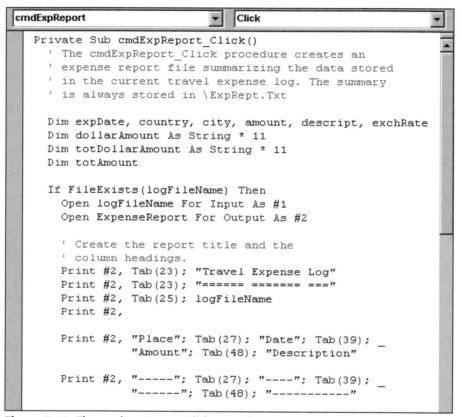

Figure 7-18: The cmdExpReport_Click procedure creates a summary report of the expenses recorded in the current file. This is the first half of the procedure.

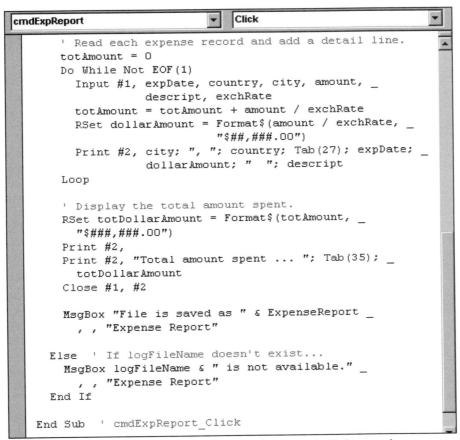

```
cmdExpReport            ▼   Click                    ▼

        ' Read each expense record and add a detail line.
        totAmount = 0
        Do While Not EOF(1)
          Input #1, expDate, country, city, amount, _
                    descript, exchRate
          totAmount = totAmount + amount / exchRate
          RSet dollarAmount = Format$(amount / exchRate, _
                    "$##,###.00")
          Print #2, city; ", "; country; Tab(27); expDate; _
                    dollarAmount; "   "; descript
        Loop

        ' Display the total amount spent.
        RSet totDollarAmount = Format$(totAmount, _
          "$###,###.00")
        Print #2,
        Print #2, "Total amount spent ... "; Tab(35); _
          totDollarAmount
        Close #1, #2

        MsgBox "File is saved as " & ExpenseReport _
          , , "Expense Report"

      Else  ' If logFileName doesn't exist...
        MsgBox logFileName & " is not available." _
          , , "Expense Report"
      End If

    End Sub  ' cmdExpReport_Click
```

Figure 7-19: This is the second half of the cmdExpReport_Click procedure.

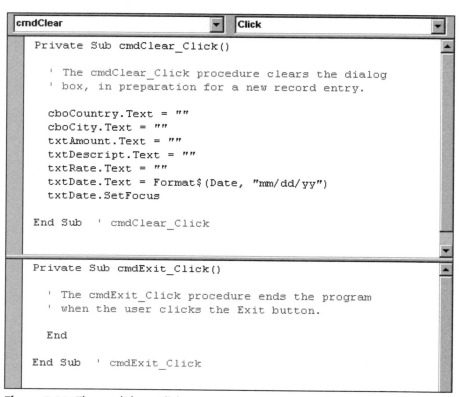

Figure 7-20: The cmdClear_Click procedure clears the text boxes on the dialog box so that the user can enter a new record. The cmdExit_Click procedure terminates the program run.

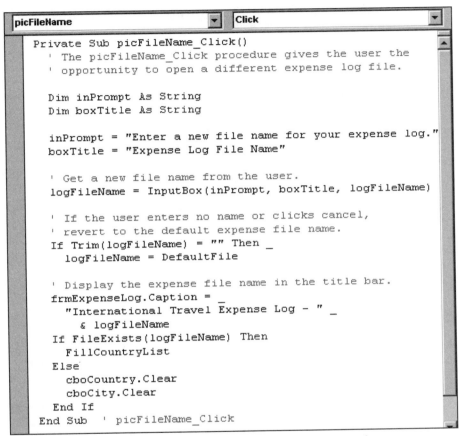

```
picFileName ▼    Click ▼

Private Sub picFileName_Click()
  ' The picFileName_Click procedure gives the user the
  ' opportunity to open a different expense log file.

  Dim inPrompt As String
  Dim boxTitle As String

  inPrompt = "Enter a new file name for your expense log."
  boxTitle = "Expense Log File Name"

  ' Get a new file name from the user.
  logFileName = InputBox(inPrompt, boxTitle, logFileName)

  ' If the user enters no name or clicks cancel,
  ' revert to the default expense file name.
  If Trim(logFileName) = "" Then _
    logFileName = DefaultFile

  ' Display the expense file name in the title bar.
  frmExpenseLog.Caption = _
    "International Travel Expense Log - " _
      & logFileName
  If FileExists(logFileName) Then
    FillCountryList
  Else
    cboCountry.Clear
    cboCity.Clear
  End If
End Sub  ' picFileName_Click
```

Figure 7-21: The picFileName_Click procedure elicits the name of a new expense log file that the user wants to create or open.

In addition to event procedures, the program contains many important sections of code known as *general procedures*. Unlike event procedures, general procedures are *not* performed directly as the result of events. Rather, a general procedure is *called* from a specific place in your code. As the result of a call, Visual Basic sends control to the procedure, performs its statements, and then returns control to the location of the call.

There are several important advantages to organizing your code into a combination of event procedures and general procedures:

✦ General procedures allow you to isolate particular operations into small, self-contained blocks of code that are easy to identify and to revise if necessary. As a rule of thumb, you should try to limit the length of each procedure you write to about a page of code. Dividing your program into many small procedures — rather than a few long ones — results in code that is easier to maintain over time.

✦ A general procedure, as the term implies, can be written to carry out operations in a variety of different contexts. A given procedure might be called from several places in your program, and might accomplish different tasks depending on the source of the call. As a result, general procedures help you avoid unnecessary duplication in your code.

✦ General procedures come in two varieties: Sub and Function procedures. A Sub procedure performs a defined operation and then returns control to the caller. A Function procedure is designed to calculate or determine a specific value, and return that value to the location of the procedure call. You'll see examples of both Sub and Function procedures as you continue examining the International Travel Expense Log program.

Because general procedures are so important to the structure of a program, Visual Basic provides convenient tools for creating and working with them. You'll look at these tools next.

Creating General Procedures

As you've seen, Visual Basic automatically creates *templates* for event procedures in a project. For example, suppose a project contains a command button that you've named cmdOpen. To create a template for the cmdOpen_Click procedure, you simply open the form that contains the button (in design mode, of course), and double-click the button. Visual Basic opens the code window for the form, and creates a template consisting of the first and last lines of the event procedure, as in Figure 7-22. To develop the event procedure itself, you begin entering lines of code between the Sub and End Sub statements.

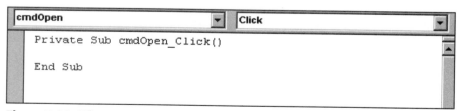

Figure 7-22: When you get ready to write an event procedure, Visual Basic automatically enters the first and last lines of the procedure into the code window.

Likewise, Visual Basic provides a tool you can use to create templates for any general procedure you want to include in the code of a project. To use this tool, you begin by deciding what kind of procedure you want to create — a Sub or Function procedure — and devising a name for the new procedure. Then follow these steps:

1. In the Project Explorer window, select the form or module in which you want to create a new procedure. Click the View Code button to open the code window.

2. Choose Tools⇨Add Procedure. The Add Procedure dialog box appears on the screen, as shown in Figure 7-23.

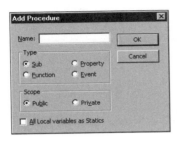

Figure 7-23: The Add Procedure dialog box provides options for creating a Sub or Function procedure in the current form or module.

3. In the Name box, enter the name of the procedure you want to create.

4. Select Sub or Function in the Type group. (Notice that there are two other options in the Type frame — Property and Event. You'll learn about Property procedures in Chapter 13.)

5. Select Public or Private in the Scope group. A Private procedure is available for use only in the form or module that contains the procedure. A Public procedure is designed to be called from any place in a project's code.

6. Click OK. In response, Visual Basic creates a template for your new procedure in the active code window.

Tip   Notice the check box labeled "All Local variables as Statics" at the bottom of the Add Procedure dialog box. If you check this option, Visual Basic adds the keyword *Static* to the top line of your procedure. The result is that all *local* variables (that is, variables that are declared inside the procedure itself) retain their values from one call to the next. Static variables can be useful in procedures that accumulate values incrementally over several calls.

Suppose you follow these steps to create a public Sub procedure named *DoCalc.* Figure 7-24 shows the lines you'll see in your code window. By contrast, if you take the same steps to create a Function procedure named *FindItem,* Visual Basic supplies the code in Figure 7-25. In either case, you're ready to begin writing the procedure, between the Sub and End Sub statements or the Function and End Function statements.

Figure 7-24: The Add Procedure command creates a new general Sub procedure for use in the current form or module.

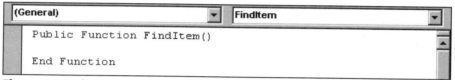

Figure 7-25: Alternatively, you can use Add Procedure to create a Function procedure.

A more direct way to create a new procedure is simply to enter a complete Sub or Function statement on a blank line in a code window. When you press Enter to complete the line, Visual Basic supplies an End Sub or End Function statement. As you develop procedures in a form or a module, you can use the code window's Object and Procedure lists to locate any general procedure or to view the names of all the general procedures you've written so far:

1. Open the code window.

2. Select the *(General)* entry in the Object list at the top of the code window.

3. Pull down the Procedure list to view the names of all the general procedures you've written for this form or module.

4. Click any name in the list to scroll directly to a particular procedure.

For example, Figure 7-26 shows the list of general procedures in the Expense Log program. You'll be examining a number of these procedures as you continue this chapter.

Figure 7-26: Viewing the list of general procedures in a form or module. Choose (General) in the Object list and then pull down the Procedure list to view the names of general Sub and Function procedures.

Understanding Procedures

A Sub procedure is designed to perform a specific, carefully defined task. The task is repeated each time your program calls the procedure. By contrast, the primary job of a Function procedure is to return a specific item of information.

As you've seen, every procedure has a name, which you supply when you first create the procedure. The name of the procedure is defined in the Sub or Function statement at the beginning of the code. A good procedure name indicates something essential about what the procedure is designed to do.

A *call* is a statement or expression that refers to a procedure by name and results in a performance of the procedure. A *private* procedure can be called from any other procedure in the same form or module; a *public* procedure can be called from anywhere in the project that contains the procedure. When a general procedure completes its task, control of the program returns to the location where the procedure was originally called.

A call to a Sub procedure is a statement by itself. For example, consider the Sub procedure named *DoCalc;* a call to the procedure may look like this:

```
DoCalc
```

By contrast, a call to a Function procedure typically appears as part of a statement designed to use the value that the function returns. For example, a call to a function named FindItem might appear at the right side of an assignment statement:

```
newItem = FindItem
```

or in a decision statement:

```
If oldItem = FindItem Then
   ...
End If
```

The more you learn about Sub and Function procedures, the more skillfully you can use them as the building blocks of a program. In the upcoming sections of this chapter, you'll review the structural elements of procedures and you'll focus on their use. In particular, you'll learn how to send information to a procedure in a call, and how to design a procedure to make use of the information it receives.

Designing Sub procedures

Here is a general format of a Sub procedure:

```
Sub ProcedureName (argument1, argument2, ...)
  ' The statements of the procedure.
End Sub
```

As you've seen, the keyword *Sub* can be preceded by Private or Public, specifying the scope of the procedure. In addition, the keyword *Static* results in a procedure in which the values of local variables are retained from one call to the next. For example, here is the general format for a private static Sub procedure:

```
Private Static Sub ProcedureName (argument1, argument2, ...)
    ' The statements of the procedure.
End Sub
```

The procedure name is followed by an optional *argument list,* enclosed in parentheses. An argument is a variable representing a data item that will be passed to the procedure at the time of a call. The argument list consists of variable names and, optionally, their type declarations. Like any variable, each argument belongs to a specified type.

You can use an As clause to define an argument's type. For example, consider the *FillCityList* procedure (Figure 7-27). This is the first line of the procedure:

```
Private Sub FillCityList(countryName As String)
```

As its name indicates, this procedure is in charge of maintaining the list of names attached to the City box in the Expense Log program. When the user chooses an entry from the Country list, a call to *FillCityList* opens the current data file, finds all the city names recorded for the selected country, and adds each name to the drop-down City list. As you can see, the procedure receives one string argument, represented by the variable *countryName*. This argument tells the procedure what country to search for in the data file. In the procedure's code, this argument looks just like any other variable. Its distinct feature is that it represents data that has been passed to the procedure from the caller.

Calling Sub procedures

A call to a Sub procedure sends items of information to the procedure's argument variables. Here is the general form of a Sub procedure call:

```
ProcedureName argument1, argument2, ...
```

Notice that the argument list is not enclosed in parentheses in the procedure call.

For example, a call to *FillCityList* sends one string argument to the procedure. The following call, which takes place from a general procedure named *ChangeCityList* (Figure 7-28), sends the current Text property of the cboCountry combo box control as the value of the argument:

```
FillCityList cboCountry.Text
```

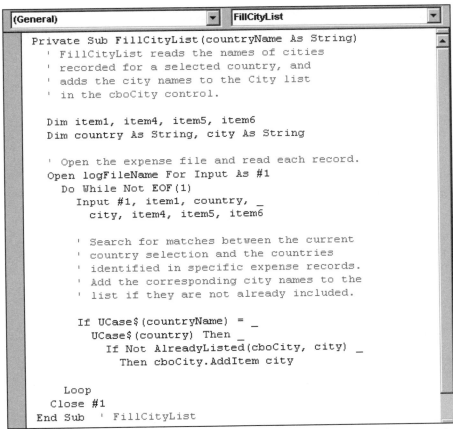

```
(General)                              ▼    FillCityList                        ▼

Private Sub FillCityList(countryName As String)
   ' FillCityList reads the names of cities
   ' recorded for a selected country, and
   ' adds the city names to the City list
   ' in the cboCity control.

   Dim item1, item4, item5, item6
   Dim country As String, city As String

   ' Open the expense file and read each record.
   Open logFileName For Input As #1
     Do While Not EOF(1)
       Input #1, item1, country, _
         city, item4, item5, item6

       ' Search for matches between the current
       ' country selection and the countries
       ' identified in specific expense records.
       ' Add the corresponding city names to the
       ' list if they are not already included.

       If UCase$(countryName) = _
         UCase$(country) Then _
           If Not AlreadyListed(cboCity, city) _
             Then cboCity.AddItem city

     Loop
   Close #1
End Sub  ' FillCityList
```

Figure 7-27: The *FillCityList* procedure receives one string argument, represented as *countryName*. The procedure uses this value to determine which country to search for in the expense log file.

In this particular example, the argument is represented by a property. But you can express an argument in any way that results in a value of the appropriate data type. For example, the argument might appear as a literal string value, enclosed in quotation marks:

```
FillCityList "France"
```

Keep in mind that the argument list is optional in the definition of a general procedure. If there is no argument list, a call consists simply of the procedure name itself. For example, the *ChangeCityList* procedure shown in Figure 7-28 arranges to rebuild the city list whenever a change occurs in the country entry. The procedure takes no arguments:

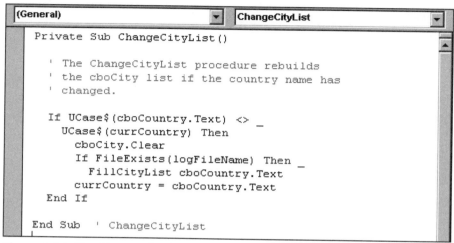

Figure 7-28: The *ChangeCityList* procedure makes a call to *FillCityList* and passes the value of the cboCountry.Text property as an argument.

```
Private Sub ChangeCityList()
```

In the Sub statement, the procedure name is followed by a pair of empty parentheses, indicating that there is no argument list. A call to the procedure is represented simply by the name itself:

```
ChangeCityList
```

As you can see in Figure 7-29, the program calls this procedure in response to either of two events:

✦ A Click event occurs when the user chooses a new entry from the Country list. This event results in a call to the cboCountry_Click procedure.

✦ An event named LostFocus occurs when the user moves the focus from the Country list to another control (by pressing the Tab key or by clicking another control with the mouse). In this case, the corresponding event procedure is cboCountry_LostFocus. (You'll see other examples of the LostFocus event shortly.)

Passing controls as arguments

Significantly, a procedure can also receive a reference to a control as an argument. This feature allows you to write procedures that perform general operations on different controls in your project. For example, consider the *ValidNumInput* procedure, shown in Figure 7-30. As you can see, the procedure receives one argument, identified as a Control object:

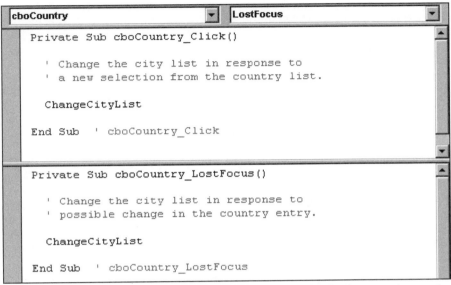

Figure 7-29: Two events can result in a call to the *ChangeCityList* procedure — the user actually selects a new country in the Country list (cboCountry_Click) or simply moves the focus from the Country list to some other control (cboCountry_LostFocus).

```
Private Sub ValidNumInput(textControl As Control)
```

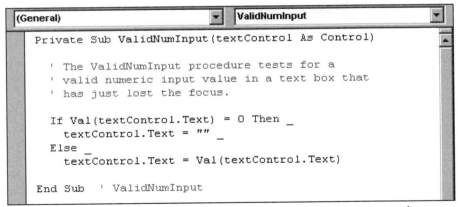

Figure 7-30: The *ValidNumInput* procedure receives a reference to a text box control as its argument. The procedure confirms that the current entry in the text box can be read as a numeric value.

The purpose of this procedure is to examine and validate the contents of a text box that is meant for numeric input. The procedure examines the box just after the control loses the focus. If the control contains a valid numeric entry, the value is left intact. But if the entry can't be read as a number, the procedure clears the value from the box. The Expense Log program uses this procedure to ensure that the Amount box (named txtAmount) and the Rate box (named txtRate) both contain numeric values. If the user inadvertently enters a nonnumeric value in one of these boxes, the *ValidNumInput* procedure removes the entry. (You can test this procedure during a program run by entering a nonnumeric value in either of these boxes and then moving the focus to another control.)

The *ValidNumInput* procedure needs to be able to operate on a control that's specified at the time of a call. Accordingly, the *textControl* argument represents the control whose contents should be examined. The procedure is called when either the Amount or the Rate box loses the focus, triggering the LostFocus event for the corresponding control. In Figure 7-31 you can see the two LostFocus event procedures that handle this situation. In each case, a call is made to the *ValidNumInput* procedure to check for numeric data entry. For example, this is the call that's made when the Amount box loses the focus:

```
ValidNumInput txtAmount
```

And here is the equivalent call for the Rate box:

```
ValidNumInput txtRate
```

In both cases, the call sends the name of a text box control as the argument of the *ValidNumInput* procedure. The procedure then performs its validation tasks on the contents of the corresponding control.

Optional arguments

Sometimes you may want to write a procedure that receives optional arguments — values that can either be included or omitted in a procedure call, depending on the requirements of the caller. In the procedure's argument list, you use the Optional keyword to identify such an argument:

```
Optional argumentName As typeName
```

You can include more than one optional item in an argument list, as long as each is declared using the Optional keyword. After the first optional argument, any subsequent arguments in the list must also be optional. In other words, you can't randomly mix the order of the required and optional arguments.

A Sub procedure named *ShowExpense,* in Figure 7-32, contains an example of an optional argument. (Note that this hypothetical procedure is not part of the Travel Expense Log project.) Designed to display a message describing a single travel expense entry, the procedure receives two required arguments, identified as *amount* and *description.* In addition, the procedure may receive an optional argument, *currencyName*. If *currencyName* is omitted, the procedure assumes that *amount* is in dollars; otherwise, the procedure uses *currencyName* as the local currency.

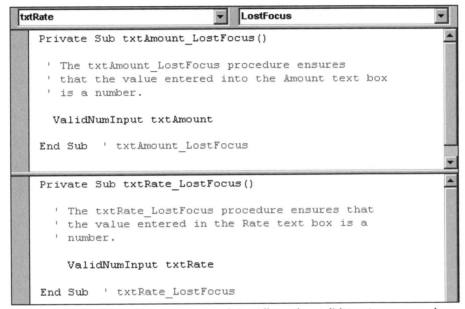

```
txtRate                          ▼   LostFocus                      ▼

    Private Sub txtAmount_LostFocus()                               ▲

     ' The txtAmount_LostFocus procedure ensures
     ' that the value entered into the Amount text box
     ' is a number.

      ValidNumInput txtAmount

    End Sub  ' txtAmount_LostFocus                                  ▼

    Private Sub txtRate_LostFocus()                                 ▲

      ' The txtRate_LostFocus procedure ensures that
      ' the value entered in the Rate text box is a
      ' number.

       ValidNumInput txtRate

    End Sub  ' txtRate_LostFocus
```

Figure 7-31: Two LostFocus events result in calls to the *ValidNumInput* procedure.

Suppose the procedure is part of a project in which the user enters information about a travel expense into a group of text boxes. If the user provides only an expense amount and a description, the program calls *ShowExpense* as follows, supplying only the two required arguments:

```
ShowExpense txtAmount.Text, txtDescription.Text
```

In this case, the procedure displays a message giving the expense amount in dollars, as shown in Figure 7-33. On the other hand, if the user provides a local currency name, the program calls the *ShowExpense* procedure and sends all three arguments, including the final optional one:

```
ShowExpense txtAmount.Text, txtDescription.Text, _
    txtCurrency.Text
```

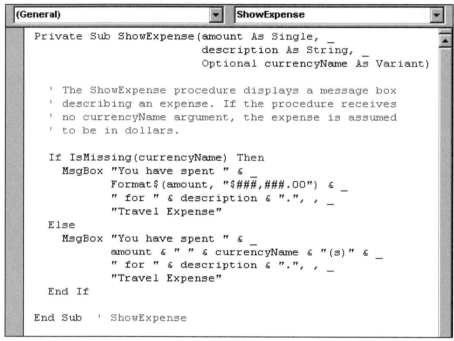

```
(General)                          ▼  ShowExpense                  ▼

Private Sub ShowExpense(amount As Single, _
                       description As String, _
                       Optional currencyName As Variant)

    ' The ShowExpense procedure displays a message box
    ' describing an expense. If the procedure receives
    ' no currencyName argument, the expense is assumed
    ' to be in dollars.

    If IsMissing(currencyName) Then
      MsgBox "You have spent " & _
             Format$(amount, "$###,###.00") & _
             " for " & description & ".", , _
             "Travel Expense"
    Else
      MsgBox "You have spent " & _
             amount & " " & currencyName & "(s)" & _
             " for " & description & ".", , _
             "Travel Expense"
    End If

End Sub  ' ShowExpense
```

Figure 7-32: The *ShowExpense* procedure illustrates the declaration syntax for an optional argument. This procedure accepts either two or three arguments, depending on the requirements of the caller.

The procedure responds with a message that cites the currency, as in Figure 7-34.

Figure 7-33: If *ShowExpense* receives only the first two arguments, the message shows the expense in dollars.

Figure 7-34: If the procedure receives the third (optional) argument, the message includes the local currency name.

Looking at the *ShowExpense* procedure itself, you can see that the optional *currencyName* argument belongs to the Variant type:

```
Private Sub ShowExpense(amount As Single, _
                       description As String, _
                       Optional currencyName As Variant)
```

Like a text box, a Variant-type variable can represent a numeric or string data item. (You'll learn much more about the Variant data type later in this chapter.) Given a Variant argument, the procedure can use a function named IsMissing to determine whether or not the optional value has been received:

```
If IsMissing(currencyName) Then
```

By this simple mechanism, the ShowExpense procedure chooses the appropriate message to display on the screen. If the expression *IsMissing(currencyName)* is true, the expense is displayed in dollars; if false, the expense appears in the named currency.

Tip In the syntax for declaring an optional item in an argument list, you can also supply a *default* value for the argument:

```
Optional argumentName As typeName = defaultValue
```

If the caller doesn't send a value for the optional argument, the default value is automatically assigned. For example the ShowExpense procedure could be redesigned to begin as follows:

```
Private Sub ShowExpense(amount As Single, _
                        description As String, _
                        Optional currencyName _
                            As Variant = "dollar")

If currencyName = "dollar" Then
```

Multiple arguments

In some applications you may want to design a procedure that accepts a list of arguments, where the number of items in the list is not known in advance. For this situation, you can use the keyword *ParamArray* to declare the argument variable:

```
ParamArray argumentName()
```

A ParamArray argument must belong to the Variant type, which is the default if you omit the As clause. The parentheses after *argumentName* indicate that this argument is an *array,* a data structure designed to represent a list of values. (You'll learn how to use arrays in Chapter 9.)

The *ShowCountries* procedure in Figure 7-35 contains an example of a ParamArray argument. (Again, this sample code is not part of the Expense Log program.) The procedure is designed to receive a list of countries that have been part of a business trip, and to display the list in a message box. The *countries* array is the ParamArray argument that represents the list of country names:

```
Private Sub ShowCountries(ParamArray countries())
```

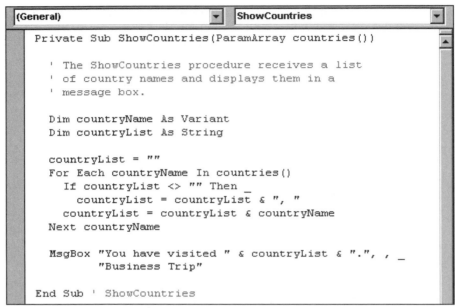

```
(General)                              ▼   ShowCountries                      ▼

   Private Sub ShowCountries(ParamArray countries())

     ' The ShowCountries procedure receives a list
     ' of country names and displays them in a
     ' message box.

     Dim countryName As Variant
     Dim countryList As String

     countryList = ""
     For Each countryName In countries()
       If countryList <> "" Then _
         countryList = countryList & ", "
       countryList = countryList & countryName
     Next countryName

     MsgBox "You have visited " & countryList & ".", , _
            "Business Trip"

   End Sub ' ShowCountries
```

Figure 7-35: The ShowCountries procedure illustrates the use of a ParamArray argument. The countries argument can receive a list of any number of country names.

A call to the procedure sends a list of strings; the length of the list can vary. For example, the following call results in the message box shown in Figure 7-36:

```
ShowCountries "France", "Italy", "Spain"
```

And this call produces the message in Figure 7-37:

```
ShowCountries "Senegal", "Ivory Coast", _
              "Mali", "Burkina Fasso", _
              "Togo", "Benin"
```

The *ShowCountries* procedure successfully handles a list of any length.

Figure 7-36: Here the procedure received a list of three names.

Figure 7-37: In this case, the procedure received a list of six names.

Tip You can define Optional or ParamArray arguments in both Sub and Function procedures. Function procedures are introduced in the next section of this chapter.

Passing arguments by value or by reference

Two other keywords that you might see in argument lists are *ByVal* and *ByRef:*

```
ByVal argumentName As
typeName
ByRef argumentName As
typeName
```

These keywords determine the mechanism for passing an argument to a procedure — specifically, when the argument is expressed as a variable name in the call statement:

✦ ByVal indicates that the argument is passed by value. The procedure receives a copy of the variable's value, not use of the variable itself. If the procedure happens to change the value of the argument, the change is local to the procedure. When control returns to the caller, the variable retains the value it had before the procedure call.

✦ ByRef indicates that the argument is passed by reference. In other words, the actual variable is available to the procedure. Any change that the procedure makes in the value of the variable is global. When control returns to the caller, the variable has the new value that was assigned by the procedure.

ByRef is the default for all arguments in a procedure. Unless you specify ByVal, a procedure can make permanent changes in the values of variables it receives as arguments. Keep this in mind as you design procedures for a project; the ByRef default sometimes results in unexpected side effects.

Designing function procedures

Like a Sub procedure, a function may include an argument list:

```
Function FunctionName (argument1, argument2, ...) As type
  ' The statements of the function procedure.
End Function
```

A Function can be declared as Private or Public. Your choice between these options depends on whether you are designing a function for use exclusively within a given form or module, or for general use across the components of a project.

A function procedure has some important features that distinguish it from a Sub procedure. Most importantly, a function is designed to return a specific value to the location of the function call:

✦ An optional As clause in the Function statement defines the type of value that the function will return. (If the As clause is omitted, the function returns a Variant value.)

✦ Within the function's code — often near the end — is an assignment statement that identifies the return value. At the left side of the equal sign in this assignment statement is the name of the function itself, and at the right side is an expression that gives the return value:

```
FunctionName = returnValue
```

The arguments that a function receives are often central to the algorithm that produces the result. For example, consider the Expense Log project's *AlreadyListed* function, shown in Figure 7-38. This function prevents duplicate entries in the Country and City lists. In an expense log file, a given country and city name may be recorded many times, but each name should appear only once in the Country or City list.

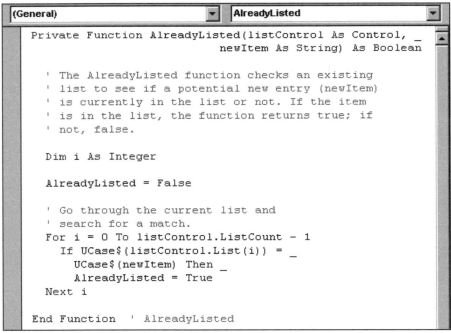

```
(General)                              AlreadyListed

Private Function AlreadyListed(listControl As Control, _
                          newItem As String) As Boolean

   ' The AlreadyListed function checks an existing
   ' list to see if a potential new entry (newItem)
   ' is currently in the list or not. If the item
   ' is in the list, the function returns true; if
   ' not, false.

   Dim i As Integer

   AlreadyListed = False

   ' Go through the current list and
   ' search for a match.
   For i = 0 To listControl.ListCount - 1
     If UCase$(listControl.List(i)) = _
       UCase$(newItem) Then _
       AlreadyListed = True
   Next i

End Function   ' AlreadyListed
```

Figure 7-38: The AlreadyListed function returns a value of True if an item already appears in a list, or False if the item is new.

The *AlreadyListed* function returns a *Boolean* value — that is, a value that the program can read as True or False:

```
Private Function AlreadyListed(listControl As Control, _
                  newItem As String) As Boolean
```

The function searches through a list for a particular entry. If the item is already in the list, the function returns a value of True; if not, False. Notice that the function takes two arguments — a Control-type argument named *listControl* and a String argument named *newItem*. The first argument tells the function which list to search through, and the second provides the string value that the function should search for.

Calling function procedures

In Visual Basic, a function call is typically part of a statement, not a statement by itself. For example, a function call might appear in an assignment statement in the following general form:

```
variableName = FunctionName(argument1, argument2, ...)
```

Unlike the argument list in a call to a Sub procedure, the arguments sent to a function are enclosed in parentheses after the function's name. The arguments may appear as literal values, variables, or expressions, as long as each value matches the data type specified in the function definition itself.

Tip Visual Basic also allows you to write a function call as a statement by itself. In this case, the call results in a performance of the Function procedure — and the return value is simply discarded. But keep in mind that the general purpose of a function is to produce and return a value; if your program doesn't need a return value, consider redesigning the procedure in Sub form rather than Function form.

The *AlreadyListed* function is called from the *FillCountryList* procedure (Figure 7-39) and the *FillCityList* procedure (Figure 7-40), which are responsible for building the Country and City lists. In each case, the function call appears in an If statement, designed to decide whether or not to add a new item to the list. Here is the statement in the *FillCountryList* procedure:

```
If Not AlreadyListed(cboCountry, countryName) _
   Then cboCountry.AddItem countryName
```

You'll learn about decision statements in detail in Chapter 7, but for now you can intuitively see how this statement works:

✦ The call to the *AlreadyListed* function checks to see whether a particular country — represented by the variable *countryName* — is already in the Country list. (Notice that a reference to the control cboCountry is sent as the first argument to the function.)

✦ If *AlreadyListed* returns a value of False, the expression *Not AlreadyListed* is True. In this case, the program uses the AddItem method to add the country name to the list.

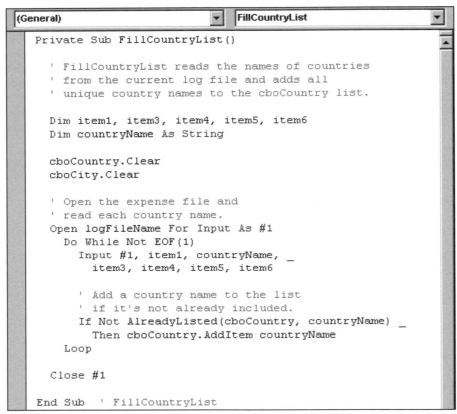

Figure 7-39: The *FillCountryList* procedure calls *AlreadyListed* to find out whether the list already contains a given country name. If *AlreadyListed* returns a value of False, *FillCountryList* adds the country to the list.

✦ If *AlreadyListed* returns a value of True — meaning that the country is already in the list — *Not AlreadyListed* is False. In this case, the country is not added again to the list.

A similar statement in the *FillCityList* procedure checks to see whether a given city name is already in the City list:

```
If Not AlreadyListed(cboCity, city) _
   Then cboCity.AddItem city
```

Examining these two decision statements closely, you can appreciate the beauty of a function like *AlreadyListed*. Once you've created the function as a general tool, you can confidently use it in many contexts — searching through various lists for different data values. When you write a call to the function, you don't need to think about the algorithmic details of the search itself; you simply focus on sending the right combination of arguments to the function.

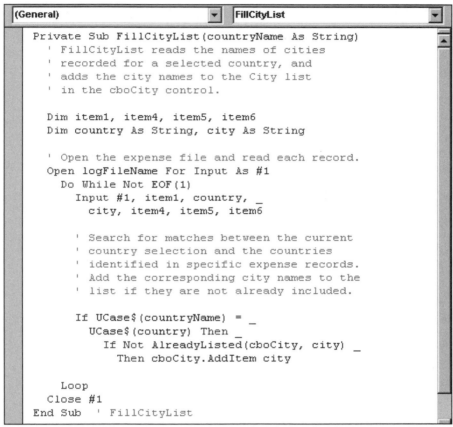

```
(General)                          ▼   FillCityList                    ▼

  Private Sub FillCityList(countryName As String)
    ' FillCityList reads the names of cities
    ' recorded for a selected country, and
    ' adds the city names to the City list
    ' in the cboCity control.

    Dim item1, item4, item5, item6
    Dim country As String, city As String

    ' Open the expense file and read each record.
    Open logFileName For Input As #1
      Do While Not EOF(1)
        Input #1, item1, country, _
          city, item4, item5, item6

        ' Search for matches between the current
        ' country selection and the countries
        ' identified in specific expense records.
        ' Add the corresponding city names to the
        ' list if they are not already included.

        If UCase$(countryName) = _
          UCase$(country) Then _
            If Not AlreadyListed(cboCity, city) _
              Then cboCity.AddItem city

      Loop
    Close #1
End Sub   ' FillCityList
```

Figure 7-40: The *FillCityList* procedure calls *AlreadyListed* to find out whether the list contains a given city name. If *AlreadyListed* returns a value of False, *FillCityList* adds the city to the list.

In summary, one important way to exchange information between different parts of your program is to pass argument values to a Sub or Function procedure. Inside the procedure, the arguments are represented by variables defined in the Sub or Function statement.

But there are other important ways to share data among procedures. You'll continue to examine this topic in the remaining sections of this chapter.

Using Variables in a Program

A program may contain many different variables to represent data. Most program-mers prefer to use meaningful variable names that clearly indicate the kind of information variables represent. For example, variables like *largeRate, smallRate, country, exchRate,* and *boxTitle* help make a program listing easy to read and understand. (Programmers who don't like to type are sometimes tempted to skimp on meaning in favor of brevity; for this reason, you may often see very short variable names like *i, j,* and *k* in a program.) As you write your own programs, you'll develop your own style of creating variable names.

An *assignment statement* is an essential way to store a value in a variable. The item you assign to a variable can be represented as a literal value, another variable, or an expression. An *expression* is a sequence of operations that result in a particular value. When you write an expression as part of an assignment statement, Visual Basic performs the operations and then assigns the result to the designated variable.

In the Expense Log program you can find many examples of variables, assignments, and expressions. You'll also see uses of the Dim statement to define variables at different levels of the program. Figure 7-41 shows the code known as the *general declarations section* of the frmExpenseLog form, which starts with a series of comment lines that describe the project itself. Notice that the first statement in this section is the following:

```
Option Explicit
```

As you know, this statement enforces the discipline of systematic variable declarations. As a result of this statement, all variables used in the program have to be declared formally. You'll see the significance of this option as you continue examining the program's code.

Declaring variables

Visual Basic sets a few simple rules for variable names: A name begins with a letter, and may contain any combination of letters and digits. Embedded periods and spaces are not allowed. A variable name can be as long as 255 characters. But once you've created a variable, you've got to spell it consistently throughout your program; the longer the name, the harder this task becomes. You should therefore try to write variable names that are as meaningful as possible within a reasonable length. Most programmers create names that are no longer than about 10 to 15 characters. You can use uppercase or lowercase letters in a variable name. The use of uppercase letters can help clarify the significance of a name, as in *logFileName* or *countryName*.

As you type variable names into the code window, Visual Basic automatically maintains consistency in alphabetic case. For example, suppose you initially declare a variable as *cityName*. Then in another part of your program you inadvertently type the variable as *cityNAME*. Visual Basic recognizes this as an existing name and changes it to *cityName*.

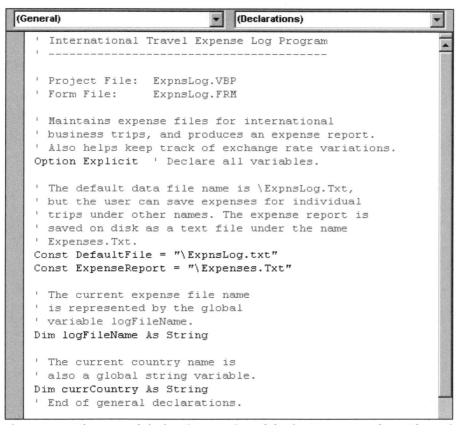

Figure 7-41: The general declarations section of the frmExpenseLog form. The variables defined in this section are available to all the procedures in the form.

In the As clause of a Dim statement you can declare a variable's data type:

```
Dim variableName As typeName
```

In this syntax, *typeName* may be one of these keywords:

✦ *Byte,* for an integer in the range 0 to 255.

✦ *Integer,* for a whole number in the range -32768 to 32767.

✦ *Long,* for an integer in a range of about -2 billion to +2 billion.

✦ *Single,* for a single-precision floating-point value.

✦ *Double,* for a double-precision floating-point value.

✦ *Currency,* for a numeric data type that supports an appropriate range and precision for large or small monetary values.

✦ *Date,* for values that Visual Basic recognizes as dates.

✦ *String,* for a string of characters, either variable length or fixed length.

✦ *Boolean,* for a value of True or False.

✦ *Object,* for a reference to an object.

✦ *Variant,* for Visual Basic's most versatile and general-purpose data type. (This is the default type if you omit the As clause from a Dim declaration.)

The Expense Log program illustrates many of these data types. For example, the following Dim statements declare string variables:

```
Dim logFileName As String
Dim dollarAmount As String * 11
```

The first of these statements declares a variable-length string named *logFileName,* and the second a fixed-length string named *dollarAmount.* A variable-length string can contain any number of characters; this is the most commonly used type of string variable. But a fixed-length string can simplify operations in some procedures. For example, the Expense Log program uses the *dollarAmount* string variable in the process of organizing columns of information in the expense report.

Note the format for declaring a fixed-length string variable. After the keyword *String,* you include an asterisk and then the length of the variable in characters:

```
Dim variableName As String * length
```

You can declare individual variables in separate Dim statements, or you can use a single Dim statement to declare several variables at once:

```
Dim expDate, country, city, amount, _
          descript, exchRate

Dim largeRate As Double, smallRate as Double
```

The first of these Dim statements declares six variables belonging to the default Variant type. The second statement declares two double-precision floating-point variables.

In short, Visual Basic allows you to declare variables formally or informally, with or without the use of Dim statements. Your choice between these two approaches may depend on the length of your programming project or just your own programming style. Most programmers prefer to declare *all* variables, and therefore appreciate the extra security supplied by the Option Explicit statement. But in some very small projects, coding may seem easier and more efficient without the requirement of variable declarations. You'll decide for yourself as you begin building your own programs.

Tip   Notice the use of the terms *range* and *precision* in the descriptions of Visual Basic's numeric data types. The *range* of a numeric data type indicates the largest and smallest values that can be represented in the type. The *precision* is the number of digits of accuracy provided in the type. (For a complete technical description of any data type, consult the appropriate Visual Basic Help topic.)

The Variant type

Most variable types are, by design, somewhat rigid in the ways they can be used. For example, a numeric variable can store a number, not a string; if you try to assign a string value to a numeric variable, an error results. By contrast, a Variant can represent values of almost any type, thereby providing greater flexibility in programs that work with data. As you know, variables that are not explicitly declared belong to the Variant type by default. You may ultimately find yourself favoring the Variant over other variable types because of the advantages it provides.

Perhaps the best way to understand a Variant is to compare it with a text box control in a Visual Basic dialog box. A text box accepts any type of entry from the keyboard — number, currency, string, or date. What a program *does* with the input is another question, but the text box itself accepts all types of values. Likewise, any type of value can be stored in a Variant-type variable.

You'll find many illustrations of Variant-type variables in the Expense Log program. For example, the procedures that read expense records from the data file use Variants to represent individual fields of data. The cmdExpReport_Click procedure (shown back in Figures 7-18 and 7-19) defines six variables for this purpose:

```
Dim expDate, country, city, amount, descript, exchRate
```

These variables then appear in the Input statement that reads each record from the open file:

```
Input #1, expDate, country, city, amount, _
          descript, exchRate
```

You'll learn more about reading data from files in Chapter 10. For now, simply notice that the Variant-type variables can receive whatever data types are stored in the file itself, including dates, strings, and numeric values.

The scope of variables

The *scope* of a variable determines where it is available for use in your program. In general, variables defined inside a Sub or Function procedure are private to that procedure, and not available to other procedures in the same form or module. If another procedure happens to have a variable of the same name, it is a *different* variable, with its own distinct values.

Tip   The keywords Private and Public are available for explicitly declaring the scope of a variable. You can use these keywords in place of Dim to specify whether you want a variable to be available locally or globally.

Private variables are one of the great advantages of procedural programming. They allow you to develop independent procedures that don't interfere with each other's data. But occasionally you may want to establish a few central variables at the *module level* — that is, available to all the procedures in a form or module. In this case, you define the variables in the general declarations section, at the top of the code and outside any procedure.

For example, back in Figure 7-41 you can see the general declarations section of the Expense Log program, where two module-level String variables are declared:

```
Dim logFileName As String
Dim currCountry As String
```

The variable *logFileName* represents the file name under which the expense records will be stored. As you know, this file is \ExpnsLog.Txt by default, but can be changed at any time by the user. Because several procedures in the program need access to this name, *logFileName* serves most usefully as a module-level variable.

The variable *currCountry* represents the current entry or selection in the Country box. Defining this as a module-level variable gives the program a simple technique for finding out when the user has changed the Country entry — and therefore when the City list has to be rebuilt.

Because the Expense Log program contains a single form, the only scope levels you need to worry about are module level and procedure level. In a project that contains multiple forms and modules, scoping rules are more detailed, as you'll learn in Chapter 8.

To overdo the use of module-level variables would be counterproductive in a procedural language. As you've learned, procedures can exchange information with each other through arguments, which is generally a more elegant way to share data. But declaring a few of a form's central variables at the module-level is always a reasonable technique, especially when a majority of the procedures in the program need access to the variables.

Once you've defined the name, type, and scope of a variable, the next step is to assign it a value.

Assigning values to variables

An assignment statement changes the value of a variable. An equal sign represents the assignment. At the left side of the equal sign is the name of the variable that receives the value; at the right is the value being assigned:

```
variableName = value
```

The expression on the right side of the equal sign can appear in any format that produces a value of the appropriate type. For example, it can be a literal numeric value:

```
numEntries = 0
```

a literal string value enclosed in quotation marks:

```
boxTitle = "Expense Log File Name"
```

another variable name:

```
smallRate = exchRate
```

or an expression that calculates a value:

```
totAmount = totAmount + amount / exchRate
```

Tip

In some old versions of BASIC, assignment statements always began with the keyword *Let:*

```
Let variableName = value
```

Although Visual Basic still allows you to write assignments in this way, the Let keyword is optional and seldom used.

Often you may want to *initialize* certain variables — that is, to assign their first values — at the very beginning of a program's performance. A good place to take care of initializations is the event procedure named Form_Load. This event is triggered when a form is first loaded into memory.

Initializing variables and defining constants

In an application that contains a window designated as the *startup* form — such as the Expense Log project — Visual Basic loads the form into memory at the beginning of the program run. (By default, the first form you create for a new project is the startup form. You'll learn more about this topic in Chapter 8.) Because Form_Load is performed when the form is first loaded into memory, this procedure is an ideal place for assigning first values to the program's module-level variables and for completing any other tasks that need to be accomplished at the outset of the program's performance.

You can examine the Expense Log program's Form_Load procedure in Figure 7-42. You'll see that this procedure does indeed initialize the program's module-level variables. For example, the logFileName variable receives a string value represented by the name DefaultFile:

```
logFileName = DefaultFile
```

```
Form                          ▼   Load                          ▼

    Private Sub Form_Load()

        ' The Form_Load procedure opens the default
        ' travel expense log file, and fills the country
        ' list with any country names stored in the file.

        logFileName = DefaultFile
        txtDate.Text = Format$(Date, "mm/dd/yy")
        currCountry = ""

        If FileExists(logFileName) Then FillCountryList

    End Sub   ' Form_Load
```

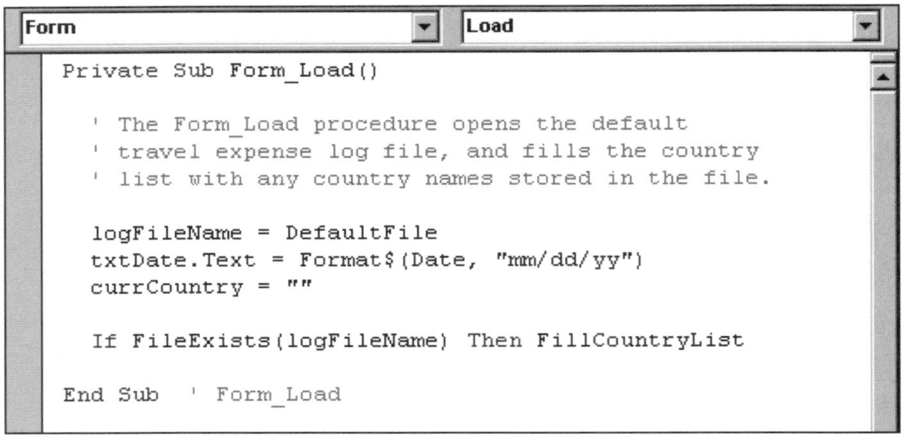

Figure 7-42: The *Form_Load* procedure is a good place to initialize variables.

DefaultFile, in turn, is a constant defined in the general declarations section. Unlike a variable, a constant is a name that represents an unchanging value throughout a program. You use the keyword *Const* to create a constant:

```
Const constantName = value
```

For example, here's the statement that defines DefaultFile in the general declarations section:

```
Const DefaultFile = "\ExpnsLog.txt"
```

Constants are convenient for representing important or frequently used values in a program.

Tip   Visual Basic 5 has a new data structure known as an *enumeration,* identified by the keyword *Enum.* An enumeration is essentially an ordered list of constants. You'll learn how to use the Enum type in Chapter 9.

Writing expressions in assignment statements

As you see, the value on the right side of an assignment statement can appear in the form of an expression. To carry out the assignment, Visual Basic first performs the calculation that the expression represents and then stores the result in the variable.

Visual Basic provides a variety of *operators* for forming arithmetic expressions. As you see in the following list, an operator is the symbol that represents a particular calculation:

✦ The ^ operator represents *exponentiation,* which raises a number to the power of an exponent. For example, the expression $x \wedge 2$ finds the value of x squared.

✦ The * operator represents multiplication.

✦ The / operator represents division, where the number at the left of the operator is the *dividend* and the number at the right is the *divisor.* The divisor may not be zero in a Visual Basic program; division by zero is not defined and results in a runtime error.

✦ The \ operator (the backslash character) represents *integer division,* which divides one integer by another and drops the remainder. For example, the expression 7 \ 3 results in a value of 2. The divisor may not be zero.

✦ The *Mod* operator returns the remainder from the division of two integers. For example, 7 *Mod* 3 is 1. This is the only arithmetic operation that is represented by a keyword rather than a symbol. Again, the divisor may not be zero.

✦ The + operator represents addition.

✦ The - operator represents subtraction. The minus sign is also used for negation or for a negative number.

You'll find some of these operations illustrated in the Expense Log program. For example, the following statement from the cmdExpReport_Click procedure (back in Figure 7-19) calculates a running total of the expense amounts recorded in the current data file:

```
totAmount = totAmount + amount / exchRate
```

To find the total, the procedure divides each expense amount by the corresponding exchange rate, and adds the result to the previous total value.

Notice that the variable *totAmount* appears on both sides of the equal sign in this assignment statement. Sometimes a program needs to assign a new value to a variable, based on the variable's *current* value. Here's a simpler example, from the cmdRate_Click procedure (shown back in Figure 7-16):

```
numEntries = numEntries + 1
```

This statement increases the value of *numEntries* by 1. The expression on the right adds a value of 1 to the current value of *numEntries;* then the statement assigns this new incremented value to *numEntries.* As always in an assignment statement, the previous value of *numEntries* is lost.

Understanding the order of precedence

When an expression contains multiple operations — as in the expression *totAmount* + *amount* / *exchRate* — Visual Basic follows a default set of precedence rules to decide which operation to perform first. Here's the order in which arithmetic operations are performed:

1. exponentiation (^)
2. negation (-)
3. multiplication (*) and division (/)
4. integer division (\)
5. the *Mod* operation
6. addition (+) and subtraction (-)

Following this order, you can see how the total expense amount is calculated in the *cmdExpRept_Click* procedure:

```
totAmount = totAmount + amount / exchRate
```

The division is performed first and then the addition, even though the operations appear in just the opposite order in the expression itself. Clearly it's important to pay close attention to the order of precedence in arithmetic expressions. Making false assumptions about the default order can result in significant calculation errors.

You can override the default order of precedence by inserting parentheses into an expression. Visual Basic performs operations that are enclosed in parentheses first. You can even place one set of parentheses inside another (sometimes known as *nested* parentheses). In this case, Visual Basic performs the operation in the innermost parentheses first, and then works its way step by step to the outermost parentheses.

For example, suppose you want to find the average of two values, *v1* and *v2*. To carry out the calculation, you need to find the sum of the values and then divide the result by 2. Here's the assignment statement you might write:

```
average = (v1 + v2) / 2
```

The parentheses in this expression specify that the addition must be performed before the division. Without the parentheses, Visual Basic would divide *v2* by 2 and then add the result to *v1,* which could produce a very different value.

You can use parentheses even when they are not strictly needed. Sometimes parentheses can help you formulate a complex expression, even when the default order of precedence is the correct way to evaluate the expression. Alternatively, you can use parentheses when you can't remember Visual Basic's default precedence rules. Nonessential parentheses are always better than an incorrect calculation.

Performing operations on strings

Visual Basic also defines specific operations for other types of data. For example, you can use an operation known as *concatenation* to combine two strings. The preferred operator for concatenation is the ampersand character (&). Here's an example from the *cmdRate_Click* procedure (Figure 7-17):

```
boxTitle = "Exchange Rates for " & cboCountry.Text
```

The expression on the right side of the equal sign combines a literal string with the current value of the *cboCountry.Text* property. This value is then displayed in the title bar of a message box. For example, you might see the following text in the title bar:

```
Exchange Rates for France
```

Turn back to Figure 7-10 to see exactly what this message box looks like.

Significantly, the & operator can be used with data values that don't belong to the same type — for example, a string and a number. In this case, Visual Basic converts the numeric value to a string before completing the concatenation. The cmdRate_Click procedure illustrates this technique in the following statement:

```
msg = "   Lowest: " & smallRate & _
      "   Highest: " & largeRate
```

Here the variables *smallRate* and *largeRate* are both declared as double-precision values:

```
Dim largeRate As Double, smallRate As Double
```

But the concatenation successfully combines string versions of these two numeric values with two literal strings. Again, you can turn back to Figure 7-10 to see an example of the resulting string.

An alternative operator for performing concatenations is the plus symbol (+). But unlike the ampersand, the + operator works only on strings. An attempt to combine a string and a number using + results in an error.

Using other types of operations

Visual Basic has other important categories of operations:

✦ The *relational* operators (also known as *comparison* operators) perform comparisons between values. For example, the expression $x > y$ is true if x is greater than y, or false if y is greater than or equal to x.

✦ The *logical* operators (sometimes known as Boolean operators) provide ways to combine true or false values. The most commonly used logical operators are *And, Or,* and *Not.*

If you continue examining the code of the Expense Log program, you'll find several examples of both relational and logical operators. You'll study these operations in detail in Chapter 9.

Projects, Forms, and Modules

As you've seen, you can build a practical application around a single form. A project that presents all of its features and operations in one window can be an appropriate solution to a particular programming task. For example, in the International Travel Expense Log program (Chapter 7), all the action takes place in one dialog box, where you enter your expense records and then request information about the data you've recorded. Likewise, the two currency exchange programs (Chapters 1 to 4) provide varieties of information about international currencies in single windows.

But some applications are more complex and require more than one form to present all their features. Even if most of a program's activities take place in one major window, additional forms and dialog boxes may appear on the screen when the user chooses menu commands or performs other operations in the program.

To develop such a program in Visual Basic, you create a project consisting of multiple forms. One form may become the program's primary window, displaying the controls and options that are most closely associated with the program's main features. But other forms may serve secondary purposes — for example, eliciting information from the user, offering additional sets of options, or presenting information in useful formats.

Tip As you've seen, the forms and modules of a project are listed in the Project Explorer window. But the hierarchy of objects outlined in this window can become even more complex. Specifically, in the Professional and Enterprise editions of Visual Basic 5, you can open two or more projects at once, to form a *group* of projects. From the File menu, choose the Add Project command to include a project in a group, or the Remove Project command to take a project out of a group. The Save Project Group As command guides you through the steps of saving each file component of a group, and finally supplying a name for the group file itself, which is saved with a VBG extension. The Project Explorer depicts the contents of the group you're building. A group allows you to develop and test an application consisting of different types of project components. You'll learn more about this topic in Chapter 17.

Visual Basic provides some important properties and methods for designing and working with multiple forms in a project. For example, you can use properties to establish several important characteristics of a form in your application:

✦ The title bar caption, which your program can change at any time during a performance

✦ The buttons available on the title bar, including the Minimize, Maximize, and Close buttons, and the control-menu box

✦ The form's border style, which determines whether the user can resize the form during runtime

✦ The form's reaction to keystrokes — that is, whether specific keystrokes will trigger form events rather than control events

✦ The three-dimensional quality of a form's appearance

These properties help to define a form's specific role in your project.

Also central to the use of forms are two methods named *Show* and *Hide*. As you'll recall, a *method* is a built-in Visual Basic procedure that applies to a specific object and performs a basic operation on that object. The format for a call to a method is *objectName.methodName*. Show and Hide are two important methods that apply to forms:

✦ The Show method loads a form into memory (if it's not already loaded) and displays the form on the screen. This method gives you the option of specifying whether the form will be *modal* (the exclusive form available for use at a given time) or *modeless* (a nonexclusive form). You'll learn more about these two form styles later. The Show method triggers a form event named *Activate*. The Form_Activate procedure is therefore a good place to write code that initializes the conditions for a newly displayed form.

✦ The Hide method removes the form window from the desktop — temporarily or permanently, depending on the plan of your program.

In this chapter you'll begin learning about these and other features as you examine a project named the Restaurant Review application. The program builds a personal restaurant database for locations anywhere in the world. If you're a frequent business traveler, the database helps you keep track of restaurants you like — or don't like — wherever you go. In each restaurant record you can keep information about varieties of cuisines, food quality, price, and suitable ambiance for business meetings. Closer to home, you can also use the database to record information about favorite restaurants in your own neighborhood. The program provides several techniques for retrieving information from the database whenever you need it.

Running the Restaurant Review Program

The Restaurant Review program is stored on the program disk as RestRevu.Vbp. Open the application now. In the Project Explorer window (Figure 8-1) you'll see that it contains two forms and one module:

✦ RestRevu.Frm (named frmRestRevu) is the program's main dialog box, where the user enters individual restaurant records and retrieves records for inspection or revision.

✦ RestList.Frm (named frmRestList) is a secondary dialog box, enabling the user to scroll through all the restaurant records for a selected city.

✦ RestRevu.Bas (modRestRevu) is a module that contains declarations and other code relevant to the entire program.

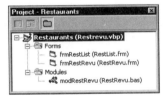

Figure 8-1: The Project Explorer window for the Restaurant Review program shows the two forms and one module that make up the project.

The startup form

In this application, RestRevu.Frm is known as the *startup form*, which means it is the first window to appear on the desktop when you run the program. By default, the first form you create when you're developing a project is defined as the startup form. Alternatively, you can designate any form in your application as the startup form by following these simple steps:

1. Pull down Visual Basic's Project menu and choose the Properties command at the bottom of the menu list. (This command shows the name of the current project; for example, the command appears as Restaurant Properties for the Restaurant Review application.) When the General tab is selected, the dialog box appears as in Figure 8-2.

2. The Startup Object list shows all the forms you've added to your project. Pull down the list and choose the name of the form you want to designate as the startup.

3. Click OK.

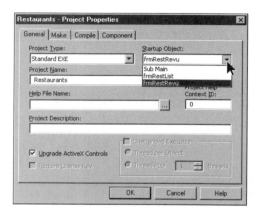

Figure 8-2: The General tab of the Project Properties dialog box allows you to designate a startup form for the project.

When you run a program, Visual Basic immediately loads the startup form into memory, triggering the Load event for the form. If you've written a Form_Load procedure in your startup form, this code is performed.

Tip   If you want to begin a program by running a procedure instead of loading a form, designate Sub Main as the startup object. Choose Project⇨Properties, and select Sub Main in the Startup Object list. (In Figure 8-2 you can see Sub Main at the top of the Startup Object list.) Then add a module file to your project and create a procedure named Sub Main. This startup procedure can perform any variety of initial actions and it can use the Show method to open and display the forms of your project. You'll see an example of a program that uses the Sub Main procedure in Chapter 13.

Try running the Restaurant Review program now, by pressing F5 or clicking the Start button on the Visual Basic toolbar. The Restaurants dialog box appears on the screen, as shown in Figure 8-3. This window contains a variety of controls that allow you to enter the information for a new restaurant record or ultimately to view the fields of an existing record:

✦ The City combo box is where you enter the restaurant's location. As you begin entering records and building a database, the attached list shows the names of all the cities currently in your file. You'll see how this works shortly.

✦ The Restaurant box is for the name of a new restaurant entry. When you've built a database, the attached list shows specific lists of restaurants — for a given city, a selected food type, or both. But the Restaurant list remains empty until you choose a city or a food type that's already represented in your database.

✦ The box labeled Type of Food is for identifying the restaurant's cuisine specialty, such as French, Mexican, Chinese, Italian, California, barbecue, or fast food. The program develops an attached list of all food types represented in your database.

✦ The Comments box allows you to enter any brief notes you might want to include in a given restaurant record. (The Comments field in each record may contain up to 65 characters.)

✦ The Quality option buttons give you the opportunity to rate the restaurant, from four stars (****) down to one star (*).

✦ The Price option buttons allow you to specify the price range of a meal at the restaurant, from very expensive ($$$$) down to inexpensive ($).

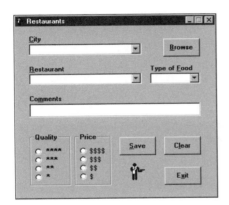

Figure 8-3: The Restaurants dialog box displays controls representing the fields of a restaurant record, including the city location, the restaurant name, the cuisine specialty, comments, and the quality and price ratings.

Entering a restaurant record

Suppose you've just returned from a business trip to Washington, D.C., and you want to record information about a small French restaurant you tried while you were there. You start up the Restaurant Review program and begin entering the relevant data: the city, the name of the restaurant, the type of food, and a brief description in the Comments box. You liked the food and the atmosphere, so you click the three-star option in the Quality box. The price was moderate, so you click the $$ option in the Price box. When all of these fields are complete, the Restaurants dialog box might appear as shown in Figure 8-4. To save the record, you click the Save button, or press Alt+S. In response, the program writes your new record to the database and then clears the dialog box for your next record entry.

The database is saved under the file name RestRevu.DB, in the root directory of your hard disk. The program creates this file the first time you run the program, and adds a new record to it when you click the Save button.

Significantly, the program requires that each record be complete. In other words, you have to enter information in all four text fields and you must select Quality and Price options before you click the Save button. (As you can see in Figure 8-4, a ToolTip reminds you of this fact when you move the mouse pointer to the Save button.) If you omit a field, an error message appears on the screen, as shown in Figure 8-5. To continue your work, click OK and then finish the record before clicking Save again.

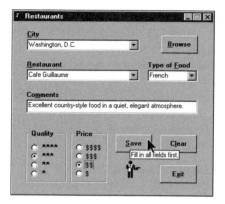

Figure 8-4: Entering a restaurant record. Click Save after entering all the information for the record.

Figure 8-5: The error message for an incomplete record. The program requires entries for each field before saving a record.

Retrieving records from the database

The Restaurants dialog box serves not only as a form for entering new records, but also as a window for viewing existing records. Once you begin developing your database, the City, Type of Food, and Restaurant boxes are designed to display lists of the information you've stored.

For example, suppose you've been using the program for some time to record your reviews of restaurants in the many cities you've visited on business trips. Now you're anticipating a trip to California and you want to search for the restaurants you've recorded in your database for San Francisco. To do so, begin by clicking the Clear button, if necessary, to clear any information currently displayed in the dialog box. Then click the down-arrow button displayed at the right side of the City box. As you can see in Figure 8-6, the resulting list displays all the cities currently represented in the records of your Restaurant database. The cities are arranged in alphabetical order. Click San Francisco as your city selection. When you do so, this name is copied to the City box.

Once you've chosen a city, the program automatically searches through the database for all the restaurants corresponding to your selection. To view the list of restaurants in San Francisco, you simply click the down-arrow button at the right side of the Restaurant box. As shown in Figure 8-7, the list of restaurants appears in alphabetical order.

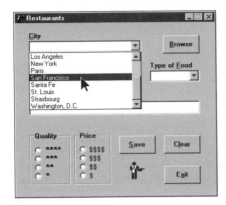

Figure 8-6: The City list shows the names of all the cities you've recorded in your restaurant database.

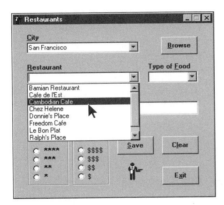

Figure 8-7: The Restaurant list. When you make a selection from the City list, the program searches through the database for all the restaurant records for that city.

You can now select any entry in this list to view the entire restaurant record. For instance, if you want to see the information you've recorded about a restaurant called Cambodian Cafe, you click this name in the Restaurant list. In response, the program retrieves this record and displays all of its fields in the Restaurant dialog box, as in Figure 8-8. (Keep in mind that the program can display only the information that's actually available in your own database. You can view a specific restaurant record only after you've entered it into the database.)

Alternatively, you can search for restaurants by cuisine type. If you want to see a list of all the French restaurants in your database, begin by clicking the Clear button to clear any existing data in the dialog box. Then pull down the Type of Food list. The program displays all the unique cuisine types that are currently represented in your database, as in Figure 8-9. Select an entry from this list. Then pull down the Restaurant list to see the names of all the restaurants in this category. For example, Figure 8-10 shows a list of French restaurants in the database.

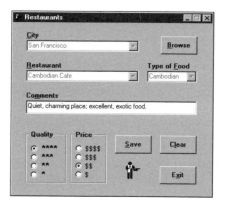

Figure 8-8: Retrieving a restaurant record from the database. When you make a selection from the Restaurant list, the program finds and reads the entire record and displays the fields of information.

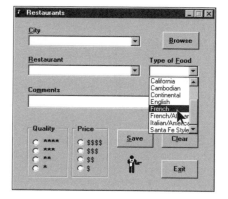

Figure 8-9: The Type of Food list shows all the different cuisine types recorded in the database.

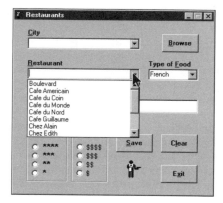

Figure 8-10: When you make a selection from the Type of Food list, the program retrieves the names of all the restaurants that match this selection. Pull down the Restaurant list to view the names.

Another option is to search for specific types of food in a selected city — in other words, to select all the records that match both a city name and a cuisine type. To do so, follow these steps:

1. Click Clear to clear the dialog box.

2. Pull down the City list and select a city.

3. Pull down the Type of Food list and select a cuisine.

4. Pull down the Restaurant list. The program displays all the restaurants that match the two criteria you've specified. (Note that the Restaurant list remains empty if the program finds no matches for the combination of City and Type of Food entries you've selected. This is an *and* condition — a record must match *both* fields to be selected.)

For example, Figure 8-11 shows a list of all the French restaurants recorded for San Francisco in one version of the database.

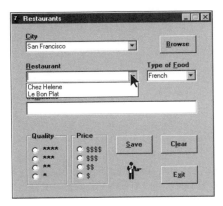

Figure 8-11: When you choose both a city and a food type, the program retrieves the names of all the restaurants that match both of these selections. Pull down the Restaurant list to view the matching records.

Browsing through restaurant records

The program gives you a convenient way to examine all the records you've recorded for a given city in your personal restaurant database. This is where the project's second form comes in: You can select a name from the City list and then click the Browse button, located near the upper-right corner of the dialog box. When you do so, the program temporarily hides the main dialog box and displays a new window in which you can quickly scroll through the restaurant descriptions for the selected city.

For example, suppose you've recently taken a short business trip to Paris, during which you recorded descriptions of three good restaurants for meeting with clients. Now, back home again, you want to take a look at these records. To do so, you follow these steps:

1. Click the down-arrow button at the right side of the City box, and select Paris from the resulting list.

2. Click the Browse button. (As you can see in Figure 8-12, a ToolTip reminds you that you need to select a city before clicking Browse.) In response, the program hides the Restaurants dialog box and displays a new window, entitled *Restaurants in PARIS*. This window displays one complete restaurant record at a time, in a format that's easy to read, as shown in Figure 8-13.

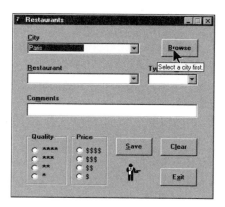

Figure 8-12: For easy access to all the restaurants you've recorded for a given city, make a selection from the City list and then click the Browse button.

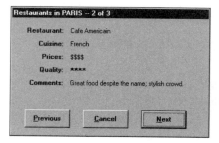

Figure 8-13: The resulting dialog box gives you the opportunity to browse through the records of the selected city, one at a time. Click Previous or Next (or press PgUp or PgDn) to move backward or forward through the records.

3. The new dialog box contains buttons labeled Previous and Next. To scroll forward to the next restaurant record, click the Next button with the mouse, or simply press the PgDn key on your keyboard. Likewise, to scroll backward to the previous record, click Previous or press PgUp on your keyboard. Each time you take one of these actions, the program displays a new restaurant record in the window.

4. When you reach the last record in this selection, the program disables the Next button. As shown in Figure 8-14, the button's caption is *dimmed*, or displayed in gray text; the button no longer responds to a mouse click. (Likewise, pressing PgDn produces no response.) Click Previous repeatedly to go back to the first record in the selection; when you do so, you'll see that the program disables the Previous button.

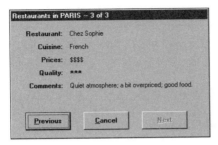

Figure 8-14: When you reach the end of the selection of restaurant records for a given city, the program dims the Next button. (Likewise, when you scroll back to the beginning of the selection, the program dims the Previous button.)

5. When you've finished examining this particular set of records, click the Cancel button or press Escape at the keyboard. The program closes the Restaurants in PARIS box and reopens the main Restaurants dialog box.

You can now click the Clear button to clear the dialog box so you can continue entering new records or examining existing records. By the way, if you click the Browse button at a time when the City box is empty, the program displays an error message, shown in Figure 8-15. The Browse operation is designed to display restaurant records from a particular city; you therefore can't use this feature until you select a city name.

Figure 8-15: An error message appears if you click the Browse button before selecting an entry from the City list.

Revising restaurant records

The program also lets you revise the information in any record you've already stored in your restaurant database. To do so, follow these steps:

1. To find the restaurant record that you want to revise, make appropriate selections from the City and Type of Food lists.

2. Pull down the Restaurant list and select the name of the target restaurant. The program displays the fields of the selected record in the Restaurants dialog box.

3. Make any changes you want in the Comments box, or to the Quality and Price options. (The program disables the City, Restaurant, and Type of Food boxes to prevent revisions in these key fields.)

4. Click the Save button. In response, the program displays the Existing Record box (Figure 8-16), asking you to confirm that you want to overwrite an existing record in your database.

5. Click Yes to save the revised record. The program writes the revised record over the existing record in the database. (Alternatively, you can click No if you change your mind about revising the record.)

Figure 8-16: To revise a restaurant record, select the restaurant, make any necessary changes, and click the Save button. The program asks you to confirm your action before carrying out the revision.

When you finish entering, examining, and revising restaurant records, click the Exit button (or press Alt+X) to end the program. As you see, this program makes effective use of its two forms to provide different views of the information in a database. In the upcoming sections of this chapter you'll examine the techniques for handling these forms and the controls they contain.

Inside the Restaurant Review Program

Each of the files identified in this application's Project Explorer window — the two forms and the module — contains part of the program's code:

✦ The code in the RestRevu.Bas module includes a Type statement that defines the program's central data structure — the fields of a restaurant record. It also declares a single record variable named *RestRecord* to represent individual restaurant records read from or written to the database on disk. (You'll learn much more about record structures in Chapters 9 and 10.) A constant named *DatabaseFile* represents the name of the database on disk, and a string variable named *currCity* is used to communicate an essential piece of information between the program's two forms. You'll see exactly how the program uses this variable later. Finally, the module contains one general procedure, a function named *StrFix*. Like everything else defined or declared in the module, this function is available for use anywhere in the program.

✦ The code in the frmRestRevu form includes event procedures for all the form's command buttons and combo boxes, plus a large collection of general procedures designed to carry out specific operations on the form. Of particular interest in this chapter is the cmdBrowse_Click procedure, which takes care of hiding the Restaurants window and displaying the browse window. As you'll see, these changes are carried out by the Hide and Show methods.

✦ The code in the frmRestList form includes the Form_Activate procedure, which initializes conditions in the dialog box; and Click event procedures for each command button. Significantly, there is also a Form_KeyDown procedure that enables the program to recognize the PgUp and PgDn keys while this form is displayed on the desktop.

You'll examine a number of listings from the two forms and the module as you complete this chapter. Keep in mind that the program's entire code listing is printed in Appendix A; alternatively, you can always examine the program by scrolling through procedures in the code window on your screen.

As you develop a project that contains more than one form, you'll find yourself paying close attention to the properties of the forms. You've seen already that some form properties define characteristics that are more cosmetic than functional. But others establish conditions that are central to the program's operations, and have significant implications for the design and content of your project's code. Before jumping directly into the code of the Restaurant program, you should therefore take a brief detour to the Properties window. You'll examine a few property settings for this program's two forms and several of the controls they contain.

Understanding form properties

To set up the Visual Basic environment conveniently for a review of form properties, follow these steps:

1. Activate the Project Explorer and select frmRestRevu in the file list. Click the View Form button at the top of the Project window to display the form. By default, the form window may be maximized inside the development environment. If so, click the Restore button (at the right side of the Visual Basic menu bar) to produce a form window that you can resize and move to a convenient location on the desktop.

2. Now select frmRestList in the Project Explorer and click View Form again. Use your mouse to resize and reposition the window that contains this form.

3. Drag the Properties window away from its docked position at the right side of the desktop. Click the Categorized tab. For the moment, the window shows the property settings for the frmRestList form. With both forms open (as in Figure 8-17), you can easily switch between them to compare their properties.

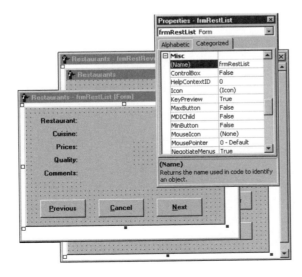

Figure 8-17: Arranging the form windows and the Properties window so that you can conveniently examine the properties of each form.

Try scrolling through the Properties list and studying the variety of properties available for a form. Keep in mind that you can jump to a help topic for any property by selecting the property's name in the list and pressing F1. This is a useful way to learn quickly about the properties of any object in Visual Basic.

In the upcoming sections you'll examine the settings of a half-dozen form properties. At least one of them is purely visual in its effect, and several others govern small but significant details in the presentation and function of a form. But two of the properties have important effects on the program's overall design.

Changing the appearance of a form and its controls

The Appearance property (in the Appearance category), provides a useful way to change the look of a form and many of its controls in one simple setting. One setting of this property gives the form a gray background, and adds subtle shadings to the controls in a form to enhance the three-dimensional effect of the form's display on the desktop.

The Appearance property has two possible settings, identified as Flat and 3D, as you can see in Figure 8-18. (The default setting is 3D.) Figure 8-19 shows what the Restaurants dialog box would look like with Flat settings for the form and its controls. Comparing this to Figure 8-3, you can see that the 3D setting provides a richer, more typical Windows-like appearance for the form. In the Restaurant project, both forms have Appearance settings of 3D.

Figure 8-18: The Appearance property has two settings: Flat and 3D.

Keep this property in mind whenever you create a new form, and decide for yourself how you want the form to appear on the screen.

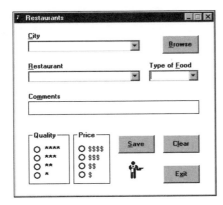

Figure 8-19: A form's look with an Appearance setting of Flat.

Displaying control buttons on a form's title bar

In Windows 95, as in previous versions of the Windows operating environment, a window typically contains certain visual elements that help the user manipulate its shape and appearance:

✦ The control menu is represented by an icon at the left side of a window's title bar. By clicking this icon, you pull down a menu of basic control commands, which may include Restore, Move, Size, Minimize, Maximize, and Close.

✦ The Minimize, Maximize, and Close buttons are clustered together at the right side of the window's title bar. (Or, if a window is maximized, the Minimize, Restore, and Close buttons may appear either on the window's title bar, or — if the window is contained within an application window — on the application's menu bar.) These buttons enable you to reduce a window to a button, expand or restore the window's size, or close a window.

By default, each new form you create in Visual Basic possesses all of these elements. But sometimes you may have reasons to exclude or disable one or more of these features, to restrict the operations available for a given window. For example, the Restaurants window contains an active Minimize button, but an inactive Maximize button. This combination allows the user to reduce the window to a button on the Windows 95 taskbar, but not to expand the window's dimensions, which are initially set appropriately for the window's contents.

Visual Basic provides several form properties that you can use to define the control elements of a window, and thereby expand or restrict the user's ability to change the window's appearance:

✦ The ControlBox property in the Misc category (Figure 8-20) has values of True or False, for including or excluding the control-menu icon. By the way, the Icon property in the Misc category enables you to select the icon that represents the control menu. The Vb\Graphics\Icons folder in the Visual Basic directory contains a large library of files — with ICO extensions — that are appropriate for this use. If this collection doesn't exist on your hard disk, you can install it from the Visual Basic setup disk.

✦ The MinButton or MaxButton properties in the Misc category (also shown in Figure 8-20) have values of True or False to include or exclude the Minimize and Maximize buttons at the upper-right corner of the window.

✦ The BorderStyle control in the Appearance category (Figure 8-21) is somewhat more complex. For a form, it has six settings, numbered 0 to 5:

• A setting of 0 - None produces no border, no title bar, and therefore none of the elements that usually appear on the title bar.

• A setting of 1 - Fixed Single produces a fixed border, and a title bar that may contain a control-menu icon and all the other usual buttons (depending on the settings of the ControlBox, MaxButton, and MinButton properties). With a fixed single border, the window can't be resized by dragging the border with the mouse.

• A setting of 2 - Sizable, the default, results in a sizable border. This means the user can drag any border with the mouse to resize the window. Under this setting, the window has a title bar that can include any of its usual control elements.

• A value of 3 - Fixed Dialog gives a fixed border. The window has a title bar and may include a control-menu icon, but not a Minimize or Maximize button. The window isn't resizable.

• A setting of 4 - Fixed ToolWindow is similar to the Fixed Single setting, except that the resulting form contains no Minimize or Maximize button and does not appear on the Windows 95 taskbar.

• A setting of 5 - Sizeable ToolWindow is similar to the Sizable setting, except that the form has no Minimize or Maximize button and does not appear on the taskbar.

Figure 8-20: The ControlBox, MaxButton, and MinButton properties determine which buttons will appear along a window's title bar and how much control the user will have over the window's shape and status.

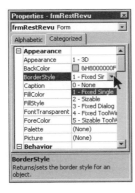

Figure 8-21: The BorderStyle property controls the appearance and sizability of a window. It also determines whether the window's name will appear on the Windows 95 taskbar.

Take a look at the settings of these four properties for the two forms in the Restaurant program, and consider their effects on the resulting windows:

✦ The frmRestRevu form has a BorderStyle setting of 1 - Fixed Single, which means that the window cannot be resized, but any combination of buttons is possible on the title bar. Accordingly, the form has ControlBox and MinButton settings of True so that the window can be minimized, but a MaxButton setting of False so that the window cannot be maximized. Interestingly enough, clicking the Close button on the title bar (or choosing Close from the control menu) is an alternate way of ending the program, and has the same effect as clicking the Exit button on the form itself.

✦ The frmRestList form has a BorderStyle setting of 3 - Fixed Dialog, which means that the resulting window cannot be sized, maximized, or minimized. Although this setting does not necessarily preclude the presence of a control-menu icon, the form has a ControlBox setting of False so that the control menu will not be available. Consequently, the only way to close the browse window is to click the Cancel button, which the program takes as a signal to switch back to the main dialog box. (As you'll see later, the cmdCancel_Click procedure contains the code for making a successful switch between these two windows.) Note that the frmRestList form has MaxButton and MinButton settings of False; with a BorderStyle setting of 3, these other settings are automatic.

In short, you can see that these four properties — BorderStyle, MaxButton, MinButton, and ControlBox — enable you to specify exactly how much control your user will have over the shape and status of a window, and how many operations will be reserved for your program to control. In the Restaurant Review application, which carefully orchestrates a particular display sequence between two windows, this is an important distinction.

Changing properties in code

When you first begin designing a new project, the Properties window, with its long lists of properties for any selected object, is always a main focus of your attention.

But properties may also play prominent roles in the code you eventually write for your project. Their names may appear explicitly in expressions and statements, or their influence may implicitly affect your program's design.

As you know, a reference to a property in code generally takes the form *objectName.propertyName*. In an assignment statement, this reference may appear on the left side of the equal sign:

```
objectName.propertyName = value
```

The result of this statement is to change the property setting to a new value. As you learn about the properties of a given object, you'll come to recognize the varieties of usage:

✦ Some property settings can be changed only at design time, not at runtime. The ControlBox, MaxButton, and MinButton properties are three examples. The settings of these properties are *read-only* at runtime; by referencing the property name, your program can read the current setting, but cannot change it.

✦ Conversely, a few properties are available only at runtime. For example, a property named ActiveForm supplies the name of the form that is active at a given point during runtime. ActiveForm is not listed in the Properties window, because it has no relevance at design time.

✦ A large selection of properties can be changed either at design time or at runtime. For example, the Caption property for a form specifies the text displayed along the form's title bar. At design time you create a form's title by selecting Caption in the Properties window and entering a line of text. In your code, you can change the caption at any time by assigning a new value to the Form.Caption property.

Changing the Caption property at runtime

In the Restaurant Review program, the title of the main dialog box is simply *Restaurants*. This caption remains unchanged throughout the program. But the second dialog box is a different story. When this second window is on the screen, its title displays the name of the city you've selected, the current record number, and the total number of restaurant records for this city; for example:

```
Restaurants in PARIS — 2 of 3
```

While the second dialog box is active, this title changes each time you click the Next or Previous button. (Look back at Figures 8-13 and 8-14 to confirm that this is the case.) As you might guess, the code responsible for this change is in cmdNext_Click (Figure 8-22) and cmdPrevious_Click (Figure 8-23), the event procedures — in the frmRestList form — that respond to clicks of the Next and Previous buttons. Near the top of each of these procedures, the following assignment statement changes the Caption property:

```
frmRestList.Caption = "Restaurants in " _
   & currCity & " — " & _
   currRec & " of " & recCount
```

As you can see, the caption is a concatenation of several literal strings and variables.

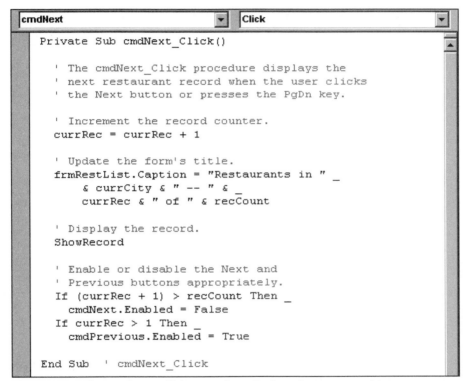

```
cmdNext                          ▼   Click                        ▼

   Private Sub cmdNext_Click()

      ' The cmdNext_Click procedure displays the
      ' next restaurant record when the user clicks
      ' the Next button or presses the PgDn key.

      ' Increment the record counter.
      currRec = currRec + 1

      ' Update the form's title.
      frmRestList.Caption = "Restaurants in " _
          & currCity & " -- " & _
          currRec & " of " & recCount

      ' Display the record.
      ShowRecord

      ' Enable or disable the Next and
      ' Previous buttons appropriately.
      If (currRec + 1) > recCount Then _
        cmdNext.Enabled = False
      If currRec > 1 Then _
        cmdPrevious.Enabled = True

   End Sub  ' cmdNext_Click
```

Figure 8-22: The cmdNext_Click procedure displays the next matching restaurant record when the user clicks the Next button. In addition, this procedure changes the caption on the title bar of the browse window, and may disable the Next button if the final matching record has been reached.

Changing the Enabled property at runtime

These same event procedures contain another important example of a property whose setting is changed frequently at runtime, the Enabled property. Enabled determines whether a given object will respond to the user's actions, such as clicks of the mouse or entries from the keyboard. This property applies to forms and to most controls displayed in a form. Its default value is True, which means events may occur around a given form or object.

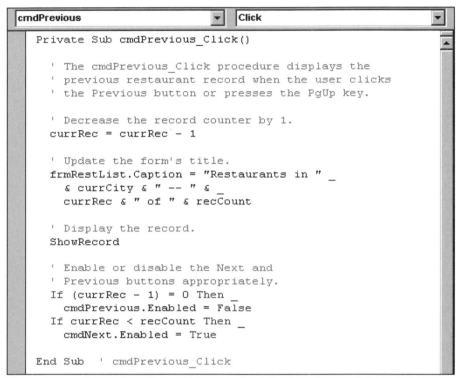

Figure 8-23: The cmdPrevious_Click procedure displays the previous matching restaurant record when the user clicks the Previous button. In addition, the procedure changes the caption on the title bar of the browse window, and may disable the Previous button if the first matching record has been displayed.

In the frmRestList form, the Restaurant Review program uses the Enabled property explicitly to activate or deactivate the Next and Previous buttons. For example, examine the following code from the cmdPrevious_Click procedure (Figure 8-23):

```
If (currRec - 1) = 0 Then _
  cmdPrevious.Enabled = False
If currRec < recCount Then _
  cmdNext.Enabled = True
```

If the current restaurant record displayed in the form is the first one available for the selected city, the program sets the cmdPrevious.Enabled setting to False. As a result, the Previous button is dimmed on the dialog box, and will no longer respond to mouse clicks. But as long as the current record is not the only restaurant available for the selected city, the cmdNext.Enabled setting is assigned a value of True, so that the user can click the Next button to examine the next record.

You'll find another important use of the Enabled property in a general procedure named *FindRestaurantRecord*, which is part of the frmRestRevu form (Figures 8-24 and 8-25). This procedure searches for a particular restaurant record when the user pulls down the Restaurant list and selects an entry. When the record is located, the procedure displays its fields in the Restaurants dialog box. At this point, the user has the option of changing certain fields in the record — the Comments entry, the Quality rating, or the Price rating — and then clicking the Save button to save a revised version of the record. But the program does not permit changes in certain key fields that identify a record: the City, Restaurant, and Type of Food entries. To prevent the user from making changes in these three fields, the program simply switches the Enabled settings to False for the corresponding controls:

```
cboCity.Enabled = False
cboFoodType.Enabled = False
cboRestaurant.Enabled = False
```

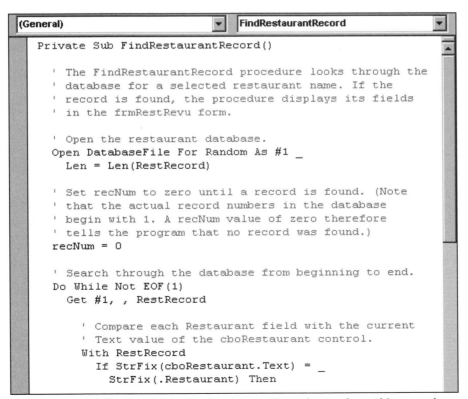

Figure 8-24: The first half of the *FindRestaurantRecord* procedure. This procedure searches through the database for the restaurant record that the user has requested; if a match is found, the procedure displays the fields of the record in the controls of the frmRestRevu form.

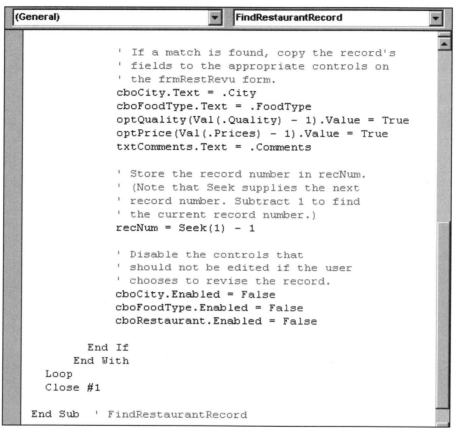

```
(General)                    ▼    FindRestaurantRecord              ▼

            ' If a match is found, copy the record's
            ' fields to the appropriate controls on
            ' the frmRestRevu form.
            cboCity.Text = .City
            cboFoodType.Text = .FoodType
            optQuality(Val(.Quality) - 1).Value = True
            optPrice(Val(.Prices) - 1).Value = True
            txtComments.Text = .Comments

            ' Store the record number in recNum.
            ' (Note that Seek supplies the next
            ' record number. Subtract 1 to find
            ' the current record number.)
            recNum = Seek(1) - 1

            ' Disable the controls that
            ' should not be edited if the user
            ' chooses to revise the record.
            cboCity.Enabled = False
            cboFoodType.Enabled = False
            cboRestaurant.Enabled = False

        End If
      End With
  Loop
  Close #1

End Sub  ' FindRestaurantRecord
```

Figure 8-25: The second half of the *FindRestaurantRecord* procedure. After displaying a restaurant record, the procedure disables the three combo box controls, preventing the user from revising their contents (although the contents are still readable on the screen).

After the user completes the save operation — or clears the record from the dialog box without revising it — the *cmdClear_Click* procedure (Figure 8-26) restores the original True settings of these properties:

```
cboCity.Enabled = True
cboFoodType.Enabled = True
cboRestaurant.Enabled = True
```

In short, the ability to control the property settings of forms and controls at runtime is one of the important features of Visual Basic programming. You'll see further examples in other projects presented in this book.

```
cmdClear                              ▼    Click                              ▼

    Private Sub cmdClear_Click()
      ' The cmdClear_Click procedure clears all the fields
      ' of information on the main dialog box, so that the
      ' user can enter a new restaurant record.
      Dim i

      ' Assign empty strings to the Text properties and
      ' set all the option buttons to False.
      cboCity.Text = ""
      cboRestaurant.Text = ""
      cboFoodType.Text = ""
      txtComments.Text = ""
      For i = 0 To 3
        optQuality(i).Value = False
        optPrice(i).Value = False
      Next i

      ' Enable the combo boxes that may have been disabled.
      cboCity.Enabled = True
      cboFoodType.Enabled = True
      cboRestaurant.Enabled = True

      ' Clear the restaurant list and variables, and move
      ' the focus to the City box.
      cboRestaurant.Clear
      prevCity = ""
      prevFoodType = ""
      cboCity.SetFocus
    End Sub  ' cmdClear_Click
```

Figure 8-26: In response to a click on the Clear button, the *cmdClear_Click* procedure removes the display of the current restaurant record from the dialog box. It also enables the three combo boxes so the user can select or enter a new restaurant record.

Properties and program design

Some properties are so influential that they may affect the way you design your program, and even dictate the selection of procedures you decide to write. One example of this is the form property named MDIChild. When you set this property to its nondefault True setting, it creates an instance of a *child* form in a *multiple-document interface* (MDI) application. In an MDI program, a primary background window serves as the container for any number of document windows; familiar examples are spreadsheet programs such as Excel and Lotus 1-2-3, and word processing programs like Word. You'll explore the topic of MDI programming in Chapter 14.

But even in simpler applications you can find properties that have special pro-gramming significance. An interesting example is the use of the KeyPreview property in the Restaurant Review program.

Using the KeyPreview property

The KeyPreview property is in the Misc category in the Properties window, and has settings of True and False (Figure 8-27). False is the default. When applied to a form, it allows the form to override its own controls in intercepting and reacting to keyboard activity. This property is especially important when you're designing a form that needs to recognize certain keystrokes, regardless of the control that has the focus at a given moment.

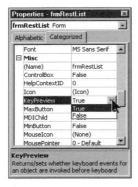

Figure 8-27: The KeyPreview property for a form allows the form to recognize and respond to keyboard activity, regardless of which control has the focus.

The frmRestList form has three command buttons, any one of which might have the focus at a point when the form is displayed on the screen. Normally a key-stroke event is captured by the control that has the focus. But in this case, the form itself needs to recognize two keys — PgUp and PgDn — as signals to move to the next or previous record in the current selection of restaurant descriptions.

The event that occurs when the user presses a key is named KeyDown. A related event, KeyUp, occurs when the user releases the key. By default, these events apply to the object that currently has the focus. Because the frmRestList form has three buttons — cmdPrevious, cmdCancel, and cmdNext — that may have the focus, one approach to capturing the PgUp and PgDn keys would be to write a KeyDown event procedure for each of these objects; the procedures would be named

- ✦ cmdPrevious_KeyDown
- ✦ cmdCancel_KeyDown
- ✦ cmdNext_KeyDown

Each procedure would have the identical task of translating the PgUp and PgDn keys into the equivalent mouse events — that is, making calls to the Click event procedures that are normally performed when the user clicks the Previous or Next button.

Fortunately, the KeyPreview property allows the program to avoid this redundancy. The KeyPreview property is set to True for the frmRestList form, ensuring that the PgUp and PgDn keystrokes will be captured first by the form itself rather than by any one of the controls on the form. Consequently, a single event procedure — Form_KeyDown, shown in Figure 8-28 — is enough to define the program's reaction to these keys.

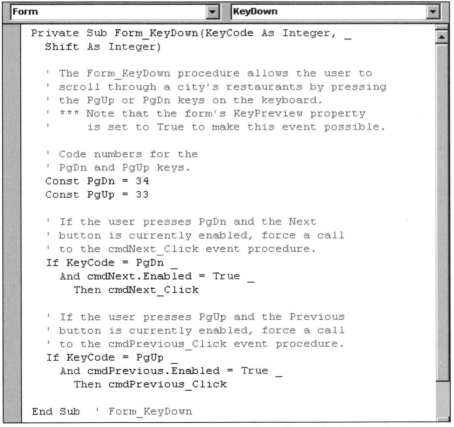

```
Form                        ▼   KeyDown                      ▼

   Private Sub Form_KeyDown(KeyCode As Integer, _
     Shift As Integer)

     ' The Form_KeyDown procedure allows the user to
     ' scroll through a city's restaurants by pressing
     ' the PgUp or PgDn keys on the keyboard.
     ' *** Note that the form's KeyPreview property
     '      is set to True to make this event possible.

     ' Code numbers for the
     ' PgDn and PgUp keys.
     Const PgDn = 34
     Const PgUp = 33

     ' If the user presses PgDn and the Next
     ' button is currently enabled, force a call
     ' to the cmdNext_Click event procedure.
     If KeyCode = PgDn _
       And cmdNext.Enabled = True _
         Then cmdNext_Click

     ' If the user presses PgUp and the Previous
     ' button is currently enabled, force a call
     ' to the cmdPrevious_Click event procedure.
     If KeyCode = PgUp _
       And cmdPrevious.Enabled = True _
         Then cmdPrevious_Click

   End Sub  ' Form_KeyDown
```

Figure 8-28: The Form_KeyDown event procedure allows the frmRestList form to recognize the PgUp and PgDn keys for scrolling through selected restaurant records. A True setting for the form's KeyPreview property is what makes this possible.

The KeyDown event procedure automatically receives an argument named KeyCode:

```
Private Sub Form_KeyDown(KeyCode As Integer, _
   Shift As Integer)
```

KeyCode is an integer that represents the key that the user has pressed. The codes for the PgDn and PgUp keys are 34 and 33, respectively:

```
Const PgDn = 34
Const PgUp = 33
```

The Form_KeyDown procedure does its work in two simple statements. If the user has pressed the PgDn key and the Next button is currently available for use, a call to the cmdNext_Click procedure displays the next restaurant record:

```
If KeyCode = PgDn _
   And cmdNext.Enabled = True _
      Then cmdNext_Click
```

Likewise, if the user has pressed PgUp and the Previous button is available, a call to cmdPrevious_Click displays the previous record:

```
If KeyCode = PgUp _
   And cmdPrevious.Enabled = True _
      Then cmdPrevious_Click
```

Keep in mind that the form's KeyPreview property setting is partially responsible for the economy of this event procedure. The properties you set for forms and their objects are not always merely cosmetic; they sometimes have important meaning to the program as a whole.

Tip   The Form_KeyDown procedure (Figure 8-28) shows that event procedures can be called explicitly from code. As you know, a Click procedure is normally performed in response to a specific event — when the user clicks a command button. But sometimes you may want to force a performance of an event procedure even when the corresponding event has not taken place. To do so, you simply write a call statement to the appropriate procedure — such as cmdNext_Click or cmdPrevious_Click.

As you continue exploring the Restaurant Review application, you'll learn more about how a program can manage forms and promote communication between them.

Managing multiple forms in a project

When the user clicks the Browse button, the program calls the Hide method to remove the main window temporarily from the desktop, and calls the Show method to display the secondary window, which is designed for browsing through the records of a selected city. Both of these methods are easy to use; they appear in the following general formats:

```
formName.Hide
formName.Show
```

For example, you'll find these two statements in the cmdBrowse_Click procedure in Figure 8-29:

```
frmRestRevu.Hide
frmRestList.Show
```

These statements make the switch between one window and the other in response to a click of the Browse button.

```
cmdBrowse                    ▼  Click                         ▼

    Private Sub cmdBrowse_Click()

       ' The cmdBrowse_Click procedure activates
       ' the frmRestList form so that the user can
       ' browse through the restaurants for a
       ' selected city.

       ' If the City box contains a selection,
       ' hide the program's main dialog box and
       ' activate the browse dialog box.
       If StrFix(cboCity.Text) <> "" Then
         currCity = StrFix(cboCity.Text)
         frmRestRevu.Hide
         frmRestList.Show

       ' Otherwise, if the user hasn't yet
       ' selected a restaurant, display an
       ' error message.
       Else
         MsgBox "You must select a city first.", , _
           "Browse through Restaurants"
       End If

    End Sub  ' cmdBrowse_Click
```

Figure 8-29: When the user clicks the Browse button, the cmdBrowse_Click procedure uses the Hide and Show methods to switch from the program's main window to the browse dialog box.

Interestingly, the Show method takes an optional argument, style, an integer equal to 0 or 1:

```
formName.Show style
```

If *style* is 0, *formName* appears on the desktop as a *modeless* form. This means that the user can activate and work with any other form in the program, even while the newly displayed form remains on the desktop. No specific response to *formName* is required before another form can be activated. By contrast, a *style* value of 1 produces a *modal* form. A modal form requires the user's full attention as long as the form is displayed; no other form can be activated until the user responds to the modal form in whatever way the program requires. Only when the modal form is removed from the desktop can the user activate other forms.

The modal style is useful for creating dialog boxes in an application. Before the user can resume other activities in the application, the modal dialog box requires a response. You'll notice, though, that the Restaurant Review program does not use the *style* argument. There is no need in this case, because the program presents only one window on the screen at a time. This is an alternative approach to capturing the user's attention for a particular activity.

Note that a modal window does not prevent the user from activating a different application on the Windows 95 desktop.

Exchanging information between forms

In a program that contains multiple forms and modules, the code in one form may need to read information available on a different form. There are several ways that you can conveniently exchange information between forms in a program.

For example, consider the frmRestList form. To display a selection of records from the database, it needs to know which city the user has selected on the main Restaurants window. Without this key piece of information, the secondary form has no way of knowing which set of records to read from the database.

One simple way to get information from another form is to refer directly to a specific control on the target form. The general format for this kind of reference is

```
formName.controlName.propertyName
```

or, alternatively

```
formName!controlName.propertyName
```

Either format supplies the current setting of a specific property of a control on the target form. This reference works successfully even if the target form is not currently displayed on the desktop.

For example, the frmRestList form could use the following format to read the current city selection from the City box in the Restaurants dialog box:

```
frmRestRevu.cboCity.Text
```

The first part of this reference identifies the form that contains the control, the second identifies the control itself, and the third is the name of the property that is to be read.

Another way to exchange information between the forms of a project is to establish one or more global variables — that is, variables available anywhere in the program. If one form assigns a specific value to a global variable, another form can read the value by referring to the variable.

This second approach is used in the Restaurant Review program to make the current city selection available to the frmRestList form. In the general declarations section of the RestRevu.Bas module (Figure 8-30), a public variable named *currCity* is declared to represent the user's city selection:

```
Public currCity As String
```

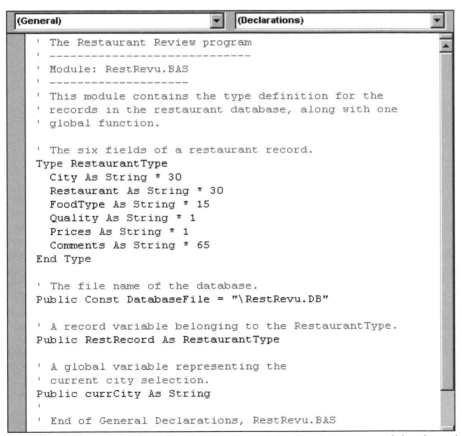

```
(General)                          (Declarations)
' The Restaurant Review program
' -----------------------------
' Module: RestRevu.BAS
' --------------------
' This module contains the type definition for the
' records in the restaurant database, along with one
' global function.

' The six fields of a restaurant record.
Type RestaurantType
  City As String * 30
  Restaurant As String * 30
  FoodType As String * 15
  Quality As String * 1
  Prices As String * 1
  Comments As String * 65
End Type

' The file name of the database.
Public Const DatabaseFile = "\RestRevu.DB"

' A record variable belonging to the RestaurantType.
Public RestRecord As RestaurantType

' A global variable representing the
' current city selection.
Public currCity As String
'
' End of General Declarations, RestRevu.BAS
```

Figure 8-30: The general declarations section of the RestRevu.Bas module. The public variable named currCity serves as a means of communication between the project's two forms.

When the user clicks the Browse button on the main dialog box, the cmdBrowse_Click procedure (shown back in Figure 8-29) assigns the current value of the cboCity control to the variable *currCity*:

```
currCity = StrFix(cboCity.Text)
```

The *StrFix* function (Figure 8-31), also defined in the RestRevu.Bas module, simply removes leading and trailing blanks from a string and converts it to all uppercase letters. This conversion results in reliable comparisons between strings throughout the program.

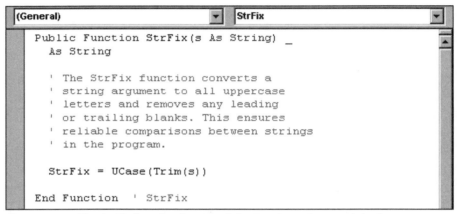

Figure 8-31: The StrFix function is part of the RestRevu.Bas module. It serves to standardize the format of strings to ensure reliable comparisons.

When the frmRestList form is activated, it uses the variable *currCity* to find out which city's restaurant records the user wants to see. It opens the restaurant database and calls the *CountMatches* function (Figure 8-32) to select only those records whose City fields match the value of *currCity*:

```
If currCity = StrFix(RestRecord.City) Then
```

Your choice of techniques for exchanging data between forms is largely a matter of personal preference and convenience. As an exercise, you might want to try revising the Restaurant Review program to eliminate the global *currCity* variable and use *formName.controlName.propertyName* references instead.

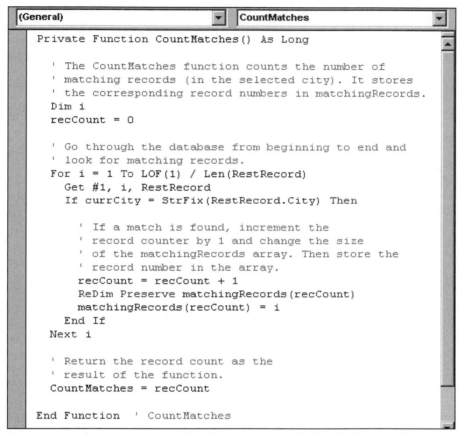

```
(General)                          ▼    CountMatches                      ▼

  Private Function CountMatches() As Long

     ' The CountMatches function counts the number of
     ' matching records (in the selected city). It stores
     ' the corresponding record numbers in matchingRecords.
     Dim i
     recCount = 0

     ' Go through the database from beginning to end and
     ' look for matching records.
     For i = 1 To LOF(1) / Len(RestRecord)
       Get #1, i, RestRecord
       If currCity = StrFix(RestRecord.City) Then

         ' If a match is found, increment the
         ' record counter by 1 and change the size
         ' of the matchingRecords array. Then store the
         ' record number in the array.
         recCount = recCount + 1
         ReDim Preserve matchingRecords(recCount)
         matchingRecords(recCount) = i
       End If
     Next i

     ' Return the record count as the
     ' result of the function.
     CountMatches = recCount

  End Function   ' CountMatches
```

Figure 8-32: The CountMatches function loops through the database and selects the restaurants that match the user's city selection. It stores the record numbers for these selections in the matchingRecords array.

Looking Further at the Restaurant Review Program

The Restaurant Review application illustrates many other programming techniques that you'll study in later chapters. Before you go on, you may want to survey a few highlights in the program's code:

✦ *Dynamic arrays.* An array is an indexed variable that represents a list or table of data values. A *dynamic* array is an array whose dimensions may change one or more times at runtime. The Restaurant Review program uses a dynamic array to represent the list of records that match any given city selection when the user clicks Browse. The array named *matchingRecords* is declared in the general declarations section of the frmRestList form (Figure 8-33) and used in the general procedure named *CountMatches* (back in Figure 8-32). You'll learn about arrays and other data structures in Chapter 9.

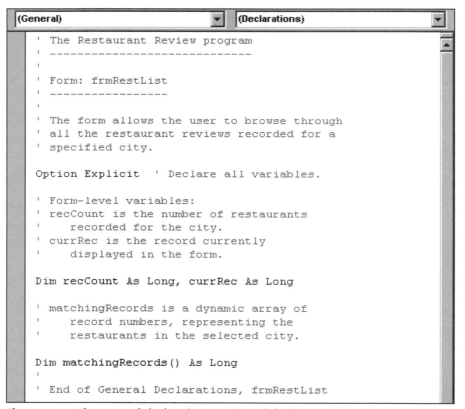

```
(General)                          ▼    (Declarations)                      ▼

     ' The Restaurant Review program
     ' -----------------------------
     '
     ' Form: frmRestList
     ' -----------------
     '
     ' The form allows the user to browse through
     ' all the restaurant reviews recorded for a
     ' specified city.

Option Explicit   ' Declare all variables.

     ' Form-level variables:
     ' recCount is the number of restaurants
     '     recorded for the city.
     ' currRec is the record currently
     '     displayed in the form.

Dim recCount As Long, currRec As Long

     ' matchingRecords is a dynamic array of
     '     record numbers, representing the
     '     restaurants in the selected city.

Dim matchingRecords() As Long
     '
     ' End of General Declarations, frmRestList
```

Figure 8-33: The general declarations section of the frmRestList form declares a dynamic array named *matchingRecords*. The program uses this array to keep track of record numbers for restaurants in a selected city.

✦ *Random-access files.* A random-access file gives a program direct access to any record in the file, thereby simplifying operations that read, write, or revise records. The Restaurant Review database is a random-access file, which streamlines the program's capability to retrieve and store restaurant records. You'll examine the various techniques of data file programming in Chapter 10.

✦ *Data structures and record variables.* A *data structure* is a way of representing the multiple fields in a record. As you've seen, the RestRevu.Bas module (Figure 8-30) uses a Type statement to define a structure that matches the fields of a Restaurant record, and a Public statement to declare a variable that will represent individual records. You'll learn more about these statements in Chapters 9 and 10.

✦ *Control arrays.* Sometimes it's convenient to define a group of controls as an array, so that they can be identified under a single indexed name. In the Restaurant Review program, the two sets of option buttons (Quality and Price) are both defined as control arrays. Chapter 11 discusses this kind of array.

✦ *MsgBox function and statement.* As you've seen, several message boxes pop up onto the desktop at various points in the Restaurant program. (Look back at Figures 8-5, 8-15, and 8-16 to review this feature.) These boxes are not defined as individual forms in the program, but rather are created by Visual Basic's built-in MsgBox tool. MsgBox is available both as a statement and a function. In either case, it displays a modal box on the screen, and waits for a specific reaction from the user. You can see how these boxes are displayed and used in the cmdSave_Click procedure (Figures 8-34, 8-35, and 8-36) and the cmdBrowse_Click procedure (shown back in Figure 8-29).

✦ *Other built-in functions.* Visual Basic has a large library of built-in functions that perform calculations and operations on specific types of data. These functions save time and effort; as you learn to use them, you'll avoid reinventing procedures that already exist in the language itself. Like all the programs in this book, the Restaurant Review application contains many illustrations of built-in functions.

You'll continue learning about these programming topics as you examine other applications presented in this book.

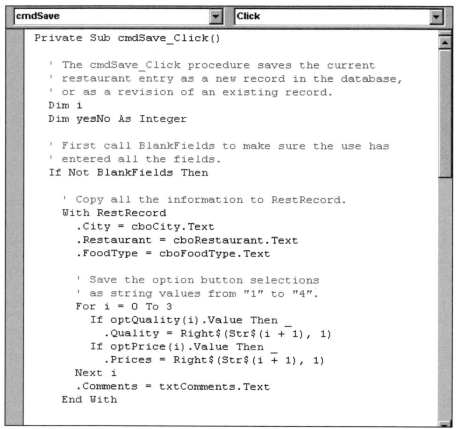

```
cmdSave                    ▼      Click                       ▼

Private Sub cmdSave_Click()

    ' The cmdSave_Click procedure saves the current
    ' restaurant entry as a new record in the database,
    ' or as a revision of an existing record.
    Dim i
    Dim yesNo As Integer

    ' First call BlankFields to make sure the use has
    ' entered all the fields.
    If Not BlankFields Then

        ' Copy all the information to RestRecord.
        With RestRecord
            .City = cboCity.Text
            .Restaurant = cboRestaurant.Text
            .FoodType = cboFoodType.Text

            ' Save the option button selections
            ' as string values from "1" to "4".
            For i = 0 To 3
                If optQuality(i).Value Then _
                    .Quality = Right$(Str$(i + 1), 1)
                If optPrice(i).Value Then _
                    .Prices = Right$(Str$(i + 1), 1)
            Next i
            .Comments = txtComments.Text
        End With
```

Figure 8-34: The cmdSave_Click event procedure (part 1 of 3). This procedure saves the current entry as a new restaurant record, or — if the user so instructs — writes it back to the database as a revision of an existing record.

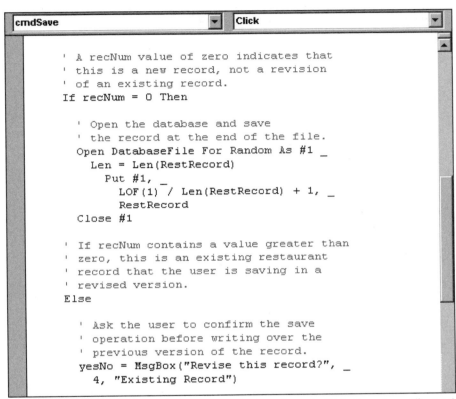

```
cmdSave                    ▼    Click                         ▼

   ' A recNum value of zero indicates that
   ' this is a new record, not a revision
   ' of an existing record.
   If recNum = 0 Then

      ' Open the database and save
      ' the record at the end of the file.
      Open DatabaseFile For Random As #1 _
        Len = Len(RestRecord)
          Put #1, _
            LOF(1) / Len(RestRecord) + 1, _
            RestRecord
      Close #1

   ' If recNum contains a value greater than
   ' zero, this is an existing restaurant
   ' record that the user is saving in a
   ' revised version.
   Else

      ' Ask the user to confirm the save
      ' operation before writing over the
      ' previous version of the record.
      yesNo = MsgBox("Revise this record?", _
        4, "Existing Record")
```

Figure 8-35: The cmdSave_Click event procedure (part 2 of 3). Here is an illustration of MsgBox used as a function. The procedure uses a call to MsgBox to elicit a yes-or-no response from the user — confirming or canceling a record revision.

```
cmdSave                              ▼    Click                              ▼

        ' If the user confirms, open the database and save
        ' the record at the same position as the original.
        If yesNo = vbYes Then
          Open DatabaseFile For Random As #1 _
            Len = Len(RestRecord)
              Put #1, recNum, RestRecord
          Close #1
        End If
      End If

      ' If the new record contains a new city or food type,
      ' add this information to the combo box list.
      If Not AlreadyListed(cboCity, cboCity.Text) _
        Then cboCity.AddItem cboCity.Text
      If Not AlreadyListed(cboFoodType, cboFoodType.Text) _
        Then cboFoodType.AddItem cboFoodType.Text

      ' Clear the dialog box for the next record entry.
      cmdClear_Click
    Else
      ' Display an error message if the user
      ' hasn't filled in all the fields of a new
      ' restaurant record.
      MsgBox "You must fill in all the fields.", _
        0, "Save"
    End If
End Sub ' cmdSave_Click
```

Figure 8-36: The cmdSave_Click event procedure (part 3 of 3). Here is an illustration of MsgBox used as a statement, to display a reminder message on the desktop.

Data Structures and Control Structures

In a programming language, the word *structure* has several important meanings. A structured language encourages a modular approach to writing code, where programs are organized into small, self-contained tasks. The practical result is that programmers can confidently create longer and more elaborate projects. Although the earliest versions of BASIC were anything but structured, the language has evolved. Visual Basic has all the elements of a well-structured language, including a productive variety of data structures and control structures. These are the topics of this chapter.

A *data structure* gives you convenient ways to organize and store information in a program. Two commonly used data structures in Visual Basic are *arrays* and *user-defined types*.

+ An *array* is a list, a table, or another multidimensional arrangement of data items, all represented by a single variable name. In programs that work with large amounts of interrelated information, arrays are an indispensable way of organizing data.

+ A *user-defined type* enables you to create variables that represent multiple values of different types. A variable belonging to a user-defined type is sometimes known as a *record* variable. This type of structure is ideal for use in database applications.

In addition to these standard data types, Visual Basic now offers a somewhat more enigmatic structure known as an *enumeration*, declared by the keyword *Enum*. An enumeration is, in essence, a list of numeric constants represented by distinct names. The values in an enumeration may typically be consecutive, though this is not a requirement. As you'll learn in this chapter, you can use an enumeration to improve the readability of your code by giving names to a sequence of related numeric values.

A programming language also has control structures that you can use to define the direction and flow of your program. Control structures include procedures, loops, and decisions:

✦ As you know, *procedures* allow you to divide your code into small, cogent, usable blocks of code that are easy to understand and revise if necessary. A Sub procedure in Visual Basic performs a discrete well-defined task; a Function procedure typically produces a return value. A *call* results in a performance of a procedure.

✦ *Loops* are structures that perform repetition in a program. During a loop, a block of code is performed over and over until a particular condition is met or until a counter reaches a specified value. Visual Basic has several convenient loop structures, each suited to particular needs.

✦ *Decisions* are structures that choose among alternative courses of action available in a program. A simple decision might determine whether or not a single line of code should be performed. More complex decisions involve many alternative blocks of code and many elaborate conditions. But the idea is always the same: Given what has happened so far in a program, what direction should the action take next?

Control structures and data structures are often closely related in the code of a program. For example, certain kinds of loops are ideally designed to process all the data elements in an array. Other control structures are perfect for working with the information stored in a record variable.

The best way to explore these language elements is to examine them in working examples. This chapter's project, called the Meetings program, illustrates a variety of structures and shows how they operate together. The program is designed to help you keep records about the business meetings you conduct or attend during your travels. It saves meeting records in a database file on disk, and gives you the opportunity to retrieve records and view them on the screen.

You'll begin your work in this chapter with a close look at the Meetings program. Then you'll examine parts of the program's code in detail as you review Visual Basic's data structures and control structures.

Running the Meetings Program

The Meetings application is stored on the program disk as Meetings.Vbp. When you open the project, you'll see that it contains two forms and a module, as shown in Figure 9-1:

✦ The form named frmMeetings (Meetings.Frm) is the program's startup window. In this form, you enter the information about a particular meeting — the place, date, and time; the names of the people who attended the meeting; the main subject or purpose of the meeting; and any brief notes that you want to store about what took place or what was discussed.

✦ The form named frmMeetFind (MeetFind.Frm) is a secondary dialog box that allows you to search for a particular set of meeting records. The key for each search is the name of any person who attended a particular meeting.

✦ The modMeetings module (Meetings.Bas) contains the program's central data structure definitions, along with two short procedures available for use anywhere in the project.

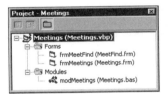

Figure 9-1: The Meetings project includes two forms and a module, as shown in the Project Explorer window.

Run the program now by pressing F5 or by clicking the Run button on the toolbar. A dialog box named Business Meetings appears on the screen, as shown in Figure 9-2. The window is divided into four areas. At the upper-left corner are four text boxes in which you can enter the place, date, and time of the meeting. In the area below, you can enter a list of as many as five people who were present at the meeting; there are separate boxes for each person's first and last names. Then at the upper-right corner of the dialog box you can see a space for the subject of the meeting and a large scrollable text box for your own notes and observations about the meeting. The program accepts a 400-character block of text (about 80 words) in the Notes box. As you type text in the box, word wrap takes place at the end of each line. To scroll the text in the box up and down, you can use the PgUp and PgDn keys or you can click inside the scroll bar at the right side of the box.

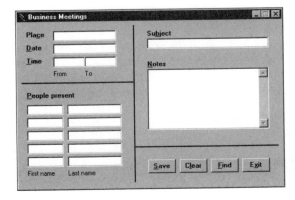

Figure 9-2: The Business Meetings dialog box contains text boxes for the fields of a meeting record, including the place, date, and time of a meeting; the names of people present; the subject of the meeting; and any brief notes you want to record about the meeting.

Finally, at the lower-right corner of the dialog box you see a panel containing four command buttons. When you poise the mouse pointer over a button, a ToolTip provides a brief description of the resulting action, as shown in Figure 9-3. Here is what these buttons do:

✦ The Save button saves your current meeting record as part of a database file named Meetings.DB, stored in the root directory of your hard disk. Before you click Save, you should fill in the Place, Date, Time, Subject, and Notes text boxes, and at least one pair of boxes in the People list. If you click Save before filling in all the boxes, the program displays a message reminding you that a complete record is required (Figure 9-4). After a Save operation, the program clears the dialog box for your next record entry.

✦ The Clear button erases all the information currently displayed in the dialog box. You might want to click this button if you begin an entry and then decide you want to start over without saving the current information. But as you'll see shortly, the program also uses the Business Meetings dialog box to display an existing meeting record that you've requested; in this case, the Clear button allows you to clear the record and return to data-entry mode.

✦ The Find button switches to a different dialog box, where you can search for specific meeting records by entering the name of a person who attended the target meetings. You'll explore this feature shortly.

✦ The Exit button stops the program's performance.

Figure 9-3: The Business Meetings dialog box contains command buttons representing the database operations you can perform.

Figure 9-4: The program requires a complete record entry for a Save operation, as indicated by this message.

Entering and retrieving meeting records

Figure 9-5 shows a sample record that's been entered into the Business Meetings dialog box. As you can see, this record contains a list of four people who were present at the meeting and several lines of notes about the discussion that took place. Try entering this record — or a meeting record of your own — into the Business Meetings dialog box on your screen. Then click Save to save the record. The program clears the record and moves the focus to the Place box. Continue experimenting with the program by entering several more meeting records, real or imaginary. Remember that you can click the Clear button at any time to remove the current entry from the dialog box and start over again.

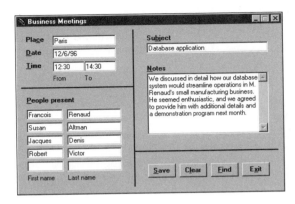

Figure 9-5: Entering a meeting record to describe a meeting you've attended. Notice that a record entry may contain from one to five names of people in attendance; the other name fields may remain blank.

Once you've begun developing a database of meeting records, you'll want to be able to retrieve the information and review the notes you've kept. To do so, you begin by clicking the Find button. In response, the program displays a new dialog box titled Find a Meeting Record. As you can see in Figure 9-6, this window contains text boxes in which you can identify a person you want to search for in the Meetings database. For a successful search, you have to enter the person's first and last name in the same way you stored it in one or more database records. (The program ignores differences in alphabetic case; you can enter the name in all uppercase or lowercase letters, or any combination.) Then click the Search button, or simply press Enter.

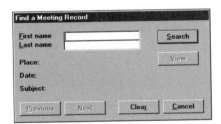

Figure 9-6: The Find a Meeting Record dialog box allows you to look for particular meeting records, using the name of a participant as the key to the search.

In response, the program searches for all the records in which this person's name appears, and displays information from the first record it finds. This dialog box displays only three fields of information from a given record: the place of the meeting, the date, and the subject. If the target name appears in more than one record, the program activates the Next button so you can scroll through the records that match the name you've entered.

For example, in Figure 9-7 you can see a name that the program has searched for in the database. Because the Next button is available, you know that multiple records have been found for this name. To scroll forward through the records one at a time, you can click Next or press PgDn at the keyboard. To scroll backward, click Previous or press PgUp. When the program reaches the first or last matching record, the Previous or Next button is disabled. Figure 9-8 shows the last record for this particular search; as you can see, the Previous button is available but the Next button is not.

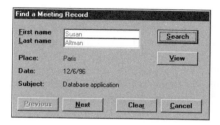

Figure 9-7: To search for a meeting record, enter the name of a participant and then click Search (or press Enter). The dialog box shows the place, date, and subject of a given record, and allows you to scroll through other records that contain the name you've entered.

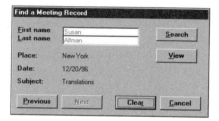

Figure 9-8: To scroll through matching records, click the Previous or Next button, or press PgUp or PgDn at the keyboard.

If you enter a name that cannot be found in the database, the program displays an appropriate message on the screen, as shown in Figure 9-9. To try again, click OK in the message box and then click Clear in the Find a Meeting Record dialog box. Enter a new search name and click Search.

Figure 9-9: The program displays a message like this one if you enter a name that can't be found in the Meetings database.

Once you've completed a successful search — and located a set of matching records — you may want to view a particular record in its entirety. To do so, you simply click the View button at the right side of the Find a Meeting Record dialog box. In response, the program immediately switches back to the Business Meetings dialog box and shows all the fields of the record you've selected, as in Figure 9-10. At this point, the dialog box is in its read-only mode. You can examine the record, but you can't change it or save it again. (Notice that the Save button is dimmed.) Click the Clear button when you've finished reading the information, or click Find to search for yet another record.

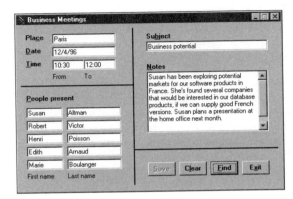

Figure 9-10: When you retrieve an entire record from a Find operation, the program disables the text boxes that supply the record. You can view the record but you can't revise it or save it again.

If you decide that you want to close the Find dialog box without retrieving a record, simply click Cancel or press the Escape key. The program returns to the empty Business Meetings dialog box and prepares to accept a new record entry. Click Exit when you're ready to quit the program. Of course, the Meetings database is retained on disk; you can retrieve and view records from it any time you run the program.

Inside the Meetings program

The program's code is contained in the two forms and the module. In the remainder of this chapter you'll examine many individual procedures in detail. (To examine the entire listing in one place, turn to Appendix A. Alternatively, scroll through the listing in the code window on your screen.)

Here's a summary of what you'll find in the module and the two forms:

✦ **The modMeetings module (Meetings.Bas).** The module's general declarations section contains Type definitions for the program's two major data structures, and Public declarations for global constants, variables, and arrays. In particular, the *Meeting* variable represents a meeting record that's been read from the database or is about to be written to the file. The *NameList* array stores a special index structure that the program uses to search for records. You'll see a lot of these two structures as you examine the program. The modMeetings module also contains two short string functions used to standardize names and ensure reliable comparisons.

✦ **The frmMeetings form (Meetings.Frm).** This is the startup form. In its general declarations section you'll find an Enum type that defines names (Place, Date, StartTime, EndTime, Subject, and Notes) to identify the input fields for a meeting record. The form contains a variety of event procedures, including Form_Load, which initially opens the Meetings database and creates an index of participant names; and Form_Activate, which displays a selected record from the database when the program returns to this form from the secondary frmMeetFind form. Click procedures respond to each of the form's command buttons.

✦ **The frmMeetFind form (MeetFind.Frm).** Again, you'll find event procedures that carry out the operations corresponding to each of the form's command buttons. You'll also see a variety of general procedures that help in the process of searching for records and displaying them in the dialog box.

The program contains many interesting illustrations of decisions, loops, arrays, records, and enumerations. It also contains examples of the With statement, which helps to simplify code by allowing you to abbreviate the names of record elements and object properties. In upcoming sections of this chapter, you'll look in detail at many passages from the program's code as you review the use of control structures and data structures in Visual Basic.

Decisions

Decision statements give your program the power to choose between options available in your code and to react appropriately to situations that occur during a run. For example, decisions may take place when a program responds correctly to a request made from the keyboard or provides relevant information based on a particular condition.

The *If* statement is the most common way to express decisions in Visual Basic programs. At the heart of every If decision is a *condition* — an expression that your program evaluates as true or false. If the condition is true, the program follows one course of action; if false, another.

Writing If statements

Depending on the complexity of the decision, you can use If either as a one-line statement or as a multiline block structure. Both formats make use of the keywords If, Then, and Else:

✦ **If** introduces the condition on which the decision will be based.

✦ **Then** identifies the action that will be performed if the condition is true.

✦ **Else** specifies an alternate action, to be performed if the condition is false.

A block structure uses some additional keywords:

✦ **ElseIf** introduces another condition that the program will evaluate if no previous condition has turned out to be true. (ElseIf is an optional clause; it may be included one or more times in a single decision structure.)

✦ **End If** marks the end of the decision structure.

The one-line If statement is the simplest decision format. It presents a condition and a choice of actions all in a single statement:

```
If condition Then action1 Else action2
```

In this format, *condition* is an expression that Visual Basic evaluates as true or false; and *action1* and *action2* are statements — such as assignments, procedure calls, or any other Visual Basic statement. If *condition* is true, the program performs *action1* and skips *action2;* conversely, if *condition* is false, the program skips *action1* and performs *action2.*

The Else clause is optional in the If statement. If you leave it out, the one-line If statement becomes simply:

```
If condition Then action
```

In this case, the *action* is performed if the *condition* is true. If the *condition* is false, this If statement results in no action at all. For example, the following statement appears near the end of the Form_Load procedure of the frmMeetings module (Figures 9-11 and 9-12):

```
If listLength > 1 Then SortNameList
```

To prepare for retrieving records from the Meetings database, the Form_Load procedure reads through the entire file and copies the names of the people in each record to the index array called *NameList.* When this process is complete, the program needs to alphabetize the name list, but only if the list contains more than one entry. Accordingly, this If statement decides whether alphabetization is necessary. The variable *listLength* represents the number of names in the list. If *listLength* is greater than 1, the program makes a call to the SortNameList procedure to alphabetize the list.

Take a look at the condition in this decision. In the expression *listLength > 1*, the > symbol represents *greater than*, one of Visual Basic's *comparison operations*. If *listLength* contains a value that is greater than 1, Visual Basic evaluates this expression as True, and the action of the If statement is carried out. Otherwise, if *listLength* contains a value of 0 or 1, the condition is False, and no action takes place.

To write successful decisions, you need to be familiar with the various operators available for expressing conditions.

Conditional expressions

You've learned to write arithmetic expressions in Visual Basic, using operations such as multiplication (*), division (/), addition (+), and subtraction (-). An arithmetic expression produces a value belonging to one of Visual Basic's numeric data types. By contrast, a conditional expression results in a *Boolean* value, also sometimes known as a *logical* value. The Boolean data type represents two values, True and False, which are themselves keywords in Visual Basic. (This data type is named after the 19th-century English mathematician and logician George Boole.)

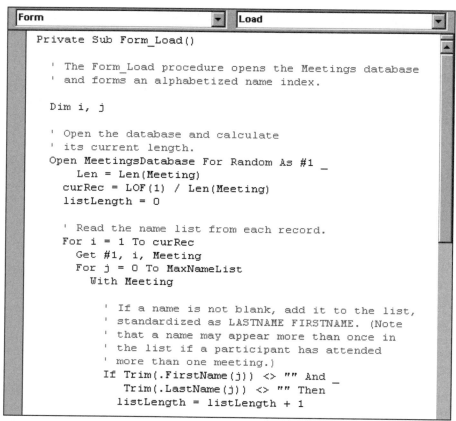

```
Form                          ▼   Load                              ▼

   Private Sub Form_Load()                                        ▲

    ' The Form_Load procedure opens the Meetings database
    ' and forms an alphabetized name index.

   Dim i, j

    ' Open the database and calculate
    ' its current length.
   Open MeetingsDatabase For Random As #1 _
      Len = Len(Meeting)
    curRec = LOF(1) / Len(Meeting)
    listLength = 0

     ' Read the name list from each record.
    For i = 1 To curRec
      Get #1, i, Meeting
      For j = 0 To MaxNameList
        With Meeting

          ' If a name is not blank, add it to the list,
          ' standardized as LASTNAME FIRSTNAME. (Note
          ' that a name may appear more than once in
          ' the list if a participant has attended
          ' more than one meeting.)
          If Trim(.FirstName(j)) <> "" And _
            Trim(.LastName(j)) <> "" Then
            listLength = listLength + 1
```

Figure 9-11: The first half of the Form_Load procedure from the frmMeetings form. This procedure opens the Meetings database and creates a list of all the names (of meeting participants) contained in each record. The list is stored in the *NameList* array. This array of records has fields for the name *(FullName)* and the record number *(RecordNum)* of each entry.

Two special sets of operations are available for conditional expressions: comparison operations and logical operations. The *comparison* operations perform comparisons between two values. For example, the *equal to* (=) operation is true if two operands have the same value; *less than* (<) is true if the first operand has a smaller value than the second. The *logical* operations combine or modify Boolean expressions to produce results of True or False. The most commonly used among Visual Basic's logical operations are And, Or, and Not.

Understanding the logic of conditional expressions is not hard; the only difficulty is in learning to use the operators themselves. Note the distinction between the terms *operator* and *operation*. An operator is a symbol or keyword that represents an operation. For example, the + symbol is the operator that represents addition;

likewise, < represents the comparison operation *less than*. An operand is a value that is the object of an operation. In the expressions $a + b$ and $a < b$, the values a and b are operands.

```
Form                              ▼    Load                              ▼

             ' Resize the NameList array, preserving
             ' its current contents.
             ReDim Preserve NameList(listLength)

             ' Standardize the name format.
             NameList(listLength).FullName = _
                FixName(.FirstName(j), .LastName(j))

             ' In the RecordNum field save the
             ' record number where the name can be found.
             NameList(listLength).RecordNum = i
          End If
       End With
    Next j
  Next i
Close #1

' If the index contains more than one name,
' sort the list.
If listLength > 1 Then SortNameList

' Set the global curRec pointer to zero, indicating
' that no record has been selected yet.
curRec = 0

End Sub   ' Form_Load
```

Figure 9-12: The second half of the Form_Load procedure from the frmMeetings form. At the end of the procedure, a call to the *SortNameList* routine alphabetizes the contents of the *NameList* array by the *FullName* field. The call is made only if the array contains more than one record.

Comparison operations

There are six comparison operations, represented by the following symbols:

Symbol	Comparison Operation
<	less than
<=	less than or equal to

Symbol	Comparison Operation
>	greater than
>=	greater than or equal to
=	equal to
<>	not equal to

You use these operators to compare two values in a conditional expression. The expression is true if the comparison is accurate, or false if it is inaccurate. For example, suppose a equals 1, b equals 2, and c equals 3; the following comparisons are all True:

```
a < c
c >= a + b
c - a = b
```

And the following are all False:

```
a > c
b = a * 3
c <= b
```

In an expression that contains both arithmetic and comparison operations, Visual Basic performs the arithmetic first, and then the comparison. For example, in the expression $c >= a + b$, Visual Basic first finds the value of $a + b$ and then compares the sum with the value of c. (You'll learn more about the order of operations later in this chapter.)

You'll find many illustrations of comparison operations in the Meetings program. One simple example appears in the Form_Activate procedure of the frmMeetings module, shown in Figures 9-13 and 9-14. This is the event procedure that takes control whenever the program's startup form is activated or reactivated during a run. When the user selects a record in the secondary frmMeetFind form and then clicks the View button, the program stores the target record number in a public variable named *curRec*. The frmMeetings form is then activated, and the program reads the *curRec* record from the database and displays it in the form. But if the user clicks the Cancel button on the frmMeetFind form, the program assigns a value of 0 to *curRec*. This is a signal that the user has not requested a record search. Accordingly, before reading a record from the database, the Form_Activate procedure checks the value of *curRec*:

```
If curRec <> 0 Then
```

If *curRec* is not equal to 0, the program opens the database and retrieves the target record. By contrast, if *curRec* is 0, the program clears the frmMeetings form and stands ready for the user's next action.

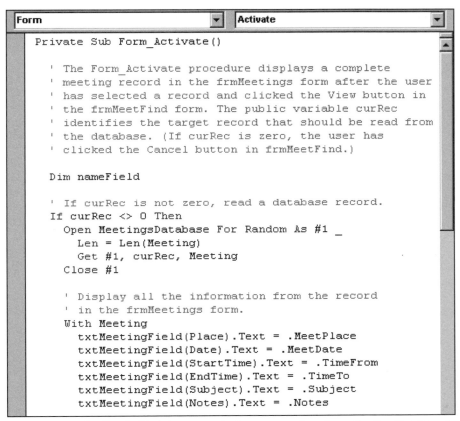

Figure 9-13: The first half of the Form_Activate procedure from the frmMeetings form. This event procedure is responsible for displaying a meeting record in the Business Meetings dialog box after a Find operation. A record is displayed only if the global variable *curRec* is not zero. A nonzero value represents the record that the procedure should read and display.

Logical operations

Visual Basic's six logical operations are represented by the keywords Not, And, Or, Xor, Eqv, and Imp. Five of the logical operators — And, Or, Xor, Eqv, and Imp — are designed to work with pairs of operands; you use them to combine two logical values in an expression. By contrast, Not is a *unary* operator; it works on a single value. Each of these operators produces a logical result. In the following descriptions, assume that the operands *v1* and *v2* represent values of True or False.

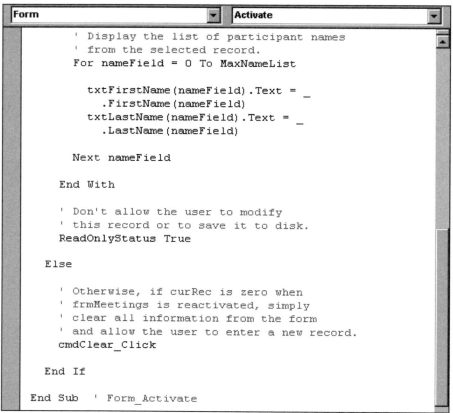

```
Form                          ▼   Activate                    ▼

        ' Display the list of participant names
        ' from the selected record.
        For nameField = 0 To MaxNameList

          txtFirstName(nameField).Text = _
            .FirstName(nameField)
          txtLastName(nameField).Text = _
            .LastName(nameField)

        Next nameField

      End With

      ' Don't allow the user to modify
      ' this record or to save it to disk.
      ReadOnlyStatus True

    Else

      ' Otherwise, if curRec is zero when
      ' frmMeetings is reactivated, simply
      ' clear all information from the form
      ' and allow the user to enter a new record.
      cmdClear_Click

    End If

  End Sub  ' Form_Activate
```

Figure 9-14: The second half of the Form_Activate procedure from the frmMeetings form. A block If structure governs this procedure's action. If *curRec* is zero, the procedure skips down to the Else clause and simply clears all the text boxes in the Business Meetings dialog box; subsequently the program is ready to accept a new record.

Not produces the reverse value of its operand:

```
Not v1
```

If *v1* is True, Not *v1* results in a value of False; if *v1* is False, Not *v1* is True.

And results in a value of True only if both of its operands are True:

```
v1 And v2
```

If both *v1* and *v2* are True, the And operation produces a value of True. If either value is False or if both are False, the And operation results in False.

Or results in a value of True if either or both of its operands are True:

```
v1 Or v2
```

If *v1* is True, or *v2* is True, or both are True, the Or operation results in True. Only if *v1* and *v2* are both False does Or result in False.

Xor is True only if its two operands have different values:

```
v1 Xor v2
```

If one of the operands is True and the other is False, Xor results in True. If both *v1* and *v2* are True or if both are False, Xor is False.

Eqv is True if its two operands are the same:

```
v1 Eqv v2
```

If both *v1* and *v2* are True or both are False, Eqv results in True. If one of the operands is True and the other is False, Eqv is False.

Imp is False if its first operand is True and the second is False. Otherwise, Imp is True:

```
v1 Imp v2
```

If *v1* is True and *v2* is False, Imp produces a value of False. For all other combinations of values, Imp is True.

The simplest and most commonly used of Visual Basic's six logical operators are And and Or. The Form_KeyDown event procedure from the frmMeetFind form (Figure 9-15) contains some interesting examples. While the frmMeetFind form is displayed on the desktop, this procedure captures any keyboard activity and determines whether the user has pressed PgUp or PgDn as an instruction to scroll to a new record. If one of these keys has been pressed *and* the equivalent command button — Previous or Next — is currently enabled, the program makes a call to the appropriate procedure to display a new record:

```
If KeyCode = PgDn _
   And cmdNext.Enabled = True _
      Then cmdNext_Click
```

The resulting action takes place only if both of these conditions are true. If one condition is false or both are false, the action is skipped.

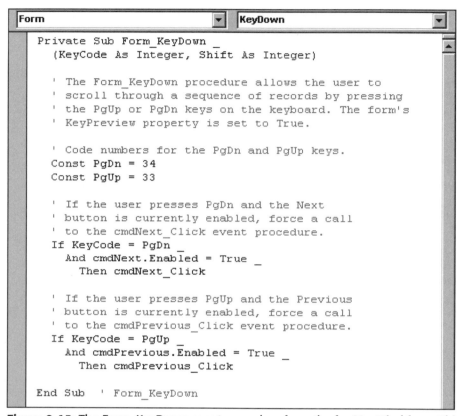

```
Form                              ▼    KeyDown                          ▼

Private Sub Form_KeyDown _
  (KeyCode As Integer, Shift As Integer)

  ' The Form_KeyDown procedure allows the user to
  ' scroll through a sequence of records by pressing
  ' the PgUp or PgDn keys on the keyboard. The form's
  ' KeyPreview property is set to True.

  ' Code numbers for the PgDn and PgUp keys.
  Const PgDn = 34
  Const PgUp = 33

  ' If the user presses PgDn and the Next
  ' button is currently enabled, force a call
  ' to the cmdNext_Click event procedure.
  If KeyCode = PgDn _
    And cmdNext.Enabled = True _
      Then cmdNext_Click

  ' If the user presses PgUp and the Previous
  ' button is currently enabled, force a call
  ' to the cmdPrevious_Click event procedure.
  If KeyCode = PgUp _
    And cmdPrevious.Enabled = True _
      Then cmdPrevious_Click

End Sub  ' Form_KeyDown
```

Figure 9-15: The Form_KeyDown event procedure from the frmMeetFind form. This procedure captures PgUp and PgDn keypresses and calls the appropriate Click procedures, allowing the user to scroll through selected records.

Sometimes a conditional test may require the use of two or more logical operators. For example, consider the *OKRecord* function from the frmMeetings form (Figure 9-16). This function has the job of determining whether a new record entry is complete and therefore suitable for saving to the database. First the function loops through all the input text boxes except for the participant names. When this test is done, a Boolean variable named *fieldsComplete* has a value of True if all the text boxes contain entries.

Then the *OKRecord* function checks through the name entries. A For loop examines the five pairs of name text boxes. The Boolean variables *firstOK* and *lastOK* together indicate whether or not a given pair of text boxes contain entries:

```
For nameBox = 0 To MaxNameList
  firstOK = Trim(txtFirstName(nameBox).Text) <> ""
  lastOK = Trim(txtLastName(nameBox).Text) <> ""
```

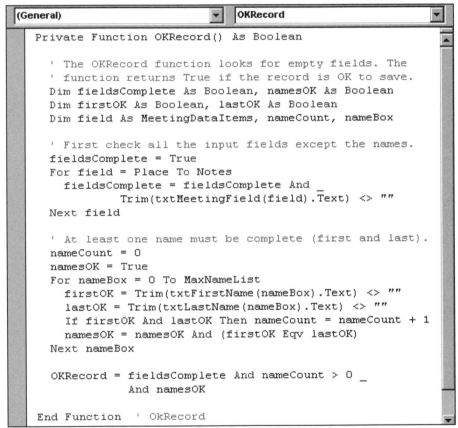

```
(General)                        ▼    OKRecord                          ▼

  Private Function OKRecord() As Boolean

    ' The OKRecord function looks for empty fields. The
    ' function returns True if the record is OK to save.
    Dim fieldsComplete As Boolean, namesOK As Boolean
    Dim firstOK As Boolean, lastOK As Boolean
    Dim field As MeetingDataItems, nameCount, nameBox

    ' First check all the input fields except the names.
    fieldsComplete = True
    For field = Place To Notes
      fieldsComplete = fieldsComplete And _
              Trim(txtMeetingField(field).Text) <> ""
    Next field

    ' At least one name must be complete (first and last).
    nameCount = 0
    namesOK = True
    For nameBox = 0 To MaxNameList
      firstOK = Trim(txtFirstName(nameBox).Text) <> ""
      lastOK = Trim(txtLastName(nameBox).Text) <> ""
      If firstOK And lastOK Then nameCount = nameCount + 1
      namesOK = namesOK And (firstOK Eqv lastOK)
    Next nameBox

    OKRecord = fieldsComplete And nameCount > 0 _
              And namesOK

  End Function   ' OkRecord
```

Figure 9-16: The *OKRecord* function checks to make sure a new record entry is valid before the program saves the record to the Meetings database. The place, date, time, subject, and notes entries must all be complete, and at least one participant's name must be complete.

The function counts the number of complete name entries. If both *firstOK* and *lastOK* are True, the value of *nameCount* is increased by 1:

```
If firstOK And lastOK Then nameCount = nameCount + 1
```

If the user has entered at least one complete name, the other pairs of name boxes may be blank. But the function disallows any incomplete names; if the user enters only a first name or only a last name in a given pair of name boxes, the record cannot be saved. Using a combination of And and Eqv operations, the following statement checks to make sure that all pairs of name boxes are either complete (first name *and* last name) or empty:

```
namesOK = namesOK And (firstOK Eqv lastOK)
```

To be saved to the database, a record must pass all three tests that the *OKRecord* function performs:

```
OKRecord = fieldsComplete And nameCount > 0 _
           And namesOK
```

Notice that this last statement contains both comparison and logical operations. When you write a condition that includes two or more operations, you have to be aware of the default order in which Visual Basic evaluates the operations.

Order of precedence

In an expression that contains a combination of arithmetic, comparison, and logical operations, Visual Basic performs the operations in this order, by default:

1. All the arithmetic operations first, following the usual order of arithmetic precedence

2. All the comparison operations, from left to right

3. All the logical operations, in this order: Not, And, Or, Xor, Eqv, Imp

Thanks to this preset order, many expressions you write will automatically be evaluated in the way you would expect. For example, in the following expressions, Visual Basic performs the arithmetic operations before the comparison ones:

```
c >= a + b
c - a = b
b = a * 3
```

And in this expression, the comparison operations are evaluated before the logical operation:

```
x >= 5 And x < 32
```

But sometimes the default order of operations gives the wrong answer for a particular application. Just as with arithmetic operations, you can use parentheses to override Visual Basic's default order of precedence. Simply place parentheses around the operation that you want Visual Basic to evaluate first. In addition, you may sometimes decide to use parentheses simply to make an expression more readable.

Writing decision structures

A one-line decision statement makes a simple choice between one action or another. By contrast, a decision structure allows your program to choose between two or more *blocks* of code, where a block consists of several Visual Basic statements in sequence. One form of the decision structure can be represented as follows:

```
If condition Then
   ' Block of code to be performed
   ' if the condition is true.
Else
   ' Block of code to be performed
   ' if the condition is false.
End If
```

In this format, the keywords of the decision structure itself serve to define distinct blocks of code. The statements located between the If line and the Else line make up the block that will be performed if the condition is true, and the statements between Else and End If make up the block that the decision will select if the condition is false. Each block may contain any number of statements.

For example, a decision structure in the Form_Activate procedure (shown back in Figures 9-13 and 9-14) determines whether or not to retrieve a record and display it on the frmMeetings form:

```
If curRec <> 0 Then
   Open MeetingsDatabase For Random As #1 _
     Len = Len(Meeting)
     Get #1, curRec, Meeting
   Close #1

   With Meeting
     txtMeetingField(Place).Text = .MeetPlace
     txtMeetingField(Date).Text = .MeetDate
     txtMeetingField(StartTime).Text = .TimeFrom
     txtMeetingField(EndTime).Text = .TimeTo
     txtMeetingField(Subject).Text = .Subject
     txtMeetingField(Notes).Text = .Notes

     For nameField = 0 To MaxNameList
       txtFirstName(nameField).Text = _
         .FirstName(nameField)
       txtLastName(nameField).Text = _
         .LastName(nameField)
     Next nameField
   End With
   ReadOnlyStatus True

Else
   cmdClear_Click
End If
```

In this passage, the If-Then block contains many statements that carry out the task of opening the database, reading a record, displaying its fields on the form, and switching to the read-only status. By contrast, the Else block contains a single statement that simply clears all information from the form in preparation for the user's next action.

As you know, the Else clause is optional. In the following example from the frmMeetings form's *SortNameList* procedure (Figure 9-17), the If condition compares two string values in the *NameList* array. If the two items are out of alphabetical order, the procedure swaps their positions in the list; otherwise, if they are already in the correct order, no action takes place:

```
If NameList(i).FullName > _
    NameList(j).FullName Then

    temp = NameList(i)
    NameList(i) = NameList(j)
    NameList(j) = temp
End If
```

Using the ElseIf clause

Finally, the ElseIf clause gives you the opportunity to write decisions based on multiple conditions. A decision structure may contain any number of ElseIf clauses, each with its own condition and corresponding block of code:

```
If condition1 Then

    ' Block of code to be performed
    ' if condition1 is true.

ElseIf condition2 Then

    ' Block of code to be performed
    ' if condition2 is true.

ElseIf condition3 Then

    ' Block of code to be performed
    ' if condition3 is true.

Else

    ' Block of code to be performed
    ' if none of the conditions is true.

End If
```

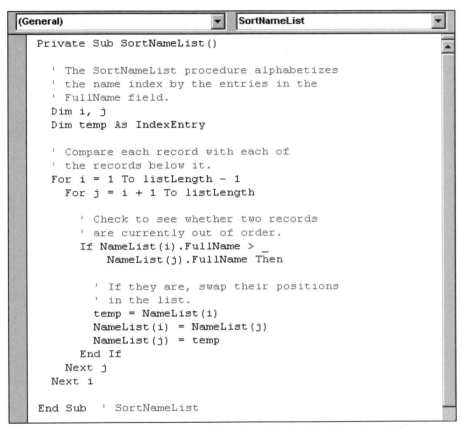

```
(General)                    ▼    SortNameList                  ▼

   Private Sub SortNameList()

     ' The SortNameList procedure alphabetizes
     ' the name index by the entries in the
     ' FullName field.
     Dim i, j
     Dim temp As IndexEntry

     ' Compare each record with each of
     ' the records below it.
     For i = 1 To listLength - 1
       For j = i + 1 To listLength

         ' Check to see whether two records
         ' are currently out of order.
         If NameList(i).FullName > _
             NameList(j).FullName Then

           ' If they are, swap their positions
           ' in the list.
           temp = NameList(i)
           NameList(i) = NameList(j)
           NameList(j) = temp
         End If
       Next j
     Next i

   End Sub  ' SortNameList
```

Figure 9-17: The *SortNameList* procedure from the frmMeetings form. The program uses this procedure to keep the name index in alphabetical order.

In this structure, Visual Basic evaluates each condition in sequence — first the condition in the If statement at the top of the decision, then each of the ElseIf conditions in turn. If any condition is True, the corresponding block of code is performed, and then the remainder of the decision structure is skipped. But if none of the conditions is True, Visual Basic performs the block located between Else and End If, if the structure contains an Else clause.

You can find an example of the ElseIf clause in the function procedure named *SearchForName*, shown in Figure 9-18. When the user enters a name into the frmMeetFind form and clicks the Search button, this procedure searches through the alphabetized name index to see if the target name exists in the database.

Rather than look through the entire list from beginning to end, the function carries out an efficient algorithm known as a *binary search*. In this technique, the program divides the alphabetized list into progressively smaller sections in an effort to focus in on the part of the list that will contain the name, if it exists. Along the way, the following If structure determines which of three conditions is true:

```
(General)                        ▼    SearchForName                    ▼

  Private Function SearchForName(findName As String) As Long
    ' The SearchForName function performs a binary search.
    Dim pos1 As Long, pos2 As Long
    Dim posX As Long, midPos As Long

    ' Search for the target name in portions of the list.
    pos1 = 1
    pos2 = listLength
    posX = 0
    Do While pos1 <= pos2 And posX = 0
      midPos = (pos1 + pos2) / 2
      If findName = NameList(midPos).FullName Then
        posX = midPos
      ElseIf findName > NameList(midPos).FullName Then
        pos1 = midPos + 1
      Else
        pos2 = midPos - 1
      End If
    Loop

    ' If the name is found, check for other instances.
    If posX > 1 Then
      Do While NameList(posX).FullName _
          = NameList(posX - 1).FullName
        posX = posX - 1
      Loop
    End If
    SearchForName = posX
End Function  ' SearchForName
```

Figure 9-18: The *SearchForName* function from the frmMeetFind form. This routine performs a binary search on the name index to search for the name of a participant that the user has requested. If the name is found, the function returns its record number in the database. (Note that the function also checks for multiple instances of the name in the index, and returns the position of the first instance.)

```
If findName = NameList(midPos).FullName Then
  posX = midPos
ElseIf findName > NameList(midPos).FullName Then
  pos1 = midPos + 1
Else
  pos2 = midPos - 1
End If
```

If the name has been found, the variable *posX* records its position in the list. Otherwise, the search continues either in a lower or higher portion of the list, depending on a comparison between the target name and the name at the current position. This fairly complex decision is carried out gracefully in the If-Then-ElseIf structure.

The Select Case structure

Visual Basic provides a second decision structure, identified by the keywords *Select Case*. Like the If structure, Select Case allows you to divide a decision into blocks of code representing different options that the decision can choose among. The Select Case decision bases its choice on a match between a *test expression* and individual Case expressions located at the top of each block of code.

A Select Case decision chooses at most one block of code to perform, among the multiple blocks you include in the structure. Each block of code is marked by a Case clause. The decision works by comparing the value of a test expression with expressions that appear at the top of each Case block. When a match is found, the decision performs the corresponding block of code.

Here is one way to represent the general format of the Select Case structure:

```
Select Case testExpression

Case expression1
   ' Block of code to be performed
   ' if a match is found between
   ' testExpression and expression1.

Case expression2
   ' Block of code to be performed
   ' if a match is found between
   ' testExpression and expression2.

Case expression3
   ' Block of code to be performed
   ' if a match is found between
   ' testExpression and expression3.
```

```
' Any number of additional Case
' blocks may be included.

Case Else
    ' Block of code to be performed
    ' if no match is found between
    ' testExpression and any of the
    ' previous Case expressions.

End Select
```

This is how the Select Case decision proceeds:

1. The decision begins by comparing the value of *testExpression* with *expression1* in the first Case clause.

2. If there is a match between the two expressions, Visual Basic performs the first block of code — that is, the statements between the first and second Case clauses.

3. If there is no match, the program goes on to the next Case expression.

4. Whenever a match is found, the corresponding block of code is performed. Then the action of the decision is complete; no further Case expressions are compared.

5. If the decision reaches the final Case clause — identified as Case Else — without having found a match in any of the previous Case clauses, the Case Else block is performed. (But note that the Case Else clause is optional. If it is not present, the decision results in no action if no match is found between *testExpression* and a Case expression.)

Understanding Case expressions

The Case clause can contain lists or ranges of values, in the following formats:

✦ A list, where each value is separated from the next by a comma:

```
Case expression1, expression2, ...
```

A match occurs when *testExpression* equals any of the values in the list.

✦ A range of values, expressed with the keyword To:

```
Case expression1 To expression2
```

A match occurs when *testExpression* equals any value within the range.

✦ A comparison expression, introduced by the keyword Is, and employing one of Visual Basic's six comparison operators (<, <=, >, >=, =, <>):

```
Case Is comparisonOperator expression
```

A match occurs if the value of *testExpression* is correctly described by the relation.

Tip A Case expression may also consist of a combination of these formats — lists, ranges, and comparisons.

Sometimes Select Case may result in clearer code than an If structure with a long sequence of ElseIf clauses. For example, the decision you've already examined from the *SearchForName* procedure could just as well have been written as a Select Case structure:

```
Select Case findName
   Case Is = NameList(midPos).FullName
     posX = midPos
   Case Is > NameList(midPos).FullName
     pos1 = midPos + 1
   Case Else
     pos2 = midPos - 1
End Select
```

Your choice between the If and Select Case structures is often a matter of personal preference.

Nested decisions

Sometimes one decision leads to another. When this happens in a program, you may find yourself organizing your code in a series of *nested* decisions. This means that an inner decision is contained within one of the blocks of code belonging to an outer decision. If the outer decision selects that particular block for performance, the program will have yet another decision structure to perform. You'll find an example of this in the *cmdSave_Click* procedure shown in Figures 9-19 and 9-20. The outer decision determines whether the current record is complete and therefore suitable for saving to the database:

```
If OKRecord Then
```

If the call to OKRecord returns a value of True, one nested decision checks for name entries that should be added to the name index, and another determines whether the index needs to be realphabetized.

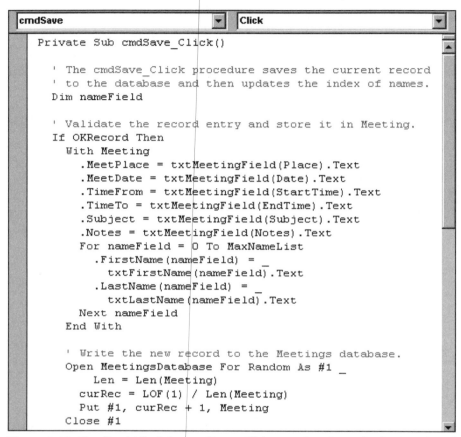

Figure 9-19: The first half of the *cmdSave_Click* procedure from the frmMeetings form. If a call to OKRecord confirms that the current record can be saved, this event procedure writes the record to the Meetings database, and updates the name index.

As you'll learn in the upcoming sections, decisions are not the only structures that can be nested. You can write nested loops, decisions nested within loops, loops within decisions, and a variety of other powerful combinations.

Loops

Repetition is a central feature of programming. To carry out repetition in a program, you organize a block of code in a *loop* structure. Whatever the task — processing hundreds of database records, performing scores of calculations, or printing dozens of copies of nearly identical documents — a well-designed loop controls the repetition reliably and efficiently.

```
cmdSave                        ▼    Click                        ▼
        ' Update the name index.
     For nameField = 0 To MaxNameList

        ' Add any complete name entry to the index.
      If Trim(txtFirstName(nameField).Text) <> "" And _
         Trim(txtLastName(nameField).Text) <> "" Then

           ' Resize the name list, and add the new name.
           listLength = listLength + 1
           ReDim Preserve NameList(listLength)
           NameList(listLength).FullName = _
             FixName(txtFirstName(nameField).Text, _
                    txtLastName(nameField).Text)
           NameList(listLength).RecordNum = _
             curRec + 1
      End If
    Next nameField

      ' If the index is longer than 1 sort the names.
      If listLength > 1 Then SortNameList

      ' Clear the frmMeetings form for a new entry.
      cmdClear_Click
    Else
      ' If the current record is incomplete, don't save it.
      MsgBox "Can't save an incomplete record.", , "Save"
    End If

End Sub  ' cmdSave_Click
```

Figure 9-20: The second half of the *cmdSave_Click* procedure from the frmMeetings form. One nested decision is responsible for adding new names to the *NameList* index, and another realphabetizes the index if the list is longer than one entry.

A loop has two basic components:

✦ The block of code that you want the computer to perform repeatedly

✦ An instruction that controls the duration of the looping

In the design of a loop, your typical goal is to provide the computer with distinct information to work with during each *iteration* of the loop. The code remains the same, but the data changes. This is what makes repetition truly powerful: Each time around the loop, the computer can process the *next* record in a database, perform a calculation on a *different* set of data, or conduct a *new* output operation.

Visual Basic has two major varieties of loops, known by the keywords *Do* and *For*.

Understanding Do loops

The first requirement of a loop structure is to identify the block of code that will be performed repeatedly during the looping. You meet this requirement by writing specific statements at the beginning and the end of the loop. In a Do loop, a *Do* statement always marks the top of the loop and a *Loop* statement marks the bottom. The statements located between Do and Loop make up the body of the loop — that is, the code that will be performed once for each iteration.

The conditional expression that controls the duration of the looping can appear either in the Do statement at the top of the loop or in the Loop statement at the bottom. Furthermore, the condition can appear in either of two clauses, introduced by the keywords *While* or *Until*. In the two most commonly used Do loop formats, a While clause appears in the Do statement at the top of the loop, or an Until clause appears in the Loop statement at the bottom. Here is a loop with the condition at the top:

```
Do While condition

   ' The block of statements that the
   ' computer will perform repeatedly
   ' as long as the condition is true.

Loop
```

And here is a loop with the condition located at the bottom:

```
Do

   ' The block of statements that the
   ' computer will perform repeatedly
   ' until the condition is true.

Loop Until condition
```

In both cases, the *condition* is an expression that results in a value of True or False.

Visual Basic evaluates the condition once for each iteration of the loop. A change in the condition's value ultimately causes the loop to stop. In a While clause, the looping continues as long as the condition remains True; looping stops when the condition becomes False. In an Until clause, the looping continues as long as the condition is False; looping stops when the condition becomes True.

Just as in decision statements, you can use a variety of operations to build conditions. The comparison operations (represented by <, <=, >, >=, =, <>) and the logical operations (represented by Not, And, Or, Xor, Eqv, and Imp) are all available for use in Do loop conditions.

The placement of the condition at the top or the bottom of a loop can be an important factor in the loop's behavior. With the expression located at the top of the loop, Visual Basic evaluates the condition *before* the first iteration; if the condition has the wrong value — False in a While clause, or True in an Until clause — Visual Basic immediately skips the entire loop without performing a single iteration. By contrast, if the expression is located at the bottom of the loop, Visual Basic always performs the block of code at least one time. *After* the first iteration, Visual Basic evaluates the condition and determines whether to continue the looping.

The actual mechanism for controlling the duration of the loops clearly depends on your choice of a While clause or an Until clause for a Do loop.

Using the While clause

When you want the repetition to continue as long as a condition remains true, use a While clause in your Do loop. With the While clause in the Do statement at the top of the loop, Visual Basic evaluates the condition before the first iteration. For example, the following loop, found in the frmMeetFind form's cmdSearch_Click procedure (Figures 9-21 and 9-22), looks to see if the name index contains more than one instance of a target name:

```
Do While inName = _
    NameList(curPos + 1).FullName
  timesCount = timesCount + 1
  curPos = curPos + 1
  If curPos = listLength Then Exit Do
Loop
```

For each iteration of the loop, a counter variable, *timesCount*, is increased by 1.

Using the Until clause

An Until clause stops the looping when a condition becomes True. As long as the value of the condition is False, the iterations continue. For example, consider the following hypothetical input operation:

```
prompt = "Enter a value from 1 to 10"

Do
  inValue = InputBox(prompt, "Input Value")
Loop Until inValue >= 1 And inValue <= 10
```

This loop uses Visual Basic's built-in InputBox function to display a prompt on the screen and elicit a numeric input value. Because the required value must be between 1 and 10, the loop iterates until the user enters a number in the appropriate range. As you can see, the Until condition is True only when the user meets the input requirement; a False condition results in another iteration of the loop.

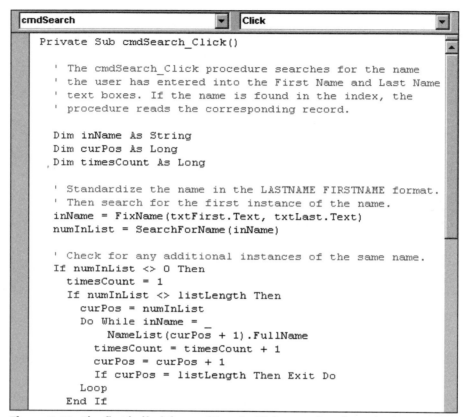

| cmdSearch ▼ | Click ▼ |

```
Private Sub cmdSearch_Click()

    ' The cmdSearch_Click procedure searches for the name
    ' the user has entered into the First Name and Last Name
    ' text boxes. If the name is found in the index, the
    ' procedure reads the corresponding record.

    Dim inName As String
    Dim curPos As Long
    Dim timesCount As Long

    ' Standardize the name in the LASTNAME FIRSTNAME format.
    ' Then search for the first instance of the name.
    inName = FixName(txtFirst.Text, txtLast.Text)
    numInList = SearchForName(inName)

    ' Check for any additional instances of the same name.
    If numInList <> 0 Then
        timesCount = 1
        If numInList <> listLength Then
            curPos = numInList
            Do While inName = _
                NameList(curPos + 1).FullName
                timesCount = timesCount + 1
                curPos = curPos + 1
                If curPos = listLength Then Exit Do
            Loop
        End If
```

Figure 9-21: The first half of the cmdSearch_Click procedure from the frmMeetFind form. When the user clicks Search on the Find a Meeting Record dialog box, this procedure looks through the index for the first instance of the target name. If the name is found, the procedure looks further down the index for any additional instances of the name.

In short, a Do loop is based on a condition; the looping stops when the value of the condition changes from True to False or from False to True. By contrast, a traditional For loop contains a numeric counter variable that controls the duration of the looping. The loop completes one iteration for each change in the value of this counter variable. When the counter moves beyond a specified range, the looping stops.

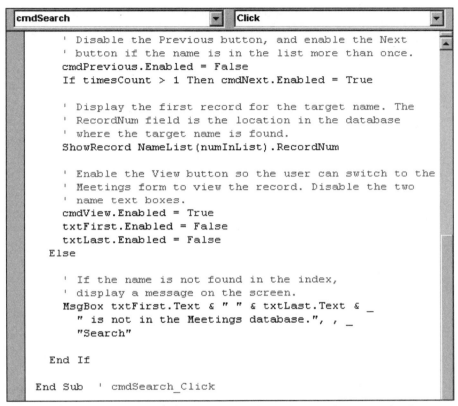

```
cmdSearch                          ▼    Click                                ▼

        ' Disable the Previous button, and enable the Next
        ' button if the name is in the list more than once.
        cmdPrevious.Enabled = False
        If timesCount > 1 Then cmdNext.Enabled = True

        ' Display the first record for the target name. The
        ' RecordNum field is the location in the database
        ' where the target name is found.
        ShowRecord NameList(numInList).RecordNum

        ' Enable the View button so the user can switch to the
        ' Meetings form to view the record. Disable the two
        ' name text boxes.
        cmdView.Enabled = True
        txtFirst.Enabled = False
        txtLast.Enabled = False
    Else

        ' If the name is not found in the index,
        ' display a message on the screen.
        MsgBox txtFirst.Text & " " & txtLast.Text & _
            " is not in the Meetings database.", , _
            "Search"

    End If

End Sub  ' cmdSearch_Click
```

Figure 9-22: The second half of the cmdSearch_Click procedure from the frmMeetFind form. The procedure displays the target record, and enables or disables command buttons and text boxes.

Understanding For loops

For loops are useful in a variety of programming contexts. You should consider using a For loop whenever you can

- ✦ Specify in advance the exact number of iterations that the loop should go through.

- ✦ Define a variable that represents the correct number of iterations. (The value of this variable can be determined during the program run, so that each performance of a loop may result in a different number of iterations.)

- ✦ Write an expression that calculates the appropriate number of iterations. (Again, the number of iterations may vary from one run to the next.)

As in a Do structure, the For loop contains a block of code that will be performed repeatedly during the looping. Two parts of a For loop serve as markers for the beginning and the end of the code. The *For* statement always marks the beginning of the loop. This statement also identifies the counter variable and specifies the range of values it will go through during the looping. The *Next* statement marks the end of the loop. The statements between For and Next are performed once for each iteration of the loop.

In many For loops, the counter variable itself becomes a useful data item in the performance of the loop. You can display this counter on the screen, perform calculations with it, or use it as an *index* to access other information. The more you learn about using For loops, the more important this counter variable can become in the design of your program.

In its simplest form, the For loop uses an integer counter that increases by 1 for each iteration. The loop's syntax can be represented as follows:

```
For counter = v1 To v2

    ' The block of statements that the
    ' computer will perform repeatedly
    ' as counter increases from v1 to v2.

Next counter
```

In this format, *counter* is the name of a variable, and *v1* and *v2* specify the range of values that counter will represent during the looping. You can write *v1* and *v2* as literal numeric values, variables, or expressions. Here are the steps Visual Basic goes through to perform a For loop:

1. Assign the value of *v1* to *counter*.

2. Compare the value of *counter* with *v2*. If *counter* is greater than *v2*, terminate the loop and jump down to the statement located after Next. If *counter* is less than or equal to *v2,* perform all the statements located between For and Next once.

3. If the looping hasn't terminated, increase the value of *counter* by 1 and continue again as described in Step 2, above.

Consider the following simple example from the frmMeetings form's cmdClear_Click procedure (Figure 9-23):

```
For nameField = 0 to MaxNameList
    txtFirstName(nameField).Text = ""
    txtLastName(nameField).Text = ""
Next nameField
```

This loop clears any text entries in all five pairs of name text boxes in the frmMeetings form. As you may notice, the text boxes themselves — txtFirstName and txtLastName — are indexed, or numbered sequentially, from 0 to 4.

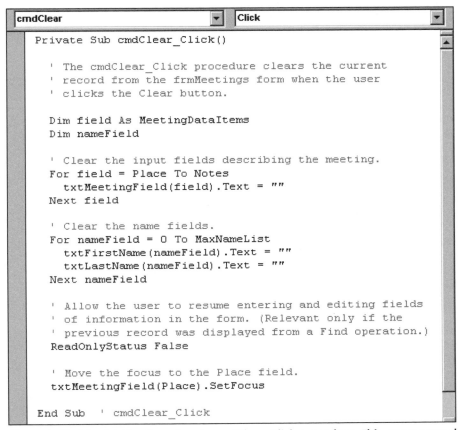

| cmdClear | ▼ | Click | ▼ |

```
Private Sub cmdClear_Click()

  ' The cmdClear_Click procedure clears the current
  ' record from the frmMeetings form when the user
  ' clicks the Clear button.

  Dim field As MeetingDataItems
  Dim nameField

  ' Clear the input fields describing the meeting.
  For field = Place To Notes
    txtMeetingField(field).Text = ""
  Next field

  ' Clear the name fields.
  For nameField = 0 To MaxNameList
    txtFirstName(nameField).Text = ""
    txtLastName(nameField).Text = ""
  Next nameField

  ' Allow the user to resume entering and editing fields
  ' of information in the form. (Relevant only if the
  ' previous record was displayed from a Find operation.)
  ReadOnlyStatus False

  ' Move the focus to the Place field.
  txtMeetingField(Place).SetFocus

End Sub   ' cmdClear_Click
```

Figure 9-23: The frmMeetings form's cmdClear_Click procedure. This event procedure clears all the text boxes in the startup form, preparing the program for a new record entry.

(*MaxNameList* is a named constant defined in the general declarations section of the modMeetings module. Its value is 4.) These text boxes are established as *control arrays* — that is, two groups of controls that have common names. This arrangement considerably simplifies the program's processing of the information in these particular text boxes, as shown in this example. You can create a control array at design time by assigning the same Name property setting to two or more controls in a form. You'll see other examples later in this chapter, and you'll examine control arrays more formally in Chapter 11.

Using the Step clause

Sometimes you'll want to increase the counter variable by a value other than 1 for each iteration of a For loop. In this case, you can use the Step clause in the For statement to indicate the increment amount. Here is a general format for the For loop with a Step clause:

```
For counter = v1 To v2 Step incr

  ' The block of statements that the
  ' computer will perform repeatedly.

Next counter
```

As a result of the Step clause, Visual Basic increases the value of *counter* by *incr* instead of 1 after each iteration. You can express the incrementation amount as a literal value, a variable, or an expression.

The Step clause also allows you to *decrease* the value of the counter variable as the iterations progress. If this is what you want to do, you write the For statement as follows:

```
For counter = v2 To v1 Step decr
```

where *v2* is greater than *v1* and the Step clause provides a *decrement* amount — that is, a negative value.

Under two sets of circumstances, a For loop results in no iterations:

✦ The starting value you specify for the counter variable is greater than the ending value, and the Step value is positive.

✦ The starting value is less than the ending value and the Step value is negative.

Although the use of integer counters is common in For loops, you are free to use counters belonging to any of Visual Basic's numeric data types — including integer, long integer, single-precision, or double-precision variables. Using a noninteger counter allows you to increase or decrease the variable by fractional values as the iterations proceed.

Nested loops

Like decisions, Do loops and For loops can be nested, resulting in powerful patterns of repetition. When one loop is nested inside another, the inner loop goes through its entire cycle of iterations once for each iteration of the outer loop. Carefully planned, nested loops allow you to accomplish a lot of work in a very compact amount of code.

A simple but classic example of nested loops appears in the SortNameList procedure (shown back in Figure 9-17), which alphabetizes the program's name index:

```
For i = 1 To listLength - 1
  For j = i + 1 To listLength
    If NameList(i).FullName > _
        NameList(j).FullName Then
      temp = NameList(i)
      NameList(i) = NameList(j)
```

```
        NameList(j) = temp
      End If
    Next j
  Next i
```

The outer loop uses the variable *i* as its counter, and the inner loop uses *j*. The outer loop goes through the list of names, from the beginning to the second-to-last element (represented by *listLength - 1*). For each iteration of the outer loop, the inner loop goes through all the elements located *below* the current *i* position. If any two names, represented by the positions *i* and *j*, are found to be out of order, the decision structure swaps their positions. When the looping is complete, the list is alphabetized. (This algorithm is known as the *bubble sort*. Although it's a rather inefficient way to alphabetize a list, it's one of the easiest sorting algorithms to code and to understand. As an exercise, you might want to try replacing this procedure with a more efficient routine, such as the Shell sort.)

The For Each loop

Visual Basic has another loop structure known by the keywords *For Each*. Although you can use a For Each loop to process an array, its ideal application is with a type of object known as a *collection*. You'll learn about collections and the For Each loop in Chapter 11.

As you now turn your attention to Visual Basic's major data structures, you'll continue to see how control structures are suited for working with arrays and records.

Arrays

An *array* is a list, a table, or another multidimensional arrangement of data items, all represented by a single variable name. The Dim statement (or a Private or Public statement) declares an array and defines its characteristics.

An array has some features in common with a simple variable; both represent values belonging to a consistent data type, and both have a designated *scope* that determines where they are available for use in your program. But an array has some additional characteristics. Most importantly, every array has a specific number of *dimensions*, which determine how the array's data items are organized. Arrays containing one, two, or three dimensions are probably the most commonly used data structures in Visual Basic programs:

✦ A one-dimensional array represents a list of data.

✦ A two-dimensional array represents a table of data, conceptually arranged in rows and columns.

✦ A three-dimensional array represents several data tables, each with the same number of rows and columns.

Declaring arrays

You can use Dim, Private, or Public to declare the characteristics of an array, including its name, scope, data type, and dimensions. For example, you can declare a one-dimensional array as follows:

```
Dim arrayName(length) As dataType
```

Here are the components of this declaration:

✦ *arrayName* is a name that conforms to Visual Basic's rules for variable names; it begins with a letter and may contain a combination of letters and digits.

✦ *length* specifies the number of data items the array can represent. By default, the actual size is *length* + *1* because items are numbered from 0 to *length* in the array.

✦ *dataType* is a keyword representing one of Visual Basic's data types or a user-defined type.

If you omit the As clause, the array belongs to the Variant type by default.

For example, the following Dim statement declares a one-dimensional string array named *MeetingPlace*, and specifies its length as 5:

```
Dim MeetingPlace(5) As String
```

Once you've declared an array, you can use Visual Basic statements to assign values to the *elements* of the array. You identify each element by specifying a subscript in parentheses immediately after the array name. For example, the *MeetingPlace* array has six elements, with subscripts ranging from 0 to 5:

```
MeetingPlace(0)
MeetingPlace(1)
MeetingPlace(2)
MeetingPlace(3)
MeetingPlace(4)
MeetingPlace(5)
```

Although the length of the *MeetingPlace* array is specified as 5, the array contains six elements, because the subscripts begin at 0. The array can therefore store a list of six strings. Of course you're free to use these array elements in any way that suits the data requirements of your program. For example, you might decide to store values only in *MeetingPlace(1)* to *MeetingPlace(5)*, leaving *MeetingPlace(0)* unused.

As you've already begun to see, the For loop is an extremely convenient structure for handling arrays. The loop's counter variable serves perfectly as the subscript for accessing the elements of an array. For example, in the SortNameList procedure, which you examined earlier in this chapter, the counter variables of two loops are used to access pairs of elements from the *NameList* array.

Visual Basic also allows you to establish a custom range of subscripts for an array. In the Dim statement that declares the array, you use the keyword *To* to specify the range:

```
Dim arrayName(sub1 To sub2)
```

In this format, the elements of the array range from *arrayName(sub1)* to *arrayName(sub2)*. Another way to control the range of indexes for an array is to include an Option Base statement in the general declarations section of a form or module. This statement can take one of the following two forms:

```
Option Base 0
```

or

```
Option Base 1
```

Depending on the value specified in the Option Base statement, all array indexes start at either 0 or 1.

Multidimensional arrays

To create an array of more than one dimension, you specify the length of each dimension in a Dim statement. The dimensions appear in parentheses just after the array name. Here is the general format for declaring a two-dimensional array:

```
Dim arrayName2(length1, length2)
```

And here is the format for a three-dimensional array:

```
Dim arrayName3(length1, length2, length3)
```

A pair of nested For loops presents the ideal structure for processing a two-dimensional array. For example, the following pair of loops assigns values to all the elements of a two-dimensional array:

```
Dim test(3, 4)

For i = 0 To 3
  For j = 0 To 4
    test(i, j) = i * j
  Next j
Next i
```

Likewise, a nested sequence of three loops can efficiently handle the elements of a three-dimensional array.

Dynamic arrays

When you use a literal numeric value to declare the length of an array, Visual Basic creates an array whose length cannot be changed at runtime. For example, *MeetingPlace* is a fixed-length array (also known as a *static* array):

```
Dim MeetingPlace(5) As String
```

Visual Basic allocates the memory space required for this array when you first start the program. The allocation remains unchanged throughout the program run.

A fixed-length array works fine whenever you know in advance how many data items you want to store in the array. But sometimes the size requirements are determined during a program run. In this case, you need to create a *dynamic* array. Visual Basic allocates memory space for a dynamic array during a run. The initial size of the array can therefore be based on information that's not available until the program begins. Furthermore, Visual Basic allows dynamic arrays to be redimensioned any number of times during a program run. The size of the array can change if a program needs to accommodate specific data.

Here is the general approach to creating and working with a dynamic array: Begin by declaring the array (in a Dim, Private, or Public statement) using empty parentheses in place of the array's dimensions:

```
Public arrayName() as dataType
```

At the point when the program is ready to store data in the array, use a ReDim statement to define the array's size:

```
ReDim arrayName(length)
```

To change the array's size later without losing any of the data already stored in the array, use the *Preserve* keyword in another ReDim statement:

```
ReDim Preserve arrayName(length)
```

The Meetings program contains a good example of a dynamic array. As you know, the program creates an array called *NameList* to store an index of all the participant's names that appear in the Meetings database. (The array also stores the record number where each person's name can be found in the database; you'll see exactly how the array is organized later in this chapter.) The program initially creates *NameList* at the very beginning of a performance, by opening the database file and reading the names of all the people stored in each record. But the length of *NameList* may change many times during the performance, as the user adds new meeting records to the database. *NameList* is therefore defined as a dynamic array whose length can be changed at any time.

The array is declared as a Public variable in the general declarations section of the Meetings.Bas module (Figure 9-24):

```
Public NameList() As IndexEntry
```

As you'll see shortly, *IndexEntry* is a user-defined type. Notice the empty parentheses in the *NameList* declaration; whenever you see these in a variable declaration, you can expect to find one or more ReDim statements to define the program's length.

```
(General)                              (Declarations)

' The Meetings program
' Module: modMeetings (Meetings.BAS)
' Contains types for the Meetings record and its index.

Public Const MeetingsDatabase = "\Meetings.DB"
Public Const MaxNameList = 4     ' Length of a name list.


' Meeting represents a database record.
Type MeetingRec
  MeetPlace As String * 18
  MeetDate As String * 10
  TimeFrom As String * 10
  TimeTo As String * 10
  FirstName(MaxNameList) As String * 10
  LastName(MaxNameList) As String * 18
  Subject As String * 35
  Notes As String * 400
End Type
Public Meeting As MeetingRec     ' The record variable.
Public curRec As Integer         ' The record pointer.


' The NameList array stores all the names in the database.
Type IndexEntry
  FullName As String
  RecordNum As Long
End Type
Public NameList() As IndexEntry   ' The index array.
Public listLength As Long         ' The index length.
' End of general declarations, modMeetings module.
```

Figure 9-24: The top of the modMeetings module contains declarations for many of the application's key data structures, arrays, variables, and constants. For example, *NameList* is declared as a dynamic array; it will represent the name index, which the program uses to search for meeting records by the names of participants.

The Form_Load procedure in the *frmMeetings* module (shown back in Figures 9-11 and 9-12) performs the program's first ReDim statement. The procedure opens the Meetings database file and reads each record from beginning to end. Because a given meeting record may contain from one to five names of people who attended the meeting, the number of names in the database is unpredictable, even though the number of records can be calculated from the size of the file. The program therefore redimensions the *NameList* array each time a new name is read from the database:

```
listLength = listLength + 1
ReDim Preserve NameList(listLength)
```

The *listLength* variable keeps a running count of the number of names that have been read. For each new name, the count is increased by 1 and then the array is redimensioned to accommodate the new data. Finally, the new name is stored in the array. Thanks to the Preserve keyword, none of the previous names are lost.

The *cmdSave_Click* procedure (shown back in Figures 9-19 and 9-20) goes through a similar process each time the user adds a new meeting record to the database. As you've seen, the program sorts the *NameList* array after each increase in its length. Whenever the user requests a particular record from the database, the array serves as a convenient index for locating the target record.

Keep in mind that ReDim works only with dynamic arrays. An attempt to redimension a fixed-length (static) array results in an error.

Tip In some cases you can use ReDim to adjust the number of dimensions in an array. For example, you can change a two-dimensional array to a three-dimensional array. But this kind of change is not possible if you use the Preserve keyword in the ReDim statement. In fact, in a ReDim Preserve statement you can change the length of only the last dimension in a multidimensional array. All other dimensions must retain their original lengths if you wish to preserve the values of the array.

Now it's time to turn to the final topics of this chapter, user-defined types, record variables, and enumerations.

User-Defined Types

An array contains multiple data values, all belonging to one data type. In a string array all the elements are strings, and in a numeric array all the values are numbers. By contrast, the *user-defined type* allows you to create variables that represent multiple values of different types.

The user-defined type is ideal for use in database applications, as is clearly illustrated in the Meetings program. A database is a collection of records in which information is organized in a consistent way. The individual data items in a record are known as *fields*. For example, the fields of a meeting record include the meeting's place, date, starting time, ending time, and subject, the list of people who attended, and the notes recorded about the meeting.

Tip Because the user-defined type is so closely associated with database programs, Visual Basic programmers commonly use database terminology to describe the components of the data structure itself. Most programmers refer to a user-defined type as a *record structure*. In this terminology, the elements of a user-defined type are known as the *fields* of the record structure. A variable belonging to a user-defined type is simply a *record variable*. An array belonging to a user-defined type is an *array of records*.

Creating a record variable is a two-step process in a Visual Basic program:

1. Use a Type statement to define a record structure. The definition consists of a type name followed by a list of field names. Each field belongs to a specific data type.

2. Write a Dim statement to declare a record variable or an array of records.

Defining a record structure

The general form of the Type statement is as follows:

```
Type TypeName
   Element1 As dataType
   Element2 As dataType
   Element3 As dataType

      ' ... additional field definitions

   End Type
```

In this statement, *TypeName* is the name you devise for the record structure, and *Element1*, *Element2*, *Element3* (and so on) are the names you give to the fields in the structure. You must also identify a data type for each field. The *dataType* may be any of Visual Basic's predefined types. An element may also be typed as an array or as another user-defined type.

The Type statement may appear only in the general declarations section of a form or module. User-defined types are global by default, but you can use the keyword Public or Private just before Type to specify an explicit scope for your type definition.

In the modMeetings module of the Meetings program (shown back in Figure 9-24), two user-defined types are declared. The first defines the structure of a meeting record:

```
Type MeetingRec
   MeetPlace As String * 18
   MeetDate As String * 10
   TimeFrom As String * 10
   TimeTo As String * 10
   FirstName(MaxNameList) As String * 10
   LastName(MaxNameList) As String * 18
   Subject As String * 35
   Notes As String * 400
End Type
```

The first four elements of the MeetingRec type correspond to the Place, Date, and From Time, and To Time fields of a meeting record. The next two are arrays of strings, *FirstName* and *LastName*, designed to store as many as five names of people who attended a meeting. The last two elements are for the Subject and Notes fields. Notice that the Notes field is a fixed string of length 400.

The Type statement defines a new data structure, but does not create any variables belonging to this data type. You use Dim, Public, or Private for this task. For example, here is the general form of a Dim statement for declaring a record variable:

```
Dim RecordVar As TypeName
```

The Meetings program uses Public rather than Dim to declare a variable belonging to the *MeetingRec* type:

```
Public Meeting As MeetingRec
```

Given this variable declaration, Visual Basic supplies a special notation for referring to the elements of the Meeting record. This notation is a combination of the record name and an element name, separated by a period, as in the general form *RecordVar.Element*. For example, here are the names of the first four fields in the Meeting record variable:

```
Meeting.MeetPlace
Meeting.MeetDate
Meeting.TimeFrom
Meeting.TimeTo
```

You can use the *RecordVar.Element* notation in assignment statements or any other kind of statement in which you normally include variable names.

The With statement

Visual Basic has an important control structure you can use to simplify any code that refers to the elements of a user-defined type. The With statement enables you to abbreviate the names of any user-defined data elements. Here is the general form of the With structure for use with a variable belonging to a user-defined type:

```
With RecordVar

    ' Statements that may refer to
    ' the elements of RecordVar.

End With
```

Inside the With block, you refer to *RecordVar.Element* simply as:

```
.Element
```

The Meetings program uses the With statement frequently to streamline references to elements of the *Meeting* record variable. For example, here is how the *cmdSave_Click* procedure (Figures 9-19 and 9-20) copies data from text boxes to the corresponding elements of the *Meeting* variable:

```
With Meeting
   .MeetPlace = txtMeetingField(Place).Text
   .MeetDate = txtMeetingField(Date).Text
   .TimeFrom = txtMeetingField(StartTime).Text
   .TimeTo = txtMeetingField(EndTime).Text
   .Subject = txtMeetingField(Subject).Text
   .Notes = txtMeetingField(Notes).Text
   For nameField = 0 To MaxNameList
     .FirstName(nameField) = _
       txtFirstName(nameField).Text
     .LastName(nameField) = _
       txtLastName(nameField).Text
   Next nameField
End With
```

The abbreviated names for the elements of the *Meeting* record appear on the left side of the equal signs in a sequence of assignment statements. Conversely, here is how the Form_Activate procedure (Figures 9-13 and 9-14) displays the elements of a newly retrieved record in the text boxes of the Business Meetings dialog box:

```
With Meeting
   txtMeetingField(Place).Text = .MeetPlace
   txtMeetingField(Date).Text = .MeetDate
   txtMeetingField(StartTime).Text = .TimeFrom
   txtMeetingField(EndTime).Text = .TimeTo
   txtMeetingField(Subject).Text = .Subject
   txtMeetingField(Notes).Text = .Notes

   For nameField = 0 To MaxNameList
     txtFirstName(nameField).Text = _
       .FirstName(nameField)
     txtLastName(nameField).Text = _
       .LastName(nameField)
   Next nameField
End With
```

In this case, the abbreviated names appear on the right side of the equal signs.

Creating an array of records

The *Meeting* variable can store only a single record at a time. But it's also possible to declare an array that belongs to a user-defined type, or in other words, an array of records. Here is the general format for declaring such an array:

```
Dim RecordArray(length) As TypeName
```

As you would expect, *length* indicates the number of records that the array can store. (Actually, the array can contain *length + 1* records, because the subscripts of the array begin at 0.) Once this array is declared, your program uses the following notation to identify the fields of a single record in the array:

```
RecordArray(i).FieldName1
RecordArray(i).FieldName2
RecordArray(i).FieldName3
```

where *i* is a subscript for one of the elements of the array.

The Meetings application creates an array of records to represent the name index that the program uses to retrieve individual meeting records from the database. The second user-defined type in the modMeetings module (Figure 9-24) is named *IndexEntry*:

```
Type IndexEntry
  FullName As String
  RecordNum As Long
End Type
```

This is the type on which the *NameList* array is based. The following Public statement declares the array:

```
Public NameList() As IndexEntry
```

As you can see, each element of the array has two fields, which are identified as

```
NameList(i).FullName
NameList(i).RecordNum
```

The *FullName* field contains the name of each person who is added to the *NameList* array, and the *RecordNum* field is the record number where the person's name can be found in the database. When the program locates a name in this array, it can simply look at the *RecordNum* field of the same array element to find out which database record contains the name.

To see how this is accomplished, take a look at the cmdView_Click procedure in Figure 9-25. This procedure takes control when the user chooses a record in the frmMeetFind form and then clicks the View button. Before switching back to the program's original dialog box, this procedure assigns the target record number to the Public variable named *curRec*:

```
curRec = NameList(numInList).RecordNum
```

The variable *numInList* serves as the index into the *NameList* array. The program sets the value of *numInList* when a target name is located in the list. (For example, see the cmdSearch_Click procedure in Figures 9-21 and 9-22.) Back in the frmMeetings form, the Form_Activate procedure (Figures 9-13 and 9-14) uses the value of *curRec* to retrieve a record directly from the database — and then displays its fields in the text boxes of the form.

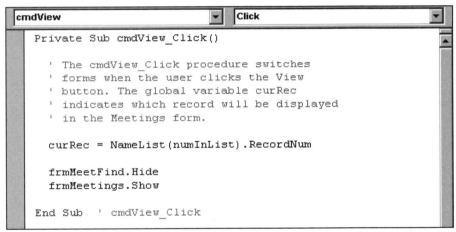

Figure 9-25: The cmdView_Click procedure takes control when the user clicks the View button on the frmMeetFind form. It assigns the record number of the current meeting record to the global variable *curRec*. Then it hides the frmMeetFind form and displays the frmMeetings form.

Using the Enum type

One final data type that is illustrated in the Meetings application is Visual Basic's new Enum structure. In its simplest form, the Enum statement creates a list of named constants representing a sequence of integers. For example, the general declarations section of the frmMeetings form (Figure 9-26) contains the following enumeration:

```
Enum MeetingDataItems
    Place
    Date
    StartTime
    EndTime
    Subject
    Notes
End Enum
```

By default, the first name in an enumeration represents a value of zero, and subsequent names represent integers in sequence. In this example, the names *Place*, *Date*, *StartTime*, *EndTime*, *Subject*, and *Notes* represent values from 0 to 5.

Figure 9-26: The global declarations section of the frmMeetings form creates an enumeration named *MeetingDataItems*. The program uses the constants in this enumeration to identify the individual text boxes in the txtMeetingField array.

As you may have noticed, the six text boxes displayed in the upper portions of the frmMeetings form all have the same name, txtMeetingField. They make up a control array in which the individual text boxes have indexes from 0 to 5. Conveniently, these are the same default values represented by the six constants in the *MeetingDataItems* enumeration. Accordingly, the program can use the Enum constants to represent individual controls in the txtMeetingField array. For example, here is the notation you've seen for identifying the Text property of each box in the array:

```
txtMeetingField(Place).Text
txtMeetingField(Date).Text
txtMeetingField(StartTime).Text
txtMeetingField(EndTime).Text
txtMeetingField(Subject).Text
txtMeetingField(Notes).Text
```

The Enum constants give the program a clear, understandable way to identify the six elements of the control array named txtMeetingField.

But this isn't the only use the program makes of these constants. A variable belonging to the *MeetingDataItems* type can be used as the counter in a For loop. For example, look back at the cmdClear_Click procedure in Figure 9-23. This procedure declares a variable named *field*, belonging to the *MeetingDataItems* type:

```
Dim field As MeetingDataItems
```

Using this variable, the procedure can loop through the entire *txtMeetingField* array, from the first control (identified by the constant *Place*) to the last (identified by *Notes*):

```
For field = Place To Notes
  txtMeetingField(field).Text = ""
Next field
```

With this short and elegant loop, the procedure clears all the text boxes in the array.

Tip Enumeration constants need not represent a only sequence of integers. In the Enum statement itself, you can assign any numeric value to a name in the enumeration, using the notation *enumName = value*. Whether you use the default values or specific values that you assign in the Enum statement, no other statement in your program can change the value assigned to an Enum member.

You'll continue exploring data structures and control structures as you turn to the topic of data file programming in Chapter 10.

Data Files and Database Management

Data file management is an essential skill for all programmers. Files on disk serve a variety of purposes in Visual Basic projects:

+ Applications often create files as permanent records of the information they generate; data produced during one program run can be retrieved during the next.

+ A data file may become a medium for exchanging information between different applications.

+ Programs can produce text files designed for *people* to read; these files may contain information that a user can view, modify, incorporate into larger documents, and print.

Every project you've worked with so far in this book has used data files to store or retrieve information. The Travel Guide and Currency Exchange programs (Chapters 1 through 4) are both designed to read a data file containing international currency exchange rates. The programs use this information to provide a variety of currency calculation tools for the business traveler.

The Travel Expense Log program (Chapter 7) creates a text file to record expense records from business trips. The program also creates a readable text file containing a summary of travel expenses.

The Restaurant Review program (Chapter 8) develops a database for storing your comments about restaurants in your city or around the world. The database format makes it easy for the program to retrieve any restaurant record on request.

The Meetings program (Chapter 9) saves information about meetings that you conduct or attend during business trips. Again, the database file is designed for efficient retrieval of any record that you need to review.

These programs illustrate two kinds of files you can create in Visual Basic — text files and random-access files:

✦ In the context of these applications, a *text file* consists of characters that you can view and read in a text editor. For the purposes of data storage, a text file is generally arranged as a *sequential access* structure; a program typically reads a text file's data from beginning to end. But text files can also be formatted as reports designed for people to read.

✦ A *random-access file* contains individual records in a fixed-length format. Individual data items in a random-access file are stored in special formats that give each item a predictable length. Thanks to this structure, a Visual Basic program can go directly to any record in the file without having to read other records first. The random-access file format is often used in database management applications.

Text files and random-access files require different programming techniques for reading and writing data. You'll study these techniques in this chapter, as you examine a sample project called the Phone Directory program.

The Phone Directory Program

A program in charge of a database typically gives you simple ways to perform several important operations on individual records. Two of the most basic operations are saving and retrieving records. You'll want be able to add new records at any point during your work with the database, and you'll want the program to find and display records that you request. You may also need to revise records when information changes over time, and scroll through records one by one as a direct means of searching for particular data.

The database managed by the Phone Directory program is a collection of names, phone numbers, and e-mail addresses. The records in the database have fields for a person's name (first and last), three phone numbers (home, work, and fax), and an e-mail address. Open the project now from the program disk; the project file is named Phone.Vbp. When you press F5 to run the program for the first time, the Phone Directory window appears on the desktop, as shown in Figure 10-1. As you can see, the boxes where you enter the fields of a new record are clearly labeled in the window.

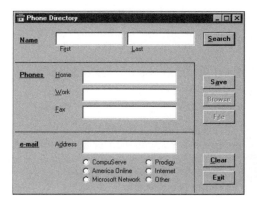

Figure 10-1: The Phone Directory window. You can use this window for entering new phone records and for viewing existing records.

You can use this program on business trips, when your primary tool for communication with the outside world is the telephone, and your laptop computer is never far from reach. The program gives you a quick way to look up people's phone numbers and e-mail addresses whenever you need them. You find a record simply by typing a person's name and clicking the Search button. You can also add phone records to your database at any time, and you can revise any record when necessary. Finally, you may occasionally want to produce a directory of all the telephone numbers in your database. To provide this feature, the program creates a text file containing all the records in the database, alphabetized by last names. You can print this file — or incorporate it into a larger document — by loading it into your word processor, or a text editor such as Notepad.

Simplicity is always the key to an effective database management program. People want fast and easy ways to find information so they can get on with their work. Paradoxically, from your point of view as a programmer, simplicity can be difficult to provide. Although the Phone Directory application is easy to use — allowing the user to add, retrieve, and revise phone records, and to produce a directory — the program has many detailed procedures to perform in the background.

Running the Program

When you run this program, your initial task is data entry. To enter a new record, you begin by typing the first and last name of a person whose phone numbers you want to save. Then you type the other fields of the record. When you arrive at the e-mail address field, you enter the address and then select one of the online services listed below the address.

The phone number fields are long enough to accommodate area codes, extensions, and international telephone numbers. If you have no number to enter for a particular field, leave the text box blank. (You can fill in a missing number later by revising the record.) When you complete the fields for a given entry, as in Figure 10-2, click the Save button at the right side of the Phone Directory window.

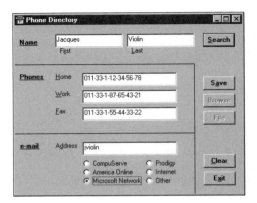

Figure 10-2: Saving a Phone Directory record. You must enter a first and last name to identify the new record, but other text boxes may be left blank and completed at a later time.

Note that the program requires entries for both the first and last name in order to save a new record in the database. If you attempt to enter a record in which one of these fields is missing, the program displays the message box shown in Figure 10-3, reminding you to enter both name fields before trying to save a record. The first and last names are the keys by which the program organizes and retrieves information from the database; for consistency and reliability, the program therefore needs both entries.

Figure 10-3: This message appears if you try to save a phone record without both name entries. The program needs a full name to maintain a reliable index for the database.

To begin another new entry, click the Clear button to remove the previous record from the window, and then begin typing the fields of the next record.

Once your database contains a collection of records, you can begin using the program to look up phone numbers. To do so, enter the first and last names of the person you want to look up, and click the Search button, as in Figure 10-4. (Alternatively, you can simply press the Enter key after you type the person's name. Because Search is designated as the default command button, its Click procedure is performed automatically in response to the Enter key.) The program immediately searches for the name in the database, and assuming the name is found, displays the complete record in the Phone Directory window. Like other database management programs you've seen in this book, the main dialog box serves both as a location for entering new records and as a window for retrieving and viewing existing records.

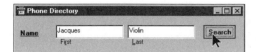

Figure 10-4: Searching for a record. Again, you need to enter both a first and a last name for a successful search.

If you misspell a name — or otherwise enter a name that's not in the database — the program displays a "Can't find" message, as in Figure 10-5.

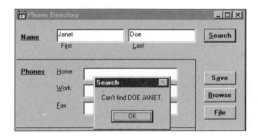

Figure 10-5: Searching for a name that's not in the database. If you misspell a name or enter a name that isn't in the database, the program displays this message.

When you need to revise a phone number or e-mail address, begin by retrieving the target record, following the steps you've just seen: Enter the person's name and click the Search button. The program retrieves the target record and displays its fields in the Phone Directory window. You can then revise the information in any of the phone, fax, or e-mail boxes, and in the list of network services if necessary.

When you've completed the revisions, click the Save button. The program recognizes that the current name already exists in the database and displays the message box shown in Figure 10-6. If you're sure you want to revise the current record, click the Yes button in response to the prompt. The next time you retrieve this record, you'll see that the revision has been saved. (If you change your mind about making a revision, click No in the Revise a Record box.)

Figure 10-6: Revising a Phone Directory record. The program displays this message to confirm that you want to revise an existing record.

Sometimes you may prefer to select a record by browsing through all the names currently stored in your database. In this case, you can click the Browse button to open a new dialog box entitled Browse through Phone Directory, as shown in Figure 10-7. (By the way, the Browse and File buttons are both disabled until you've entered at least one record in your database.) In the Browse dialog box you can click the Previous and Next buttons (or press PgUp and PgDn at the keyboard) to move alphabetically through the names in your database. When you find the name you want to retrieve, click the View button. In response, the program closes the Browse window and displays the record you've requested in the main Phone Directory window (Figure 10-8).

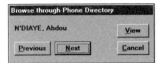

Figure 10-7: Using the Browse window to search for a record. Click Previous or Next — or press PgUp or PgDn on the keyboard — to scroll alphabetically through all the names in your phone database.

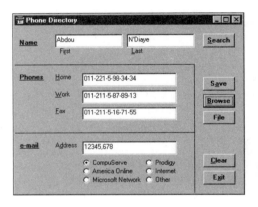

Figure 10-8: After you click the View button in the Browse window, the program switches to the main Phone Directory window and displays the phone record you've requested.

Finally, you can create a text listing of all the phone records in your database by clicking the File button (Figure 10-9). In response, the program produces a file named Phones.Txt in the root directory of your hard disk; the message box shown in Figure 10-10 appears on the desktop to confirm that the file has been created. Open this file into any text editor, as shown in Figure 10-11. You can reformat the information it contains, incorporate the list into another document, or simply print the file directory from the text editor.

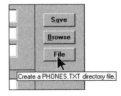

Figure 10-9: The File button is for creating a phone directory file. A ToolTip appears when you poise the mouse pointer over the button.

Figure 10-10: Creating the Phones.Txt directory file. The program notifies you when the file has been created.

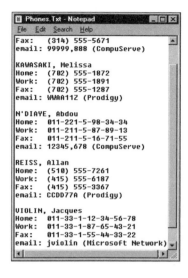

```
Phones.Txt - Notepad                    _ □ ×
File  Edit  Search  Help
Fax:    (314) 555-5671                        ▲
email: 99999,888 (CompuServe)

KAWASAKI, Melissa
Home:   (702) 555-1872
Work:   (702) 555-1891
Fax:    (702) 555-1287
email: WWAA11Z (Prodigy)

N'DIAYE, Abdou
Home:   011-221-5-98-34-34
Work:   011-211-5-87-89-13
Fax:    011-211-5-16-71-55
email: 12345,678 (CompuServe)

REISS, Allan
Home:   (510) 555-7261
Work:   (415) 555-6187
Fax:    (415) 555-3367
email: CCDD77A (Prodigy)

VIOLIN, Jacques
Home:   011-33-1-12-34-56-78
Work:   011-33-1-87-65-43-21
Fax:    011-33-1-55-44-33-22
email: jviolin (Microsoft Network) ▼
◄                                 ► │
```

Figure 10-11: Loading the Phones.Txt file into a text editor. You can also open this file in your word processing program, and print the phone records onto gummed labels. Notice that each record takes up five lines of text, followed by a blank line.

You'll find that the Phone Directory program continues to work effectively and efficiently as your phone database increases in size. Whether you have a few dozen or a few hundred records in the database, the database operations work the same.

The phone database is stored on disk as a random-access file named PhoneVB.DB. (The name identifies this as a database file that's created by a Visual Basic application.) As you've just seen, the program also creates a text file named Phones.Txt. In the upcoming sections of this chapter, you'll examine the Visual Basic tools for creating and working with both kinds of files, starting with random-access. As shown in Figure 10-12, the program includes two forms and one code module; these three files contain the program's code:

✦ The modPhone module (Phone.Bas) contains the program's central data type definitions and public declarations for key variables and arrays.

✦ The code from the frmPhone form (Phone.Frm) includes a variety of event procedures, most notably the Click procedures that respond to command-button clicks. This module also has several important general procedures: *CreateIndex* continually updates and sorts the Index array that the program uses for retrieving records from the database. The *Search* function efficiently searches through the index for a particular name in the database.

✦ Finally, the code from the frmBrowse form (PhonBrow.Frm) controls activities on the program's secondary dialog box, and coordinates the transition back to the main Phone Directory window when the user clicks the View or Cancel button.

You'll examine selections from many of these procedures as you continue through this chapter. You can read through the entire code listing by turning to Appendix A or by scrolling through procedures in the code window on your screen.

Figure 10-12: The Phone Directory application contains two forms and one code module. These three files contain the declarations, event procedures, and general procedures that define the program's behavior at runtime.

Working with Random-Access Files

A random-access file contains individual records of information. Each record is a collection of data items organized in a consistent format. The most important feature of this file type is *access;* after opening a file, a program can go directly to any record and read the information it contains. Data access is efficient and reliable.

To create a random-access file in Visual Basic, you begin by declaring a user-defined record structure. As you learned in Chapter 9, the Type statement defines the name of a structure and provides a list of individual field names and their data types. In a subsequent Dim statement you declare a record variable belonging to the user-defined type. This variable becomes the ideal medium for writing records to — or reading records from — a random-access file. Each write operation stores an entire record, with all its fields of data, in the file; likewise, each read operation retrieves a complete record from the file and gives your program access to the data in the record.

A program refers to records in a random-access file by number, from 1 up to the current number of records. The record number indicates a record's position in the file. Keeping track of the numbers for specific records is one of the challenging problems in a database management program. Programmers devise a variety of ways to solve this problem. In some applications, the record number itself may have special significance to the user — for example, it may be a part number or an invoice number. In this special case, the user's request for a particular record number may correspond precisely to the record's position in the file.

But more typically, the user needs to request records by some item of information other than the record number. For example, in the Phone Directory database, the programming goal is to give the user easy access to any *name* in the file. When the user provides the name of a person to look up in the file, the program retrieves the corresponding record. To achieve this goal, the program has to maintain an index of all the names in the file and their corresponding record numbers. If the user requests the address for Mary Doe, your program looks up "DOE MARY" in the index, finds the record number, and then reads the correct record from the file. You'll see exactly how the indexing system works as you begin exploring the program.

Designing a random-access file

Visual Basic supplies a variety of tools for working with random-access files; three of the most important are

- ✦ Open, to open a file in the Random mode
- ✦ Put #, to write a record to the file
- ✦ Get #, to read a record from the file

In addition, you use Type and Dim to prepare data structures for the file. Here are the typical programming steps you follow to create and work with a random-access file in Visual Basic:

1. Write a Type statement to define the structure of the records you intend to store in the file.

2. Write a Dim statement to declare a record variable for storing information on its way to or from the file.

3. Use the Open statement to open the file in the Random mode. In this mode, a file is available for both writing and reading information.

4. Assign field values to the elements of the record variable. Then use the Put # statement to write individual records to the file.

5. Use the Get # statement to read individual records from the file. Then access the fields of the record from the elements of the record variable.

In the Phone Directory program, the modPhone module (Figure 10-13) defines the record structure for the database:

```
Type PhoneType
    FirstName As String * 20
    LastName As String * 20
    WorkPhone As String * 25
    HomePhone As String * 25
    FaxNumber As String * 25
    EmailAddress As String * 25
    ServiceType As Byte
End Type
```

The structure has seven fields, including six fixed-length strings and a Byte item. The *FirstName* and *LastName* fields store a person's full name; *WorkPhone, HomePhone,* and *FaxNumber* are for the three phone numbers; *EmailAddress* is for the text of an online address; and *ServiceType* is an integer from 0 to 5 representing one of the e-mail types listed in the Phone Directory window.

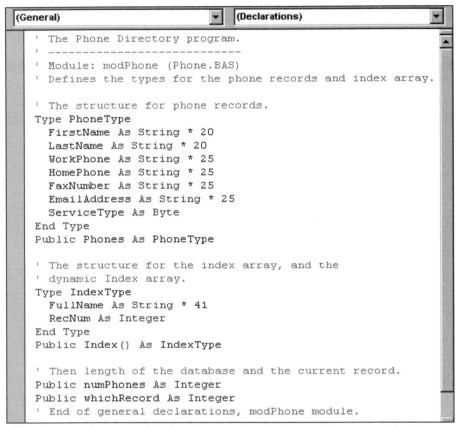

| (General) ▾ | (Declarations) ▾ |

```
' The Phone Directory program.
' --------------------------
' Module: modPhone (Phone.BAS)
' Defines the types for the phone records and index array.

' The structure for phone records.
Type PhoneType
  FirstName As String * 20
  LastName As String * 20
  WorkPhone As String * 25
  HomePhone As String * 25
  FaxNumber As String * 25
  EmailAddress As String * 25
  ServiceType As Byte
End Type
Public Phones As PhoneType

' The structure for the index array, and the
' dynamic Index array.
Type IndexType
  FullName As String * 41
  RecNum As Integer
End Type
Public Index() As IndexType

' Then length of the database and the current record.
Public numPhones As Integer
Public whichRecord As Integer
' End of general declarations, modPhone module.
```

Figure 10-13: The general declarations section of the modPhone module. The declarations include Type statements for the phone fields and the index structure; and Public variable declarations for the phone record (*Phones*) and the dynamic *Index* array.

After defining this structure, the program declares a record variable belonging to the user-defined type:

```
Public Phones As PhoneType
```

When a program reads a record from the database file, or prepares to write a record to the file, the following names represent the seven fields of the record:

```
Phones.FirstName
Phones.LastName
Phones.WorkPhone
Phones.HomePhone
Phones.FaxNumber
Phones.EmailAddress
Phones.ServiceType
```

As you'll recall from Chapter 7, these names can be abbreviated inside a With structure. For example, here is how the *cmdSave_Click* procedure (Figures 10-14 and 10-15) copies the user's field entries to the elements of the *Phones* record:

```
cmdSave                                    Click

Private Sub cmdSave_Click()

  ' The cmdSave_Click procedure stores the current record
  ' entry in the databse and updates the index.
  Dim isFound As Integer, i
  Dim answer As Integer, lf As String
  lf = Chr(13) & Chr(10) ' Represents a linefeed.

  ' Display a reminder message if either name is missing.
  If Not FullNameOK Then
    MsgBox "Enter first and last names.", , "Add a Record"

  ' Otherwise, search for this name in an existing record
  ' and copy the entry to the Phones record variable.
  Else
    isFound = Search(MakeName(txtFirstName.Text, _
                              txtLastName.Text))
    With Phones
      .FirstName = txtFirstName.Text
      .LastName = txtLastName.Text
      .HomePhone = txtHomePhone.Text
      .WorkPhone = txtWorkPhone.Text
      .FaxNumber = txtFaxNumber.Text
      .EmailAddress = txtEMailAddress.Text
      For i = 0 To 5
        If optService(i).Value Then _
          .ServiceType = i
      Next i
    End With
```

Figure 10-14: The first half of the cmdSave_Click procedure from the frmPhone form. When the user clicks the Save button, this event procedure confirms that the name entry is valid, checks for an existing record under this name, and writes the record to the file.

```
With Phones
  .FirstName = txtFirstName.Text
  .LastName = txtLastName.Text
  .HomePhone = txtHomePhone.Text
  .WorkPhone = txtWorkPhone.Text
  .FaxNumber = txtFaxNumber.Text
  .EmailAddress = txtEMailAddress.Text

  For i = 0 To 5
    If optService(i).Value Then _
```

```
        .ServiceType = i
    Next i
End With
```

The program also uses the *Phones* variable in Open, Put #, and Get # statements, as you'll see in upcoming examples.

```
cmdSave                        ▼    Click                           ▼
    ' If the name doesn't already exist, add the record.
    If isFound = 0 Then
      numPhones = numPhones + 1

      ' Enable the Browse and File buttons.
      If numPhones > 0 Then
        cmdBrowse.Enabled = True
        cmdFile.Enabled = True
      End If

      ' Write the record to the file and update the index.
      Put #1, numPhones, Phones
      ReDim Index(numPhones)
      CreateIndex

    ' If the name already exists allow the user to
    ' revise the record (overwriting the previous entry).
    Else
      answer = MsgBox("This name is already on file." _
        & lf & "Do you want to save " & lf & _
        "a revised record?", 4, "Revise a Record")

      ' If the user confirms, store the revised record.
      If answer = 6 Then _
        Put #1, Index(isFound).RecNum, Phones
    End If
  End If

End Sub  ' cmdSave_Click
```

Figure 10-15: The second half of the cmdSave_Click procedure from the frmPhone form. If the name is new to the database, the procedure writes it to the end of the file. If the name already exists — and the user confirms — the program writes the revised record back to its original position.

Opening a file in the Random mode

An open random-access file is available for both reading and writing. The Visual Basic keyword that represents this file mode is *Random*. The Open statement for a random-access file normally contains a Len clause that indicates the total length of each record in the file. Keep in mind that access to information in the file is based on the fact that all records have a consistent structure. Thanks to this structure, Visual Basic can determine where a given record begins and ends. Accordingly, the Len clause tells Visual Basic the length of records in the file:

```
Open fileName For Random As #fileNum Len = recordLength
```

In this statement, *fileName* is the name and path of the file on disk, and *fileNum* is an integer that identifies the file in subsequent input and output statements. In the Len clause, *recordLength* is the length, in bytes, of a record in the file.

To supply a *recordLength* value for the Len clause, you can use Visual Basic's Len function. Given a record variable as its argument, Len returns the total length of all the fields in the record. Consequently, you can write the Len clause as follows:

```
Len = Len(recordVariable)
```

The first Len is a keyword in the Open statement itself; the second Len refers to Visual Basic's built-in function that supplies the length of a variable.

For example, here's how the Form_Load procedure (in the frmPhone form, Figure 10-16) opens the phone database as a random-access file:

```
Open PhoneDB For Random As #1 Len = Len(Phones)
```

In this Open statement the name of the database file is represented by the named constant, *PhoneDB*. The constant is defined in the general declarations section of frmPhone (Figure 10-17):

```
Const PhoneDB = "\PhoneVB.DB"
```

Because the record variable *Phones* has already been declared in a Dim statement, and its structure defined in a Type statement, the expression *Len(Phones)* tells Visual Basic the length of records in the PhoneVB.DB file. Once the file is open, the program is ready to write records to the database or read records from it.

After opening a random-access file, an application typically needs to find out the number of records currently stored in the file. Visual Basic's built-in LOF (length of file) function returns the total length, in bytes, of an open file. LOF takes one argument, the file number assigned to the file in the corresponding Open statement. If you divide the length of the file by the length of a single record in the file, the result is the number of records. For example, here's how the Form_Load procedure (shown in Figure 10-16) calculates the current number of records in the database:

```
numPhones = LOF(1) / Len(Phones)
```

Once again notice the use of the expression *Len(Phones)* to find the length of a single record.

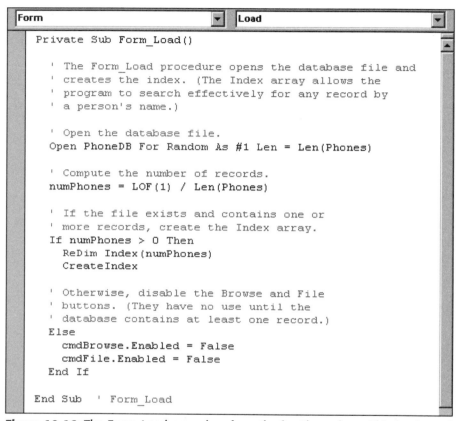

Figure 10-16: The Form_Load procedure from the frmPhone form. This is where the database is originally opened, and the first version of the index is created.

A program uses Put # to write records to an open random-access file and Get # to read records from the file.

Using Put # to write records to a file

The Put # statement sends a complete data record to a particular position in an open random-access file. Here is the usual syntax for this statement:

```
Put #fileNum, recordNum, recordVariable
```

In this format, *fileNum* is the integer that identifies the open file; this is the same number assigned to the file in the corresponding Open statement. The next value, *recordNum,* is an integer specifying the position where the record will be stored in the file. Finally, *recordVariable* is the variable containing the record that Put # writes to the file. Before the Put # statement, your program assigns values to the fields of *recordVariable*.

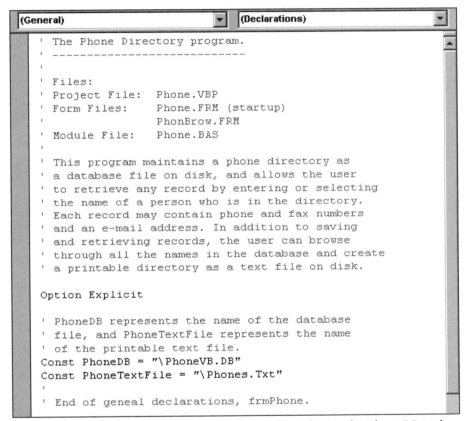

```
(General)                    ▼   (Declarations)                    ▼
' The Phone Directory program.
' ----------------------------
'
' Files:
' Project File:   Phone.VBP
' Form Files:     Phone.FRM (startup)
'                 PhonBrow.FRM
' Module File:    Phone.BAS
'
' This program maintains a phone directory as
' a database file on disk, and allows the user
' to retrieve any record by entering or selecting
' the name of a person who is in the directory.
' Each record may contain phone and fax numbers
' and an e-mail address. In addition to saving
' and retrieving records, the user can browse
' through all the names in the database and create
' a printable directory as a text file on disk.

Option Explicit

' PhoneDB represents the name of the database
' file, and PhoneTextFile represents the name
' of the printable text file.
Const PhoneDB = "\PhoneVB.DB"
Const PhoneTextFile = "\Phones.Txt"
'
' End of geneal declarations, frmPhone.
```

Figure 10-17: The general declarations section of frmPhone. The PhoneDB and PhoneTextFile constants represent the names of the database file and the text directory file. These names are used only in the frmPhone form.

Of the three items you supply in the Put # statement, the second, *recordNum,* is probably the trickiest. Depending on the value of *recordNum,* Put # does one of two things:

✦ If *recordNum* is a value from 1 up to the current number of records in the file, Put # overwrites an existing record in the file. For example, suppose a file contains 10 records, and you supply a value of 5 as the *recordNum.* Your Put # statement stores a new record to position 5 in the file, overwriting the previous data at this position.

✦ If *recordNum* is equal to 1 greater than the current number of records in the file, Put # appends a new record to the file. For example, in the file containing 10 records, you would supply a *recordNum* value of 11 to append a new record. As a result of this Put # statement, the length of your file increases by one record.

The cmdSave_Click procedure (shown in Figures 10-14 and 10-15) allows the user to append new records to the end of the phone database at any time during a run. As you've seen, the variable *numPhones* (Figure 10-13) specifies the number of records currently in the file. Before writing a new record, the program copies the seven fields of information from the Phone Directory window to the elements of the *Phones* record and then increases the value of numPhones by 1:

```
numPhones = numPhones + 1
```

Then the following Put # statement appends the record to the end of the database file:

```
Put #1, numPhones, Phones
```

In other words, the next new record number will be 1 greater than the current number of records in the file. In this way, each Put # statement adds a new record to the file. Careful management of the *numPhones* variable prevents the possibility of inadvertently overwriting any existing records in the database.

Tip

Visual Basic allows you to omit the *recordNum* argument in the Put # statement:

```
Put #fileNum, , recordVariable
```

If you write the statement in this way, each succeeding Put # automatically writes a record to the next position in the file. This can be a convenient way to store an initial set of records in a new file. But if your program opens an existing file that already contains records, Visual Basic initially sets the current record number at 1. If you don't specify a new starting record number, a series of Put # statements can therefore overwrite the existing records. To avoid loss of data, you should always make sure you know where Put # will be writing data in your file.

Using Get # to read records from a file

Get # reads a complete data record from a particular position in an open random-access file. Here is the syntax:

```
Get #fileNum, recordNum, recordVariable
```

Again, *fileNum* is the integer that identifies the open file, and *recordNum* is the position from which the record will be read. In this case, *recordVariable* receives the record from the file. After Get #, your program refers to the individual fields of *recordVariable* to gain access to the information that's been read from the file.

One of the first tasks in the Phone Directory program is to create an index for the phone database. The Form_Load procedure (Figure 10-16) opens the file and calculates the current number of records, *numPhones*. Then, if *numPhones* is greater than 0, the program resizes the Index array appropriately and makes a call to the *CreateIndex* procedure to develop the index for the first time:

```
If numPhones > 0 Then
   ReDim Index(numPhones)
   CreateIndex
```

The *CreateIndex* procedure (Figure 10-18), in turn, uses a For loop to read each record from the beginning to the end of the file:

```
For i = 1 To numPhones
   Get #1, i, Phones
```

During the iterations of this loop, the counter variable *i* represents record numbers from 1 to the last record in the file. The Get # statement therefore reads each record in turn. After each Get #, the fields of the newly accessed record are represented by *Phones.FirstName, Phones.LastName,* and so on.

```
(General)                          ▼     CreateIndex                         ▼

   Sub CreateIndex()

     ' The CreateIndex procedure develops the Index array
     ' when the program begins and after each record is added.
     Dim indexEntry As IndexType, i, j, temp As String

     ' Read each record, from the beginning to the end.
     For i = 1 To numPhones
       Get #1, i, Phones

       ' Standardize the name entry in each record, and store
       ' the full name and record number as the fields.
       temp = MakeName(Phones.FirstName, Phones.LastName)
       Index(i).FullName = temp
       Index(i).RecNum = i
     Next i

     ' Sort the index array by the FullName field.
     For i = 1 To numPhones - 1
       For j = i + 1 To numPhones
         If Index(i).FullName > Index(j).FullName Then
           indexEntry = Index(i)
           Index(i) = Index(j)
           Index(j) = indexEntry
         End If
       Next j
     Next i

   End Sub    ' CreateIndex
```

Figure 10-18: The *CreateIndex* procedure from the frmPhone form. This procedure reads the records from the beginning to the end of the file and copies the names to the *Index* array. Then the procedure sorts the index by the *FullName* field.

Tip

Just as in Put #, the *recordNum* is optional in the Get # statement:

```
Get #fileNum, , recordVariable
```

If you write the statement this way, each succeeding Get # reads the *next* record in the file. In a program that doesn't otherwise need to know the number of records in the file, you can use a Do loop to read the records from beginning to end:

```
Do While Not EOF(1)
  Get #1, , Phones
  ' ...
Loop
```

In this loop, Visual Basic automatically increments the record number after each Get #. When the loop reaches the end of the file, the built-in EOF function returns a value of True, and the program stops reading records.

Using Seek # to select the current record number

In some applications you may want to begin by specifying a particular starting point in your database for subsequent Put # or Get # operations. Visual Basic's Seek # statement allows you to do this. Seek # sets the position for a particular open file:

```
Seek #fileNum, recordNum
```

After Seek #, you can use the Put # statement to write a record to the *recordNum* position in the database:

```
Put #fileNum, , recordVariable
```

Alternatively, use a Get # statement to read a record from the Seek # position:

```
Get #fileNum, , recordVariable
```

Designing an index for a random-access file

The order in which records are entered into a database is often random. For example, as you develop your phone database you're unlikely to enter all the records in alphabetical order by people's names. Instead, you'll probably enter a particular record into the database when the information becomes available.

There's nothing unusual about randomly ordered entries in a database. But when you get ready to use the information, you want it to be presented systematically in a planned order. For example, you'll want to print your phone directory in alphabetical order by people's names.

As you know, the task of rearranging records in a particular order is called *sorting*. A practical way to present database records in a sorted order is to create an index for the database and then to sort the index rather than the database itself. This technique enables you to leave a potentially large database file in its original order, and focus on sorting the smaller data set represented by the index.

The Phone Directory program creates an index consisting of all the names in the database and their corresponding record numbers. The program sorts the index in alphabetical order by names, and produces a sorted list of records by retrieving each record from the database in the order presented by the index. The index is stored in memory as an array of records — a smaller array than the one that would have been needed to store the entire database in memory. Here are the steps the program follows to create and manage this index:

1. A Type statement in the modPhone module (shown in Figure 10-13) declares a special structure for the elements of the index array. The structure contains two fields: *FullName* to represent the name in each phone record, and *RecNum* to represent the corresponding record number:

```
Type IndexType
  FullName As String * 41
  RecNum As Integer
End Type
```

2. After defining the record structure, the program declares a dynamic array of *IndexType* records to represent the index:

```
Public Index() As IndexType
```

Before creating or updating the index, the program always resizes this array, as shown in the cmdSave_Click procedure (Figure 10-15) and the Form_Load procedure (Figure 10-16):

```
ReDim Index(numPhones)
CreateIndex
```

The index thus contains one element for each record in the array.

3. The *CreateIndex* procedure (Figure 10-18) then builds the index by storing the name and record number of each phone record in the database:

```
For i = 1 to numPhones
  Get #1, i, Phones
  temp = MakeName(Phones.FirstName, Phones.LastName)
  Index(i).FullName = temp
  Index(i).RecNum = i
Next i
```

The *MakeName* function (Figure 10-19) simply creates a standard format for all the names in the index: last name first, all capital letters, and no extraneous spaces.

4. The CreateIndex procedure then sorts the index by the *FullName* field:

```
For i = 1 to numPhones - 1
```

```
      For j = i + 1 to numPhones
        If Index(i).FullName > Index(j).FullName Then
          indexEntry = Index(i)
          Index(i) = Index(j)
          Index(j) = indexEntry
        End if
      Next j
    Next i
```

5. When the user enters a name and clicks the Search button to find a record in the phone directory, the cmdSearch_Click procedure (Figure 10-20) standardizes the name and then calls the *Search* procedure (Figure 10-21) to look for the name in the index:

```
searchName = MakeName(txtFirstName.Text, _
                      txtLastName.Text)

rec = Search(searchName)
```

The variable *rec* represents the element in the index array where the name is located. The corresponding record number is provided by the expression *Index(rec).RecNum*. In other words, the *RecNum* field in the index array represents the database position from which the program reads the record. Once this record number is known, the cmdSearch_Click procedure calls the *ShowRecord* procedure (Figure 10-22) to display the phone record on the screen:

```
inFileRec = Index(rec).RecNum
ShowRecord inFileRec
```

In this way the program allows the user to view any record in the database.

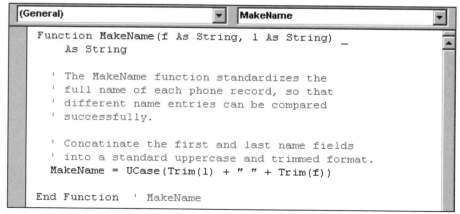

Figure 10-19: The *MakeName* function from the frmPhone form. The program uses this short function to standardize each name into the LASTNAME FIRSTNAME format.

```
cmdSearch                    ▼   Click                        ▼
  Private Sub cmdSearch_Click()

    ' The cmdSearch_Click procedure searches for a name in
    ' the phone directory, and retrieves the record.

    Dim searchName As String
    Dim rec As Integer, inFileRec As Integer

    If Not FullNameOK Then
      MsgBox "Enter the first and last names.", , "Search"
    Else

      ' Standardize the format and search for the name.
      searchName = MakeName(txtFirstName.Text, _
                            txtLastName.Text)
      rec = Search(searchName)

      ' If the name is found, display the record.
      If rec > 0 Then
        inFileRec = Index(rec).RecNum
        ShowRecord inFileRec

      ' Otherwise, tell the user that the search failed.
      Else
        MsgBox "Can't find " & searchName & ".", , "Search"

      End If
    End If
End Sub  ' cmdSearch_Click
```

Figure 10-20: The cmdSearch_Click procedure from the frmPhone form. When the user enters a name and clicks the Search button, this procedure searches for the name in the index. If the name is found, a call to *ShowRecord* displays the complete record in the Phone Directory window.

Using the Index for other database operations

The Phone Directory program also uses the *Index* array in several other important contexts. When the user clicks the Save button to add a record to the database, the cmdSave_Click procedure (Figures 10-14 and 10-15) calls the *Search* function to look for the name in the index:

```
isFound = Search(MakeName(txtFirstName.Text, _
                          txtLastName.Text))
```

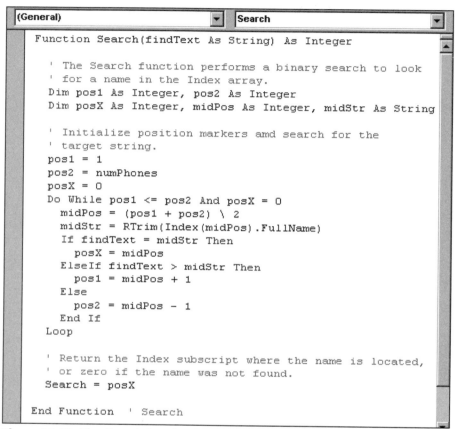

```
(General)                          ▼   Search                        ▼

  Function Search(findText As String) As Integer

     ' The Search function performs a binary search to look
     ' for a name in the Index array.
     Dim pos1 As Integer, pos2 As Integer
     Dim posX As Integer, midPos As Integer, midStr As String

     ' Initialize position markers amd search for the
     ' target string.
     pos1 = 1
     pos2 = numPhones
     posX = 0
     Do While pos1 <= pos2 And posX = 0
       midPos = (pos1 + pos2) \ 2
       midStr = RTrim(Index(midPos).FullName)
       If findText = midStr Then
         posX = midPos
       ElseIf findText > midStr Then
         pos1 = midPos + 1
       Else
         pos2 = midPos - 1
       End If
     Loop

     ' Return the Index subscript where the name is located,
     ' or zero if the name was not found.
     Search = posX

  End Function   ' Search
```

Figure 10-21: The *Search* function from the frmPhone form. This function performs a binary search through the *Index* array to locate the target name. If the name is found, the function returns its position in the index; if not, a return value of zero indicates a failed search.

If the *Search* function (Figure 10-21) returns a value of 0, the current name does not already exist in the *Index* array. Accordingly, the program can safely add the record to the end of the database:

```
If isFound = 0 Then
  numPhones = numPhones + 1

  ' ...

  Put #1, numPhones, Phones
```

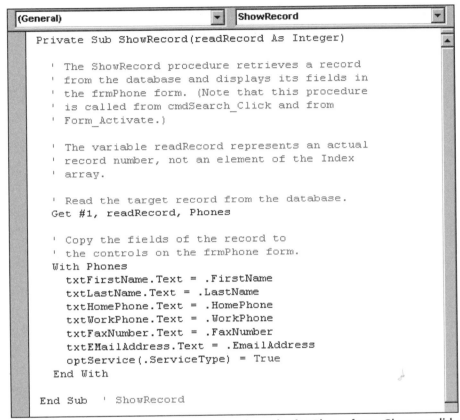

```
(General)                          ▼   ShowRecord                        ▼

    Private Sub ShowRecord(readRecord As Integer)

      ' The ShowRecord procedure retrieves a record
      ' from the database and displays its fields in
      ' the frmPhone form. (Note that this procedure
      ' is called from cmdSearch_Click and from
      ' Form_Activate.)

      ' The variable readRecord represents an actual
      ' record number, not an element of the Index
      ' array.

      ' Read the target record from the database.
      Get #1, readRecord, Phones

      ' Copy the fields of the record to
      ' the controls on the frmPhone form.
      With Phones
        txtFirstName.Text = .FirstName
        txtLastName.Text = .LastName
        txtHomePhone.Text = .HomePhone
        txtWorkPhone.Text = .WorkPhone
        txtFaxNumber.Text = .FaxNumber
        txtEMailAddress.Text = .EmailAddress
        optService(.ServiceType) = True
      End With

    End Sub   ' ShowRecord
```

Figure 10-22: The *ShowRecord* procedure from the frmPhone form. Given a valid record number, this procedure reads the record from the database and copies its fields to the appropriate text boxes in the Phone Directory window.

But if *isFound* receives a value other than 0, the *Search* function has located the current name in the *Index* array. In this case, *isFound* represents the position in *Index* where the name was found. The cmdSave_Click procedure's first step is to ask the user whether this Save operation is intended as a revision of the record:

```
Else

  answer = MsgBox("This name is already on file." _
    & lf & "Do you want to save " & lf & _
    "a revised record?", 4, "Revise a Record")
```

If the user confirms (as indicated by a return value of 6 from the MsgBox function), the program writes the record back to its original position, represented by *Index(isFound).RecNum*:

```
If answer = 6 Then
```

```
Put #1, Index(isFound).RecNum, Phones
```

The procedures in the frmBrowse form illustrate another use of the *Index* array, allowing the user to scroll alphabetically through the database records. Throughout this form's code, the variable *whichRecord* represents the Index number of the name currently displayed in the dialog box. If the user clicks the Next button, the cmdNext_Click procedure increases the value of *whichRecord* by 1 (Figure 10-23):

```
whichRecord = whichRecord + 1
```

Conversely, if the user clicks Previous, the cmdPrevious_Click procedure decreases the value of *whichRecord* by 1 (also in Figure 10-23):

```
whichRecord = whichRecord - 1
```

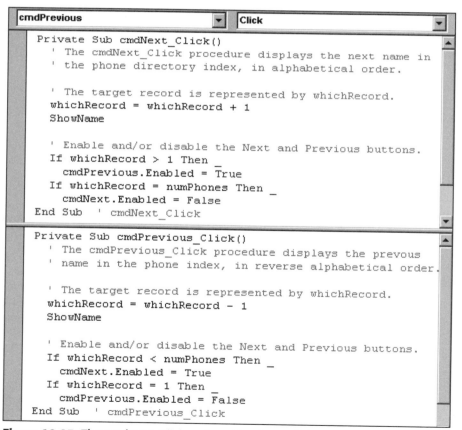

```
cmdPrevious                      ▼  |  Click                        ▼

   Private Sub cmdNext_Click()                                    ▲
     ' The cmdNext_Click procedure displays the next name in
     ' the phone directory index, in alphabetical order.

     ' The target record is represented by whichRecord.
     whichRecord = whichRecord + 1
     ShowName

     ' Enable and/or disable the Next and Previous buttons.
     If whichRecord > 1 Then _
       cmdPrevious.Enabled = True
     If whichRecord = numPhones Then _
       cmdNext.Enabled = False
   End Sub  ' cmdNext_Click                                       ▼

   Private Sub cmdPrevious_Click()                                ▲
     ' The cmdPrevious_Click procedure displays the prevous
     ' name in the phone index, in reverse alphabetical order.

     ' The target record is represented by whichRecord.
     whichRecord = whichRecord - 1
     ShowName

     ' Enable and/or disable the Next and Previous buttons.
     If whichRecord < numPhones Then _
       cmdNext.Enabled = True
     If whichRecord = 1 Then _
       cmdPrevious.Enabled = False
   End Sub  ' cmdPrevious_Click
```

Figure 10-23: The cmdNext_Click and cmdPrevious_Click procedures from the frmBrowse form. These procedures increase or decrease the value of *whichRecord* by 1, and then display the name from the corresponding record. (The variable *whichRecord* represents a position in the index, not a record number.)

Whenever the value of *whichRecord* is changed, a call to the *ShowName* procedure (Figure 10-24) displays the new name. This procedure reads the target record from the database file and displays the name from the record as the Caption property of a label named lblFullName:

```
Get #1, Index(whichRecord).RecNum, Phones
With Phones
   lblFullName.Caption = Trim(UCase(.LastName)) _
                         & ", " & _
                         Trim(.FirstName)
End With
```

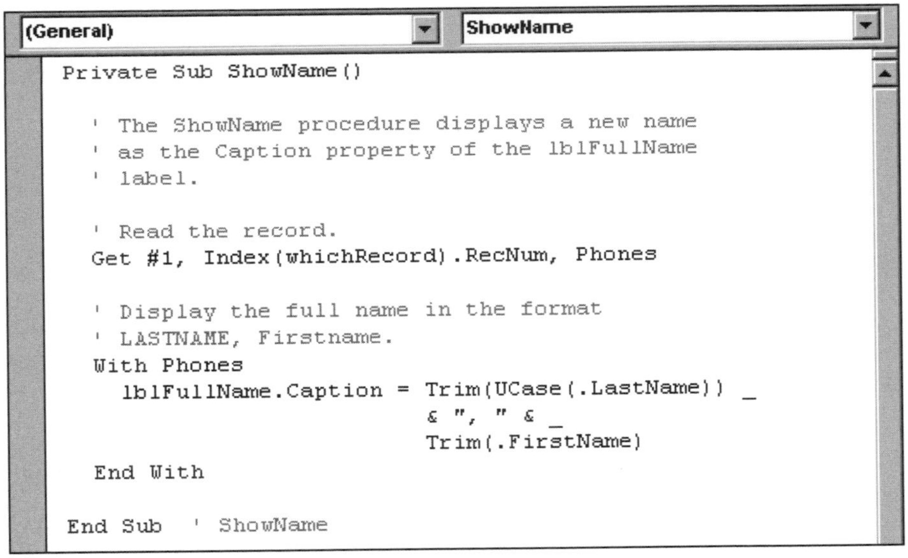

```
(General)                             ▼   ShowName                          ▼

   Private Sub ShowName()

     ' The ShowName procedure displays a new name
     ' as the Caption property of the lblFullName
     ' label.

     ' Read the record.
     Get #1, Index(whichRecord).RecNum, Phones

     ' Display the full name in the format
     ' LASTNAME, Firstname.
     With Phones
        lblFullName.Caption = Trim(UCase(.LastName)) _
                              & ", " & _
                              Trim(.FirstName)
     End With

   End Sub  ' ShowName
```

Figure 10-24: The *ShowName* procedure from the frmBrowse form. Given a new value for *whichRecord* (a position in the index), this procedure reads a record and displays the full name in the Browse window.

In yet another use of the *Index* array, the cmdFile_Click procedure (from the frmPhone form) creates a text file containing an alphabetical listing of the entire phone directory. You'll examine this procedure in upcoming sections of this chapter, as you now turn to the subject of text files.

Working with Text Files

You can use a text file to store individual data items in an order and structure that a Visual Basic program can read conveniently. Alternatively, a text file might contain a table of text and numbers, ready to be printed or incorporated into a larger document for people to read. As you'll see, Visual Basic provides two sets of input and output commands for use with a text file, depending on the purpose of the file.

Opening a text file for writing

You use Visual Basic's Open statement to open a text file for any of three purposes:

✦ To create a new file

✦ To append information to an existing file

✦ To read data from a file

For text files, the Open statement typically appears in the following format:

```
Open fileName For mode As #fileNum
```

This statement supplies three essential items of information. The name of the file on disk is *fileName*. The name is always expressed as a string value in the Open statement — a literal string enclosed in quotation marks, a string variable, or a string expression. The string may include the file's directory path. The file *mode* identifies the kind of operation you intend to perform on the file. For text files, the most common modes are identified by the Visual Basic keywords Output, Append, and Input. The file number, *fileNum,* is an integer that identifies the open file in subsequent input or output statements.

For output to a text file, the Open command can create a new file or open an existing file. This important distinction is represented by the keywords *Output* and *Append:*

✦ The Output mode creates a new file and prepares to write data to the file. If a file by the same name already exists on disk, the Open statement overwrites that file in the Output mode. In other words, the previous file will be deleted and its data lost.

✦ The Append mode opens an existing file and prepares to add new data to the end of the file. Any data already in the file is safely retained. If the named file does not exist yet, the Append mode is the same as the Output mode; Open creates the file and prepares to write the first data to the file.

Your choice between these operations depends on the design of the program you're creating. For example, the Phone Directory program opens the Phones.Txt file — represented by the named constant *PhoneTextFile* — in the Output mode, as you can see in the cmdFile_Click procedure (Figure 10-25):

```
Open PhoneTextFile For Output As #2
```

This means that the program creates a new alphabetized phone directory in text format each time the user clicks the File button. Any previous version of the Phones.Txt file is overwritten. The new file is based on the entire data set currently stored in the phone database.

```
cmdFile                    ▼    Click                        ▼

  Private Sub cmdFile_Click()

    ' The cmdFile_Click procedure creates a phone directory.
    Dim i

    ' If the file already exists, overwrite it. Using
    ' the index, read records in alphabetical order.
    ' Then write the fields to the text file.
    Open PhoneTextFile For Output As #2
    For i = 1 To numPhones
      Get #1, Index(i).RecNum, Phones
      With Phones
        Print #2, UCase(Trim(.LastName)); ", ";
        Print #2, .FirstName
        Print #2, "Home:   "; .HomePhone
        Print #2, "Work:   "; .WorkPhone
        Print #2, "Fax:    "; .FaxNumber
        Print #2, "email: "; Trim(.EmailAddress);
        Print #2, " (";
        Print #2, optService(.ServiceType).Caption;
        Print #2, ")"
        Print #2,
      End With
    Next i
    Close #2

    MsgBox UCase(PhoneTextFile) & " has been created.", , _
      "Save a Text File"
  End Sub  ' cmdFile_Click
```

Figure 10-25: The cmdFile_Click procedure from the frmPhone form. Each time it's called, the procedure creates a new version of the phone directory under the file name Phones.Txt. It uses the index to read records from the database in alphabetical order. A sequence of Print # statements write the data to the text file.

By contrast, the Travel Expense Log program presented in Chapter 7 creates a different kind of text file for saving the chronological expense records that the user enters into the program's dialog box. To ensure that each new record is added to the end of the file, without destroying any existing records, the program opens the file in the Append mode, as shown in Figure 10-26:

```
Open logFileName For Append As #1
```

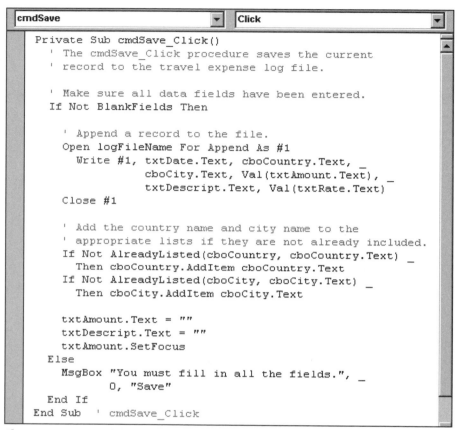

Figure 10-26: A review of the cmdSave_Click from the Travel Expense Log program. This procedure illustrates the effect of the Append keyword in the Open statement, and the use of the Write # statement to store data in an open text file.

Once a file is open in the Output or the Append mode, your program can use either the Write # statement or the Print # statement to begin sending data to the open file. Write # is ideal for storing raw data in a format that a Visual Basic program can easily read back. By contrast, the Print # statement gives you the ability to save data in formats that people can read easily. As you'll see in the upcoming sections of this chapter, these commands use the # notation to identify by number the file to which they are sending data.

Using the Write # statement

Write # sends a line of data items to an open file. This statement automatically supplies important punctuation to separate data items inside the file:

   ✦ A string is enclosed in double quotation marks in the file.

✦ Data items in a given line are separated by commas.

✦ Each line of data ends with a carriage-return/line-feed sequence (ASCII characters 13 and 10, respectively).

As you'll learn shortly, Visual Basic's Input # statement uses this punctuation to distinguish between one data item and the next as it reads information from a text file.

In the Travel Expense Log program, the cmdSave_Click procedure contains a good example of the Write # statement. After opening the expense log file, the program uses the following statement to write the user's current input to the file:

```
Write #1, txtDate.Text, cboCountry.Text, _
        cboCity.Text, Val(txtAmount.Text), _
        txtDescript.Text, Val(txtRate.Text)
```

The output file is identified in the Write # statement by the notation #1. This is the file number assigned to the open file in the previous Open statement. Each successive Write # statement sends a new line of comma-delimited data to the file. For example, Figure 10-27 shows how a sequence of records might appear in the file. Each line consists of four string items and two numeric items.

```
ExpnsLog.txt - Notepad
File   Edit   Search   Help
"11/27/96","France","Strasbourg",665,"Miscellaneous supplies",5.22
"11/27/96","Switzerland","Basel",485,"Dinner with buyers",1.29
"11/28/96","Switzerland","Geneva",185,"l'Hotel du lac, one night",1.29
"11/28/96","Switzerland","Geneva",295,"Lunch with agents",1.29
"11/29/96","Italy","Florence",240000,"English Hotel, one night",1510
"11/30/96","Italy","Florence",210000,"Dinner with buyers",1510
"12/01/96","France","Paris",1850,"Car rental",5.28
"12/02/96","France","Caen",1750,"Conference room, l'Hotel du Chateau",5.25
"12/03/96","France","Caen",850,"l'Hotel du Chateau, one night",5.25
```

Figure 10-27: An example of the output from the Write# statement. Text items are enclosed in quotes, and the data items on a given line are separated by commas.

Using the Print # statement

Print # sends output to an open text file, identified by the # notation. This statement gives you greater control over the format and appearance of the output. Normally you'll use Print # when you're writing a procedure that creates a report.

Each Print # statement sends one or more undelimited text items to the designated file. In the Phone Directory program, the cmdFile_Click procedure (shown in Figure 10-25) contains a sequence of examples:

```
For i = 1 To numPhones
   Get #1, Index(i).RecNum, Phones
   With Phones
```

```
            Print #2, UCase(Trim(.LastName)); ", ";
            Print #2, .FirstName
            Print #2, "Home:   "; .HomePhone
            Print #2, "Work:   "; .WorkPhone
            Print #2, "Fax:    "; .FaxNumber
            Print #2, "email: "; Trim(.EmailAddress);
            Print #2, " (";
            Print #2, optService(.ServiceType).Caption;
            Print #2, ")"
            Print #2,
        End With
    Next i
```

As this passage illustrates, Visual Basic allows a program to open multiple files at the same time, each identified with a different *fileNum* value. In this case, the phone database is already open as file #1; the procedure reads records from the file one by one from beginning to end. The Phones.Txt file is open as file #2. The sequence of Print #2 statements writes phone directory records to the text file, in the following format:

```
KAWASAKI, Melissa
Home:   (702) 555-1872
Work:   (702) 555-1891
Fax:    (702) 555-1287
email: WWAA11Z (Prodigy)
```

Notice some of the syntactical elements of the Print # statement. Multiple data items are separated by semicolons (;) in the statement. Normally each Print # statement results in a new line of text in the file, but a semicolon at the end of the statement suppresses the usual carriage-return/line-feed sequence so that additional output can be sent to the same line. For additional examples of the Print # statement, examine the cmdExpReport_Click procedure from the Expense Log program (Figures 10-28 and 10-29).

Opening a text file for reading

To read a text file, you open it in the Input mode:

```
Open fileName For Input As #fileNum
```

For example, in the Travel Expense Log program, the cmdExpReport_Click procedure opens the expense file for input in order to read its records one by one:

```
Open logFileName For Input As #1
```

Using the Input mode presupposes that the file exists on disk. If the file is missing, the Open statement causes a runtime error known as the "File not found" error. In the next section you'll learn how to avoid an interruption in your program when a text file doesn't exist.

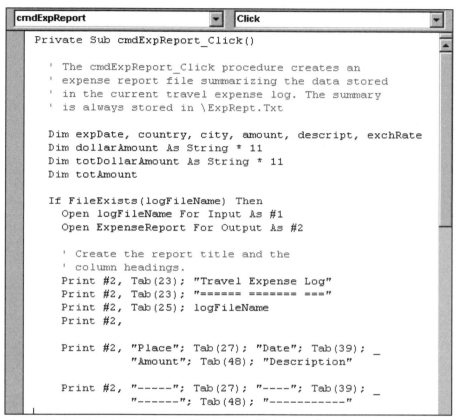

Figure 10-28: A review of the cmdExpReport_Click procedure from the Travel Expense Log program. In this first half of the procedure the program opens the data file for reading (Input) and creates the expense report file for writing (Ouput).

Trapping the "File not found" runtime error

If Visual Basic cannot find the disk file named in an Open *fileName* For Input statement, the program run is interrupted by default, and the "File not found" error message appears in a message box on the screen, as shown in Figure 10-30. This error may occur when a program asks the user to supply a file name interactively from the keyboard. If the user misspells the file name, or otherwise supplies a name that doesn't exist on disk, the "File not found" error takes place and the program run is interrupted.

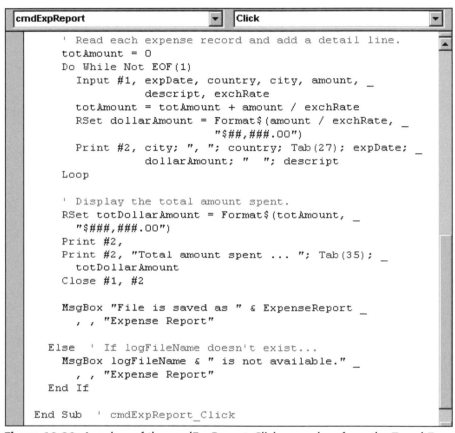

```
cmdExpReport ▼          Click ▼

     ' Read each expense record and add a detail line.
     totAmount = 0
     Do While Not EOF(1)
       Input #1, expDate, country, city, amount, _
               descript, exchRate
       totAmount = totAmount + amount / exchRate
       RSet dollarAmount = Format$(amount / exchRate, _
                        "$##,###.00")
       Print #2, city; ", "; country; Tab(27); expDate; _
               dollarAmount; "  "; descript
     Loop

     ' Display the total amount spent.
     RSet totDollarAmount = Format$(totAmount, _
       "$###,###.00")
     Print #2,
     Print #2, "Total amount spent ... "; Tab(35); _
       totDollarAmount
     Close #1, #2

     MsgBox "File is saved as " & ExpenseReport _
       , , "Expense Report"

   Else  ' If logFileName doesn't exist...
     MsgBox logFileName & " is not available." _
       , , "Expense Report"
   End If

 End Sub  ' cmdExpReport_Click
```

Figure 10-29: A review of the cmdExpReport_Click procedure from the Travel Expense Log program. In the second half of the procedure you can see the use of the Input # statement for reading data items from a text file. You can also see many examples of the Print # statement for creating the text of the expense report.

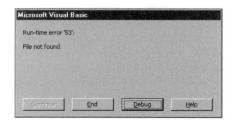

Figure 10-30: When a program attempts to open a text file for reading, the "File not found" error can occur if the file does not exist on disk. By creating an error trap in your code, you can avoid the interruption that this error creates.

You can prevent the interruption by creating a special control structure known as an *error trap*. An error trap puts Visual Basic on alert for a potential runtime error. If an error occurs that would normally interrupt the program, the error trap instead directs control of the program to a special block of code — an *error routine* — designed to handle the error more gracefully.

You create an error trap by placing an On Error Goto statement above the code where you're anticipating a possible runtime error. On Error Goto refers by name to an error routine located in the same procedure. The routine is identified by a *label*, a name that marks a particular location in the listing. A label ends in a colon, which distinguishes it from other kinds of names that you write in a Visual Basic program.

A good example of the On Error Goto statement — and a corresponding error routine — appears in the Travel Expense Log program in a function named *FileExists* (Figure 10-31). This function is designed specifically to find out whether a given expense file can be found on disk — before the program attempts to read data from the designated file. The function receives a string argument that identifies the target file by name, and returns a Boolean value — True if the file exists or False if it does not.

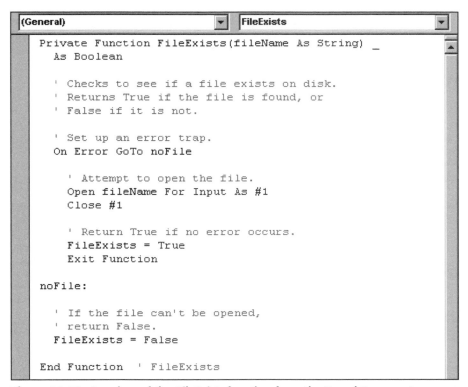

```
(General)                          ▼   FileExists                          ▼

  Private Function FileExists(fileName As String) _
    As Boolean

    ' Checks to see if a file exists on disk.
    ' Returns True if the file is found, or
    ' False if it is not.

    ' Set up an error trap.
    On Error GoTo noFile

      ' Attempt to open the file.
      Open fileName For Input As #1
      Close #1

      ' Return True if no error occurs.
      FileExists = True
      Exit Function

  noFile:

    ' If the file can't be opened,
    ' return False.
    FileExists = False

  End Function   ' FileExists
```

Figure 10-31: A review of the *FileExists* function from the Travel Expense Log program. The function sets up an error trap and then attempts to open a text file for reading. If the file opens successfully, the function returns a value of True; if not, False.

An Open statement at the top of the function tries to open the file for reading. If the operation is not successful — that is, if Visual Basic can't find the designated file — the On Error Goto statement redirects control of the program to the routine labeled *noFile*, and the function returns a value of False. On the other hand, if the program finds the file, the error trap is not triggered, and the function returns a value of True. Elsewhere in the program, you'll find several procedures that make calls to the *FileExists* function before attempting to open the expense log file:

```
If FileExists(logFileName) Then
```

Once a program has successfully opened a file for Input, the Input # statement can be used to read individual data items from the file. You'll learn about this statement next.

Using the Input # statement

Input # identifies the number of the open file from which this statement will read data, and provides a list of variables that will receive the input data:

```
Input #fileNum, varName1, varName2, varName3, ...
```

For example, here is an Input # statement from the cmdExpReport_Click procedure in the Travel Expense Log program (Figure 10-29) that reads a line of data from the open expense log file:

```
Input #1, expDate, country, city, amount, _
              descript, exchRate
```

As you can see, the statement reads six data items from the file — the date, country, city, amount of the expense, description, and exchange rate. The program can then use these variables to work with this data in any appropriate way.

When the Input # statement reads data from a text file, it recognizes a comma as a delimiter between one data item and the next. In addition, it reads a value enclosed in quotation marks as a string — even if the string contains commas or other punctuation characters that would normally serve as delimiters between data items. The Write # statement is therefore the perfect counterpart to Input #. Write # organizes data in a file in just the way that Input # expects to find it.

Using the Line Input # statement

Another way to get information from a text file is to read entire lines at a time, with the Line Input # statement. Line Input # recognizes only the end-of-line markers (ASCII characters 13 and 10) as delimiters in the text. The statement therefore reads a line of text and stores it in a string variable:

```
Line Input #fileNum, stringVarName
```

Line Input # is perfect for reading text files that contain unpredictable combinations of text and numbers, in tables or in other formats. In this sense, Line Input # is often a good way to read a file that has been created with the Print # statement. You'll find an example in the International Sales program, presented in Chapter 11.

Closing a file

When your program is finished with a file, you can use the Close statement to close the file:

```
Close #fileNum
```

For example, here is how the Phone Directory program closes the two files that it works with:

```
Close #1
```

and

```
Close #2
```

These statements also release the file numbers so they can be used for opening a different file.

Alternatively, you can use the Close statement without a file number:

```
Close
```

This statement closes all open files. Likewise, the End statement that terminates a program performance closes any files that remain open.

You'll find more examples of database management applications and data file programming techniques as you continue through this book. Note that Visual Basic also contains important data access features for connecting a project to a database created by an external application such as Microsoft Access or dBASE. You can read about this topic in Chapter 16.

Effective Input and Output Techniques

Input and output are the defining activities of almost any Visual Basic application. In a well-designed program, input techniques are simple, convenient, reliable, and even self-correcting; and the resulting output is clear, intuitive, useful, and immediate. To achieve these programming goals, you may spend more time on input and output procedures than on any other part of your code.

Input is information that a program receives from an outside source. For example, input operations take place when the user enters values from the keyboard or selects options with the mouse. As a programmer, you always need to think carefully about the problems of getting input from the user:

+ What types of information should the user supply, and how will your program prompt the user to enter the data?

+ What are the easiest and most reliable ways to accept information and instructions from the keyboard and the mouse?

+ How will the program react when the user makes a mistake during data entry? What techniques will your program provide for correcting mistakes?

+ Once the user has entered a particular input item, will your program reformat the data in convenient ways so that the user can verify the input?

+ How will the user select among the options available in a given application?

These design issues take time to resolve. You may find yourself spending many hours with your code — writing, revising, and fine-tuning — before you're happy with the details of the data-entry process.

Output is the information a program provides for the user. It can be sent to devices such as the display screen, the printer, a disk, or a modem. A program can supply information in various forms, including text, tables of numbers, charts, graphs, or files.

For the user, the output *is* the program. The essence of a program is the information it provides. An important goal in programming is to separate the process from the outcome. A user has no interest in the detailed steps of producing information; only the result matters.

In the graphical interface of a Visual Basic application, input and output sometimes seem to merge into one simultaneous operation. The user's mouse and keyboard activities may produce multiple and instantaneous results on the screen, giving the impression that a keystroke or a mouse click is the *instrument* for creating impressive results from the application.

To help you explore a variety of input and output techniques in Visual Basic, this chapter presents a programming project named the International Sales program. In this application, the user enters a table of sales figures into a small worksheet on the screen. The table is organized into rows of sales regions and columns representing sales periods. As each individual data entry is completed, the program instantly supplies output information in a variety of forms:

✦ It calculates and displays the regional totals in a column at the right side of the sales table, and the period totals in a row at the bottom.

✦ It updates the grand total of all the data.

✦ It draws a chart to represent the sales data pictorially. This display can take the form of a column chart or a pie chart, depending on the user's current selections in a menu of chart options.

The numbers in the sales table are the user's input, and the totals and charts are the program's output. But input and output operations take place simultaneously, providing an instant tool for analyzing sales data.

The International Sales program also illustrates other input and output techniques. For example, the application window contains menus of commands and options that the user can choose with simple mouse or keyboard techniques. The menus include commands to send the sales table to a variety of output destinations; choices between different chart presentations; and options that help the user clarify the meaning of the data table itself. You'll explore these menus as you begin working with the program.

The International Sales Program

The project file is stored on disk as IntSales.Vbp. Start Visual Basic now, open the application, and press F5 to begin a first run. The application window initially appears on your screen as shown in Figure 11-1. As you can see, it contains a grid arrangement of text boxes in which you can enter annual sales totals for five regions. These entries become your sales table.

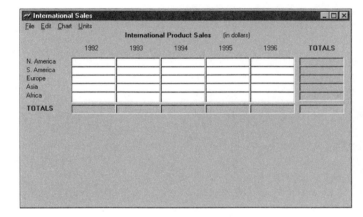

Figure 11-1: The International Sales application window. The grid of text boxes is empty when you first begin a program run, but the program supplies default row labels and column headings.

Although the program starts out by providing region labels at the left side of the sales table and year headings at the top of the table, you can change these headings to any text that identifies your sales data. You can also give the table a more specific title. For example, in Figure 11-2, the region labels have been changed to the names of countries and the period labels appear as months. A new title identifies a specific category of regional sales. To make changes like these, use your mouse to select the text you want to modify, and then enter the new label from the keyboard.

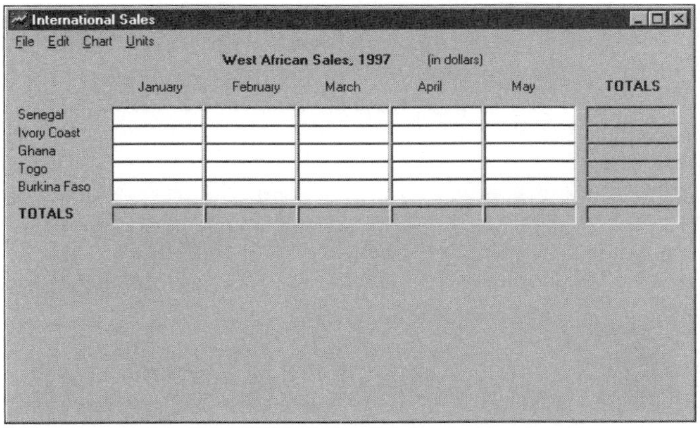

Figure 11-2: To change the title and the row and column headings, use your mouse to highlight the text that you want to revise, and enter a new title or label from the keyboard.

You can begin entering data anywhere in the sales table. Simply select a text box and begin typing the digits of the entry. To complete the entry, you can press an arrow key, the Tab key, or the Enter key to move the focus to another text box in the table. When you do so, you'll see several changes take place at once, as in Figure 11-3.

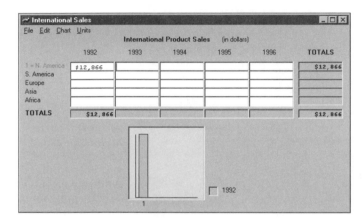

Figure 11-3: As soon as you enter a first numeric sales value, the program begins building a chart. It also displays row and column totals.

First, the program changes your sales entry into a dollar format. For example, an entry of **12865** becomes $12,865. If you inadvertently include nonnumeric characters in your entry, the program ignores them. An entry of **12865abc** becomes $12,865. (An entry that *begins* with a nonnumeric character, such as **a123**, is ignored altogether; the program clears the entry when you move to another text box. Likewise, the program ignores negative numbers.)

You'll also see three totals appear in the application window. At the right of the sales table, the program displays the total sales for the current row. Below the table, the program shows the total sales for the current column. And at the lower-right corner of the table you'll see the grand total of all the sales figures you've entered up to this point. These totals are for display only; you can't edit them or select the boxes in which they appear.

Finally, in the lower half of the application window, the program begins creating a chart to represent the numeric data you've entered into the table. Initially, the program displays a column chart. When the table contains only one entry (as in Figure 11-3), it is represented as a single column in the chart. But as you continue entering values in a given row of the sales table, the chart displays a multicolored stacked column. Each colored portion of a column represents the periodic sales figure for a given sales region. For example, in Figure 11-4, the column contains proportionally sized stacks representing the annual North American sales figures for 1992, 1993, and 1994.

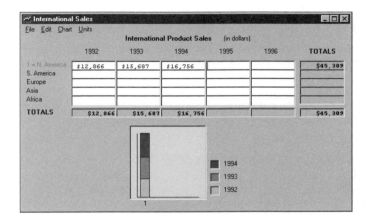

Figure 11-4: Each new data entry results in an additional chart element and in newly calculated totals.

Notice that the program displays a legend at the right side of the chart to identify the stack colors. Just below a given column in the chart, a number identifies the entire column; the same number appears next to one of the labels displayed to the left of the sales table. For example, in Figure 11-5, the first column (identified as 1) represents North American sales and the second column (2) represents South American sales. At the left of the sales table, the program displays the row labels as follows:

```
1 = N. America
2 = S. America
```

In this simple way, the program identifies each column and each stack that appears in the chart.

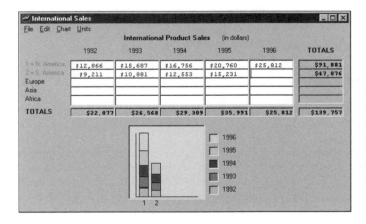

Figure 11-5: The legend identifies the colored elements of the column chart, here representing years. Labels along the horizontal axis (just below each column of the chart) identify the regional categories by number.

Finish entering a set of sample data values into the sales table now, using the data shown in Figure 11-6. A complete column chart appears in the lower half of the application window. Now pull down the program's Chart menu by clicking Chart with the mouse or by pressing Alt+C at the keyboard. The Chart menu (Figure 11-7) contains four chart options. As you can see, the initial selections are By Years and Column Chart. This means that the program starts out by creating a chart in which each column contains stacks representing annual (or other periodic) sales; an entire column thus represents the total sales for a given region.

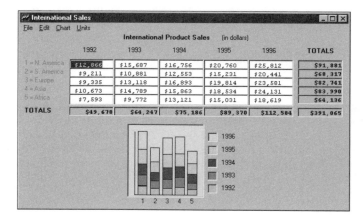

Figure 11-6: When you fill the sales grid with numbers, the program builds a complete bar chart. Initially each column in the chart represents the total sales for a given region.

Figure 11-7: You can make dramatic changes in the chart presentation by choosing options from the Chart menu.

To experiment with the chart, select the By Region entry. In response, the program instantly redraws the chart, producing columns in which the stacks represent individual regions and each column represents the total sales for a given year, as in Figure 11-8. Notice also that the labels displayed in the legend are adjusted accordingly.

The Chart menu also offers another chart type known as the pie chart. Choose Chart⇨Pie Chart to switch to this display type. When you do so, the program redraws the chart as shown in Figure 11-9. In this chart, each wedge represents the total sales for one of the regions and the entire pie represents the total sales for all the regions. To reorient the pie chart, choose Chart⇨By Years. Figure 11-10 shows the resulting chart; each wedge represents the total sales for a given year, as indicated by the new labels in the legend. Again, all the wedges together represent total sales for all the years in the sales table.

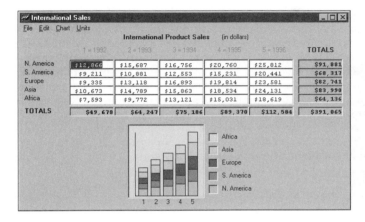

Figure 11-8: Changing the orientation of the chart. When you choose Chart⇨By Region, the program redraws the chart so that each column represents the total sales for a given year, and each colored portion represents a region.

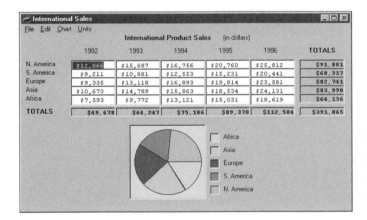

Figure 11-9: When you choose Chart⇨Pie Chart, the resulting pie chart contains wedges representing the regional sales.

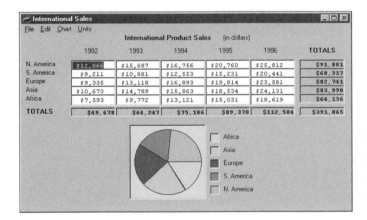

Figure 11-10: To reorient the pie chart, choose Chart⇨By Years. Now each wedge represents the total sales for a given year.

The International Sales program offers several techniques for printing the sales table or transferring it to other software environments. If you simply want a printed copy of the application window, choose File⇨Print Window, as shown in Figure 11-11. (Alternatively, press Ctrl+P from the keyboard.) In response, the program sends an image of the current sales table to your printer. You can also create a text file of the sales data alone by choosing File⇨Save Report or pressing Ctrl+S. As shown in Figure 11-12, a small message box informs you that a file named IntSales.Txt has been created in the root directory of your hard disk. Note that the program creates a new version of this file each time you choose the Save Report command; if you want to save the report from a particular data set, you should rename the file or insert it into another document.

Figure 11-11: To send an image of the application window to your printer, choose File⇨Print Window.

Figure 11-12: To create a text file containing the sales data, choose File⇨Save Report. The program saves this file as \IntSales.Txt.

Alternatively, to place a copy of the sales table on the Clipboard, choose Edit⇨Copy (or press Ctrl+C), as shown in Figure 11-13. You can then paste the sales table into your word processing program or to some other software environment if you want to incorporate the sales data into a larger document. Figure 11-14 shows how the table might appear in a Word for Windows document.

Figure 11-13: The Edit⇨Copy command places a copy of the current sales data on the Clipboard. From there, you can paste the data into a document in your word processing program.

Notice that the Edit menu also contains a Clear command. Choose this command (or press Ctrl+L) when you're ready to clear the current sales table and begin entering a new set of data.

The program offers one additional set of menu commands, under the name Units. The options in this menu enable you to change the units label displayed just to the right of the title at the top of the sales table. When you pull down the Units menu, you can choose among three options for this label, as shown in Figure 11-15.

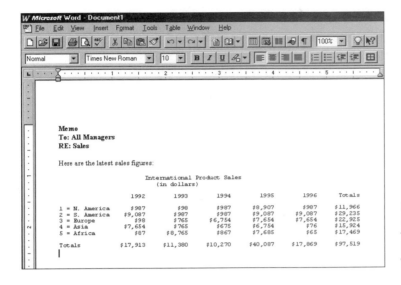

Figure 11-14: Here the data table has been incorporated into a Word document.

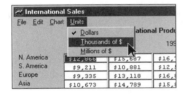

Figure 11-15: The Units menu contains three options for modifying the units label displayed at the right of the sales table title.

The units label helps you clarify the meaning of the data you enter into the sales table. Because the individual text boxes in the table are relatively small — and because the sales table doesn't necessarily need to be accurate to the last dollar — the program allows entries up to only six digits long. If you want to represent sales figures of a larger magnitude, you should reduce them by powers of 10, and then choose an appropriate label from the Units menu. For example, rather than entering a sales figure as $9,355,443, you could enter it as $9,355 and change the Units selection to "Thousands of $." In response, the program displays a new units label, as shown in Figure 11-16. Alternatively, enter the value as $9 and change the Units selection to "Millions of $." The units label is revised accordingly.

Continue experimenting with the International Sales program if you like. When you're ready to quit, choose File⇨Exit, or press Ctrl+X. All the code for this program is contained in the application's single form, named frmIntSales. You can examine the entire listing in Appendix A; alternatively, scroll through the code window on your screen. During the course of this chapter, you'll focus on procedures designed to manage the program's detailed input and output techniques.

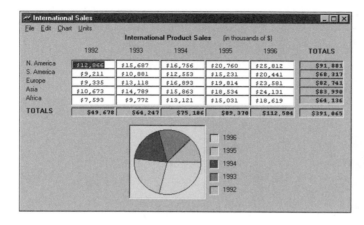

International Product Sales					(in thousands of $)	
	1992	1993	1994	1995	1996	TOTALS
N. America	$12,866	$15,687	$16,756	$20,760	$25,812	$91,881
S. America	$9,211	$10,881	$12,553	$15,231	$20,441	$68,317
Europe	$9,335	$13,118	$16,893	$19,814	$23,581	$82,741
Asia	$10,673	$14,789	$15,863	$18,534	$24,131	$83,990
Africa	$7,593	$9,772	$13,121	$15,031	$18,619	$64,136
TOTALS	$49,678	$64,247	$75,186	$89,370	$112,584	$391,065

Figure 11-16: The units label, displayed just to the right of the table's title, specifies the magnitude of the sales data.

But before turning your attention to the program's code, you should explore two important components of the program's interface: the menu bar and the control arrays.

Defining a Menu

As you've seen, the International Sales application has a menu bar containing four main menus, named File, Edit, Chart, and Units. Each of these top-level names, in turn, represents a list of commands and options. For example, the File menu contains commands for saving and printing sales data and for exiting the program; and the Chart menu contains options for changing the appearance of the sales chart. Defining a menu system like this one is remarkably easy in Visual Basic. To do so, you use a feature called the Menu Editor. The Menu Editor window contains all the tools you need to develop the elements of a menu for any form in an application. To open this window, click the Menu Editor button on the toolbar (Figure 11-17), or choose Tools⇨Menu Editor. (Alternatively, press Ctrl+E from the keyboard.)

Figure 11-17: There are three ways to open the Menu Editor: Click the Menu Editor button on the toolbar, choose Tools⇨Menu Editor, or press Ctrl+E.

Here are the basic steps for creating a menu:

1. Select and open the form on which you want the menu to appear.

2. Click the Menu Editor button on the toolbar, or choose Tools⇨Menu Editor. The Menu Editor dialog box appears on the screen, as shown in Figure 11-18.

3. In the Caption box, type the first main menu entry, just as you want it to appear on the menu bar. Optionally, use the ampersand character (&) to provide keyboard access to the menu. For example, **&File** means that the user will be able to press Alt+F to pull down the File menu. In the menu bar itself, the letter *F* will be underlined.

4. In the Name box, enter the name by which this menu entry will be identified in your code. If you normally use standard prefixes to identify different types of controls in a project, consider starting each menu name with the letters *mnu*. For example, the control name for the File menu may be *mnuFile*. (As you'll see shortly, the control name for a menu is used in the same ways as any other control name in a program.)

5. As appropriate, fill in other properties for the current menu entry. In particular, the Shortcut property allows you to select a shortcut key for a particular menu command. For example, you may choose Ctrl+P as the shortcut for a Print command. (You'll learn about other menu properties as you continue in this chapter.)

6. Click the Next button to begin the next menu entry. If you want the new entry to be defined as a command in a pull-down menu list, click the right-arrow button, as illustrated in Figure 11-19. In the large box located in the lower half of the Menu Editor, Visual Basic displays an outline of the menu you're developing. A command within a menu is indented and preceded by four dots.

7. Begin again at Step 3, and define the caption, name, and other properties of the new menu entry. Continue this process until you've defined all the main menu entries and their corresponding command lists. After you've developed a list of commands within a menu, click the left-arrow button to define the next caption as a new menu-bar entry.

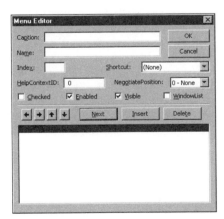

Figure 11-18: The Menu Editor window contains the tools you need to develop menus for any of the forms in an application.

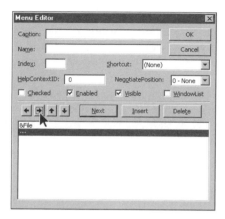

Figure 11-19: As you develop the menus for a form, the large box in the lower half of the Menu Editor window displays an outline of your work. Different levels of menus and commands are represented by sets of dots before their indented names.

Figures 11-20 and 11-21 show the complete menu definition for the International Sales project. (You can view the program's menu definition on your screen by opening the frmIntSales form in design mode and clicking the Menu Editor button on the Visual Basic toolbar.) As you can see, each of the four main menu entries is followed by its own list of indented commands. Notice the use of the ampersand character to define access keys throughout. In addition, the Menu Editor displays the Ctrl+key shortcuts that have been defined for particular menu commands (as in Figure 11-20). When you complete a menu definition like this one, click the OK button to confirm. In response, the current form displays the menu system you've created. You can view the menu both in design mode and in run mode.

Figure 11-20: The first part of the menu definition for the frmIntSales form. You can see the Ctrl+key shortcuts that have been established for some of the menu commands.

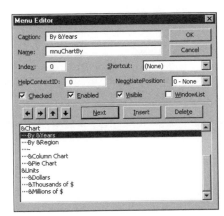

Figure 11-21: By scrolling down the window, you can see the remainder of the menu definition for the frmIntSales form.

Like any other control in a project, menu entries have event procedures and properties that become part of your program's code. The Click event for a menu control takes place when the user pulls down a menu and chooses a particular command. (Click is the only event defined for a menu control.) Figure 11-22 shows the code window for the frmIntSales form. As you can see, the object list contains the names of all the menu entries defined for the program. To create an event procedure for one of these objects, you simply select its name in the object list. As you examine the code of the International Sales program, you'll find Click event procedures that define the action of all the program's menu commands.

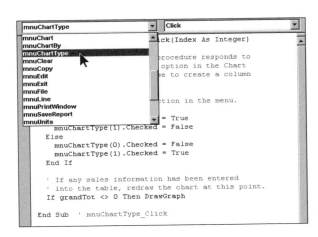

Figure 11-22: Like any other object in an application, menu commands have properties and event procedures that become part of your program's code. To create an event procedure for a menu command, select the name in the object list at the top of the code window. The Click event occurs when the user chooses a menu command.

You may have noticed that one of the properties available in the Menu Editor is named Index. You can use this property to define an *array* of menu controls. You've seen examples of control arrays in applications presented in previous chapters. Now you'll take a closer look at the techniques for defining and using control arrays in Visual Basic.

Defining Control Arrays

A *control array* is a group of objects that belong to the same type and share a common name. The International Sales application contains several control arrays. For example, the 25 text boxes of the sales table make up an array named txtAmount.

Like the elements of ordinary data arrays, each object in a control array is identified by a numeric index. As you may guess, the property named Index defines the index of each control in an array. For instance, the txtAmount text boxes have Index values from 0 to 24.

You create a control array in a form simply by assigning the same Name property to two or more controls. When you do so, Visual Basic displays a dialog box asking you to confirm the definition.

For example, suppose you've created a text box and given it the name txtAmount. Then you add a second text box to the same form and once again enter txtAmount as the object's Name property. As soon as you confirm the new Name property, the dialog box shown in Figure 11-23 appears on the desktop, asking you if you want to create a control array. To confirm the definition, you simply click Yes. In response, Visual Basic automatically assigns appropriate Index values to each object in the array; the first text box has an Index property of 0, the second 1, and so on. Each new control you add to the array is assigned the next available Index value.

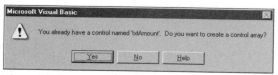

Figure 11-23: When you assign the same name to two controls of the same type, Visual Basic assumes that you want to create a control array. To confirm, click Yes on the message box that appears on the screen. This message box does not reappear for any subsequent controls you add to the array.

There are many advantages to creating control arrays for groups of objects that have a common purpose in your project. Because the controls in the array are indexed, you can conveniently use For loops to process all the elements of the array. Here is the general syntax for identifying the properties of a control array:

```
controlName(Index).propertyName
```

As usual, the control name and property name are separated by a period, but here the control name is followed by an index number enclosed in parentheses.

For example, consider the mnuClear_Click procedure, shown in Figure 11-24. When the user chooses Edit⇨Clear, this procedure is responsible for clearing all the sales data from the txtAmount controls. It does so in a simple For loop:

```
For i = 0 to 24
    txtAmount(i).Text = ""
    ' ...
Next i
```

As the loop increments the value of *i* from 0 to 24, the program assigns an empty string value to the Text property of each control in the txtAmount array. When the looping is complete, the entire sales table is blank.

```
mnuClear                          ▼    Click                          ▼

    Private Sub mnuClear_Click()

      ' The mnuClear_Click procedure clears the sales data
      ' and temporarily hides the chart.
      Dim i

      ' Reinitialize the text boxes, totals,
      ' arrays, and labels.
      For i = 0 To 24
        txtAmount(i).Text = ""
        amounts(i) = 0
        amountStr(i) = ""
      Next i
      For i = 0 To 4
        lblPeriodTotal(i).Caption = ""
        lblRegionTotal(i).Caption = ""
        periodTots(i) = 0
        regionTots(i) = 0
        txtPlace(i).Text = regionLabels(i)
        txtYear(i).Text = periodLabels(i)
      Next i
      lblGrandTotal.Caption = ""
      grandTot = 0

      ' Hide the graph objects and set the focus.
      HideGraph
      txtAmount(0).SetFocus

    End Sub  ' mnuClear_Click
```

Figure 11-24: The mnuClear_Click procedure illustrates one of the advantages of a control array. You can conveniently use a For loop to assign new property settings all at once to the objects in the array.

Event procedures for a control array apply to any object in the array. In other words, you can write a single procedure to define an event for the entire array. When the event occurs, Visual Basic supplies the Index value of the control that was the object of the event.

For example, the txtAmount_GotFocus procedure in Figure 11-25 is responsible for highlighting the current contents of a txtAmount text box whenever the user selects a value in the sales table. To do so, it makes a call to a general procedure named *SelectText* (also shown in Figure 11-25):

```
Private Sub txtAmount_GotFocus(Index As Integer)

  SelectText txtAmount(Index)

End Sub  ' txtAmount_GotFocus
```

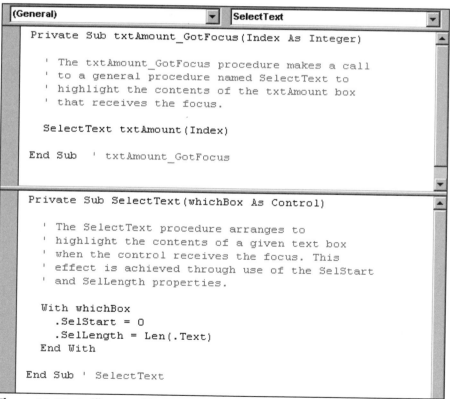

```
(General)                               SelectText

  Private Sub txtAmount_GotFocus(Index As Integer)

    ' The txtAmount_GotFocus procedure makes a call
    ' to a general procedure named SelectText to
    ' highlight the contents of the txtAmount box
    ' that receives the focus.

    SelectText txtAmount(Index)

  End Sub  ' txtAmount_GotFocus


  Private Sub SelectText(whichBox As Control)

    ' The SelectText procedure arranges to
    ' highlight the contents of a given text box
    ' when the control receives the focus. This
    ' effect is achieved through use of the SelStart
    ' and SelLength properties.

    With whichBox
      .SelStart = 0
      .SelLength = Len(.Text)
    End With

  End Sub ' SelectText
```

Figure 11-25: As illustrated by txtAmount_GotFocus, a single event procedure applies to all the elements of a control array. When the event occurs, Visual Basic automatically passes an Index argument to the procedure, identifying a specific object in the control array.

When you create an event procedure for a control array, Visual Basic automatically includes an Index argument as part of the procedure definition. This argument identifies the object of the event. Each time the event is triggered, Visual Basic passes the appropriate Index value to the event procedure. You use Index in your code to specify the control that the code will act upon. In this case, txtAmount_GotFocus uses the *SelectText* procedure to highlight the contents of the control that has just received the focus.

You'll see many more examples of control arrays as you examine the code of the International Sales program. Here is a list of all the control arrays in the frmIntSales form:

✦ The txtAmount array, with Index values from 0 to 24, provides the text boxes in which the user enters the data for the sales table.

✦ The txtYear and txtPlace arrays display the column and row headings at the top and left side of the sales table, respectively. Each of these arrays contains five text boxes, indexed from 0 to 4.

✦ The lblPeriodTotal and lblRegionTotal arrays represent the row of totals at the bottom of the sales table and the column of totals at the right side of the table. Because these are arrays of labels, the user cannot change their contents; the program is responsible for supplying any information that each label displays. The arrays have index values from 0 to 4.

✦ The lblLegendColor array is a group of labels located just to the right of the chart. (The program draws the chart itself in a picture box control named picSalesChart.) These labels display the colors that identify the stacks of a column chart or the wedges of a pie chart. Just to the right of these labels, the corresponding lblLegendText array displays the regions or sales periods represented by the chart colors. Again, these arrays have indexes from 0 to 4.

✦ The lblxAxis array displays integers from 1 to 5 along the chart's horizontal axis, identifying the five columns of a column chart.

✦ The mnuChartBy and mnuChartType arrays, in the project's menu definition, identify the two sets of charting options. To create a control array in the Menu Editor, you simply assign the same Name property to two or more menu entries and then enter appropriate Index values for each object in the array, as shown in Figure 11-26. In these examples, each array contains two controls, indexed 0 and 1.

✦ Finally, the mnuUnitType array, also part of the menu definition, identifies the options that the user can select from the Units menu. This array contains three controls, indexed from 0 to 2.

You'll learn how the application uses these various arrays as you now turn to the program's code.

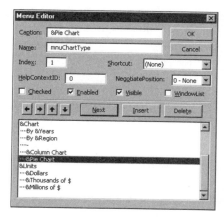

Figure 11-26: To create an array of menu commands, assign the same Name property to all the commands in the array and set the Index property appropriately.

Input Techniques

You've seen how the International Sales program manages the data-entry process in the sales table:

♦ In any of the txtAmount text boxes, the program accepts positive numeric values up to six digits long. Once the focus moves to another control, the program redisplays the previous input in a dollar format, right-aligned within its column.

♦ Any nonnumeric characters entered in a txtAmount box are ignored. If the nonnumeric characters occur at the end of an entry (such as **1234abc**), they are simply truncated from the numeric part of the value. But if an entry *begins* with a nonnumeric character (such as **abc1234**) the entire value is ignored and the program empties the text box when the focus moves to another control.

♦ The program gives the user a variety of techniques for moving from one text box to another within the sales table. The arrow keys, Enter, and Tab are all available for selecting a text box. Of course, the user can also click any box with the mouse to select it. When the focus moves to a text box that already contains an entry, the program highlights the entry. Unless you first use the mouse or the keyboard to undo the highlighting, any new information typed from the keyboard completely replaces the current contents of the box.

These details are all handled by the event procedures written for the txtAmount array. Specifically, the txtAmount_LostFocus procedure validates and reformats each new numeric entry when the focus moves to another text box. The txtAmount_KeyDown procedure defines the keyboard techniques for moving from one text box to another. And, as you've already seen, the txtAmount_GotFocus procedure arranges to highlight the text box that receives the focus. In the upcoming sections, you'll learn how these procedures work.

Validating and formatting the input

For convenience, the program uses several data arrays to keep track of the current contents of the sales table. The Dim statements for all these arrays are located in the general declarations section of the frmIntSales form shown in Figure 11-27:

```
Dim amounts(24)
Dim amountStr(24) As String
Dim periodTots(4)
Dim periodLabels(4) As String
Dim regionTots(4)
Dim regionLabels(4) As String
```

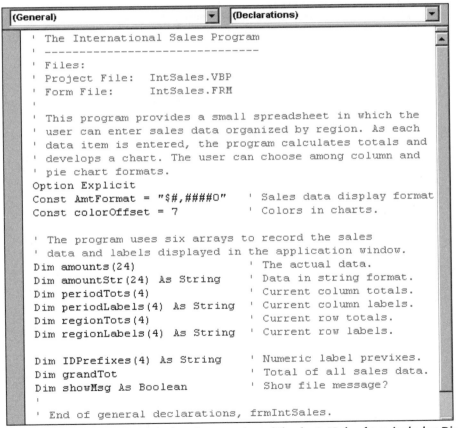

```
(General) ▼          (Declarations) ▼

' The International Sales Program
' -------------------------------
'
' Files:
' Project File:   IntSales.VBP
' Form File:      IntSales.FRM
'
' This program provides a small spreadsheet in which the
' user can enter sales data organized by region. As each
' data item is entered, the program calculates totals and
' develops a chart. The user can choose among column and
' pie chart formats.
Option Explicit
Const AmtFormat = "$#,####0"    ' Sales data display format
Const colorOffset = 7          ' Colors in charts.


' The program uses six arrays to record the sales
' data and labels displayed in the application window.
Dim amounts(24)                ' The actual data.
Dim amountStr(24) As String    ' Data in string format.
Dim periodTots(4)              ' Current column totals.
Dim periodLabels(4) As String  ' Current column labels.
Dim regionTots(4)              ' Current row totals.
Dim regionLabels(4) As String  ' Current row labels.


Dim IDPrefixes(4) As String    ' Numeric label previxes.
Dim grandTot                   ' Total of all sales data.
Dim showMsg As Boolean         ' Show file message?
'
' End of general declarations, frmIntSales.
```

Figure 11-27: The general declarations section of the frmIntSales form includes Dim statements for several structures that the program uses to keep track of the current sales table.

The *amounts* array records the numeric values that the user has entered into the 25 text boxes of the sales table, and the *amountStr* array records the formatted dollar displays. The other four arrays record the sales totals (*periodTots* and *regionTots*) and the row and column labels (*periodLabels* and *regionLabels*). Throughout the code, these arrays help the program manage the content and appearance of the sales table and the corresponding chart.

For example, the txtAmount_LostFocus procedure (Figures 11-28 and 11-29) begins by determining whether the target text box contains a *new* data entry:

```
If amountStr(Index) <> txtAmount(Index).Text Then
```

In other words, if the current entry in the text box is different from the entry recorded in the *amountStr* array, the procedure has a new data item to work with. Notice the use of the Index argument to identify the specific text box that has lost the focus.

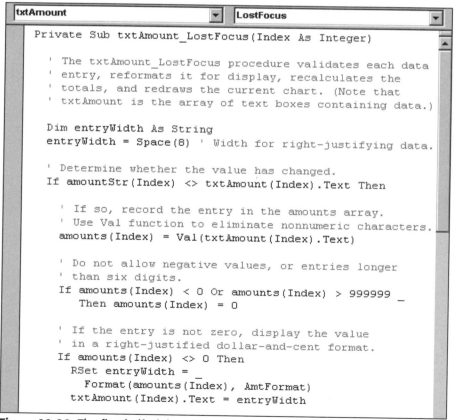

```
txtAmount                          ▼   LostFocus                        ▼

   Private Sub txtAmount_LostFocus(Index As Integer)

     ' The txtAmount_LostFocus procedure validates each data
     ' entry, reformats it for display, recalculates the
     ' totals, and redraws the current chart. (Note that
     ' txtAmount is the array of text boxes containing data.)

     Dim entryWidth As String
     entryWidth = Space(8) ' Width for right-justifying data.

     ' Determine whether the value has changed.
     If amountStr(Index) <> txtAmount(Index).Text Then

       ' If so, record the entry in the amounts array.
       ' Use Val function to eliminate nonnumeric characters.
       amounts(Index) = Val(txtAmount(Index).Text)

       ' Do not allow negative values, or entries longer
       ' than six digits.
       If amounts(Index) < 0 Or amounts(Index) > 999999 _
         Then amounts(Index) = 0

       ' If the entry is not zero, display the value
       ' in a right-justified dollar-and-cent format.
       If amounts(Index) <> 0 Then
         RSet entryWidth = _
           Format(amounts(Index), AmtFormat)
         txtAmount(Index).Text = entryWidth
```

Figure 11-28: The first half of the txtAmount_LostFocus procedure. If a new data item has been entered into the sales table, this procedure begins by recording, validating, and reformatting the input.

txtAmount	▼	LostFocus	▼

```
        Else
          ' Otherwise, if the entry is zero,
          ' display it as a blank entry.
          txtAmount(Index).Text = ""
        End If

        ' Record the formatted value in the
        ' string array named amountStr.
        amountStr(Index) = txtAmount(Index).Text

        ' Recaculate the totals for the row and
        ' column where this new entry is located.
        CalculateTotals Index

        ' If the current grand total is not zero,
        ' redraw the current chart. Otherwise,
        ' hide the chart controls.
        If grandTot <> 0 Then
          DrawGraph
        Else
          HideGraph
        End If

    End If

End Sub  ' txtAmount_LostFocus
```

Figure 11-29: The second half of the txtAmount_LostFocus procedure. After displaying the new entry in dollar format, the procedure recalculates the appropriate totals and redraws the chart in the current format and orientation.

The procedure assigns the numeric value of this new entry to the appropriate element of the *amounts* array:

```
amounts(Index) = Val(txtAmount(Index).Text)
```

On the surface, this may seem like an unnecessary use of Visual Basic's Val function, which simply converts a string of digits into a numeric value. But Val serves an important purpose here. If the numeric value contains trailing characters that are not numeric, Val ignores them. Furthermore, if the entry *begins* with a nonnumeric character, Val returns a value of 0. This simple tool is therefore a central part of the program's input validation procedure.

The program next checks the numeric range of the input. If the user has entered a negative number or a value that's longer than six digits, the entry is rejected:

```
If amounts(Index) < 0 Or amounts(Index) > 999999 _
  Then amounts(Index) = 0
```

Now if the entry is not 0, the procedure reformats the value for display. There are two parts to this task. First the value is converted to a dollar display and then it's right-aligned within the text box. These are accomplished by use of the Format function and the RSet statement, respectively:

```
RSet entryWidth = _
   Format(amounts(Index), AmtFormat)
txtAmount(Index).Text = entryWidth
```

The variable *entryWidth* is assigned a string of eight spaces at the beginning of the procedure; the RSet statement therefore right-aligns the entry within this width. *AmtFormat* is a named constant that contains the formatting string for converting a value to a dollar display. The constant is defined in the program's general declarations:

```
Const AmtFormat = "$#,###0"
```

If the entry is 0, the program empties the text box that has lost the focus:

```
Else
   txtAmount(Index).Text = ""
```

Once the formatted value has been displayed in the text box, the string value is recorded in the *amountStr* array:

```
amountStr(Index) = txtAmount(Index).Text
```

In short, the txtAmount_LostFocus procedure carries out its input validation and formatting tasks through the use of three built-in tools: the Val function, the RSet statement, and the Format function. You can read more about these tools in Visual Basic's online help.

After confirming and redisplaying each entry, the procedure makes a call to the *CalculateTotals* procedure to update the sales totals, and then a call to the *DrawGraph* procedure to redraw the chart. You'll read about these two procedures later in this chapter.

Moving the focus

The txtAmount_KeyDown procedure (Figures 11-30 and 11-31) is designed to recognize special keystrokes for moving the focus from one text box to another in the sales table. These keystrokes include the arrow keys (up, down, left, and right) and the Enter key, as defined in the Const statements at the beginning of the procedure:

```
Const leftKey = 37
Const upKey = 38
Const rightKey = 39
Const downKey = 40
Const enter = 13
```

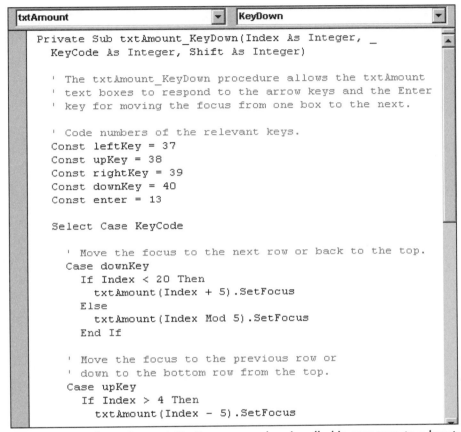

```
txtAmount ▼    KeyDown ▼

Private Sub txtAmount_KeyDown(Index As Integer, _
  KeyCode As Integer, Shift As Integer)

  ' The txtAmount_KeyDown procedure allows the txtAmount
  ' text boxes to respond to the arrow keys and the Enter
  ' key for moving the focus from one box to the next.

  ' Code numbers of the relevant keys.
  Const leftKey = 37
  Const upKey = 38
  Const rightKey = 39
  Const downKey = 40
  Const enter = 13

  Select Case KeyCode

    ' Move the focus to the next row or back to the top.
    Case downKey
      If Index < 20 Then
        txtAmount(Index + 5).SetFocus
      Else
        txtAmount(Index Mod 5).SetFocus
      End If

    ' Move the focus to the previous row or
    ' down to the bottom row from the top.
    Case upKey
      If Index > 4 Then
        txtAmount(Index - 5).SetFocus
```

Figure 11-30: The txtAmount_KeyDown procedure is called in response to a keystroke when a txtAmount control has the focus. The procedure recognizes the four cursor-movement keys as tools for changing the focus from one text box to another. Code numbers for these keys are recorded as named constants at the beginning of the routine.

Visual Basic passes a KeyCode argument to a KeyDown event procedure to identify the key that the user has pressed. In txtAmount_KeyDown, a Select Case structure uses this argument to decide which direction to move the focus:

```
Select Case KeyCode
```

For example, if the user has pressed the right-arrow key or the Enter key, the focus is moved to the *next* text box in the txtAmount array:

```
Case rightKey, enter
  If Index <> 24 Then
    txtAmount(Index + 1).SetFocus
  Else
    txtAmount(0).SetFocus
  End If
```

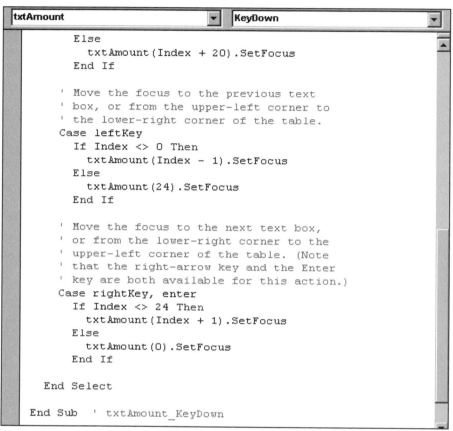

```
txtAmount                  ▼    KeyDown                              ▼
        Else
           txtAmount(Index + 20).SetFocus
        End If

     ' Move the focus to the previous text
     ' box, or from the upper-left corner to
     ' the lower-right corner of the table.
     Case leftKey
        If Index <> 0 Then
           txtAmount(Index - 1).SetFocus
        Else
           txtAmount(24).SetFocus
        End If

     ' Move the focus to the next text box,
     ' or from the lower-right corner to the
     ' upper-left corner of the table. (Note
     ' that the right-arrow key and the Enter
     ' key are both available for this action.)
     Case rightKey, enter
        If Index <> 24 Then
           txtAmount(Index + 1).SetFocus
        Else
           txtAmount(0).SetFocus
        End If

  End Select

End Sub  ' txtAmount_KeyDown
```

Figure 11-31: The second half of the txtAmount_KeyDown procedure completes the Select Case statement for responding to arrow keys. Notice that the final Case block defines the response to two keys: right-arrow and Enter.

The procedure uses the SetFocus method to make the move. Also notice the one contingency: If the last text box in the txtAmount array currently has the focus, the procedure moves the focus up to the first control in the array in response to the right-arrow or Enter key.

Once a text box receives the focus, the txtAmount_GotFocus procedure arranges to highlight the contents of the control, as you saw back in Figure 11-25. In the *SelectText* procedure, the SelStart method establishes the starting point of the highlight:

```
.SelStart = 0
```

Then the SelLength method defines the length of the highlight:

```
.SelLength = Len(.Text)
```

The procedure uses Visual Basic's built-in Len function to determine the length of the entry.

The program's menu commands represent another important input technique. In menus, the purpose of the user's input is to issue specific instructions to the program rather than to enter data. You'll look at the menu procedures in the next section.

Responding to the user's menu choices

Conveniently, some menu techniques are built into the definition of the menu, and therefore require no extra code. For example, the Menu Editor allows you to define shortcut keys for carrying out menu commands directly from the keyboard. In addition, you can use the ampersand character to define Alt keys for pulling down menus and choosing specific commands or options.

But other menu events are controlled by the program itself. Each menu command in the International Sales application is represented by a Click procedure. These procedures take control when the user pulls down a menu and chooses an option or presses a shortcut key to perform a menu command. You'll be examining several of these procedures later in this chapter.

Using the Checked property

Two of the program's menus — the Chart menu and the Units menu — contain lists of options rather than commands. As you'll recall, the Chart menu has two pairs of options that allow the user to choose the orientation and format of the chart display. The Units menu contains three options for defining the dollar units represented by the sales figures themselves. When the user selects an option in either of these menus, the new selection is *checked* — that is, a check mark is displayed just to the left of the currently selected option. Appropriately enough, a menu property named Checked determines which option will display a check mark in a given menu list. The property has two settings, True or False.

For example, consider the two chart-type options in the Chart menu. These options are displayed as *Column Chart* and *Pie Chart* in the menu list itself, but in the program they are represented as a control array named mnuChartType. This array contains two elements, with indexes of 0 and 1. When the user pulls down the Chart menu and chooses one of these options, the mnuChartType_Click procedure in Figure 11-32 takes control.

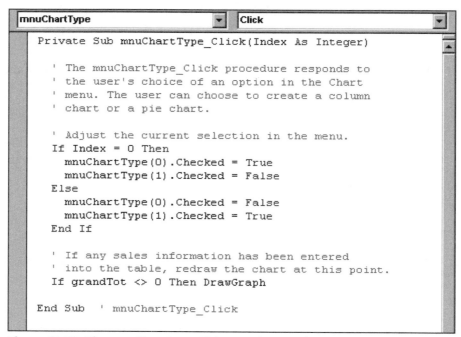

```
mnuChartType                    ▼    Click                                ▼

Private Sub mnuChartType_Click(Index As Integer)

  ' The mnuChartType_Click procedure responds to
  ' the user's choice of an option in the Chart
  ' menu. The user can choose to create a column
  ' chart or a pie chart.

  ' Adjust the current selection in the menu.
  If Index = 0 Then
    mnuChartType(0).Checked = True
    mnuChartType(1).Checked = False
  Else
    mnuChartType(0).Checked = False
    mnuChartType(1).Checked = True
  End If

  ' If any sales information has been entered
  ' into the table, redraw the chart at this point.
  If grandTot <> 0 Then DrawGraph

End Sub   ' mnuChartType_Click
```

Figure 11-32: The mnuChartType_Click procedure marks the user's choice in the Chart menu and then redraws the chart under this new setting.

The procedure's first task is to display a check next to the option that the user has selected, and remove the check from the other option. The following If structure accomplishes this task by changing the settings of the Checked properties appropriately:

```
If Index = 0 Then
  mnuChartType(0).Checked = True
  mnuChartType(1).Checked = False
Else
  mnuChartType(0).Checked = False
  mnuChartType(1).Checked = True
End If
```

Once this is done, the procedure makes a call to the *DrawGraph* routine to redraw the chart itself, following the new instructions the user has issued for the chart's format:

```
If grandTot <> 0 Then DrawGraph
```

Notice that this call is made only if the total of all the sales data (represented by the variable *grandTot*) is not 0. If the sales table is currently empty, the program draws no chart.

You'll find similar steps in other menu procedures. The mnuChartBy_Click procedure in Figure 11-33 changes between the *By Years* and *By Region* selections in the Chart menu; and the mnuUnitType_Click procedure selects one of the three dollar units in the Units menu.

```
mnuChartBy                              ▼    Click                              ▼

  Private Sub mnuChartBy_Click(Index As Integer)

    ' The mnuChartBy_Click procedure responds to the user's
    ' choice of an option in the Chart menu. The user can
    ' choose a chart by region or by years.
    Dim i

    ' Adjust the selection within the menu itself.
    If Index = 0 Then
      mnuChartBy(0).Checked = True
      mnuChartBy(1).Checked = False
    Else
      mnuChartBy(0).Checked = False
      mnuChartBy(1).Checked = True
    End If

    ' Restore the original column and row labels.
    For i = 0 To 4
      txtYear(i).Text = periodLabels(i)
      txtYear(i).Enabled = True
      txtPlace(i).Text = regionLabels(i)
      txtPlace(i).Enabled = True
    Next i

    ' Redraw the chart if any sales entries exist.
    If grandTot <> 0 Then DrawGraph

  End Sub  ' mnuChartBy_Click
```

Figure 11-33: The mnuChartBy_Click procedure responds to the user's selection for the chart's orientation (by region or by year), and redraws the chart accordingly.

In the mnuUnitType_Click procedure (Figure 11-34) the control array mnuUnitType represents all three options in the menu, indexed from 0 to 2. Here's how the procedure determines which option should be checked:

```
For i = 0 To 2
  If i = Index Then
    mnuUnitType(i).Checked = True
  Else
    mnuUnitType(i).Checked = False
  End If
Next i
```

A call to the *ShowUnits* procedure (also in Figure 11-34) then makes the appropriate change in the unit display, represented by the lblUnits label:

```
Select Case True
  Case mnuUnitType(0).Checked
    lblUnits.Caption = "(in dollars)"
  Case mnuUnitType(1).Checked
    lblUnits.Caption = "(in thousands of $)"
  Case mnuUnitType(2).Checked
    lblUnits.Caption = "(in millions of $)"
End Select
```

The program reads the values of the Checked properties in the Units menu to decide which units label to display on the form.

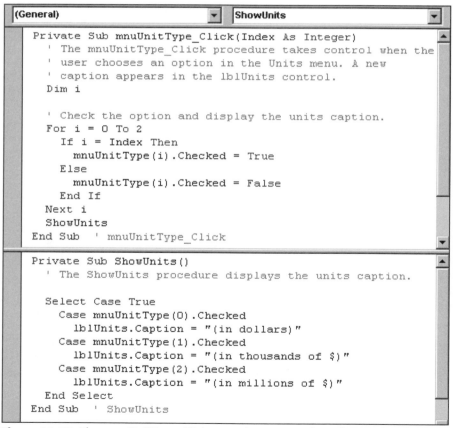

Figure 11-34: The mnuUnitType_Click procedure responds to the user's selection in the Units menu. A call to the ShowUnits procedure then displays the selected units caption.

Next you'll look at a variety of output techniques illustrated in the International Sales program.

Output Techniques

Each time the user enters a new figure into the sales table, the International Sales program displays instant output in the controls of the frmIntSales form. The two arrays of labels named lblPeriodTotal and lblRegionTotal receive the updated total sales figures for the current sales period and region. A label named lblGrandTotal displays the total of all the sales. And a picture box control named picSalesChart displays either a column chart or a pie chart representing the current sales data.

In addition, the program's menu commands offer the user several ways to send the data to other destinations:

✦ The Save Report command in the File menu creates a text file to store the numeric data on disk. The mnuSaveReport_Click procedure performs this output operation.

✦ The Print Window command in the File menu sends an image of the application window to the printer. The mnuPrintWindow_Click procedure takes care of this step.

✦ The Copy command in the Edit menu sends a copy of the sales table to the Windows 95 Clipboard. The mnuCopy_Click procedure takes control when the user chooses this command.

You'll examine all of these output procedures in the sections ahead.

Calculating and displaying sales totals

The txtAmount_LostFocus procedure makes a call to the *CalculateTotals* procedure whenever the user completes a new data entry in the sales table:

```
CalculateTotals Index
```

As shown in Figures 11-35 and 11-36, *CalculateTotals* needs to recalculate only those totals that are affected by the new entry — the total regional sales in the current row, the total period sales in the current column, and the grand total at the lower-right corner of the table. For this reason, a call to the procedure sends the index number of the current entry as an argument. The procedure receives this value in the variable *amtIndex:*

```
Private Sub CalculateTotals(amtIndex As Integer)
```

As you know, the txtAmount array has index values from 0 to 24, but the two totals arrays (lblPeriodTotal and lblRegionTotal) have index values from 0 to 4. To determine the relevant indexes for the totals arrays, the program uses the Mod and integer division operations:

```
periodIndex = amtIndex Mod 5
regionIndex = amtIndex \ 5
```

Then the procedure needs to calculate the indexes corresponding to the first text boxes in the row and column of the new entry:

```
firstRowIndex = regionIndex * 5
firstColIndex = periodIndex
```

These indexes allow the procedure to loop through all the values in the target row and column to calculate the corresponding totals.

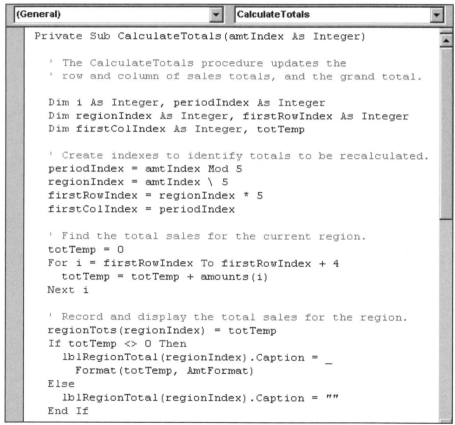

```
(General)                              CalculateTotals

    Private Sub CalculateTotals(amtIndex As Integer)

      ' The CalculateTotals procedure updates the
      ' row and column of sales totals, and the grand total.

      Dim i As Integer, periodIndex As Integer
      Dim regionIndex As Integer, firstRowIndex As Integer
      Dim firstColIndex As Integer, totTemp

      ' Create indexes to identify totals to be recalculated.
      periodIndex = amtIndex Mod 5
      regionIndex = amtIndex \ 5
      firstRowIndex = regionIndex * 5
      firstColIndex = periodIndex

      ' Find the total sales for the current region.
      totTemp = 0
      For i = firstRowIndex To firstRowIndex + 4
        totTemp = totTemp + amounts(i)
      Next i

      ' Record and display the total sales for the region.
      regionTots(regionIndex) = totTemp
      If totTemp <> 0 Then
        lblRegionTotal(regionIndex).Caption = _
          Format(totTemp, AmtFormat)
      Else
        lblRegionTotal(regionIndex).Caption = ""
      End If
```

Figure 11-35: The *CalculateTotals* procedure updates selected totals in response to a new sales entry. The procedure begins by converting the current txtAmount index (received as the argument *amtIndex*) into indexes identifying the row and column that will be the objects of the new calculations.

(General)	▼	CalculateTotals	▼

```
  ' Calculate the total sales for the current period.
  totTemp = 0
  For i = firstColIndex To firstColIndex + 20 Step 5
    totTemp = totTemp + amounts(i)
  Next i

  ' Record and display the total sales for the period.
  periodTots(periodIndex) = totTemp
  If totTemp <> 0 Then
    lblPeriodTotal(periodIndex).Caption = _
      Format(totTemp, AmtFormat)
  Else
    lblPeriodTotal(periodIndex).Caption = ""
  End If

  ' Calculate the new grand total.
  totTemp = 0
  For i = 0 To 24
    totTemp = totTemp + amounts(i)
  Next i

  ' Record and display the calculated grand total.
  grandTot = totTemp
  If totTemp <> 0 Then
    lblGrandTotal.Caption = Format(totTemp, AmtFormat)
  Else
    lblGrandTotal.Caption = ""
  End If
End Sub  ' CalculateTotals
```

Figure 11-36: The *CalculateTotals* procedure recalculates and displays the current row total, column total, and grand total.

For example, here's how the procedure finds the total of all the sales entries in the target row:

```
totTemp = 0
For i = firstRowIndex To firstRowIndex + 4
  totTemp = totTemp + amounts(i)
Next i
```

Likewise, here is the code for calculating the total of all the sales amounts in the target column:

```
totTemp = 0
For i = firstColIndex To firstColIndex + 20 Step 5
  totTemp = totTemp + amounts(i)
Next i
```

Once these totals are computed, the program formats them and displays them in the appropriate label controls:

```
lblRegionTotal(regionIndex).Caption = _
   Format(totTemp, AmtFormat)
```

and

```
lblPeriodTotal(periodIndex).Caption = _
   Format(totTemp, AmtFormat)
```

Finally, the procedure calculates the new grand total of all the sales figures:

```
totTemp = 0
For i = 0 To 24
   totTemp = totTemp + amounts(i)
Next i
```

This amount is displayed in the label control named lblGrandTotal:

```
lblGrandTotal.Caption = Format(totTemp, AmtFormat)
```

Along the way, the *CalculateTotals* procedure records the numeric totals in the data arrays *regionTots* and *periodTots,* and in the variable named *grandTot*. As you'll see shortly, the charting procedures make use of these totals to determine the correct proportions for drawing the elements of a column or pie chart.

Drawing charts

The txtAmount_LostFocus procedure also makes a call to the *DrawGraph* procedure after confirming each new entry in the sales table. As shown in Figure 11-37, *DrawGraph* has the job of determining which of four charting procedures to call, depending on the current selections in the Chart menu. The procedure uses a Select Case structure to make this decision:

```
Select Case True
   Case mnuChartBy(0).Checked And mnuChartType(0).Checked
      DrawAxes
      ColumnByYears
   Case mnuChartBy(0).Checked And mnuChartType(1).Checked
      PieByYears
   Case mnuChartBy(1).Checked And mnuChartType(0).Checked
      DrawAxes
      ColumnByRegion
   Case mnuChartBy(1).Checked And mnuChartType(1).Checked
      PieByRegion
End Select
```

As you can see, the decision depends on the specific combination of Chart menu options that the user has selected. A column chart is drawn by either the *ColumnByYears* or *ColumnByRegion* procedure, and a pie chart is drawn by either the *PieByYears* or the *PieByRegion* procedure. In the case of a column chart, the program also makes a call to the *DrawAxes* procedure to draw the horizontal x-axis and the vertical y-axis for the chart.

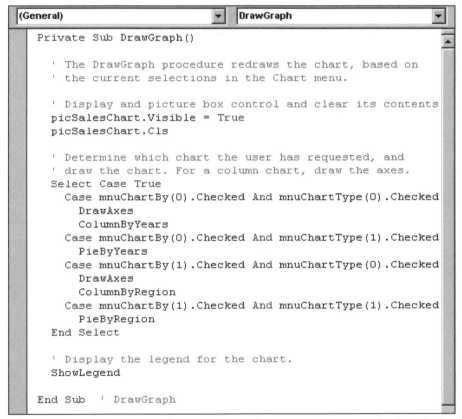

```
(General)                            ▼    DrawGraph                       ▼

    Private Sub DrawGraph()

      ' The DrawGraph procedure redraws the chart, based on
      ' the current selections in the Chart menu.

      ' Display and picture box control and clear its contents
      picSalesChart.Visible = True
      picSalesChart.Cls

      ' Determine which chart the user has requested, and
      ' draw the chart. For a column chart, draw the axes.
      Select Case True
        Case mnuChartBy(0).Checked And mnuChartType(0).Checked
          DrawAxes
          ColumnByYears
        Case mnuChartBy(0).Checked And mnuChartType(1).Checked
          PieByYears
        Case mnuChartBy(1).Checked And mnuChartType(0).Checked
          DrawAxes
          ColumnByRegion
        Case mnuChartBy(1).Checked And mnuChartType(1).Checked
          PieByRegion
      End Select

      ' Display the legend for the chart.
      ShowLegend

    End Sub   ' DrawGraph
```

Figure 11-37: The *DrawGraph* procedure reads the user's current selections in the Chart menu and calls on the appropriate charting procedures to create either a column chart or a pie chart in the selected orientation.

The actual charting procedures make use of properties and methods defined for a picture box control — in this case the picSalesChart object. For example, the Line method draws the rectangular "stack" elements of a column chart, and the Circle method draws the wedges of a pie chart. In addition, the Scale method defines a coordinate system within the picture box, with the goal of making the chart as easy to draw as possible. You'll see how these methods work as you examine the procedures.

Drawing a column chart

Before the program draws a column chart, a call to the *DrawAxes* procedure (Figure 11-38) accomplishes two tasks. First, the procedure uses the Scale method to establish an appropriate coordinate system. Here is the general format of this method:

```
objectName.Scale (x1, y1)-(x2, y2)
```

where (*x1*, *y1*) is the coordinate address of the control's upper-left corner, and (*x2*, *y2*) is the address of the lower-right corner. The *DrawAxes* procedure uses this method to establish the *picSalesChart* coordinates as follows:

```
picSalesChart.Scale (-1, 11)-(11, -0.25)
```

Under this coordinate system, the *origin* of the chart — that is, the point that has the coordinate address (0, 0) — is located slightly above and to the right of the control's lower-left corner. Furthermore, this call to the Scale method makes room for a drawing area that is 10 units high and 10 units across, as you can see by the lengths of the two axes:

```
picSalesChart.Line (0, 0)-Step(10, 0)
picSalesChart.Line (0, 0)-Step(0, 10)
```

This means that the maximum height of any column in the chart is 10 units.

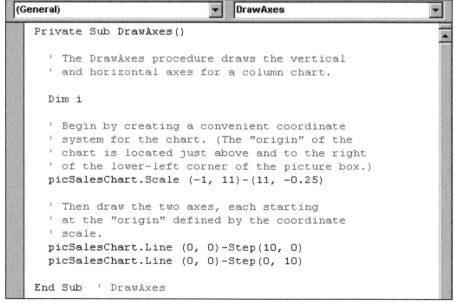

Figure 11-38: The *DrawAxes* procedure sets the scale for a column chart and draws the vertical and horizontal axes.

The major arithmetic problem in a column chart is determining the scale factor by which each sales value should be multiplied to calculate the proportional height of the corresponding chart stack. This scale factor is based on two values:

✦ The height of the drawing area (which, as you've now seen, is 10 in this program)

✦ The tallest column that will be drawn within this area

Both the *ColumnByRegion* and *ColumnByYears* procedures must therefore begin their work by determining the largest total value that will be represented in the chart.

For example, here is how the *ColumnByRegion* procedure (Figure 11-39) finds the value of *maxPeriod*, the largest annual sales total:

```
maxPeriod = 0
For i = 0 To 4
  If periodTots(i) > maxPeriod Then _
    maxPeriod = periodtots(i)
Next i
```

Given *maxPeriod*, the following statement calculates the scale factor:

```
scaleFactor = 10 / maxPeriod
```

Multiplying this scale factor by the largest annual total results in a product of 10, the total height of the drawing area.

The *ColumnByRegion* procedure draws the columns of the chart in a pair of For loops, one nested within the other. The outer loop contains the code for drawing each complete column, and the inner loop draws the stacks in a given column. Thanks to the scale factor, the height of each individual stack appropriately represents the corresponding sales value:

```
y2 = scaleFactor * amounts(j)
```

Before drawing a given stack, the program uses the FillColor property to select a color. A convenient built-in function named QBColor identifies colors by numeric arguments from 0 to 15:

```
picSalesChart.FillColor = _
  QBColor(j \ 5 + colorOffset)
```

To draw a rectangle filled with color, the program uses the Line method in the following form:

```
object.Line (x1, y1)-Step(x2, y2), outlineColor, B
```

```
(General)                              ColumnByRegion

Private Sub ColumnByRegion()
  ' The ColumnByRegion procedure draws a column chart.
  Dim i, j, x, y, y2, maxPeriod, scaleFactor

  ' Determine the largest total and compute the scale.
  maxPeriod = 0
  For i = 0 To 4
    If periodTots(i) > maxPeriod Then _
      maxPeriod = periodTots(i)
  Next i
  scaleFactor = 10 / maxPeriod

  For i = 0 To 4
    x = 0.5 + 2 * i
    y = 0

    ' Draw a "stack" for each sales entry.
    For j = i To i + 20 Step 5
      If amounts(j) <> 0 Then
        y2 = scaleFactor * amounts(j)
        picSalesChart.FillColor = _
          QBColor(j \ 5 + colorOffset)
        picSalesChart.FillStyle = 0
        picSalesChart.Line (x, y)-Step(1.5, y2), 0, B
        y = y + y2
      End If
    Next j
  Next i
End Sub    ' ColumnByRegion
```

Figure 11-39: The *ColumnByRegion* procedure draws a column chart if the user has selected the "By Region" orientation in the Chart menu.

The keyword Step indicates that (*x2, y2*) is an offset measurement from the starting point (*x1, y1*). The *outlineColor* defines the color around the rectangle's perimeter. The letter *B* is an instruction to draw a box rather than a line. For example, here is how the *ColumnByRegion* procedure draws each stack in a given column:

```
picSalesChart.Line (x, y)-Step(1.5, y2), 0, B
```

Notice that the vertical offset is *y2,* the calculated height of the stack. The vertical starting point is *y*, which is the top coordinate of the *previous* stack. The width of each column is specified as 1.5 units in the coordinate scale. The outline color is 0, which represents black. After drawing each stack, the program increases the value of *y* by the height of the previous stack:

```
y = y + y2
```

If you take a look at the *ColumnByYears* procedure (Figure 11-40), you'll see that the steps for producing the other chart orientation are about the same, except that the scale factor is based on the regional sales totals rather than the annual sales.

```
(General)                          ColumnByYears

Private Sub ColumnByYears()
  ' The ColumnByYears procedure draws a column chart.
  Dim i, x, y, y2, maxRegion, scaleFactor

  ' Determine the largest total and compute the scale.
  maxRegion = 0
  For i = 0 To 4
    If regionTots(i) > maxRegion Then _
      maxRegion = regionTots(i)
  Next i
  scaleFactor = 10 / maxRegion

  For i = 0 To 24
    If i Mod 5 = 0 Then
      x = 0.5 + 2 * (i / 5)
      y = 0
    End If

    ' Compute the height, choose a color, and draw.
    If amounts(i) <> 0 Then
      y2 = scaleFactor * amounts(i)
      picSalesChart.FillColor = _
        QBColor(i Mod 5 + colorOffset)
      picSalesChart.FillStyle = 0
      picSalesChart.Line (x, y)-Step(1.5, y2), 0, B
      y = y + y2
    End If
  Next i
End Sub  ' ColumnByYears
```

Figure 11-40: The *ColumnByYears* procedure draws a column chart if the user has selected the "By Years" orientation in the Chart menu.

Drawing a pie chart

In a pie chart, the angle of a given wedge represents one value in relation to the total of all the values. Here's the general formula for calculating the angle to represent a value, *x*, which is part of a total, *t:*

$$360 * (x / t)$$

For example, suppose the sales total for a five-year period is $120,000 and the sales total for the year 1996 is $40,000. Because the 1996 sales are one-third of the overall total, the year is represented by a pie-chart wedge with an angle of 120 degrees, or one-third of a full circle.

In Visual Basic's Circle method, angles are measured in *radians* rather than degrees. A full circle of 360 degrees is equal to a radian measurement of 2π. To draw a wedge, you supply the starting and ending angles as *negative* radian values in the Circle method:

```
Object.Circle (x, y), radius, outlineColor, -angle1, -angle2
```

In this general format, (x, y) represents the circle's center; *radius* is the length of the radius; *outlineColor* is a color selection for the perimeter of the wedge; and *angle1* and *angle2* are the starting and ending angles in radians.

By convention, an angle of 0 is defined as the radius that extends horizontally to the right from the circle's center point. Interestingly, the Circle method has a quirk: Using 0 or 2π as one of the angles of a wedge produces unexpected results. You should therefore substitute values that are slightly offset from 0 or 2π to represent these angles.

The *PieByYears* procedure (Figure 11-41) begins by calculating a value of π, using a standard formula that includes a call to Visual Basic's built-in Atn (arctangent) function:

```
pi = 4 * Atn(1)
```

Then the procedure establishes a coordinate scale for the picture box in which the chart will be drawn:

```
picSalesChart.Scale (-1, 1)-(1, -1)
```

Under this coordinate system, the origin of the chart $(0, 0)$, is located at the center of the picture box. This simplifies the use of the Circle method to draw the wedges of the pie chart.

The wedges are drawn in a For structure that loops through the total sales figures for each year in the five-year period. The starting angle of the first wedge is set at a small nonzero value:

```
a1 = 0.00001
```

Then the ending angle is calculated as a portion of the full 2π sweep of the circle:

```
a2 = a1 + (2 * pi) * (periodTots(i) / grandTot)
```

```
(General)                              ▼   PieByYears                    ▼

   Private Sub PieByYears()                                              ▲
     ' The PieByYears procedure draws a pie chart.
     Dim i, pi, a1, a2

     ' Calculate pi, set the scale and the starting point.
     pi = 4 * Atn(1)
     picSalesChart.Scale (-1, 1)-(1, -1)
     a1 = 0.00001

     ' Draw a wedge for the total sales of each year.
     For i = 0 To 4
       If periodTots(i) <> 0 Then

         ' Calculate the ending angle of the wedge.
         a2 = a1 + (2 * pi) * (periodTots(i) / grandTot)

         ' Select a color and draw the wedge.
         picSalesChart.FillColor = QBColor(i + colorOffset)
         picSalesChart.FillStyle = 0
         If periodTots(i) < grandTot Then
           picSalesChart.Circle (0, 0), 0.9, _
             0, -a1, -a2 + 0.00001
         Else      ' If this is the only sales value.
           picSalesChart.Circle (0, 0), 0.9, 0
         End If
         a1 = a2   ' The starting angle for the next wedge.
       End If
     Next i
   End Sub  ' PieByYears
```

Figure 11-41: The *PieByYears* procedure draws a pie chart if the user has selected the "By Years" orientation in the Chart menu.

As you'll recall, the data array *periodTots* contains the total annual sales figures, and the variable *grandTot* contains the grand total of all the sales.

Once the angles have been calculated, the procedure uses the FillColor property to select a color for the wedge:

```
picSalesChart.FillColor = QBColor(i + colorOffset)
```

Then a call to the Circle method draws the wedge itself:

```
picSalesChart.Circle (0, 0), 0.9, _
  0, -a1, -a2 + 0.00001
```

Notice that the center of the circle is (0, 0) and the radius is 0.9, slightly less than half the width of the picture box itself. Also notice that the procedure adds a small nonzero value to *a2* to avoid using an angle of 2π.

When one wedge has been drawn, the starting angle of the next wedge is defined as the ending angle of the current wedge:

```
a1 = a2
```

You'll find that the *PieByRegion* procedure (Figure 11-42) uses these same techniques to draw its version of the pie chart, except that it bases the wedge calculations on the regional sales totals rather than the annual totals.

```
(General)                           PieByRegion

Private Sub PieByRegion()
  ' The PieByRegion procedure draws a pie chart.
  Dim i, pi, a1, a2

  ' Calculate pi, set the scale and the starting point.
  pi = 4 * Atn(1)
  picSalesChart.Scale (-1, 1)-(1, -1)
  a1 = 0.00001

  ' Draw a wedge for the total sales of each year.
  For i = 0 To 4
    If regionTots(i) <> 0 Then

      ' Calculate the ending angle of the wedge.
      a2 = a1 + (2 * pi) * (regionTots(i) / grandTot)

      ' Select a color and draw the wedge.
      picSalesChart.FillColor = QBColor(i + colorOffset)
      picSalesChart.FillStyle = 0
      If regionTots(i) < grandTot Then
        picSalesChart.Circle (0, 0), 0.9, _
          0, -a1, -a2 + 0.00001
      Else      ' If this is the only sales value.
        picSalesChart.Circle (0, 0), 0.9, 0
      End If
      a1 = a2    ' The starting angle for the next wedge.
    End If
  Next i
End Sub  ' PieByRegion
```

Figure 11-42: The *PieByRegion* procedure draws a pie chart if the user has selected the "By Region" orientation in the Chart menu.

Performing other output tasks

The mnuSaveReport_Click procedure (Figures 11-43 and 11-44) responds to the user's selection of the Save Report command in the File menu. The procedure creates a file named IntSales.Txt in the root directory of the current disk:

```
Open "\IntSales.Txt" For Output As #1
```

The procedure then uses a sequence of Print # statements to send the sales data and totals to the file. (Refer back to Chapter 10 for more information about data file commands.) This file can then be printed or incorporated into a larger document.

```
mnuSaveReport                              Click

  Private Sub mnuSaveReport_Click()

    ' The mnuSaveReport_Click procedure takes control when
    ' the user chooses Save Report from the File menu. It
    ' creates a text file (\IntSales.Txt) for the numeric
    ' data currently displayed in the sales table.
    Dim i, j
    Dim f As String, b As String

    f = "$#,####0"
    b = Space(12)

    ' Create the file. (If the file already
    ' exists, overwrite the previous version.)
    Open "\IntSales.Txt" For Output As #1

      ' Write the title and the column labels
      ' to the file.
      Print #1, b; b; txtTitle
      Print #1, b; b; Space(3); lblUnits
      Print #1,

      Print #1, b;
      For i = 0 To 4
        RSet b = txtYear(i)
        Print #1, b;
      Next i
      Print #1, Space(6); "Totals"
      Print #1,
```

Figure 11-43: The mnuSaveReport_Click procedure creates a text file to store the current sales table. An Open statement creates the file for output, and a sequence of Print # statements write data to the file.

```
mnuSaveReport                    ▼    Click                              ▼
        ' Write the table of sales data to the file.                      ▲
        For i = 0 To 4
          LSet b = txtPlace(i).Text
          Print #1, b;
          For j = i * 5 To i * 5 + 4
            RSet b = txtAmount(j).Text
            Print #1, b;
          Next j
          RSet b = lblRegionTotal(i).Caption
          Print #1, b
        Next i

        ' Write the totals to the file.
        Print #1,
        Print #1, "Totals"; Space(6);
        For i = 0 To 4
          RSet b = lblPeriodTotal(i).Caption
          Print #1, b;
        Next i
        RSet b = lblGrandTotal
        Print #1, b

      Close #1
      If showMsg Then _
        MsgBox "Created \IntSales.Txt", , "Report"

    End Sub   ' mnuSaveReport_Click
```

Figure 11-44: The second half of the mnuSaveReport_Click procedure illustrates techniques for creating a formatted table of numbers, suitable for incorporating into a document.

The mnuPrintWindow_Click procedure (Figure 11-45) makes a call to Visual Basic's PrintForm method to send an image of the International Sales window to the printer. This procedure responds to the user's selection of the Print Window command in the File menu.

Finally, the mnuCopy_Click procedure (Figure 11-46) arranges to send a copy of the sales table to the Clipboard. To do so, it begins by forcing a call to the mnuSaveReport_Click procedure to make sure that the IntSales.Txt file exists in the root directory. Then the procedure opens the file, reads it line by line, and assigns its entire contents to a string variable named *temp:*

```
temp = ""
Open "\IntSales.Txt" For Input As #1
  Do While Not EOF(1)
    Line Input #1, inTemp
    temp = temp + inTemp + Chr(13) + Chr(10)
  Loop
Close #1
```

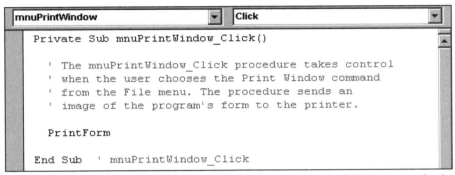

Figure 11-45: The mnuPrintWindow_Click procedure uses the PrintForm method to print a copy of the application window.

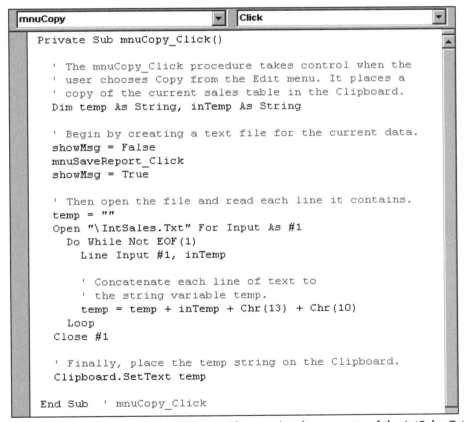

Figure 11-46: The mnuCopy_Click procedure copies the contents of the IntSales.Txt file to the Clipboard. It illustrates the use of the SetText method for the Clipboard object.

Notice the use of the Line Input command to read entire lines at a time from the file. Also note that the procedure adds a carriage-return/line-feed combination (Chr(13) and Chr(10)) to each line stored in *temp*.

The procedure uses the SetText method to store this string value in the Clipboard:

```
Clipboard.SetText temp
```

When this operation is complete, the user can paste the sales table to a word processed document or to another software environment.

In summary, the International Sales application illustrates several interesting input and output techniques, including data validation and formatting, menu procedures, numeric and graphical output to the screen, and output to a variety of other destinations. You'll continue to explore these techniques in other programs presented in this book.

Beyond Standard Controls

Up to this point, you've worked with the standard controls initially shown in the Visual Basic Toolbox, as in Figure 12-1. Text boxes, labels, command buttons, check boxes, option buttons, picture boxes, lists, scroll bars — these and a few others are among the most familiar objects in Windows dialog boxes, and are generally the controls that most Visual Basic programmers learn to use first.

Figure 12-1: The standard controls that are initially represented as icons in the Toolbox. While these controls are among the most familiar to Windows users, Visual Basic provides many other tools that you can include in projects.

But a number of other significant tools are available. In particular, the Components dialog box, which you can examine in Figure 12-2, lists a collection of additional controls that you can add to any project. There are three convenient ways to gain access to this important list:

- ✦ Click inside the Toolbox with the right mouse button, and choose Components from the resulting shortcut menu, as in Figure 12-3.
- ✦ Choose Project⇨Components, as shown in Figure 12-4.
- ✦ Press Ctrl+T, the keyboard shortcut for the Components command.

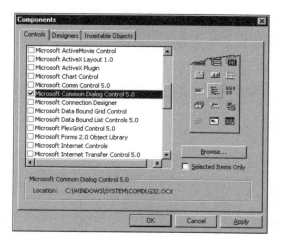

Figure 12-2: The Controls tab in the Components dialog box (from the Components command in the Project menu) lists additional controls that you can add to a project. To add a control to the current project, simply click the check box next to any name in the scrollable list.

Figure 12-3: One way to open the Components dialog box is to click inside the Toolbox with the right mouse button and choose Components from the resulting shortcut menu.

Figure 12-4: Two other ways to open the Components dialog box are to choose the corresponding command from the Project menu, or to press the Ctrl+T shortcut from the keyboard.

Formerly called custom controls, the tools shown in the Controls tab of the Components dialog box are now known as ActiveX controls. When you install an edition of Visual Basic, the available ActiveX controls are stored on disk as separate files with OCX extension names. (Libraries of objects, which may also appear in the Components list, are identified by DLL extensions.) They may be provided by Microsoft or by other developers who create tools for use in Visual Basic. In general, these controls serve more complex roles — and meet more sophisticated programming requirements — than the standard controls you've worked with up to now.

As you'll learn in Part III of this book, ActiveX technology has special significance in a personal computing environment that includes connections to the Internet. But for now you can simply think of ActiveX controls as additional components available to expand the scope of your own Visual Basic projects.

For example, the highlighted item back in Figure 12-2 is named the common dialog control. This particular control gives your projects access to standard Windows 95 dialog boxes, including Save As, Open, Print, Font, and Color. By using this control, you avoid having to recreate these dialog boxes, and you ensure that your application will have the same basic operations as other Windows programs. In this chapter, you'll explore the use of the common dialog control as an example of an additional component you can add to a project.

Adding Components to a Project

To add controls to the Toolbox for use in a particular project, you simply make a selection from the Components dialog box. Here is an outline of the steps:

1. Start a new project, or open the existing project in which you want to use new controls.
2. Choose Project⇨Components.
3. Scroll through the list of controls, and click the check box for any controls you want to include in the current project.
4. Click OK.

When you complete these steps, the Toolbox displays new icons representing the components you've added. If you wish, you can resize the Toolbox (by dragging its right border) to display its contents in a more convenient arrangement. For example, Figure 12-5 shows a Toolbox containing an expanded selection of controls, selected from the Components dialog box.

Figure 12-5: When you select items from the Components dialog box, the selected controls are represented as icons in the Toolbox. You can resize the Toolbox to display these icons conveniently.

All of the ActiveX controls included in the Visual Basic editions are extensively documented in online help. You can find information about events, properties, and methods that apply to a selected control, as well as general instructions for using the control. Some components are as easy to use as any of the intrinsic controls; others can be complex and detailed, almost like small programming environments in themselves.

As an example of a component that you can add to a project, you'll examine the common dialog control in this chapter's application example, named the Transportation Planner program. The program is designed to help you record information about the various modes of transportation you might use on multiple legs of a business trip or vacation. For trips by plane, train, bus, or car, the Transportation Planner program helps you keep track of travel reservations and schedules. You can use the program to create any number of itinerary databases on disk. As you'll see shortly, the program's file-handling interface is provided by the common dialog control.

The Transportation Planner Program

The project's name on disk is TranPlan.Vbp. When you open it, you'll see that the application consists of one form, named frmTranPlan. Before you run the program for the first time, open the form in design mode to take a look at the controls it contains. In Figure 12-6 you can see the assortment of controls representing various fields of a single transportation record; you'll examine these controls in detail shortly. For now, take a close look at the small, perhaps unfamiliar, control located at the right side of the form, beneath the check boxes labeled Reserved and Paid. This is the common dialog control. Although it has no associated events and offers no direct interaction with the user, its presence on the form gives the application access to Windows-style dialog boxes for opening and saving files.

Adding Tabs to the Toolbox

If you find yourself adding many new components to the Toolbox, you might want to organize controls in separate tabbed groups. In the Toolbar, a tab is simply a button that represents a category of controls you've selected from the Components dialog box. To view the contents of a particular group, you click the corresponding tab button.

To add a tab, click inside the Toolbox with the right mouse button, and choose the Add Tab command from the resulting pop-up menu, as in Figure 12-6. In the resulting dialog box, shown in Figure 12-7, enter a short name for the tab you're creating and then click OK. As you can see in Figure 12-8, the new tab button appears at the bottom of the Toolbox.

Figure 12-6

The next step is to select a group of controls to place in this new tab. To do so, click the tab button at the bottom of the Toolbox; as a result, the tab button moves to the top of the Toolbox and becomes the current tab. Then press Ctrl+T to open the Components dialog box. Select the controls you want to add, and click OK. The selection of controls appears under the current tab, as shown in Figure 12-9.

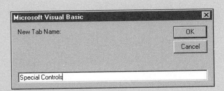

Figure 12-7

Add more tabs to the Toolbox if you wish. To work with a particular group of controls that you've added, simply click the corresponding tab in the Toolbox.

To remove a tab, click it with the right mouse button and choose Delete Tab. You cannot delete the General tab.

Figure 12-8

Figure 12-9

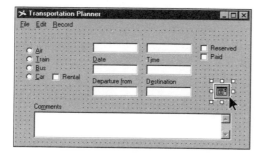

Figure 12-10: The Transportation Planner form in design mode. The common dialog control (here surrounded by selection handles, at the right side of the form) represents the availability of standard Windows dialog boxes for use in this project.

Now press F5 or click the Start button on the toolbar to begin a performance of the program. During a run, the common dialog control disappears completely from the dialog box, as you can see in Figure 12-11. Nonetheless, you'll experience the benefit of its presence as you explore the program's features.

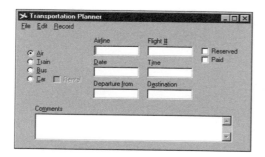

Figure 12-11: The Transportation Planner dialog box during a run. Notice that the common dialog control no longer appears on the form.

The program's dialog box is designed to accept or display one complete transportation record. The fields of a record include:

◆ The transportation mode, which you indicate by selecting one of the four option buttons at the left side of the form — Air, Train, Bus, or Car. (If you select the Car option, you can also specify whether or not the car is a rental; this option is itself a separate field in the travel record.)

◆ The name of the airline, train line, bus line, or car rental agency

◆ The flight number, or the number associated with the train or bus route. If the Car Rental option is selected, this field is available for a reservation number.

◆ The reservation status (reserved or not)

◆ The payment status (paid or not)

✦ The date of departure

✦ The time of departure

✦ The place where your trip begins

✦ The destination of the trip

✦ A set of notes, comments, reminders, plans, or ideas that you want to record about this particular leg of the trip

For example, Figure 12-12 shows a first record that has been entered into the application window. In this case, the record describes an airline flight that has been reserved and paid for in advance. Of the application's seven text boxes, six are designed to accept short text entries, but the seventh (at the bottom of the window) is a multiline box in which you can enter as many as 200 characters, or approximately 40 words.

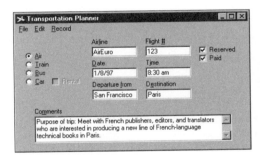

Figure 12-12: Entering a first travel record into the Transportation Planner window. As you begin entering records, you'll notice that the labels for some fields change when you select a new transportation mode.

A transportation file that you create with this program may contain any number of individual travel records like this one. Together, these records are meant to describe a complete itinerary — that is, all the segments of an upcoming business trip or vacation that you're planning.

The program allows you to enter one initial travel record for any trip without first specifying a file name for saving the itinerary database. But to continue your work, you need to save the file to disk. As you might expect in this menu-driven application, the Save As command is located in the File menu. As indicated in Figure 12-13, you can invoke this command either by choosing it directly from the menu list or by pressing Ctrl+A at the keyboard. Either way, the Save As dialog box appears on the screen, as in Figure 12-14.

Take a moment to examine the features of the Save As window. This dialog box is the same one that appears when you choose the Save As command in any other Windows 95 application. In the center of the window is a large box that shows the folders on your hard disk; when you begin creating travel files, this window will

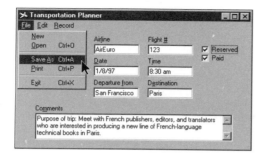

Figure 12-13: Choosing the Save As command from the File menu. You can pull down the File menu and choose the command, or you can press Ctrl+A to open the Save As dialog box.

Figure 12-14: The Save As dialog box contains all the elements familiar to Windows 95 users, including navigation tools and directory format options.

also list them. Above the file list you can see a variety of tools designed for navigating to different directories, creating new folders, or changing the way the file list is displayed. Beneath the file list is a text box where you'll enter the name for the new file you're about to create. The Save as type box indicates the type of file that the program will create. As you can see, the Transportation Planner application automatically adds a TRV extension to any file name you enter.

There are other features to notice in the Save As dialog box. If you position the mouse pointer over certain objects in the box (in particular, the buttons located above the file list), a small ToolTip box appears, explaining the purpose of the object. For additional help, you can click the **?** button at the right side of the title bar and then click any other object in the window; a help box appears on the screen. All of these features are built-in elements of the Windows 95 Save As dialog box. The Transportation Planner application inherits the benefit of these features automatically through the services of the common dialog control.

To complete the Save operation, enter a name for the travel file you want to create and click the Save button. By default, the program saves TRV files in the root directory of your hard disk. When you complete the Save As operation, the program's dialog box returns to view. But now the title bar displays the name of the file you're creating and the record number of the travel segment currently displayed in the window. For example, in Figure 12-15 you can see the new title bar caption:

```
Transportation Planner — C:\Paris.trv, #1
```

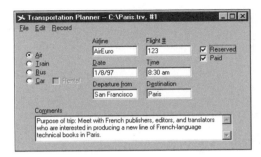

Figure 12-15: When you complete a Save As operation, the current file name appears on the program's title bar.

Now that you've saved your work as a TRV file, the program allows you to create new records and scroll from one record to the next. At the moment, the file contains only the one record that you initially entered into the dialog box, but you can scroll one record further, to the blank record #2. To do so, choose Record⇨Next, or simply press the PgDn key at the keyboard. As you can see in Figure 12-16, the program presents a blank set of controls, ready for you to enter the fields of the second travel record. To view the first record again, simply choose Record⇨Previous, or press PgUp at the keyboard.

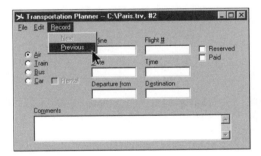

Figure 12-16: After a Save As operation, record #2 contains blank fields, ready for you to enter information for the second leg of your trip. To scroll back to the first record, choose Record⇨Previous, or press PgUp.

Figures 12-17, 12-18, and 12-19 show three additional records that have been entered into a travel file, each illustrating a different mode of transportation. If you examine these figures carefully, you'll see that the program makes a variety of small but important changes in the dialog box itself in response to your selection of a transportation mode. Most obviously, the labels displayed above the first two text boxes are adjusted to represent the travel mode selection. When you choose the Car option (Figure 12-19), the program activates the Rental check box, allowing you to specify whether or not you're planning to rent a car. If you check this box, the Rental Agency and Reservation number text boxes are available to accept your entries; if not, these fields are dimmed.

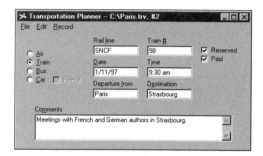

Figure 12-17: Traveling by train. The dialog box supplies fields for the rail line and the train number.

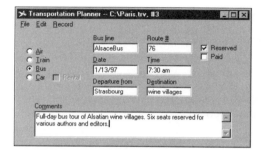

Figure 12-18: Traveling by bus. The program provides fields for the bus line and the route number.

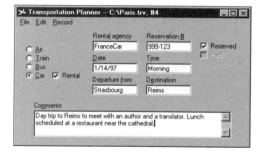

Figure 12-19: Traveling by car. If the car is a rental, the program supplies fields for the name of the rental agency, the reservation status, and a reservation number (available only if the Reserved box is checked).

Each time you enter a new travel record and scroll forward (or backward) in your itinerary database, the program automatically saves the new record to the file on disk. Furthermore, you can scroll to an existing record in the file at any time and make changes in the information that the record contains. Again, when you scroll to a different record, the program automatically saves your revisions to disk. For this reason, the program doesn't provide a Save command for saving individual records. Whenever you work with a travel file, the program always makes sure that any new or revised records are saved to the file.

Over time, you may find yourself creating a number of TRV files to record the details of business trips or vacation travel. When each trip is over, these files remain on disk as a record of your travels. To review any existing file for a past or future trip, you can open the corresponding TRV file from disk and examine its records one by one. Simply pull down the program's File menu and choose the Open command. The Open dialog box appears on the screen, as shown in Figure 12-20. This window provides a list of all the TRV files you've created. (By default the program shows the contents of the root directory of your hard disk.) To open a file, choose its name in the list and click Open. Then, back in the program's main dialog box, choose the Previous command (or press PgUp repeatedly) to scroll back through the existing records in the file you've opened. Of course, you're always free to revise existing records or add new records to the file.

Figure 12-20: The Open dialog box shows a list of all the TRV files you've created using the Transportation Planner program. The elements of this dialog box are familiar to anyone who has used application software in Windows 95.

Like the Save As window, the Open dialog box is the same as the one used for all standard Windows 95 applications. Thanks to the common dialog control, you don't have to redesign these dialog boxes for each application you create; rather, you can incorporate them automatically into the operations of your program, and take advantage of all their built-in features.

As in many applications, the Save As command has two possible uses. The first, as you've seen, is to create a new file on disk to save a new set of travel records that you're planning to enter. But you can also use Save As to create a *duplicate* file containing the same records as a file you've already created and opened. Consider this scenario: You and a colleague are planning a sales trip to Europe. You're traveling together to France, but then you're planning to split up and proceed in different directions. The first several records in your itinerary files will therefore be identical, but the remaining records will be different. Here are the steps you might take to create the two travel files for yourself and your colleague:

1. Start the Transportation Planner program and enter the first travel record.

2. Choose the Save As command and create a file for your own itinerary records.

3. Continue entering travel records up until the point where your own travel plans diverge from your colleague's.

4. Choose the Save As command again, but this time enter a different file name to create your colleague's travel file, as in Figure 12-21. When you complete the Save operation, there will be two travel files on disk — your file and your colleague's file — containing the same set of travel records.

5. Continue developing each of the travel files independently, entering the remaining records for each trip.

Figure 12-21: Using the Save As command to create a duplicate of an existing travel file. After this step, you can continue adding records to each travel file individually.

The Save As dialog box also lets you overwrite an existing TRV file. If you do so, the information in the original file will be replaced by the new records you're storing under the existing name. To avoid any inadvertent loss of data, the Save As dialog box displays a warning dialog box on the screen and asks you to confirm that you really want to replace an existing file, as you can see in Figure 12-22. Again, this warning box is a built-in feature of the Save As dialog box; when you examine the code of the Transportation Planner application, you'll see exactly how this warning is produced.

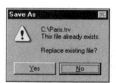

Figure 12-22: A warning box for replacing an existing file. You have the option of going ahead with the Save operation, in which case the new version of the file will overwrite the previous version; or canceling the operation, in which case the original version of the file remains on disk.

The menus of the Transportation Planner program contain several other useful commands. For example, you can clear the contents of any record by choosing Edit⇨Clear. Alternatively, you can close the current Travel file completely — and then start again with a new file of travel records if you want — by choosing File⇨New. By the way, you might notice a couple of apparent conflicts among the shortcut keys defined for menus and controls in the Transportation Planner window: The File menu and the "Departure from" text box both use Alt+F, and the Edit menu and the Destination text box both use Alt+E. You can work around these conflicts by using Alt,F and Alt,E to pull down the menus (that is, press the Alt key, release it, and then press the letter key) and Alt+F and Alt+E to activate the text box controls (press Alt and the letter key concurrently).

Finally, you can use the Print command to produce a printed copy of all the records in any travel file. Begin by opening the file you want to print. Turn on your printer and then choose File⇨Print, as shown in Figure 12-23.

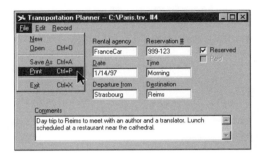

Figure 12-23: To print all the records of a travel file, open the file and then choose File⇨Print. Make sure your printer is ready to operate before you choose this command.

The program prints formatted copies of each record in the file, as in the two printed records in Figure 12-24.

```
Airline -- AirEuro
     #123

   Date:     1/8/97
   Time:     8:30 am
   From:     San Francisco
   To:       Paris

   Reserved: Yes
   Paid:     Yes

   Comments:
   Purpose of trip: Meet with French
   publishers, editors, and translators
   who are interested in producing a new
   line of French-language technical books
   in Paris.


Train Line -- SNCF
     #98

   Date:     1/11/97
   Time:     9:30 am
   From:     Paris
   To:       Strasbourg

   Reserved: Yes
   Paid:     Yes

   Comments:
   Meetings with French and German authors
   in Strasbourg.
```

Figure 12-24: When you print a travel file, the program arranges each record in a convenient and readable format.

As you now turn to the program's code, you'll focus particularly on the use of the common dialog control, and then on the procedures that perform printing operations.

Inside the Transportation Planner Program

The program's code is contained completely within the frmTranPlan form. To examine the code, you can scroll through the procedures in the code window on your screen, or you can turn to Appendix A for a printed copy of the program. In upcoming sections of this chapter, you'll be examining selected procedures in detail. Here is an overview of the code.

In the general declarations section of the frmTranPlan form, shown in Figures 12-25 and 12-26, you can see the structure of the travel records that this program works with:

```
Type TranRecType
   TranMode As Integer
   RentalCar As Boolean
   Carrier As String * 30
   TripNumber As String * 30
   ReservedStatus As Boolean
   PaidStatus As Boolean
   TripDate As String * 30
   TripTime As String * 30
   TripFrom As String * 30
   TripTo As String * 30
   Comments As String * 200
End Type
```

This Type statement contains field definitions for all of the data items in the application window. Notice that the transportation mode (TranMode) is represented as an integer. The three check box fields (RentalCar, ReservedStatus, and PaidStatus) are Boolean values. The remaining fields are fixed-length strings, including the Comments field, which accommodates entries as long as 200 characters.

Figure 12-26 shows the program's global variable declarations. Notice the record variable named *TranRecord,* which belongs to the *TranRecType* record type. In addition, the program declares several variables that keep track of essential conditions and data items during a program run:

```
Dim TranRecord As TranRecType
Dim tranFileOpen As Boolean
Dim tranFileName As String
Dim curTranRecord As Integer
Dim titleBarText As String
Dim recordChanged As Boolean
```

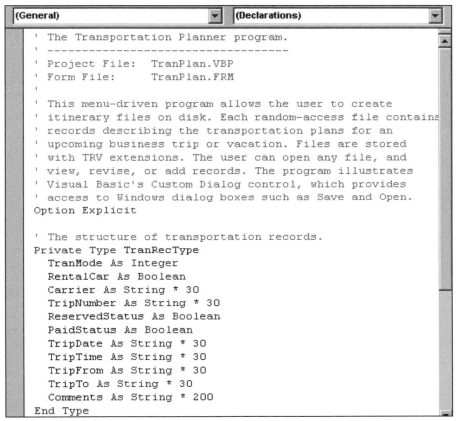

```
(General)                        ▼   (Declarations)                      ▼
  ' The Transportation Planner program.
  ' -----------------------------------
  ' Project File:   TranPlan.VBP
  ' Form File:      TranPlan.FRM
  '
  ' This menu-driven program allows the user to create
  ' itinerary files on disk. Each random-access file contains
  ' records describing the transportation plans for an
  ' upcoming business trip or vacation. Files are stored
  ' with TRV extensions. The user can open any file, and
  ' view, revise, or add records. The program illustrates
  ' Visual Basic's Custom Dialog control, which provides
  ' access to Windows dialog boxes such as Save and Open.
  Option Explicit

  ' The structure of transportation records.
  Private Type TranRecType
    TranMode As Integer
    RentalCar As Boolean
    Carrier As String * 30
    TripNumber As String * 30
    ReservedStatus As Boolean
    PaidStatus As Boolean
    TripDate As String * 30
    TripTime As String * 30
    TripFrom As String * 30
    TripTo As String * 30
    Comments As String * 200
  End Type
```

Figure 12-25: The general declarations section of the frmTranPlan form contains a Type statement to define the structure of transportation records.

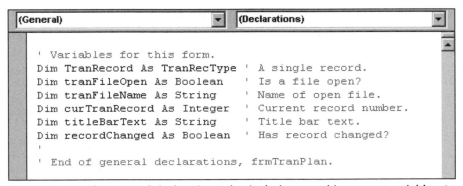

```
(General)                        ▼   (Declarations)                      ▼
    ' Variables for this form.
  Dim TranRecord As TranRecType   ' A single record.
  Dim tranFileOpen As Boolean     ' Is a file open?
  Dim tranFileName As String      ' Name of open file.
  Dim curTranRecord As Integer    ' Current record number.
  Dim titleBarText As String      ' Title bar text.
  Dim recordChanged As Boolean    ' Has record changed?
  '
  ' End of general declarations, frmTranPlan.
```

Figure 12-26: The general declarations also include several important variables. In particular, *TranRecord* is a record variable that represents the current record as it is written to or read from a transportation file.

The Boolean variables *tranFileOpen* and *recordChanged* are among the most important; the first of these indicates whether a Travel file is currently open, and the second keeps track of whether the current record has been changed. The program uses these variables in many contexts to decide how to respond to the user's actions. In addition, *curTranRecord* is an integer that represents the number of the current record. The variables *tranFileName* and *titleBarText* keep track of the name of the open file and the caption displayed on the program's title bar, respectively. Some of these variables are initialized in the program's Form_Load procedure, shown in Figure 12-27.

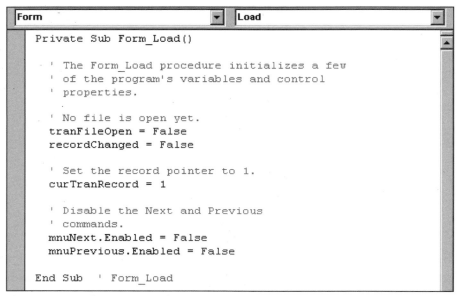

```
Form                          ▼    Load                          ▼

    Private Sub Form_Load()

        ' The Form_Load procedure initializes a few
        ' of the program's variables and control
        ' properties.

        ' No file is open yet.
        tranFileOpen = False
        recordChanged = False

        ' Set the record pointer to 1.
        curTranRecord = 1

        ' Disable the Next and Previous
        ' commands.
        mnuNext.Enabled = False
        mnuPrevious.Enabled = False

    End Sub    ' Form_Load
```

Figure 12-27: The Form_Load procedure initializes several key variables and properties. In particular, notice that the variable named *curTranRecord* is set at a value of 1. This variable represents the number of the current record.

A variety of procedures are devoted to the tasks of creating a new travel file or a duplicate of an existing file. First, the mnuSaveAs_Click procedure takes charge when the user chooses the Save As command. This procedure illustrates the essential characteristics of the common dialog control, which is employed here to display the Save As dialog box. Then several related procedures play important roles in the process of saving or copying a travel database. Conversely, the mnuOpen_Click procedure responds when the user invokes the Open command. Like mnuSaveAs_Click, this event procedure uses the common dialog control and a variety of general procedures to complete its task. You'll have an opportunity to examine these procedures later in this chapter.

The mnuNext_Click and mnuPrevious_Click routines appear in Figures 12-28 and 12-29. These are the event procedures that allow the user to scroll through the records of an open travel database. In Figure 12-30, the Form_KeyDown procedure (versions of which you've seen in other applications) allows the user to press PgUp or PgDn at the keyboard as an alternative to choosing the Previous or Next command. Once the program has read the next or previous record from the database on disk (a task performed in the mnuNext_Click or mnuPrevious_Click procedure), the *ShowRecord* procedure — shown in Figures 12-31 and 12-32 — is called to display the new record in the application window.

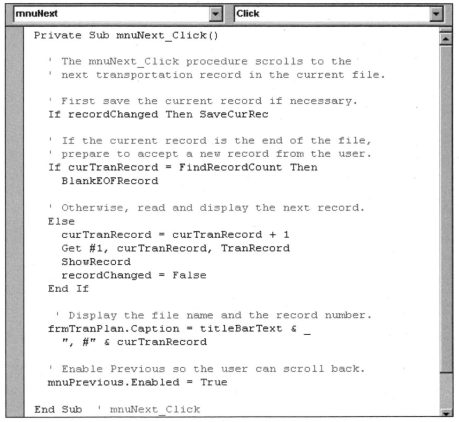

```
mnuNext                          ▼    Click                          ▼

    Private Sub mnuNext_Click()

      ' The mnuNext_Click procedure scrolls to the
      ' next transportation record in the current file.

      ' First save the current record if necessary.
      If recordChanged Then SaveCurRec

      ' If the current record is the end of the file,
      ' prepare to accept a new record from the user.
      If curTranRecord = FindRecordCount Then
        BlankEOFRecord

      ' Otherwise, read and display the next record.
      Else
        curTranRecord = curTranRecord + 1
        Get #1, curTranRecord, TranRecord
        ShowRecord
        recordChanged = False
      End If

      ' Display the file name and the record number.
      frmTranPlan.Caption = titleBarText & _
        ", #" & curTranRecord

      ' Enable Previous so the user can scroll back.
      mnuPrevious.Enabled = True

    End Sub   ' mnuNext_Click
```

Figure 12-28: The mnuNext_Click procedure is called when the user chooses the Next command or presses PgDn. The procedure saves the current record and displays the next one.

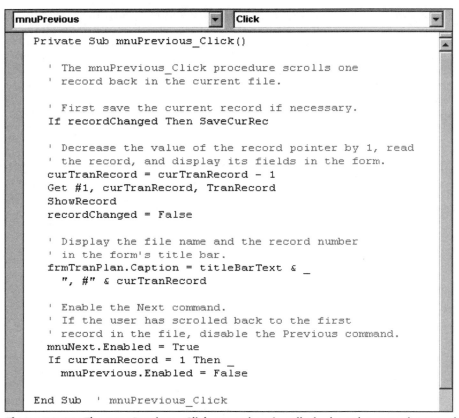

| mnuPrevious | ▼ | Click | ▼ |

```
Private Sub mnuPrevious_Click()

  ' The mnuPrevious_Click procedure scrolls one
  ' record back in the current file.

  ' First save the current record if necessary.
  If recordChanged Then SaveCurRec

  ' Decrease the value of the record pointer by 1, read
  ' the record, and display its fields in the form.
  curTranRecord = curTranRecord - 1
  Get #1, curTranRecord, TranRecord
  ShowRecord
  recordChanged = False

  ' Display the file name and the record number
  ' in the form's title bar.
  frmTranPlan.Caption = titleBarText & _
    ", #" & curTranRecord

  ' Enable the Next command.
  ' If the user has scrolled back to the first
  ' record in the file, disable the Previous command.
  mnuNext.Enabled = True
  If curTranRecord = 1 Then _
    mnuPrevious.Enabled = False

End Sub  ' mnuPrevious_Click
```

Figure 12-29: The mnuPrevious_Click procedure is called when the user chooses the Previous command or presses PgUp. The procedure saves the current record and displays the previous one.

When the user chooses File⇨Print, the event procedure named mnuPrint_Click takes charge of printing each record of the current file, from beginning to end. This procedure reads each record in turn, and then calls the *PrintRecord* proce-dure to carry out the printing operation. The *PrintComments* procedure carries out the somewhat complex task of dividing the Comments field into manageable lines of printed output. As you'll see later in this chapter, these procedures illustrate the use of Visual Basic's important Printer object.

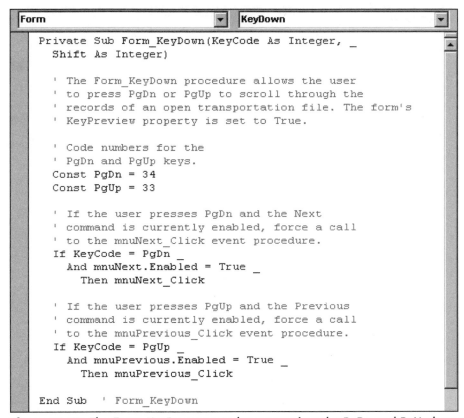

```
Form                          ▼    KeyDown                        ▼
    Private Sub Form_KeyDown(KeyCode As Integer, _
      Shift As Integer)

      ' The Form_KeyDown procedure allows the user
      ' to press PgDn or PgUp to scroll through the
      ' records of an open transportation file. The form's
      ' KeyPreview property is set to True.

      ' Code numbers for the
      ' PgDn and PgUp keys.
      Const PgDn = 34
      Const PgUp = 33

      ' If the user presses PgDn and the Next
      ' command is currently enabled, force a call
      ' to the mnuNext_Click event procedure.
      If KeyCode = PgDn _
        And mnuNext.Enabled = True _
          Then mnuNext_Click

      ' If the user presses PgUp and the Previous
      ' command is currently enabled, force a call
      ' to the mnuPrevious_Click event procedure.
      If KeyCode = PgUp _
        And mnuPrevious.Enabled = True _
          Then mnuPrevious_Click

    End Sub   ' Form_KeyDown
```

Figure 12-30: The Form_KeyDown procedure recognizes the PgDn and PgUp keys as signals for a record change.

Several event procedures are designed to respond to menu commands or to the user's activities in the dialog box itself. For example, the mnuNew_Click procedure, in Figure 12-33, closes the current file and prepares the dialog box for the possible creation of a new database. Other Click procedures keep track of any changes in the travel mode option buttons or the application's three check boxes. And a sequence of Change event procedures allow the program to keep track of whether the user has modified the current record.

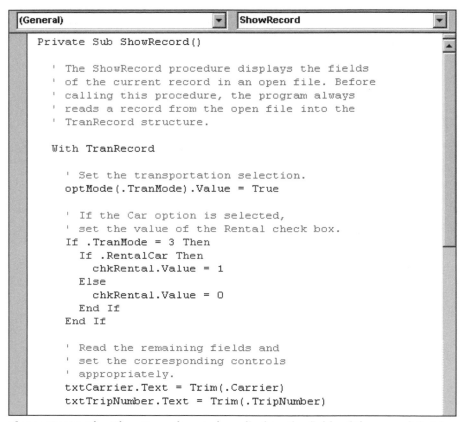

Figure 12-31: The *ShowRecord* procedure displays the fields of the record that have been most recently read from the current database.

Among the program's most interesting techniques are the two different uses it makes of the common dialog control. You'll learn about this control in the next section.

Using the common dialog control

To use the common dialog control in an application, you begin by placing an instance of the object on a form. As with any other control, you can accomplish this task by opening the form and double-clicking the appropriate button in the Toolbox. Because this control isn't visible at runtime, its precise location in the form is unimportant; you can drag it to any out-of-the-way corner of your form. Unlike most controls, the common dialog icon can't be resized, but its presence on your form at design time serves to remind you that the considerable resources of this control are available to your program.

```
(General)                    ▼   ShowRecord                    ▼
        If .ReservedStatus Then
          chkReserved.Value = 1
        Else
          chkReserved.Value = 0
        End If

        If .PaidStatus Then
          chkPaid.Value = 1
        Else
          chkPaid.Value = 0
        End If

        txtDate.Text = Trim(.TripDate)
        txtTime.Text = Trim(.TripTime)
        txtFrom.Text = Trim(.TripFrom)
        txtTo.Text = Trim(.TripTo)

        txtNotes.Text = Trim(.Comments)

      End With

    End Sub  ' ShowRecord
```

Figure 12-32: Some of the information that the *ShowRecord* procedure displays depends on the transportation mode selection and the Boolean values of the reserved and paid fields.

As you'll see shortly, the common dialog control has several important properties. Some of these you'll want to set at design time; others, in your program's code. To ensure that you can identify the control consistently in your code, the first property you should assign is Name. (Select the control, scroll to the Name property in the Properties window, and enter a name for the control.) In the Transportation Planner application, the common dialog control is named cdlFileManager.

The control has several associated methods, each designed to display and activate one of the standard Windows dialog boxes. These methods include ShowPrint, ShowColor, ShowFont, ShowOpen, and ShowSave. (An additional method, ShowHelp, is available to invoke the Windows online Help facility.) To open a particular dialog box, you simply make a call to one of these methods in your code. For example, the following call appears in the mnuSaveAs_Click procedure, which you can examine in Figures 12-34 and 12-35:

```
cdlFileManager.ShowSave
```

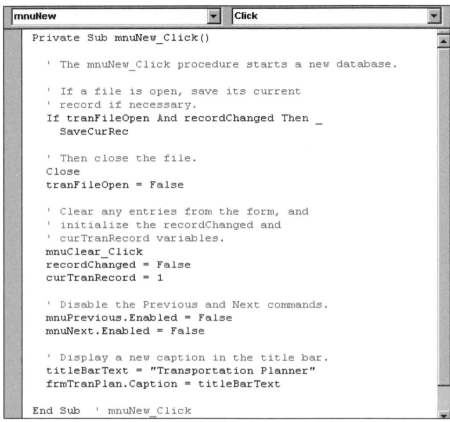

```
mnuNew                              ▼   Click                              ▼

      Private Sub mnuNew_Click()

        ' The mnuNew_Click procedure starts a new database.

        ' If a file is open, save its current
        ' record if necessary.
        If tranFileOpen And recordChanged Then _
          SaveCurRec

        ' Then close the file.
        Close
        tranFileOpen = False

        ' Clear any entries from the form, and
        ' initialize the recordChanged and
        ' curTranRecord variables.
        mnuClear_Click
        recordChanged = False
        curTranRecord = 1

         ' Disable the Previous and Next commands.
        mnuPrevious.Enabled = False
        mnuNext.Enabled = False

         ' Display a new caption in the title bar.
        titleBarText = "Transportation Planner"
        frmTranPlan.Caption = titleBarText

      End Sub  ' mnuNew_Click
```

Figure 12-33: The mnuNew_Click procedure is called when the user chooses the New command from the File menu. It closes the current database and prepares for the creation of a new one.

And this call is in the mnuOpen_Click procedure, shown in Figures 12-36 and 12-37:

```
cdlFileManager.ShowOpen
```

During a program run, these calls give the user access to the Save As and Open dialog boxes, respectively.

Setting the properties of the common dialog control

Among the properties available for the common dialog control, certain settings apply specifically to particular Windows dialog boxes. For example, the following five properties have important meanings for the Save As and Open dialog boxes, invoked by the ShowSave and ShowOpen methods:

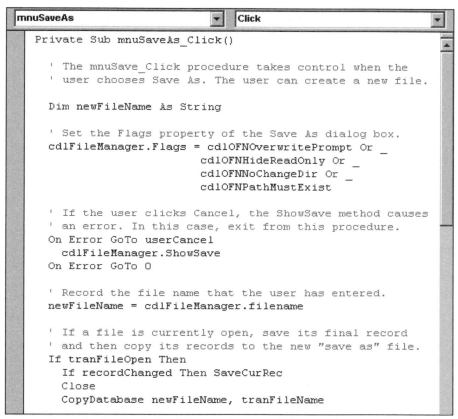

```
mnuSaveAs                    ▼   Click                        ▼

Private Sub mnuSaveAs_Click()

  ' The mnuSave_Click procedure takes control when the
  ' user chooses Save As. The user can create a new file.

  Dim newFileName As String

  ' Set the Flags property of the Save As dialog box.
  cdlFileManager.Flags = cdlOFNOverwritePrompt Or _
                         cdlOFNHideReadOnly Or _
                         cdlOFNNoChangeDir Or _
                         cdlOFNPathMustExist

  ' If the user clicks Cancel, the ShowSave method causes
  ' an error. In this case, exit from this procedure.
  On Error GoTo userCancel
    cdlFileManager.ShowSave
  On Error GoTo 0

  ' Record the file name that the user has entered.
  newFileName = cdlFileManager.filename

  ' If a file is currently open, save its final record
  ' and then copy its records to the new "save as" file.
  If tranFileOpen Then
    If recordChanged Then SaveCurRec
    Close
    CopyDatabase newFileName, tranFileName
```

Figure 12-34: In the first half of the mnuSaveAs_Click procedure, a call to the ShowSave method opens the Save As dialog box. Notice the error trap, which is triggered if the user clicks Cancel on the dialog box.

✦ The InitDir property designates the directory that will be displayed when the Save As or Open dialog box first appears on the screen. In the Transportation Planner program, this property has a setting of \ so that the dialog boxes will initially show the contents of the root directory.

✦ The DefaultExt property provides a default extension for file names entered into the Save As dialog box. For example, the setting of *trv* provides the default extension name for files created from the Transportation Planner program.

✦ The Filter property determines the types of files that will be displayed in the Open and Save As dialog boxes. A filter setting includes a file-type description and a file name extension, in the form *description|extension*. (Notice that the two parts of this definition are separated by the vertical line character, |, sometimes known as the *pipe symbol*.) The Filter property setting in the Transportation Planner program is *Travel (*.trv)|*.trv*. You can see the

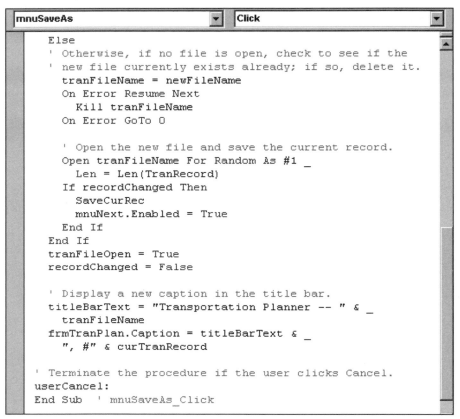

```
mnuSaveAs          ▼    Click              ▼

      Else
      ' Otherwise, if no file is open, check to see if the
      ' new file currently exists already; if so, delete it.
        tranFileName = newFileName
        On Error Resume Next
          Kill tranFileName
        On Error GoTo 0

        ' Open the new file and save the current record.
        Open tranFileName For Random As #1 _
          Len = Len(TranRecord)
        If recordChanged Then
          SaveCurRec
          mnuNext.Enabled = True
        End If
      End If
      tranFileOpen = True
      recordChanged = False

      ' Display a new caption in the title bar.
      titleBarText = "Transportation Planner -- " & _
        tranFileName
      frmTranPlan.Caption = titleBarText & _
        ", #" & curTranRecord

    ' Terminate the procedure if the user clicks Cancel.
    userCancel:
    End Sub  ' mnuSaveAs_Click
```

Figure 12-35: The second half of the mnuSaveAs_Click procedure creates the new file and saves the current record.

results of this setting back in Figures 12-14 and 12-20. The "Files of type" box displays the text *Travel (*.trv),* and the file list (in Figure 12-20) includes only those files that have TRV extensions.

✦ The CancelError property is a Boolean setting that indicates whether an error will be generated when the user clicks the Cancel button on a Windows dialog box. When you assign a value of True to this property, your program can read the resulting error as a signal that the Cancel button has been clicked; in response, your program should be prepared to skip the subsequent file operation. You'll see exactly how the Transportation Planner program makes use of this property a little later in this chapter.

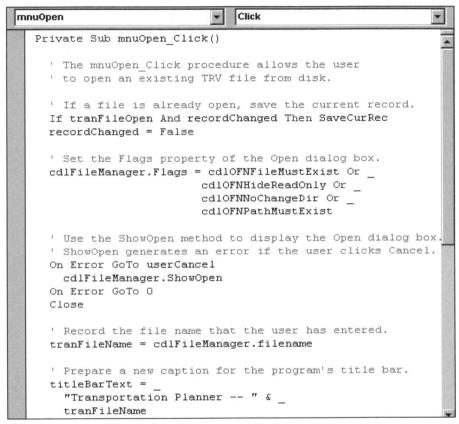

```
mnuOpen ▼    Click ▼

Private Sub mnuOpen_Click()

    ' The mnuOpen_Click procedure allows the user
    ' to open an existing TRV file from disk.

    ' If a file is already open, save the current record.
    If tranFileOpen And recordChanged Then SaveCurRec
    recordChanged = False

    ' Set the Flags property of the Open dialog box.
    cdlFileManager.Flags = cdlOFNFileMustExist Or _
                           cdlOFNHideReadOnly Or _
                           cdlOFNNoChangeDir Or _
                           cdlOFNPathMustExist

    ' Use the ShowOpen method to display the Open dialog box.
    ' ShowOpen generates an error if the user clicks Cancel.
    On Error GoTo userCancel
        cdlFileManager.ShowOpen
    On Error GoTo 0
    Close

    ' Record the file name that the user has entered.
    tranFileName = cdlFileManager.filename

    ' Prepare a new caption for the program's title bar.
    titleBarText = _
        "Transportation Planner -- " & _
        tranFileName
```

Figure 12-36: In the first half of the mnuOpen_Click procedure, a call to the ShowOpen method displays the Open dialog box. An error trap is triggered if the user clicks Cancel. Before the call to ShowOpen, the procedure sets flags to define the features of the Open dialog box.

✦ The MaxFileSize property is an integer setting that specifies the maximum *name* length, in characters, of a file you can open or save from one of the Windows dialog boxes. (The setting applies to the length of the path name and the file name together.) In the Transportation Planner application, this property has a fairly low setting of 20, allowing the program to display the entire file name and path in the title bar. But this setting may restrict not only the length of the file names you devise, but also the directory locations in which you can save your transportation files. If you don't like these restrictions, enter a larger setting for the MaxFileSize property. (The default setting is 256.)

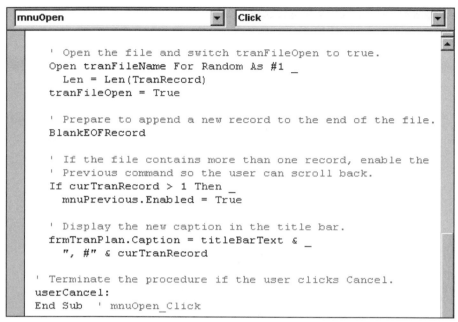

```
mnuOpen                            ▼   Click                              ▼

      ' Open the file and switch tranFileOpen to true.
      Open tranFileName For Random As #1 _
        Len = Len(TranRecord)
      tranFileOpen = True

      ' Prepare to append a new record to the end of the file.
      BlankEOFRecord

      ' If the file contains more than one record, enable the
      ' Previous command so the user can scroll back.
      If curTranRecord > 1 Then _
        mnuPrevious.Enabled = True

      ' Display the new caption in the title bar.
      frmTranPlan.Caption = titleBarText & _
        ", #" & curTranRecord

    ' Terminate the procedure if the user clicks Cancel.
    userCancel:
    End Sub  ' mnuOpen_Click
```

Figure 12-37: The second half of the mnuOpen_Click procedure opens the new file and prepares to accept a new record entry from the user.

As always, you can enter settings for these and other properties directly into the Properties window. But Visual Basic provides a convenient alternative for working with the properties of the common dialog control. In the Misc category of the Properties window, you'll find an entry identified as "(Custom)", as shown in Figure 12-38. Select this entry and click the small button that appears at the right side of the settings box. In response, Visual Basic displays the Property Pages box, which you can see in Figure 12-39. This tabbed dialog box gives you a quick way to set the properties for any of the functional categories of this control.

Figure 12-38: In the Misc category of the Properties window for the common dialog control, the (Custom) entry gives you access to a convenient window for setting properties.

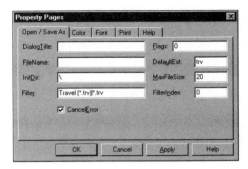

Figure 12-39: The Property Pages dialog box is a tabbed window in which you can choose settings for the common dialog control.

One additional property, named Flags, is essential for defining the behavior and characteristics of the dialog boxes for a particular application. You'll learn about the Flags property next.

Working with the common dialog control in code

In both the mnuSaveAs_Click and mnuOpen_Click procedures, the use of the common dialog control requires three main steps:

1. Set the Flags property to establish the characteristics of the Save As or Open dialog box.

2. Call the ShowSave or ShowOpen method within the control of an error trap. (If the user clicks the Cancel button on the resulting dialog box, the error trap allows the procedure to avoid any further action.)

3. Read the value of the FileName property to find out the name of the file that the user has entered or selected in the dialog box.

The Flags property is the key to ensuring that a Windows dialog box will work just the way you want it to in a particular application. For example, in the Transportation Planner program, the Save As dialog box provides a warning message if the user selects an existing file name. Look back at Figure 12-22 to review this feature. The warning is a result of a specific setting of the Flags property.

Visual Basic defines a variety of flags for each common dialog box. Each flag is represented by a constant whose name begins with *cdl*. The setting that produces an *existing file* warning message in the Save As dialog box is a flag named cdlOFNOverwritePrompt. This is one of four flags that the mnuSaveAs_Click procedure uses, as you can see back in Figure 12-34:

```
cdlFileManager.Flags = cdlOFNOverwritePrompt Or _
                       cdlOFNHideReadOnly Or _
                       cdlOFNNoChangeDir Or _
                       cdlOFNPathMustExist
```

The other three flags specify a variety of characteristics: omitting the Read Only check box (cdlOFNHideReadOnly); ensuring a consistent directory location for the Save operation (cdlOFNNoChangeDir); and validating the directory path (cdlOFNPathMustExist).

The mnuOpen_Click procedure (shown back in Figure 12-36) uses a slightly different set of flags to specify the behavior of the Open dialog box:

```
cdlFileManager.Flags = cdlOFNFileMustExist Or _
                       cdlOFNHideReadOnly Or _
                       cdlOFNNoChangeDir Or _
                       cdlOFNPathMustExist
```

The first of these flags, cdlOFNFileMustExist, prevents an attempt to open a nonexistent file; if the user enters a file name that can't be found on disk, the Open dialog box displays an error message. The other three flags are the same as those used for the Save As dialog box.

After setting the Flags property, each event procedure is ready to make a call to the appropriate common dialog method, ShowSave or ShowOpen. Thanks to the True setting assigned to the CancelError property, the method generates an error if the user clicks the Cancel button. To recognize this error, each method is called within an error trap. For example, here is how the mnuSaveAs_Click procedure calls the ShowSave method (Figure 12-34):

```
On Error GoTo userCancel
  cdlFileManager.ShowSave
On Error GoTo 0
```

If the error occurs — that is, if the user clicks Cancel instead of Save on the dialog box — the On Error GoTo statement arranges to send control to the *userCancel* label, located at the very end of the procedure (Figure 12-35):

```
userCancel:
End Sub   ' mnuSaveAs_Click
```

In this way, the action of the procedure is skipped completely if the user decides to cancel the Save As operation.

But if the user enters a valid file name and clicks Save, the procedure's next step is to find out the name of the file. As you might expect, a common dialog property named FileName supplies this essential piece of information:

```
newFileName = cdlFileManager.FileName
```

Eliciting this file name from the user is the whole purpose of the Save As or Open dialog box. Once the name is available, the program continues with the file operation, either creating a new travel database on disk or opening an existing database. You can continue exploring the mnuSaveAs_Click and mnuOpen_Click procedures to see exactly how these tasks are carried out.

Common dialog is only one of many components that you might decide to incorporate into the applications you design. Each control listed in the Components dialog box has specific properties, methods, and events that you need to learn about in detail before you can use the object successfully.

The Transportation Planner application illustrates a variety of other programming techniques that are worth exploring. Among these is the use of the Printer object to produce a printed copy of the current travel file. You'll take a look at the printing procedures in the final section of this chapter.

Using the Printer object

The Printer object represents the default system printer in a Visual Basic application. Using the various properties and methods defined for this object, you can prepare a document for printing. Then your program makes a call to a method named EndDoc to release your document to the printer.

In the Transportation Planner application, the mnuPrint_Click procedure (Figure 12-40) is designed to print all the records of the current travel database. Assuming a file is open, the procedure reads each record from the beginning to the end of the file, and calls a procedure named *PrintRecord* to carry out the printing:

```
For i = 1 To FindRecordCount
   Get #1, i, TranRecord
   PrintRecord
Next i
```

The *PrintRecord* procedure (Figures 12-41 and 12-42) in turn uses the Print method to send individual lines of text to the Printer object, as in the following example:

```
Printer.Print
Printer.Print Tab(t1); "Date:";
Printer.Print Tab(t2); .TripDate
Printer.Print Tab(t1); "Time:";
Printer.Print Tab(t2); .TripTime
Printer.Print Tab(t1); "From:";
Printer.Print Tab(t2); .TripFrom
Printer.Print Tab(t1); "To:";
Printer.Print Tab(t2); .TripTo
Printer.Print
```

Notice the various formats of the Print method. The Tab function allows you to specify where the horizontal position of the line will begin. A semicolon separates one element from the next in the list of values that will be printed. If a call to the Print method ends in a semicolon, the line-feed/carriage-return is suppressed; as a result, the *next* Print method sends information to the same line of text. Finally, a Printer.Print statement by itself results in a blank line.

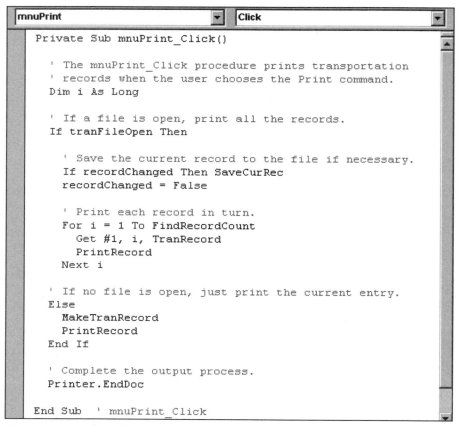

```
mnuPrint                          ▼   Click                              ▼

  Private Sub mnuPrint_Click()

    ' The mnuPrint_Click procedure prints transportation
    ' records when the user chooses the Print command.
    Dim i As Long

    ' If a file is open, print all the records.
    If tranFileOpen Then

      ' Save the current record to the file if necessary.
      If recordChanged Then SaveCurRec
      recordChanged = False

      ' Print each record in turn.
      For i = 1 To FindRecordCount
        Get #1, i, TranRecord
        PrintRecord
      Next i

    ' If no file is open, just print the current entry.
    Else
      MakeTranRecord
      PrintRecord
    End If

    ' Complete the output process.
    Printer.EndDoc

  End Sub  ' mnuPrint_Click
```

Figure 12-40: When the user chooses File⇨Print, the mnuPrint_Click procedure arranges to print each record in the current transportation file. Notice the use of the Printer.EndDoc method to complete the print operation.

When all the records have been sent to the Printer object, the mnuPrint_Click procedure makes a call to the EndDoc method to release the document to the printer:

```
Printer.EndDoc
```

The Print and EndDoc methods are only two of those associated with the Printer object. Other methods are available for a variety of printing operations, including graphic output and document formatting. You can explore these methods by searching for the Printer Object topic in the Visual Basic Help window and then clicking Methods in the resulting Help page.

(General)	▼	PrintRecord	▼

```
Private Sub PrintRecord()
  ' The PrintRecord procedure prints the current record.
  Const t1 = 5    ' First tab stop.
  Const t2 = 15   ' Second tab stop.

  With TranRecord
    Select Case .TranMode ' Print the transportation mode.
      Case 0
        Printer.Print "Airline";
      Case 1
        Printer.Print "Train Line";
      Case 2
        Printer.Print "Bus Line";
      Case 3
        If .RentalCar Then
          Printer.Print "Car Rental Agency";
        Else
          Printer.Print "Private Car"
        End If
    End Select

    ' Print the remaining fields.
    If .TranMode < 3 Then
      Printer.Print " -- "; .Carrier
      Printer.Print Tab(t1); " #"; .TripNumber
    Else
      If .RentalCar Then
        Printer.Print " -- "; .Carrier;
        If .ReservedStatus Then
```

Figure 12-41: The *PrintRecord* procedure illustrates the use of the Printer.Print method to send lines of text to the printer.

In its current version, the Transportation Planner application prints the records of the travel database just as soon as the user chooses the Print command from the File menu. An intervening Print dialog box would give the user much greater control over the process — allowing device selection, multiple copies, and so on. As a hands-on programming exercise with this project, you might consider using the common dialog control to display a Print dialog box before the program goes forward with the printing procedure.

```
(General)                              ▼   PrintRecord                          ▼

                Printer.Print Tab(t1); " #"; .TripNumber
          Else
              Printer.Print
          End If
        End If
      End If
    Printer.Print
    Printer.Print Tab(t1); "Date:";
    Printer.Print Tab(t2); .TripDate
    Printer.Print Tab(t1); "Time:";
    Printer.Print Tab(t2); .TripTime
    Printer.Print Tab(t1); "From:";
    Printer.Print Tab(t2); .TripFrom
    Printer.Print Tab(t1); "To:";
    Printer.Print Tab(t2); .TripTo
    Printer.Print
    If .TranMode < 3 Then
      Printer.Print Tab(t1); "Reserved:";
      Printer.Print Tab(t2); YesNo(.ReservedStatus)
      Printer.Print Tab(t1); "Paid:";
      Printer.Print Tab(t2); YesNo(.PaidStatus)
    End If
    Printer.Print
    Printer.Print Tab(t1); "Comments:"
    PrintComments (RTrim(.Comments))
    Printer.Print
    Printer.Print
  End With
End Sub  ' PrintRecord
```

Figure 12-42: In the second half of the *PrintRecord* procedure, you can see how the program prints each field of the current record.

More Programming Techniques

O nce you've mastered the essentials of Visual Basic programming and project design, there are several interesting new directions to investigate as you continue to expand your understanding of the language. The techniques covered in this final part of the book are some of the most useful ones.

Chapter 13 reviews the significance of classes and objects in Visual Basic. You'll learn the techniques for creating class modules in a project, and you'll see how an application creates instances of objects from a class definition. Along the way, you'll learn how and why to develop property procedures as part of a class module, and you'll see examples of the useful collection object. This chapter's Travel Reminders application illustrates class modules, property procedures, and collections. The program provides check lists to help you keep track of the tasks you need to complete before, during, and after a business trip.

Chapter 14 discusses the use of multiple-document interface (MDI) forms in a Visual Basic application. With an MDI form, a program can allow the user to open and work with more than one document file at a time. A program creates instances of a child form inside the parent MDI form. This technique is illustrated in an MDI version of the Transportation Planner application, which displays as many as five windows to represent the contents of open itinerary files.

Chapter 15 introduces the use of ActiveX components in a Visual Basic project. By creating instances of the objects "exposed" by an ActiveX component — and by setting the properties and calling the methods of these objects — you can exploit the resources of other Windows applications from within your own program. To illustrate ActiveX components, this chapter presents a new version of the International Sales program, which transfers sales data to an Excel worksheet and then issues the instructions necessary to generate an Excel chart from the data.

Chapter 16 shows you how to use the data control and bound controls to create a connection between a Visual Basic form and an external database. The source of the database can be any one of several database and spreadsheet programs, including Access, dBase, or Excel. Remarkably enough, the data control can be used without a single line of code to produce a form in which the user views, edits, and appends records to the attached database. You'll see an example of this approach in the Currency Input program, which you'll develop as a hands-on exercise. Alternatively, you can use programming techniques to work with the records of a connected database, as illustrated in the database version of the Currency Exchange program.

Chapter 17 guides you through the initial steps of developing, testing, and compiling your own ActiveX components in Visual Basic. You'll learn that Visual Basic provides simple starting points for several categories of ActiveX components, including ActiveX EXE, ActiveX DLL, ActiveX Control, and ActiveX Document projects. In this chapter you'll examine a working ActiveX DLL component, along with a project designed to test its behavior. After running the component as part of a project group, you'll learn how to create and use a compiled DLL file.

Chapter 18 introduces the ActiveX Document project, a versatile new tool designed to simplify many programming tasks in today's online environment. Running in Microsoft's Internet Explorer, an ActiveX document provides Internet functionality in the context of a full-featured Visual Basic application. This final chapter provides a simple demonstration for you to run, examine, and compile.

Introduction to Objects, Classes, and Collections

An *object* is a unit of code and data, packaged for convenient use in developing new applications. Objects are the essence of Visual Basic programming. A control is one example of an object. As you work with controls, you quickly develop an intuitive understanding of what objects are about. Each control you place on a form is an object with a consistent and predictable set of characteristics, including:

✦ The *properties* that define the object's appearance and behavior in your application

✦ The *methods* that your program can call to perform specific actions on the object

✦ The *events* that can occur around the object, triggering automatic calls to specific event procedures in your application's code

For example, consider the text box, one of the commonly used objects in Visual Basic programs. When you place a text box on a form, you know in advance that you'll find a specific list of properties for this control in the Properties window. The list includes Name, Text, Width, Height, Font, Multiline, and other text box properties that you've become familiar with. Although you may set the values of these properties independently for each different text box that you create, every text box control has the same list of properties. Likewise, Visual Basic defines a list of methods that your program can call to perform specific operations on text boxes; for example, you can use the SetFocus method to move the focus to a specific text box at runtime.

Furthermore, you can expect each text box to react to particular events during a program performance. One such event, named LostFocus, takes place when the user moves the focus away from the target text box. In your program you can write a txtBox_LostFocus event procedure, presenting specific code that will be performed whenever this event occurs.

Finally, a text box has a variety of built-in characteristics that the user quickly learns to depend on. For example, every text box has editing capabilities such as selection control, deletion, insertion, and cut-and-paste. Because these are part of the definition of a text box, you don't need to write any code to supply these features in your application; they are automatically part of every text box.

A *class* is the actual definition of a specific type of object. For example, the TextBox button in the Visual Basic Toolbox represents the class that defines all text boxes. Each time you place a text box on a form, you are creating an *instance* of the TextBox class. All text box controls belong to this same class; they all have a common set of properties, methods, events, and characteristics defined by the class.

Up to now you've worked with classes of objects that are defined as part of the Visual Basic development environment. In this chapter you'll learn that you can create classes of your own, defining new types of objects for use in applications. You begin defining a class by adding a *class module* to a project. Unlike a form module, a class module has no predefined visual appearance in your running application. Inside a class module you write code to create the characteristics of the class itself:

 ✦ Public variables in the module represent the properties of the class.

 ✦ Special property procedures can define additional class properties. A property procedure contains a block of code that is performed whenever the property setting is changed or accessed.

 ✦ Other public procedures serve as the methods of your class.

The programming techniques for developing the procedures of a class are similar to the steps you've learned for creating the other code components of a Visual Basic project.

Once you've defined a class, your application can create any number of objects belonging to the class. In a program's code, you can use the *New* keyword in a Dim statement to create an instance of a class and to declare a variable to represent the object. You can also define *collections* of objects belonging to one or more classes. A collection is analogous in some ways to an array; but a collection provides different ways of gathering, handling, identifying, and accessing the objects that it contains.

To introduce the use of class modules, procedure properties, objects, and collections in Visual Basic, this chapter presents a simple demonstration program named the Travel Reminders application. When you open this project and run it, the program displays three different check lists of travel reminders in separate forms inside a containing window. The lists contain brief descriptions of tasks that you may typically need to complete before, during, and after a business trip. You can customize these lists to match your own travel habits. In short, the application is designed to help you become a more efficient business traveler.

As you'll learn, this application creates and manages these three lists as instances of a class named ReminderPage, which is defined as a class module in the Reminder project.

The Travel Reminders Application

The project is stored on disk as Reminder.Vbp. Open the application now and take a first look at the Project Explorer window, as shown in Figure 13-1. Three files are listed:

✦ A form module named frmReminder (saved on disk as Reminder.Frm). The program uses this form to display the lists.

✦ A second form named MDIReminder (saved as ReminMDI.Frm). This is a special type of object known as a *multiple-document interface* (or MDI) form. It's designed as a container form for displaying and managing any number of document windows at runtime. In this context, the MDI form is known as the *parent* and any window it contains is known as a *child* form. You'll learn much more about MDI applications in Chapter 14. For now, note that an application may contain only one MDI form. In this program, MDIReminder is the startup form. The code contained in the MDIForm_Load procedure is performed first when the program begins.

✦ A class module named ReminderPage (saved as Reminder.Cls). This module is a self-contained definition for a new class of objects. Once an instance of the ReminderPage class is created at runtime, the module's code is designed to display a frmReminder window at a specified location on the screen, to read the list itself from a text file on disk, and to provide a set of basic operations for managing the list. You'll examine the details of this class module in this chapter.

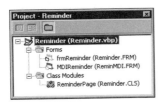

Figure 13-1: The Project Explorer window for the Travel Reminders application. The application contains an MDI form, a standard form module, and a class module.

Before running the program for the first time, select the frmReminder form, the first entry in the Project Explorer window, and click the View Object button. As you can see in Figure 13-2, the form contains a vertically-arranged array of command buttons and a corresponding array of check-box controls. The check boxes are designed to display the list of travel reminders for each ReminderPage object that the program creates. The command buttons give the user the opportunity to change the text of any reminder in the list.

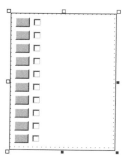

Figure 13-2: The frmReminder form contains two arrays of controls — an array of command buttons named cmdChange, and an array of check boxes named chkReminder. These controls give the user convenient ways to develop and use the lists of travel reminders.

Adding an MDI form and a class module to a project

This project contains two types of files that you haven't worked with before — the MDI form and the class module. Visual Basic's Project menu (Figure 13-3) contains the commands for inserting both of these into a new application that you're developing.

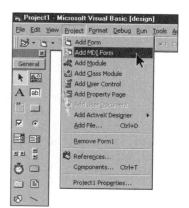

Figure 13-3: The Project menu contains commands for adding file components to a project, including Add MDI Form and Add Class Module. Although you can add any number of class modules to a project, you can add only one MDI form; after the first, the Add MDI Form command is dimmed.

To add an MDI form to a project, choose Project➪Add MDI Form, and click Open on the resulting dialog box. Because a project may have only one such form, the Add MDI Form command is dimmed after you've chosen it for the current project. Like a standard form, an MDI form is saved on disk with an extension name of Frm.

But the MDI form is a different class from an ordinary form; it has its own list of properties and events. If you open the code window for an MDI form, as in Figure 13-4, you'll discover that the names of the form's event procedures begin with the object name MDIForm. For example, the MDI form in the Travel Reminders project contains event procedures named MDIForm_Load, MDIForm_DblClick, and MDIForm_QueryUnload.

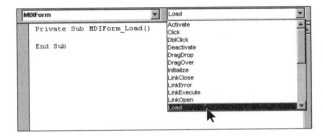

Figure 13-4: The object name for MDI event procedures is MDIForm. For example, MDIForm_Load is the procedure that's called when an MDI form is loaded into memory.

To add a class module to a project, choose Project⇨Add Class Module, and click Open on the resulting dialog box. As you've seen, Visual Basic saves a class module with an extension name of Cls. A project may include one or more class modules. At design time, a class module is represented as a code window in which you develop the declarations, general procedures, and event procedures that define the class. If you open the class module and examine the Properties window, you'll see that the module has only one property, Name, which defines the name of the class.

Visual Basic recognizes two Class events, as you can see in Figure 13-5:

✦ The Class_Initialize event takes place when a program creates a new instance of the class.

✦ The Class_Terminate event takes place when an instance of a class is released from memory.

In the ReminderPage class, the Class_Terminate event is used to perform some important final operations before a given list window is closed. You'll learn more about this event when you examine the program's code.

Figure 13-5: Two event procedures are associated with a class: Class_Initialize and Class_Terminate. In addition to these, you can write any number of general procedures to include in the code of a class module.

Running the Travel Reminders program

Now press F5 to start a first run of the application. A maximized window named Travel Reminders appears on the screen; within this window, the program displays three smaller windows labeled "Before Trip," "During Trip," and "After Trip." (As you'll discover later in this chapter, each of these is produced by an instance of the ReminderPage class.) At the outset, the reminder lists are all empty and all the check boxes are unchecked, as you can see in Figure 13-6.

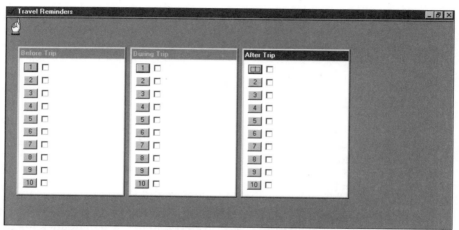

Figure 13-6: The three reminder pages, displayed as windows inside the Travel Reminders application window. Initially the lists are empty and the check boxes unchecked.

To begin developing your reminder lists, follow these steps:

1. Activate any one of the three windows. You can activate a list window by clicking its title bar with the mouse, or by pressing Ctrl+Tab repeatedly until the target window is active.

2. Click one of the numbered command buttons (or press Tab repeatedly until the target button is active, and press the spacebar to "click" it). When you do, the program displays an input box on the screen, prompting you to enter the text of a new reminder.

3. Type the reminder into the text box, as in Figure 13-7, and then click OK.

As you can see in Figure 13-8, the reminder you've just created now appears in the list. If the text you've entered turns out to be too long to display on a single line within the width of the reminder window, try re-entering the reminder text in a shorter version.

Figure 13-7: The input box for a new reminder. This box appears when you click any of the numbered buttons in a reminder window.

Figure 13-8: When you click OK in the Reminder input box, the text you've entered for a new reminder appears in the current list.

You can complete a list by performing these steps once for each numbered command button in a given window. When you finish developing all three lists, the windows may appear as shown in Figure 13-9. Creating these lists is a one-time task that you perform during your first run of the program. Subsequently, the program records your lists on disk in text files named Before.Txt, During.Txt, and After.Txt, all stored in the root directory of your hard disk. (In fact, if you want to use the lists shown in Figure 13-9, you can copy these three files to your hard disk from the program disk supplied with this book, and then run the program.) Of course, you're free to revise your reminder lists at any time during a program run. Just click a numbered command button and enter the new reminder in the resulting text box.

You can now begin using the lists to keep track of the activities surrounding a business trip. To show that you've completed a particular task described in a list, click the corresponding check box in the appropriate window. As you can see in Figure 13-10, a check appears, indicating that the job has been accomplished.

For convenience, the program allows you to change the order in which the reminders appear in the lists. At the upper-left corner of the Travel Reminders window, a pointing-hand icon represents this feature. To alphabetize the list in any one of the three windows, double-click the pointing hand (or double-click the mouse pointer anywhere in the background of the Travel Reminders window). In response, the program immediately changes the order of all three reminder lists, as shown in Figure 13-11. If any of the lists have fewer than ten reminders, the blank items "float" to the top of the list window as a result of the sort.

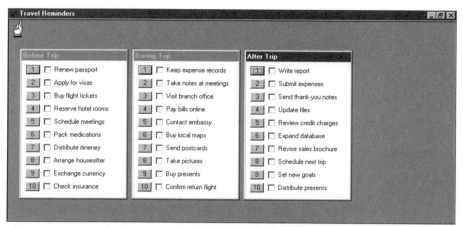

Figure 13-9: Developing the reminder lists. The lists are stored as text files under the names Before.Txt, During.Txt, and After.Txt. You can revise any reminder in the list by clicking the corresponding numbered button.

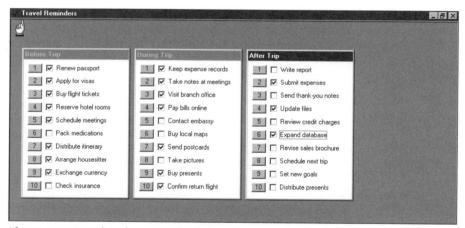

Figure 13-10: Using the reminder lists to keep track of business trip activities. A check indicates that you've completed a particular task described in one of the three windows.

If you want to restore the original order of the lists, double-click the pointing-hand icon again. The program assumes that the unalphabetized order may be significant to you — for example, you may have originally entered the tasks in their order of importance or in chronological order. Accordingly, the program keeps track of the sequence as you first entered it, and is always prepared to restore this order.

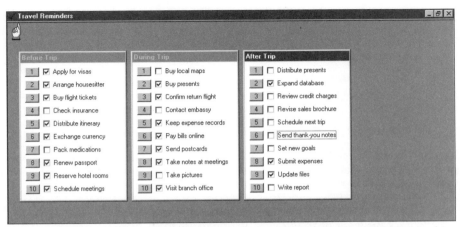

Figure 13-11: To alphabetize the reminder lists, double-click the pointing hand icon at the upper-left corner of the application window. To restore the original order, double-click again.

When you eventually quit the program — by clicking the Close button at the upper-right corner of the Travel Reminders window, or by pulling down the window's control menu and choosing Close — the reminders and the current check box values (checked or not checked) are all saved together in the three text files associated with this program. For example, Figure 13-12 shows the contents of the After.Txt file. As you can see, each line in the file contains the text of a reminder, followed by a value of 0 (for unchecked) or 1 (for checked), representing the current value of the corresponding check box. Because this is a text file, you can view and revise it in a text editor such as the Windows Notepad program. The next time you run the Travel Reminders application, the program displays the contents of these files in the three reminder lists.

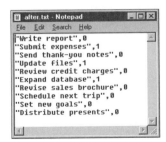

Figure 13-12: The contents of a reminder list text file. Each line of the file contains the text of a reminder item enclosed in quotes, followed by a value of 0 or 1, representing the current status of the corresponding check box.

Examining the program's code

The code for the Travel Reminders application appears in the MDI form, the standard form, and the class module:

✦ MDIReminder, the startup form, contains some key declarations and event procedures. In particular, the MDIForm_Load procedure, performed at the beginning of each run, creates instances of the ReminderPage class and assigns property values to each new object.

✦ The frmReminder form contains one Click procedure, which takes control when the user clicks a command button on one of the reminder pages.

✦ ReminderPage, the class module, contains procedures defining the properties, methods, and events of the ReminderPage class.

You may want to use Visual Basic's Object Browser to examine the contents of this project — particularly the procedures and properties of the ReminderPage class; to do so, follow these steps:

1. Choose View⇨Object Browser to open this window. (Alternatively, click the Object Browser button on the Visual Basic toolbar or simply press F2 at the keyboard.) If the window is maximized, click the Restore Window button at the right side of the Visual Basic menu bar to view the Object Browser in a window that you can move and resize.

2. Pull down the Project/Library list (at the upper-left corner of the Object Browser) and choose the Reminder project.

3. In the Classes list (at the left side of the Object Browser) select ReminderPage.

As you can see in Figure 13-13, the Object Browser lists the contents of the ReminderPage class, including its procedures, methods, properties, and events.

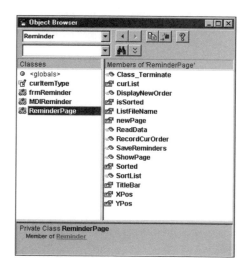

Figure 13-13: The Object Browser lists the contents of the current project. Select a class in the list on the left; the Members list shows the procedures, methods, properties, and events of the selected class.

The Object Browser is a useful tool for making your way around the code of a detailed project. For example, when you double-click the name of any procedure listed in the Members list, a code window displays the procedure you've selected. You'll experiment further with the Object Browser in Chapter 15.

Developing Classes and Collections

The code of the Travel Reminders application introduces several important programming techniques related to objects, collections, classes, and property procedures. Specifically, as you examine the listings, you'll learn how to

+ Develop the code inside a class module

+ Create instances of a class you've defined

+ Organize a group of class objects as a collection

+ Loop through the objects in a collection

+ Create instances of a form

+ Develop methods and property procedures in a class module

+ Make calls to property procedures by setting or accessing property values

+ Make use of the events that Visual Basic defines for classes

+ Release an object from memory when your program is finished with it

Before you begin exploring these techniques in detail, here's an overview of how the program works. As you know, the MDIForm_Load procedure in the MDIReminder module is the first code to be performed. This procedure creates three instances of the ReminderPage class and then organizes these three objects as a collection. This collection object, represented as *colReminderPages,* provides access to the three ReminderPage objects throughout the program.

Each ReminderPage object in its turn creates an instance of the frmReminder form. You may be surprised to learn that Visual Basic recognizes each form that you add to a project as a class. You can therefore create new form objects from any standard form (but not from an MDI form). Each instance of a form contains all the characteristics defined in the original form class, including properties, controls, and code.

The ReminderPage class contains a method (that is, a public procedure) named *ShowPage,* which is designed to display the current instance of the frmReminder form on the screen. The MDIForm_Load procedure calls this method once for each instance of the ReminderPage class, thus displaying all three reminder pages on the screen. But before calling the *ShowPage* method, the program sets the relevant properties of the new ReminderPage object. These include *TitleBar,* which specifies the title bar caption; *ListFileName,* which provides the name of the text file that contains the list of reminders; and *XPos* and *YPos,* two integer arguments that give the position coordinates of the window.

Once the three reminder pages are displayed, event procedures respond to the user's subsequent actions. For example, the cmdChange_Click procedure in the frmReminder form displays an input box on the screen — with the prompt "Enter a new reminder" — when the user clicks any one of the numbered command buttons. The MDIForm_DblClick procedure takes control when the user double-clicks inside the MDI form. This procedure changes a property named *Sorted* on all three ReminderPage objects. The property change itself results in a call to a property procedure in the class module, which in turn performs the sort.

Finally, when the user closes the application window, the program initiates the process of releasing all three ReminderPage objects from memory. This event triggers a call to a procedure named Class_Terminate in each object. To complete the program's action appropriately, the event procedure writes the current reminder lists back to disk, saving any changes that may have been made during the current run.

You'll begin learning how the program uses the ReminderPage class in the next section.

Working with a class

Each ReminderPage object — along with the form object that it creates — is a self-contained unit of code, data, and displayable objects. Part of the design of a class is that it should be easy to transport for use in any application. Accordingly, you can add the Reminder.Cls and Reminder.Frm files to any project that contains an MDI form, and successfully create instances of the ReminderPage class. To use a ReminderPage object, you perform the following tasks in your code:

1. In the code of the MDI form, create an instance of the ReminderPage class.

2. In the MDIForm_Load procedure, assign settings to the new object's properties, including *TitleBar, ListFileName, XPos,* and *YPos.*

3. Call the *ShowPage* method to display the object as a child of the MDI parent form.

4. Write procedures for the MDIForm events that may occur while the object is active, and use these events as opportunities to manipulate the object itself. For example, change the object's Sorted property in response to an MDIForm_DblClick event; and release the object from memory in response to the MDIForm_QueryUnload event.

Thanks to the ReminderPage class, you can manage all these tasks economically, with very few lines of code. Once the class itself is available, you don't need to concern yourself with the details of its implementation. All you need to know is how to use the properties, methods, and events that the class defines.

Creating a class object

The first step for your code is to create an instance of the class. This is accomplished with the Dim statement and the New keyword:

```
Dim objectVariable As New ClassName
```

This statement does two things. First, it creates a new object belonging to the class identified as *ClassName*. This is analogous to the step you take when you double-click a button on the Toolbox to place a new control on a form; the result is a new object belonging to a particular class of controls. Second, the Dim statement declares a variable name, *objectVariable,* to represent the new object in your program. This second task is parallel to the step of assigning a value to the Name property for a control in a form; the name represents the object in your program's code.

Consider the examples from the MDIForm_Load procedure, in Figures 13-14 and 13-15. The following statements create instances of the ReminderPage class:

```
Dim Before As New ReminderPage
Dim During As New ReminderPage
Dim After As New ReminderPage
```

The variables named *Before, During,* and *After* represent the new ReminderPage objects. Once the program has created these objects and given them names, *Before, During,* and *After* can be used in several familiar ways. Given the list of properties defined in the ReminderPage class, you can assign specific settings to the objects. For example, the following statement assigns a string value to the *Before* object's TitleBar property:

```
Before.TitleBar = "Before Trip"
```

Likewise you can make calls to any method defined in the class. This statement calls the *ShowPage* method, displaying a reminder list on the screen:

```
Before.ShowPage
```

You can also use Visual Basic's With structure to simplify references to the properties and methods of the object. Taking advantage of With, here is how the MDIForm_Load procedure assigns property values to the *Before* object and displays the resulting reminder page on the screen:

```
With Before
  .TitleBar = "Before Trip"
  .ListFileName = "\Before.TXT"
  .XPos = 300
  .YPos = 800
  .ShowPage
End With
```

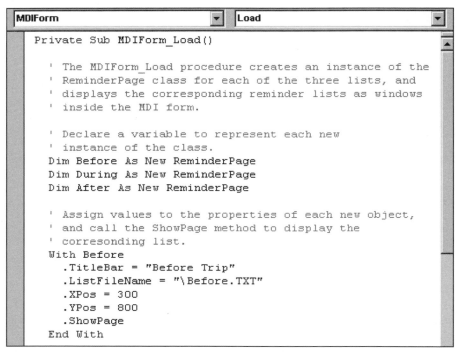

Figure 13-14: In the first half of the MDIForm_Load procedure you can see how the program creates the three new ReminderPage objects and declares variables to represent them.

As previewed earlier in this chapter, the properties of a ReminderPage object include the *TitleBar* caption, the *ListFileName* text file name, and the *XPos* and *YPos* coordinates. Once these properties have been set, the *ShowPage* method displays the list in the application window. (The fifth property, *Sorted,* isn't used until a list is already displayed on the screen.)

The MDIForm_Load procedure uses similar sequences of code to define the properties of the other two ReminderPage objects, first *During*:

```
With During
  .TitleBar = "During Trip"
  .ListFileName = "\During.TXT"
  .XPos = 3300
  .YPos = 800
  .ShowPage
End With
```

and then *After:*

```
With After
  .TitleBar = "After Trip"
  .ListFileName = "\After.TXT"
  .XPos = 6300
  .YPos = 800
  .ShowPage
End With
```

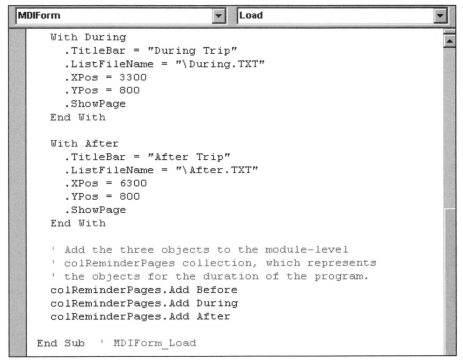

```
With During
  .TitleBar = "During Trip"
  .ListFileName = "\During.TXT"
  .XPos = 3300
  .YPos = 800
  .ShowPage
End With

With After
  .TitleBar = "After Trip"
  .ListFileName = "\After.TXT"
  .XPos = 6300
  .YPos = 800
  .ShowPage
End With

' Add the three objects to the module-level
' colReminderPages collection, which represents
' the objects for the duration of the program.
colReminderPages.Add Before
colReminderPages.Add During
colReminderPages.Add After

End Sub  ' MDIForm_Load
```

Figure 13-15: After creating the ReminderPage objects, the MDIForm_Load procedure assigns property settings and makes a call to the *ShowPage* method to display each reminder list window. Finally, the procedure develops a collection to represent all three objects conveniently.

When the MDIForm_Load procedure is finished, the three reminder lists are displayed on the screen, as shown back in Figure 13-6 (if the Before.Txt, During.Txt, and After.Txt files have not yet been created) or in Figure 13-9 (if the three files exist). At this point, the application is ready for the user to begin interacting with the objects on the screen — developing or revising the reminder lists, checking or unchecking individual tasks in the lists, changing the sort order, and eventually ending the program performance so that the lists can be recorded again on disk.

Declaring Object Variables — Early and Late Binding

Sometimes you may want a way to declare an object variable without creating a new object. Perhaps the object itself already exists, and you simply need a new variable to represent it. Or you may want to organize your code in a particular way, declaring the object variable before creating the object that the variable will eventually represent.

To create an object variable belonging to a certain class, use the following familiar format of the Dim statement:

```
Dim objectVariable As _
        ClassName
```

Without the New keyword, this statement declares a variable but does not create a new instance of *ClassName*. At this point, the value of the object variable is represented by the keyword Nothing; the variable does not yet refer to any object.

To assign the variable a reference to an existing object, you use Visual Basic's Set statement:

```
Set objectVariable = _
        objectName
```

This statement assumes that an object called *objectName* already exists as an instance of *ClassName*. For example, suppose your program creates a ReminderPage object named *Sometime*:

```
Dim Sometime As New _
        ReminderPage
```

Later in the program you want to refer to this same object as *Before* rather than *Sometime*. The following statements create *Before* as a ReminderPage variable and then assign the variable a reference to the *Sometime* object:

```
Dim Before As ReminderPage _
Set Before = Sometime
```

You can also use the Set statement to *create* a new object, in the following format:

```
Dim objectVariable As _
        ClassName
Set objectVariable = New _
        ClassName
```

Finally, you can use Set to disassociate the variable from the object it currently refers to:

```
Set objectVariable = Nothing
```

After this statement, *objectVariable* no longer refers to any object. Furthermore, if *objectVariable* was previously the only existing variable referring to this object, assigning Nothing to the variable is a way to release the object itself from memory, thus triggering the Class_Terminate event. You'll see an example of this in the Travel Reminders program.

It's important to keep in mind the difference between *early* and *late* binding in the creation of objects. When you use early binding to declare an object, Visual Basic defines the object at the time your program is compiled rather than during a run. Early binding ensures maximum efficiency in the handling of an object. To implement early binding, write a Dim statement that refers to the specific class to which the new object belongs:

```
Dim objectVariable As New _
        ClassName
```

Alternatively, declare an object variable belonging to the class, and use a Set statement to create the object itself:

```
Dim objectVariable As _            Dim objectVariable As Object
    ClassName                      Set objectVariable = New _
Set objectVariable = New _             ClassName
    ClassName
```

By contrast, the use of the generic Object class results in late binding:

Late binding is a less efficient way to handle objects at runtime, and may slow down your program performance.

Creating and using a collection of objects

In some applications, a *collection* proves to be a convenient way to refer to a group of objects and to gain access to individual objects in the group. A collection is itself an object, which you can create using the Dim statement and the New keyword:

```
Dim collectionName As New Collection
```

For example, a collection object named *colReminderPages* is created in the general declarations section of the MDIReminder form, as shown in Figure 13-16:

```
Dim colReminderPages As New Collection
```

Because this object has a module-level scope, it is available to represent a group of objects throughout the life of the MDI form, which is to say during the entire program run. In general, the objects in a collection need not all belong to the same class; you can use a collection to represent any assortment of related objects in your application. But the *colReminderPages* collection — as its name implies — is created to represent a set of objects that all belong to a single class, ReminderPage.

Once a collection exists, you can add any number of members, using a method named Add. Here is the syntax of the Add method in its simplest form:

```
collectionName.Add objectName
```

The MDIForm_Load procedure uses this format to add the three ReminderPage objects — *Before*, *During*, and *After* — to the *colReminderPages* collection, as you can see back in Figure 13-15:

```
colReminderPages.Add Before
colReminderPages.Add During
colReminderPages.Add After
```

(See the sidebar named "Organizing a Collection" for more information about the Add method.)

Figure 13-16: In the general declarations section of the MDIReminder form, a Dim statement creates a collection to represent the three ReminderPage objects.

Significantly, the *Before*, *During*, and *After* object variables are declared locally in the MDIForm_Load procedure. When the procedure relinquishes control, these three variables go out of scope, and are no longer available as references to ReminderPage objects. But the *colReminderPages* collection is declared at the module level of the MDIReminder form. For the remainder of the program, this collection is therefore the only way to refer to the set of three ReminderPage objects.

Visual Basic provides an important variation on the For loop that is ideal for working with a collection. Here is a general format of the For Each loop:

```
For Each objectVariable In collectionName

    ' Inside the loop, use objectVariable to refer
    ' to each successive member of the collection.

Next objectVariable
```

This loop provides ordered access to each member of the collection. For each new iteration of the loop, *objectVariable* is assigned a reference to the next member in the collection.

For example, the MDIForm_DblClick procedure in Figure 13-17 uses a For Each loop to change the Sorted property of each object in the *colReminderPages* collection:

```
Dim Reminder As Object
For Each Reminder In colReminderPages
  With Reminder
    .Sorted = Not .Sorted
  End With
Next Reminder
```

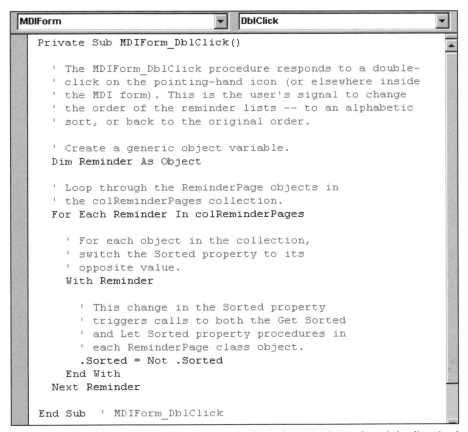

Figure 13-17: The MDIForm_DblClick procedure changes the order of the lists in the reminder windows. If they are currently unsorted, the procedure alphabetizes them. If they are currently displayed in alphabetical order, the procedure returns them to their original order.

Notice the use of a *generic* object variable — *Reminder* — to serve as the reference to objects in the collection. Because collections may contain objects of diverse classes, it's often necessary to use a generic object variable in the For Each loop. Of course, in this particular application, the *colReminderPages* collection contains only objects that belong to the ReminderPage class. In this special case, *Reminder* could therefore have been declared as a ReminderPage variable:

```
Dim Reminder as ReminderPage
```

The MDIReminder module illustrates one more convenient use of the *colReminderPages* collection. When the user clicks the Close button to close the Travel Reminders window, the MDIForm_QueryUnload event procedure in Figure 13-18 is performed. (The QueryUnload event takes place just *before* the actual closing of a form, and thus gives an application the opportunity to perform final operations while the form is still open.) This procedure contains a single statement:

```
Set colReminderPages = Nothing
```

Because *colReminderPages* is the only module-level reference to the program's three ReminderPage objects, this statement has the effect of releasing all three objects from memory. But before they are released, a Class_Terminate event procedure is triggered for each instance of the class. As you'll see shortly, this event procedure completes the action of the program by making appropriate arrangements for saving the three reminder lists.

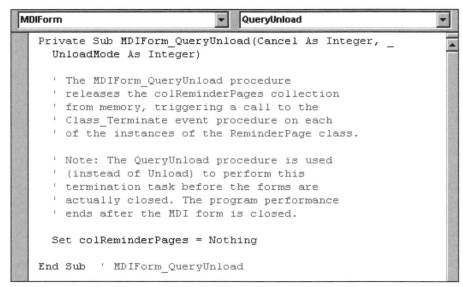

Figure 13-18: The MDIForm_QueryUnload procedure assigns a value of Nothing to the *colReminderPages* collection. This action results in a call to the Class_Terminate event for each of the objects belonging to the ReminderPage class.

Organizing a Collection

A collection is an *ordered* group of objects. Each time you add an object to a collection, the object is assigned an index value from 1 to the number of objects in the collection. You can use this index number to access a particular member in the collection. Although the For Each loop is clearly the most convenient way to access the members of a collection, you can also use a traditional For loop with an index. For example, the loop in MDIForm_DblClick could be redesigned as follows:

```
Dim i
For i = 1 To _
      colReminderPages.Count
   With colReminderPages(i)
      .Sorted = Not .Sorted
   End With
Next i
```

Notice the use of the Count property at the top of the For loop. This property indicates the current number of members in a collection.

Another way to identify the members of a collection is to assign a key string to each object at the time the object is added to the collection. Use the following format of the Add method to accomplish this:

```
collectionName.Add
      objectName, keyString
```

You can subsequently refer to a collection member by using the key string:

```
collectionName(keyString)
```

For example, suppose you were to use the following statement to add the *Before* object to the *colReminderPages* collection:

```
colReminderPages.Add Before, _
      "BeforeTrip"
```

Later in the program you can refer to this member of the collection as

```
colReminderPages("BeforeTrip")
```

This format can be an important alternative to the use of numeric indexes for accessing members in the collection.

Inside the class module

You've seen how the MDIReminder form makes use of the ReminderPage class — creating instances of the class, setting properties, calling the ShowPage method, and carrying out other operations that trigger specific events. Now you're ready to look inside the class module itself to see how all these class-related resources are defined.

The general declarations for the ReminderPage class module appear in Figure 13-19. The first thing to keep in mind about this module is that it uses the frmReminder form as its own visual component. In fact, each instance of the ReminderPage class creates a new instance of the frmReminder form. In this sense, the ReminderPage class and the frmReminder form are two parts of the same package. If you want to use this class in another program, you have to make sure to add both the Reminder.Frm and Reminder.Cls files to the project.

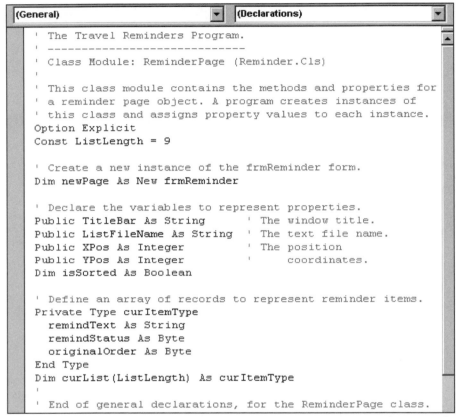

| (General) | ▼ | (Declarations) | ▼ |

```
' The Travel Reminders Program.
' --------------------------------
' Class Module: ReminderPage (Reminder.Cls)
'
' This class module contains the methods and properties for
' a reminder page object. A program creates instances of
' this class and assigns property values to each instance.
Option Explicit
Const ListLength = 9

' Create a new instance of the frmReminder form.
Dim newPage As New frmReminder

' Declare the variables to represent properties.
Public TitleBar As String        ' The window title.
Public ListFileName As String    ' The text file name.
Public XPos As Integer           ' The position
Public YPos As Integer           '    coordinates.
Dim isSorted As Boolean

' Define an array of records to represent reminder items.
Private Type curItemType
  remindText As String
  remindStatus As Byte
  originalOrder As Byte
End Type
Dim curList(ListLength) As curItemType
'
' End of general declarations, for the ReminderPage class.
```

Figure 13-19: The general declarations section of the ReminderPage class module. The module declares and creates a new instance of the frmReminder form.

Near the top of the general declarations, you'll find the following Dim statement:

```
Dim newPage As New frmReminder
```

As this statement demonstrates, Visual Basic regards each form in a project as a class definition, and therefore allows the application to create multiple instances of the form. Each instance contains all of the form's controls and all of its code. If the form is designed to present a certain dialog box on the screen and react to particular events, each instance of the form will behave in the same way.

In the Reminder.Cls module, *newPage* is a module-level object variable that retains its scope throughout the life of a given ReminderPage object. The class object and its associated *newPage* form are designed to work together to provide the visual interface for each instance of the ReminderPage class. You'll find references to *newPage* throughout the class module.

Several interesting techniques are worth investigating in the code of a class module. How does the module define the properties of the class? How are the methods designed? And what is the role of event procedures in the behavior of class objects? These are the questions you'll explore in the upcoming sections of this chapter.

Defining the properties of the class

There are two ways to define properties inside a class module. The easy way is to create one or more public variables in the module's general declarations section. The more difficult — but also more powerful — approach is to write property procedures. A property procedure is automatically called every time a particular property setting is changed or accessed.

The ReminderPage class contains examples of both these approaches. Four of the class properties are defined as public variables in the general declarations section of the class module:

```
Public TitleBar As String       ' The window title.
Public ListFileName As String   ' The text file name.
Public XPos As Integer          ' The position
Public YPos As Integer          '     coordinates.
```

As you've seen, the Travel Reminders program assigns values to these properties immediately after creating instances of the ReminderPage class, but before making a call to the ShowPage method:

```
With During
  .TitleBar = "During Trip"
  .ListFileName = "\During.TXT"
  .XPos = 3300
  .YPos = 800
  .ShowPage
End With
```

In short, the values of these properties determine the appearance and content of each new reminder list: *TitleBar* is the caption, *ListFileName* identifies the text file that contains the reminder list itself, and *XPos* and *YPos* specify the position of the window.

Developing property procedures

But the ReminderPage class has a fifth property, named *Sorted*. Unlike the other four properties, this property is meant to be used after a given list is already displayed on the screen. As you've seen, the MDIForm_DblClick procedure changes the value of the *Sorted* property each time the user double-clicks the mouse in the background of the form. The ReminderPage class takes any change in the value of this property as a signal to sort the list displayed in a particular instance of the class. The *Sorted* property procedures, shown in Figure 13-20, make this possible.

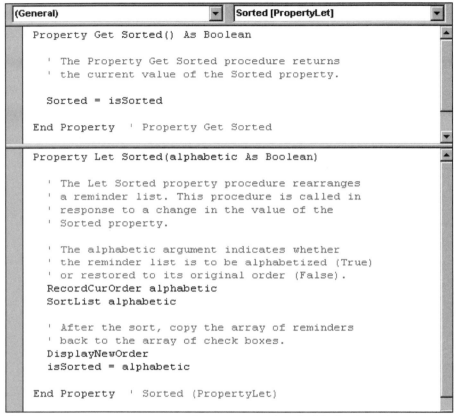

Figure 13-20: Two property procedures are associated with the *Sorted* property. Property Get Sorted is called when a statement reads the Sorted property, and Property Let Sorted is called when a statement changes the Sorted property.

As you can see, two property procedures are related to the *Sorted* property. The longer of the two, Property Let Sorted, is called in response to any statement that changes the current value of the property:

```
Property Let Sorted(alphabetic As Boolean)
```

The other, named Property Get Sorted, is called in response to any statement that *reads* the value of the Sorted property:

```
Property Get Sorted() As Boolean
```

The Property Let Sorted procedure receives as its argument the new value that is assigned to the property. For example, consider this hypothetical statement:

```
During.Sorted = False
```

In response to this statement, the Property Let Sorted procedure is called and a value of False is sent to its *alphabetic* argument.

By contrast, the role of the Property Get Sorted procedure is to supply the current value of the *Sorted* property. In response to a statement that reads the value of *Sorted*, the Property Get Sorted procedure is called and returns the current value of the *Sorted* property. For example, the following statement results in a call to Property Get Sorted; the property value is then assigned to the variable *isAlpha*:

```
isAlpha = During.Sorted
```

Take a quick look at the design of these two property procedures in the class module. The Property Let Sorted procedure uses its *alphabetic* argument to determine whether the target list should be alphabetized or returned to its original order. To accomplish either of these tasks, the routine makes three procedure calls of its own:

```
Property Let Sorted(alphabetic As Boolean)

    RecordCurOrder alphabetic
    SortList alphabetic

    DisplayNewOrder
    isSorted = alphabetic

End Property  ' Sorted (PropertyLet)
```

The *RecordCurOrder* procedure in Figure 13-21 makes a copy of the current list in an array named *curList*. This procedure also keeps track of the original order of the list so that this order can be restored if the *Sorted* property is changed to False again. The *SortList* procedure in Figure 13-22 performs the sort, either alphabetizing the text entries of the reminder list if the program has requested an alphabetical sort, or sorting by the *originalOrder* field if the program has requested a return to the original order of the list. Finally, the *DisplayNewOrder* procedure in Figure 13-23 redisplays the list in its newly sorted order.

After these three procedure calls, the Property Let Sorted procedure changes the value of a module-level variable named *isSorted*. The Property Get Sorted procedure simply returns the value of this variable, supplying the current value of the *Sorted* property itself:

```
Property Get Sorted() As Boolean

  Sorted = isSorted

End Property  ' Property Get Sorted
```

You may want to spend some time studying these two property procedures — and the three procedures called by the Property Get Sorted routine — to learn exactly how the sort operations are carried out in a ReminderPage object.

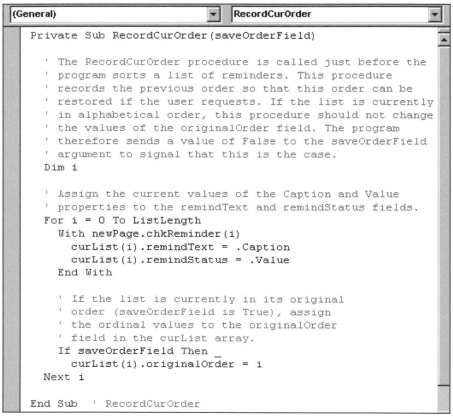

Figure 13-21: The *RecordCurOrder* procedure keeps track of the original order of the current list.

Tip   A third type of property procedure is available in Visual Basic, defined by the keywords *Property Set*. This procedure is called when an object is assigned to an object-type property. For more information, search for *Property Set* in the Visual Basic Help Topics window.

Designing a method for the class

Looking through the procedures in the ReminderPage class module, you'll find that all but three of them are labeled Private. By design, the bulk of the code inside the module is invisible to a program that creates instances of the class.

```
(General)                              ▼    SortList                              ▼

    Private Sub SortList(byReminders As Boolean)
      ' The SortList procedure rearranges a list of reminders.
      ' If byReminders is true, the procedure alphabetizes the
      ' list; if false, the list returns to its original order.
    Dim i, j
    Dim tempItem As curItemType

      ' Use a bubble sort to arrange the list alphabetically
      ' or to its original order.
    For i = 0 To ListLength - 1
      For j = i + 1 To ListLength
        If byReminders Then
          If curList(i).remindText > _
            curList(j).remindText Then
              tempItem = curList(i)
              curList(i) = curList(j)
              curList(j) = tempItem
          End If
        Else
          If curList(i).originalOrder > _
            curList(j).originalOrder Then
              tempItem = curList(i)
              curList(i) = curList(j)
              curList(j) = tempItem
          End If
        End If
      Next j
    Next i
    End Sub  ' SortList
```

Figure 13-22: The *SortList* procedure performs the alphabetic sort or restores the original order of the current list.

Of the three procedures available for use outside the class module itself, two are the property procedures that you've just looked at, Property Let Sorted and Property Get Sorted. The third is the *ShowPage* procedure in Figure 13-24, the one method defined for this class. After creating a ReminderPage object and assigning values to its properties, a program uses the *ShowPage* method to display the reminder list on the screen. As you've seen, a call to this method looks like this:

```
During.ShowPage
```

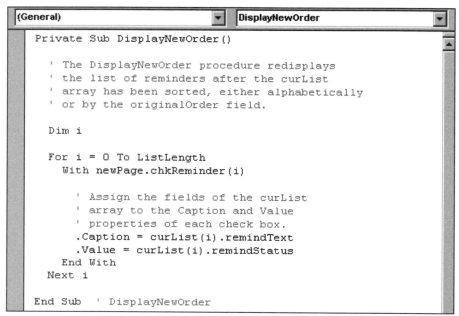

```
(General)                              DisplayNewOrder

   Private Sub DisplayNewOrder()

     ' The DisplayNewOrder procedure redisplays
     ' the list of reminders after the curList
     ' array has been sorted, either alphabetically
     ' or by the originalOrder field.

     Dim i

     For i = 0 To ListLength
       With newPage.chkReminder(i)

         ' Assign the fields of the curList
         ' array to the Caption and Value
         ' properties of each check box.
         .Caption = curList(i).remindText
         .Value = curList(i).remindStatus
       End With
     Next i

   End Sub  ' DisplayNewOrder
```

Figure 13-23: The *DisplayNewOrder* procedure redisplays the current list after a sort operation.

The *ShowPage* procedure itself is surprisingly simple:

```
Sub ShowPage()

   ReadData ListFileName

   newPage.Caption = TitleBar
   newPage.Top = YPos
   newPage.Left = XPos

   newPage.Show

End Sub  ' ShowPage
```

The procedure begins by making a call to the *ReadData* procedure in Figure 13-25, which has the task of opening the appropriate text file on disk and copying its contents to the control arrays on the *newPage* form. (If this procedure doesn't find the target file on disk, the check box captions remain blank.) Then *ShowPage* sets the caption and position properties of the *newPage* form. Finally, a call to the Show method displays the form on the screen.

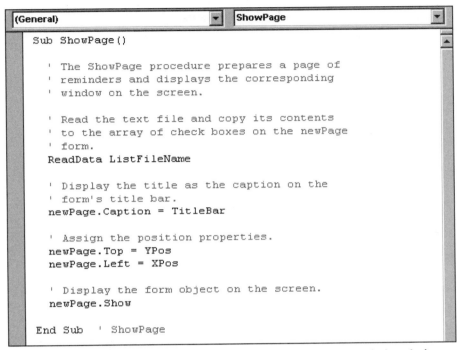

Figure 13-24: The *ShowPage* procedure displays a reminder page in its window.

Responding to events around the ReminderPage objects

Once the reminder lists are displayed, three kinds of events can take place:

✦ The user can click one of the numbered command buttons located at the left side of all three lists (see Figure 13-6). In response, the program elicits a new text entry for the current reminder (Figure 13-7) and then displays this new value as part of the list. This particular event is handled by a procedure contained in the frmReminder form itself. The cmdChange_Click procedure (Figure 13-26) uses Visual Basic's InputBox function to display the prompt, and then assigns the input to the appropriate chkReminder control:

```
newStr = InputBox("Enter a new reminder", Me.Caption)
If Trim(newStr) <> "" Then _
  chkReminder(Index).Caption = newStr
```

✦ The user can double-click inside the MDI form to request a change in the sort order. As you've seen, the MDIForm_DblClick procedure responds to this event by changing the value of the *Sorted* property for all three ReminderPage objects. In response, the property procedures in the Reminder.Cls module are called.

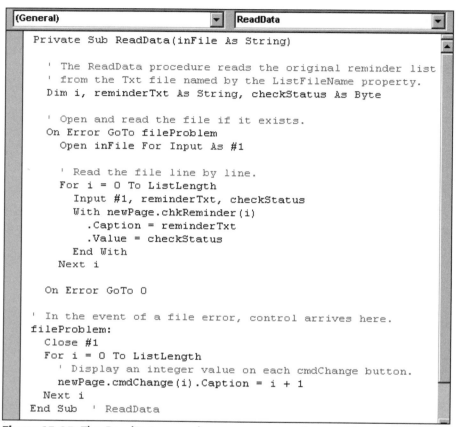

```
(General)                          ▼    ReadData                              ▼

  Private Sub ReadData(inFile As String)

    ' The ReadData procedure reads the original reminder list
    ' from the Txt file named by the ListFileName property.
    Dim i, reminderTxt As String, checkStatus As Byte

    ' Open and read the file if it exists.
    On Error GoTo fileProblem
      Open inFile For Input As #1

      ' Read the file line by line.
      For i = 0 To ListLength
        Input #1, reminderTxt, checkStatus
        With newPage.chkReminder(i)
          .Caption = reminderTxt
          .Value = checkStatus
        End With
      Next i

    On Error GoTo 0

  ' In the event of a file error, control arrives here.
  fileProblem:
    Close #1
    For i = 0 To ListLength
      ' Display an integer value on each cmdChange button.
      newPage.cmdChange(i).Caption = i + 1
    Next i
  End Sub    ' ReadData
```

Figure 13-25: The *ReadData* procedure opens and reads a text file of reminders, if the file exists.

✦ The user can click the Close button at the upper-right corner of the MDI form, a signal to terminate the program. In response, theMDIForm_ QueryUnload procedure (shown back in Figure 13-18) assigns a value of Nothing to the *colReminderPages* collection, releasing all three of the ReminderPage objects from memory. But before the objects can be released, this assignment triggers a call to the Class_Terminate procedure in the class module (Figure 13-27).

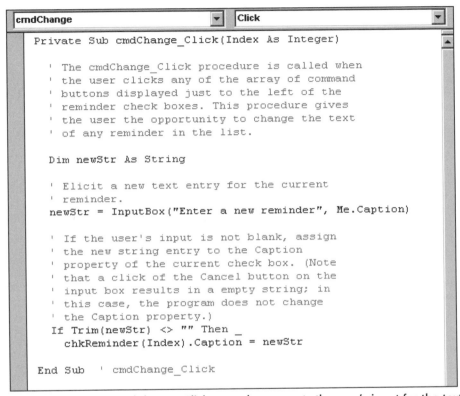

```
cmdChange                          ▼   Click                          ▼

    Private Sub cmdChange_Click(Index As Integer)

        ' The cmdChange_Click procedure is called when
        ' the user clicks any of the array of command
        ' buttons displayed just to the left of the
        ' reminder check boxes. This procedure gives
        ' the user the opportunity to change the text
        ' of any reminder in the list.

        Dim newStr As String

        ' Elicit a new text entry for the current
        ' reminder.
        newStr = InputBox("Enter a new reminder", Me.Caption)

        ' If the user's input is not blank, assign
        ' the new string entry to the Caption
        ' property of the current check box. (Note
        ' that a click of the Cancel button on the
        ' input box results in a empty string; in
        ' this case, the program does not change
        ' the Caption property.)
        If Trim(newStr) <> "" Then _
            chkReminder(Index).Caption = newStr

    End Sub  ' cmdChange_Click
```

Figure 13-26: The cmdChange_Click procedure accepts the user's input for the text of a new reminder item and then displays the item as the Caption property of the corresponding check box.

The Class_Terminate procedure has two tasks to perform before releasing an object from memory. If the current list is in alphabetical order, this procedure restores it to its original order before writing the list back to disk:

```
If Me.Sorted Then Me.Sorted = False
```

Notice the use of the keyword Me. Me can be used anywhere inside a class module to refer to the current instance of the class. Because a program may create many objects from a given class definition, Me is an easy way to refer to the instance that is currently the target of operations. (You can see another example of Me in the cmdChange_Click procedure back in Figure 13-26.)

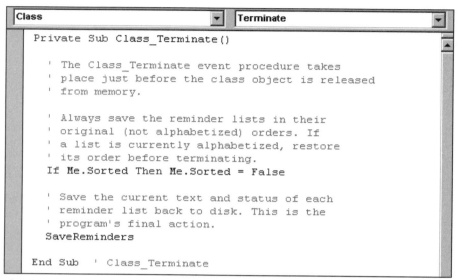

| Class | ▼ | Terminate | ▼ |

```
Private Sub Class_Terminate()

    ' The Class_Terminate event procedure takes
    ' place just before the class object is released
    ' from memory.

    ' Always save the reminder lists in their
    ' original (not alphabetized) orders. If
    ' a list is currently alphabetized, restore
    ' its order before terminating.
    If Me.Sorted Then Me.Sorted = False

    ' Save the current text and status of each
    ' reminder list back to disk. This is the
    ' program's final action.
    SaveReminders

End Sub   ' Class_Terminate
```

Figure 13-27: The Class_Terminate procedure restores the original order of the current list and saves the reminder list back to its text file before the program ends.

Finally, the Class_Terminate procedure saves the current reminder list back to its text file on disk. A call to the *SaveReminders* procedure, shown in Figure 13-28, accomplishes this task:

```
SaveReminders
```

The procedure saves not only the text of the current reminder list, but also the checked or unchecked setting of each check box. This ensures that the user will see the same list at the beginning of the next program run.

Tip Note that you can also add event definitions to the code of a class. To do so, you use the Event statement to declare the event in the class module. You also write a Dim WithEvents statement to declare an object variable used to respond to events. Within a procedure in the class module, you use the RaiseEvent statement to "fire" the event. Search for the Event, RaiseEvent, and WithEvents keywords in the Visual Basic Help Topics window for more information.

Objects, classes, collections, methods, property procedures, and class events — all of these features give you powerful ways to organize Visual Basic projects. As you move beyond the scope of this brief introduction, you'll find many additional techniques to explore under the general topic of object-oriented programming. In addition, Chapter 17 shows you how to organize and compile a class of objects as an ActiveX DLL (*dynamic link library*) component. Working with a generalized version of the ReminderPage class, you'll begin to see the advantages of creating ActiveX components for use in your Visual Basic projects.

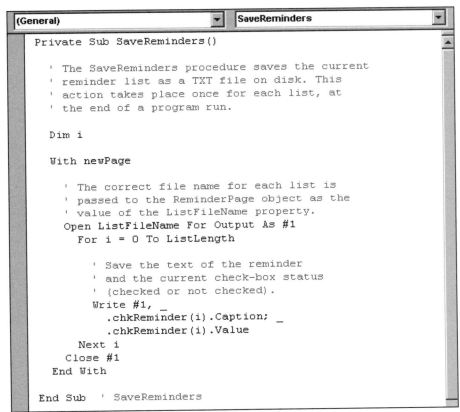

```
(General)                              ▼   SaveReminders                    ▼

    Private Sub SaveReminders()

        ' The SaveReminders procedure saves the current
        ' reminder list as a TXT file on disk. This
        ' action takes place once for each list, at
        ' the end of a program run.

        Dim i

        With newPage

          ' The correct file name for each list is
          ' passed to the ReminderPage object as the
          ' value of the ListFileName property.
          Open ListFileName For Output As #1
            For i = 0 To ListLength

              ' Save the text of the reminder
              ' and the current check-box status
              ' (checked or not checked).
              Write #1, _
                .chkReminder(i).Caption; _
                .chkReminder(i).Value
            Next i
          Close #1
        End With

    End Sub   ' SaveReminders
```

Figure 13-28: The *SaveReminders* procedure performs the task of writing an entire list of reminders to the correct text file.

Multiple-
Document
Interface

Many Windows applications are designed to let you work with more than one file at a time. For example, in a word processing program such as Microsoft Word you can open multiple documents concurrently. This gives you a convenient way to compare the information contained in different documents and to move or copy text from one file to another.

Similarly, you can create Visual Basic programs that permit the user to open multiple instances of a given form inside an appropriately designed application window. This feature is known as *multiple-document interface*, or simply MDI. A Visual Basic application may contain one MDI form, along with any number of standard forms from which the program can create instances. The MDI form is known as the *parent* and the windows displayed inside it are known as *child* forms.

An MDI form can provide familiar tools designed to help the user open and work with documents:

◆ A set of menu commands often appears at the top of the MDI form. These commands generally apply to the child document that is active at a given moment during a program run.

◆ The MDI form may also display a toolbar, containing single-click shortcuts for carrying out the most common menu commands.

✦ A Window menu on the MDI form typically lists the names of all the open windows inside the form and provides an easy way to select and activate a given document.

✦ The Window menu may also contain commands designed to rearrange the open documents within the MDI form. For example, the Cascade command places the open windows in an overlapping stack, and the Tile command arranges them side-by-side.

✦ The programming resources of the MDI environment allow you to write code that carries out common operations on all open files. For instance, before the end of a performance your program can ensure that all changes will be saved to disk from open documents.

In Chapter 13 you saw a simple example of an MDI application, called the Travel Reminders program. That program presents three check lists of typical travel-related activities — tasks that you need to accomplish before, during, and after a business trip. The windows for these lists are created as three instances of the same form definition, all displayed inside an MDI form.

In this chapter you'll work with a somewhat more elaborate application example, an MDI version of the Transportation Planner application. First presented in Chapter 12, the Transportation Planner is designed to create files describing the travel arrangements for the various parts of a business trip. The files are saved on disk as random-access databases with Trv extensions; each record in a file contains information about one leg of a trip. In the fields of a record you specify the mode of transportation, the reservation status and number, the date and time of departure, the origin and destination of the trip and any brief notes that you want to keep about the trip.

The original version of the program consists of a single form in which you can enter or review a record. Using this one form, you can open any Trv file and scroll through its existing records; and you can save new Trv files to disk. By contrast, the MDI version presented in this chapter enables you to open several travel files at once in a convenient working environment. In this case, the "documents" of the MDI application are travel databases; each window that you open in the program becomes a scrollable display of a particular Trv file that you're creating or reviewing. This program illustrates the potential of MDI in Visual Basic applications.

The Transportation Planner, MDI Version

The program is stored on disk as TranMDI.Vbp. (Don't confuse its component files with the original version of the program, which is stored as TranPlan.Vbp.) Open the program now and take a look at its project window. As you can see in Figure 14-1, the program contains two form files. The MDI parent form is named frmTranParent (saved as TranMDIp.Frm). The child form is named frmTranPlan (saved as TranMDIc.Frm).

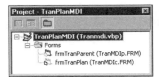

Figure 14-1: The Project Explorer window for the Transportation Planner program, MDI version. The project contains an MDI form and one child form. Notice the slightly different form icons that Visual Basic uses in the Project Explorer to distinguish between parent and child.

Both forms contain important sections of code. In general, the code in the parent form deals with MDI events and processing tasks that apply to all child windows. By contrast, the code in the child form focuses on operations for an open travel file. As you know, each instance of a child form contains its own copy of the code from the form definition and keeps track of its own data. In other words, each new instance of the frmTranPlan form operates as an independent window for a particular open travel file. You'll see exactly how this works as you run the program for the first time.

Running the program

Press F5 or click the Start button on the Visual Basic toolbar to begin the program. When you do, you'll see the Transportation Planner window take over the screen, as shown in Figure 14-2. The MDI window starts out in a maximized state and initially displays one instance of the child form with the generic name Trip1; at this point, no file is open. Like the original version of the program, this form displays an assortment of option buttons, text boxes, and check boxes representing the fields of a transportation record.

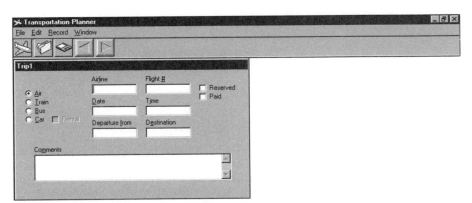

Figure 14-2: The Transportation Planner program at the beginning of a run. The parent form displays a menu bar and a toolbar. Initially one child form is open, with a generic name of Trip1.

Examining the elements of the application, you'll find that the program's menu bar is displayed at the top of the application window, not inside the trip window. The menu bar identifies four lists of commands: The File menu contains commands for creating new trip windows, opening travel files, saving a file to disk, printing the records of an open travel file, and exiting from the program. The Edit menu has a Clear command that erases the information from the current record. The Record menu contains Next and Previous commands for scrolling through the records of a travel file. The Window menu, as discussed earlier, presents a list of all the open windows and provides commands for rearranging trip windows within the application window.

Just below the menu line you can see the toolbar. As shown in Figure 14-3, a ToolTip appears when you position the mouse pointer over any of the icons in the toolbar. In this application the toolbar contains a row of five buttons providing one-click shortcuts for specific menu operations:

✦ The New Trip Window button, showing an image of an airplane, adds a new trip window to the group of open windows.

✦ The Open Trip File button displays the Open dialog box on the screen so that you can open an existing travel file in the active trip window.

✦ The Save Trip File button displays the Save As dialog box so you can save the contents of the active trip window as a new travel file on disk.

✦ The Scroll Back and Scroll Forward buttons are for scrolling through the records of an open travel file, taking you one record back or one record forward in the file.

You'll have a chance to experiment with the program's menu commands and toolbar buttons in the upcoming exercises.

Figure 14-3: The toolbar of the Transportation Planner program, MDI version. A ToolTip appears when you position the mouse pointer over any icon in the toolbar.

Adding trip windows and opening files

You can open additional trip windows by clicking the New Trip Window button on the toolbar or by choosing File⇨New, as shown in Figure 14-4. The program gives each new window a generic name (Trip2, Trip3, and so on) and initially displays the windows in a cascade arrangement. In its current version, the program enables you to open as many as five trip windows. When you reach that maximum, as in Figure 14-5, the program dims the New command in the File menu and the New Trip Window button on the toolbar.

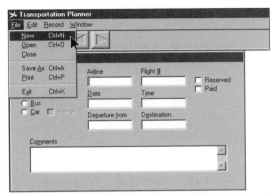

Figure 14-4: Choose File⇨New to open an additional trip window. Alternatively, you can click the New Trip Window button on the toolbar or press Ctrl+N.

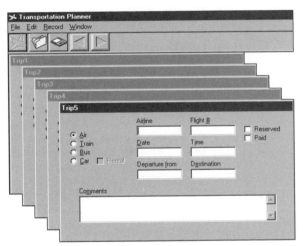

Figure 14-5: When you open the maximum number of windows, the New command in the File menu and the New Trip Window button on the toolbar are dimmed.

The five-window maximum is an arbitrary limitation, set in the interest of simplicity for this sample program. Later in this chapter you'll find out how to adjust the program's code if you want to increase the number of files that can be opened at one time.

Initially, each new trip window contains no data and displays no open file. To open an existing TRV file from disk, follow these steps:

1. Click the title bar of the trip window in which you want to open the file. This becomes the *active* window.

2. Choose File⇨Open or click the Open Trip File button on the toolbar. The Open dialog box appears on the screen, as shown in Figure 14-6.

3. Choose the name of the file that you want to open or type the name into the File name text box. Then click Open.

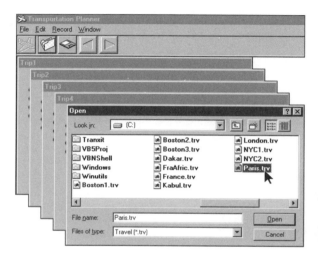

Figure 14-6: Opening a travel file. To view the Open dialog box, click the Open Trip File button on the toolbar, choose File⇨Open, or press Ctrl+O.

In response, the program opens the file you've selected and displays its path and file name in the title bar of the active trip window. (Initially, the trip window displays a blank form in which you can enter the fields of a new record to be stored in the file; to scroll backward through existing records, click the Scroll Back button on the toolbar or press PgUp.) If you want to open files in other trip windows, repeat these three steps, activating a different window each time. For example, Figure 14-7 shows the five trip windows at a moment when each one contains an open travel file. Notice that the title bar of each window displays not only the file name but the number of the current record that's displayed in the window.

By the way, the program prevents you from opening the same file twice in two different trip windows. If you choose the Open command and select the name of a file that's already open, the program simply ignores the operation.

Whether a trip window contains a single new record that you've just entered or a file that you've opened, you can use the Save As operation to save the information in the window under a new file name. Here are the steps:

1. Click the title bar of the target trip window. This becomes the active window.

2. Choose File⇨Save As, or click the Save Trip File button on the toolbar. The Save As dialog box appears on the screen, as shown in Figure 14-8.

3. Enter the name of the file you want to create. Alternatively, select the name of an existing file that you want to overwrite. In this case, the program displays a warning ("This file already exists") and asks you to confirm that you want to replace the existing file; click Yes if you do. Then click Save to complete the operation.

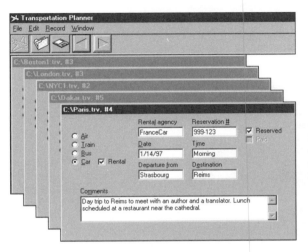

Figure 14-7: Opening a different file in each of the five trip windows. By opening several travel files at once, you can compare the itineraries of different trips, and you can copy information from one window to another.

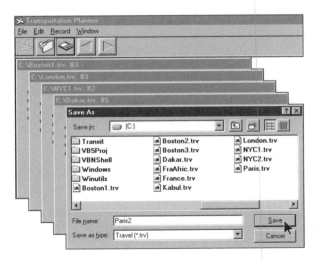

Figure 14-8: Saving a travel file under a new name on disk. If you choose an existing Trv file name, the program asks you to confirm your intention to overwrite the existing file.

After these steps, the program displays the name of the new file in the title bar of the active trip window. There are three ways to scroll through the records of an open file. You can choose the Previous or Next command from the Record menu; you can click the Scroll Back or Scroll Forward button on the toolbar; or you can press PgUp or PgDn to scroll backward or forward through the file.

Using the Window menu

The Window menu gives you an easy way to activate any of the open trip windows using the keyboard or the mouse. You can pull down the menu either by clicking Window with the mouse or by pressing Alt,W from the keyboard. As shown in Figure 14-9, the menu displays a list of all the open windows. For each window that contains an open file, the list displays the file name — that is, the full text from the window's title bar. For a window that does not contain an open file, the list displays a generic name such as Trip1 or Trip2. To activate a window, click any name in the list or press the corresponding number (from 1 to 5) at the keyboard.

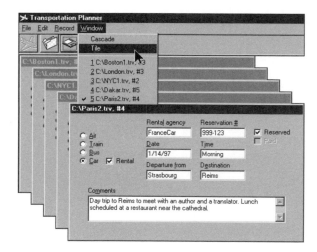

Figure 14-9: The Window menu provides a simple way to activate any open trip window, or to rearrange the child windows within the parent MDI form.

For example, suppose you want to close the file displayed in a particular trip window so you can begin recording a new itinerary. Here's how you can use the Window menu to select the window and then choose the Close command to close the file:

1. Using the mouse or the keyboard, pull down the Window menu and select the name of the file you want to close. The trip window containing this file becomes the active form.

2. Choose File⇨Close. The program saves the current record if it has been revised in any way and then closes the file. The active window returns to its generic title, such as Trip1 or Trip2.

3. Now you can begin entering the first record of a new travel file. Choose Save As when you're ready to create the file on disk.

At the top of the Window menu you can see two additional entries, the Cascade and Tile commands. As you know, Cascade is the program's default arrangement for new trip windows that you open. To change this arrangement, choose Window⇨ Tile. The program rearranges the open windows in a side-by-side format, as shown in Figure 14-10. Notice that you can also move any window to a new position inside the MDI form simply by dragging the target window by its title bar. To return to the original cascade arrangement, choose Window⇨Cascade.

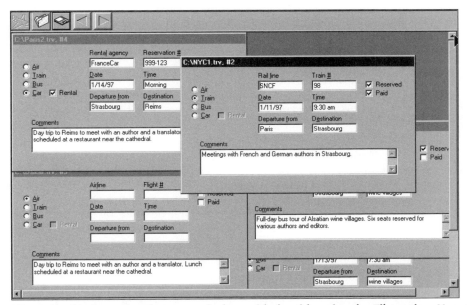

Figure 14-10: Arranging the open windows side-by-side using the Tile option. You can also reposition a trip window by dragging it by its title bar.

When you've finished working with travel files, you can end the program performance by choosing File⇨Exit or by clicking the Close button at the upper-right corner of the Transportation Planner window. Either way, the program ensures that any unsaved records are written to their respective files before the performance ends.

Inside the MDI Application

In the steps for developing a successful MDI application, you begin by setting form properties, defining menus, and designing a toolbar. Then you write the code to manage specific operations in the multiple-document environment.

At the outset, you need to understand several important points about an MDI form:

✦ An MDI form may contain its own menu definition. But whenever a child form is active within the MDI form, the child's menu is displayed at the top of the application window, completely taking the place of the MDI parent menu. Only when no child form is open does the parent menu appear. This arrangement allows an application to adjust its menus according to the context of particular runtime events. In the Transportation Planner program, at least one child form is always open; the menu bar therefore derives from the menu definition of the child form, frmTranPlan. The MDI form in this program contains no menu definition.

✦ To create a Window menu — displaying the names of all open child forms in the MDI form — you simply check the WindowList property in the Menu Editor at design time. At runtime, Visual Basic automatically builds and updates the window list as changes occur in the number of open windows. Figure 14-11 shows the menu definition for the child form, frmTranPlan, in the Transportation Planner application. The WindowList property is checked for the Window menu. You can review the result of this setting by looking again at Figure 14-9.

✦ An MDI form cannot contain the same variety of controls that are available for a standard form. In fact, one of the few standard controls that you can place on an MDI form is the picture box. (The other two are the Timer control and the Data control.) A picture box works as the container for a toolbar. Inside the picture box you can add an assortment of command buttons or image controls, as you'll learn a little later in this chapter. The Align property for the picture box control specifies where the box will be displayed within the form. The default Align setting for a picture box in an MDI form is 1-Top.

✦ You define a child form by assigning a setting of True to the property named MDIChild on a standard form in your application. If a child form is designated as the startup form in an MDI application, Visual Basic displays the child form inside the MDI form at the beginning of a program run. But if the MDI form is the startup, no child form is automatically loaded into the parent. In the Transportation Planner, the MDI form is the startup. An MDIChild setting of True designates the frmTranPlan form as the child, as shown in Figure 14-12. The MDIForm_Load procedure arranges to display the first instance of frmTranPlan in the application window. You'll see how this works when you examine the program's code.

Figure 14-11: Setting the WindowList property for the Window menu. Thanks to this setting, the application's Window menu contains a list of all current trip windows. If a window contains an open file, the Window list shows the file's name.

Figure 14-12: Using the MDIChild property to designate a child form in an MDI application. Setting this Form property to True establishes the child relationship.

Creating a toolbar on the MDI form

To prepare a toolbar for an MDI form, you begin by placing a picture box on the form. Then you can add any number of command button controls to the containing picture box. (Keep in mind that the command button controls may not be placed directly on the MDI form, only inside the picture box control.) Here's an outline of the steps for creating a toolbar like the one that appears in the Transportation Planner:

1. Open your project's MDI form at design time and double-click the PictureBox button in the Toolbox. The picture box control automatically appears just beneath the title bar of the MDI form, in the typical position of a toolbar.

2. Select the CommandButton control in the Toolbox. Carefully draw a row of command button controls inside the picture box. Each control you draw will become a button in the toolbar.

3. Select the first command button and activate the Properties window. Scroll to the Style property and change the setting to 1-Graphical. This setting allows you to display an icon on the face of the command button. Next, scroll to the Caption property and delete its setting, so that no text appears on the button.

4. Select the Picture property and click the small button displayed at the right side of the property setting. In the Load Picture dialog box, navigate to the VB\Graphics\Icons folder and select the folder that contains the icon you want to display on the face of the command button. For example, Figure 14-13 shows the Plane icon in the Industry folder. Select the icon file and click Open. The image you've selected appears on the face of the control. Repeat this step for each of the other command buttons you've placed inside the picture box.

5. Set other properties of each individual command button. Begin by selecting the Name property and entering a meaningful name for each control. If necessary, adjust the Left, Top, Height, and Width properties to correct the position and dimensions of each control within the picture box.

6. Finally, write a Click event procedure for each command button in the toolbar you've created. Typically these procedures make calls to corresponding menu procedures; as a result, the toolbar buttons perform the same operations as the menu commands that they represent. For example, in the Transportation Planner, the cmdOpen_Click procedure — the Click event for the Open button on the toolbar — simply calls the mnuOpen_Click procedure for the active trip window, as you can see in Figure 14-14.

You'll learn more about the event procedures for toolbar buttons as you now turn to the code of the Transportation Planner MDI application.

Figure 14-13: The Load Picture dialog box allows you to choose an image for an icon in your application's toolbar. To view this dialog box, select the Picture property for a command button.

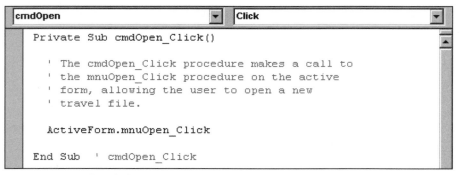

Figure 14-14: The Click event procedure for a command button on the toolbar can simply make a call to the Click procedure for the corresponding menu command. For example, cmdOpen_Click calls the mnuOpen_Click procedure.

Exploring the program's code

The declarations, event procedures, and general procedures of the MDI parent form, frmTranParent, will be the main focus of your attention in this chapter. You can examine the entire program listing in Appendix A, or you can scroll through the procedures in the code window on your screen.

Other Ways to Create a Toolbar

The image control is an alternative object for creating buttons along your application's toolbar. Its property settings are a little easier to establish for the purposes of the toolbar. But it also has a disadvantage. When the user clicks an image control with the mouse, the object doesn't behave quite like a typical Windows button. The satisfying push-button effect — the action that normally takes place on the screen when a button is clicked — doesn't happen with an image control. For this reason, you might favor the command button control for toolbox icons, even though it requires slightly more planning than an image control.

A more sophisticated approach for creating a toolbar is to use the Toolbar control, supplied as part of a group of ActiveX controls in a file named COMCTL32.OCX. (These controls are identified as Microsoft Windows Common Controls 5.0 in the Controls list of the Components dialog box.) The Toolbar control and its associated ImageList control enable you to create the visual elements of a Windows-style toolbar in an application. To use the Toolbar control, you place an instance of it on a form. Then click the control with the right mouse button and choose Properties from the resulting shortcut menu. In the Property Pages dialog box, you can add a collection of Button objects to the Toolbar control and set other important properties of the control.

For more information about this ActiveX control, search for *Toolbar control* in Visual Basic's Help Topics window.

In addition, the program's code includes the declarations and procedures of the child form, frmTranPlan. Although these procedures are similar to the code of the original program, as presented in Chapter 12, there are several significant revisions. (Notice again that the child form for the MDI program is saved as TranMDIc.Frm; the corresponding form in the original Transportation Planner program is TranPlan.Frm.) Here are some of the differences that you should keep in mind as you examine the code of the MDI program:

✦ The child form now has a public variable named *fileNumber,* which represents the number that the program assigns to the open travel file in a particular trip window. The variable is declared in the general declarations section of the child form, shown in Figures 14-15 and 14-16:

```
Public fileNumber As Integer
```

After creating an instance of the child form, the program assigns a unique integer value from 1 to 5 to the new form's *fileNumber* property. This avoids any conflicts among the multiple files that may be open at one time. Procedures that work with an open file in the child form use this variable to identify the file; for example, here is how a file is opened in the mnuOpen_Click procedure, shown in Figures 14-17 and 14-18:

```
Open tranFileName for Random As #fileNumber _
    Len = Len(TranRecord)
```

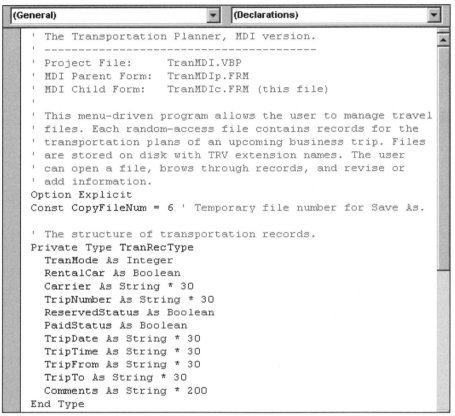

```
(General)                    ▼   (Declarations)                ▼

 ' The Transportation Planner, MDI version.
 ' -----------------------------------------
 ' Project File:      TranMDI.VBP
 ' MDI Parent Form:   TranMDIp.FRM
 ' MDI Child Form:    TranMDIc.FRM (this file)
 '
 ' This menu-driven program allows the user to manage travel
 ' files. Each random-access file contains records for the
 ' transportation plans of an upcoming business trip. Files
 ' are stored on disk with TRV extension names. The user
 ' can open a file, brows through records, and revise or
 ' add information.
 Option Explicit
 Const CopyFileNum = 6 ' Temporary file number for Save As.


 ' The structure of transportation records.
 Private Type TranRecType
   TranMode As Integer
   RentalCar As Boolean
   Carrier As String * 30
   TripNumber As String * 30
   ReservedStatus As Boolean
   PaidStatus As Boolean
   TripDate As String * 30
   TripTime As String * 30
   TripFrom As String * 30
   TripTo As String * 30
   Comments As String * 200
 End Type
```

Figure 14-15: The general declarations section of the child form. For the MDI version, the child form contains a variety of public variables used by the parent form.

✦ Three other key variables are declared publicly in the child form so that the parent form can read the data they contain for each instance of the child. Specifically, the variable *tranFileOpen* indicates whether a file is open in a given child form; *tranFileName* is the name of the open file; and *recordChanged* indicates whether the current record has been revised and therefore needs to be saved to disk:

```
Public tranFileOpen As Boolean
Public tranFileName As String
Public recordChanged as Boolean
```

✦ Likewise, several key routines in the child form are defined as Public procedures. This allows the parent form to call procedures as methods of a particular instance of the child form. In particular, several major menu procedures in the child form are declared publicly; when the user clicks a button on the toolbar, the parent form makes a call to the appropriate menu procedure on the child form.

◆ Finally, several new menu procedures are included in the code of the child form. Keep in mind that the application's menu is defined on the child form, not the parent form. As a result, each instance of the child form displays and responds to its own menu commands. The new menu procedures include the two event procedures for Window commands, mnuCascade_Click and mnuTile_Click, which rearrange the open windows within the parent form, as shown in Figure 14-19. These two procedures use Visual Basic's Arrange method to rearrange the windows. For example, this statement produces a cascade arrangement:

```
frmTranParent.Arrange 0
```

And this statement creates a tiled arrangement:

```
frmTranParent.Arrange 1
```

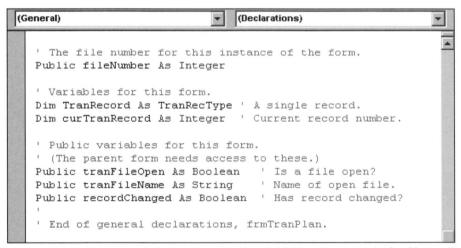

```
(General)                    ▼   (Declarations)                ▼

   ' The file number for this instance of the form.
   Public fileNumber As Integer

   ' Variables for this form.
   Dim TranRecord As TranRecType ' A single record.
   Dim curTranRecord As Integer  ' Current record number.

   ' Public variables for this form.
   ' (The parent form needs access to these.)
   Public tranFileOpen As Boolean   ' Is a file open?
   Public tranFileName As String    ' Name of open file.
   Public recordChanged As Boolean  ' Has record changed?
   '
   ' End of general declarations, frmTranPlan.
```

Figure 14-16: The general declarations for the child form, continued. The *fileNumber* variable represents the number of the Trv file open in the current child.

The parent form contains procedures designed to carry out the general operations of the multiple-document application. These operations include creating and displaying new instances of the child form, responding to clicks on the toolbar buttons, checking to see whether a requested file is already open in an existing child form, and ensuring that all records are saved to their respective files on disk before the program performance ends. You'll examine each of these MDI techniques in the sections ahead.

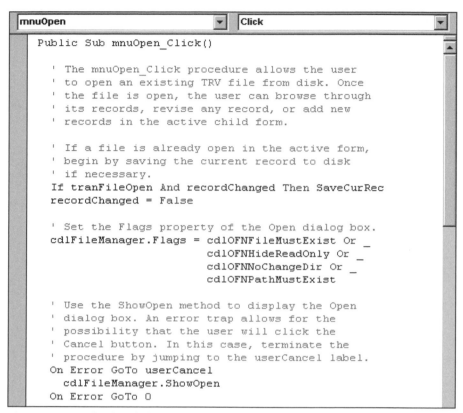

```
mnuOpen                                  ▼    Click                                              ▼

    Public Sub mnuOpen_Click()

        ' The mnuOpen_Click procedure allows the user
        ' to open an existing TRV file from disk. Once
        ' the file is open, the user can browse through
        ' its records, revise any record, or add new
        ' records in the active child form.

        ' If a file is already open in the active form,
        ' begin by saving the current record to disk
        ' if necessary.
        If tranFileOpen And recordChanged Then SaveCurRec
        recordChanged = False

        ' Set the Flags property of the Open dialog box.
        cdlFileManager.Flags = cdlOFNFileMustExist Or _
                               cdlOFNHideReadOnly Or _
                               cdlOFNNoChangeDir Or _
                               cdlOFNPathMustExist

        ' Use the ShowOpen method to display the Open
        ' dialog box. An error trap allows for the
        ' possibility that the user will click the
        ' Cancel button. In this case, terminate the
        ' procedure by jumping to the userCancel label.
        On Error GoTo userCancel
          cdlFileManager.ShowOpen
        On Error GoTo 0
```

Figure 14-17: The first half of the mnuOpen_Click procedure from the child form. After setting the Flags property, the procedure makes a call to the ShowOpen method of the common dialog control to display the Open dialog box.

Creating new instances of the child form

The *NewTranChild* procedure in Figure 14-20 is responsible for creating each new instance of the frmTranPlan form and displaying it inside the parent form as a trip window. This procedure is called once at the beginning of the program by the MDIForm_Load procedure shown in Figure 14-21, and again from the mnuNew_Click procedure in Figure 14-22 — each time the user chooses the New command from the File menu. Because mnuNew_Click is located in the child form, a reference to the parent form indicates the location of the called procedure:

```
frmTranParent.NewTranChild
```

```
mnuOpen                          ▼    Click                          ▼
' Check to see if the requested file is already open in
' another child form. (The IsAlreadyOpen function on the
' parent form returns a value of True if this is the
' case.) If so, ignore the user's request and exit.
If frmTranParent.IsAlreadyOpen _
  (cdlFileManager.filename) Then Exit Sub

' If a file is currently open in this child form, close
' it. Then record the requested file name as tranFileName.
If tranFileOpen Then Close #fileNumber
tranFileName = cdlFileManager.filename

' Open the file and switch tranFileOpen to true.
Open tranFileName For Random As #fileNumber _
   Len = Len(TranRecord)
tranFileOpen = True

' Prepare to append a new record to the end of the file.
BlankEOFRecord

' Enable the Previous command for multiple records.
If curTranRecord > 1 Then mnuPrevious.Enabled = True

' Display the new caption in the title bar.
Caption = tranFileName & ", #" & curTranRecord

' Terminate the procedure if the user clicks Cancel.
userCancel:
End Sub  ' mnuOpen_Click
```

Figure 14-18: The second half of the mnuOpen_Click procedure from the child form. Before opening a file to display in the current child, this procedure checks to see if the requested file is already open. If so, an Exit Sub statement aborts the procedure.

The *NewTranChild* procedure uses a module-level variable named *tripNum* to keep track of the current number of open trip windows. At the same time, a constant named *MaxTrips* represents the maximum number of trip windows that the program allows. If *tripNum* is less than or equal to *MaxTrips* at the time *NewTranChild* is called, the procedure's first action is to create a new instance of the frmTranPlan form:

```
If tripNum <= MaxTrips Then
   Dim newTranPlan As New frmTranPlan
```

As you can see, the object variable *newTranPlan* represents the form for the procedure's remaining operations.

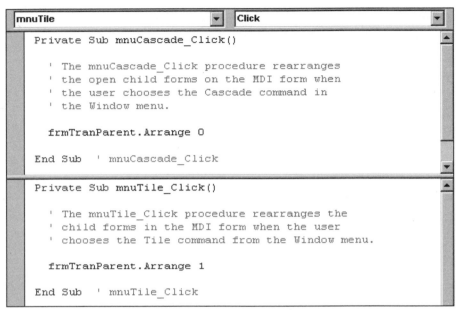

Figure 14-19: The mnuCascade_Click and mnuTile_Click procedures from the child form. These procedures use the Arrange method to rearrange child forms within the parent form.

The first task is to assign values to the properties of the new form. The procedure concatenates the current value of *tripNum* to the word "Trip" to create a generic title for the form, such as Trip1, Trip2, and so on:

```
newTranPlan.Caption = "Trip" & tripNum
newTranPlan.Tag = newTranPlan.Caption
```

This value is assigned first to the Caption property so that it will appear on the form's title bar. But in addition, a copy of the generic title is stored in the form's Tag property, where it will be available when the program needs to restore the original generic title to the form. Specifically, this happens in the mnuClose_Click procedure in Figure 14-23, after the program closes the file currently displayed in a given trip window. On the title bar, the program replaces the name of the newly closed file with the generic title:

```
Caption = Tag
```

The Tag property is a useful place to store items of information that are related to a particular form or control.

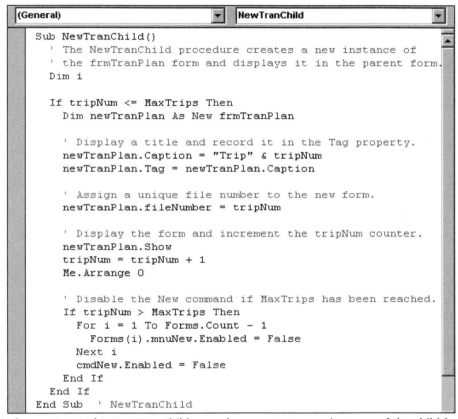

```
(General)                              NewTranChild

Sub NewTranChild()
  ' The NewTranChild procedure creates a new instance of
  ' the frmTranPlan form and displays it in the parent form.
  Dim i

  If tripNum <= MaxTrips Then
    Dim newTranPlan As New frmTranPlan

    ' Display a title and record it in the Tag property.
    newTranPlan.Caption = "Trip" & tripNum
    newTranPlan.Tag = newTranPlan.Caption

    ' Assign a unique file number to the new form.
    newTranPlan.fileNumber = tripNum

    ' Display the form and increment the tripNum counter.
    newTranPlan.Show
    tripNum = tripNum + 1
    Me.Arrange 0

    ' Disable the New command if MaxTrips has been reached.
    If tripNum > MaxTrips Then
      For i = 1 To Forms.Count - 1
        Forms(i).mnuNew.Enabled = False
      Next i
      cmdNew.Enabled = False
    End If
  End If
End Sub  ' NewTranChild
```

Figure 14-20: The *NewTranChild* procedure creates a new instance of the child form, sets its properties, and displays it inside the parent MDI form.

The *NewTranChild* procedure's next task is to assign a file number to the newly created instance of the child form:

```
newTranPlan.fileNumber = tripNum
```

As you've seen already, each child form uses *fileNumber* to identify an open file; it's therefore essential that each child possess a unique value for this variable. Assigning the value of *tripNum* to *fileNumber* is a simple way to meet this requirement.

Next, the procedure displays the new form inside the parent form and increments the value of *tripNum*:

```
newTranPlan.Show
tripNum = tripNum + 1
```

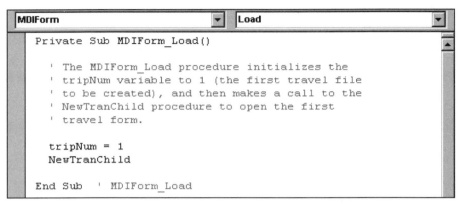

Figure 14-21: The MDIForm_Load procedure is the first routine to make a call to the *NewTranChild* procedure. Notice that *tripNum* is set to 1 for this first child form.

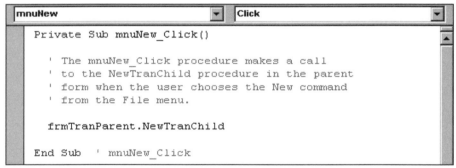

Figure 14-22: The mnuNew_Click procedure calls the *NewTranChild* procedure each time the user chooses File⇨New or clicks the New Trip Window button on the toolbar.

When *tripNum* goes past the value of *MaxTrips* — that is, when the user has opened the maximum number of trip windows that the application allows — the procedure disables the New command in the File menu and the New button in the toolbar:

```
If tripNum > MaxTrips Then
  For i = 1 To Forms.Count - 1
    Forms(i).mnuNew.Enabled = False
  Next i
  cmdNew.Enabled = False
End If
```

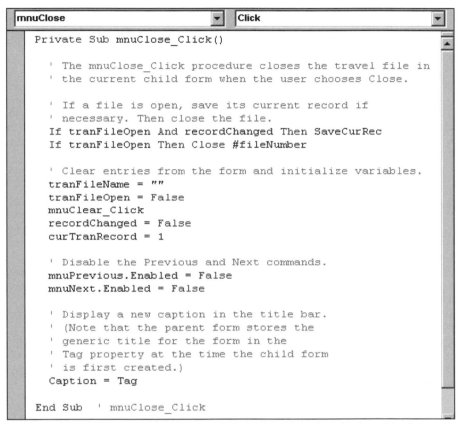

| mnuClose | ▼ | Click | ▼ |

```
Private Sub mnuClose_Click()

   ' The mnuClose_Click procedure closes the travel file in
   ' the current child form when the user chooses Close.

   ' If a file is open, save its current record if
   ' necessary. Then close the file.
   If tranFileOpen And recordChanged Then SaveCurRec
   If tranFileOpen Then Close #fileNumber

   ' Clear entries from the form and initialize variables.
   tranFileName = ""
   tranFileOpen = False
   mnuClear_Click
   recordChanged = False
   curTranRecord = 1

   ' Disable the Previous and Next commands.
   mnuPrevious.Enabled = False
   mnuNext.Enabled = False

   ' Display a new caption in the title bar.
   ' (Note that the parent form stores the
   ' generic title for the form in the
   ' Tag property at the time the child form
   ' is first created.)
   Caption = Tag

End Sub   ' mnuClose_Click
```

Figure 14-23: The mnuClose_Click procedure closes the file displayed in the current child form and reinitializes the variables that represent the child's properties. The generic form caption is copied from its storage place in the Tag property.

Keep in mind that the menu definition belongs to the child form, not the parent form. In fact, each child form has its own menu, which is displayed when the child is active. Because all the child forms are designed to behave identically, this is not an obvious issue until the program needs to make a change in the menu. But to disable the New command, the program has to loop through all the open child forms and disable the command on each form. It uses Visual Basic's built-in Forms collection to do the job. A reference to Forms(i).mnuNew identifies the target menu command for each open form. By contrast, the toolbar is defined on the MDI parent form. A simple reference to cmdNew.Enabled identifies the button property that the procedure needs to switch to False in order to disable the toolbar button.

By the way, you can change the program's maximum number of trip windows by assigning new values to two important constants. In the general declarations section of the MDI parent form, frmTranParent, change the value assigned to *MaxTrips*:

```
Const MaxTrips = 5
```

Then, in the general declarations of the child form, frmTranPlan, change the value of a constant named *CopyFileNum*:

```
Const CopyFileNum = 6
```

The constant *CopyFileNum* represents an extra file number that's available for the Save As operation. *CopyFileNum* needs a value that is 1 greater than *MaxTrips*. So, for example, if you change the value of *MaxTrips* to 10, change *CopyFileNum* to 11; these changes would allow a maximum of 10 open trip windows during a program run.

Responding to clicks on the toolbar buttons

Figures 14-24 and 14-25 show four of the five Click event procedures that handle toolbar operations. (The fifth, cmdOpen_Click, appears back in Figure 14-14.) The first of these, cmdNew_Click, makes a call to the *NewTranChild* procedure when the user clicks the New button. As you've just seen, the program removes the New button from the toolbar when the user has opened the maximum number of trip windows, so this Click procedure cannot be called again after that point.

The cmdOpen_Click and cmdSaveAs_Click procedures both make calls to menu commands on the active child form. To identify the child window that's active when the user clicks the Open or Save As button, the program uses Visual Basic's ActiveForm property. Using this important keyword, the following statements make calls to the menu commands belonging to the active child form:

```
ActiveForm.mnuOpen_Click
ActiveForm.mnuSaveAs_Click
```

Likewise, the cmdPrevious_Click and cmdNext_Click procedures need to make calls to menu procedures for the active form. But here there is an added complication. As you might recall from Chapter 12, the program is careful to disable the Previous and Next commands in the Record menu whenever their use is not appropriate. For example, if the active trip window is already displaying the first record in an open file, the Previous command is disabled.

Accordingly, the Click procedures for the Scroll Back and Scroll Forward toolbar buttons need to avoid making calls to the mnuPrevious_Click or mnuNext_Click procedures if the corresponding menu command has been disabled. To conform to this requirement, the event procedures for the toolbar buttons read the Enabled property of the appropriate menu command and use this Boolean value as the condition in a decision statement. For example, here is how the cmdPrevious_Click procedure decides whether or not to make a call to the mnuPrevious_Click procedure:

```
If ActiveForm.mnuPrevious.Enabled Then _
  ActiveForm.mnuPrevious_Click
```

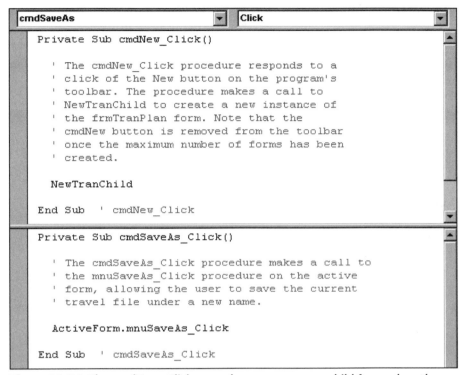

Figure 14-24: The cmdNew_Click procedure opens a new child form when the user clicks the New Trip Window button on the toolbar. The cmdSaveAs_Click procedure simply makes a call to the corresponding menu procedure when the user clicks the Save Trip File button.

Once again notice the use of the ActiveForm property to identify the form to which this operation applies.

Finding out whether a file is already open

The program does not permit the user to open the same file in more than one trip window. To enforce this rule, the program has to examine the files that are open whenever the user chooses a file from the Open or Save As dialog box. If the selected file name matches the name of a file that is already displayed in one of the trip windows, the file operation is denied.

A function named *IsAlreadyOpen*, shown in Figure 14-26, is responsible for carrying out this check. The function receives, as its single argument, the name of the file that the user has requested:

```
Function IsAlreadyOpen(testFileName As String) As Boolean
```

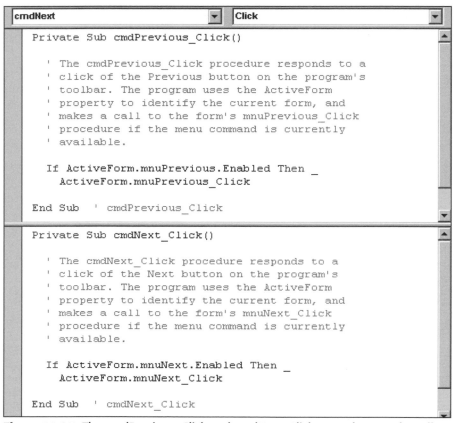

Figure 14-25: The cmdPrevious_Click and cmdNext_Click procedures make calls to the corresponding menu commands unless those commands are currently disabled.

The function returns a Boolean value of True if the file is already open, or False if not.

On each child form, the public variable *tranFileName* represents the name of the current file. (If no file is open, *tranFileName* contains an empty string.) To see whether or not a given file is open, the *IsAlreadyOpen* function loops through the Forms collection and examines the value of *tranFileName* on each child form:

```
IsAlreadyOpen = False
For i = 1 To Forms.Count - 1
  With Forms(i)
    If Trim(.tranFileName) = Trim(testFileName) _
      Then IsAlreadyOpen = True
  End With
Next i
```

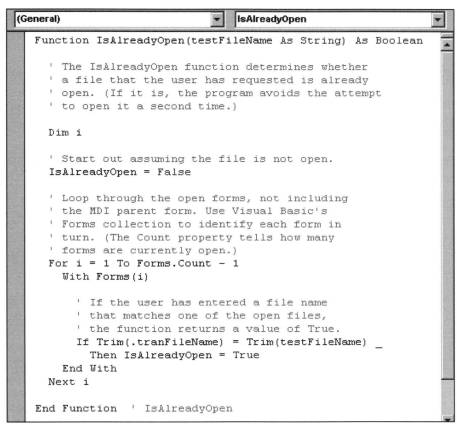

```
(General)                              ▼   IsAlreadyOpen                      ▼

Function IsAlreadyOpen(testFileName As String) As Boolean

   ' The IsAlreadyOpen function determines whether
   ' a file that the user has requested is already
   ' open. (If it is, the program avoids the attempt
   ' to open it a second time.)

   Dim i

   ' Start out assuming the file is not open.
   IsAlreadyOpen = False

   ' Loop through the open forms, not including
   ' the MDI parent form. Use Visual Basic's
   ' Forms collection to identify each form in
   ' turn. (The Count property tells how many
   ' forms are currently open.)
   For i = 1 To Forms.Count - 1
     With Forms(i)

        ' If the user has entered a file name
        ' that matches one of the open files,
        ' the function returns a value of True.
        If Trim(.tranFileName) = Trim(testFileName) _
          Then IsAlreadyOpen = True
     End With
   Next i

End Function  ' IsAlreadyOpen
```

Figure 14-26: The *IsAlreadyOpen* function returns a value of True if a requested file is already open in another child. The routine loops through the open forms (represented by the Forms collection) and compares each open file name with the argument *testFileName*.

If the comparison between Forms(i).tranFileName and the *testFileName* argument produces a match for any form in the collection, the function returns a value of True.

In the child form, *IsAlreadyOpen* is called from two menu procedures, mnuOpen_-Click and mnuSaveAs_Click. The call takes place just after the Open or Save As dialog box disappears from the screen. The file name provided by the common dialog control, cdlFileManager, is passed as an argument to *IsAlreadyOpen*:

```
If frmTranParent.IsAlreadyOpen _
  (cdlFileManager.FileName) Then Exit Sub
```

If *IsAlreadyOpen* returns a value of True, this statement simply terminates the current procedure, skipping the Open or Save As operation.

Saving all files before the end of a run

Finally, the MDI parent form is responsible for making sure that all open travel files are saved properly to disk before the end of a program performance. If the user has revised the current records in any of the trip windows, those records must be written to their corresponding files before the windows are closed. To arrange this, the program uses the MDIForm_QueryUnload procedure in Figure 14-27. This event procedure is triggered when the user clicks the Close button at the upper-right corner of the application window.

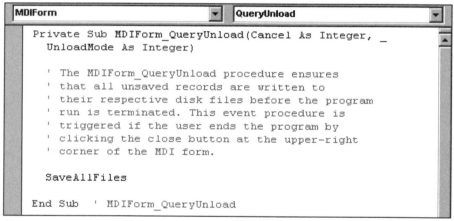

Figure 14-27: The MDIForm_QueryUnload procedure ensures that all open files are saved to disk before the program terminates.

The QueryUnload event gives the program the opportunity to perform final operations on any open child forms before the MDI form is actually closed. In this program, the event procedure makes a call to a general procedure named SaveAllFiles, shown in Figure 14-28. This procedure in turn loops through all the open trip windows and checks to see whether the current record has changed in each case; if so, a call is made to the *SaveCurRec* procedure in the child form to save the current record to disk:

```
For i = 1 To Forms.Count - 1
  With Forms(i)
    If .tranFileOpen And .recordChanged Then _
      .SaveCurRec
  End With
Next i
```

Once again, the program uses Visual Basic's built-in Forms collection to address each open child form in turn. As you'll recall, the *tranFileOpen* and *recordChanged* variables are declared as public variables on the child form. If both of these Boolean variables have values of True, the current record has been changed and must be saved before the trip window is closed.

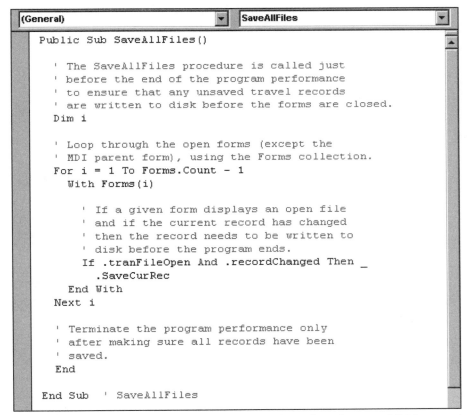

```
(General)                          ▼   SaveAllFiles                          ▼
    Public Sub SaveAllFiles()

        ' The SaveAllFiles procedure is called just
        ' before the end of the program performance
        ' to ensure that any unsaved travel records
        ' are written to disk before the forms are closed.
        Dim i

        ' Loop through the open forms (except the
        ' MDI parent form), using the Forms collection.
        For i = 1 To Forms.Count - 1
          With Forms(i)

            ' If a given form displays an open file
            ' and if the current record has changed
            ' then the record needs to be written to
            ' disk before the program ends.
            If .tranFileOpen And .recordChanged Then _
              .SaveCurRec
          End With
        Next i

        ' Terminate the program performance only
        ' after making sure all records have been
        ' saved.
        End

    End Sub  ' SaveAllFiles
```

Figure 14-28: The *SaveAllFiles* procedure loops through each open child form and examines the *tranFileOpen* and *recordChanged* properties to determine whether the form contains an open file that has been revised. If so, the file is saved before the program terminates.

As shown in Figure 14-29, the mnuExit_Click procedure in the child form also makes a call to the *SaveAllFiles* procedure on the parent form. This ensures that the final save operation will be performed no matter what technique the user chooses to terminate the program performance.

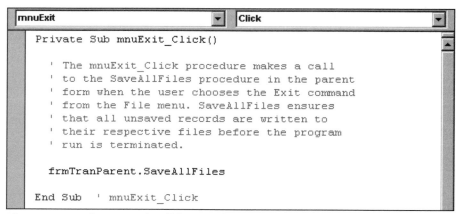

Figure 14-29: The mnuExit_Click procedure calls *SaveAllFiles* to make sure all open files are saved before the end of the program run.

As a programming exercise, you might want to try developing a new MDI application from another project presented earlier in this book. For example:

✦ An MDI version of the International Travel Expense Log program (Chapter 7) could enable the user to open expense files from several different business trips at once.

✦ Similarly, an MDI version of the International Sales program (Chapter 11) could give the user the opportunity to compare sales data for different products, time periods, or geographical regions.

MDI is clearly an important feature that adds to the value to your Visual Basic applications.

ActiveX Components and the OLE Control

✦ ✦ ✦ ✦

In This Chapter

Using the OLE control to link or embed an application in a form

Adding application objects to a project from the Components dialog box

Creating a reference to an object library

Viewing the classes and members of a library in the Object Browser

Using an ActiveX component in a Visual Basic program

Creating instances of objects, setting properties, and calling methods

Understanding Excel as an ActiveX component

✦ ✦ ✦ ✦

An ActiveX component is an application, a control, or a code library that provides programmable objects you can use in Visual Basic projects. To include such an object in an application, you begin by making sure that the component itself is available on your system. Then you follow steps that by now are strikingly familiar:

1. Declare a variable to represent the object in code.

2. Create an instance of the object, and assign the object's reference to the variable.

3. Use this reference to access the object's properties, methods, and events.

An ActiveX component that provides objects is sometimes known as a *server* and the application that uses the objects is a *client*. For example, this chapter presents a Visual Basic program that employs Microsoft Excel as an ActiveX component. As a server, Excel provides objects such as worksheets and charts. A client application can make use of these objects — and carry out detailed worksheet operations — by calling on the properties and methods of the Excel objects. In this scenario, the Excel application is an *out-of-process* server; its use results in the appearance of an additional application button on the Windows 95 Taskbar when you run the client program.

Tip   The programming techniques for using ActiveX components were previously known as *OLE automation*. (OLE, pronounced *OH-lay*, stands for Object Linking and Embedding.) ActiveX is the new name for a technology that includes OLE controls,

OLE servers, and a variety of important new features. Perhaps most significantly, you can use ActiveX components to build Internet-ready applications. You'll learn more about ActiveX technology in Chapters 17 and 18.

Visual Basic also includes a tool called the OLE container control. This control represents an alternative approach for including an application such as Excel in a Visual Basic project. Before turning specifically to the subject of ActiveX components, this chapter begins with a brief look at the OLE control.

Using the OLE Control

With the OLE control, you can provide access to existing Windows applications within the context of a Visual Basic program. OLE defines two basic ways of attaching objects to a host — *embedding* and *linking:*

✦ An embedded object is contained within the host document. When you want to develop or edit the data of an embedded object, you can activate the source application without leaving the document. The resulting object is saved in the host document, not in a separate file.

✦ By contrast, a linked object is stored in an external file. The host document contains a reference to the data and an image of the linked object, but does not store the data. When you revise the object's data, the changes are displayed in the host document but saved in the external file.

Using the OLE control, shown in Figure 15-1, you can link or embed objects inside a form. During a run, the user can view and edit the object's data, employing the resources of the source application.

Figure 15-1: The OLE container control represents a simple technique for adding the resources of an OLE-enabled Windows application to a Visual Basic project.

When you add an OLE control to a form at design time, Visual Basic immediately displays the Insert Object dialog box on the screen, giving you the opportunity to select the object that the control will contain. In the process, you can choose between embedding or linking the object. Here are the steps for placing an OLE control on a form and then choosing an object:

1. Open the form and double-click the OLE container control in the Toolbox. A box representing the control appears in the center of your form, and the Insert Object dialog box opens onto the desktop as in Figure 15-2.

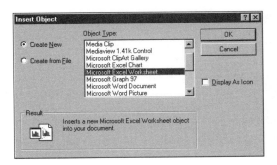

Figure 15-2: The Insert Object dialog box appears when you add an OLE container control to any form in your project. In the Object Type list you select the object that you want to display within the control.

2. If you want to create a new object, keep the Create New option selected. In the Object Type list, select the application object that you want your OLE control to display. Notice that one application might provide two or more types of items in the Object Type list. For example, Excel provides worksheet objects and chart objects.

3. If you want the object to show the data from an existing file, choose the Create from File option. As you can see in Figure 15-3, the dialog box displays a File text box in which you can enter the complete path and name of the file you want to attach. (If you don't know the file's exact location, click the Browse button; in the resulting Browse dialog box, you can select the appropriate folder and look for the file.)

4. By default, the Insert Object dialog box assumes you want to attach the file as an embedded object in your form. Notice that the Result box at the bottom of Figure 15-3 provides a brief description of an embedded object. If you instead want to link the object to your file, click the Link option. A check appears in the adjacent box, and a general description of a linked object appears in the Result box, as shown in Figure 15-4.

5. Click OK to complete the process. Back on your form, the object appears inside the OLE container control. You can now move and resize the object box to create a convenient presentation of its contents.

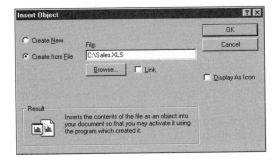

Figure 15-3: To attach the data from an existing file, select the Create from File option and enter the full path name of the file. If the Link option is unchecked, the Result box provides a description of an embedded object.

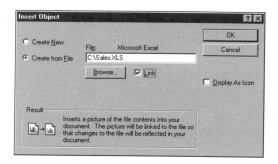

Figure 15-4: To link the object to your form, select the Link option. When Link is checked, the Result box provides a description of a linked object.

For example, the Visual Basic application in Figure 15-5 illustrates the use of the OLE control to display a linked object. The object is an Excel worksheet, displayed inside the large box at the bottom of the form. In addition to the OLE container, the form contains a multiline text box control and command buttons representing operations that the program provides for working with the linked object.

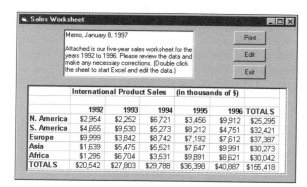

Figure 15-5: A program illustrating the use of the OLE container control to display a linked object. Here the OLE control displays the contents of an Excel worksheet file. During a run of the program, the user double-clicks inside the sheet to start Excel and edit the file.

During a program run, the user can double-click inside the OLE container control to start Excel. In response, the Excel application appears in a window of its own and displays the complete source worksheet, as you can see in Figure 15-6. The user then has the opportunity to scroll through all the data and make necessary changes. When the user exits from Excel and returns to the Visual Basic application, any changes in the linked data are displayed in the OLE container control.

Another way to provide access to Windows applications in a Visual Basic program is to add specific application objects to the Toolbox from the Components dialog box. Then you can insert these objects in a form directly from the Toolbox. For example, you can create Toolbox buttons representing Excel worksheets and charts, Paint drawings, or WordPad documents. These tools are then available as insertable application objects for your current Visual Basic project. Here are the steps:

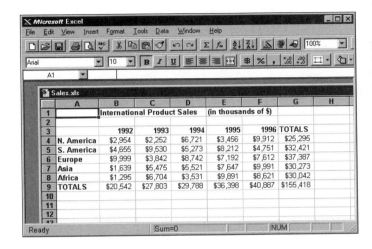

Figure 15-6: When the user double-clicks inside the OLE container control, the source application appears in its own application window and displays the contents of the linked file. Any changes that the user makes and saves in the file are then displayed in the Visual Basic application.

1. Choose Project⇨Components to open the Components dialog box. (Alternatively, press Ctrl+T, or click the Toolbox with the right mouse button and choose Components from the shortcut menu.)

2. Click the Insertable Objects tab. In the resulting list, click the check box next to each application object that you want to include in your Toolbox. A check appears next to each selection, as in Figure 15-7. Click OK when you've completed your selection.

3. The Toolbox now displays buttons for each of the application objects you've added. For example, the buttons in the bottom rows of the Toolbox in Figure 15-8 represent a variety of Windows application objects. To place an instance of any of these objects in the current project, open a form and double-click the target object in the Toolbox.

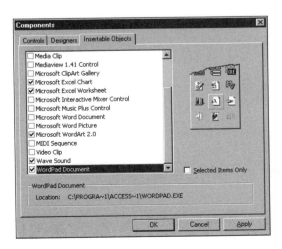

Figure 15-7: To add application objects to the Visual Basic Toolbox, click the Insertable Objects tab in the Components dialog box, and check any combination of objects that you want to add.

Figure 15-8: The new insertable objects appear at the bottom of the Toolbox. To add any of these objects to a form, open the form and double-click the appropriate Toolbox icon.

Using the OLE container control or individual application controls, you can quickly build a project that provides access to the resources of other Windows applications. But to exert direct control in your code over the features of a server application, you instead employ specific programming techniques designed for ActiveX components and their objects. This approach, formerly known as OLE activation, is the main topic of this chapter.

Programming with ActiveX Components

An ActiveX component provides programmable objects whose methods and properties can be used in the client program's code. The client creates new instances of these objects at runtime and makes calls to the methods and properties, thereby controlling the server's operations. In this case, the objects are not embedded or linked to the client application at design time; rather, the program creates instances of the objects in code. The upcoming sections of this chapter show you how to build a Visual Basic project that works with ActiveX components.

Only ActiveX applications — which "expose" their objects to the client — may be used in this way. Other applications may be linked or embedded in a Visual Basic form. But if an application is not designed as an ActiveX component, its objects, methods, and properties are not available for programming.

Creating a reference to an object library

An application like Excel has an associated *object library*, with complete information about the programmable objects it provides. To develop a Visual Basic program that works with these objects, you begin by creating a reference to the appropriate object library. You can then use the Object Browser to help you develop your application, as in the following steps:

1. Choose Project⇨References. The References dialog box provides a list of available object library files, as you can see in Figure 15-9.

2. To add a reference to a particular library for use in the project you're currently developing, click the check box next to the library's name in the list. A check indicates that a particular object library is available to your current project. For example, if you're planning to write a program that works with Excel objects, you should select the Microsoft Excel Object Library entry in the list. Click OK to confirm the new reference.

3. Once a given library is referenced in your project, you can view lists of its objects, methods, and properties in Visual Basic's Object Browser. Press F2 to open the Object Browser — or click the Object Browser button on the Toolbar — and then select the appropriate library from the drop-down list at the upper-left corner of the window. The Classes and Members lists show the contents of the library, as in Figure 15-10.

4. To learn how to use a particular method or property in the object library, select the class to which the object belongs and then select an item in the Members list. The syntax of the method or property appears at the bottom of the Object Browser dialog box.

5. For more information, click the Help button at the top of the Object Browser window. A help window appears on the desktop, displaying the topic you've requested. For example, Figure 15-11 shows the Excel help window for a method named Add.

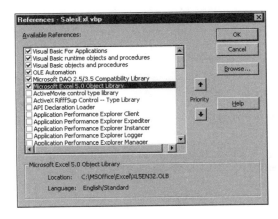

Figure 15-9: The References dialog box with its list of object libraries. Place a check next to a library that you want to make available to the current project.

Figure 15-10: The Object Browser dialog box, displaying the classes and members of a library. When you select a class and then choose an item from the Members list, the Object Browser displays the syntax of the item.

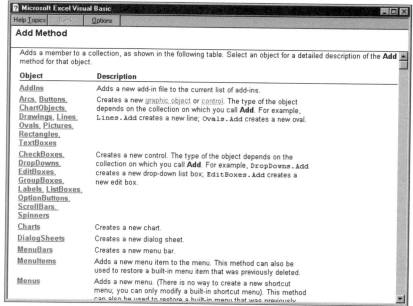

Figure 15-11: By clicking the Help button you can open a help topic for a particular method or property in the object library.

To illustrate ActiveX programming, this chapter presents an expanded version of the International Sales program, which was first presented in Chapter 11. Like the original project, this new program provides an arrangement of text boxes in which you create a table of sales data. As you enter each row and column of figures, the program calculates totals and develops a graph depicting the data. You can choose between a column chart or a pie chart, oriented to depict rows of regional data or columns of periodic data.

This version's main new feature is a technique for copying the sales data to an external application, Microsoft Excel. Once you've developed a sales table and chart, you can choose a single menu command to copy the entire data set to an Excel worksheet. In response to your menu choice, the program takes steps to perform the following tasks:

✦ Create and display an Excel worksheet

✦ Copy all the sales data to the sheet, along with titles and headings

✦ Enter formulas for calculating row and column totals on the worksheet

✦ Instruct Excel to create a chart, equivalent to the one currently displayed in the International Sales application window

When all these tasks are complete, you can save a copy of the worksheet object to disk as a file that you can later use directly in Excel.

Tip This application is designed to run on a system that contains an installation of Microsoft Excel for Windows 95, or a later version of the spreadsheet. If Excel is not installed on your computer, you won't be able to test this version of the International Sales project. But you can follow the program's action by examining the screen illustrations presented in this chapter. And, of course, you can review the program's basic operations by opening and running the original version, IntSales.Vbp.

If you do have Excel, take a moment now to run the expanded version of the program and experiment with its new features.

Running the International Sales program, Excel version

The project is stored on disk as SalesExl.Vbp. Open the application and take a look at the Project window, shown in Figure 15-12. It contains a single form named frmIntSales, which is saved as SalesExl.Frm.

Figure 15-12: The Excel version of the International Sales program contains one form, stored on disk as SalesExl.Frm. This form contains all the program's code.

Press F5 to run the new version of the International Sales program. Initially the application window seems unchanged from the original version. To see the new features, take a look at the File and Edit menus:

✦ In the File menu, the Save Report and Print Window commands have been replaced by the Transfer to Excel command, as you can see in Figure 15-13.

✦ The Edit menu, in Figure 15-14, contains a new command called Random Data, which fills the sales table with random four-digit figures. (This feature gives you a quick way to generate sample data so you can explore the Transfer to Excel command.)

Figure 15-13: The new Transfer to Excel command in the program's File menu is a one-step tool for copying any data set and graph from the International Sales form to an Excel worksheet.

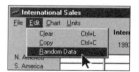

Figure 15-14: The new Random Data command in the Edit menu provides a quick way to generate a sample data set so you can focus on the program's new feature — the Transfer to Excel command. In response to this command, the program fills the sales grid with randomly generated four-digit values.

Pull down the Edit menu now and choose Random Data. The program provides an experimental data set, as in Figure 15-15. You can use these data values as they are, or you can revise them selectively to make the data seem more realistic. Either way, you are ready to begin trying out the main new feature of this program, the Transfer to Excel command. Pull down the File menu and choose the command.

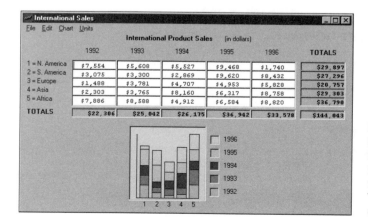

Figure 15-15: Filling the sales table with random data. At this point you're ready to begin experimenting with the Transfer to Excel command.

When you do so, the program immediately starts Microsoft Excel and begins creating a new worksheet. The entire sales table is copied to the worksheet. Summation formulas produce the totals in the last column and the bottom row. Finally, the program generates an Excel chart and arranges it below the worksheet data. All this activity takes a few seconds. When the action is complete, the Excel worksheet and chart appear as shown in Figure 15-16. The Windows 95 Taskbar contains buttons for running the International Sales program and for Microsoft Excel, showing that Excel is an out-of-process server.

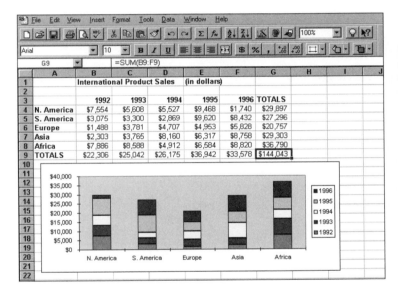

Figure 15-16: An Excel worksheet showing the sales data and the corresponding column chart. Note that the program has generated formulas to compute the totals in row 9 and column G. In the formula bar you can see the formula entry for cell G9.

Significantly, this worksheet is now a self-contained object with its own data, formulas, and charting methods. As you'll learn shortly, you can save this worksheet — or a different version of it — to disk for future work in Excel. But for now, suppose you've finished looking at the worksheet and you want to return to the International Sales program. Follow these steps:

1. Choose the Exit command from Excel's File menu to close the program. In response to the "Save changes" prompt, click the No button. The International Sales program reappears as the active program on the Windows desktop. In front of the program window a message box displays brief instructions along with an OK button, as shown in Figure 15-17. (These instructions will have greater relevance later when you decide to save an Excel worksheet.) Click the OK button. The original sales data from which the worksheet was generated remains in the application window.

2. Now choose Chart⇨By Region. This selection changes the orientation of the column chart. As shown in Figure 15-18, the legend at the right side of the chart now displays the names of the sales regions, and each column represents the sales for a particular year.

3. Choose File⇨Transfer to Excel again. The program generates a new Excel worksheet and chart to represent the sales data. But this time the Excel chart is oriented differently. As you can see in Figure 15-19, the new chart corresponds to the By Region chart option you selected in the International Sales window.

When you've finished examining the worksheet, close Excel and click the OK button in the message box provided by the International Sales program.

Figure 15-17: A message box produced by the International Sales program alerts you to the possibility of saving a worksheet file to disk before you close the Excel application.

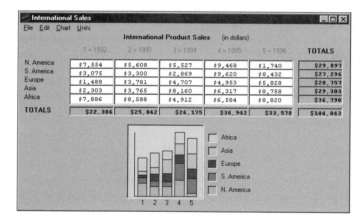

Figure 15-18: Pull down the Chart command and choose By Region to change the chart orientation in the International Sales window. The program redraws the column chart, and displays the names of the regions in the legend at the right side of the chart.

You may want to continue experimenting with the program now by choosing the Pie Chart option in the application's Chart menu and then choosing the Transfer to Excel command to view the resulting worksheet. In Figures 15-20 and 15-21, you can see how the pie chart looks when the By Years option is selected. Figures 15-22 and 15-23 show the pie chart when the By Region option is selected. Notice that Excel has its own approach to building a pie chart; you can see differences in the order of the legend entries and the starting angle for the first wedge in the pie. But a close examination confirms that the two pairs of pie charts represent the same sales data. Later in this chapter, you'll examine the code that creates a particular chart type in the Excel worksheet, depending on the current settings in the Chart menu of the International Sales window.

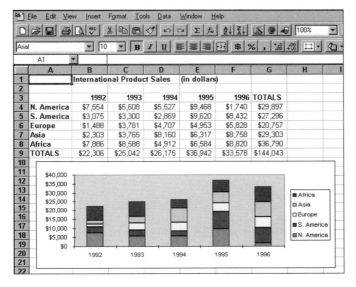

Figure 15-19: When you again choose the Transfer to Excel command, the chart on the resulting spreadsheet matches the format displayed in the International Sales window.

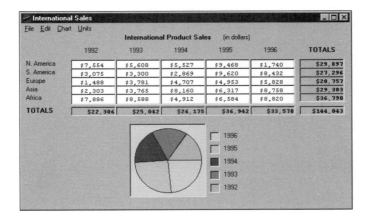

Figure 15-20: When the By Years option is selected, the wedges of a pie chart represent annual sales totals.

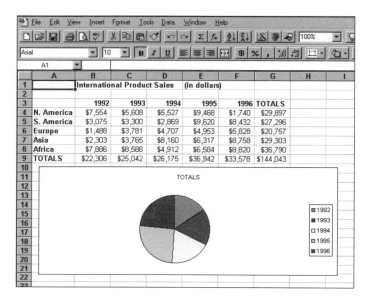

Figure 15-21: The Excel chart arranges the wedges in a different order than that of the International Sales program, but a close inspection shows that the magnitude of the wedges is the same in both versions of the chart.

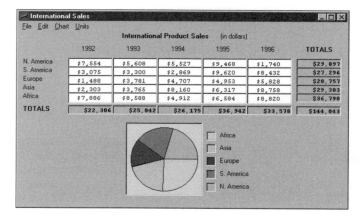

Figure 15-22: When the By Region option is selected, the wedges of a pie chart represent total regional sales.

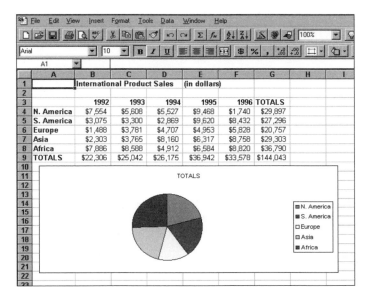

	File	Edit	View	Insert	Format	Tools	Data	Window	Help

	A	B	C	D	E	F	G	H	I
1		International Product Sales			(in dollars)				
2									
3		1992	1993	1994	1995	1996	TOTALS		
4	N. America	$7,554	$5,608	$5,527	$9,468	$1,740	$29,897		
5	S. America	$3,075	$3,300	$2,869	$9,620	$8,432	$27,296		
6	Europe	$1,488	$3,781	$4,707	$4,953	$5,828	$20,757		
7	Asia	$2,303	$3,765	$8,160	$6,317	$8,758	$29,303		
8	Africa	$7,886	$8,588	$4,912	$6,584	$8,820	$36,790		
9	TOTALS	$22,306	$25,042	$26,175	$36,942	$33,578	$144,043		

Figure 15-23: Excel arranges the chart's legend in the opposite order from that of the International Sales program, but the chart itself represents the same data set.

As you noticed at the beginning of your work, the Excel version of the International Sales program is missing two of the File commands that were available in the original application: The Save Report command was designed to create a text file containing the sales data, and the Print Window command sent an image of the application window to the printer. Why are these two commands both replaced by the Transfer to Excel command in the Excel version? Because Excel provides good alternatives for printing and saving the sales data.

As a final exercise with this program, generate a new set of sales data by entering individual sales figures yourself or by choosing the Random Data command from the Edit menu. Then choose Transfer to Excel one last time to create a worksheet and chart from the data. When the worksheet is complete, pull down the File menu from the Excel menu bar and look at the available commands, as shown in Figure 15-24.

You can choose the Print command to send a copy of the worksheet data and the chart to your printer. Alternatively, choose the Save As command to create an XLS file on disk. When you do so, the Save As dialog box (Figure 15-25) allows you to select a folder location for the file and enter a file name. Furthermore, you can use tools in the dialog box to navigate through the folder hierarchy on your hard disk, and you can click the Options button to set the properties of the file you're about to create. When you save the worksheet, it becomes an independent record of the sales data. You can later start Excel, open the worksheet, and work with the data in any way you want.

Figure 15-24: Excel's File menu provides Save As and Print commands for the worksheet and chart objects.

Figure 15-25: Creating a new XLS file, using Excel's Save As dialog box.

After saving an Excel worksheet file, click the International Sales button on the Windows 95 Taskbar. Click OK in the message box; in response, the program takes care of closing the Excel application window. To complete your work, choose File➪Exit.

In summary, the Excel version of the International Sales program presents some significant enhancements in the original design of the application. It uses Excel as an ActiveX component to produce a worksheet object and a chart object for the current sales data. The program copies the sales table to the worksheet and generates formulas for the totals. The chart type and chart orientation in the International Sales window are duplicated in the resulting Excel chart.

Keep in mind that the frmIntSales form does not contain a linked or embedded Excel object. Rather the program creates new worksheet objects at runtime. As you now turn to the program's code, you'll see how a Visual Basic program works with the objects of an ActiveX component.

Inside the Excel Version of the Sales Program

You can examine the program's code by turning to Appendix A or by scrolling though procedures in the code window on your screen. Your main focus here will be on the declarations and procedures related to the ActiveX component:

✦ The general declarations section of the frmIntSales form includes module-level declarations for the key Excel object variables, including an Application object, a Workbook object, and a Worksheet object.

✦ The mnuExcel_Click event procedure creates instances of Excel objects and then makes calls to procedures that copy the data (*CopyToExcel*) and generate the chart (*DrawExcelChart*).

✦ The procedure named *CopyToExcel* takes care of several tasks — formatting the worksheet appropriately; copying the data, titles, and headings; and creating formulas for the sales totals.

✦ The procedure named *DrawExcelChart* then creates a chart object and uses a method named ChartWizard to draw the chart. The properties of the Excel chart depend on the current settings of the mnuChartBy and mnuChartType menus in the International Sales window.

In the upcoming sections you'll examine the code from each of these listings.

Declaring object variables for the Excel component

Objects in Excel are organized in a hierarchy of containers and collections. At the top of the hierarchy is the Application object, which represents the Excel application itself. Next in line is the Workbooks collection and the Workbook object, and then the Worksheets collection and Worksheet object. To refer to a specific object, you begin with the Application object and then work your way down the hierarchy to the target level. For example, you can access the Workbooks collection through a call to the Workbooks method of the Application object. Likewise, you can access the Worksheets collection via a call to the Worksheets method.

To work successfully within this hierarchy, the program declares three object variables belonging to the Application, Workbook, and Worksheet classes. The following three Dim statements appear in the general declarations section of the frmIntSales form, in Figure 15-26:

```
Dim ExcelApp As Excel.Application
Dim ExcelWorkbook As Excel.Workbook
Dim ExcelSheet As Excel.Worksheet
```

Because these statements are in the general declarations, the three object variables are available anywhere in the program. As you'll see shortly, the mnuExcel_Click procedure creates instances of these objects. The *ExcelSheet* variable subsequently represents the worksheet in all the procedures that perform operations on the objects of the Excel component.

```
(General)                    ▼   (Declarations)                ▼

' The International Sales Program, Excel Version
' ------------------------------------------------
' Project File:   SalesEx1.VBP
' Form File:      SalesEx1.FRM
'
' In this version of the International Sales program, the
' File menu contains a command that allows the user to
' transfer the current data set to an Excel worksheet
' (assuming Excel is installed).
Option Explicit
Const AmtFormat = "$#,####0"   ' Dollar-and-cents format.
Const colorOffset = 7          ' Color selection for charts.

' Variables to represent Excel objects.
Dim ExcelApp As Excel.Application
Dim ExcelWorkbook As Excel.Workbook
Dim ExcelSheet As Excel.Worksheet

' Arrays and variables to represent sales data.
Dim amounts(24)
Dim amountStr(24) As String
Dim periodTots(4)
Dim periodLabels(4) As String
Dim regionTots(4)
Dim regionLabels(4) As String
Dim IDPrefixes(4) As String
Dim grandTot
'
' End of general declarations, SalesEx1.Frm.
```

Figure 15-26: The general declarations section of the frmIntSales form contains Dim statements for three key object variables used in the program — *ExcelApp*, *ExcelWorkbook*, and *ExcelSheet*. Turn to the mnuExcel_Click procedure to see how these variables are initialized.

Certain other objects in the hierarchy are dependent on the Worksheet; for example:

+ ✦ A Range object represents a range of cells on a worksheet.
+ ✦ A ChartObject object is a container for a chart, embedded on a sheet.
+ ✦ A Chart object represents the chart displayed inside a ChartObject.

These dependent objects can be referenced indirectly, using the methods and properties of an existing Worksheet object.

As you examine more of the program's code, you'll see examples of dependent objects and gain a clearer understanding of Excel's object hierarchy.

Creating and managing the Worksheet object

The mnuExcel_Click event procedure in Figure 15-27 takes charge when the user chooses the Transfer to Excel command from the File menu. The procedure initializes the three module-level object variables:

```
Set ExcelApp = CreateObject("Excel.Application")
Set ExcelWorkbook = ExcelApp.Workbooks.Add
Set ExcelSheet = ExcelWorkbook.Worksheets(1)
```

```
mnuExcel                              ▼    Click                              ▼

    Private Sub mnuExcel_Click()

      ' The mnuExcel_Click procedure takes control when the
      ' user chooses the Transfer to Excel command.
      Dim i, x, y

      ' If an error occurs, skip to the end of the procedure.
      On Error GoTo ActiveXProblem

      ' Create the objects, copy the data, and draw the chart.
      Set ExcelApp = CreateObject("Excel.Application")
      Set ExcelWorkbook = ExcelApp.Workbooks.Add
      Set ExcelSheet = ExcelWorkbook.Worksheets(1)
      ExcelApp.Visible = True
      CopyToExcel
      DrawExcelChart

      ' Pause to let the user examine and save the sheet.
      MsgBox "Save the Excel document if you wish. Then " & _
             "click OK to quit Excel.", , "International Sales"
      ExcelSheet.Application.Quit

    ActiveXProblem:
      ' Release object references from memory.
      Set ExcelApp = Nothing
      Set ExcelWorkbook = Nothing
      Set ExcelSheet = Nothing

    End Sub  ' mnuExcel_Click
```

Figure 15-27: Three Set statements in the mnuExcel_Click procedure create objects and assign references to the corresponding object variables. Then the program makes calls to *CopyToExcel* and *DrawExcelChart* to create the worksheet and chart. All this action takes place within the control of an error trap.

Here is how these three Set statements work:

✦ The CreateObject function creates an object belonging to a specified class. In this case, the class is identified as Excel.Application. CreateObject returns a reference to the newly created Application object. The first Set statement stores the reference in *ExcelApp.*

✦ In the next step down the hierarchy of objects, the Workbooks method returns a reference to the Workbooks collection. The Add method creates a new Workbook and returns a reference to the object, which is assigned to the variable *ExcelWorkbook.*

✦ Finally, the Worksheets method returns a reference to the first sheet in the container workbook; the third Set statement stores a reference to this sheet in *ExcelSheet.*

At this point, the application has not yet appeared on the desktop. To display Excel, the following statement changes the application's Visible property to True:

```
ExcelApp.Visible = True
```

The Visible property applies to the application itself.

Next the mnuExcel_Click procedure makes calls to the two general procedures that create the data and the chart on the new worksheet object:

```
CopyToExcel
DrawExcelChart
```

As you'll see shortly, the first of these copies all the sales data to the worksheet, and the second makes calls to an Excel method that draws charts.

Next a MsgBox statement creates a pause in the program, giving the user a chance to examine the contents of the worksheet — and optionally, to print or save the data. When the user eventually clicks the OK button on the message box, the program calls the Quit method to exit from Excel, and then assigns Nothing to the three object variables, releasing the references from memory:

```
ExcelSheet.Application.Quit

Set ExcelApp = Nothing
Set ExcelWorkbook = Nothing
Set ExcelSheet = Nothing
```

As you've seen, the program performance continues. At this juncture the user is free to enter new data into the International Sales window and then transfer the data to Excel again.

Notice that all the action of the mnuExcel_Click procedure takes place under the watch of an error trap:

```
On Error GoTo ActiveXProblem
```

This trap is triggered if an ActiveX operation fails. Control then jumps down to the end of the procedure, to the *ActiveXProblem* label.

Copying data to the worksheet

The *CopyToExcel* procedure — shown in Figures 15-28 and 15-29 — formats the worksheet, copies the sales data, and creates summation formulas. To refer to Range objects, this procedure uses three Worksheet methods:

✦ The Columns method returns a Range object consisting of one or more columns.

✦ The Cells method returns a Range object consisting of a single cell.

✦ The Range method returns a Range object consisting of a specific range on the worksheet.

```
(General)                                    CopyToExcel

  Private Sub CopyToExcel()

    ' The CopyToExcel procedure is called by mnuExcel_Click
    ' when the user chooses the Transfer to Excel command.
    ' It copies the sales data, titles, and formulas to
    ' the sheet. It also formats specific worksheet cells
    ' as appropriate.

    Dim i, x, y

    ' Apply the boldface style to titles and labels.
    ExcelSheet.Range("$A$1:$G$3,$A$3:$A$9").Font.Bold = True

    ' Adjust the width of column A.
    ExcelSheet.Columns("A").ColumnWidth = 10.29

    ' Copy the chart title and the units to the sheet.
    ExcelSheet.Cells(1, 2).Value = txtTitle.Text
    ExcelSheet.Cells(1, 5).Value = lblUnits.Caption

    ' Copy the entire table of numeric data.
    For i = 0 To 24
      y = i Mod 5 + 2
      x = i \ 5 + 4
      ExcelSheet.Cells(x, y).Value = txtAmount(i).Text
    Next i
```

Figure 15-28: The first half of the *CopyToExcel* procedure contains examples of the Range, Columns, and Cells methods. The procedure formats the sheet, adjusts a column width, and copies the numeric data from the International Sales form.

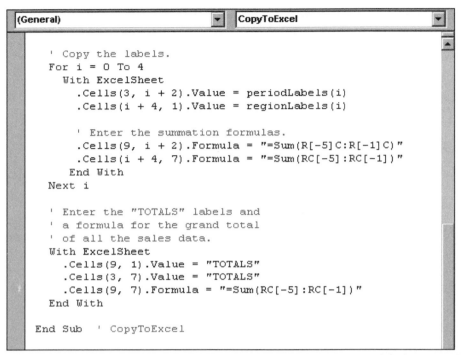

```
(General)                                  ▼    CopyToExcel                              ▼

     ' Copy the labels.
     For i = 0 To 4
       With ExcelSheet
         .Cells(3, i + 2).Value = periodLabels(i)
         .Cells(i + 4, 1).Value = regionLabels(i)

         ' Enter the summation formulas.
         .Cells(9, i + 2).Formula = "=Sum(R[-5]C:R[-1]C)"
         .Cells(i + 4, 7).Formula = "=Sum(RC[-5]:RC[-1])"
       End With
     Next i

     ' Enter the "TOTALS" labels and
     ' a formula for the grand total
     ' of all the sales data.
     With ExcelSheet
       .Cells(9, 1).Value = "TOTALS"
       .Cells(3, 7).Value = "TOTALS"
       .Cells(9, 7).Formula = "=Sum(RC[-5]:RC[-1])"
     End With

   End Sub   ' CopyToExcel
```

Figure 15-29: The second half of the *CopyToExcel* procedure copies labels to the sheet and develops the summation formulas to compute the row and column totals.

Range is a dependent object that can be referenced only indirectly. These three methods are convenient ways of identifying specific ranges on the active worksheet.

For example, the procedure begins with two formatting operations. First, the following statement applies the bold type style to multiple ranges on the sheet:

```
ExcelSheet.Range("$A$1:$G$3,$A$3:$A$9").Font.Bold = True
```

In this statement, the Range method returns a reference to a specific Range object. The Font method returns a reference to the corresponding Font object. Bold is a property of the Font object.

The next formatting task is to increase the width of column A. In the following statement, the Columns method returns a reference to a Range object that represents a single column:

```
ExcelSheet.Columns("A").ColumnWidth = 10.29
```

The ColumnWidth property applies to a Range object.

To copy the sales data, the program uses the Cells method to identify individual cells in the worksheet. (Or, more precisely, the Cells method returns a reference to a Range object that consists of a single cell.) The Value property, when applied to a Range object, represents the value stored in a cell. For example, the following statements begin by copying the title and the dollar units from the International Sales window to the worksheet:

```
ExcelSheet.Cells(1, 2).Value = txtTitle.Text
ExcelSheet.Cells(1, 5).Value = lblUnits.Caption
```

Then the following loop copies the sales figures from the application window to the worksheet:

```
For i = 0 To 24
  y = i Mod 5 + 2
  x = i \ 5 + 4
  ExcelSheet.Cells(x, y).Value = txtAmount(i).Text
Next i
```

Inside the loop, the program calculates the location of each individual worksheet cell and then assigns the txtAmount(i).Text setting to the Value property of the resulting Range object.

The Formula property of a Range object allows the program to store a formula in a particular cell or range of cells. For example, this loop enters the summation formulas into the last column and bottom row of the sales table in the worksheet:

```
For i = 0 To 4
  With ExcelSheet
    ' ...
    .Cells(9, i + 2).Formula = "=Sum(R[-5]C:R[-1]C)"
    .Cells(i + 4, 7).Formula = "=Sum(RC[-5]:RC[-1])"
  End With
Next i
```

Notice the use of Visual Basic's With structure to simplify the references to the Cells method in this loop.

When the work of the *CopyToExcel* procedure is complete, all the data, formulas, titles, and labels have been entered into the worksheet, and the program is ready to generate the chart.

Creating an embedded chart on the worksheet

The *DrawExcelChart* procedure — shown in Figures 15-30 and 15-31 — works with references to two new objects. ChartObject is a container object for a chart that's embedded on a worksheet. (The ChartObjects collection represents all the embedded charts on a Worksheet object.) The Chart object identifies the chart drawn within a ChartObject object. The procedure declares object variables to represent references to each of these objects:

```
Dim newChartObj As ChartObject
Dim newChart As Chart
```

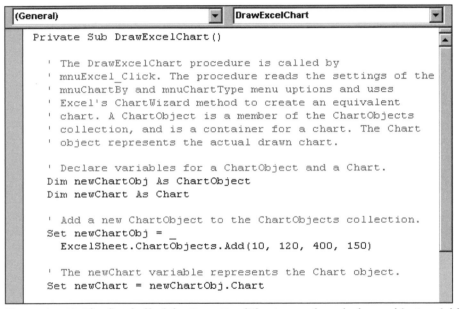

```
(General)                ▼    DrawExcelChart              ▼

    Private Sub DrawExcelChart()

      ' The DrawExcelChart procedure is called by
      ' mnuExcel_Click. The procedure reads the settings of the
      ' mnuChartBy and mnuChartType menu uptions and uses
      ' Excel's ChartWizard method to create an equivalent
      ' chart. A ChartObject is a member of the ChartObjects
      ' collection, and is a container for a chart. The Chart
      ' object represents the actual drawn chart.

      ' Declare variables for a ChartObject and a Chart.
      Dim newChartObj As ChartObject
      Dim newChart As Chart

      ' Add a new ChartObject to the ChartObjects collection.
      Set newChartObj = _
        ExcelSheet.ChartObjects.Add(10, 120, 400, 150)

      ' The newChart variable represents the Chart object.
      Set newChart = newChartObj.Chart
```

Figure 15-30: The first half of the *DrawExcelChart* procedure declares object variables to represent a ChartObject container and its Chart object. Two Set statements assign object references to these variables.

To create a new ChartObject, the program uses the Add method to add a member to the ChartObjects collection on the current worksheet:

```
Set newChartObj = _
  ExcelSheet.ChartObjects.Add(10, 120, 400, 150)
```

In this statement, the ChartObjects method returns a reference to the ChartObjects collection for the ExcelSheet object. The Add method creates a new object in the collection and displays the chart container at specified coordinates and in a specified size. (The numeric arguments of the Add method represent the Left, Top, Width, and Height properties of the ChartObject.) Finally, the Add method returns a reference to the new ChartObject; this reference is stored in the variable *newChartObj*.

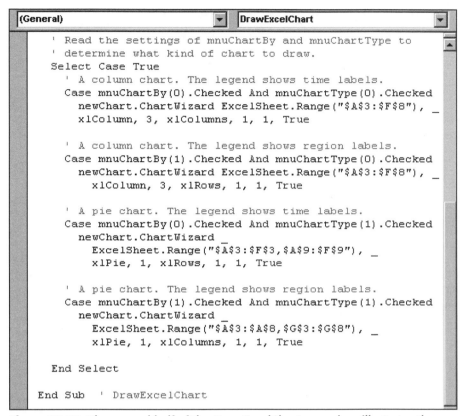

```
(General)                          ▼   DrawExcelChart                        ▼

      ' Read the settings of mnuChartBy and mnuChartType to
      ' determine what kind of chart to draw.
      Select Case True
         ' A column chart. The legend shows time labels.
         Case mnuChartBy(0).Checked And mnuChartType(0).Checked
            newChart.ChartWizard ExcelSheet.Range("$A$3:$F$8"), _
            xlColumn, 3, xlColumns, 1, 1, True

         ' A column chart. The legend shows region labels.
         Case mnuChartBy(1).Checked And mnuChartType(0).Checked
            newChart.ChartWizard ExcelSheet.Range("$A$3:$F$8"), _
               xlColumn, 3, xlRows, 1, 1, True

         ' A pie chart. The legend shows time labels.
         Case mnuChartBy(0).Checked And mnuChartType(1).Checked
            newChart.ChartWizard _
               ExcelSheet.Range("$A$3:$F$3,$A$9:$F$9"), _
               xlPie, 1, xlRows, 1, 1, True

         ' A pie chart. The legend shows region labels.
         Case mnuChartBy(1).Checked And mnuChartType(1).Checked
            newChart.ChartWizard _
               ExcelSheet.Range("$A$3:$A$8,$G$3:$G$8"), _
               xlPie, 1, xlColumns, 1, 1, True

      End Select

End Sub   ' DrawExcelChart
```

Figure 15-31: The second half of the *DrawExcelChart* procedure illustrates the use of the ChartWizard method to draw a chart in a Chart object.

The Chart property represents the Chart object contained within a ChartObject. The program uses this property to assign a reference to *newChart*:

```
Set newChart = newChartObj.Chart
```

As a result of this statement, *newChart* contains a reference to the Chart object inside *newChartObj*. The procedure's final task is to assign appropriate properties to this Chart object, resulting in the display of a chart.

The ChartWizard method is a shortcut technique for assigning properties to a Chart object, in effect defining the chart that the object displays. ChartWizard takes a long list of arguments, including:

✦ A reference to the range containing the source data for the chart

✦ A value identifying the chart type

✦ A numeric value identifying the chart format

✦ A value specifying the row or column orientation of the chart

✦ Two integers specifying the number of rows and columns of labels that are included in the source data

✦ A Boolean value specifying whether the chart should include a legend

You can see examples of all these arguments in the following call to the ChartWizard method:

```
newChart.ChartWizard ExcelSheet.Range("$A$3:$F$8"), _
    xlColumn, 3, xlColumns, 1, 1, True
```

This particular statement creates a stacked column chart in which each column represents the total sales for a given region (as you can see back in Figure 15-16).

To decide what kind of chart to draw, the *DrawExcelChart* procedure uses a Select Case structure. Each Case statement inside the structure examines the current Checked settings of the mnuChartBy and mnuChartType menu options. The Select structure chooses the Case in which both Checked settings are True; for example:

```
Select Case True

    Case mnuChartBy(0).Checked And mnuChartType(0).Checked
```

As you examine this Select Case structure, look again at Figures 15-15 through 15-23; they demonstrate the relationship between the Checked settings in the International Sales window and the chart type drawn in the Excel worksheet.

For a final programming exercise with this program, consider the following scenario: Suppose the user makes changes in the sales data displayed inside the Excel worksheet and wants these changes to be transferred *back* to the original application window. Write a loop in the mnuExcel_Click procedure (just before the call to the Quit method) to copy a revised sales table from the worksheet back to the International Sales window. This new code completes the connection between the Visual Basic form and the Excel worksheet.

Database Connections

You've seen several Visual Basic applications that create database files on disk for storing and retrieving information. These programs illustrate the traditional Basic-language techniques for working with databases:

✦ The Open statement creates a data file or opens an existing file in one of several modes. In particular, the Random mode provides direct access to structured records in a database file.

✦ The user-defined data type gives you a clear way to represent the record structure for a random-access file. In a Type statement you list the fields and their types; then in a Dim statement you declare a record variable to serve as the medium for reading records from an open file or for writing new records to the file.

✦ The Get# statement reads an entire record from a random-access file, and the Put# statement writes a record to the file.

✦ An array of records, appropriately designed and managed, serves as an effective index for a random-access file, allowing a program to locate records by specific key fields.

✦ A variety of other tools are available to help you work with the file, including the end-of-file function, EOF; the length-of-file function, LOF; and the Len function, which can be used to measure the size of a record variable. Using LOF and Len together, your program can calculate the number of records in an open file.

These techniques produce a database file in a specific random-access format. Any program that uses the same techniques can read or revise the file. A database on disk thereby becomes a medium for exchanging information between programs.

This chapter introduces a dramatically different approach to database management. Visual Basic provides a tool called the *data control* that is designed to provide access to files created by major database applications such as Microsoft Access, dBASE, and Paradox as well as spreadsheet programs such as Lotus 1-2-3 and Microsoft Excel. This control is the central topic of this chapter.

Figure 16-1 shows how the data control appears in the Toolbox. One of the control's most interesting features is its versatility as a programming tool. Using this control, you can develop database programs with or without writing code. To be sure, the data control has an important group of methods, properties, and events that you can use in a program's code to conduct sophisticated database-related activities. But this control is intrinsically so powerful that its presence on a form is enough to define a usable connection to an existing database.

Figure 16-1: The data control as it appears in the Toolbox. You can use this control to create effective database access programs, even without writing code.

The data control represents a database technology known as the Microsoft Jet database engine. Also the basis for Microsoft Access, this technology provides database techniques for a variety of application-specific formats.

You'll explore the features of the data control in two Visual Basic projects presented in this chapter. Both programs are designed to improve upon an application that first appeared in Chapter 4: The Currency Exchange program is a simple calculation tool for converting between U.S. dollars and the currencies of other countries. The original version of the program (CurrExch.Vbp) gets its data from a text file (Currency.Txt) that contains a list of countries, currencies, and exchange rates.

The two projects in this chapter together produce a broader version of this application:

✦ The Currency Input project is a convenient data-entry program for creating and updating the records of a currency exchange file. The program works with an Access database named Currency.Mdb, which in turn contains a table named Exchange. The Exchange table has fields for country names, currencies, and exchange rates. You'll develop this program, along with the associated database definition, in an extended hands-on exercise presented near the beginning of this chapter. This program is an example of a database application that requires no code of its own.

✦ The database version of the Currency Exchange application appears to be nearly identical to the first version of the program presented in Chapter 4. It provides a drop-down list of countries to choose from and a simple way to calculate exchange equivalents for specific currencies. The significant difference is that the program uses the Currency.Mdb database file as its source for currency exchange information. This program's code introduces several of the important methods and properties associated with the data control.

If Microsoft Access is installed on your computer, you can use it to develop the Currency.Mdb database for this chapter's programming exercises. If not, Visual Basic supplies an add-in program called the Visual Data Manager, which is conveniently available for defining databases in the Access format. As you work through the steps of creating a database file with the Visual Data Manager, you'll have the opportunity to review a number of general database concepts.

Using the Visual Data Manager

The Visual Data Manager is represented by a command in Visual Basic's Add-Ins menu. To start the program, simply pull down the menu and choose the command, as shown in Figure 16-2. When you do so, an empty application window appears on the desktop (Figure 16-3). As you'll discover shortly, the program's File menu contains commands for creating or opening a database.

Figure 16-2: To start the Visual Data Manager, pull down the Add-Ins menu and choose the corresponding command in the menu list.

Reviewing database terminology

Take this opportunity to review some of the basic terminology of database management. In a *relational database*, information is organized — visually or conceptually — in rows and columns. A row contains a complete record, and a column represents a particular field of information. A group of records arranged in this way is called a table. An Access database may contain many related tables. To retrieve information efficiently from multiple tables, you define relationships between key fields. Access uses the relationships to correlate records and to combine information from multiple tables in a useful way.

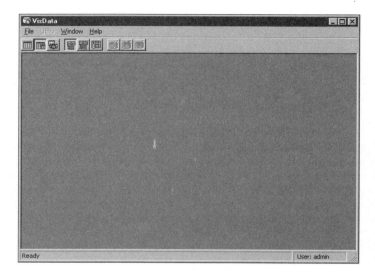

Figure 16-3: The Visual Data Manager window is empty at first, although you can see the program's menu bar and toolbar. The File menu contains an assortment of commands for getting started with a database.

Access databases are identified on disk with an extension name of MDB (for Microsoft Database). The database you're about to create, Currency.Mdb, will contain a single table, named Exchange, with three fields, Country, Currency, and InDollars. Each record you enter into the table will provide the dollar exchange rate for the currency of a particular country. You can use the Visual Data Manager program to define the field structure for a database table and to begin entering records into the table. In the upcoming exercise, you'll enter only one record into the table. Then you'll return to Visual Basic, where you'll develop the Currency Input program as a more convenient tool for data entry into the Currency.Mdb database.

Creating the Currency.Mdb database

With the Visual Data Manager window open on the desktop, you can create a new MDB file, add a table to the database, and define the table's record structure. Here are the steps:

1. Choose File⇨New⇨Microsoft Access⇨Version 7.0 MDB, as shown in Figure 16-4. These selections identify the type of database you want to create. A dialog box named Select Microsoft Access Database to Create appears on the screen. Navigate up to the root directory of your hard disk.

2. In the File name text box, near the bottom of the window, enter **Currency** as the name of the new database file you'll be creating, as in Figure 16-5. Click Save to create the database file. The Visual Data Manager automatically adds an extension of MDB to the file name, indicating that the file will be stored in the Microsoft Access database format.

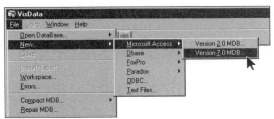

Figure 16-4: Choose these commands to create a new Access database.

Figure 16-5: Choose the folder where you want to save the database file, and enter a name for the Access database you're creating. The Visual Data Manager adds MDB as the file's extension.

3. Two new windows appear inside the Visual Data Manager application — one named Database Window and another named SQL Statement. Click inside the Database Window with the right mouse button, and choose New Table from the resulting shortcut menu, as shown in Figure 16-6. The Table Structure dialog box appears on the desktop. You use this dialog to define the field structure of the new table.

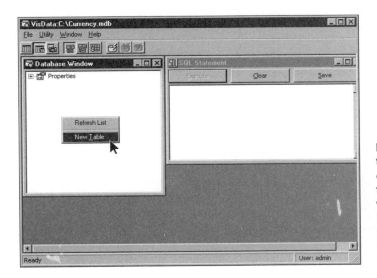

Figure 16-6: To add a table to the new database, click inside the Database Window with the right mouse button, and choose New Table from the resulting shortcut menu.

4. In the Table Name text box at the top of the dialog box, enter **Exchange** as the name for the new table as in Figure 16-7. Then click the Add Field button located just beneath the empty Field List box. Your next task is to use the Add Field dialog box to define the fields of the table.

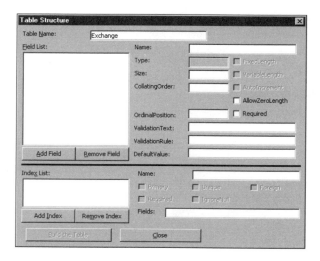

Figure 16-7: In the Table Structure dialog box, begin by entering a name for the new table. Then click the Add Field button to begin defining the field structure for the table.

5. Enter **Country** as the first field name. Keep Text as the Type selection, and enter **15** in the Size box (Figure 16-8). Click OK to continue.

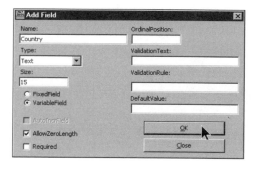

Figure 16-8: In the Add Field dialog box you can define any number of fields in sequence. For each field, enter a name, a data type, and a size. Other properties are also available, as you can see in the dialog box.

6. The Add Field dialog box remains open. Use it to define two other fields: **Currency**, a Text field with a size of 15; and **InDollars**, a Single-precision numeric field. Click OK after entering each field definition, and then click Close when you're done.

7. The Table Structure dialog box appears as in Figure 16-9. The Field List box now shows the names of the three fields you've defined for the Exchange table. Click the Build the Table button at the lower-left corner of the dialog box. This action closes the Table Structure window and returns you to the Visual Data Manager application window. By opening up the levels of outlining in the Database Window, you can confirm that the Currency database file now contains one table named Exchange, which in turn contains three fields named Country, Currency, and InDollars; all this is shown in Figure 16-10.

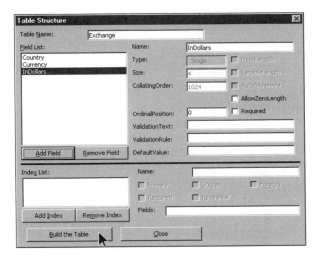

Figure 16-9: When you complete the field structure, the Table Structure dialog box lists the names of all the fields that you've created. Click the Build the Table button to save the table definition as part of the Access database. In this example, the Currency database has only one table. (Note that an Access database may typically contain multiple tables.)

Figure 16-10: The Database Window shows the structure of your database in outline form, including the name of the table and its fields. Double-click the table name to begin entering records into the table.

8. On the Visual Data Manager toolbar, click the first button — identified by its ToolTip as the Table type Recordset option. Then position the mouse pointer over the Exchange entry in the Database Window outline, and double-click the left mouse button. A window named Table:Exchange opens onto the desktop. You can use this window to append one or more records to the database table.

9. Begin entering the fields of this first record: **Britain** in the Country field; **pound** in the Currency field; and **1.6449** as a sample exchange rate in the InDollars field.

10. The Table:Exchange window now appears as shown in Figure 16-11. Click the Update button and then click OK on the resulting message box to confirm the entry of the first record into the database table. Click Close to close the Table:Exchange window. You could continue adding records to the table, but instead you'll now return to Visual Basic to create the Currency Input program. Close the Visual Data Manager window by choosing File⟳Exit. The Currency.Mdb database file, containing one table named Exchange, is now stored in the root directory of your hard disk.

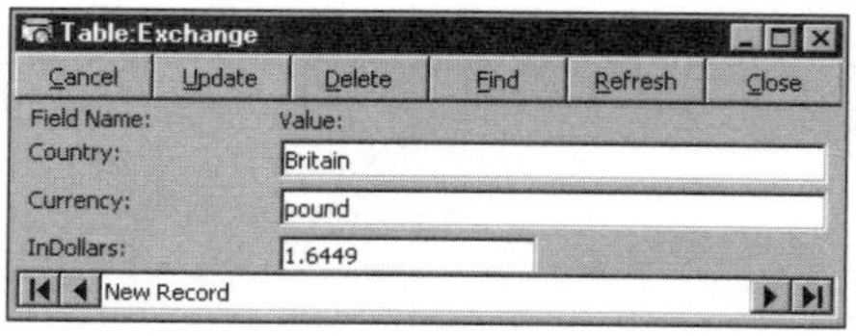

Figure 16-11: The Table:Exchange dialog box contains text boxes for each of the fields you've defined in the Exchange table. To enter a record, type values for the three fields and then click Update.

Tip   You can choose the Data Form Designer command from the Visual Data Manager's Utility menu to create a database input form for use in a Visual Basic program. In the Data Form Designer dialog box, enter a name for the form you're creating. From the list box labeled RecordSource, choose the name of the database table for which you want to create the input form. The names of all the fields defined for the table appear in the Available Fields list. Click the > button to move any number of field names to the Included Fields list. Then click the Build the Form button. The result is a Visual Basic form that contains a data control and is similar in appearance to the Table:Exchange window shown back in Figure 16-11. The form includes all the code necessary to make it a functional input window for the target database table. You can incorporate this form into any Visual Basic program that works with the database. You could follow these steps to create an input form for the Exchange table. But the upcoming exercise guides you through an alternate approach, allowing you to focus on the use of the data control itself — and on its built-in features that require no code.

The Data Control and Bound Controls

To use the data control in a Visual Basic program, you add an instance of the control to a form and then set three essential properties that define a specific database connection:

✦ The Connect property indicates the type of database you'll attach to the program; Access is the default.

✦ The DatabaseName property is the file name of the database on disk.

✦ The RecordSource property is the name of a table in the database.

Other properties are also related to the database connection. For example, the EOFAction property determines whether you will be able to use your Visual Basic program to append new records to the end of the database. You'll learn more about this property later.

After setting the properties of the data control, you next begin adding *bound* controls to the same form. Each bound control is designated to represent a field from the table you've selected as the RecordSource property of the data control. For example, you can add bound labels to display field data, or bound text boxes to allow editing of fields. Two important properties define a bound control:

✦ The DataSource property is the name of the data control to which the control is bound. In other words, the bound control will display a field from the data control's RecordSource table.

✦ The DataField property is the name of the field that the bound control represents.

A variety of Visual Basic controls can serve as bound controls in a program. In addition to the label and text box, you can use the list box, combo box, picture box, image, and check box as bound controls. In addition, the Components dialog box lists several controls that have special data-bound capabilities in connection with the data control — including DBCombo, DBList, and DBGrid.

Once you've designed a form that contains a data control and one or more bound controls, your program is ready to run. When you start the program, the bound controls display field information from the first record in the designated table. The data control provides buttons for scrolling from one record to the next in the database. The operations you can perform on the database depend on the properties of the data control and the types of bound controls you've added to your form. Some bound controls, such as labels, simply display field data; others, such as text boxes, provide both read and write capabilities.

In the following exercise you'll use this approach to create a currency input program as a tool for entering and revising records in the Exchange table of the Currency.Mdb database. The application consists of a form displaying a data control, three bound text boxes, and three labels. The program contains no code. To develop the project, you simply add the controls to a form and set the appropriate properties:

1. Start a new project in Visual Basic. Add seven controls to the project's Form1: One data control, three labels, and three text boxes. Arrange the controls and resize the form approximately as they appear in Figure 16-12. Notice that the widened data control contains a central area where a caption appears.

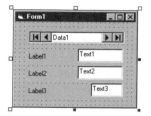

Figure 16-12: Begin your work by adding a data control, three labels, and three text boxes to the form. Arrange the controls as shown here, and resize the form appropriately. When you widen the data control, you'll see a central space that displays the control's Caption property.

2. In the Properties window, change the form's Caption setting to **Currency Exchange**. Then set the Caption properties of the data control and the three labels as you see them in Figure 16-13. Delete the default Text properties of the three text boxes.

Figure 16-13: In the Properties window, enter new captions for the form, the labels, and the data control. Delete the default Text property settings for the three text boxes.

3. Pull down the File menu and choose the Save Form1 As command. Enter **CurrInDB** as the file name for the form, and click Save; as usual, Visual Basic adds FRM as the extension. Then pull down the File menu again and choose Save Project As. Enter **CurrInDB** as the name for the project, and click Save; Visual Basic adds VBP as the extension.

4. Select the data control and activate the Properties window. Click the Categorized tab for convenient access to the control's properties. Notice the visual features of the data control. It contains four buttons designed for scrolling through the records of a database. At the far left and right sides of the control are buttons for jumping to the first and last record. Next to these are buttons for scrolling one record at a time to the previous or next record. As you've already noticed, the control's Caption property is displayed in the space between these buttons.

5. In the Properties window, scroll down to the Data category, as shown in Figure 16-14. Notice that the default setting of the Connect property is Access; you'll leave this setting unchanged. Select the DatabaseName property for the data control, and click the small button displayed at the right side of the property setting. The DatabaseName dialog box appears, giving you the opportunity to select an Access database file to connect to your program. Navigate to the root directory of your hard disk, and select the Currency file (or enter **\Currency** in the file name text box). The

DatabaseName dialog box appears as shown in Figure 16-15. Click the Open button to complete your database selection. Visual Basic copies the name of the file to the DatabaseName property in the Properties window.

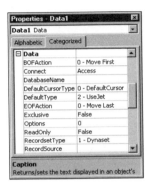

Figure 16-14: The Data properties of the data control are the essential tools for connecting the Access database to the application. In particular, you focus on the Connect, Database, EOFAction, and RecordSource properties in this exercise.

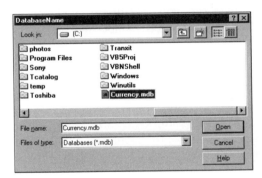

Figure 16-15: In the DatabaseName dialog box, select the name of the Access database that you've created.

6. Now select the EOFAction property. Pull down the list of property settings, and choose 2–Add New. This setting allows you to use the program to append new records to the database table.

7. Select the RecordSource property. Once you've set the DatabaseName, the RecordSource property provides a list of all the tables contained in the database. Click the down-arrow button at the right side of the property setting to view the list. In this case, the list contains the name of only one table, Exchange, as you can see in Figure 16-16. As you know, this is the only table defined in the Currency database. Select this table name as the setting for the RecordSource property. You've now set all the properties needed to define the database connection.

Figure 16-16: Once the DatabaseName property is set, the RecordSource property provides a list of the tables in the database. In this case, only one table exists.

8. Scroll down to the Misc category and select the Name property. Enter **dbCurrency** as the name of the data control. When you complete the entry, this name appears in the title bar of the Properties window. You'll use references to this name to define the program's three bound controls.

9. Select the first of the three text boxes that you've added to the form and once again activate the Properties window. Scroll to the Name property in the Misc category and enter **txtCountry** as the name for this control.

10. In the Data category, select the DataSource property. Click the down-arrow button to view the attached list. The list contains the name of the data control you've added to this form, dbCurrency. Select this name as the setting for the DataSource property.

11. Select the DataField property, and pull down its attached list. As you can see in Figure 16-17, this list displays the names of the three fields in the Exchange table — Country, Currency, and InDollars. Select Country as the DataField setting for the first text box.

Figure 16-17: To create a bound control — a text box in this case — select the name of the data control as the DataSource property, and then choose a field name for the DataField property.

12. Repeat Steps 9, 10, and 11 to set the Name, DataSource, and DataField properties for the other two text boxes. Enter **txtCurrency** as the name for the second text box, and choose Currency as the DataField property. Enter **txtDollars** as the name for the third text box, and choose InDollars as the DataField property.

13. Assign a name of **frmCurrencyInput** to the form itself. Then select the Project1 line in the Project Explorer window, reactivate the Properties window, and assign a Name property of **CurrencyInput** to the project. Your program is now complete. Click the Save Project button on the toolbar to save the final version to disk.

Now you're ready to run the program and use it to append records to the Exchange table of the Currency.Mdb database. Press F5 or click the Start button on the toolbar. The program connects to the database and, as you can see in Figure 16-18, displays the record that you've already entered into the table. To add a new record, click the *next record* button, the right-pointing arrowhead on the data control. The program presents a set of blank fields in which you can enter the information for a new record.

Figure 16-18: When you run the program, the database connection is established, thanks to the various property settings you've defined for the data control and the bound text box controls. The first record entry appears in the text boxes.

Spend a few moments appending a set of new records to the database table. Look up today's actual currency exchange rates and enter those values — or, if you prefer, use the data shown in Figure 16-19 instead. When you finish entering the last record, click the Close button at the upper-right corner of the window to end the program performance.

Figure 16-19: Optionally, use this sample data to complete the record entries into the Access database. To confirm each new record entry, click the *next record* button at the right side of the data control. In response, the program presents three blank text boxes for the next record entry.

Now you may want to open the database table in the Visual Data Manager application to confirm that the records have been saved in the database file. Choose Visual Data Manager from Visual Basic's Add-Ins menu. In the resulting application window, choose File⇨Open DataBase⇨Microsoft Access. Open the Currency database file from the root directory of your hard disk. In the Database Window, double-click the name of Exchange table to open the "Table:Exchange" window. Now you can scroll through the records that you've just appended and confirm that each of them has been saved in the table. For example, Figure 16-20 shows the record for France. Exit from the Visual Data Manager when you've finished examining the table.

Figure 16-20: By scrolling through the Exchange table in the Visual Data Manager program you can confirm that all the record entries have been successfully saved in your Access database. The notation "9 rows" in the data control indicates that the table contains nine records.

In summary, you've used the Visual Data Manager to develop an Access database. The format of this database is the same as it would be if you'd actually created it in the Microsoft Access database application. You've also designed a simple Visual Basic application — containing no code — to manage data input for the one table in the database. Now this input program can serve as a convenient tool for daily updates of currency exchange information. Keep in mind that you can use the program to view or revise the existing records or to append new records to the Exchange table.

The database version of the International Currency Exchange program, presented next in this chapter, uses Currency.Mdb as its data source. As you'll see, this program contains a data control to connect it to the database. But unlike the input program that you've just developed, this new program contains no bound controls. Instead, it uses the methods and properties of the data control to carry out specific database operations.

Programming with the Data Control

During a program run, a data control is associated with a Recordset object, which represents all the records in the corresponding database table. In code, you use the data control's Recordset property to refer to this object:

```
Data1.Recordset
```

The Recordset object has properties and methods that your program can use to scroll through the table, to locate specific records, and to read fields of information:

✦ The Move methods (MoveNext, MovePrevious, MoveFirst, MoveLast) change the *current record* in the RecordSet.

✦ The Find methods (FindNext, FindPrevious, FindFirst, FindLast) look for a record that matches a particular search criterion. When a matching record is found, it becomes the current record.

✦ The EOF property indicates whether the program has moved past the last record in the database table.

✦ The Fields property represents the collection of all the fields in the table. You can use the Fields("*fieldName*") notation to identify a specific field. The Value property of a field provides access to a data item stored in the current record.

You'll see examples of all these tools in this chapter's version of the International Currency Exchange program. But before examining the program's code, take a moment to run the program and review its operations.

The database version of the Currency Exchange program

The new version of the program is saved on disk as CurrExDB.Vbp. Open it now and take a look at the Project Explorer window, shown in Figure 16-21. The program contains one form, named frmCurrExch (saved on disk as CurrExDB.Frm). Click the View Object button to open the form onto the desktop. As you can see in Figure 16-22, there is a data control at the upper-left corner of the form. This control's Name property is dbCurrency. Its Visible property is set to False, so it does not appear on the form at all during a run. But other properties of this control define the program's connection to the Currency.Mdb database. Specifically, the DatabaseName setting is \Currency.MDB and the RecordSource setting is Exchange.

Figure 16-21: The database version of the Currency Exchange application has one form, which contains all the program's code.

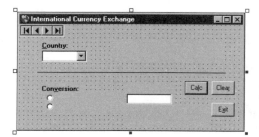

Figure 16-22: The data control, named dbCurrency, appears on the frmCurrExch form at design time. But the control's Visible property is set to False so it disappears from the form during a program run.

Press F5 or click the Start button on the toolbar to run the program. The program window appears on the desktop as in Figure 16-23. Notice that the data control is no longer visible. Also note that the program displays the database name just after the application name on the title bar. This serves as a reminder that this program gets its data from an Access database.

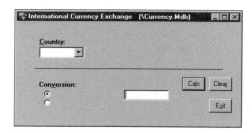

Figure 16-23: During a run, the application window looks about the same as the original program presented back in Chapter 4. The only indication that this is a different version is the appearance of the Access database name on the form's title bar.

Click the down-arrow button at the right side of the Country list to view the list of country names. As you can see in Figure 16-24, the list contains all the names you've entered into the Country field in the Exchange table. Try selecting a country from the list. When you do so, the program finds the corresponding record in the database, reads the fields of the record, and displays the information in the program window. For example, in Figure 16-25 you see the basic exchange-rate data for converting from dollars to a selected currency or from the currency to dollars.

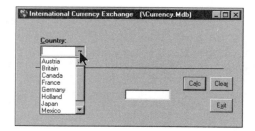

Figure 16-24: The program reads the list of countries from the Country field of the Exchange table. This is your first confirmation that the program has successfully connected to the Access database.

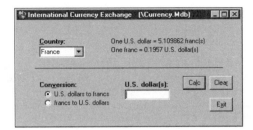

Figure 16-25: The program displays field items from the current record in the table.

The calculation feature works the same in this program as it did in the original version. To find the equivalent of a particular monetary amount, begin by choosing a Conversion option, and then enter an amount in the adjacent text box. Click the Calc button (or press Enter), and the program displays the calculated exchange amount. For example, Figure 16-26 shows a conversion from French francs to U.S. dollars.

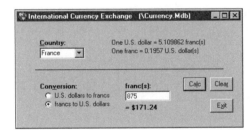

Figure 16-26: The currency calculations work the same as in the original version of the application. For example, here you can see a conversion from francs to dollars.

Continue experimenting with the program if you like. To terminate the run, click the Exit button or press Escape. Next you'll turn your attention to the program's code and to the methods and properties of the data control.

Inside the database version of the Currency Exchange program

As usual, you can find the complete code listing for the program in Appendix A, or you can scroll through the procedures in the code window on your screen. Here is a brief preview of the procedures that are central to the Access database connection:

✦ The Form_Load procedure activates the database connection and then reads through all the records in the Exchange table, from beginning to end. It copies the Country field from each record to the program's Country list.

✦ The cboCountry_Click procedure takes control when the user pulls down the Country list and chooses an entry. The procedure begins by searching for the record that contains the selected country. This becomes the current record. Then the procedure reads all three fields — Country, Currency, and InDollars — from the record, and uses these data items to fill in the various labels and captions on the application window.

✦ Other event procedures respond to the user's button clicks and option selections, taking care to check the current record status before undertaking any action that depends on a record selection: The cmdCalc_Click procedure performs the calculation for a currency conversion if the user has entered a valid monetary amount. The optCurrTo_Click and optDollarsTo_Click procedures make changes in label captions and text box contents when the user switches from one Conversion option to the other.

The final sections of this chapter discuss all of these procedures in detail.

As you've seen, the name of the data control in this program is dbCurrency. The Recordset object associated with this control is therefore referenced as

```
dbCurrency.Recordset
```

Certain methods of the Recordset object have the effect of changing the current record — or, in other words, moving the "record pointer" to a new record. Any field value that the program reads from the database table always comes from the current record. Note that there is no current record when the EOF property is True; consequently, the program has to avoid trying to read a record when the record pointer is beyond the last record of the file. You'll learn more about the *current record* concept as you examine the program's code.

Stepping through the database records

The Form_Load procedure in Figures 16-27 and 16-28 begins its work by adding the database name to the title bar of the application window:

```
frmCurrExch.Caption = frmCurrExch.Caption & _
   "   (" & dbCurrency.DatabaseName & ")"
```

The data control's DatabaseName property supplies the file name. The program then calls a data control method named Refresh:

```
dbCurrency.Refresh
```

The Refresh method builds the Recordset object associated with the data control.

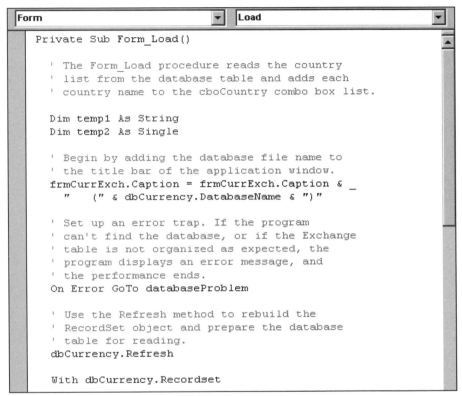

Figure 16-27: In the first half of the Form_Load procedure the program establishes an error trap that takes control if any trouble occurs in the database connection. A call to the Refresh method builds the Recordset object, making the table of records available to the program.

The main task of the Form_Load procedure is to read the Country field from each record of the Recordset and to copy the field to the drop-down list of the cboCountry combo box. This takes place in a Do loop that steps through the database table from the first record to the last:

```
With dbCurrency.Recordset

  Do While Not .EOF
    cboCountry.AddItem .Fields("Country").Value
    ' ...
    .MoveNext
  Loop

End With
```

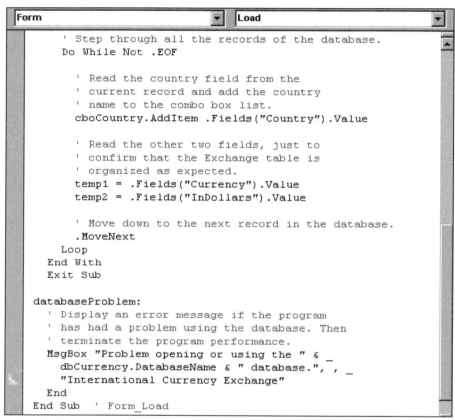

```
Form                          ▼   Load                          ▼
        ' Step through all the records of the database.
        Do While Not .EOF

          ' Read the country field from the
          ' current record and add the country
          ' name to the combo box list.
          cboCountry.AddItem .Fields("Country").Value

          ' Read the other two fields, just to
          ' confirm that the Exchange table is
          ' organized as expected.
          temp1 = .Fields("Currency").Value
          temp2 = .Fields("InDollars").Value

          ' Move down to the next record in the database.
          .MoveNext
        Loop
      End With
      Exit Sub

    databaseProblem:
      ' Display an error message if the program
      ' has had a problem using the database. Then
      ' terminate the program performance.
      MsgBox "Problem opening or using the " & _
        dbCurrency.DatabaseName & " database.", , _
        "International Currency Exchange"
      End
    End Sub   ' Form_Load
```

Figure 16-28: In the second half of the Form_Load procedure the program reads all the values stored in the Country field, and stores them in the cboCountry list. If the error trap is triggered, the procedure displays an error message and terminates the program run.

The Do loop continues reading records as long as the Recordset's EOF property is False. Notice the use of the With structure to simplify references to the Recordset object.

The Fields("Country").Value notation supplies the data item stored in the Country field of the current record. There are actually several ways to refer to this value. The complete reference is

```
dbCurrency.Recordset.Fields("Country").Value
```

But you can abbreviate this reference in the following ways:

```
dbCurrency.Recordset.Fields("Country")
```

or

```
dbCurrency.Recordset("Country")
```

Fields and Value are default properties in this expression, so they can be omitted. Another alternative is to refer to the field itself by index number rather than by name.

The procedure uses the AddItem method of the combo box control to add each country name to the drop-down list:

```
cboCountry.AddItem .Fields("Country").Value
```

Then the record pointer needs to be moved down to the next record in the database table. A call to the MoveNext method performs this task:

```
.MoveNext
```

Thanks to this method, each succeeding iteration of the loop reads the next record in the table. When the MoveNext method moves the record pointer to a position past the end of the last record, the Recordset.EOF property becomes True, and the looping stops. Consequently, there is no current record when Form_Load finishes its work. Other procedures in the program will have to check for this condition, as you'll see shortly.

A variety of circumstances could potentially cause runtime errors during the program's work with the currency database. For example, suppose one of these conditions is true:

✦ The program can't find the Currency.Mdb database file on disk.

✦ The database is found, but it doesn't contain an Exchange table.

✦ The Exchange table exists, but it doesn't have the three anticipated fields — Country, Currency, and InDollars.

Any one of these problems results in an error that prevents the program from continuing. To handle such an error gracefully, the Form_Load procedure sets up an error trap just before the call to the Refresh method:

```
On Error GoTo databaseProblem
```

If an error occurs, control of the procedure jumps down to the *databaseProblem* label. A MsgBox statement displays an error message on the screen, as in Figure 16-29, and then the program is terminated.

More Data-Bound Controls

DBList, DBCombo, and DBGrid are additional data-bound controls for use in database applications. The DBList and DBCombo controls have the following special features:

✦ Their lists can be filled automatically with data from a specified field. (Your program doesn't have to use the AddItem method to fill the list.)

✦ They can be used to coordinate activities between two different database tables. Data from one table can be used to update a field on another table.

To add these ActiveX controls to a project, choose Project⇨Components and then select Microsoft Data Bound Grid Control and Microsoft Data Bound List Controls. There is also a new Microsoft FlexGrid Control, which offers even greater flexibility in database applications.

Despite the extra features, you might sometimes still favor the more familiar controls, ListBox and ComboBox — especially in a simple database application like the one presented in this chapter.

To find out more about the data-bound controls, search for DBList, DBCombo, or DBGrid in the Visual Basic Help window. You'll find complete lists of properties and methods, along with examples.

Figure 16-29: If a problem occurs in the database connection, the program displays this error message. An error trap in the Form_Load procedure is designed to respond gracefully to a database error.

Searching for a database record

When the user pulls down the Country list and chooses the name of a country, the event procedure named cboCountry_Click (Figures 16-30 and 16-31) takes control. This procedure's first job is to find the record corresponding to the user's selection from the list. Then it reads the three fields of that record and uses the field data to display specific information in the application window.

The procedure calls the Recordset.FindFirst method to perform the search. FindFirst steps through a database table, starting from the first record, and searches for a record that meets a specific search criterion. In this case, the criterion is simple. The Country field of the target record should have the same value as cboCountry.Text — that is, the country that the user has selected from the list.

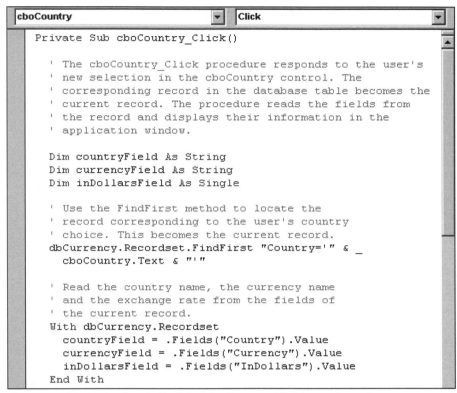

Figure 16-30: In the first half of the cboCountry_Click procedure, the program uses the FindFirst method to search for a requested country record. Then the procedure reads all three fields from the target record.

Here is how the procedure expresses this search criterion in the call to the FindFirst method:

```
dbCurrency.Recordset.FindFirst "Country='" & _
    cboCountry.Text & "'"
```

The search criterion in this example is a concatenation of three strings, making the expression a little difficult to understand at first glance. The criterion is actually a simple equality. For example, suppose the user pulls down the Country list and chooses France from the list; in effect, the FindFirst method works like this:

```
dbCurrency.Recordset.FindFirst Country='France'
```

The record that meets the criterion becomes the current record in the database table. Subsequent statements in the cboCountry_Click procedure refer to the fields of this current record.

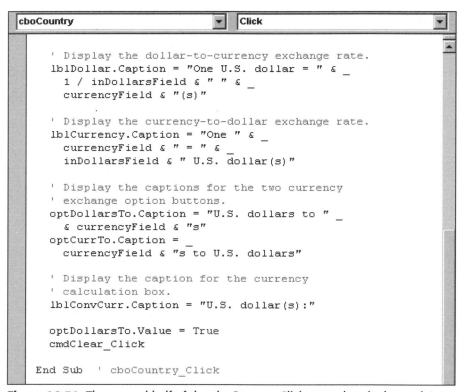

```
cboCountry              ▼    Click                    ▼

        ' Display the dollar-to-currency exchange rate.
        lblDollar.Caption = "One U.S. dollar = " & _
          1 / inDollarsField & " " & _
          currencyField & "(s)"

        ' Display the currency-to-dollar exchange rate.
        lblCurrency.Caption = "One " & _
          currencyField & " = " & _
          inDollarsField & " U.S. dollar(s)"

        ' Display the captions for the two currency
        ' exchange option buttons.
        optDollarsTo.Caption = "U.S. dollars to " _
          & currencyField & "s"
        optCurrTo.Caption = _
          currencyField & "s to U.S. dollars"

        ' Display the caption for the currency
        ' calculation box.
        lblConvCurr.Caption = "U.S. dollar(s):"

        optDollarsTo.Value = True
        cmdClear_Click

    End Sub   ' cboCountry_Click
```

Figure 16-31: The second half of the cboCountry_Click procedure is devoted to displaying the fields of the current record in the label and option controls of the application window.

Specifically, the procedure goes on to read the data from all three fields of the target record and to assign the data to variables:

```
With dbCurrency.Recordset
  countryField = .Fields("Country").Value
  currencyField = .Fields("Currency").Value
  inDollarsField = .Fields("InDollars").Value
End With
```

Once again, the Fields notation identifies a field by name, and the Value property supplies the data item stored in that field. These variables represent the field data throughout the procedure. For example, here is how the procedure displays the dollar-to-currency exchange rate in the lblDollar label:

```
lblDollar.Caption = "One U.S. dollar = " & _
  1 / inDollarsField & " " & _
  currencyField & "(s)"
```

Using SQL

SQL (Structure Query Language) is a common idiom for working with relational databases. If you're familiar with SQL, you can use it in the code of a Visual Basic database application. For example, queries in SQL are performed with the Select statement. Here is how you might use SQL in the cboCountry_Click procedure instead of the call to the FindFirst method:

```
SqlStr = "Select * from "_
    &Exchange Where " _
    & "Country = '" & _
    cboCountry.Text & "'"
dbCurrency.RecordSource = _
```

```
        SqlStr
dbCurrency.Refresh
```

This code uses a Select statement to change the setting of the RecordSource property. Then a call to the Refresh method rebuilds the Recordset. (If you want to try this approach, include a Dim statement at the top of the procedure to declare the string variable named SqlStr. Also, don't forget to delete the call to the FindFirst method, which these lines replace.)

For more information, search for *SQL* in the Visual Basic Help window.

Notice that the exchange rate in this case is calculated as the inverse of the currency-to-dollar rate.

Reading the EOF property

Once the user chooses an entry from the Country list, the Recordset.EOF property is False for the rest of the program performance. But before the first selection from the list, the EOF condition is True, thanks to the action of the Do loop in the Form_Load procedure. If the user happens to select a new Conversion option or click the Calc button before making a country selection, the corresponding event procedures need to avoid any action. Because there is no current record, a reference to Recordset.Fields would result in a runtime error.

When the user enters a specific currency amount into the text box at the bottom of the application window and clicks Calc, the cmdCalc_Click procedure in Figure 16-32 normally performs the currency calculation that the user has requested. The procedure begins by reading the Currency and InDollars fields from the current record in the database table:

```
With dbCurrency.Recordset
  currencyField = .Fields("Currency").Value
  inDollarsField = .Fields("InDollars").Value
End With
```

Then it performs either a dollar-to-currency conversion:

```
If optDollarsTo.Value Then
  lblConvText.Caption = "= " & _
    Format(txtConvAmount.Text / _
    inDollarsField, "###,###.00") & " " & _
    currencyField & "(s)"
```

or a currency-to-dollar calculation:

```
lblConvText.Caption = "= " & _
  Format(txtConvAmount.Text * _
  inDollarsField, "$###,###.00")
```

```
cmdCalc                                    Click

Private Sub cmdCalc_Click()
  ' Perform a currency exchange calculation.
  Dim currencyField As String, inDollarsField As Single

  ' First make sure that the user has entered a number
  ' (greater than zero) in the txtConvAmount text box.
  txtConvAmount.Text = Val(txtConvAmount.Text)
  If txtConvAmount.Text = 0 _
    Or dbCurrency.Recordset.EOF Then
      cmdClear_Click
  Else
  ' If the entry is valid, read fields from the record
  ' and display the results of the requested calculation.
    With dbCurrency.Recordset
      currencyField = .Fields("Currency").Value
      inDollarsField = .Fields("InDollars").Value
    End With
    If optDollarsTo.Value Then
      lblConvText.Caption = "= " & _
      Format(txtConvAmount.Text / _
      inDollarsField, "###,###.00") & " " & _
      currencyField & "(s)"
    Else
      lblConvText.Caption = "= " & _
        Format(txtConvAmount.Text * _
        inDollarsField, "$###,###.00")
    End If
  End If
End Sub  ' cmdCalc_Click
```

Figure 16-32: The cmdCalc_Click procedure checks the status of the RecordSet.EOF property before attempting to read fields from the database table. If EOF is True, there is no current record, and an attempt to read fields would result in an error.

But under some conditions, the cmdClick_Calc procedure skips the calculation:

✦ If the user has entered a nonnumeric value into the text box, the program uses the Val function to convert the Text value to zero, and no calculation is performed.

✦ If the user has not yet selected a name from the Country list, the Recordset.EOF property is still True. Because there is no current record, the currency calculation cannot take place.

The following If statement examines both of these conditions:

```
If txtConvAmount.Text = 0 _
  Or dbCurrency.Recordset.EOF Then
    cmdClear_Click
```

If either condition is True, the procedure simply clears the text box and performs no further action.

Similarly, the optCurrTo_Click and optDollarsTo_Click procedures in Figure 16-33 avoid responding to a change in the option button selection if Recordset.EOF is still True. For example, the optCurrTo_Click procedure checks the value of EOF before changing the label caption displayed above the text box:

```
With dbCurrency.Recordset
  If Not .EOF Then _
    lblConvCurr = .Fields("Currency").Value & "(s):"
End With
```

This precaution averts the runtime error that would occur if the program were to try reading a field value at a time when there is no current record.

Other Database Exercises

As you've seen, the data control — and the external database connection that it represents — requires programming techniques that are very different from the traditional Basic-language approach to database management. If you want to experiment further with the data control and its associated methods and properties, you might consider converting one of the other programs in this book to a database application using a data control.

One good candidate for this kind of exercise is the Restaurant Review program, presented in Chapter 8. Try using the Visual Data Manager program to create an Access-format version of the RestRevu database. Then redesign the application to take advantage of this new format.

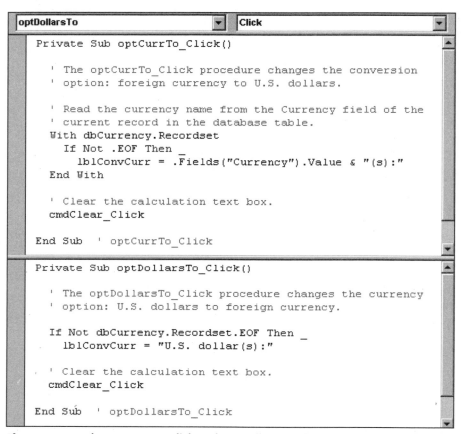

```
optDollarsTo          ▼      Click                                 ▼

  Private Sub optCurrTo_Click()

    ' The optCurrTo_Click procedure changes the conversion
    ' option: foreign currency to U.S. dollars.

    ' Read the currency name from the Currency field of the
    ' current record in the database table.
    With dbCurrency.Recordset
      If Not .EOF Then _
        lblConvCurr = .Fields("Currency").Value & "(s):"
    End With

    ' Clear the calculation text box.
    cmdClear_Click

  End Sub   ' optCurrTo_Click

  Private Sub optDollarsTo_Click()

    ' The optDollarsTo_Click procedure changes the currency
    ' option: U.S. dollars to foreign currency.

    If Not dbCurrency.Recordset.EOF Then _
      lblConvCurr = "U.S. dollar(s):"

    ' Clear the calculation text box.
    cmdClear_Click

  End Sub   ' optDollarsTo_Click
```

Figure 16-33: The optCurrTo_Click and optDollarsTo_Click procedures also check the value of Recordset.EOF before continuing with their respective actions.

ActiveX Component Development

ActiveX components provide classes of objects that you can use in Visual Basic projects. For example, in Chapter 15 you saw how Microsoft Excel serves as an ActiveX component, exposing objects — and their properties and methods — as programmable tools for a new application. The Excel version of the International Sales program transfers sales data to an Excel worksheet and then directs Excel to produce a chart from the data. This feat is possible because Excel provides a library of ActiveX objects that are available for use by other programs.

This chapter and the next introduce techniques for building your own ActiveX components. ActiveX programming is a rich and detailed topic, easily the subject of a book by itself. But Visual Basic 5.0 provides several very accessible starting points for developing ActiveX components. By experimenting with these tools, you quickly begin to appreciate the power of ActiveX technology, and you lay the foundation for mastering advanced techniques.

To start, pull down Visual Basic's File menu and choose the New Project command. In the resulting dialog box, shown in Figure 17-1, you can see icons representing the categories of ActiveX components you can create in Visual Basic. Here are brief descriptions of these categories:

    ◆ An ActiveX EXE project is a standalone application that exposes objects for use in other programs. Microsoft Excel is an example of a major ActiveX EXE application. An EXE application is an *out-of-process* server; it runs as a separate program when its objects are created. For example, when the International Sales program creates a worksheet object, a new Excel application button appears on the Windows 95 Taskbar.

✦ An ActiveX DLL project is a *dynamic-link library* that provides classes of programmable objects. This chapter presents an example of an ActiveX DLL component and a project that uses it. As this example illustrates, an ActiveX DLL component is an *in-process* server; it runs in the same process as the client program that uses its resources.

✦ An ActiveX Control project defines one or more controls that can be added to a Visual Basic application.

✦ An ActiveX Document project is a program designed to run in the Microsoft Internet Explorer. Although an ActiveX document may look like a typical Web page, this type of project combines Internet functionality with the characteristic features of Visual Basic applications. As you can see in Figure 17-1, ActiveX documents can be implemented in either EXE or DLL form. Chapter 18 presents an example of an ActiveX document.

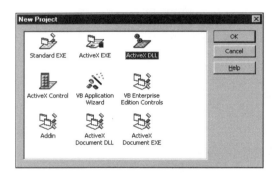

Figure 17-1: The New Project dialog box contains icons representing the categories of ActiveX projects you can develop in Visual Basic 5.0. These include ActiveX EXE, ActiveX DLL, ActiveX Control, and two types of ActiveX Document components.

By selecting one of the ActiveX icons in the New Project dialog box, you begin building a new component. For example, the ActiveX DLL icon results in a DLL project containing one class module. In the following short exercise you'll open a project of this type:

1. If necessary, choose File⇨Remove Project to close any project that is currently open.

2. Choose File⇨New Project. The New Project dialog box appears.

3. Select the ActiveX DLL icon and click OK. In response, Visual Basic creates a Project1 file containing one module named Class1.

4. Select Class1 in the Project Explorer window, and examine the class properties in the Properties window. As you can see in Figure 17-2, the default setting of the property named Instancing is 5 - MultiUse. This setting allows a client application to create instances of the object that the class defines.

5. Select Project1 in the Project Explorer window. In the Properties window enter **DLLSample** as an experimental name for the ActiveX component project. You'll continue this exercise shortly.

Figure 17-2: When you create a new ActiveX DLL component, Visual Basic automatically opens a new class module for the project. The default setting for the Instancing property is MultiUse, meaning that a client application will be able to create instances of the object that the class defines.

Tip The Toggle Folders button at the top of the Project Explorer window allows you to switch between two ways of listing the modules of a project. When this feature is turned on, the Project Explorer organizes program files into folders, where each folder represents a category of modules. When the feature is off, modules are simply listed beneath each project name. If you are designing a project that contains multiple projects and many modules, you may want to turn the Toggle Folders feature off, as shown back in Figure 17-2.

When you use Visual Basic to create and compile an ActiveX project, the end result is an EXE or DLL component that is available for use in client programs. (A compiled ActiveX document project additionally produces a document file — with a VBD extension — that can be loaded into the Internet Explorer.) But while you are developing an ActiveX component, and before you compile it, you may want to test its performance in the context of a client program — that is, an application that makes use of the component's objects. In other words, you may need to work with two different applications at once:

✦ The ActiveX component that is the main focus of your programming effort

✦ A standard Visual Basic project that uses the resources provided by the ActiveX component project

For this situation, the Visual Basic development environment allows you to open two or more projects at once and to designate them as a group. When multiple files are open, one of them is selected as the startup project. A standard project can make use of the objects in an ActiveX component when both projects are open as a group.

Returning now to the DLLSample project you've opened, the following exercise shows you how to create a group:

1. Choose File➪Add Project. In the Add Project dialog box, keep the default Standard EXE selection and click Open. Visual Basic opens a project containing one form module named Form1.

2. Select Project1 in the Project Explorer. Then select the Name property in the Properties window and enter **DLLTest** as the project's name. Figure 17-3 shows the Project Explorer window at this point in your work. Two projects

are open at once — the ActiveX DLL component that you've named DLLSample, and the standard project named DLLTest. Notice that the title bar identifies these projects together as Group1.

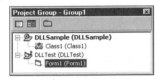

Figure 17-3: When you add a second project to your current work, the two open projects form a group. In this example, the group consists of an ActiveX DLL component named DLLSample and a standard project named DLLTest.

3. Imagine now that you've developed DLLSample as a working ActiveX component — defining one or more classes of objects — and you want to make these objects available to the DLLTest project. Select DLLTest in the Project Explorer window. Then pull down Visual Basic's Project menu and choose the References command. In the References dialog box, DLLSample appears as one of the available components. Click the box next to this reference to select the component, as in Figure 17-4. Then click OK to confirm the new reference. This action ensures that the objects of the DLLSample component will be available to the DLLTest program.

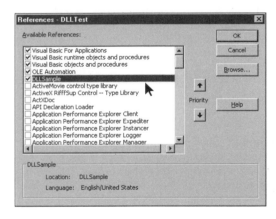

Figure 17-4: If you want the objects of an ActiveX DLL component to be available to a project, you must establish a reference appropriately. Choose Project⇨References. Then select the component reference that you want to use in your project.

4. Now suppose you've designed DLLTest as an application that uses the objects of the DLLSample component. To run the program — and test the ActiveX project — you need to establish the DLLTest application as the startup project. In the Project Explorer window, click DLLTest with the right mouse button, and choose Set as Start Up in the resulting shortcut menu, as shown in Figure 17-5. When you do so, the name of the DLLTest project is displayed in bold type in the Project Explorer window, as in Figure 17-6. The boldfacing confirms that DLLTest is now the startup project in the group.

Figure 17-5: To designate the standard application as the startup project in the group, click the application's name with the right mouse button and choose the Set as Start Up command in the resulting shortcut menu.

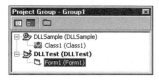

Figure 17-6: The name of the startup application appears in bold type in the Project Explorer window.

If you were developing an actual application in this exercise, you could now choose File⇨Save Project Group As. In response, Visual Basic creates a group file — identified by a VBG extension — to record the elements of the project group. (Before saving the group file, Visual Basic guides you step-by-step through the process of saving each file in the group, including the class and form module files and the two project files.) But you're now finished with this short exercise, and you can close it without saving it. The easiest way to do this is to choose File⇨Exit and click the No button when Visual Basic asks you if you want to save changes to the files you've opened.

This chapter's sample program is made up of two projects. The first, named CheckLists, is an ActiveX DLL component that defines a class named CheckList. This class is a generalized version of the class definition included in the Travel Reminders program, back in Chapter 13. Objects belonging to the CheckList class are designed to display varieties of useful lists — identifying tasks, events, places, people, or any group of items you want to work with. Among the methods defined in the CheckList class are procedures designed to display a list on the desktop and to sort the list alphabetically. (Unlike the lists presented in the Travel Reminders program, a window produced from the CheckList class is a standalone object, not a child in an MDI form.)

The second project is called the List Maker program. Essentially designed as a demonstration program for the CheckLists component, the List Maker gives you the opportunity to define a set of interrelated check lists and to work with them on the Windows desktop. Both the CheckLists component and the List Maker program are presented in the upcoming section.

The CheckLists Component and the List Maker

Restart Visual Basic now and open the project group named Lists.Vbg. You can find this file in the directory where you've stored the projects from this book's program disk. As shown in Figure 17-7, the Lists group contains the projects named CheckLists and ListMaker. Here are brief descriptions of these projects and their contents:

✦ The CheckLists project (stored as ChkList.Vbp) is an ActiveX DLL component. It contains the class module named CheckList (ChkList.Cls) and a form module named frmCheckList (ChkList.Frm). A client program can create instances of the CheckList class and then access the properties and methods defined by the class. For each new CheckList object, the code in the class module also creates an instance of the frmCheckList form as a visual display of a check list.

✦ The ListMaker project (ListMake.Vbp) is a standard Visual Basic application that demonstrates the use of the CheckLists project as an ActiveX component. As indicated by its boldface name in the Project Explorer window, ListMaker is the startup project in the group. The project includes a code module and two forms. The code module, named modListName (ListName.Bas) contains the startup code in a procedure named Sub Main. The frmListData form (ListData.Frm) is designed to elicit information about a new set of lists, and the frmListOpen form (ListOpen.Frm) is a primary window for opening, sorting, and closing the actual lists.

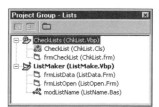

Figure 17-7: The Lists group contains two projects. CheckLists is an ActiveX DLL component, which provides a class named CheckList. ListMaker is a standard Visual Basic project, designed to demonstrate the use of the CheckLists component.

Each time you run the List Maker application, you can define and create a new *set* of lists. In this program, a set consists of one, two, or three lists, each with an associated text file that stores the actual contents of the list. The program also creates a separate text file to define the list set itself; this file contains the name of each list in the set and the associated file name. You'll see examples of all the text files shortly.

At the beginning of each program run you have the option of opening an existing list set or creating a new one. The program's startup code, which elicits the name of a new or existing list set, is contained in a procedure named Sub Main in the modListName module.

You can create a Sub Main procedure whenever you are designing a project in which no single form is the ideal startup object. As always, you designate an application's startup code in the Project Properties window. To examine this window for the List Maker application, click the project's name with the right mouse button and choose ListMaker Properties from the resulting shortcut menu. As shown in Figure 17-8, the Sub Main option has been selected in the Startup Object list.

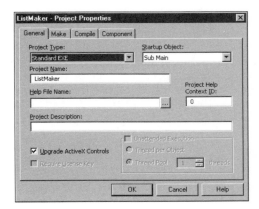

Figure 17-8: Open the Project Properties window by clicking the name of a project with the right mouse button and choosing Properties from the resulting shortcut menu (or by choosing Project⇨Properties). In the Startup Object box you can choose the name of the startup form. Alternatively, as in this example, you can designate Sub Main as the startup code; write the Sub Main procedure in a code module included in your project.

A sample run of the List Maker program

For a sample run of the List Maker application, imagine the following scenario: You're planning an extended stay in France this summer, with excursions to as many of the regions as you can find time to visit. To help finance your trip, you've agreed to write a series of magazine articles about historical sites that prove attractive to discerning American travelers. Specifically, you're planning to write about French medieval art and architecture, a longtime personal interest. Before you begin your trip you want to do some research on a number of the locations that you plan to visit. To help organize your research, you'll begin by developing check lists for three categories of sites — Romanesque churches, Gothic cathedrals, and other locations of interest. You plan to use the List Maker application to produce the check lists.

Press F5 or click the Start button to run the List Maker program. When you do so, an input box provides a brief description of the program and elicits the file name for the list set that you want to open. Enter **Medieval.LST**, as shown in Figure 17-9. (Although the program allows you to store list files wherever you want, the root directory of your hard disk is a convenient location. The program does not specify a particular extension name for list set files, but the LST extension is a good way to identify these files.) If the program does not find this file on your hard disk, the file name is assumed to represent a new list set. Accordingly, the program opens the List Maker dialog box, in which you next provide the file names and captions for the lists that will be included in the Medieval list set.

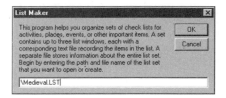

Figure 17-9: In the opening input box, enter a file name for the list set that you want to open or create. If the file already exists, the List Maker program immediately prepares to open the lists. Otherwise, if the file you identify here does not exist, the List Maker dialog box appears on the desktop so you can plan the contents of a new list set.

Figure 17-10 shows the List Maker dialog box as it first appears on the desktop. As you can see, the form contains text boxes for defining as many as three lists. To add a list, you begin by clicking the corresponding check box — List 1, List 2, or List 3. (The program ensures that you define these lists in sequence; notice that List 2 and List 3 are disabled until you check the previous check box.) For each list, you enter the name of the text file that will eventually store the list items and you supply the caption that will appear on the title bar for the list. At the top of the dialog box you enter a caption to identify the entire list set.

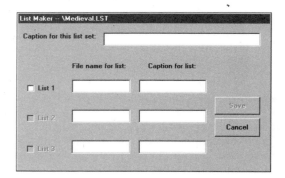

Figure 17-10: The List Maker dialog box elicits the necessary information for defining a set of lists. You enter a caption to identify the entire set, and captions for each individual list in the set. You also supply names for the text files that the program will create to record list items.

To prepare for the Medieval list set, fill in the List Maker dialog box as you see it in Figure 17-11. (Again, the program does not specify standard locations or extension names for the list files. In this example, all three files are saved in the root directory with TXT extensions.) Click the Save button when you've completed and reviewed all the entries. The sole purpose of the List Maker dialog box is to create a text file that defines the list set. Figure 17-12 shows the contents of the file that results from the information you've entered. Next time you run the program, you can skip the List Maker dialog box — and go directly to your lists — by entering **\Medieval.LST** as the name of the list set that you want to open.

After you specify the names for your lists, the program opens a second dialog box from which you can open the lists themselves. As you see in Figure 17-13, the window's title bar shows the caption you supplied to describe the list set; and

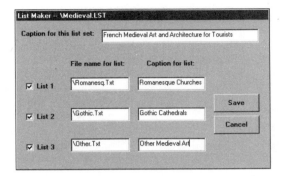

Figure 17-11: To define the Medieval list set, enter this information into the List Maker dialog box. Note that the three list files are saved in the root directory. After you've reviewed your entries for accuracy, click the Save button.

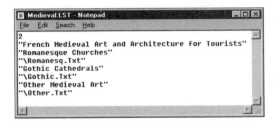

Figure 17-12: The List Maker creates a text file defining the contents of a particular list set. Here is the Medieval.LST file. To open this list set in future runs of the program, simply enter **\Medieval.LST** in the opening input box, as shown back in Figure 17-9.

each command button gives the name of one of the lists. To open a list, you simply click the appropriate command button. Each button is actually a toggle — click a button once to open a list, and click it again to hide the list. This feature allows you to focus on any combination of lists you wish to examine. You can open the lists in any order; or you can leave one or more of the lists unopened for the entire program run.

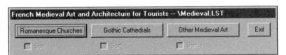

Figure 17-13: The command buttons on the second dialog box allow you to open the lists. Click a button once to open the corresponding list; click the button again to hide the list. You can open any combination of lists during a run, depending on the information that you want to work with.

The three lists are empty when you first open them, as you can see in Figure 17-14. To add an item to a list, click one of the numbered command buttons arranged in a column at the left side of a list window. In the resulting input box, enter the text of a list item. For example, Figure 17-15 shows how you might enter one of the sites into the list of Romanesque churches.

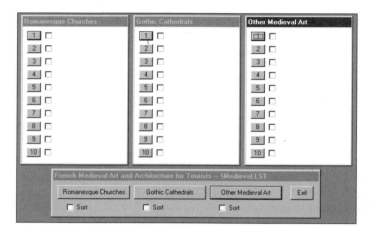

Figure 17-14: When you first open a new list window, the list itself is empty. To begin developing a list, click any one of the numbered command buttons at the left side of the list window, and enter a list item in the resulting input box.

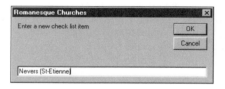

Figure 17-15: In the input box, enter the text for an individual list item. When you click OK the item appears in the list. If the text turns out to be too long to fit on a single line in the list window, try re-entering the item in a shorter form.

Once you've completed the text entries for a list, you can begin using the check boxes that appear next to the list items. In the Medieval list examples, a checked box might indicate that you've completed the necessary research for a particular site visit. For example, Figure 17-16 shows the complete Romanesque Churches list; as you can see, several of the list items are checked.

Figure 17-16: Once you've developed a list, the check boxes take on a significance that is unique to the context of the list itself. In the example of the Medieval lists, a checked item might mean that you've completed the research for a particular tourist site.

To sort a list alphabetically, check the Sort box located just beneath the list button on the dialog box. In Figure 17-17, these boxes have been checked for all three lists in the Medieval set.

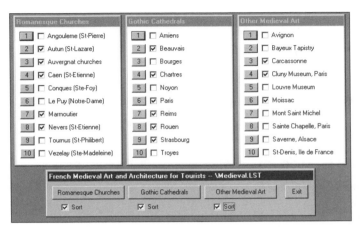

Figure 17-17: By checking the Sort box that appears beneath a list's command button, you can instruct the program to alphabetize the items in the list. To return the items to their original order, clear the check from the box.

When you click the Exit button to end the program run, the contents of the open lists are automatically saved — in their original order — to their respective text files. Figure 17-18 shows the Romanesq.Txt file; notice that each line of the file contains the text of a list item along with a value of 0 or 1, representing the checked or unchecked status of the item.

Figure 17-18: At the end of a program run, the items in a list are saved to the appropriate text file. Each line in the file contains the text of a list item, along with a value of 0 or 1 to represent the checked or unchecked status of the item.

You've noticed that the list windows seem to operate in a manner that's very similar to the reminder lists in the Travel Reminders program from Chapter 13. But there are a few important differences. First, the lists are displayed in standalone windows, not in a containing MDI form. More significantly, you can specify the subject of each list interactively at runtime, and you can work with a different set of lists each time you run the program.

The most important difference does not become clear until you take the next step in the ActiveX DLL development process — compiling the component to create an actual DLL file. Typically you postpone this step until you've had the chance to test the performance of the component adequately in the context of one or more client projects. When you've confirmed that the ActiveX component is working the way you want it to, compilation requires only one quick step. Afterwards you can remove the component from the project group; the client subsequently includes a direct reference to the compiled DLL file.

Compiling the ActiveX DLL component

To complete your work with the CheckList component, proceed with the following steps:

1. Select the name of the CheckLists project in the Project Explorer window.

2. Choose Project⇨CheckLists Properties. In the Project Description box of the resulting dialog box, you can enter a brief description of the component you're about to compile. (In this example, the description "CheckList class" has already been supplied, as shown in Figure 17-19.) This text entry subsequently appears as a description in the References dialog box, as you'll see shortly. Click OK to close the Project Properties box.

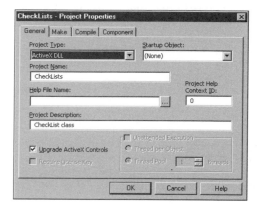

Figure 17-19: The Project Description entry in the Project Properties dialog box is a brief description of the component you're about to compile. This description subsequently identifies the component in the References dialog box.

3. Choose File⇨Make ChkList.dll, as in Figure 17-20. In the resulting Make Project dialog box, specify the folder location where you want to save the DLL file and click OK. Visual Basic compiles the project, creates the Dynamic Link Library file, and registers it properly for your system.

4. Next you can remove the ActiveX DLL project from the Lists group. Once again select the name of the CheckLists project in the Project Explorer window. Then choose File⇨Remove Project. A warning box appears; click Yes to confirm that you want to carry out this operation. Now if you choose the References command from the Project menu, you can confirm that the CheckList class reference is provided by the DLL file you've just created, as shown in Figure 17-21.

Figure 17-20: Use the File menu's Make ChkList.dll command to compile the ActiveX DLL project. When you do so, Visual Basic creates the DLL file and registers the dynamic link library appropriately on your system.

5. Press F5 to run the program. Although the ActiveX DLL component is no longer part of the project group, the List Maker program works just the same as it did before.

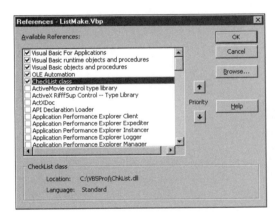

Figure 17-21: When you remove the ActiveX DLL project from the project group, the client program retains a reference to the new DLL file that you've created. As you can see at the bottom of the References dialog box, the reference location shows the path and file name of the DLL.

The ChkList.DLL component is now available for use in any project you develop. To create CheckList objects in a new project, begin by establishing a reference to the ChkList.DLL file. Then in the code of your project you can write statements that create instances of the object and use the object's properties and methods.

The final sections of this chapter examine the code of both the CheckLists ActiveX component and the ListMaker project. As always, you can turn to Appendix A to see the complete code listings from these two projects, or you can scroll through the listings in the code window on your screen. Reopen the original Lists.Vbg group so that you can view the code of both projects.

Inside the CheckLists and ListMaker Projects

The code contained in the two modules of the CheckLists component define the properties, methods, and events associated with CheckList objects. For a preview of the CheckList properties and methods available to a client program, you can open the Object Browser window:

1. Select ListMaker in the Project Explorer window.

2. Choose View➪Object Browser, or click the Object Browser icon on Toolbar.

3. In the Project/Library list at the upper-left corner of the Object Browser window, select the CheckLists component.

4. In the Classes list at the left side of the window, select the CheckList class. The Members list shows the properties and methods available for working with an instance of the CheckList class.

As you can see in Figure 17-22, the class defines four properties and four methods for use with CheckList objects. You can use the Object Browser to locate the code for any property or method that you want to investigate. Simply double-click the name of any item in the Members list; in response, Visual Basic opens the code window and displays the corresponding declaration or procedure. (Of course, the CheckLists project must be open as part of the current project group for this technique to work.)

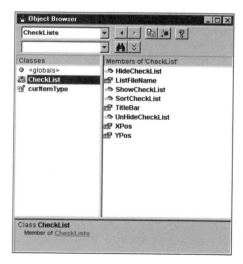

Figure 17-22: The Object Browser shows the four properties and four methods available for CheckList objects. Double-click the name of any item in the Members list to view the corresponding code in the CheckList class.

Properties and methods of the CheckList class

The general declarations section of the CheckList class, shown in Figure 17-23, declares an instance of the frmCheckList form. The variable *newList* represents this object. In addition, a Boolean variable named *newListActive* indicates whether the form has been displayed:

```
Private newList As New frmCheckList
Private newListActive As Boolean
```

As you'll discover shortly, the program uses *newListActive* to determine whether certain actions can be performed, given the current status of the *newList* form.

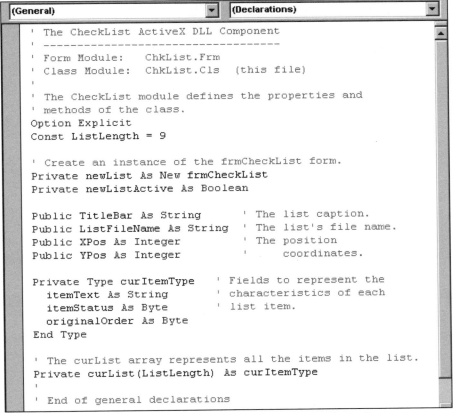

```
(General)                          (Declarations)
' The CheckList ActiveX DLL Component
' -----------------------------------
' Form Module:    ChkList.Frm
' Class Module:   ChkList.Cls   (this file)
'
' The CheckList module defines the properties and
' methods of the class.
Option Explicit
Const ListLength = 9

' Create an instance of the frmCheckList form.
Private newList As New frmCheckList
Private newListActive As Boolean

Public TitleBar As String       ' The list caption.
Public ListFileName As String   ' The list's file name.
Public XPos As Integer          ' The position
Public YPos As Integer          '     coordinates.

Private Type curItemType        ' Fields to represent the
   itemText As String           ' characteristics of each
   itemStatus As Byte           ' list item.
   originalOrder As Byte
End Type

' The curList array represents all the items in the list.
Private curList(ListLength) As curItemType
'
' End of general declarations
```

Figure 17-23: The general declarations section of the CheckList class creates an instance of the frmCheckList form and declares the Public variables that represent the properties of a CheckList object.

Four Public statements represent the properties of a CheckList object:

```
Public TitleBar As String
Public ListFileName As String
Public XPos As Integer
Public YPos As Integer
```

You may recall these same property names from the Travel Reminders program in Chapter 13. The *TitleBar* property is the caption displayed at the top of a list window. *ListFileName* is the name of the text file that stores the list items. *XPos* and *YPos* are the position coordinates of the list window on the desktop.

The *ShowCheckList* method, in Figure 17-24, uses the values of all these properties to display the list. A call to a procedure named *ReadData* opens the *ListFileName* file and copies its contents to the list window. Then the Caption, Top, and Left properties of the *newList* form are set, and a call to the Show method displays the list:

```
newList.Caption = TitleBar

newList.Top = YPos
newList.Left = XPos

newList.Show
```

Finally, the *newListActive* variable is assigned a value of True. This value indicates that the program has now read the list items and displayed the object on the desktop for the first time.

A pair of methods named *HideCheckList* and *UnHideCheckList* have the job of hiding or redisplaying the list window. To do so, they simply toggle the Visible property of the *newList* form, as you can see in Figure 17-25. For example, here is how the *HideCheckList* procedure temporarily removes the list from the desktop:

```
If newListActive Then newList.Visible = False
```

Notice that this action is performed only if the list has been initialized — that is, if *newListActive* is true.

Finally, the method named *SortCheckList* alphabetizes the list or returns it to its original order — but once again, only if *newListActive* is true. As shown in Figure 17-26, the specific action depends on the Boolean value received in the *alphabetic* argument:

```
Public Sub SortCheckList(alphabetic As Boolean)
```

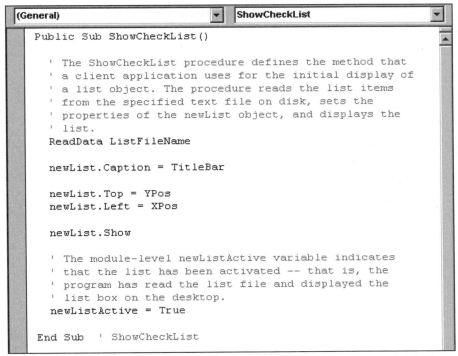

```
(General)                              ShowCheckList

   Public Sub ShowCheckList()

     ' The ShowCheckList procedure defines the method that
     ' a client application uses for the initial display of
     ' a list object. The procedure reads the list items
     ' from the specified text file on disk, sets the
     ' properties of the newList object, and displays the
     ' list.
     ReadData ListFileName

     newList.Caption = TitleBar

     newList.Top = YPos
     newList.Left = XPos

     newList.Show

     ' The module-level newListActive variable indicates
     ' that the list has been activated -- that is, the
     ' program has read the list file and displayed the
     ' list box on the desktop.
     newListActive = True

   End Sub  ' ShowCheckList
```

Figure 17-24: The *ShowCheckList* method uses the four properties — *ListFileName*, *TitleBar*, *YPos*, and *XPos* to initialize and display the CheckList object. Once this action is complete, the procedure switches the value of *newListActive* to True.

If *alphabetic* is true, the method sorts the list; if false, the list is returned to its original order. To carry out this action, *SortCheckList* makes calls to three procedures: *RecordCurOrder* makes a copy of the list items in their current order; *SortList* establishes the new order; and *DisplayNewOrder* redisplays the items in the list. These three procedures are private to the CheckList class; a client program cannot call them directly.

Events for the CheckList class

Three event procedures are associated with an instance of the CheckList class. The standard Class events — Class_Initialize and Class_Terminate, shown in Figure 17-27 — occur when an instance of the class is first created and when the object is released from memory. In this program, the Class_Initialize procedure simply assigns an initial value of False to the variable named *newListActive*. As you've seen, this value isn't changed until the *ShowCheckList* method reads the list file and displays the list on the desktop.

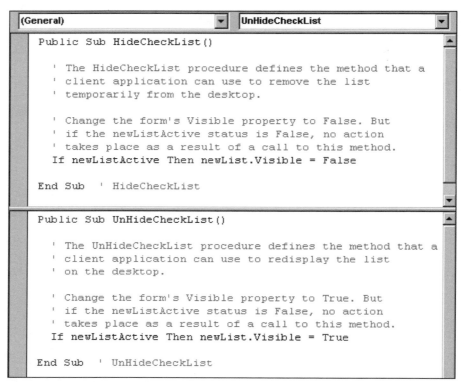

Figure 17-25: The *HideCheckList* and *UnHideCheckList* methods toggle the Visible property of the *newList* form. But these actions take place only if *newListActive* contains a value of True.

The Class_Terminate procedure has more to do. If *newListActive* is true by the time the client program is ready to release the CheckList object from memory — that is, if the list has ever been displayed — the procedure restores the list's original order and saves the current list items back to the text file. These actions are performed by calls to the *SortCheckList* and *SaveCheckList* procedures. Finally, the Class_Terminate procedure releases the corresponding *newList* form from memory:

```
Set newList = Nothing
```

Another event takes place when the user clicks one of the numbered buttons in a list window. These command buttons are defined as a control array named cmdChange. The cmdChange_Click procedure (in the frmCheckList form) takes control when one of the buttons is clicked. As shown in Figure 17-28, the procedure displays an input box on the screen, and assigns the user's input to the Caption property of the corresponding chkListItem check box.

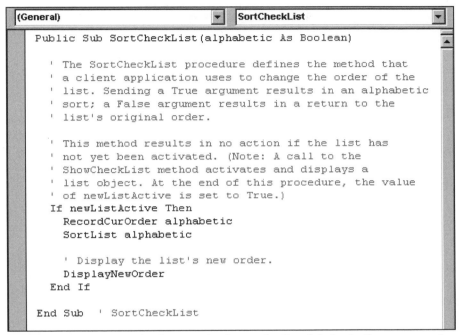

```
(General)                              ▼  SortCheckList                    ▼

   Public Sub SortCheckList(alphabetic As Boolean)

      ' The SortCheckList procedure defines the method that
      ' a client application uses to change the order of the
      ' list. Sending a True argument results in an alphabetic
      ' sort; a False argument results in a return to the
      ' list's original order.

      ' This method results in no action if the list has
      ' not yet been activated. (Note: A call to the
      ' ShowCheckList method activates and displays a
      ' list object. At the end of this procedure, the value
      ' of newListActive is set to True.)
      If newListActive Then
        RecordCurOrder alphabetic
        SortList alphabetic

        ' Display the list's new order.
        DisplayNewOrder
      End If

   End Sub   ' SortCheckList
```

Figure 17-26: The *SortCheckList* method sorts the list alphabetically, or returns it to its original order — but only if *newListActive* is True.

A new copy of the CheckList code is created for each instance of the class. When the client program changes a property setting or calls a method, the property or method always applies to a specific instance of the class. The elegance of this arrangement becomes clear as you examine the code for the ListMaker project.

The procedures of the ListMaker project

As you've seen, Sub Main is the startup code for the ListMaker project. Shown in Figure 17-29, Sub Main is the only procedure in the modListName module. After setting up a lengthy input prompt, the procedure begins the program's action by displaying an input box on the screen:

```
listSetFileName = InputBox(inputPrompt, "List Maker")
```

The string variable named *listSetFileName* is declared in a Public statement in the global declarations section of the modListName module. Its value is therefore available to both the frmListData and frmListOpen forms. When the user enters a file name, Sub Main makes an attempt to open the file, under the control of an error trap:

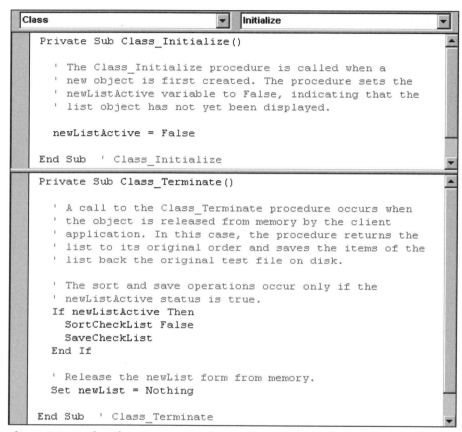

Figure 17-27: The Class event procedures are performed when an instance of the CheckList class is first created and when the object is released from memory.

```
On Error GoTo noSuchFile
  Open listSetFileName For Input As #1
  Close #1
```

If no error occurs, the file exists. Accordingly, the procedure opens the frmListOpen form so that the user can immediately begin working with the target lists:

```
frmListOpen.Show
Exit Sub
```

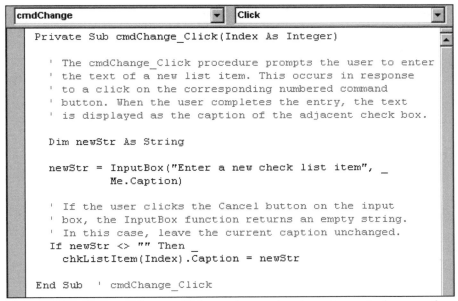

```
cmdChange                              ▼    Click                          ▼

    Private Sub cmdChange_Click(Index As Integer)

       ' The cmdChange_Click procedure prompts the user to enter
       ' the text of a new list item. This occurs in response
       ' to a click on the corresponding numbered command
       ' button. When the user completes the entry, the text
       ' is displayed as the caption of the adjacent check box.

       Dim newStr As String

       newStr = InputBox("Enter a new check list item", _
                Me.Caption)

       ' If the user clicks the Cancel button on the input
       ' box, the InputBox function returns an empty string.
       ' In this case, leave the current caption unchanged.
       If newStr <> "" Then _
          chkListItem(Index).Caption = newStr

    End Sub   ' cmdChange_Click
```

Figure 17-28: The cmdChange_Click event procedure is performed whenever the user clicks one of the numbered command buttons in a list window. The procedure gives the user the opportunity to change the caption of the corresponding list item.

But if the error trap is triggered, the program can assume that the list set file doesn't exist yet. In this case, Sub Main opens the frmListData form so that the user can begin entering the specifications for a new list set:

```
noSuchFile:
  frmListData.Show
```

Defining a list set — the frmListData form

The frmListData form contains only a few event procedures, designed to respond to the user's activities on the List Maker dialog box. For example, the procedure named chkListNum_Click enables or disables controls on the form according to the number of list check boxes the user selects.

When the user completes the input on the form and clicks the Save button, the cmdSave_Click procedure, shown in Figure 17-30, creates the list set file and copies information to it from the form. The procedure begins by opening the new text file for output. The first two data items written to the file are the value of *lastListIndex*, which specifies the number of lists to be created; and the value of txtListSetCaption.Text, the text item that the user has entered to describe the list set:

```
(General)                          ▼    Main                          ▼

Sub Main()
  ' The Sub Main procedure elicits the name of a list
  ' set file. If the file exists, the program opens the
  ' frmListOpen form; if not, the frmListData form.
  Dim inputPrompt As String

  inputPrompt = "This program helps you organize sets " & _
  "of check lists for activities, places, events, or " & _
  "other important items. A set contains up to three " & _
  "list windows, each with a corresponding text file " & _
  "recording the items in the list. A separate file " & _
  "stores information about the entire list set. Begin " & _
  "by entering the path and file name of the list set " & _
  "that you want to open or create."
  listSetFileName = InputBox(inputPrompt, "List Maker")
  If Trim(listSetFileName) = "" Then End   ' Cancel button.

  On Error GoTo noSuchFile

    ' Try to open the file. If no error, show frmListOpen.
    Open listSetFileName For Input As #1
    Close #1
    frmListOpen.Show
    Exit Sub

noSuchFile:
  ' If an error has taken place, display frmListData.
  frmListData.Show
End Sub   ' Sub Main
```

Figure 17-29: Sub Main is the startup code for the ListMaker project. It elicits the name of a list set file. If the file exists, the frmListOpen form is opened so the user can work with existing lists. If not, the frmListData form is opened so the user can specify the characteristics of a new list set.

```
Open listSetFileName For Output As #1

Write #1, lastListIndex
Write #1, txtListSetCaption.Text
```

Then a For loop writes two data items for each new list — the caption for the list window and the file name for saving the list items:

```
For i = 0 To lastListIndex
  Write #1, txtListCaption(i).Text
  Write #1, txtListFileName(i).Text
Next i
```

With this, the job of the frmListData form is complete. The program closes the file, hides the current form, and opens the frmListOpen form so the user can begin working with the lists:

```
Close #1
Me.Hide
frmListOpen.Show
```

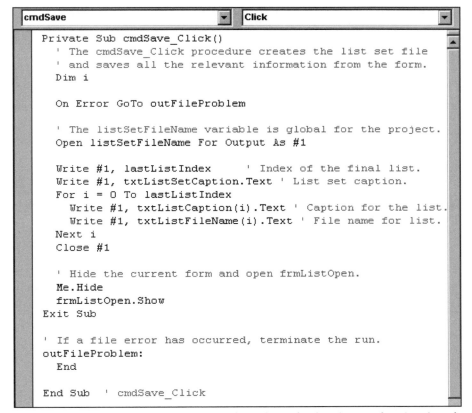

```
cmdSave                          ▼   Click                              ▼

    Private Sub cmdSave_Click()
       ' The cmdSave_Click procedure creates the list set file
       ' and saves all the relevant information from the form.
       Dim i

       On Error GoTo outFileProblem

       ' The listSetFileName variable is global for the project.
       Open listSetFileName For Output As #1

       Write #1, lastListIndex       ' Index of the final list.
       Write #1, txtListSetCaption.Text ' List set caption.
       For i = 0 To lastListIndex
          Write #1, txtListCaption(i).Text ' Caption for the list.
          Write #1, txtListFileName(i).Text ' File name for list.
       Next i
       Close #1

       ' Hide the current form and open frmListOpen.
       Me.Hide
       frmListOpen.Show
    Exit Sub

    ' If a file error has occurred, terminate the run.
    outFileProblem:
       End

    End Sub  ' cmdSave_Click
```

Figure 17-30: The cmdSave_Click procedure (from the frmListData form) writes the user's input to a new list set file. This file subsequently provides the definition for a list set that can be opened by the frmListOpen form.

Managing the CheckList objects — the frmListOpen form

The code in the frmListOpen form has the tasks of creating the CheckList objects, setting their properties, and calling their various methods according to the user's interactive instructions during the program run. In this context, several parts of this form module are worth examining:

✦ The general declarations section, shown in Figure 17-31, declares an array of CheckList objects to represent instances of the CheckList class. The name of the array is simply *List*:

```
Dim List(MaxListIndex) As CheckList
```

✦ The Form_Load procedure, in Figures 17-32 and 17-33, opens the list set file, creates the correct number of CheckList objects to represent the user's lists, and sets the properties according to the user's specifications. Each CheckList object is created as an element of the *List* array; property settings are read directly from the open file:

```
For Index = 0 to lastListIndex
  Input #1, inTitle
  Input #1, inFileName

  Set List(Index) = New(CheckList)
  With List(Index)
    .TitleBar = inTitle
    .ListFileName = inFileName
    .XPos = 300 + Index * 3000
    .YPos = 800
End With
```

✦ When the user clicks the command button for a particular list, the cmdList_Click procedure in Figure 17-34 makes a call to the *ShowCheckList*, *HideCheckList*, or *UnHideCheckList* method for the current CheckList object. The status of the object itself — *Unopened, Hidden,* or *Displayed* — determines which method is called. The three command buttons on the frmListOpen form are arranged as a control array with the common name cmdList. The current status of a given object is stored as the Tag property of the corresponding command button on the frmListOpen form:

```
List(Index).ShowCheckList
List(Index).UnHideCheckList
List(Index).HideCheckList
```

✦ When the user changes the checked or unchecked status of a Sort check box, the chkListSort_Click procedure in Figure 17-35 makes a call to the *SortCheckList* method for the appropriate CheckList object. The three Sort check boxes are arranged as a control array with the common name chkListSort:

```
List(Index).SortCheckList chkListSort(Index).Value
```

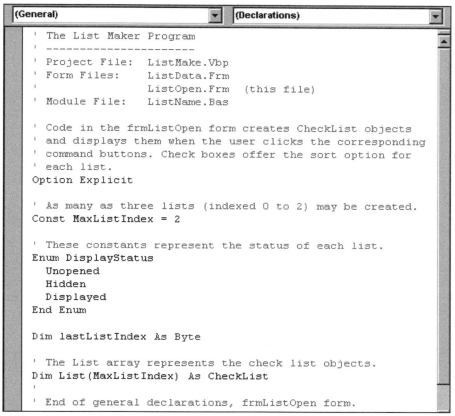

```
(General)                          ▼   (Declarations)                    ▼

' The List Maker Program
' ---------------------
' Project File:   ListMake.Vbp
' Form Files:     ListData.Frm
'                 ListOpen.Frm  (this file)
' Module File:    ListName.Bas

' Code in the frmListOpen form creates CheckList objects
' and displays them when the user clicks the corresponding
' command buttons. Check boxes offer the sort option for
' each list.
Option Explicit

' As many as three lists (indexed 0 to 2) may be created.
Const MaxListIndex = 2

' These constants represent the status of each list.
Enum DisplayStatus
  Unopened
  Hidden
  Displayed
End Enum

Dim lastListIndex As Byte

' The List array represents the check list objects.
Dim List(MaxListIndex) As CheckList
'
' End of general declarations, frmListOpen form.
```

Figure 17-31: The general declarations section of the frmListOpen form creates an array of CheckList objects named *List*. Also note the list of Enum constants, *Unopened,* *Hidden,* and *Displayed.* These constants are used to represent the status of a given CheckList object.

✦ Finally, the cmdExit_Click procedure, also in Figure 17-35, releases the CheckList objects from memory when the user clicks the Exit button. As you know, this action triggers the Class_Terminate event for each object.

```
For Index = 0 To lastListIndex
  Set List(Index) = Nothing
Next Index
```

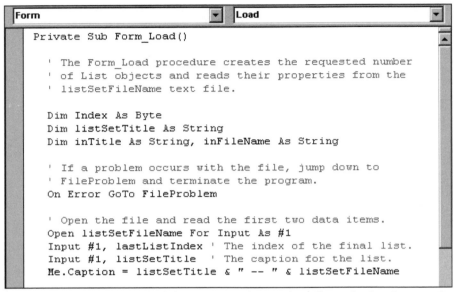

```
Form                          ▼   Load                          ▼
Private Sub Form_Load()                                          ▲

    ' The Form_Load procedure creates the requested number
    ' of List objects and reads their properties from the
    ' listSetFileName text file.

    Dim Index As Byte
    Dim listSetTitle As String
    Dim inTitle As String, inFileName As String

    ' If a problem occurs with the file, jump down to
    ' FileProblem and terminate the program.
    On Error GoTo FileProblem

    ' Open the file and read the first two data items.
    Open listSetFileName For Input As #1
    Input #1, lastListIndex  ' The index of the final list.
    Input #1, listSetTitle   ' The caption for the list.
    Me.Caption = listSetTitle & " -- " & listSetFileName
```

Figure 17-32: The first part of the Form_Load procedure (from the frmListOpen form) opens a list set file and begins reading its data.

In summary, the List Maker program uses the CheckLists ActiveX DLL component to create and manage any set of lists that you specify. Here is a recap of this program's essential design elements:

1. A reference to the CheckLists component is established for the List Maker program in the References dialog box.

2. The program creates one, two, or three instances of the CheckList class, according to the user's specifications. Each list is displayed inside an instance of the frmCheckList form, a module that is defined as part of the CheckLists component.

3. The four properties of each CheckList object provide the title bar caption, the name of the file containing the list items, and the position coordinates of the check list on the desktop.

4. The four methods of the CheckList object allow the client program to display a list on the desktop, hide the list temporarily or restore it to the screen, and sort the list items it contains.

5. When the List Maker program releases a CheckList object from memory, a Class_Terminate event procedure in the class code ensures that the current list will be saved back to the appropriate text file on disk.

```
Form                            ▼    Load                          ▼
       ' Read the title and file name for each List object.
     For Index = 0 To lastListIndex
       Input #1, inTitle
       Input #1, inFileName

       ' Create a new List object and set its properties.
       Set List(Index) = New CheckList
       With List(Index)
         .TitleBar = inTitle
         .ListFileName = inFileName
         .XPos = 300 + Index * 3000
         .YPos = 800
       End With

       ' Set the properties of the corresponding button.
       With cmdList(Index)
         .Enabled = True
         .Caption = inTitle
         .Tag = Unopened
       End With
     Next Index
     Close #1
     On Error GoTo 0
   Exit Sub

   ' End the program run if a file problem has occurred.
   FileProblem:
     End
   End Sub  ' Form_Load
```

Figure 17-33: The second part of the Form_Load procedure creates new CheckList objects and assigns settings to their properties. It reads the property settings from the list set file.

Significantly, the List Maker program can work successfully with the CheckLists component in either of two ways. The ActiveX component can be open at the same time as the ListMaker project, as part of a Lists group; or the ActiveX component can be compiled and saved as a DLL file on disk. Both approaches require an appropriate reference to the component in the References dialog box.

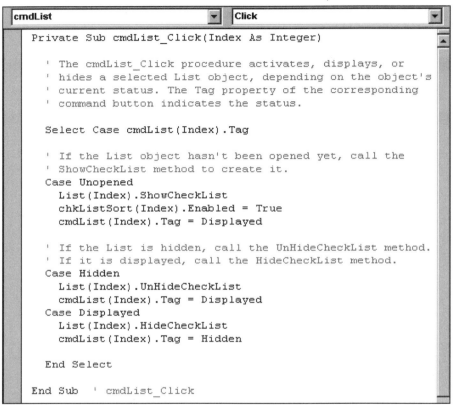

```
cmdList                              ▼   Click                                ▼

    Private Sub cmdList_Click(Index As Integer)                              ▲

      ' The cmdList_Click procedure activates, displays, or
      ' hides a selected List object, depending on the object's
      ' current status. The Tag property of the corresponding
      ' command button indicates the status.

      Select Case cmdList(Index).Tag

      ' If the List object hasn't been opened yet, call the
      ' ShowCheckList method to create it.
      Case Unopened
        List(Index).ShowCheckList
        chkListSort(Index).Enabled = True
        cmdList(Index).Tag = Displayed

      ' If the List is hidden, call the UnHideCheckList method.
      ' If it is displayed, call the HideCheckList method.
      Case Hidden
        List(Index).UnHideCheckList
        cmdList(Index).Tag = Displayed
      Case Displayed
        List(Index).HideCheckList
        cmdList(Index).Tag = Hidden

      End Select

    End Sub  ' cmdList_Click
```

Figure 17-34: The cmdList_Click procedure (from the frmListOpen form) responds to a click on one of the three list buttons. It calls one of three methods for the current CheckList object — *ShowCheckList*, *HideCheckList*, or *UnHideCheckList*.

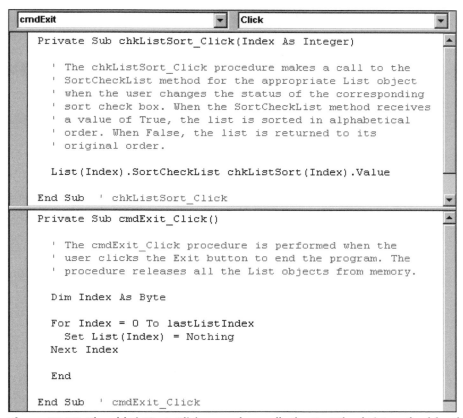

```
cmdExit                              ▼  Click                              ▼

    Private Sub chkListSort_Click(Index As Integer)

      ' The chkListSort_Click procedure makes a call to the
      ' SortCheckList method for the appropriate List object
      ' when the user changes the status of the corresponding
      ' sort check box. When the SortCheckList method receives
      ' a value of True, the list is sorted in alphabetical
      ' order. When False, the list is returned to its
      ' original order.

      List(Index).SortCheckList chkListSort(Index).Value

    End Sub  ' chkListSort_Click

    Private Sub cmdExit_Click()

      ' The cmdExit_Click procedure is performed when the
      ' user clicks the Exit button to end the program. The
      ' procedure releases all the List objects from memory.

      Dim Index As Byte

      For Index = 0 To lastListIndex
        Set List(Index) = Nothing
      Next Index

      End

    End Sub  ' cmdExit_Click
```

Figure 17-35: The chkListSort_Click procedure calls the *SortCheckList* method for the current CheckList object. As a result, the list is either sorted alphabetically or returned to its original order. The cmdExit_Click procedure releases all CheckList objects from memory. This triggers the Class_Terminate event for each object in turn.

ActiveX Documents and Web Connections

An *ActiveX document* project generates an application that you can run inside Microsoft's Internet Explorer. This new and versatile project category is designed to simplify many programming tasks in today's online environment. An ActiveX document can include general features that are characteristic of all Visual Basic applications, such as command buttons, text boxes, labels, lists, options, pictures, and all the events and methods that are associated with these controls. In addition, an ActiveX document provides Internet functionality, including links to Web sites. In the context of the Internet Explorer, an ActiveX document looks and operates like a Web page. But thanks to the tools available to you in Visual Basic, the design possibilities for this type of application are vast.

ActiveX documents are listed among the options you choose from Visual Basic's New Project window. As you can see in Figure 18-1, two types are available: An ActiveX Document DLL is an *in-process* component, and an ActiveX Document EXE is an *out-of-process* component. When you choose either of these options, Visual Basic opens a new project and a type of module known as a UserDocument. For example, Figure 18-2 shows an ActiveX document project, saved under the file name Test. As always, the project file name has a default extension of VBP. The UserDocument module has an extension name of DOB.

To develop the features of a UserDocument module, you proceed through the familiar sequence of programming steps: Add a group of controls, set their properties, and write code to define their behavior. All the standard controls in Visual Basic's Toolbox are available for use in a UserDocument module, except for the OLE control. (Embedded OLE objects such as Excel worksheets or Word documents are also excluded.)

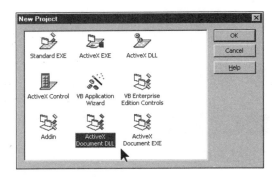

Figure 18-1: The New Project dialog box offers two types of ActiveX document projects. ActiveX Document DLL is the in-process version, and ActiveX Document EXE is the out-of-process version.

Figure 18-2: When you create a new ActiveX document project, Visual Basic automatically adds a UserDocument module. When saved to disk, this type of module has a file name extension of DOB.

Significantly, a UserDocument module provides access to an important object named Hyperlink. This object's NavigateTo method allows your program to make links to Internet sites. You'll see examples in this chapter's sample application.

When you run an ActiveX document project inside the development environment, Visual Basic creates a temporary document file with an extension of VBD (for "Visual Basic Document"). This file initially appears in the same directory as the Visual Basic application itself. To test your program, you start the Internet Explorer and open the VBD document.

When the document is working the way want it to, you can compile the ActiveX project. A compilation results in two files:

✦ A DLL file and a VBD file if you're developing an in-process component

✦ An EXE file and a VBD file if you're creating an out-of-process component

You can save these files in any directory you choose. After compilation, the VBD file is available for use in the Internet Explorer. The associated DLL or EXE file is the ActiveX component behind the document.

This chapter presents a sample ActiveX Document DLL project named France.Vbp. To set the scene for this program, imagine the following situation: You've joined an informal circle of enthusiastic Francophiles who meet monthly to practice speaking French. Most of the participants take trips in France every year or so. As your special contribution to this group's interests, you've been asked to create a tool that will help people find information about France on the Internet. In particular, the group is interested in Web sites that provide useful travel services. The France.Vbp project represents the initial version of your application. It generates an Internet Explorer document named FranceGo.Vbd.

The France Project and the FranceGo Document

Open France.Vbp from the directory where you've copied the applications from the program disk. Figure 18-3 shows the program's components in the Project Explorer window, including France.Vbp and FranceGo.Dob. (Two additional files associated with the application are France.Vbw and FranceGo.Dox; these are also provided on the program disk.)

Figure 18-3: The France.Vbp project contains a UserDocument module named FranceGo. The document is saved on disk with a default extension of DOB.

Before you run the application, open the FranceGo module and take a first look at the controls it contains:

✦ At the upper-left corner is a picture control that displays a digital photograph in bitmap (BMP) form. As you can see in Figure 18-4, the photograph shows a typical *petit déjeuner*, a French breakfast. (By the way, Visual Basic stores this image in the FranceGo.Dox file while you're developing the application. When the application is compiled, the image is included in the resulting DLL file.)

✦ Beneath the photograph is a group of labels, command buttons, and text boxes that together provide a simplified Currency Converter program, similar to projects you worked on in the early chapters of this book. This feature demonstrates an essential point: An ActiveX document is not merely an Internet Explorer tool; it is also a program that can include any variety of Visual Basic elements.

✦ Scrolling to the right side of the UserDocument, you can see a column of command buttons, as shown in Figure 18-5. When you run the program you'll see that these buttons provide links to specific commercial Web sites that may be of interest to a person who is planning a trip to France.

Running the project and viewing the document

Unlike other types of projects you've developed up to now, an ActiveX document project cannot be tested inside the Visual Basic development environment. When you run the application, your next step is to start the Internet Explorer and open the document that the program generates. In this example, you'll look for the FranceGo.Vbd document in the directory where Visual Basic itself resides.

Figure 18-4: The picture box at the upper-left corner of the FranceGo document contains a photo of a *petit déjeuner*, a familiar sight to anyone who has visited France. Beneath the photo is a simple Currency Converter program, designed to calculate equivalents between francs and dollars.

Follow these steps to run the France program, open its document, and experiment with its features:

1. In Visual Basic, press F5 or click the Start button on the toolbar to run the program. When you do so, the development environment seems atypically inactive. You don't see any sign of the FranceGo document.

2. Minimize Visual Basic on the Windows 95 desktop and start the Internet Explorer. (You can select Internet Explorer from the Start menu, or you can double-click the Internet icon on the desktop.) When you see the Sign In window, go ahead and log onto the Internet.

3. In the Address box near the top of the Explorer window, you now need to enter the complete path location and file name of the FranceGo.Vbd file. For a typical installation of Visual Basic, this entry might look like this:

```
c:\program files\devstudio\vb\francego.vbd
```

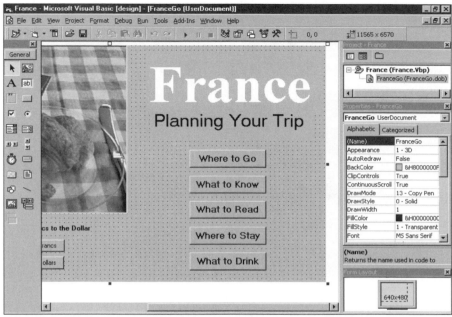

Figure 18-5: At the right side of the FranceGo document is a column of command buttons representing links to specific commercial Web sites.

4. When you complete this entry, the FranceGo document appears in the Explorer window, as shown in Figure 18-6. You can see all the controls that you examined in the UserDocument, but now the document is a running project. Position the mouse pointer over any one of the command buttons at the right side of the document. The mouse pointer turns into an upward-pointing hand, and a ToolTip indicates the Web link that the command button represents, as in Figure 18-7.

5. Try clicking one of the command buttons. When you do so, the Internet Explorer should jump to the target Web site. For example, Figure 18-8 shows the home page that appears when you click the "Where to Stay" button. (Don't worry too much if the FranceGo document doesn't work quite as expected at this point on your own system. When you later take steps to complete a full compilation of the component, the document will become fully functional.)

6. To return to the FranceGo page, pull down the Address list near the top of the Explorer window and choose the file's path address. Take a moment to experiment with the Currency Converter. For example, type an amount in the Francs box and press Enter. The program calculates the equivalent dollar amount and displays the result in the Dollars box, as in Figure 18-9.

Figure 18-6: The FranceGo document appears in the Internet Explorer window when you enter its path location and file name into the Address box.

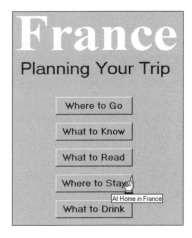

Figure 18-7: The mouse pointer changes to an upward-pointing hand icon when positioned over any of the command buttons that represent Web sites. A ToolTip identifies the linked site.

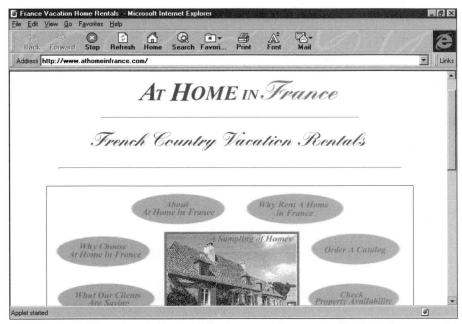

Figure 18-8: When you click one of the buttons, the Internet Explorer jumps to the target site. For example, this Web page belongs to an agency for country-home vacation rentals in France.

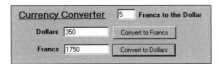

Figure 18-9: Back in the FranceGo page, you can test the Currency Converter by entering a currency amount and pressing Enter. The program calculates and displays the resulting conversion.

7. Exit from the Internet Explorer and log off. (Close all Explorer windows if more than one is open.) Then restore the Visual Basic window and click the End button on the toolbar to stop the run of the France program.

Compiling the project

After you've finished testing the France program and its ActiveX document in the Internet Explorer, you're ready to compile the project. Compilation results in two files:

✦ The France.Dll file contains the compiled code for the application.

✦ The FranceGo.Vbd file is the document that you can open in the Internet Explorer.

You can save these files in any directory of your choice. Visual Basic places both files in the same directory.

Compilation is a quick process:

1. With the France project still open in the Visual Basic environment, choose File⇨Make France.DLL.

2. In the Make Project dialog box, navigate to the directory where you want to store the DLL and VBD files. The root directory of your hard disk may be the most convenient location.

3. Click OK. Visual Basic requires only a few seconds to compile the project.

Now you can exit from Visual Basic and start up the Internet Explorer again. To open the FranceGo document, enter the path location where you've saved the DLL and VBD files, along with the name of the document file; for example:

```
c:\francego.vbd
```

The document appears in the Internet Explorer window. Take this opportunity to experiment further with the program. In particular, try out all of the Web site buttons and see where they take you. Now that the program is compiled, you can use the Internet Explorer's Back button to go directly back to the FranceGo page from a linked Web site. (This button may not have worked properly while you were running the France program from the Visual Basic environment.)

Exit from the Internet Explorer and log off when you've finished working with the FranceGo page. The final task ahead of you is to examine the project's code.

Inside the UserDocument

Like a form module, a UserDocument includes code — declarations, event procedures, and general procedures — that you can view in the code window. In this chapter's example, the FranceGo module contains all the code for the France project. Examine the code by scrolling through procedures in the code window, or turn to Appendix A for a complete listing.

Using the Hyperlink object

The most interesting part of the code is the procedure that implements the Web site links. The command buttons representing these links are organized as a control array with the common name cmdWebLink. Accordingly, the cmdWebLink_ Click procedure, shown in Figure 18-10, responds to clicks on any of the buttons. As usual, the Index argument indicates which button in the array has been clicked. Given this value, the procedure uses a Select Case structure to assign one of five Web addresses to a string variable named URL:

```
Select Case Index
  Case 0
    URL = "WWW.France.COM"
  Case 1
    URL = "WWW.ParisMatch.COM"
  Case 2
    URL = "WWW.IHT.COM"
  Case 3
    URL = "WWW.AtHomeInFrance.COM"
  Case 4
    URL = "WWW.WineCollection.COM"
End Select
```

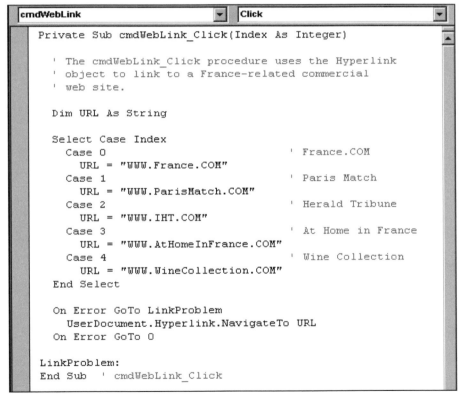

Figure 18-10: The cmdWebLink_Click procedure responds to a click on any one of the command buttons representing Web site connections. A call to the Hyperlink.NavigateTo method initiates the jump to a new Web page.

A subsequent statement in the cmdWebLink_click procedure is responsible for performing the jump to a new site:

```
UserDocument.Hyperlink.NavigateTo URL
```

Hyperlink is a property of the UserDocument object. A reference to this property provides access to the Hyperlink object. The Hyperlink object, in turn, has several methods, including NavigateTo. As a result of this method, the Internet Explorer finds and displays the Web page represented by the string stored in URL. Notice that NavigateTo is called within the control of an error trap; if something goes wrong, the cmdWebLink_Click procedure ends without completing the jump.

With the code organized in this way, you can easily add more Web connections to the program. To add a new Web link, follow these steps:

1. Add a command button to the UserDocument and assign it a Name property of cmdWebLink. This setting adds the new button to the existing control array. (You may want to rearrange the existing command buttons on the UserDocument to make room for a new button.)

2. Assign an appropriate Caption property for the new button. To make the new button operate consistently with the other buttons, you should also enter settings for three other properties: A MousePointer setting of 99-Custom allows you to choose a customized icon for the mouse icon. Select the icon itself as the setting of the MouseIcon property. (You'll find the pointing hand icon in a folder named Arrows.) In the ToolTipText property, enter a brief description of the target Web site.

3. In the cmdWebLink_Click procedure, add a Case clause for the new button, and write an assignment statement to store the appropriate Web address in the variable named URL. For example, the next button in the list might be handled as follows:

```
Case 5
   URL = "WWW.EnProvence.COM"
```

Event procedures for the Currency Converter

Because the Currency Converter in the FranceGo document deals only with francs and dollars, it doesn't require a database of international currencies. Instead it includes a simple text box — named txtConversion — in which the user can simply enter the latest franc-to-dollar exchange rate. (The default value in this box is 5.) Given this value, the program easily performs the calculations between francs and dollars.

The command buttons for currency conversions are named cmdToDollars and cmdToFrancs. The corresponding Click event procedures, shown in Figures 18-11 and 18-12, use the Val function to ensure that the user has entered positive numbers in the relevant text boxes. If so, the conversion is performed in one of two ways — francs to dollars:

```
txtDollars.Text = txtFrancs.Text / txtConversion.Txt
```

or dollars to francs:

```
txtFrancs.Text = txtDollars.Text * txtConversion.Txt
```

On the other hand, if the user has typed an invalid value in the Dollars or Francs box — such as a nonnumeric entry or a negative number — the program simply removes the entries from both boxes:

```
txtFrancs.Text = ""
txtDollars.Text = ""
```

```
cmdToDollars                    ▼   Click                            ▼

    Private Sub cmdToDollars_Click()                                 ▲

      ' The cmdToDollars_Click procedure is part of the
      ' Currency Converter. Given valid input values, it
      ' converts from francs to dollars.

      ' Make sure the conversion rate entry is valid.
      If Val(txtConversion.Text) <= 0 Then
        txtConversion.Text = ""
        Exit Sub
      End If

      ' If the Francs entry is valid, perform the calculation.
      If Val(txtFrancs.Text) > 0 Then
        txtDollars.Text = txtFrancs.Text / txtConversion.Text
      Else
        txtFrancs.Text = ""
        txtDollars.Text = ""
      End If

    End Sub ' cmdToDollars_Click
```

Figure 18-11: The cmdToDollars_Click procedure does some data checking and then performs the franc-to-dollar conversion.

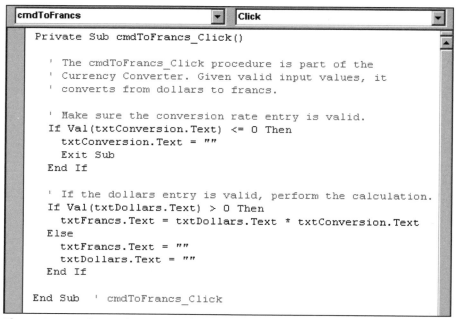

```
cmdToFrancs          ▼   Click                        ▼

Private Sub cmdToFrancs_Click()

    ' The cmdToFrancs_Click procedure is part of the
    ' Currency Converter. Given valid input values, it
    ' converts from dollars to francs.

    ' Make sure the conversion rate entry is valid.
    If Val(txtConversion.Text) <= 0 Then
      txtConversion.Text = ""
      Exit Sub
    End If

    ' If the dollars entry is valid, perform the calculation.
    If Val(txtDollars.Text) > 0 Then
      txtFrancs.Text = txtDollars.Text * txtConversion.Text
    Else
      txtFrancs.Text = ""
      txtDollars.Text = ""
    End If

End Sub    ' cmdToFrancs_Click
```

Figure 18-12: The cmdToFrancs_Click procedure checks the entries for the conversion rate and the dollar amount; if both entries are valid, the procedure performs the dollar-to-franc conversion.

The program also contains GotFocus and LostFocus event procedures for both the Dollars and Francs text boxes, as shown in Figures 18-13 and 18-14. When one of these boxes receives the focus, the corresponding GotFocus procedure highlights the current contents and assigns a value of True to the Default property of the adjacent command button. This small detail is a convenience for the user: To perform a currency conversion the user simply types a dollar or franc amount and presses Enter. Because the corresponding command button is the default, the Enter key is equivalent to a button click.

This short demonstration program is no more than an introduction to ActiveX documents. There are many other techniques to learn. For example:

✦ Like a form, a UserDocument can have its own menu, designed in Visual Basic's menu editor. The menu commands you provide are merged into the Internet Explorer's menu.

✦ A variety of important methods and events are defined for the UserDocument. A program can use these to affect the object's behavior as a document.

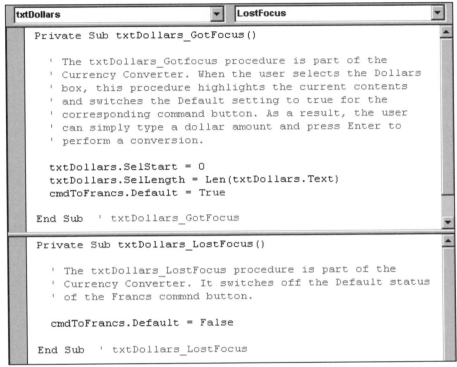

```
txtDollars                              LostFocus

Private Sub txtDollars_GotFocus()

    ' The txtDollars_Gotfocus procedure is part of the
    ' Currency Converter. When the user selects the Dollars
    ' box, this procedure highlights the current contents
    ' and switches the Default setting to true for the
    ' corresponding command button. As a result, the user
    ' can simply type a dollar amount and press Enter to
    ' perform a conversion.

    txtDollars.SelStart = 0
    txtDollars.SelLength = Len(txtDollars.Text)
    cmdToFrancs.Default = True

End Sub  ' txtDollars_GotFocus
```

```
Private Sub txtDollars_LostFocus()

    ' The txtDollars_LostFocus procedure is part of the
    ' Currency Converter. It switches off the Default status
    ' of the Francs commnd button.

    cmdToFrancs.Default = False

End Sub  ' txtDollars_LostFocus
```

Figure 18-13: The txtDollars_GotFocus procedure temporarily makes "Convert to Francs" the default command button. This technique simplifies the use of the Currency Converter.

You can explore these and other topics as you continue to work with ActiveX documents. In the meantime, the FranceGo document illustrates a basic and essential point: ActiveX documents operate not only as Internet Explorer "pages" with links to Web sites, but also as full-featured Visual Basic programs.

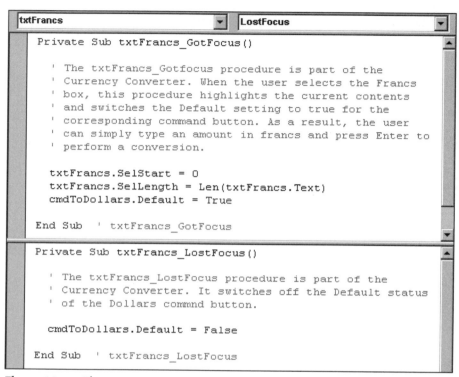

```
txtFrancs                    ▼    LostFocus                    ▼

   Private Sub txtFrancs_GotFocus()                            ▲

      ' The txtFrancs_Gotfocus procedure is part of the
      ' Currency Converter. When the user selects the Francs
      ' box, this procedure highlights the current contents
      ' and switches the Default setting to true for the
      ' corresponding command button. As a result, the user
      ' can simply type an amount in francs and press Enter to
      ' perform a conversion.

      txtFrancs.SelStart = 0
      txtFrancs.SelLength = Len(txtFrancs.Text)
      cmdToDollars.Default = True

   End Sub   ' txtFrancs_GotFocus                              ▼

   Private Sub txtFrancs_LostFocus()                           ▲

      ' The txtFrancs_LostFocus procedure is part of the
      ' Currency Converter. It switches off the Default status
      ' of the Dollars commnd button.

      cmdToDollars.Default = False

   End Sub   ' txtFrancs_LostFocus
```

Figure 18-14: The txtFrancs_GotFocus procedure temporarily makes "Convert to Dollars" the default command button. The txtFrancs_LostFocus procedure removes this status.

What's on the CD-ROM

◆　◆　◆　◆

In This Appendix

Examining the Project Explorer window for each application in this book

Reviewing the runtime behavior of each progam

Studying the complete code listings

◆　◆　◆　◆

The CD–ROM that is found in the back pocket of this book is a valuable resource, containing Microsoft Internet Explorer 3.0 and all the source code from this book in a collection of working program examples. These examples are ready for you to load into your computer and run. They are all built around an ongoing theme: developing applications that can prove useful to the business traveler. Converting international currencies, planning transportation, recording expenses, developing a restaurant database, organizing notes from business meetings, tracking international sales, keeping reminder lists, getting travel information from the Internet — these and other travel-related tasks are automated and simplified by the programs available in this book.

Think of each program as a hands-on exercise. As you work with a program — and read the text in the corresponding chapter — your goal is to master the tools and techniques illustrated in the project's design and code. Once you've seen how a program works and what it does, you should feel free to revise it in any way you like. Adjust the interface and new features, change the steps of procedures, refine the input and output techniques, replace operations that you don't like — in short, do anything you want to make the progam conform to your own progamming style.

The Currency Exchange Travel Guide Program

Chapter 1

The Travel Guide application (TrvlGde.Vbp) provides convenient exchange rate tables for converting between U.S. dollars and the local currency of a selected country. To operate the program, you simply pull down the Country list and select a name. For example, Figure A-1 shows the tables for Switzerland.

The program reads a text file named Currency.Txt, containing up-to-date exchange rates for a list of countries. You can create this file in any text editor, then save the file in the root directory of your hard disk. Figure A-2 illustrates the required format. Each line of the file shows the name of a country, the name of the local currency, and the dollar value of one unit of the currency.

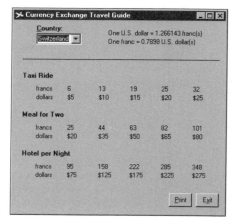

Figure A-1: The Currency Exchange Travel Guide program provides convenient exchange rate tables for a selected country.

Figure A-2: The program reads a text file named Currency.Txt, containing exchange rates for a list of countries.

As shown in the Project Explorer window for this application (Figure A-3), the program's files include the project file (Trvlgde.Vbp), a form file (TrvlGde.Frm), and a module file (CurrExch.Bas). The program's code is located in the module and the form file, as you can see in the following listings.

Figure A-3: The Travel Guide program contains one form and one module.

Travel Guide Program — CurrExch.Bas Module

```
' Currency Exchange.
' Module: CurExch.BAS
'
' Type definition for country and
' currency records.
'
Type CurrRec
  country As String
  currName As String
  inDollars As Single
End Type
```

Travel Guide Program — TrvlGde.Frm Form

```
' Travel Guide Program
' TrvlGde.VBP
'
' Produces currency exchange tables
' for likely price ranges in three
' categories: taxis, meals, and hotels.

' Reads current exchange rates from
' a text file named \Currency.Txt.

Dim CurrArray(30) As CurrRec
Dim countryNdx As Integer
Dim currCountry As Integer

Private Sub cboCountry_Click()
  ' Read the user's country choice
  ' and display the exchange rates
  ' for the currency of the selected
  ' country.

  Dim i As Integer
  Dim curr As String

  For i = 0 To countryNdx
    If cboCountry.Text = CurrArray(i).country Then
      lblDollar.Caption = "One U.S. dollar = " & _
        1 / CurrArray(i).inDollars & " " & _
        CurrArray(i).currName

      If CurrArray(i).currName <> "yen" Then _
        lblDollar.Caption = lblDollar.Caption & "(s)"

      lblCurrency.Caption = "One " & _
        CurrArray(i).currName & " = " & _
        CurrArray(i).inDollars & _
        " U.S. dollar(s)"
      currCountry = i
    End If
  Next i
```

(continued)

(continued)

```
    ' Create the three tables.

    For i = 0 To 4

        ' The range of prices for a taxi ride.

        lblTaxi2(i).Caption = _
          Format$(i * 5 + 5, "$##")
        lblTaxi1(i).Caption = _
          CLng((i * 5 + 5) / _
          CurrArray(currCountry).inDollars)

        ' The range of prices for a meal.

        lblMeal2(i).Caption = _
          Format$(i * 15 + 20, "$##")
        lblMeal1(i).Caption = _
          CLng((i * 15 + 20) / _
          CurrArray(currCountry).inDollars)

        ' The range of prices for a night
        ' in a hotel.

        lblHotel2(i).Caption = _
          Format$(i * 50 + 75, "$##")
        lblHotel1(i).Caption = _
          CLng((i * 50 + 75) / _
          CurrArray(currCountry).inDollars)
    Next i

    ' Display the name of the currency
    ' at the left of each price table.

    For i = 0 To 2
      curr = CurrArray(currCountry).currName
      If curr <> "yen" Then _
        curr = curr & "s"
      lblCurr(i).Caption = curr
    Next i


End Sub    ' cboCountry_Click


Private Sub cmdExit_Click()

    ' Terminate the program when
    ' the user clicks the Exit button.

    End
```

```vb
End Sub   ' cmdExit_Click

Private Sub cmdPrint_Click()

   PrintForm

End Sub

Private Sub Form_Load()

   ' Open the Currency.Txt file and
   ' read its contents into CurrArray,
   ' an array of records. Also create
   ' the list of countries in the
   ' cboCountry combo box.

   Dim i As Integer
   On Error GoTo cantReadFile
     Open "\Currency.Txt" For Input As #1

     i = 0

     ' Read the file.

     Do While Not EOF(1)
        Input #1, CurrArray(i).country
        Input #1, CurrArray(i).currName
        Input #1, CurrArray(i).inDollars

        ' Build the country list.

        cboCountry.AddItem CurrArray(i).country

        i = i + 1
     Loop
   Close #1

   ' Keep a record of the last country index.

   countryNdx = i - 1
   Exit Sub

' End the program if file can't be read.
cantReadFile:
   MsgBox "Have you created a CURRENCY.TXT file?" _
     , , "Travel Guide"
   End

End Sub   ' Form_Load
```

The International Currency Exchange Program

Chapters 2, 3, and 4

The Currency Exchange program (CurrExch.Vbp) is a simple tool for converting specific monetary values between U.S. dollars and the local currency of a selected country. To operate the program, begin by selecting a name from the Country list, then select a conversion option (dollars to local currency or local currency to dollars) and enter an amount. Click Calc or press Enter to compute the currency equivalent. For example, Figure A-4 shows a currency calculation from pesos to dollars, where Mexico is the current country selection.

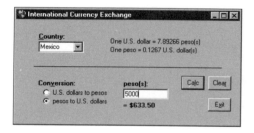

Figure A-4: The Currency Exchange program is a convenient tool for calculating exchange between dollars and the local currency of a selected country.

Like the Travel Guide application, the Currency Exchange program relies on the existence of a Currency.Txt file containing up-to-date currency rate information for a list of countries. (See Figure A-3, for an example of this file.) Each line in the file contains the name of a country, the local currency name, and the current value in dollars of one currency unit.

The files for this application include the project file (CurrExch.Vbp) and one form file (CurrExch.Frm), as shown in the Project Explorer for the application, Figure A-5. All of the program's code is in the single form file.

Figure A-5: The Currency Exchange project includes one form, which contains all the program's code.

The Currency Exchange Program — CurrExch.Frm Form

```
' Currency Exchange Program
' CurrExch.VBP
'
' Converts between dollars and
' the currencies of other countries.
' The daily exchange rates are stored in
' a text file named \Currency.Txt.

' Type definition for country and
' currency records.
Private Type CurrRec
   country As String
   currName As String
   inDollars As Single
End Type

Dim CurrArray(100) As CurrRec
Dim countryNdx As Integer
Dim currCountry As Integer

Private Sub cboCountry_Click()
   ' Read the user's country choice
   ' and display the exchange rates
   ' for the currency of the selected
   ' country.

   Dim i As Integer
   For i = 0 To countryNdx
      If cboCountry.Text = CurrArray(i).country Then
         lblDollar.Caption = "One U.S. dollar = " & _
            1 / CurrArray(i).inDollars & " " & _
            CurrArray(i).currName & "(s)"
         lblCurrency.Caption = "One " & _
            CurrArray(i).currName & " = " & _
            CurrArray(i).inDollars & _
            " U.S. dollar(s)"
         currCountry = i
      End If
   Next i

   ' Display captions for the conversion
   ' option buttons.

   optDollarsTo.Caption = "U.S. dollars to " & _
      CurrArray(currCountry).currName & "s"
   optCurrTo.Caption = CurrArray(currCountry).currName & _
      "s to U.S. dollars"

   lblConvCurr.Caption = "U.S. dollar(s):"
   optDollarsTo.Value = True
   cmdClear_Click

End Sub  ' cboCountry_Click
```

(continued)

(continued)

```
Private Sub cmdCalc_Click()

    ' Perform the currency exchange calculation
    ' that the user requests.

    ' First make sure that the user has entered
    ' a numeric value in the txtConvAmount
    ' text box.
    If Val(txtConvAmount.Text) = 0 Then
        cmdClear_Click
        Exit Sub
    End If

    ' If so, the calculation is based on
    ' the user's choice of conversion options.
    With CurrArray(currCountry)
        If optDollarsTo.Value Then
            lblConvText.Caption = "= " & _
                Format$(Val(txtConvAmount.Text) / _
                .inDollars, "###,###.##") & _
                    " " & .currName & "(s)"
        Else
            lblConvText.Caption = "= " & _
                Format$(Val(txtConvAmount.Text) * _
                .inDollars, "$###,###.00")
        End If
    End With

End Sub   ' cmdCalc_Click

Private Sub cmdClear_Click()

    ' Clear the previous conversion
    ' calculation.

    txtConvAmount.Text = ""
    lblConvText.Caption = ""

    ' Return the focus to the
    ' txtConvAmount text box.

    txtConvAmount.SetFocus

End Sub   ' cmdClear_Click

Private Sub cmdExit_Click()

    ' Terminate the program when
    ' the user clicks the Exit button.

    End

End Sub   ' cmdExit_Click
```

```
Private Sub Form_Load()
  ' Open the Currency.Txt file and read its contents
  ' into CurrArray, an array of records. Also create
  ' the list of countries in the cboCountry combo box.
  Dim i As Integer

  On Error GoTo cantReadFile
    Open "\Currency.Txt" For Input As #1
    i = 0
    ' Read the file.
    Do While Not EOF(1)
      Input #1, CurrArray(i).country
      Input #1, CurrArray(i).currName
      Input #1, CurrArray(i).inDollars
      ' Build the country list.
      cboCountry.AddItem CurrArray(i).country
      i = i + 1
    Loop
  Close #1
  ' Keep a record of the last country index.
  countryNdx = i - 1
  Exit Sub

' End the program if file can't be read.
cantReadFile:
  MsgBox "Have you created a CURRENCY.TXT file?" _
  , , "Currency Exchange"
  End
End Sub  ' Form_Load
Private Sub optCurrTo_Click()

  ' Change the conversion option:
  ' foreign currency to U.S. dollars.

  lblConvCurr = CurrArray(currCountry).currName & "(s):"
  cmdClear_Click

End Sub  ' optCurrTo_Click

Private Sub optDollarsTo_Click()

  ' Change the currency option:
  ' U.S. dollars to foreign currency.

  lblConvCurr = "U.S. dollar(s):"
  cmdClear_Click

End Sub  ' optDollarsTo_Click
```

The International Travel Expense Log Program

Chapter 7

The Travel Expense Log program (ExpnsLog.Vbp) is designed to help you keep track of expenses on an international business trip. For each expense record, you enter the date, the country, the city, the amount spent in local currency, a brief description of the expenditure, and the applicable exchange rate. Click the Save button to store the record in the expense log file. For example, Figure A-6 shows a complete record of a hotel expense, ready to be saved to the expense log.

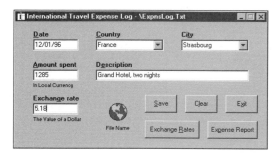

Figure A-6: The Travel Expense Log program is a tool for recording business trip expenses. To complete a record, enter the information and click Save. To generate a summary report of all the expenses you've recorded in the current expense log file, click the Expense Report button.

By default, the program stores expense information in a text file named ExpnsLog.Txt, but you can designate a different file by clicking the globe icon (labeled "File Name"). For historical information about the range of expense rates you've recorded for a given country, click the Exchange Rates button. To generate a report of all the expenses recorded in the current expense log file, click Expense Report; the program saves the report as an expense file (Expenses.Txt), which you can incorporate into any word-processed document.

As shown in Figure A-7, the application files include the project file (ExpnsLog.Vbp) and one form file (ExpnsLog.Frm). All of the program's code is in the form file.

Figure A-7: The Project Explorer window for the Travel Expense Log program. The program includes one form file, which contains all the code.

The Travel Expense Log Program — ExpnsLog.Frm Form

```
' International Travel Expense Log Program
'

' Project File:  ExpnsLog.VBP
' Form File:     ExpnsLog.FRM

' Maintains expense files for international
' business trips, and produces an expense report.
' Also helps keep track of exchange rate variations.
Option Explicit  ' Declare all variables.

' The default data file name is \ExpnsLog.Txt,
' but the user can save expenses for individual
' trips under other names. The expense report is
' saved on disk as a text file under the name
' Expenses.Txt.
Const DefaultFile = "\ExpnsLog.txt"
Const ExpenseReport = "\Expenses.Txt"

' The current expense file name
' is represented by the global
' variable logFileName.
Dim logFileName As String

' The current country name is
' also a global string variable.
Dim currCountry As String
' End of general declarations.


Private Function FileExists(fileName As String) _
  As Boolean

   ' Checks to see if a file exists on disk.
   ' Returns True if the file is found, or
   ' False if it is not.

   ' Set up an error trap.
   On Error GoTo noFile

     ' Attempt to open the file.
     Open fileName For Input As #1
     Close #1

     ' Return True if no error occurs.
     FileExists = True
     Exit Function

noFile:
```

(continued)

(continued)

```
      ' If the file can't be opened,
      ' return False.
      FileExists = False

End Function  ' FileExists
Private Sub FillCityList(countryName As String)
      ' FillCityList reads the names of cities
      ' recorded for a selected country, and
      ' adds the city names to the City list
      ' in the cboCity control.

    Dim item1, item4, item5, item6
    Dim country As String, city As String

    ' Open the expense file and read each record.
    Open logFileName For Input As #1
       Do While Not EOF(1)
          Input #1, item1, country, _
            city, item4, item5, item6

          ' Search for matches between the current
          ' country selection and the countries
          ' identified in specific expense records.
          ' Add the corresponding city names to the
          ' list if they are not already included.

          If UCase$(countryName) = _
            UCase$(country) Then _
               If Not AlreadyListed(cboCity, city) _
                  Then cboCity.AddItem city

       Loop
    Close #1
End Sub  ' FillCityList

Private Sub FillCountryList()

      ' FillCountryList reads the names of countries
      ' from the current log file and adds all
      ' unique country names to the cboCountry list.

    Dim item1, item3, item4, item5, item6
    Dim countryName As String

    cboCountry.Clear
    cboCity.Clear

    ' Open the expense file and
    ' read each country name.
    Open logFileName For Input As #1
       Do While Not EOF(1)
          Input #1, item1, countryName, _
            item3, item4, item5, item6
```

```
            ' Add a country name to the list
            ' if it's not already included.
            If Not AlreadyListed(cboCountry, countryName) _
              Then cboCountry.AddItem countryName
         Loop

      Close #1

End Sub   ' FillCountryList
Private Function AlreadyListed(listControl As Control, _
                             newItem As String) As Boolean

   ' The AlreadyListed function checks an existing
   ' list to see if a potential new entry (newItem)
   ' is currently in the list or not. If the item
   ' is in the list, the function returns true; if
   ' not, false.

   Dim i As Integer

   AlreadyListed = False

   ' Go through the current list and
   ' search for a match.
   For i = 0 To listControl.ListCount - 1
     If UCase$(listControl.List(i)) = _
       UCase$(newItem) Then _
       AlreadyListed = True
   Next i

End Function   ' AlreadyListed


Private Sub cboCountry_Click()

   ' Change the city list in response to
   ' a new selection from the country list.

   ChangeCityList

End Sub   ' cboCountry_Click

Private Sub cboCountry_LostFocus()

   ' Change the city list in response to
   ' possible change in the country entry.

   ChangeCityList

End Sub   ' cboCountry_LostFocus


Private Sub cmdClear_Click()

   ' The cmdClear_Click procedure clears the dialog
   ' box, in preparation for a new record entry.
```

(continued)

(continued)

```vb
      cboCountry.Text = ""
      cboCity.Text = ""
      txtAmount.Text = ""
      txtDescript.Text = ""
      txtRate.Text = ""
      txtDate.Text = Format$(Date, "mm/dd/yy")
      txtDate.SetFocus

  End Sub   ' cmdClear_Click

  Private Sub cmdExit_Click()

    ' The cmdExit_Click procedure ends the program
    ' when the user clicks the Exit button.

    End

  End Sub   ' cmdExit_Click

  Private Sub cmdExpReport_Click()
    ' The cmdExpReport_Click procedure creates an
    ' expense report file summarizing the data stored
    ' in the current travel expense log. The summary
    ' is always stored in \ExpRept.Txt

    Dim expDate, country, city, amount, descript, exchRate
    Dim dollarAmount As String * 11
    Dim totDollarAmount As String * 11
    Dim totAmount

    If FileExists(logFileName) Then
      Open logFileName For Input As #1
      Open ExpenseReport For Output As #2

      ' Create the report title and the
      ' column headings.
      Print #2, Tab(23); "Travel Expense Log"
      Print #2, Tab(23); "====== ======= ==="
      Print #2, Tab(25); logFileName
      Print #2,

      Print #2, "Place"; Tab(27); "Date"; Tab(39); _
                "Amount"; Tab(48); "Description"

      Print #2, "---"; Tab(27); "--"; Tab(39); -
                "---"; Tab(48); "-----"


      ' Read each expense record and add a detail line.
      totAmount = 0
      Do While Not EOF(1)
        Input #1, expDate, country, city, amount, _
                  descript, exchRate
```

```
        totAmount = totAmount + amount / exchRate
        RSet dollarAmount = Format$(amount / exchRate, _
                          "$###,###.00")
        Print #2, city; ", "; country; Tab(27); expDate; _
                dollarAmount; "  "; descript
    Loop

    ' Display the total amount spent.
    RSet totDollarAmount = Format$(totAmount, _
      "$###,###.00")
    Print #2,
    Print #2, "Total amount spent ... "; Tab(35); _
      totDollarAmount
    Close #1, #2

    MsgBox "File is saved as " & ExpenseReport _
      , , "Expense Report"

  Else  ' If logFileName doesn't exist...
    MsgBox logFileName & " is not available." _
      , , "Expense Report"
  End If

End Sub  ' cmdExpReport_Click

Private Sub cmdRate_Click()
  ' The cmdRate_Click procedure finds the range of
  ' exchange rates recorded for the current country,
  ' and displays the range in a message box.

  Dim numEntries As Integer
  Dim largeRate As Double, smallRate As Double
  Dim item1, item3, item4, item5
  Dim country As String, exchRate As Double
  Dim msg As String, boxTitle As String

  numEntries = 0
  If FileExists(logFileName) Then
    If Trim$(cboCountry.Text) <> "" Then

      ' Open the expense file and read each record.
      Open logFileName For Input As #1
      Do While Not EOF(1)
        Input #1, item1, country, item3, item4, _
                item5, exchRate
        ' Look for matches between the current
        ' country selection, and the countries
        ' identified in specific expense records.
        If UCase$(country) = UCase$(cboCountry.Text) Then
          numEntries = numEntries + 1
          If numEntries = 1 Then
            smallRate = exchRate
            largeRate = exchRate
          Else
```

(continued)

(continued)

```
                    ' Compare each exchange rate to locate
                    ' the smallest and largest rates on record.
                    If exchRate < smallRate Then _
                        smallRate = exchRate
                    If exchRate > largeRate Then _
                        largeRate = exchRate
                End If
            End If
        Loop
        Close #1

        boxTitle = "Exchange Rates for " & cboCountry.Text
        If numEntries > 0 Then
            msg = "   Lowest: " & smallRate & _
                  "   Highest: " & largeRate
        Else   ' If no country matches were found...
            msg = "No entries for " & cboCountry.Text & "."
        End If
    Else   ' If no country is currently selected...
        msg = "Please select or enter a country name."
        boxTitle = "Exchange Rates"
    End If
  Else   ' If logFileName doesn't exist...
    msg = logFileName & " is not available."
    boxTitle = "Exchange Rates"
  End If
  MsgBox msg, , boxTitle
End Sub   ' cmdRate_Click

Private Sub cmdSave_Click()
  ' The cmdSave_Click procedure saves the current
  ' record to the travel expense log file.

  ' Make sure all data fields have been entered.
  If Not BlankFields Then

    ' Append a record to the file.
    Open logFileName For Append As #1
      Write #1, txtDate.Text, cboCountry.Text, _
              cboCity.Text, Val(txtAmount.Text), _
              txtDescript.Text, Val(txtRate.Text)
    Close #1

    ' Add the country name and city name to the
    ' appropriate lists if they are not already included.
    If Not AlreadyListed(cboCountry, cboCountry.Text) _
      Then cboCountry.AddItem cboCountry.Text
    If Not AlreadyListed(cboCity, cboCity.Text) _
      Then cboCity.AddItem cboCity.Text

    txtAmount.Text = ""
    txtDescript.Text = ""
    txtAmount.SetFocus
  Else
```

```vb
    MsgBox "You must fill in all the fields.", _
        0, "Save"
  End If
End Sub    ' cmdSave_Click

Private Sub Form_Load()

  ' The Form_Load procedure opens the default
  ' travel expense log file, and fills the country
  ' list with any country names stored in the file.

  logFileName = DefaultFile
  txtDate.Text = Format$(Date, "mm/dd/yy")
  currCountry = ""

  If FileExists(logFileName) Then FillCountryList

End Sub    ' Form_Load


Private Sub picFileName_Click()
  ' The picFileName_Click procedure gives the user the
  ' opportunity to open a different expense log file.

  Dim inPrompt As String
  Dim boxTitle As String

  inPrompt = "Enter a new file name for your expense log."
  boxTitle = "Expense Log File Name"

  ' Get a new file name from the user.
  logFileName = InputBox(inPrompt, boxTitle, logFileName)

  ' If the user enters no name or clicks cancel,
  ' revert to the default expense file name.
  If Trim(logFileName) = "" Then _
    logFileName = DefaultFile

  ' Display the expense file name in the title bar.
  frmExpenseLog.Caption = _
    "International Travel Expense Log - " _
      & logFileName
  If FileExists(logFileName) Then
    FillCountryList
  Else
    cboCountry.Clear
    cboCity.Clear
  End If
End Sub    ' picFileName_Click

Private Sub txtAmount_GotFocus()

  ' The txtAmount_GotFocus procedure highlights
  ' the contents of the Amount text box whenever
  ' the box receives the focus.
```

(continued)

(continued)

```vb
    HighlightContents txtAmount

End Sub   ' txtAmount_GotFocus

Private Sub txtAmount_LostFocus()

 ' The txtAmount_LostFocus procedure ensures
 ' that the value entered into the Amount text box
 ' is a number.

  ValidNumInput txtAmount

End Sub   ' txtAmount_LostFocus

Private Sub txtDate_GotFocus()

  ' The txtDate_GotFocus procedure highlights
  ' the contents of the Date text box whenever
  ' the box receives the focus.

  HighlightContents txtDate

End Sub   ' txtDate_GotFocus

Private Sub HighlightContents(target As Control)

  ' The HighlightContents procedure uses the
  ' SelStart and SelLength properties to
  ' highlight the contents of any control
  ' that has just received the focus.

  target.SelStart = 0
  target.SelLength = Len(target.Text)

End Sub   ' HighlightContents

Private Sub txtDate_LostFocus()

  ' The txtDate_LostFocus procedure ensures that
  ' the value entered into the Date text box is
  ' a valid date.

  If IsDate(txtDate.Text) Then
    txtDate.Text = Format$(txtDate.Text, "mm/dd/yy")
  Else
    txtDate.Text = Format$(Date, "mm/dd/yy")
  End If

End Sub   ' txtDate_LostFocus

Private Sub txtDescript_GotFocus()

  ' The txtDescript_GotFocus procedure highlights
  ' the contents of the Description text box
  ' whenever the box receives the focus.
```

```
    HighlightContents txtDescript

End Sub   ' txtDescript_GotFocus

Private Sub txtRate_GotFocus()

   ' The txtRate_GotFocus procedure highlights
   ' the contents of the Rate text box
   ' whenever the box receives the focus.

   HighlightContents txtRate

End Sub   ' txtRate_GotFocus


Private Function BlankFields() As Boolean

   ' The BlankFields function tests for blank
   ' fields in the current record entry. The function
   ' returns a value of true if any entry is found
   ' to be empty; or false if all fields are complete.


   BlankFields = Trim(txtDate.Text) = "" Or _
                 Trim(cboCountry.Text) = "" Or _
                 Trim(cboCity.Text) = "" Or _
                 Trim(txtAmount.Text) = "" Or _
                 Trim(txtDescript.Text) = "" Or _
                 Trim(txtRate.Text) = ""

End Function   ' BlankFields

Private Sub txtRate_LostFocus()

   ' The txtRate_LostFocus procedure ensures that
   ' the value entered in the Rate text box is a
   ' number.

   ValidNumInput txtRate

End Sub   ' txtRate_LostFocus

Private Sub ValidNumInput(textControl As Control)

   ' The ValidNumInput procedure tests for a
   ' valid numeric input value in a text box that
   ' has just lost the focus.

   If Val(textControl.Text) = 0 Then _
      textControl.Text = "" _
   Else _
      textControl.Text = Val(textControl.Text)

End Sub   ' ValidNumInput

Private Sub ChangeCityList()
```

(continued)

(continued)

```
' The ChangeCityList procedure rebuilds
' the cboCity list if the country name has
' changed.

If UCase$(cboCountry.Text) <> _
  UCase$(currCountry) Then
    cboCity.Clear
    If FileExists(logFileName) Then _
      FillCityList cboCountry.Text
    currCountry = cboCountry.Text
End If

End Sub  ' ChangeCityList
```

The Restaurant Review Program

Chapter 8

The Restaurant Review program (RestRevu.Vbp) is designed to help you build a database of the restaurants where you dine on business trips. The program serves both as a data-entry tool for recording individual restaurant descriptions, and a browser for examining the existing records in your database. To operate the program, you simply begin entering the fields of a new record — including the city where the restaurant is located, the restaurant's name, the cuisine category (Type of Food), a brief line of comments, and ratings for quality and price. Click Save to write the current record to your database. For example, Figure A-8 shows a complete restaurant record.

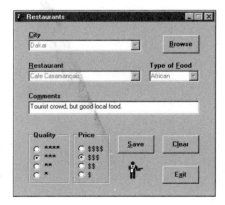

Figure A-8: The Restaurant Review program builds a restaurant database for use on business trips. You can use the program both to enter new records and to browse through existing records.

Once you've begun developing a database, you can use this program to examine any restaurant record you've saved. To locate a record, select the target city from the City list and/or select a cuisine category from the Type of Food list. The Restaurant list shows all the entries available for the place and category you've selected. Choose a name from the Restaurant list to view the entire record. Alternatively, you can use the program's Browse feature to look through all the restaurants recorded for a given city. Click the Clear button to clear any information currently displayed in the window. Then select an entry from the City list and click the Browse button. A browse window shows the records available for the city you've selected, as illustrated in Figure A-9. You can click Previous or Next to browse backward or forward through the available records.

Figure A-9: The browse window allows you to examine all the restaurant descriptions recorded for a particular city.

As shown in Figure A-10, the Restaurant Review application files include the project file, RestRevu.Vbp; two form files — RestRevu.Frm, representing the main application window, and RestList.Frm, the browse window; and the one module, RestRevu.Bas. Code is contained in both of the form files and in the module.

Figure A-10: The Restaurant Review application includes a project file, two form files, and a module. The two forms and the module all contain code.

The Restaurant Review Program — RestRevu.Frm Form

```
' The Restaurant Review program
' ─────────────
' Files:
' Project File:   RestRevu.VBP
' Form Files:     RestRevu.FRM
'                 RestList.FRM
' Module File:    RestRevu.BAS
```

(continued)

(continued)

```
' Creates a database of restaurant reviews
' for the business traveler. Allows the user
' to enter individual restaurant records, and
' to find restaurants by city and cuisine type.
' User can also browse through restaurant
' listings by city.
Option Explicit    ' Declare all variables.

' The program uses the variables
' prevCity and prevFoodType to determine
' whether the user has changed the City
' and Food Type entries. (In response, the
' program rebuilds the Restaurant list.)
Dim prevCity As String
Dim prevFoodType As String

' The variable recNum represents the
' record number of the currently selected
' restaurant.
Dim recNum As Long
' End of general declarations.


Private Sub FindRestaurantRecord()

   ' The FindRestaurantRecord procedure looks through the
   ' database for a selected restaurant name. If the
   ' record is found, the procedure displays its fields
   ' in the frmRestRevu form.

   ' Open the restaurant database.
   Open DatabaseFile For Random As #1 _
      Len = Len(RestRecord)

   ' Set recNum to zero until a record is found. (Note
   ' that the actual record numbers in the database
   ' begin with 1. A recNum value of zero therefore
   ' tells the program that no record was found.)
   recNum = 0

   ' Search through the database from beginning to end.
   Do While Not EOF(1)
      Get #1, , RestRecord

         ' Compare each Restaurant field with the current
         ' Text value of the cboRestaurant control.
         With RestRecord
           If StrFix(cboRestaurant.Text) = _
             StrFix(.Restaurant) Then

               ' If a match is found, copy the record's
               ' fields to the appropriate controls on
               ' the frmRestRevu form.
               cboCity.Text = .City
```

```
                      cboFoodType.Text = .FoodType
                      optQuality(Val(.Quality) - 1).Value = True
                      optPrice(Val(.Prices) - 1).Value = True
                      txtComments.Text = .Comments

                      ' Store the record number in recNum.
                      ' (Note that Seek supplies the next
                      ' record number. Subtract 1 to find
                      ' the current record number.)
                      recNum = Seek(1) - 1

                      ' Disable the controls that
                      ' should not be edited if the user
                      ' chooses to revise the record.
                      cboCity.Enabled = False
                      cboFoodType.Enabled = False
                      cboRestaurant.Enabled = False

            End If
          End With
      Loop
      Close #1

End Sub   ' FindRestaurantRecord

Private Sub ListRestaurants _
   (place As String, food As String)

   ' The ListRestaurants procedure builds a list
   ' of restaurants that match (1) a city selection,
   ' (2) a food type selection, or (3) a combination
   ' of city and food type. The list appears in the
   ' cboRestaurant combo box.

   Open DatabaseFile For Random As #1 _
      Len = Len(RestRecord)

      ' If the Food Type entry is blank,
      ' base the search on the City entry.
      If Len(food) = 0 Then

         ' Search through the entire database.
         Do While Not EOF(1)
            Get #1, , RestRecord

               ' Compare each City field with the
               ' current City entry. When a match is
               ' found, add the restaurant to the list
               ' if it's not already there.
               With RestRecord
                  If StrFix(.City) = place Then _
                     If Not AlreadyListed _
                        (cboRestaurant, .Restaurant) _
                           Then _
                              cboRestaurant.AddItem .Restaurant
               End With
```

(continued)

(continued)

```
            Loop

    ' If the City entry is blank, base the
    ' search on the current Food Type entry.
    ElseIf Len(place) = 0 Then

        ' Search through the entire database.
        Do While Not EOF(1)
          Get #1, , RestRecord

            ' Compare each FoodType field with
            ' the current Food Type entry. When a
            ' match is found, add the restaurant to
            ' the list if it's not already there.
            With RestRecord
              If StrFix(.FoodType) = food Then _
                If Not AlreadyListed _
                  (cboRestaurant, .Restaurant) _
                    Then _
                      cboRestaurant.AddItem .Restaurant
            End With
        Loop


    ' If the user has entered both a city and
    ' a food type, base the search on both entries.
    Else

        ' Search through the entire database.
        Do While Not EOF(1)
          Get #1, , RestRecord

            ' When a record matches both the
            ' city and the food type, add the
            ' restaurant to the list if it's not
            ' already there.
            With RestRecord
              If StrFix(.City) = place _
              And StrFix(.FoodType) = food Then _
                If Not AlreadyListed _
                  (cboRestaurant, .Restaurant) _
                    Then _
                      cboRestaurant.AddItem .Restaurant
            End With
        Loop

    End If

    Close #1

End Sub   ' ListRestaurants
```

```
Private Sub ChangeRestaurantList()

    ' The ChangeRestaurantList procedure checks
    ' to see whether the conditions are right
    ' for rebuilding the restaurant list.

    ' The variables c1 and f1 represent the
    ' current City and Food Type entries. The
    ' variables c2 and f2 represent the previous
    ' entries in these two controls.
    Dim c1 As String, c2 As String
    Dim f1 As String, f2 As String
    Dim r As String

    ' Use StrFix to standardize the string
    ' formats before attempting comparisons.
    c1 = StrFix(cboCity.Text)
    c2 = StrFix(prevCity)
    f1 = StrFix(cboFoodType.Text)
    f2 = StrFix(prevFoodType)

    ' If a change has taken place in either
    ' the City or Food Type entry, then call
    ' the ListRestaurants procedure to
    ' rebuild the list.
    If (c1 <> c2) Or (f1 <> f2) Then

        ' Save the current restaurant
        ' entry, but clear the current list.
        r = cboRestaurant.Text
        cboRestaurant.Clear
        cboRestaurant.Text = r

        ' The current City and Food Type entries
        ' become the new values of prevCity and
        ' prevFoodType.
        prevCity = c1
        prevFoodType = f1

        ' Make sure that at least one of the two
        ' controls contains an entry before
        ' attempting to build the list.
        If Not (Len(c1) = 0 And Len(f1) = 0) _
            Then ListRestaurants c1, f1
    End If

End Sub    ' ChangeRestaurantList

Private Function BlankFields() As Boolean

    ' The BlankFields function determines whether
    ' the user has entered all the fields of
    ' information required for a new record. The
    ' program calls this function before a save
```

(continued)

(continued)

```vb
          ' operation. The function returns a value of
          ' True or False. A value of True means that
          ' one or more fields are still blank, and the
          ' current record cannot yet be saved.

          BlankFields = Trim(cboCity.Text) = "" Or _
                        Trim(cboRestaurant.Text) = "" Or _
                        Trim(cboFoodType.Text) = "" Or _
                        Trim(txtComments.Text) = "" Or _
                        AllFalseOptions

End Function  ' BlankFields

Private Function AllFalseOptions() As Boolean

     ' The AllFalseOptions function examines the
     ' two arrays of option button controls to
     ' to determine whether the user has made
     ' a selection in each group. If one or both
     ' groups remains without a selection, this
     ' function returns a value of True, which
     ' indicates that the current record cannot
     ' be saved yet. The function is called by
     ' the BlankFields function, just before a
     ' save operation.

     Dim i

     ' The Boolean variables priceOpts and
     ' qualityOpts record the current status of
     ' the option button groups.
     Dim priceOpts As Boolean
     Dim qualityOpts As Boolean

     ' Initialize both variables to False.
     priceOpts = False
     qualityOpts = False

     ' Read each group of option buttons. If either
     ' group of buttons has no selection, the
     ' corresponding variable remains False.
     For i = 0 To 3
       priceOpts = priceOpts Or optPrice(i).Value
       qualityOpts = qualityOpts Or optQuality(i).Value
     Next i

     ' If either variable is still False, the
     ' function returns a value of True.
     AllFalseOptions = Not (priceOpts And qualityOpts)

End Function  ' AllFalseOptions

Private Sub ListFoodTypes()
```

```
' The ListFoodType procedure builds the
' list of cuisines (for example, French,
' Chinese, American) in the Food Type
' combo box. The procedure reads the
' food types from the records currently
' contained in the restaurant database.

Open DatabaseFile For Random As #1 _
   Len = Len(RestRecord)

' Go through the database from
' beginning to end.
Do While Not EOF(1)
   Get #1, , RestRecord

   ' Add any new food type to the list.
   If Not AlreadyListed _
      (cboFoodType, RestRecord.FoodType) _
      And Not EOF(1) _
      Then cboFoodType.AddItem RestRecord.FoodType
Loop

   Close #1

End Sub   ' ListFoodTypes

Private Sub ListCities()

' The ListCities procedure builds the list
' of cities represented in the records
' currently contained in the restaurant
' database.

   Open DatabaseFile For Random As #1 _
      Len = Len(RestRecord)

   ' Go through the database from
   ' beginning to end.
   Do While Not EOF(1)
      Get #1, , RestRecord

      ' Add any new city to the list.
      If Not AlreadyListed _
         (cboCity, RestRecord.City) _
         And Not EOF(1) _
         Then cboCity.AddItem RestRecord.City
   Loop

   Close #1

End Sub   ' ListCities

Private Function AlreadyListed(listControl As Control, _
                         newItem As String) As Boolean
```

(continued)

(continued)

```
      ' The AlreadyListed function checks an existing
      ' list to see if a potential new entry (newItem)
      ' is currently in the list or not. If the item
      ' is in the list, the function returns true; if
      ' not, false.

      Dim i As Integer

      AlreadyListed = False

      ' Go through the current list and
      ' search for a match.
      For i = 0 To listControl.ListCount - 1
        If StrFix(listControl.List(i)) = _
          StrFix(newItem) Then _
          AlreadyListed = True
      Next i

  End Function  ' AlreadyListed

  Private Sub cboCity_Click()

      ' The cboCity_Click procedure arranges
      ' to rebuild the restaurant list if the
      ' user selects a new entry from the
      ' current city list.

      ChangeRestaurantList

  End Sub  ' cboCity_Click

  Private Sub cboCity_LostFocus()

      ' The cboCity_LostFocus procedure arranges
      ' to rebuild the restaurant list if the
      ' user enters a new city and then move the
      ' focus to another control.

      ChangeRestaurantList

  End Sub  ' cboCity_LostFocus

  Private Sub cboFoodType_Click()

      ' The cboFoodType_Click procedure arranges
      ' to rebuild the restaurant list if the
      ' user selects a new entry from the
      ' current Food Type list.

      ChangeRestaurantList

  End Sub  ' cboFoodType_Click
```

```
Private Sub cboFoodType_LostFocus()

    ' The cboFoodType_LostFocus procedure arranges
    ' to rebuild the restaurant list if the
    ' user enters a new food type and then move the
    ' focus to another control.

    ChangeRestaurantList

End Sub   ' cboFoodType_LostFocus

Private Sub cboRestaurant_Click()

    ' The cboRestaurant_Click procedure searches
    ' for a restaurant record — and displays its
    ' fields in the dialog box — if the user
    ' selects an entry from the current restaurant
    ' list.

    FindRestaurantRecord

End Sub   ' cboRestaurant_Click

Private Sub cboRestaurant_LostFocus()

    ' The cboRestaurant_LostFocus procedure searches
    ' for a restaurant record — and displays its
    ' fields in the dialog box — if the user enters
    ' an existing restaurant name and then moves the
    ' focus to another control.

    FindRestaurantRecord

End Sub   ' cboRestaurant_LostFocus


Private Sub cmdBrowse_Click()

    ' The cmdBrowse_Click procedure activates
    ' the frmRestList form so that the user can
    ' browse through the restaurants for a
    ' selected city.

    ' If the City box contains a selection,
    ' hide the program's main dialog box and
    ' activate the browse dialog box.
    If StrFix(cboCity.Text) <> "" Then
       currCity = StrFix(cboCity.Text)
       frmRestRevu.Hide
       frmRestList.Show

    ' Otherwise, if the user hasn't yet
    ' selected a restaurant, display an
    ' error message.
```

(continued)

(continued)

```
    Else
      MsgBox "You must select a city first.", , _
        "Browse through Restaurants"
    End If

End Sub    ' cmdBrowse_Click

Private Sub cmdClear_Click()
    ' The cmdClear_Click procedure clears all the fields
    ' of information on the main dialog box, so that the
    ' user can enter a new restaurant record.
    Dim i

    ' Assign empty strings to the Text properties and
    ' set all the option buttons to False.
    cboCity.Text = ""
    cboRestaurant.Text = ""
    cboFoodType.Text = ""
    txtComments.Text = ""
    For i = 0 To 3
      optQuality(i).Value = False
      optPrice(i).Value = False
    Next i

    ' Enable the combo boxes that may have been disabled.
    cboCity.Enabled = True
    cboFoodType.Enabled = True
    cboRestaurant.Enabled = True

    ' Clear the restaurant list and variables, and move
    ' the focus to the City box.
    cboRestaurant.Clear
    prevCity = ""
    prevFoodType = ""
    cboCity.SetFocus
End Sub    ' cmdClear_Click

Private Sub cmdExit_Click()

    ' The cmdExit_Click terminates the
    ' program, in response to a click of
    ' the Exit button.

    End

End Sub    ' cmdExit_Click

Private Sub cmdSave_Click()

    ' The cmdSave_Click procedure saves the current
    ' restaurant entry as a new record in the database,
    ' or as a revision of an existing record.
```

```
Dim i
Dim yesNo As Integer

' First call BlankFields to make sure the use has
' entered all the fields.
If Not BlankFields Then

  ' Copy all the information to RestRecord.
  With RestRecord
    .City = cboCity.Text
    .Restaurant = cboRestaurant.Text
    .FoodType = cboFoodType.Text

    ' Save the option button selections
    ' as string values from "1" to "4".
    For i = 0 To 3
      If optQuality(i).Value Then _
        .Quality = Right$(Str$(i + 1), 1)
      If optPrice(i).Value Then _
        .Prices = Right$(Str$(i + 1), 1)
    Next i
    .Comments = txtComments.Text
  End With

  ' A recNum value of zero indicates that
  ' this is a new record, not a revision
  ' of an existing record.
  If recNum = 0 Then

    ' Open the database and save
    ' the record at the end of the file.
    Open DatabaseFile For Random As #1 _
      Len = Len(RestRecord)
        Put #1, _
          LOF(1) / Len(RestRecord) + 1, _
          RestRecord
    Close #1

  ' If recNum contains a value greater than
  ' zero, this is an existing restaurant
  ' record that the user is saving in a
  ' revised version.
  Else

    ' Ask the user to confirm the save
    ' operation before writing over the
    ' previous version of the record.
    yesNo = MsgBox("Revise this record?", _
      4, "Existing Record")

    ' If the user confirms, open the database and save
    ' the record at the same position as the original.
    If yesNo = vbYes Then
```

(continued)

(continued)

```
        Open DatabaseFile For Random As #1 _
          Len = Len(RestRecord)
            Put #1, recNum, RestRecord
        Close #1
      End If
    End If

    ' If the new record contains a new city or food type,
    ' add this information to the combo box list.
    If Not AlreadyListed(cboCity, cboCity.Text) _
      Then cboCity.AddItem cboCity.Text
    If Not AlreadyListed(cboFoodType, cboFoodType.Text) _
      Then cboFoodType.AddItem cboFoodType.Text

    ' Clear the dialog box for the next record entry.
    cmdClear_Click
  Else
    ' Display an error message if the user
    ' hasn't filled in all the fields of a new
    ' restaurant record.
    MsgBox "You must fill in all the fields.", _
      0, "Save"
  End If
End Sub ' cmdSave_Click

Private Sub Form_Load()

  ' The Form_Load procedure builds the
  ' City and Food Type lists at the beginning
  ' of the program, and also initializes
  ' some important form-level variables.

  ' Build the lists.
  ListCities
  ListFoodTypes

  ' The prevCity and prevFoodType variables
  ' are used to keep track of changes in the
  ' City and Food Type boxes. They are
  ' initialized as blank strings.
  prevCity = ""
  prevFoodType = ""

  ' The recNum variables indicates whether the
  ' dialog box is currently displaying information
  ' from an existing restaurant record. An initial
  ' value of zero means it is not. (This value is
  ' important to the cmdSave_Click procedure.)
  recNum = 0

End Sub ' Form_Load
```

The Restaurant Review Program — RestList.Frm Form

```
' The Restaurant Review program
'
'
' Form: frmRestList
'
'
' The form allows the user to browse through
' all the restaurant reviews recorded for a
' specified city.

Option Explicit    ' Declare all variables.

' Form-level variables:
' recCount is the number of restaurants
'     recorded for the city.
' currRec is the record currently
'     displayed in the form.

Dim recCount As Long, currRec As Long

' matchingRecords is a dynamic array of
'     record numbers, representing the
'     restaurants in the selected city.

Dim matchingRecords() As Long
'
' End of General Declarations, frmRestList

' End of general declarations for frmRestList.


Private Sub cmdCancel_Click()

    ' The cmdCancel_Click procedure clears
    ' the data displayed in the frmRestList form,
    ' closes the form, and activates frmRestRevu,
    ' the application's startup form.

    ' Begin by closing the restaurant database.
    Close #1

    ' Then clear the captions in the labels used
    ' for displaying restaurant records.
    lblRestaurant.Caption = ""
    lblCuisine.Caption = ""
    lblQuality.Caption = ""
    lblPrices.Caption = ""
    lblComments.Caption = ""
```

(continued)

(continued)

```
        ' Hide this form and display the startup form.
        frmRestList.Hide
        frmRestRevu.Show

    End Sub    ' cmdCancel_Click

    Private Sub cmdNext_Click()

        ' The cmdNext_Click procedure displays the
        ' next restaurant record when the user clicks
        ' the Next button or presses the PgDn key.

        ' Increment the record counter.
        currRec = currRec + 1

        ' Update the form's title.
        frmRestList.Caption = "Restaurants in " _
            & currCity & " — " & _
            currRec & " of " & recCount

        ' Display the record.
        ShowRecord

        ' Enable or disable the Next and
        ' Previous buttons appropriately.
        If (currRec + 1) > recCount Then _
          cmdNext.Enabled = False
        If currRec > 1 Then _
          cmdPrevious.Enabled = True

    End Sub    ' cmdNext_Click

    Private Sub cmdPrevious_Click()

        ' The cmdPrevious_Click procedure displays the
        ' previous restaurant record when the user clicks
        ' the Previous button or presses the PgUp key.

        ' Decrease the record counter by 1.
        currRec = currRec - 1

        ' Update the form's title.
        frmRestList.Caption = "Restaurants in " _
            & currCity & " — " & _
            currRec & " of " & recCount

        ' Display the record.
        ShowRecord

        ' Enable or disable the Next and
        ' Previous buttons appropriately.
        If (currRec - 1) = 0 Then _
          cmdPrevious.Enabled = False
```

```
      If currRec < recCount Then _
        cmdNext.Enabled = True

End Sub   ' cmdPrevious_Click

Private Sub Form_Activate()

    ' The Form_Activate procedure is called each
    ' time the frmRestList form appears on the
    ' desktop. It opens the database, finds matching
    ' records, and enables or disables the appropriate
    ' command buttons.

    Open DatabaseFile For Random As #1 _
      Len = Len(RestRecord)

    ' If any matching records are found, adjust
    ' the Next and Previous buttons appropriately.
    If CountMatches() > 0 Then

      cmdPrevious.Enabled = False
      If recCount = 1 Then
        cmdNext.Enabled = False
      Else
        cmdNext.Enabled = True
      End If

      currRec = 0

      ' Display the first record.
      cmdNext_Click

    Else

      ' Otherwise, display a message box to tell the
      ' user that no matching records were found.
      frmRestList.Caption = ""
      MsgBox "No restaurants found for " _
        & currCity, , "Browse"
      cmdCancel_Click
    End If

End Sub   ' Form_Activate

Private Function CountMatches() As Long

    ' The CountMatches function counts the number of
    ' matching records (in the selected city). It stores
    ' the corresponding record numbers in matchingRecords.
    Dim i
    recCount = 0

    ' Go through the database from beginning to end and
    ' look for matching records.
```

(continued)

(continued)

```
    For i = 1 To LOF(1) / Len(RestRecord)
      Get #1, i, RestRecord
      If currCity = StrFix(RestRecord.City) Then

        ' If a match is found, increment the
        ' record counter by 1 and change the size
        ' of the matchingRecords array. Then store the
        ' record number in the array.
        recCount = recCount + 1
        ReDim Preserve matchingRecords(recCount)
        matchingRecords(recCount) = i
      End If
    Next i

    ' Return the record count as the
    ' result of the function.
    CountMatches = recCount

End Function   ' CountMatches


Private Sub ShowRecord()

    ' The ShowRecord procedure reads the record
    ' from the position represented by the variable
    ' currRec, and copies its fields to the appropriate
    ' labels on the frmRestList form.

    ' Get the correct record.
    Get #1, matchingRecords(currRec), RestRecord

    ' Display its fields as the Caption properties
    ' of the appropriate labels on the form.
    With RestRecord
      lblRestaurant.Caption = .Restaurant
      lblCuisine.Caption = .FoodType

      ' Convert the Quality and Prices values into
      ' strings of asterisks and dollar signs.
      lblQuality.Caption = String$(Val(.Quality), "*")
      lblPrices.Caption = String$(Val(.Prices), "$")

      lblComments.Caption = .Comments
    End With

End Sub   ' ShowRecord

Private Sub Form_KeyDown(KeyCode As Integer, _
  Shift As Integer)

    ' The Form_KeyDown procedure allows the user to
    ' scroll through a city's restaurants by pressing
    ' the PgUp or PgDn keys on the keyboard.
```

```
' *** Note that the form's KeyPreview property
'      is set to True to make this event possible.

' Code numbers for the
' PgDn and PgUp keys.
Const PgDn = 34
Const PgUp = 33

' If the user presses PgDn and the Next
' button is currently enabled, force a call
' to the cmdNext_Click event procedure.
If KeyCode = PgDn _
   And cmdNext.Enabled = True _
      Then cmdNext_Click

' If the user presses PgUp and the Previous
' button is currently enabled, force a call
' to the cmdPrevious_Click event procedure.
If KeyCode = PgUp _
   And cmdPrevious.Enabled = True _
      Then cmdPrevious_Click

End Sub   ' Form_KeyDown
```

The Restaurant Review Program — RestRevu.Bas Module

```
' The Restaurant Review program
'
' Module: RestRevu.BAS
'
' This module contains the type definition for the
' records in the restaurant database, along with one
' global function.

' The six fields of a restaurant record.
Type RestaurantType
   City As String * 30
   Restaurant As String * 30
   FoodType As String * 15
   Quality As String * 1
   Prices As String * 1
   Comments As String * 65
End Type

' The file name of the database.
Public Const DatabaseFile = "\RestRevu.DB"

' A record variable belonging to the RestaurantType.
Public RestRecord As RestaurantType
```

(continued)

(continued)

```
' A global variable representing the
' current city selection.
Public currCity As String
'
' End of General Declarations, RestRevu.BAS


Public Function StrFix(s As String) _
  As String

  ' The StrFix function converts a
  ' string argument to all uppercase
  ' letters and removes any leading
  ' or trailing blanks. This ensures
  ' reliable comparisons between strings
  ' in the program.

  StrFix = UCase(Trim(s))

End Function  ' StrFix
```

The Meetings Program

Chapter 9

The Meetings program (Meetings.Vbp) creates a database in which you can store information about meetings you attend during international business trips. The main application window, shown in Figure A-11, contains text boxes for a meeting's place, date, time, and subject, and for the names of as many as five participants. There is also a scrollable box in which you can enter brief notes about the meeting.

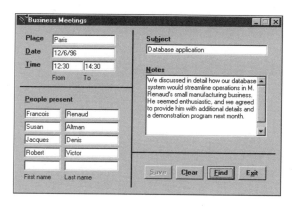

Figure A-11: The Meetings program manages a database of information about business meetings you attend. The application's main window serves as an input form and a record viewer.

After you've begun creating your own meeting database, you can use this same window to view any existing record. To search for a record, click the Find button. In the resulting Find a Meeting Record dialog box, shown in Figure A-12, enter the name of any person who attended the meeting you want to examine, and click Search. In the Find dialog box, you can scroll through all the records that contain the name you've entered. Click View to switch back to the original Meetings window, where the program shows the complete record you've requested.

Figure A-12: A secondary dialog box gives you the opportunity to search for any meeting record, using the name of a participant as the key for the search.

As you can see in Figure A-13, the Meetings application contains two forms and a code module. All three files contain parts of the program's code.

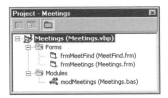

Figure A-13: The Meetings application includes a project file, two form files, and a code module. Code is contained in both forms and the module.

The Meetings Program — Meetings.Frm Form

```
' The Meetings program
'
' Project File: Meetings.VBP
' Form Files:   Meetings.FRM (startup)
'               MeetFind.FRM
' Module File:  Meetings.BAS

' This program saves information and notes about meetings
' conducted during business trips. The meeting records
' are saved on disk in a database file named \Meetings.DB.
' Each record includes the place, date, and time of the
' meeting, the names of the people (as many as five), the
' subject of the meeting, and a text field for notes about
' the meeting. The program allows the user to search for
```

(continued)

(continued)

```
' and view any meeting record, using the name of a person
' present at the meeting as the key for the search.
Option Explicit   ' Declare all variables.

' Constants for identifying the input fields in
' the txtMeetingField control array.
Enum MeetingDataItems
  Place
  Date
  StartTime
  EndTime
  Subject
  Notes
End Enum
' End of general declarations for Meetings.Frm.


Private Sub cmdClear_Click()

  ' The cmdClear_Click procedure clears the current
  ' record from the frmMeetings form when the user
  ' clicks the Clear button.

  Dim field As MeetingDataItems
  Dim nameField

  ' Clear the input fields describing the meeting.
  For field = Place To Notes
    txtMeetingField(field).Text = ""
  Next field

  ' Clear the name fields.
  For nameField = 0 To MaxNameList
    txtFirstName(nameField).Text = ""
    txtLastName(nameField).Text = ""
  Next nameField

  ' Allow the user to resume entering and editing fields
  ' of information in the form. (Relevant only if the
  ' previous record was displayed from a Find operation.)
  ReadOnlyStatus False

  ' Move the focus to the Place field.
  txtMeetingField(Place).SetFocus

End Sub   ' cmdClear_Click

Private Sub cmdExit_Click()

  ' The cmdExit_Click procedure ends
  ' the program's performance when the
  ' user clicks the Exit button.

  End
```

```
End Sub  ' cmdExit_Click

Private Sub cmdFind_Click()

    ' The cmdFind_click procedure
    ' switches forms when the user
    ' clicks the Find button.

    frmMeetings.Hide
    frmMeetFind.Show

End Sub  ' cmdFind_Click

Private Sub cmdSave_Click()

    ' The cmdSave_Click procedure saves the current record
    ' to the database and then updates the index of names.
    Dim nameField

    ' Validate the record entry and store it in Meeting.
    If OKRecord Then
        With Meeting
            .MeetPlace = txtMeetingField(Place).Text
            .MeetDate = txtMeetingField(Date).Text
            .TimeFrom = txtMeetingField(StartTime).Text
            .TimeTo = txtMeetingField(EndTime).Text
            .Subject = txtMeetingField(Subject).Text
            .Notes = txtMeetingField(Notes).Text
            For nameField = 0 To MaxNameList
                .FirstName(nameField) = _
                  txtFirstName(nameField).Text
                .LastName(nameField) = _
                  txtLastName(nameField).Text
            Next nameField
        End With

        ' Write the new record to the Meetings database.
        Open MeetingsDatabase For Random As #1 _
            Len = Len(Meeting)
          curRec = LOF(1) / Len(Meeting)
          Put #1, curRec + 1, Meeting
        Close #1

        ' Update the name index.
        For nameField = 0 To MaxNameList

            ' Add any complete name entry to the index.
            If Trim(txtFirstName(nameField).Text) <> "" And _
               Trim(txtLastName(nameField).Text) <> "" Then

                ' Resize the name list, and add the new name.
                listLength = listLength + 1
                ReDim Preserve NameList(listLength)
```

(continued)

(continued)

```
                NameList(listLength).FullName = _
                  FixName(txtFirstName(nameField).Text, _
                        txtLastName(nameField).Text)
                NameList(listLength).RecordNum = _
                  curRec + 1
         End If
      Next nameField

      ' If the index is longer than 1 sort the names.
      If listLength > 1 Then SortNameList

      ' Clear the frmMeetings form for a new entry.
      cmdClear_Click
   Else
      ' If the current record is incomplete, don't save it.
      MsgBox "Can't save an incomplete record.", , "Save"
   End If

End Sub    ' cmdSave_Click

Private Function OKRecord() As Boolean

   ' The OKRecord function looks for empty fields. The
   ' function returns True if the record is OK to save.
   Dim fieldsComplete As Boolean, namesOK As Boolean
   Dim firstOK As Boolean, lastOK As Boolean
   Dim field As MeetingDataItems, nameCount, nameBox

   ' First check all the input fields except the names.
   fieldsComplete = True
   For field = Place To Notes
      fieldsComplete = fieldsComplete And _
            Trim(txtMeetingField(field).Text) <> ""
   Next field

   ' At least one name must be complete (first and last).
   nameCount = 0
   namesOK = True
   For nameBox = 0 To MaxNameList
      firstOK = Trim(txtFirstName(nameBox).Text) <> ""
      lastOK = Trim(txtLastName(nameBox).Text) <> ""
      If firstOK And lastOK Then nameCount = nameCount + 1
      namesOK = namesOK And (firstOK Eqv lastOK)
   Next nameBox

   OKRecord = fieldsComplete And nameCount > 0 _
            And namesOK

End Function    ' OkRecord

Private Sub Form_Activate()

   ' The Form_Activate procedure displays a complete
   ' meeting record in the frmMeetings form after the user
```

```
' has selected a record and clicked the View button in
' the frmMeetFind form. The public variable curRec
' identifies the target record that should be read from
' the database. (If curRec is zero, the user has
' clicked the Cancel button in frmMeetFind.)

Dim nameField

' If curRec is not zero, read a database record.
If curRec <> 0 Then
  Open MeetingsDatabase For Random As #1 _
    Len = Len(Meeting)
    Get #1, curRec, Meeting
  Close #1

  ' Display all the information from the record
  ' in the frmMeetings form.
  With Meeting
    txtMeetingField(Place).Text = .MeetPlace
    txtMeetingField(Date).Text = .MeetDate
    txtMeetingField(StartTime).Text = .TimeFrom
    txtMeetingField(EndTime).Text = .TimeTo
    txtMeetingField(Subject).Text = .Subject
    txtMeetingField(Notes).Text = .Notes

    ' Display the list of participant names
    ' from the selected record.
    For nameField = 0 To MaxNameList

      txtFirstName(nameField).Text = _
        .FirstName(nameField)
      txtLastName(nameField).Text = _
        .LastName(nameField)

    Next nameField

  End With

  ' Don't allow the user to modify
  ' this record or to save it to disk.
  ReadOnlyStatus True

Else

  ' Otherwise, if curRec is zero when
  ' frmMeetings is reactivated, simply
  ' clear all information from the form
  ' and allow the user to enter a new record.
  cmdClear_Click

End If

End Sub  ' Form_Activate
```

(continued)

(continued)

```
Private Sub ReadOnlyStatus(onOff As Boolean)

   ' The ReadOnlyStatus procedure switches the Locked
   ' property to either true or false for all the text
   ' boxes in the frmMeetings form. (The Form_Activate
   ' procedure switches the read-only status to true in
   ' order to prevent changes in a record that's been
   ' read from the database. The cmdClear_Click procedure
   ' switches the status to false so the user can enter
   ' and save a new meeting record.)
   Dim field As MeetingDataItems
   Dim nameField

   ' Set the Locked property for input field.
   For field = Place To Notes
     txtMeetingField(field).Locked = onOff
   Next field

   For nameField = 0 To MaxNameList
     txtFirstName(nameField).Locked = onOff
     txtLastName(nameField).Locked = onOff
   Next nameField

   ' If the read-only status is true, disable the Save
   ' button. Conversely, if the read-only status is false,
   ' the Save button is available to the user.
   cmdSave.Enabled = Not onOff

End Sub   ' ReadOnlyStatus


Private Sub Form_Load()

   ' The Form_Load procedure opens the Meetings database
   ' and forms an alphabetized name index.

   Dim i, j

   ' Open the database and calculate
   ' its current length.
   Open MeetingsDatabase For Random As #1 _
      Len = Len(Meeting)
    curRec = LOF(1) / Len(Meeting)
    listLength = 0

     ' Read the name list from each record.
     For i = 1 To curRec
       Get #1, i, Meeting
       For j = 0 To MaxNameList
         With Meeting

           ' If a name is not blank, add it to the list,
           ' standardized as LASTNAME FIRSTNAME. (Note
           ' that a name may appear more than once in
```

```
            ' the list if a participant has attended
            ' more than one meeting.)
            If Trim(.FirstName(j)) <> "" And _
              Trim(.LastName(j)) <> "" Then
              listLength = listLength + 1

                ' Resize the NameList array, preserving
                ' its current contents.
                ReDim Preserve NameList(listLength)

                ' Standardize the name format.
                NameList(listLength).FullName = _
                  FixName(.FirstName(j), .LastName(j))

                ' In the RecordNum field save the
                ' record number where the name can be found.
                NameList(listLength).RecordNum = i
            End If
          End With
        Next j
      Next i
    Close #1

    ' If the index contains more than one name,
    ' sort the list.
    If listLength > 1 Then SortNameList

    ' Set the global curRec pointer to zero, indicating
    ' that no record has been selected yet.
    curRec = 0

End Sub    ' Form_Load

Private Sub SortNameList()

    ' The SortNameList procedure alphabetizes
    ' the name index by the entries in the
    ' FullName field.
    Dim i, j
    Dim temp As IndexEntry

    ' Compare each record with each of
    ' the records below it.
    For i = 1 To listLength - 1
      For j = i + 1 To listLength

        ' Check to see whether two records
        ' are currently out of order.
        If NameList(i).FullName > _
            NameList(j).FullName Then

          ' If they are, swap their positions
          ' in the list.
          temp = NameList(i)
```

(continued)

(continued)

```
        NameList(i) = NameList(j)
        NameList(j) = temp
      End If
    Next j
  Next i

End Sub   ' SortNameList
```

The Meetings Program — MeetFind.Frm Form

```
' The Meetings program
' _____
'
'
' Form: frmMeetFind (MeetFind.FRM)

' This form allows the user to search for
' the name of any person in the database
' (that is, anyone who has attended one of
' the meetings recorded in the file). If
' a given name appears in more than one
' record, the user can scroll through the
' target records, viewing the place, date,
' and subject fields for each record. To
' switch to the frmMeetings form and view
' all the fields of a selected record, the
' user simply clicks the View button after
' scrolling to the target record.

Option Explicit   ' Declare all variables.

' The numInList variable identifies
' index number of the record that is
' currently displayed in the form. Note
' that a given name may appear multiple
' times in the index list.
Dim numInList
'
' End of general declarations for the frmMeetFind form.

Private Sub cmdCancel_Click()

   ' The cmdCancel_Click procedure switches
   ' back to the Meetings form when the user
   ' clicks the Cancel button.

   ' By setting the value of the global
   ' variable curRec to zero, this procedure
   ' notifies the Meetings form that the
   ' user does not currently want to view
   ' a target record.
   curRec = 0
   frmMeetFind.Hide
   frmMeetings.Show
```

```
End Sub    ' cmdCancel_Click

Private Sub cmdClearName_Click()

    ' The cmdClearName_Click procedure
    ' clears current record information
    ' from the frmMeetFind form so that
    ' the user can search for a new name.

    ' Enable and clear the name text boxes.
    txtFirst.Enabled = True
    txtLast.Enabled = True
    txtFirst.Text = ""
    txtLast.Text = ""

    ' Clear the labels designated
    ' for displaying the place, date
    ' and subject fields.
    lblPlace.Caption = ""
    lblDate.Caption = ""
    lblSubject.Caption = ""

    ' Disable the Previous, Next,
    ' and View buttons.
    cmdPrevious.Enabled = False
    cmdNext.Enabled = False
    cmdView.Enabled = False

    ' Move the focus to the first
    ' of the text boxes in the form.
    txtFirst.SetFocus

End Sub    ' cmdClearName_Click

Private Sub cmdNext_Click()

    ' The cmdNext_Click procedure displays
    ' the next record that matches the
    ' current name entry.

    ' Increase numInList by 1 and display
    ' the corresponding record.
    numInList = numInList + 1
    ShowRecord NameList(numInList).RecordNum

    ' Enable to Previous button so that
    ' the user can go back to the previous
    ' record.
    cmdPrevious.Enabled = True
    cmdNext.Enabled = False

    ' Check to see if there is another
    ' entry of the same name in the index
    ' list. If there is, enable the Next
```

(continued)

(continued)

```
    ' button to allow the user to scroll
    ' forward through the database.
    If numInList <> listLength Then _
      If NameList(numInList + 1).FullName = _
        FixName(txtFirst.Text, txtLast.Text) Then _
          cmdNext.Enabled = True

End Sub    ' cmdNext_Click

Private Sub cmdPrevious_Click()

    ' The cmdPrevious_Click procedure displays
    ' the previous record that matches the
    ' current name entry.

    ' Decrease numInList by 1 and display
    ' the corresponding record.
    numInList = numInList - 1
    ShowRecord NameList(numInList).RecordNum

    ' Enable to Next button so that
    ' the user can go forward to the next
    ' record.
    cmdNext.Enabled = True

    ' Check to see if there is another
    ' entry of the same name earlier in the index
    ' list. If there is not, disable the Previous
    ' button to prevent the user from scrolling
    ' backward through the database.
    If NameList(numInList - 1).FullName <> _
      FixName(txtFirst.Text, txtLast.Text) Then _
        cmdPrevious.Enabled = False

End Sub    ' cmdPrevious_Click

Private Sub cmdSearch_Click()

    ' The cmdSearch_Click procedure searches for the name
    ' the user has entered into the First Name and Last Name
    ' text boxes. If the name is found in the index, the
    ' procedure reads the corresponding record.

    Dim inName As String
    Dim curPos As Long
    Dim timesCount As Long

    ' Standardize the name in the LASTNAME FIRSTNAME format.
    ' Then search for the first instance of the name.
    inName = FixName(txtFirst.Text, txtLast.Text)
    numInList = SearchForName(inName)
```

```
' Check for any additional instances of the same name.
If numInList <> 0 Then
  timesCount = 1
  If numInList <> listLength Then
    curPos = numInList
    Do While inName = _
        NameList(curPos + 1).FullName
      timesCount = timesCount + 1
      curPos = curPos + 1
      If curPos = listLength Then Exit Do
    Loop
  End If

  ' Disable the Previous button, and enable the Next
  ' button if the name is in the list more than once.
  cmdPrevious.Enabled = False
  If timesCount > 1 Then cmdNext.Enabled = True

  ' Display the first record for the target name. The
  ' RecordNum field is the location in the database
  ' where the target name is found.
  ShowRecord NameList(numInList).RecordNum

  ' Enable the View button so the user can switch to the
  ' Meetings form to view the record. Disable the two
  ' name text boxes.
  cmdView.Enabled = True
  txtFirst.Enabled = False
  txtLast.Enabled = False
Else

  ' If the name is not found in the index,
  ' display a message on the screen.
  MsgBox txtFirst.Text & " " & txtLast.Text & _
    " is not in the Meetings database.", , _
    "Search"

End If

End Sub  ' cmdSearch_Click

Private Sub ShowRecord(which As Long)

  ' The ShowRecord procedure reads a
  ' record from the Meetings database and
  ' displays the Place, Date, and Subject
  ' fields in the frmMeetFind form.

  ' Open the database and read the record.
  Open MeetingsDatabase For Random As #1 _
      Len = Len(Meeting)
    Get #1, which, Meeting
  Close #1
```

(continued)

(continued)

```
      ' Display the fields as the captions
      ' of the appropriate labels.
      With Meeting
        lblPlace.Caption = .MeetPlace
        lblDate.Caption = .MeetDate
        lblSubject.Caption = .Subject
      End With

  End Sub   ' ShowRecord

  Private Sub cmdView_Click()

      ' The cmdView_Click procedure switches
      ' forms when the user clicks the View
      ' button. The global variable curRec
      ' indicates which record will be displayed
      ' in the Meetings form.

      curRec = NameList(numInList).RecordNum

      frmMeetFind.Hide
      frmMeetings.Show

  End Sub   ' cmdView_Click

  Private Sub Form_Activate()

      ' The Form_Activate clears the frmMeetFind
      ' form at the time it is activated.

      cmdClearName_Click

  End Sub   ' Form_Activate

  Private Function SearchForName(findName As String) As Long
      ' The SearchForName function performs a binary search.
      Dim pos1 As Long, pos2 As Long
      Dim posX As Long, midPos As Long

      ' Search for the target name in portions of the list.
      pos1 = 1
      pos2 = listLength
      posX = 0
      Do While pos1 <= pos2 And posX = 0
        midPos = (pos1 + pos2) / 2
        If findName = NameList(midPos).FullName Then
          posX = midPos
        ElseIf findName > NameList(midPos).FullName Then
          pos1 = midPos + 1
        Else
          pos2 = midPos - 1
        End If
      Loop
```

```
   ' If the name is found, check for other instances.
   If posX > 1 Then
     Do While NameList(posX).FullName _
         = NameList(posX - 1).FullName
       posX = posX - 1
     Loop
   End If
   SearchForName = posX
End Function   ' SearchForName

Private Sub Form_KeyDown _
  (KeyCode As Integer, Shift As Integer)

   ' The Form_KeyDown procedure allows the user to
   ' scroll through a sequence of records by pressing
   ' the PgUp or PgDn keys on the keyboard. The form's
   ' KeyPreview property is set to True.

   ' Code numbers for the PgDn and PgUp keys.
   Const PgDn = 34
   Const PgUp = 33

   ' If the user presses PgDn and the Next
   ' button is currently enabled, force a call
   ' to the cmdNext_Click event procedure.
   If KeyCode = PgDn _
     And cmdNext.Enabled = True _
       Then cmdNext_Click

   ' If the user presses PgUp and the Previous
   ' button is currently enabled, force a call
   ' to the cmdPrevious_Click event procedure.
   If KeyCode = PgUp _
     And cmdPrevious.Enabled = True _
       Then cmdPrevious_Click

End Sub   ' Form_KeyDown
```

The Meetings Program — Meetings.Bas Module

```
' The Meetings program
' Module: modMeetings (Meetings.BAS)
' Contains types for the Meetings record and its index.

Public Const MeetingsDatabase = "\Meetings.DB"
Public Const MaxNameList = 4   ' Length of a name list.

' Meeting represents a database record.
Type MeetingRec
  MeetPlace As String * 18
  MeetDate As String * 10
  TimeFrom As String * 10
  TimeTo As String * 10
```

(continued)

(continued)

```
    FirstName(MaxNameList) As String * 10
    LastName(MaxNameList) As String * 18
    Subject As String * 35
    Notes As String * 400
End Type
Public Meeting As MeetingRec   ' The record variable.
Public curRec As Integer       ' The record pointer.

' The NameList array stores all the names in the database.
Type IndexEntry
    FullName As String
    RecordNum As Long
End Type
Public NameList() As IndexEntry   ' The index array.
Public listLength As Long         ' The index length.
' End of general declarations, modMeetings module.

Function StrFix(s As String) _
    As String

    ' The StrFix function converts a
    ' string argument to all uppercase
    ' letters and removes any leading
    ' or trailing blanks. This ensures
    ' reliable comparisons between strings
    ' in the program.

    StrFix = UCase(Trim(s))

End Function   ' StrFix

Function FixName(first As String, last As String) _
    As String

    ' The FixName function returns a name string
    ' in the standard format LASTNAME FIRSTNAME.

    FixName = StrFix(last) & " " & StrFix(first)

End Function   ' FixName
```

The Phone Directory Program

Chapter 10

The Phone Directory program (Phone.Vbp) is a simple tool for storing and retrieving phone numbers and e-mail addresses. It creates a database (PhoneVB.DB) in the root directory of your hard disk, and gives you easy access to any phone record stored in the database. It also gives you the option of creating a printable phone directory (Phones.Txt) that includes all the records currently stored in your database.

As shown in Figure A-14, the program's main window contains boxes for a first and last name, three phone numbers, and an e-mail address. Once you've entered the information for a new record, click the Save button to store the record in your database. To view an existing record, enter the name of the person you want to look up and click Search.

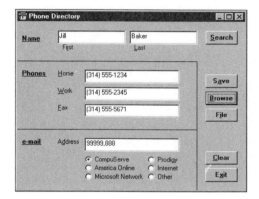

Figure A-14: The main window of the Phone Directory application contains text boxes for a first and a last name; home, work, and fax phone numbers; and an e-mail address. You can also identify the e-mail account by selecting one of the network options shown below the e-mail box.

Sometimes you may want to search for a name by scrolling through your entire phone database. To do so, click the Browse button. As shown in Figure A-15 a secondary dialog box shows each name, one by one. When you find the name you want, click View to see the entire record. The program switches you back to the main Phone Directory window, where the selected record appears.

Figure A-15: The Browse dialog box allows you to scroll alphabetically through all the names stored in your phone database.

As shown in Figure A-16, the Phone Directory application contains a project file, two form files, and a code module. The program's code is in the two forms and the module.

Figure A-16: The Phone Directory program contains two forms and a module, all of which contain code.

The Phone Directory Program — Phone.Frm Form

```
' The Phone Directory program.
'
'
' Files:
' Project File:  Phone.VBP
' Form Files:    Phone.FRM (startup)
'                PhonBrow.FRM
' Module File:   Phone.BAS
'
' This program maintains a phone directory as
' a database file on disk, and allows the user
' to retrieve any record by entering or selecting
' the name of a person who is in the directory.
' Each record may contain phone and fax numbers
' and an e-mail address. In addition to saving
' and retrieving records, the user can browse
' through all the names in the database and create
' a printable directory as a text file on disk.

Option Explicit

' PhoneDB represents the name of the database
' file, and PhoneTextFile represents the name
' of the printable text file.
Const PhoneDB = "\PhoneVB.DB"
Const PhoneTextFile = "\Phones.Txt"
'
' End of geneal declarations, frmPhone.


Private Sub ShowRecord(readRecord As Integer)

    ' The ShowRecord procedure retrieves a record
    ' from the database and displays its fields in
    ' the frmPhone form. (Note that this procedure
    ' is called from cmdSearch_Click and from
    ' Form_Activate.)

    ' The variable readRecord represents an actual
    ' record number, not an element of the Index
    ' array.

    ' Read the target record from the database.
    Get #1, readRecord, Phones

    ' Copy the fields of the record to
    ' the controls on the frmPhone form.
    With Phones
      txtFirstName.Text = .FirstName
      txtLastName.Text = .LastName
      txtHomePhone.Text = .HomePhone
      txtWorkPhone.Text = .WorkPhone
      txtFaxNumber.Text = .FaxNumber
```

```
      txtEMailAddress.Text = .EmailAddress
      optService(.ServiceType) = True
   End With

End Sub   ' ShowRecord

Private Sub cmdBrowse_Click()

   ' The cmdBrowse_Click procedure activates
   ' the frmBrowse form.

   ' The global variable whichRecord indicates
   ' which name should be displayed first in
   ' the form. If no record is current, the
   ' program simply displays the first name
   ' in alphabetical order.
   If whichRecord = 0 Then _
      whichRecord = 1

   ' Activate frmBrowse as a modal form. (In other
   ' words, the form retains control until the
   ' user takes a specific action to switch back to
   ' the other form.)
   frmBrowse.Show 1

End Sub   ' cmdBrowse_Click


Private Sub cmdClear_Click()

   ' The cmdClear_Click procedure clears all
   ' the controls on the main dialog box so
   ' that the user can begin entering a new
   ' record.

   Dim i

   ' Blank out all the text boxes.
   txtFirstName.Text = ""
   txtLastName.Text = ""
   txtHomePhone.Text = ""
   txtWorkPhone.Text = ""
   txtFaxNumber.Text = ""
   txtEMailAddress.Text = ""

   ' Deselect all the option buttons.
   For i = 0 To 5
      optService(i).Value = False
   Next i

   ' Move the focus to the first name text box.
   txtFirstName.SetFocus

End Sub   ' cmdClear_Click
```

(continued)

(continued)

```
Private Sub cmdExit_Click()

' The cmdExit_Click procedure ends the
' program performance when the user clicks
' the Exit button.

  Close #1
  End

End Sub   ' cmdExit_Click


Private Sub cmdFile_Click()

  ' The cmdFile_Click procedure creates a phone directory.
  Dim i

  ' If the file already exists, overwrite it. Using
  ' the index, read records in alphabetical order.
  ' Then write the fields to the text file.
  Open PhoneTextFile For Output As #2
  For i = 1 To numPhones
    Get #1, Index(i).RecNum, Phones
    With Phones
      Print #2, UCase(Trim(.LastName)); ", ";
      Print #2, .FirstName
      Print #2, "Home:  "; .HomePhone
      Print #2, "Work:  "; .WorkPhone
      Print #2, "Fax:   "; .FaxNumber
      Print #2, "email: "; Trim(.EmailAddress);
      Print #2, " (";
      Print #2, optService(.ServiceType).Caption;
      Print #2, ")"
      Print #2,
    End With
  Next i
  Close #2

  MsgBox UCase(PhoneTextFile) & " has been created.", , _
    "Save a Text File"
End Sub   ' cmdFile_Click


Private Sub cmdSave_Click()

  ' The cmdSave_Click procedure stores the current record
  ' entry in the database and updates the index.
  Dim isFound As Integer, i
  Dim answer As Integer, lf As String
  lf = Chr(13) & Chr(10) ' Represents a linefeed.

  ' Display a reminder message if either name is missing.
  If Not FullNameOK Then
    MsgBox "Enter first and last names.", , "Add a Record"
```

```
' Otherwise, search for this name in an existing record
' and copy the entry to the Phones record variable.
Else
   isFound = Search(MakeName(txtFirstName.Text, _
                            txtLastName.Text))
   With Phones
     .FirstName = txtFirstName.Text
     .LastName = txtLastName.Text
     .HomePhone = txtHomePhone.Text
     .WorkPhone = txtWorkPhone.Text
     .FaxNumber = txtFaxNumber.Text
     .EmailAddress = txtEMailAddress.Text
     For i = 0 To 5
       If optService(i).Value Then _
         .ServiceType = i
     Next i
   End With

   ' If the name doesn't already exist, add the record.
   If isFound = 0 Then
     numPhones = numPhones + 1

     ' Enable the Browse and File buttons.
     If numPhones > 0 Then
       cmdBrowse.Enabled = True
       cmdFile.Enabled = True
     End If

     ' Write the record to the file and update the index.
     Put #1, numPhones, Phones
     ReDim Index(numPhones)
     CreateIndex

   ' If the name already exists allow the user to
   ' revise the record (overwriting the previous entry).
   Else
     answer = MsgBox("This name is already on file." _
       & lf & "Do you want to save " & lf & _
       "a revised record?", 4, "Revise a Record")

     ' If the user confirms, store the revised record.
     If answer = 6 Then _
       Put #1, Index(isFound).RecNum, Phones
   End If
 End If

End Sub   ' cmdSave_Click

Private Sub cmdSearch_Click()

 ' The cmdSearch_Click procedure searches for a name in
 ' the phone directory, and retrieves the record.

 Dim searchName As String
 Dim rec As Integer, inFileRec As Integer
```

(continued)

(continued)

```
      If Not FullNameOK Then
        MsgBox "Enter the first and last names.", , "Search"
      Else

        ' Standardize the format and search for the name.
        searchName = MakeName(txtFirstName.Text, _
                         txtLastName.Text)
        rec = Search(searchName)

        ' If the name is found, display the record.
        If rec > 0 Then
          inFileRec = Index(rec).RecNum
          ShowRecord inFileRec

        ' Otherwise, tell the user that the search failed.
        Else
          MsgBox "Can't find " & searchName & ".", , "Search"

        End If
      End If
    End Sub   ' cmdSearch_Click

    Private Sub Form_Activate()

      ' When control returns to the frmPhone form
      ' from the frmBrowse form, display the record
      ' that the user has requested. (Note: If
      ' whichRecord is zero, the user has clicked
      ' the Cancel button rather than the View button
      ' on the frmBrowse form.)

      If whichRecord > 0 Then _
        ShowRecord Index(whichRecord).RecNum

    End Sub   ' Form_Activate

    Private Sub Form_Load()

      ' The Form_Load procedure opens the database file and
      ' creates the index. (The Index array allows the
      ' program to search effectively for any record by
      ' a person's name.)

      ' Open the database file.
      Open PhoneDB For Random As #1 Len = Len(Phones)

      ' Compute the number of records.
      numPhones = LOF(1) / Len(Phones)

      ' If the file exists and contains one or
      ' more records, create the Index array.
      If numPhones > 0 Then
        ReDim Index(numPhones)
        CreateIndex
```

```
    ' Otherwise, disable the Browse and File
    ' buttons. (They have no use until the
    ' database contains at least one record.)
    Else
      cmdBrowse.Enabled = False
      cmdFile.Enabled = False
    End If

End Sub   ' Form_Load

Sub CreateIndex()

  ' The CreateIndex procedure develops the Index array
  ' when the program begins and after each record is added.
  Dim indexEntry As IndexType, i, j, temp As String

  ' Read each record, from the beginning to the end.
  For i = 1 To numPhones
    Get #1, i, Phones

    ' Standardize the name entry in each record, and store
    ' the full name and record number as the fields.
    temp = MakeName(Phones.FirstName, Phones.LastName)
    Index(i).FullName = temp
    Index(i).RecNum = i
  Next i

  ' Sort the index array by the FullName field.
  For i = 1 To numPhones - 1
    For j = i + 1 To numPhones
      If Index(i).FullName > Index(j).FullName Then
        indexEntry = Index(i)
        Index(i) = Index(j)
        Index(j) = indexEntry
      End If
    Next j
  Next i

End Sub   ' CreateIndex

Function MakeName(f As String, l As String) _
    As String

  ' The MakeName function standardizes the
  ' full name of each phone record, so that
  ' different name entries can be compared
  ' successfully.

  ' Concatenate the first and last name fields
  ' into a standard uppercase and trimmed format.
  MakeName = UCase(Trim(l) + " " + Trim(f))

End Function   ' MakeName
```

(continued)

(continued)

```
Function Search(findText As String) As Integer

  ' The Search function performs a binary search to look
  ' for a name in the Index array.
  Dim pos1 As Integer, pos2 As Integer
  Dim posX As Integer, midPos As Integer, midStr As String

  ' Initialize position markers and search for the
  ' target string.
  pos1 = 1
  pos2 = numPhones
  posX = 0
  Do While pos1 <= pos2 And posX = 0
    midPos = (pos1 + pos2) \ 2
    midStr = RTrim(Index(midPos).FullName)
    If findText = midStr Then
      posX = midPos
    ElseIf findText > midStr Then
      pos1 = midPos + 1
    Else
      pos2 = midPos - 1
    End If
  Loop

  ' Return the Index subscript where the name is located,
  ' or zero if the name was not found.
  Search = posX

End Function   ' Search


Private Function FullNameOK() As Boolean

  ' The FullNameOK function checks to see if either
  ' of the name fields is blank. Returns True if
  ' the user has entered both names, or False if a
  ' name is missing.

  Dim blankFirst As Boolean, blankLast As Boolean

  blankFirst = (Trim(txtFirstName.Text) = "")
  blankLast = (Trim(txtLastName.Text) = "")

  FullNameOK = Not (blankFirst Or blankLast)

End Function ' FullNameOK
```

The Phone Directory Program — PhonBrow.Frm Form

```
' The Phone Directory program.
'
'
```

```
' Form: frmBrowse (PhonBrow.FRM)
' This form allows the user to browse through
' the names recorded in the phone directory, and
' to view the complete record for any selected
' name.

Option Explicit


Private Sub Form_KeyDown _
  (KeyCode As Integer, Shift As Integer)

  ' The Form_KeyDown procedure allows the user to
  ' scroll through a sequence of records by pressing
  ' the PgUp or PgDn keys on the keyboard.

  ' *** Note that the form's KeyPreview property
  '     is set to True to make this event possible.

  ' Code numbers for the
  ' PgDn and PgUp keys.
  Const PgDn = 34
  Const PgUp = 33

  ' If the user presses PgDn and the Next
  ' button is currently enabled, force a call
  ' to the cmdNext_Click event procedure.
  If KeyCode = PgDn _
    And cmdNext.Enabled = True _
      Then cmdNext_Click

  ' If the user presses PgUp and the Previous
  ' button is currently enabled, force a call
  ' to the cmdPrevious_Click event procedure.
  If KeyCode = PgUp _
    And cmdPrevious.Enabled = True _
      Then cmdPrevious_Click

End Sub   ' Form_KeyDown


Private Sub ShowName()

  ' The ShowName procedure displays a new name
  ' as the Caption property of the lblFullName
  ' label.

  ' Read the record.
  Get #1, Index(whichRecord).RecNum, Phones

  ' Display the full name in the format
  ' LASTNAME, Firstname.
  With Phones
```

(continued)

(continued)

```
          lblFullName.Caption = Trim(UCase(.LastName)) _
                                & ", " & _
                                Trim(.FirstName)
       End With

    End Sub    ' ShowName


    Private Sub cmdCancel_Click()

       ' The cmdCancel_Click procedure switches
       ' control back to the frmPhone form, without
       ' requesting a record display.

       ' A whichRecord value of zero signals to frmPhone
       ' that the user has clicked Cancel rather than
       ' the View button.
       whichRecord = 0

       frmBrowse.Hide

    End Sub    ' cmdCancel_Click


    Private Sub cmdNext_Click()
       ' The cmdNext_Click procedure displays the next name in
       ' the phone directory index, in alphabetical order.

       ' The target record is represented by whichRecord.
       whichRecord = whichRecord + 1
       ShowName

       ' Enable and/or disable the Next and Previous buttons.
       If whichRecord > 1 Then _
          cmdPrevious.Enabled = True
       If whichRecord = numPhones Then _
          cmdNext.Enabled = False
    End Sub    ' cmdNext_Click


    Private Sub cmdPrevious_Click()
       ' The cmdPrevious_Click procedure displays the previous
       ' name in the phone index, in reverse alphabetical order.

       ' The target record is represented by whichRecord.
       whichRecord = whichRecord - 1
       ShowName

       ' Enable and/or disable the Next and Previous buttons.
       If whichRecord < numPhones Then _
          cmdNext.Enabled = True
       If whichRecord = 1 Then _
          cmdPrevious.Enabled = False
    End Sub    ' cmdPrevious_Click
```

```
Private Sub cmdView_Click()

    ' The cmdView_Click procedure returns control
    ' to the frmPhone form. (Note that the global
    ' variable whichRecord indicates the index
    ' number that will be displayed in the frmPhone
    ' form. See the Form_Activate procedure in
    ' frmPhone for details.)

    frmBrowse.Hide

End Sub   ' cmdView_Click


Private Sub Form_Activate()

    ' The Form_Activate procedure shows the current
    ' name in the lblFullName label when the form
    ' is first activated.

    ShowName

    ' Enable or disable the Next and Previous
    ' buttons as appropriate.
    If whichRecord > 1 Then
       cmdPrevious.Enabled = True
    Else
       cmdPrevious.Enabled = False
    End If

    If whichRecord < numPhones Then
       cmdNext.Enabled = True
    Else
       cmdNext.Enabled = False
    End If

End Sub   ' Form_Activate
```

The Phone Directory Program — Phone.Bas Module

```
' The Phone Directory program.
'
' Module: modPhone (Phone.BAS)
' Defines the types for the phone records and index array.

' The structure for phone records.
Type PhoneType
   FirstName As String * 20
   LastName As String * 20
   WorkPhone As String * 25
   HomePhone As String * 25
   FaxNumber As String * 25
```

(continued)

(continued)

```
        EmailAddress As String * 25
        ServiceType As Byte
    End Type
    Public Phones As PhoneType

    ' The structure for the index array, and the
    ' dynamic Index array.
    Type IndexType
        FullName As String * 41
        RecNum As Integer
    End Type
    Public Index() As IndexType

    ' Then length of the database and the current record.
    Public numPhones As Integer
    Public whichRecord As Integer
    ' End of general declarations, modPhone module.
```

The International Sales Program

Chapter 11

The International Sales Program (IntSales.Vbp) presents a small grid of input boxes in which you can enter a table of sales figures organized by region and by year. When you enter the rows and columns of numeric data, the program calculates totals and develops a chart to represent the data. As you can see in Figure A-17, the program initially creates a stacked column chart, where each column represents the total regional sales over time and each colored portion represents the sales for a particular year. By choosing options from the program's Chart menu, you can change both the orientation and the format of the chart. For example, Figure A-18 shows a pie chart in which each slice represents total sales for a region.

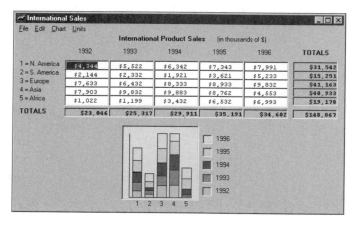

Figure A-17: As you enter sales figures into the cells of the input table, the International Sales Program calculates the regional and annual sales totals, and draws a chart to represent your data.

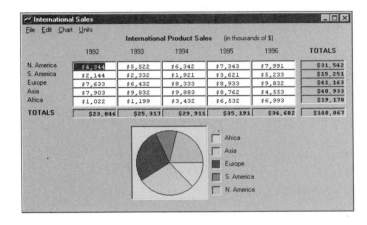

Figure A-18: You can change the appearance of the chart by choosing commands from the program's Chart menu.

Other menu commands allow you to produce various records of the sales table. In the File menu, the Save Report command creates a text file (IntSales.Txt) containing a formatted sales table, and the Print Window command sends a copy of the application window to your printer. The Copy command in the Edit menu places a copy of the sales table on the Clipboard so that you can paste the data to a document in another application.

You can revise the column headings, the row labels, and the title to provide an appropriate description of your own data. You can also choose options from the Units menu to identify the magnitude of dollar units represented by the numeric data you enter.

The application consists of the project file and a single form file, as shown in Figure A-19. All of the program's code is in the form module.

Figure A-19: The International Sales application has one form, which contains all the program's code.

The International Sales Program — IntSales.Frm

```
' The International Sales Program
'
' Files:
' Project File:   IntSales.VBP
' Form File:      IntSales.FRM
'
```

(continued)

(continued)

```
' This program provides a small spreadsheet in which the
' user can enter sales data organized by region. As each
' data item is entered, the program calculates totals and
' develops a chart. The user can choose among column and
' pie chart formats.
Option Explicit
Const AmtFormat = "$#,####0"    ' Sales data display format.
Const colorOffset = 7           ' Colors in charts.

' The program uses six arrays to record the sales
' data and labels displayed in the application window.
Dim amounts(24)                 ' The actual data.
Dim amountStr(24) As String     ' Data in string format.
Dim periodTots(4)               ' Current column totals.
Dim periodLabels(4) As String   ' Current column labels.
Dim regionTots(4)               ' Current row totals.
Dim regionLabels(4) As String   ' Current row labels.

Dim IDPrefixes(4) As String     ' Numeric label prefixes.
Dim grandTot                    ' Total of all sales data.
Dim showMsg As Boolean          ' Show file message?
'
' End of general declarations, frmIntSales.

Private Sub SelectText(whichBox As Control)

  ' The SelectText procedure arranges to
  ' highlight the contents of a given text box
  ' when the control receives the focus. This
  ' effect is achieved through use of the SelStart
  ' and SelLength properties.

  With whichBox
    .SelStart = 0
    .SelLength = Len(.Text)
  End With

End Sub ' SelectText

Private Sub Form_Load()

  ' The Form_Load procedure performs a variety
  ' of initializations at the beginning of the
  ' program's performance.

  Dim i
  Dim tempYear As String

  ' Display the initial column labels and
  ' initialize the arrays that record the
  ' current labels.
  For i = 0 To 4
    tempYear = Year(Date) - (4 - i)
    txtYear(i).Text = tempYear
    periodLabels(i) = txtYear(i).Text
```

```vb
      regionLabels(i) = txtPlace(i).Text
      IDPrefixes(i) = Format((i + 1), "# = ")
   Next i

   ' Display the current dollar unit selection.
   ' (The user can change this display by making
   ' a new selection from the Units menu.)
   ShowUnits
   showMsg = True

End Sub   ' Form_Load


Private Sub mnuChartBy_Click(Index As Integer)

   ' The mnuChartBy_Click procedure responds to the user's
   ' choice of an option in the Chart menu. The user can
   ' choose a chart by region or by years.
   Dim i

   ' Adjust the selection within the menu itself.
   If Index = 0 Then
      mnuChartBy(0).Checked = True
      mnuChartBy(1).Checked = False
   Else
      mnuChartBy(0).Checked = False
      mnuChartBy(1).Checked = True
   End If

   ' Restore the original column and row labels.
   For i = 0 To 4
      txtYear(i).Text = periodLabels(i)
      txtYear(i).Enabled = True
      txtPlace(i).Text = regionLabels(i)
      txtPlace(i).Enabled = True
   Next i

   ' Redraw the chart if any sales entries exist.
   If grandTot <> 0 Then DrawGraph

End Sub   ' mnuChartBy_Click


Private Sub mnuChartType_Click(Index As Integer)

   ' The mnuChartType_Click procedure responds to
   ' the user's choice of an option in the Chart
   ' menu. The user can choose to create a column
   ' chart or a pie chart.

   ' Adjust the current selection in the menu.
   If Index = 0 Then
      mnuChartType(0).Checked = True
      mnuChartType(1).Checked = False
   Else
```

(continued)

(continued)

```
            mnuChartType(0).Checked = False
            mnuChartType(1).Checked = True
        End If

        ' If any sales information has been entered
        ' into the table, redraw the chart at this point.
        If grandTot <> 0 Then DrawGraph

    End Sub  ' mnuChartType_Click


    Private Sub mnuClear_Click()

        ' The mnuClear_Click procedure clears the sales data
        ' and temporarily hides the chart.
        Dim i

        ' Reinitialize the text boxes, totals,
        ' arrays, and labels.
        For i = 0 To 24
            txtAmount(i).Text = ""
            amounts(i) = 0
            amountStr(i) = ""
        Next i
        For i = 0 To 4
            lblPeriodTotal(i).Caption = ""
            lblRegionTotal(i).Caption = ""
            periodTots(i) = 0
            regionTots(i) = 0
            txtPlace(i).Text = regionLabels(i)
            txtYear(i).Text = periodLabels(i)
        Next i
        lblGrandTotal.Caption = ""
        grandTot = 0

        ' Hide the graph objects and set the focus.
        HideGraph
        txtAmount(0).SetFocus

    End Sub  ' mnuClear_Click


    Private Sub mnuCopy_Click()

        ' The mnuCopy_Click procedure takes control when the
        ' user chooses Copy from the Edit menu. It places a
        ' copy of the current sales table in the Clipboard.
        Dim temp As String, inTemp As String

        ' Begin by creating a text file for the current data.
        showMsg = False
        mnuSaveReport_Click
        showMsg = True
```

```
' Then open the file and read each line it contains.
temp = ""
Open "\IntSales.Txt" For Input As #1
  Do While Not EOF(1)
    Line Input #1, inTemp

    ' Concatenate each line of text to
    ' the string variable temp.
    temp = temp + inTemp + Chr(13) + Chr(10)
  Loop
Close #1

' Finally, place the temp string on the Clipboard.
Clipboard.SetText temp

End Sub   ' mnuCopy_Click

Private Sub mnuExit_Click()

  ' The mnuExit_Click procedure takes control when
  ' the user chooses the Exit command from the
  ' File menu. The procedure simply terminates the
  ' program performance.

  End

End Sub   ' mnuExit_Click


Private Sub mnuPrintWindow_Click()

  ' The mnuPrintWindow_Click procedure takes control
  ' when the user chooses the Print Window command
  ' from the File menu. The procedure sends an
  ' image of the program's form to the printer.

  PrintForm

End Sub   ' mnuPrintWindow_Click


Private Sub mnuSaveReport_Click()

  ' The mnuSaveReport_Click procedure takes control when
  ' the user chooses Save Report from the File menu. It
  ' creates a text file (\IntSales.Txt) for the numeric
  ' data currently displayed in the sales table.
  Dim i, j
  Dim f As String, b As String

  f = "$#,####0"
  b = Space(12)

  ' Create the file. (If the file already
```

(continued)

(continued)

```
    ' exists, overwrite the previous version.)
    Open "\IntSales.Txt" For Output As #1

        ' Write the title and the column labels
        ' to the file.
        Print #1, b; b; txtTitle
        Print #1, b; b; Space(3); lblUnits
        Print #1,

        Print #1, b;
        For i = 0 To 4
          RSet b = txtYear(i)
          Print #1, b;
        Next i
        Print #1, Space(6); "Totals"
        Print #1,

        ' Write the table of sales data to the file.
        For i = 0 To 4
          LSet b = txtPlace(i).Text
          Print #1, b;
          For j = i * 5 To i * 5 + 4
            RSet b = txtAmount(j).Text
            Print #1, b;
          Next j
          RSet b = lblRegionTotal(i).Caption
          Print #1, b
        Next i

        ' Write the totals to the file.
        Print #1,
        Print #1, "Totals"; Space(6);
        For i = 0 To 4
          RSet b = lblPeriodTotal(i).Caption
          Print #1, b;
        Next i
        RSet b = lblGrandTotal
        Print #1, b

    Close #1
    If showMsg Then _
      MsgBox "Created \IntSales.Txt", , "Report"

End Sub   ' mnuSaveReport_Click

Private Sub mnuUnitType_Click(Index As Integer)
    ' The mnuUnitType_Click procedure takes control when the
    ' user chooses an option in the Units menu. A new
    ' caption appears in the lblUnits control.
    Dim i

    ' Check the option and display the units caption.
    For i = 0 To 2
```

```
      If i = Index Then
        mnuUnitType(i).Checked = True
      Else
        mnuUnitType(i).Checked = False
      End If
    Next i
    ShowUnits
End Sub   ' mnuUnitType_Click


Private Sub ShowUnits()
    ' The ShowUnits procedure displays the units caption.

    Select Case True
      Case mnuUnitType(0).Checked
        lblUnits.Caption = "(in dollars)"
      Case mnuUnitType(1).Checked
        lblUnits.Caption = "(in thousands of $)"
      Case mnuUnitType(2).Checked
        lblUnits.Caption = "(in millions of $)"
    End Select
End Sub   ' ShowUnits


Private Sub txtAmount_GotFocus(Index As Integer)

    ' The txtAmount_GotFocus procedure makes a call
    ' to a general procedure named SelectText to
    ' highlight the contents of the txtAmount box
    ' that receives the focus.

    SelectText txtAmount(Index)

End Sub   ' txtAmount_GotFocus

Private Sub txtAmount_KeyDown(Index As Integer, _
    KeyCode As Integer, Shift As Integer)

    ' The txtAmount_KeyDown procedure allows the txtAmount
    ' text boxes to respond to the arrow keys and the Enter
    ' key for moving the focus from one box to the next.

    ' Code numbers of the relevant keys.
    Const leftKey = 37
    Const upKey = 38
    Const rightKey = 39
    Const downKey = 40
    Const enter = 13

    Select Case KeyCode

      ' Move the focus to the next row or back to the top.
      Case downKey
        If Index < 20 Then
          txtAmount(Index + 5).SetFocus
```

(continued)

(continued)

```
            Else
              txtAmount(Index Mod 5).SetFocus
            End If

          ' Move the focus to the previous row or
          ' down to the bottom row from the top.
          Case upKey
            If Index > 4 Then
              txtAmount(Index - 5).SetFocus
            Else
              txtAmount(Index + 20).SetFocus
            End If

          ' Move the focus to the previous text
          ' box, or from the upper-left corner to
          ' the lower-right corner of the table.
          Case leftKey
            If Index <> 0 Then
              txtAmount(Index - 1).SetFocus
            Else
              txtAmount(24).SetFocus
            End If

          ' Move the focus to the next text box,
          ' or from the lower-right corner to the
          ' upper-left corner of the table. (Note
          ' that the right-arrow key and the Enter
          ' key are both available for this action.)
          Case rightKey, enter
            If Index <> 24 Then
              txtAmount(Index + 1).SetFocus
            Else
              txtAmount(0).SetFocus
            End If

      End Select

  End Sub    ' txtAmount_KeyDown


  Private Sub CalculateTotals(amtIndex As Integer)

    ' The CalculateTotals procedure updates the
    ' row and column of sales totals, and the grand total.

    Dim i As Integer, periodIndex As Integer
    Dim regionIndex As Integer, firstRowIndex As Integer
    Dim firstColIndex As Integer, totTemp

    ' Create indexes to identify totals to be recalculated.
    periodIndex = amtIndex Mod 5
    regionIndex = amtIndex \ 5
    firstRowIndex = regionIndex * 5
    firstColIndex = periodIndex
```

```
      ' Find the total sales for the current region.
      totTemp = 0
      For i = firstRowIndex To firstRowIndex + 4
        totTemp = totTemp + amounts(i)
      Next i

      ' Record and display the total sales for the region.
      regionTots(regionIndex) = totTemp
      If totTemp <> 0 Then
        lblRegionTotal(regionIndex).Caption = _
          Format(totTemp, AmtFormat)
      Else
        lblRegionTotal(regionIndex).Caption = ""
      End If

      ' Calculate the total sales for the current period.
      totTemp = 0
      For i = firstColIndex To firstColIndex + 20 Step 5
        totTemp = totTemp + amounts(i)
      Next i

      ' Record and display the total sales for the period.
      periodTots(periodIndex) = totTemp
      If totTemp <> 0 Then
        lblPeriodTotal(periodIndex).Caption = _
          Format(totTemp, AmtFormat)
      Else
        lblPeriodTotal(periodIndex).Caption = ""
      End If

      ' Calculate the new grand total.
      totTemp = 0
      For i = 0 To 24
        totTemp = totTemp + amounts(i)
      Next i

      ' Record and display the calculated grand total.
      grandTot = totTemp
      If totTemp <> 0 Then
        lblGrandTotal.Caption = Format(totTemp, AmtFormat)
      Else
        lblGrandTotal.Caption = ""
      End If
End Sub   ' CalculateTotals


Private Sub txtAmount_LostFocus(Index As Integer)

  ' The txtAmount_LostFocus procedure validates each data
  ' entry, reformats it for display, recalculates the
  ' totals, and redraws the current chart. (Note that
  ' txtAmount is the array of text boxes containing data.)

  Dim entryWidth As String
  entryWidth = Space(8)  ' Width for right-justifying data.
```

(continued)

(continued)

```vb
        ' Determine whether the value has changed.
        If amountStr(Index) <> txtAmount(Index).Text Then

          ' If so, record the entry in the amounts array.
          ' Use Val function to eliminate nonnumeric characters.
          amounts(Index) = Val(txtAmount(Index).Text)

          ' Do not allow negative values, or entries longer
          ' than six digits.
          If amounts(Index) < 0 Or amounts(Index) > 999999 _
            Then amounts(Index) = 0

          ' If the entry is not zero, display the value
          ' in a right-justified dollar-and-cent format.
          If amounts(Index) <> 0 Then
            RSet entryWidth = _
              Format(amounts(Index), AmtFormat)
            txtAmount(Index).Text = entryWidth

          Else
            ' Otherwise, if the entry is zero,
            ' display it as a blank entry.
            txtAmount(Index).Text = ""
          End If

          ' Record the formatted value in the
          ' string array named amountStr.
          amountStr(Index) = txtAmount(Index).Text

          ' Recaculate the totals for the row and
          ' column where this new entry is located.
          CalculateTotals Index

          ' If the current grand total is not zero,
          ' redraw the current chart. Otherwise,
          ' hide the chart controls.
          If grandTot <> 0 Then
            DrawGraph
          Else
            HideGraph
          End If

        End If

    End Sub    ' txtAmount_LostFocus


    Private Sub DrawGraph()

      ' The DrawGraph procedure redraws the chart, based on
      ' the current selections in the Chart menu.

      ' Display and picture box control and clear its contents.
      picSalesChart.Visible = True
      picSalesChart.Cls
```

```
    ' Determine which chart the user has requested, and
    ' draw the chart. For a column chart, draw the axes.
    Select Case True
      Case mnuChartBy(0).Checked And mnuChartType(0).Checked
        DrawAxes
        ColumnByYears
      Case mnuChartBy(0).Checked And mnuChartType(1).Checked
        PieByYears
      Case mnuChartBy(1).Checked And mnuChartType(0).Checked
        DrawAxes
        ColumnByRegion
      Case mnuChartBy(1).Checked And mnuChartType(1).Checked
        PieByRegion
    End Select

    ' Display the legend for the chart.
    ShowLegend

End Sub   ' DrawGraph

Private Sub DrawAxes()

    ' The DrawAxes procedure draws the vertical
    ' and horizontal axes for a column chart.

    Dim i

    ' Begin by creating a convenient coordinate
    ' system for the chart. (The "origin" of the
    ' chart is located just above and to the right
    ' of the lower-left corner of the picture box.)
    picSalesChart.Scale (-1, 11)-(11, -0.25)

    ' Then draw the two axes, each starting
    ' at the "origin" defined by the coordinate
    ' scale.
    picSalesChart.Line (0, 0)-Step(10, 0)
    picSalesChart.Line (0, 0)-Step(0, 10)

End Sub   ' DrawAxes

Private Sub ShowLegend()

    ' The ShowLegend procedure displays the labels
    ' and colors of the legend for a pie chart or a
    ' column chart. In addition, the procedure adds
    ' numeric prefixes to labels above or to the left
    ' of the sales table, to identify the individual
    ' columns of a column chart.

    Dim i

    For i = 0 To 4
```

(continued)

(continued)

```
' If the "By Years" option has been selected
' in the Chart menu, display the years as the
' legend labels.
If mnuChartBy(0).Checked Then
  If periodTots(i) <> 0 Then
    lblLegendColor(i).Visible = True
    lblLegendColor(i).BackColor = _
      QBColor(i + colorOffset)
    lblLegendText(i).Caption = periodLabels(i)

  ' But don't display a box or label for
  ' a sales table column that has a
  ' total value of zero.
  Else
    lblLegendColor(i).Visible = False
    lblLegendText(i).Caption = ""
  End If

  ' For a column chart, add a numeric
  ' prefix to the region labels to identify
  ' each column of the chart.
  If mnuChartType(0).Checked And _
      regionTots(i) <> 0 Then
    lblxAxis(i).Caption = i + 1
    txtPlace(i).Text = IDPrefixes(i) + _
      regionLabels(i)
    txtPlace(i).Enabled = False
  Else
    lblxAxis(i).Caption = ""
    txtPlace(i).Text = regionLabels(i)
    txtPlace(i).Enabled = True
  End If

Else

  ' If the "By Region" option has been
  ' selected in the Chart menu, display
  ' the regions of the legend labels.
  If regionTots(i) <> 0 Then
    lblLegendColor(i).Visible = True
    lblLegendColor(i).BackColor = _
      QBColor(i + colorOffset)
    lblLegendText(i).Caption = regionLabels(i)
  Else
    lblLegendColor(i).Visible = False
    lblLegendText(i).Caption = ""
  End If

  ' For a column chart, add numeric prefixes
  ' to the year labels to identify each
  ' column of the chart.
  If mnuChartType(0).Checked And _
      periodTots(i) <> 0 Then
```

```
            lblxAxis(i).Caption = i + 1
            txtYear(i).Text = IDPrefixes(i) + _
              periodLabels(i)
            txtYear(i).Enabled = False
          Else
            lblxAxis(i).Caption = ""
            txtYear(i).Text = periodLabels(i)
            txtYear(i).Enabled = True
          End If

      End If
    Next i

End Sub   ' ShowLegend

Private Sub HideGraph()

  ' The HideGraph procedure hides the picture box
  ' and other controls related to the chart and
  ' its legend. The program calls this routine
  ' whenever the grand total value is zero.

  Dim i

  ' Hide the picture box.
  picSalesChart.Visible = False

  For i = 0 To 4

    ' Hide all of the legend labels.
    lblLegendColor(i).Visible = False
    lblLegendText(i).Caption = ""

    ' Erase the labels arranged beneath
    ' the horizontal axis of a column chart.
    lblxAxis(i).Caption = ""

    ' Restore the original year and region
    ' labels above and to the left of the
    ' sales table.
    txtYear(i).Text = periodLabels(i)
    txtYear(i).Enabled = True
    txtPlace(i).Text = regionLabels(i)
    txtPlace(i).Enabled = True
  Next i

End Sub   ' HideGraph

Private Sub txtPlace_LostFocus(Index As Integer)

  ' The txtPlace_LostFocus procedure is called when
  ' the user completes a change in any one of the
  ' region labels displayed to the left of the
  ' sales chart. The procedure records this change
  ' in the regionLabels array.
```

(continued)

(continued)

```
       regionLabels(Index) = txtPlace(Index).Text
       If grandTot <> 0 Then ShowLegend

    End Sub   ' txtPlace_LostFocus


Private Sub ColumnByYears()
   ' The ColumnByYears procedure draws a column chart.
   Dim i, x, y, y2, maxRegion, scaleFactor

   ' Determine the largest total and compute the scale.
   maxRegion = 0
   For i = 0 To 4
     If regionTots(i) > maxRegion Then _
       maxRegion = regionTots(i)
   Next i
   scaleFactor = 10 / maxRegion

   For i = 0 To 24
     If i Mod 5 = 0 Then
       x = 0.5 + 2 * (i / 5)
       y = 0
     End If

     ' Compute the height, choose a color, and draw.
     If amounts(i) <> 0 Then
       y2 = scaleFactor * amounts(i)
       picSalesChart.FillColor = _
         QBColor(i Mod 5 + colorOffset)
       picSalesChart.FillStyle = 0
       picSalesChart.Line (x, y)-Step(1.5, y2), 0, B
       y = y + y2
     End If
   Next i
End Sub   ' ColumnByYears

Private Sub ColumnByRegion()
   ' The ColumnByRegion procedure draws a column chart.
   Dim i, j, x, y, y2, maxPeriod, scaleFactor

   ' Determine the largest total and compute the scale.
   maxPeriod = 0
   For i = 0 To 4
     If periodTots(i) > maxPeriod Then _
       maxPeriod = periodTots(i)
   Next i
   scaleFactor = 10 / maxPeriod

   For i = 0 To 4
     x = 0.5 + 2 * i
     y = 0
```

```
        ' Draw a "stack" for each sales entry.
        For j = i To i + 20 Step 5
          If amounts(j) <> 0 Then
            y2 = scaleFactor * amounts(j)
            picSalesChart.FillColor = _
              QBColor(j \ 5 + colorOffset)
            picSalesChart.FillStyle = 0
            picSalesChart.Line (x, y)-Step(1.5, y2), 0, B
            y = y + y2
          End If
        Next j
      Next i
End Sub    ' ColumnByRegion

Private Sub txtYear_LostFocus(Index As Integer)

    ' The txtYear_LostFocus procedure is called when
    ' the user completes a change in any one of the
    ' year labels displayed above the sales chart.
    ' The procedure records this change in the
    ' periodLabels array.

    periodLabels(Index) = txtYear(Index).Text
    If grandTot <> 0 Then ShowLegend

End Sub    ' txtYear_LostFocus


Private Sub PieByYears()
    ' The PieByYears procedure draws a pie chart.
    Dim i, pi, a1, a2

    ' Calculate pi, set the scale and the starting point.
    pi = 4 * Atn(1)
    picSalesChart.Scale (-1, 1)-(1, -1)
    a1 = 0.00001

    ' Draw a wedge for the total sales of each year.
    For i = 0 To 4
      If periodTots(i) <> 0 Then

        ' Calculate the ending angle of the wedge.
        a2 = a1 + (2 * pi) * (periodTots(i) / grandTot)

        ' Select a color and draw the wedge.
        picSalesChart.FillColor = QBColor(i + colorOffset)
        picSalesChart.FillStyle = 0
        If periodTots(i) < grandTot Then
          picSalesChart.Circle (0, 0), 0.9, _
            0, -a1, -a2 + 0.00001
        Else       ' If this is the only sales value.
          picSalesChart.Circle (0, 0), 0.9, 0
        End If
```

(continued)

(continued)

```
        a1 = a2   ' The starting angle for the next wedge.
      End If
    Next i
End Sub   ' PieByYears

Private Sub PieByRegion()
   ' The PieByRegion procedure draws a pie chart.
   Dim i, pi, a1, a2

   ' Calculate pi, set the scale and the starting point.
   pi = 4 * Atn(1)
   picSalesChart.Scale (-1, 1)-(1, -1)
   a1 = 0.00001

   ' Draw a wedge for the total sales of each year.
   For i = 0 To 4
     If regionTots(i) <> 0 Then

       ' Calculate the ending angle of the wedge.
       a2 = a1 + (2 * pi) * (regionTots(i) / grandTot)

       ' Select a color and draw the wedge.
       picSalesChart.FillColor = QBColor(i + colorOffset)
       picSalesChart.FillStyle = 0
       If regionTots(i) < grandTot Then
         picSalesChart.Circle (0, 0), 0.9, _
           0, -a1, -a2 + 0.00001
       Else      ' If this is the only sales value.
         picSalesChart.Circle (0, 0), 0.9, 0
       End If
       a1 = a2   ' The starting angle for the next wedge.
     End If
   Next i
End Sub   ' PieByRegion
```

The Transportation Planner Program

Chapter 12

The Transportation Planner program (TranPlan.Vbp) is designed to help you plan your itinerary for an upcoming business trip. The program creates and manages database files to record the transportation details. As you can see in Figure A-20, the fields of each transportation record include the mode of transportation, the name of the transportation company (for example, the airline or bus line), the number and reservation status, the date and time of departure, the starting point and the destination of the trip, and any brief comments you wish to include in the record.

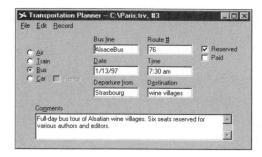

Figure A-20: The option buttons, text boxes, and check boxes of the Transportation Planner window represent the various fields of a travel record.

You can use the program to develop any number of travel files over time, each saved on disk under a unique file name. To save a new database, choose File⇨ Save As. To open an existing database, choose File⇨Open. The application uses Visual Basic's common dialog control to provide standard Windows dialog boxes for file operations. For example, Figure A-21 shows the Open dialog box, displaying a list of existing travel files.

Figure A-21: The program uses the common dialog control to provide familiar Windows dialog boxes for file operations.

As shown in Figure A-22, the program consists of the application file and a single form file, which contains all the code.

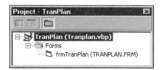

Figure A-22: All the program's code is contained in a single form module.

The Transportation Planner Program — TranPlan.Frm

```
' The Transportation Planner program.
'
' Project File:  TranPlan.VBP
' Form File:     TranPlan.FRM
'
' This menu-driven program allows the user to create
' itinerary files on disk. Each random-access file contains
' records describing the transportation plans for an
' upcoming business trip or vacation. Files are stored
' with TRV extensions. The user can open any file, and
' view, revise, or add records. The program illustrates
' Visual Basic's Custom Dialog control, which provides
' access to Windows dialog boxes such as Save and Open.
Option Explicit

' The structure of transportation records.
Private Type TranRecType
  TranMode As Integer
  RentalCar As Boolean
  Carrier As String * 30
  TripNumber As String * 30
  ReservedStatus As Boolean
  PaidStatus As Boolean
  TripDate As String * 30
  TripTime As String * 30
  TripFrom As String * 30
  TripTo As String * 30
  Comments As String * 200
End Type


' Variables for this form.
Dim TranRecord As TranRecType   ' A single record.
Dim tranFileOpen As Boolean     ' Is a file open?
Dim tranFileName As String      ' Name of open file.
Dim curTranRecord As Integer    ' Current record number.
Dim titleBarText As String      ' Title bar text.
Dim recordChanged As Boolean    ' Has record changed?
'
' End of general declarations, frmTranPlan.


Private Sub BlankEOFRecord()

  ' This procedure moves the record pointer
  ' one position past the end of the current
  ' file, in preparation for a new record entry.

  curTranRecord = FindRecordCount + 1
  mnuClear_Click
  recordChanged = False
```

```
        ' Disable the Next command until the
        ' user makes an entry into this new record.
        mnuNext.Enabled = False
    End Sub   ' BlankEOFRecord

Private Sub ChangedStatus()

    ' The ChangedStatus procedure sets the
    ' recordChanged variable and, if appropriate,
    ' enables the Next command, in response to
    ' a change in the contents of one of the
    ' program's text boxes.

    recordChanged = True
    If tranFileOpen Then _
      mnuNext.Enabled = True

End Sub   ' ChangedStatus

Private Sub CopyDatabase _
  (toFile As String, fromFile As String)

    ' The CopyDatabase procedure copies the records
    ' of the current transportation file to a new
    ' file, in response to the user's instructions
    ' in the Save As command.

    Dim i As Long

    ' If the destination file already exists,
    ' delete it from disk. (Note that the Save As
    ' dialog box provides a warning if the user
    ' chooses an existing file; the Save As
    ' operation continues only if the user confirms.)
    On Error Resume Next
       Kill toFile
    On Error GoTo 0

    ' Open the two files.
    Open toFile For Random As #1 _
       Len = Len(TranRecord)
    Open fromFile For Random As #2 _
       Len = Len(TranRecord)

    ' Copy all the records from the source file
    ' to the destination file.
    For i = 1 To LOF(2) / Len(TranRecord)
       Get #2, i, TranRecord
       Put #1, i, TranRecord
    Next i

    ' Close the source file. The destination
    ' file becomes the current tranporation
    ' database.
```

(continued)

(continued)

```
    Close #2
    tranFileName = toFile

End Sub    ' CopyDatabase

Private Sub PrintComments(noteStr As String)

    ' The PrintComments procedure arranges to
    ' print the Comments field of any record
    ' in a sequence of approximately 40-character
    ' lines, without breaking any words in the text.

    Const lineLen = 40    ' Line length.
    Const t1 = 5          ' Tab stop.

    Dim curPos As Integer
    Dim curLine As String
    Dim curChar As String

    ' Divide the text into 40-character lines.
    Do While Len(noteStr) > lineLen
      curPos = lineLen

      ' Break each line after a word.
      Do
        curChar = Mid(noteStr, curPos, 1)
        curPos = curPos - 1
      Loop Until curChar = " "

      ' Print the current line.
      Printer.Print Tab(t1); _
        Left(noteStr, curPos)

      ' Reduce the string by the line
      ' that has just been printed.
      noteStr = Mid(noteStr, curPos + 2)
    Loop

    ' Print the final line of the text.
    Printer.Print Tab(t1); noteStr

End Sub    ' PrintComments

Private Sub SaveCurRec()

    ' The SaveCurRec procedure writes the current
    ' transportation record to its correct position
    ' in the open file.

    ' Copy the user's input to the
    ' TranRecord structure.
    MakeTranRecord
```

```
' Write the record to the file. The variable
' curTranRecord keeps track of the current
' record position.
Put #1, curTranRecord, TranRecord
recordChanged = False

End Sub    ' SaveCurRec


Private Function YesNo(which As Boolean) As String

  ' The YesNo function converts a Boolean value
  ' into a string value of "Yes" or "No." This
  ' conversion is used in the process of printing
  ' transportation records.

  If which Then
    YesNo = "Yes"
  Else
    YesNo = "No"
  End If

End Function    ' YesNo


Private Sub chkPaid_Click()

  ' The chkPaid_Click procedure changes the
  ' Boolean value of the recordChanged variable
  ' if the user changes the status of the Paid
  ' check box.

  recordChanged = True

End Sub    ' chkPaid_Click

Private Sub mnuNew_Click()

  ' The mnuNew_Click procedure starts a new database.

  ' If a file is open, save its current
  ' record if necessary.
  If tranFileOpen And recordChanged Then _
    SaveCurRec

  ' Then close the file.
  Close
  tranFileOpen = False

  ' Clear any entries from the form, and
  ' initialize the recordChanged and
  ' curTranRecord variables.
  mnuClear_Click
  recordChanged = False
  curTranRecord = 1
```

(continued)

(continued)

```
        ' Disable the Previous and Next commands.
        mnuPrevious.Enabled = False
        mnuNext.Enabled = False

        ' Display a new caption in the title bar.
        titleBarText = "Transportation Planner"
        frmTranPlan.Caption = titleBarText

    End Sub    ' mnuNew_Click

    Private Sub mnuPrint_Click()

        ' The mnuPrint_Click procedure prints transportation
        ' records when the user chooses the Print command.
        Dim i As Long

        ' If a file is open, print all the records.
        If tranFileOpen Then

            ' Save the current record to the file if necessary.
            If recordChanged Then SaveCurRec
            recordChanged = False

            ' Print each record in turn.
            For i = 1 To FindRecordCount
                Get #1, i, TranRecord
                PrintRecord
            Next i

        ' If no file is open, just print the current entry.
        Else
            MakeTranRecord
            PrintRecord
        End If

        ' Complete the output process.
        Printer.EndDoc

    End Sub    ' mnuPrint_Click

    Private Sub Form_KeyDown(KeyCode As Integer, _
        Shift As Integer)

        ' The Form_KeyDown procedure allows the user
        ' to press PgDn or PgUp to scroll through the
        ' records of an open transportation file. The form's
        ' KeyPreview property is set to True.

        ' Code numbers for the
        ' PgDn and PgUp keys.
        Const PgDn = 34
        Const PgUp = 33
```

```
' If the user presses PgDn and the Next
' command is currently enabled, force a call
' to the mnuNext_Click event procedure.
If KeyCode = PgDn _
  And mnuNext.Enabled = True _
    Then mnuNext_Click

' If the user presses PgUp and the Previous
' command is currently enabled, force a call
' to the mnuPrevious_Click event procedure.
If KeyCode = PgUp _
  And mnuPrevious.Enabled = True _
    Then mnuPrevious_Click

End Sub   ' Form_KeyDown


Private Sub chkRental_Click()

  ' The chkRental_Click procedure adjusts
  ' the Enabled properties of several controls,
  ' depending on the value of the chkRental
  ' check box. (If the car option is selected,
  ' the Rental box indicates whether the
  ' car is a rental or a private vehicle.)

  ' If chkRental is checked, enable the
  ' text boxes for the rental agency (txtCarrier)
  ' and the reservation number (txtTripNumber).
  ' Also enable the chkReserved check box, which
  ' indicates whether a reservation has been made.

  If optMode(3).Value Then
    If chkRental.Value = 1 Then
      txtCarrier.Enabled = True
      lblCarrier.Enabled = True
      txtTripNumber.Enabled = True
      lblTripNumber.Enabled = True
      chkReserved.Enabled = True
      chkReserved_Click

    ' If chkRental is unchecked, disable
    ' all these controls.
    Else
      txtCarrier.Enabled = False
      lblCarrier.Enabled = False
      txtTripNumber.Enabled = False
      lblTripNumber.Enabled = False
      chkReserved.Value = 0
      chkReserved.Enabled = False
    End If
```

(continued)

(continued)

```vb
        recordChanged = True
      End If

End Sub    ' chkRental_Click

Private Sub chkReserved_Click()

   ' The chkReserved_Click procedure enables or
   ' disables the "Reservation #" text box
   ' (txtTripNumber), depending on the value of
   ' the chkReserved check box. This action
   ' occurs only if the current transporation
   ' selection is "Car."

   If optMode(3).Value Then
     If chkReserved.Value = 0 Then
       txtTripNumber.Enabled = False
       lblTripNumber.Enabled = False
     Else
       txtTripNumber.Enabled = True
       lblTripNumber.Enabled = True
     End If
   End If

   recordChanged = True

End Sub   ' chkReserved_Click


Private Sub mnuClear_Click()

   ' The mnuClear_Click procedure clears the
   ' entries from all the controls in the
   ' Transportation Planner form, preparing
   ' for a new record entry.

   optMode(0).Value = True
   txtCarrier.Text = ""
   txtTripNumber.Text = ""
   chkReserved.Value = 0
   chkPaid.Value = 0
   txtDate.Text = ""
   txtTime.Text = ""
   txtFrom.Text = ""
   txtTo.Text = ""
   txtNotes.Text = ""

   txtCarrier.SetFocus

End Sub   ' mnuClear_Click
```

```
Private Sub mnuExit_Click()

  ' The mnuExit_Click procedure ends the program
  ' performance when the user chooses the Exit
  ' command.

  ' Save the current record if a file is open.
  If tranFileOpen And recordChanged Then _
    SaveCurRec

  End

End Sub   ' mnuExit_Click


Private Sub mnuNext_Click()

  ' The mnuNext_Click procedure scrolls to the
  ' next transportation record in the current file.

  ' First save the current record if necessary.
  If recordChanged Then SaveCurRec

  ' If the current record is the end of the file,
  ' prepare to accept a new record from the user.
  If curTranRecord = FindRecordCount Then
    BlankEOFRecord

  ' Otherwise, read and display the next record.
  Else
    curTranRecord = curTranRecord + 1
    Get #1, curTranRecord, TranRecord
    ShowRecord
    recordChanged = False
  End If

    ' Display the file name and the record number.
  frmTranPlan.Caption = titleBarText & _
    ", #" & curTranRecord

    ' Enable Previous so the user can scroll back.
  mnuPrevious.Enabled = True

End Sub   ' mnuNext_Click


Private Sub mnuOpen_Click()

  ' The mnuOpen_Click procedure allows the user
  ' to open an existing TRV file from disk.

  ' If a file is already open, save the current record.
  If tranFileOpen And recordChanged Then SaveCurRec
  recordChanged = False
```

(continued)

(continued)

```
        ' Set the Flags property of the Open dialog box.
        cdlFileManager.Flags = cdlOFNFileMustExist Or _
                               cdlOFNHideReadOnly Or _
                               cdlOFNNoChangeDir Or _
                               cdlOFNPathMustExist

    ' Use the ShowOpen method to display the Open dialog box.
    ' ShowOpen generates an error if the user clicks Cancel.
    On Error GoTo userCancel
      cdlFileManager.ShowOpen
    On Error GoTo 0
    Close

    ' Record the file name that the user has entered.
    tranFileName = cdlFileManager.filename

    ' Prepare a new caption for the program's title bar.
    titleBarText = _
      "Transportation Planner - " & _
      tranFileName

    ' Open the file and switch tranFileOpen to true.
    Open tranFileName For Random As #1 _
      Len = Len(TranRecord)
    tranFileOpen = True

    ' Prepare to append a new record to the end of the file.
    BlankEOFRecord

    ' If the file contains more than one record, enable the
    ' Previous command so the user can scroll back.
    If curTranRecord > 1 Then _
      mnuPrevious.Enabled = True

    ' Display the new caption in the title bar.
    frmTranPlan.Caption = titleBarText & _
      ", #" & curTranRecord

' Terminate the procedure if the user clicks Cancel.
userCancel:
End Sub   ' mnuOpen_Click


Private Sub mnuPrevious_Click()

  ' The mnuPrevious_Click procedure scrolls one
  ' record back in the current file.

  ' First save the current record if necessary.
  If recordChanged Then SaveCurRec

  ' Decrease the value of the record pointer by 1, read
  ' the record, and display its fields in the form.
  curTranRecord = curTranRecord - 1
```

```
    Get #1, curTranRecord, TranRecord
    ShowRecord
    recordChanged = False

    ' Display the file name and the record number
    ' in the form's title bar.
    frmTranPlan.Caption = titleBarText & _
      ", #" & curTranRecord

    ' Enable the Next command.
    ' If the user has scrolled back to the first
    ' record in the file, disable the Previous command.
    mnuNext.Enabled = True
    If curTranRecord = 1 Then _
      mnuPrevious.Enabled = False

End Sub   ' mnuPrevious_Click


Private Sub mnuSaveAs_Click()

    ' The mnuSave_Click procedure takes control when the
    ' user chooses Save As. The user can create a new file.

    Dim newFileName As String

    ' Set the Flags property of the Save As dialog box.
    cdlFileManager.Flags = cdlOFNOverwritePrompt Or _
                           cdlOFNHideReadOnly Or _
                           cdlOFNNoChangeDir Or _
                           cdlOFNPathMustExist

    ' If the user clicks Cancel, the ShowSave method causes
    ' an error. In this case, exit from this procedure.
    On Error GoTo userCancel
      cdlFileManager.ShowSave
    On Error GoTo 0

    ' Record the file name that the user has entered.
    newFileName = cdlFileManager.filename

    ' If a file is currently open, save its final record
    ' and then copy its records to the new "save as" file.
    If tranFileOpen Then
      If recordChanged Then SaveCurRec
      Close
      CopyDatabase newFileName, tranFileName

    Else
    ' Otherwise, if no file is open, check to see if the
    ' new file currently exists already; if so, delete it.
      tranFileName = newFileName
      On Error Resume Next
        Kill tranFileName
      On Error GoTo 0
```

(continued)

(continued)

```
            ' Open the new file and save the current record.
            Open tranFileName For Random As #1 _
              Len = Len(TranRecord)
            If recordChanged Then
              SaveCurRec
              mnuNext.Enabled = True
            End If
        End If
        tranFileOpen = True
        recordChanged = False

        ' Display a new caption in the title bar.
        titleBarText = "Transportation Planner - " & _
          tranFileName
        frmTranPlan.Caption = titleBarText & _
          ", #" & curTranRecord

    ' Terminate the procedure if the user clicks Cancel.
    userCancel:
    End Sub   ' mnuSaveAs_Click


    Private Sub Form_Load()

        ' The Form_Load procedure initializes a few
        ' of the program's variables and control
        ' properties.

        ' No file is open yet.
        tranFileOpen = False
        recordChanged = False

        ' Set the record pointer to 1.
        curTranRecord = 1

        ' Disable the Next and Previous
        ' commands.
        mnuNext.Enabled = False
        mnuPrevious.Enabled = False

    End Sub   ' Form_Load

    Private Sub optMode_Click(Index As Integer)

        ' The optMode_Click procedure sets the properties
        ' of relevant controls whenever the user changes
        ' the selection in the optMode control array.

        ' Set the default property values for the
        ' program's three check box controls.
        chkRental.Enabled = False
        chkRental.Value = 0
        chkReserved.Enabled = True
        chkPaid.Enabled = True
```

```vb
       ' Enable the txtCarrier and txtTripNumber
       ' controls and their associated labels.
       lblTripNumber.Enabled = True
       txtTripNumber.Enabled = True
       txtCarrier.Enabled = True
       lblCarrier.Enabled = True

       ' Adjust the label captions according
       ' to the selected mode of transportion.
       Select Case Index
          Case 0
             lblCarrier.Caption = "Air&line"
             lblTripNumber.Caption = "Flight &#"

          Case 1
             lblCarrier.Caption = "Rail &line"
             lblTripNumber.Caption = "Train &#"

          Case 2
             lblCarrier.Caption = "Bus &line"
             lblTripNumber.Caption = "Route &#"

          ' If the user chooses the Car option,
          ' adjust the appropriate check boxes.
          Case 3
             lblCarrier.Caption = "Renta&l agency"
             lblTripNumber.Caption = "Reservation &#"
             chkRental.Enabled = True
             chkRental.Value = 1
             chkReserved_Click
             chkPaid.Enabled = False
       End Select

       ' Give the focus to the txtCarrier
       ' text box control.
       txtCarrier.SetFocus

End Sub    ' optMode_Click

Private Sub MakeTranRecord()

    ' The MakeTranRecord procedure copies the
    ' user's entries for the current transportation
    ' record to the TranRecord structure.
    ' Note that the TranRecType is defined in
    ' the TranPlan.Bas module, and TranRecord
    ' is declared in the general declarations section
    ' of this form.

    Dim i

    With TranRecord

       ' Determine which of the four optMode
       ' buttons is currently selected.
```

(continued)

(continued)

```
For i = 0 To 3
  If optMode(i).Value Then
    .TranMode = i
  End If
Next i

' If the selection is Car, read the
' value of the chkRental check box.
If .TranMode = 3 Then
  If chkRental.Value = 0 Then
    .RentalCar = False
  Else
    .RentalCar = True
  End If
End If

' Read the first two text boxes.
.Carrier = txtCarrier.Text
.TripNumber = txtTripNumber.Text

' Read the values of the Reserved
' and Paid check boxes.
If chkReserved.Value = 0 Then
  .ReservedStatus = False
Else
  .ReservedStatus = True
End If

If chkPaid.Value = 0 Then
  .PaidStatus = False
Else
  .PaidStatus = True
End If

' Read the remaining text boxes.
.TripDate = txtDate.Text
.TripTime = txtTime.Text
.TripFrom = txtFrom.Text
.TripTo = txtTo.Text

.Comments = txtNotes.Text

End With

End Sub  ' MakeTranRecord

Private Function FindRecordCount()

  ' The FindRecordCount function determines
  ' the number of records in the current
  ' transportation file. Note that this
  ' function is called only if a file is open.
```

```vb
    FindRecordCount = LOF(1) / Len(TranRecord)
End Function  ' FindRecordCount
Private Sub ShowRecord()

    ' The ShowRecord procedure displays the fields
    ' of the current record in an open file. Before
    ' calling this procedure, the program always
    ' reads a record from the open file into the
    ' TranRecord structure.

    With TranRecord

        ' Set the transportation selection.
        optMode(.TranMode).Value = True

        ' If the Car option is selected,
        ' set the value of the Rental check box.
        If .TranMode = 3 Then
          If .RentalCar Then
            chkRental.Value = 1
          Else
            chkRental.Value = 0
          End If
        End If

        ' Read the remaining fields and
        ' set the corresponding controls
        ' appropriately.
        txtCarrier.Text = Trim(.Carrier)
        txtTripNumber.Text = Trim(.TripNumber)

        If .ReservedStatus Then
          chkReserved.Value = 1
        Else
          chkReserved.Value = 0
        End If

        If .PaidStatus Then
          chkPaid.Value = 1
        Else
          chkPaid.Value = 0
        End If

        txtDate.Text = Trim(.TripDate)
        txtTime.Text = Trim(.TripTime)
        txtFrom.Text = Trim(.TripFrom)
        txtTo.Text = Trim(.TripTo)

        txtNotes.Text = Trim(.Comments)

    End With

End Sub  ' ShowRecord
```

(continued)

(continued)

```vb
Private Sub txtCarrier_Change()

    ' The txtCarrier_Change procedure sets
    ' recordChanged to True if the user enters
    ' new text into this text box control.

    ChangedStatus

End Sub    ' txtCarrier_Change


Private Sub txtDate_Change()

    ' The txtDate_Change procedure sets
    ' recordChanged to True if the user enters
    ' new text into this text box control.

    ChangedStatus

End Sub    ' txtDate_Change


Private Sub txtFrom_Change()

    ' The txtFrom_Change procedure sets
    ' recordChanged to True if the user enters
    ' new text into this text box control.

    ChangedStatus

End Sub    ' txtFrom_Change


Private Sub txtNotes_Change()

    ' The txtNotes_Change procedure sets
    ' recordChanged to True if the user enters
    ' new text into this text box control.

    ChangedStatus

End Sub    ' txtNotes_Change


Private Sub txtTime_Change()

    ' The txtTime_Change procedure sets
    ' recordChanged to True if the user enters
    ' new text into this text box control.

    ChangedStatus

End Sub    ' txtTime_Change
```

```
Private Sub txtTo_Change()

  ' The txtTo_Change procedure set
  ' recordChanged to True if the user enters
  ' new text into this text box control.

  ChangedStatus

End Sub   ' txtTo_Change


Private Sub txtTripNumber_Change()

  ' The txtCarrier_Change procedure sets
  ' recordChanged to True if the user enters
  ' new text into this text box control.

  ChangedStatus

End Sub   ' txtTripNumber_Change


Private Sub PrintRecord()
  ' The PrintRecord procedure prints the current record.
  Const t1 = 5   ' First tab stop.
  Const t2 = 15  ' Second tab stop.

  With TranRecord
    Select Case .TranMode ' Print the transportation mode.
      Case 0
        Printer.Print "Airline";
      Case 1
        Printer.Print "Train Line";
      Case 2
        Printer.Print "Bus Line";
      Case 3
        If .RentalCar Then
          Printer.Print "Car Rental Agency";
        Else
          Printer.Print "Private Car"
        End If
    End Select

    ' Print the remaining fields.
    If .TranMode < 3 Then
      Printer.Print " - "; .Carrier
      Printer.Print Tab(t1); " #"; .TripNumber
    Else
      If .RentalCar Then
        Printer.Print " - "; .Carrier;
        If .ReservedStatus Then
          Printer.Print Tab(t1); " #"; .TripNumber
        Else
          Printer.Print
```

(continued)

(continued)

```
        End If
      End If
    End If
    Printer.Print
    Printer.Print Tab(t1); "Date:";
    Printer.Print Tab(t2); .TripDate
    Printer.Print Tab(t1); "Time:";
    Printer.Print Tab(t2); .TripTime
    Printer.Print Tab(t1); "From:";
    Printer.Print Tab(t2); .TripFrom
    Printer.Print Tab(t1); "To:";
    Printer.Print Tab(t2); .TripTo
    Printer.Print
    If .TranMode < 3 Then
      Printer.Print Tab(t1); "Reserved:";
      Printer.Print Tab(t2); YesNo(.ReservedStatus)
      Printer.Print Tab(t1); "Paid:";
      Printer.Print Tab(t2); YesNo(.PaidStatus)
    End If
    Printer.Print
    Printer.Print Tab(t1); "Comments:"
    PrintComments (RTrim(.Comments))
    Printer.Print
    Printer.Print
  End With
End Sub  ' PrintRecord
```

The Travel Reminders Program

Chapter 13

The Travel Reminders program (Reminder.Vbp) helps you organize the travel-related tasks that you need to accomplish before, during, and after a business trip. As shown in Figure A-23, the program displays three check lists of travel reminders in which you can keep track of the tasks you've completed and the ones that still remain to be done. In this multiple-document interface, all three travel lists are displayed as document windows inside the containing application window.

When you run the program for the first time, the travel lists are empty. To begin developing the reminders for a list, click any one of the numbered command buttons inside a list window. In response, the program opens the dialog box shown in Figure A-24. Enter the brief text of a particular reminder and click OK. The reminder becomes part of the current list. You need to develop the lists of reminders only once; the program stores them on disk (in files named Before.Txt, During.Txt, and After.Txt), along with the current setting of each check box.

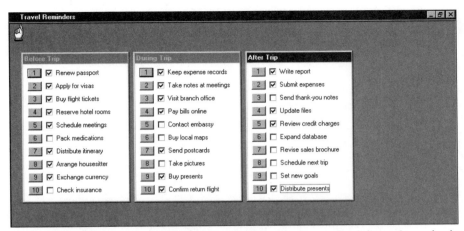

Figure A-23: The Travel Reminders program displays three check lists of travel-related tasks that you intend to complete before, during, and after a business trip.

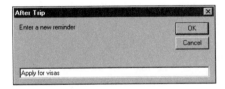

Figure A-24: You can develop or revise the reminder lists themselves during any run of the program. The application saves your lists on disk in three different text files.

The program contains a variety of files, as shown in Figure A-25. Reminder.Frm is the basis for the check list windows, and ReminMDI.Frm is the containing application window. In addition, the program includes a class module stored as Reminder.Cls. All three of these files contain code.

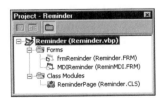

Figure A-25: The program's class module and two form modules all contain code.

The Travel Reminders Program — ReminMDI.Frm

```
' The Travel Reminders Program.
'
'
' Project File:   Reminder.VBP
' MDI Form File:  ReminMDI.FRM (MDIReminder)
' Form File:      Reminder.FRM (frmReminder)
' Class File:     Reminder.CLS (ReminderPage)

' This program illustrates the use of classes, collections,
' property procedures, and other object-related features.
' The program creates three instances of the ReminderPage
' class, which in turn display three instances of the
' frmReminder form inside the containing MDI form. Each
' of these "pages" displays a check list of travel
' reminders — tasks that need to be accomplished before,
' during, and after a business trip. The text of these
' lists is stored in three text files, Before.Txt,
' During.Txt, and After.Txt. The user may develop and
' revise these lists during any program run. Upon
' termination, the program saves the current lists back
' to the same three text files.

Option Explicit

' Create a module-level collection object
' to represent the three ReminderPage objects.
Dim colReminderPages As New Collection
'
' End of general declarations, MDIReminder.

Private Sub MDIForm_DblClick()

    ' The MDIForm_DblClick procedure responds to a double-
    ' click on the pointing-hand icon (or elsewhere inside
    ' the MDI form). This is the user's signal to change
    ' the order of the reminder lists — to an alphabetic
    ' sort, or back to the original order.

    ' Create a generic object variable.
    Dim Reminder As Object

    ' Loop through the ReminderPage objects in
    ' the colReminderPages collection.
    For Each Reminder In colReminderPages

        ' For each object in the collection,
        ' switch the Sorted property to its
        ' opposite value.
        With Reminder

            ' This change in the Sorted property
            ' triggers calls to both the Get Sorted
```

```
        ' and Let Sorted property procedures in
        ' each ReminderPage class object.
        .Sorted = Not .Sorted
      End With
   Next Reminder

End Sub    ' MDIForm_DblClick


Private Sub MDIForm_Load()

   ' The MDIForm_Load procedure creates an instance of the
   ' ReminderPage class for each of the three lists, and
   ' displays the corresponding reminder lists as windows
   ' inside the MDI form.

   ' Declare a variable to represent each new
   ' instance of the class.
   Dim Before As New ReminderPage
   Dim During As New ReminderPage
   Dim After As New ReminderPage

   ' Assign values to the properties of each new object,
   ' and call the ShowPage method to display the
   ' corresponding list.
   With Before
      .TitleBar = "Before Trip"
      .ListFileName = "\Before.TXT"
      .XPos = 300
      .YPos = 800
      .ShowPage
   End With

   With During
      .TitleBar = "During Trip"
      .ListFileName = "\During.TXT"
      .XPos = 3300
      .YPos = 800
      .ShowPage
   End With

   With After
      .TitleBar = "After Trip"
      .ListFileName = "\After.TXT"
      .XPos = 6300
      .YPos = 800
      .ShowPage
   End With

   ' Add the three objects to the module-level
   ' colReminderPages collection, which represents
   ' the objects for the duration of the program.
   colReminderPages.Add Before
```

(continued)

(continued)

```
    colReminderPages.Add During
    colReminderPages.Add After

End Sub   ' MDIForm_Load


Private Sub MDIForm_QueryUnload(Cancel As Integer, _
   UnloadMode As Integer)

   ' The MDIForm_QueryUnload procedure
   ' releases the colReminderPages collection
   ' from memory, triggering a call to the
   ' Class_Terminate event procedure on each
   ' of the instances of the ReminderPage class.

   ' Note: The QueryUnload procedure is used
   ' (instead of Unload) to perform this
   ' termination task before the forms are
   ' actually closed. The program performance
   ' ends after the MDI form is closed.

   Set colReminderPages = Nothing

End Sub   ' MDIForm_QueryUnload
```

The Travel Reminders Program — Reminder.Frm

```
' The Travel Reminders Program.
'
'
' Form File: Reminder.FRM
'
' Note: An instance of this form is created as
' part of each instance of the ReminderPage
' class. The form contains one event procedure
' Each instance of the form contains this procedure.
'


Private Sub cmdChange_Click(Index As Integer)

   ' The cmdChange_Click procedure is called when
   ' the user clicks any of the array of command
   ' buttons displayed just to the left of the
   ' reminder check boxes. This procedure gives
   ' the user the opportunity to change the text
   ' of any reminder in the list.

   Dim newStr As String

   ' Elicit a new text entry for the current
   ' reminder.
   newStr = InputBox("Enter a new reminder", Me.Caption)
```

```
' If the user's input is not blank, assign
' the new string entry to the Caption
' property of the current check box. (Note
' that a click of the Cancel button on the
' input box results in a empty string; in
' this case, the program does not change
' the Caption property.)
If Trim(newStr) <> "" Then _
   chkReminder(Index).Caption = newStr

End Sub  ' cmdChange_Click
```

The Travel Reminders Program — Reminder.Cls

```
' The Travel Reminders Program.
'
' Class Module: ReminderPage (Reminder.Cls)
'
' This class module contains the methods and properties for
' a reminder page object. A program creates instances of
' this class and assigns property values to each instance.
Option Explicit
Const ListLength = 9

' Create a new instance of the frmReminder form.
Dim newPage As New frmReminder

' Declare the variables to represent properties.
Public TitleBar As String      ' The window title.
Public ListFileName As String  ' The text file name.
Public XPos As Integer         ' The position
Public YPos As Integer         ' coordinates.
Dim isSorted As Boolean

' Define an array of records to represent reminder items.
Private Type curItemType
  remindText As String
  remindStatus As Byte
  originalOrder As Byte
End Type
Dim curList(ListLength) As curItemType
'
' End of general declarations, for the ReminderPage class.


Private Sub DisplayNewOrder()

  ' The DisplayNewOrder procedure redisplays
  ' the list of reminders after the curList
  ' array has been sorted, either alphabetically
  ' or by the originalOrder field.

  Dim i
```

(continued)

```
    For i = 0 To ListLength
      With newPage.chkReminder(i)

        ' Assign the fields of the curList
        ' array to the Caption and Value
        ' properties of each check box.
        .Caption = curList(i).remindText
        .Value = curList(i).remindStatus
      End With
    Next i

End Sub   ' DisplayNewOrder

Private Sub ReadData(inFile As String)

  ' The ReadData procedure reads the original reminder list
  ' from the Txt file named by the ListFileName property.
  Dim i, reminderTxt As String, checkStatus As Byte

  ' Open and read the file if it exists.
  On Error GoTo fileProblem
    Open inFile For Input As #1

    ' Read the file line by line.
    For i = 0 To ListLength
      Input #1, reminderTxt, checkStatus
      With newPage.chkReminder(i)
        .Caption = reminderTxt
        .Value = checkStatus
      End With
    Next i

  On Error GoTo 0

' In the event of a file error, control arrives here.
fileProblem:
  Close #1
  For i = 0 To ListLength
    ' Display an integer value on each cmdChange button.
    newPage.cmdChange(i).Caption = i + 1
  Next i
End Sub   ' ReadData


Private Sub RecordCurOrder(saveOrderField)

  ' The RecordCurOrder procedure is called just before the
  ' program sorts a list of reminders. This procedure
  ' records the previous order so that this order can be
  ' restored if the user requests. If the list is currently
  ' in alphabetical order, this procedure should not change
  ' the values of the originalOrder field. The program
  ' therefore sends a value of False to the saveOrderField
  ' argument to signal that this is the case.
  Dim i
```

```
' Assign the current values of the Caption and Value
' properties to the remindText and remindStatus fields.
For i = 0 To ListLength
  With newPage.chkReminder(i)
    curList(i).remindText = .Caption
    curList(i).remindStatus = .Value
  End With

  ' If the list is currently in its original
  ' order (saveOrderField is True), assign
  ' the ordinal values to the originalOrder
  ' field in the curList array.
  If saveOrderField Then _
    curList(i).originalOrder = i
Next i

End Sub   ' RecordCurOrder

Private Sub SaveReminders()

  ' The SaveReminders procedure saves the current
  ' reminder list as a TXT file on disk. This
  ' action takes place once for each list, at
  ' the end of a program run.

  Dim i

  With newPage

    ' The correct file name for each list is
    ' passed to the ReminderPage object as the
    ' value of the ListFileName property.
    Open ListFileName For Output As #1
      For i = 0 To ListLength

        ' Save the text of the reminder
        ' and the current check-box status
        ' (checked or not checked).
        Write #1, _
          .chkReminder(i).Caption; _
          .chkReminder(i).Value
      Next i
    Close #1
  End With

End Sub   ' SaveReminders

Sub ShowPage()

  ' The ShowPage procedure prepares a page of
  ' reminders and displays the corresponding
  ' window on the screen.

  ' Read the text file and copy its contents
  ' to the array of check boxes on the newPage
```

(continued)

(continued)

```vb
' form.
ReadData ListFileName

' Display the title as the caption on the
' form's title bar.
newPage.Caption = TitleBar

' Assign the position properties.
newPage.Top = YPos
newPage.Left = XPos

' Display the form object on the screen.
newPage.Show

End Sub    ' ShowPage


Property Get Sorted() As Boolean

' The Property Get Sorted procedure returns
' the current value of the Sorted property.

Sorted = isSorted

End Property   ' Property Get Sorted

Property Let Sorted(alphabetic As Boolean)

' The Let Sorted property procedure rearranges
' a reminder list. This procedure is called in
' response to a change in the value of the
' Sorted property.

' The alphabetic argument indicates whether
' the reminder list is to be alphabetized (True)
' or restored to its original order (False).
RecordCurOrder alphabetic
SortList alphabetic

' After the sort, copy the array of reminders
' back to the array of check boxes.
DisplayNewOrder
isSorted = alphabetic

End Property    ' Sorted (PropertyLet)

Private Sub SortList(byReminders As Boolean)
   ' The SortList procedure rearranges a list of reminders.
   ' If byReminders is true, the procedure alphabetizes the
   ' list; if false, the list returns to its original order.
   Dim i, j
   Dim tempItem As curItemType
   ' Use a bubble sort to arrange the list alphabetically
   ' or to its original order.
```

```
        For i = 0 To ListLength - 1
          For j = i + 1 To ListLength
            If byReminders Then
              If curList(i).remindText > _
                curList(j).remindText Then
                  tempItem = curList(i)
                  curList(i) = curList(j)
                  curList(j) = tempItem
              End If
            Else
              If curList(i).originalOrder > _
                curList(j).originalOrder Then
                  tempItem = curList(i)
                  curList(i) = curList(j)
                  curList(j) = tempItem
              End If
            End If
          Next j
        Next i
End Sub  ' SortList


Private Sub Class_Terminate()

   ' The Class_Terminate event procedure takes
   ' place just before the class object is released
   ' from memory.

   ' Always save the reminder lists in their
   ' original (not alphabetized) orders. If
   ' a list is currently alphabetized, restore
   ' its order before terminating.
   If Me.Sorted Then Me.Sorted = False

   ' Save the current text and status of each
   ' reminder list back to disk. This is the
   ' program's final action.
   SaveReminders

End Sub   ' Class_Terminate
```

The Transportation Planner, MDI Version

Chapter 14

The MDI version of the Transportation Planner program (TranMDI.Vbp) allows you to view as many as five open travel files at once. As in the original Transportation Planner application (Chapter 12), each travel file contains individual records describing the transportation details of a business trip. In the MDI version, you can open multiple files as separate documents inside the application window, shown in Figure A-26. This arrangement allows you to compare the travel details of different trips, and even to copy information from one file to another.

The application window displays a menu bar and a toolbar representing the various operations you can perform. As you can see in Figure A-27, the toolbar contains five buttons, identified by their individual functions: New Trip Window, Open Trip File, Save Trip File, Scroll Back, and Scroll Forward.

As shown in Figure A-28, the application contains two forms, the *parent* MDI form and the *child* form. Both of these contain code.

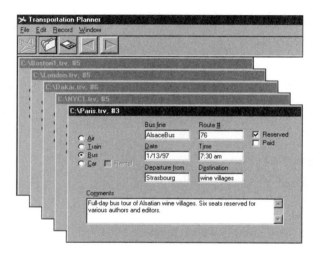

Figure A-26: The MDI version of the Transportation Planner program allows you to open as many as five travel files at once. Each file appears as a document window inside the application window.

Figure A-27: The application window includes a toolbar with five buttons representing the program's main operations.

Figure A-28: The project includes two forms, a parent MDI form and a child form. Both modules contain code.

The Transportation Planner, MDI — TranMDIp.Frm

```
' The Transportation Planner, MDI version.
'
'
' Files:
'
' Project File:     TranMDI.VBP
' MDI Parent Form:  TranMDIp.FRM (this file)
```

```
' MDI Child Form:   TranMDIc.FRM
'
' This MDI version of the Transportation Planner
' program allows the user to open as many as five
' itinerary files at once, and view them within
' the environment of a contining window. The MDI
' window includes a menu bar and a Toolbar designed
' to simplify the program's various operations.
' There is also a Windows menu that lists the
' names of the open files and offers the
' opportunity of displaying them in cascade or
' tiled arrangements.

Option Explicit

' The maximum number of open files.
Const MaxTrips = 5

' The number of the active file.
Dim tripNum As Integer
'
' End of general declarations, TranMDIp.FRM.


Function IsAlreadyOpen(testFileName As String) As Boolean

    ' The IsAlreadyOpen function determines whether
    ' a file that the user has requested is already
    ' open. (If it is, the program avoids the attempt
    ' to open it a second time.)

    Dim i

    ' Start out assuming the file is not open.
    IsAlreadyOpen = False

    ' Loop through the open forms, not including
    ' the MDI parent form. Use Visual Basic's
    ' Forms collection to identify each form in
    ' turn. (The Count property tells how many
    ' forms are currently open.)
    For i = 1 To Forms.Count - 1
      With Forms(i)

        ' If the user has entered a file name
        ' that matches one of the open files,
        ' the function returns a value of True.
        If Trim(.tranFileName) = Trim(testFileName) _
          Then IsAlreadyOpen = True
      End With
    Next i

End Function   ' IsAlreadyOpen
```

(continued)

(continued)

```
Public Sub SaveAllFiles()

    ' The SaveAllFiles procedure is called just
    ' before the end of the program performance
    ' to ensure that any unsaved travel records
    ' are written to disk before the forms are closed.
    Dim i

    ' Loop through the open forms (except the
    ' MDI parent form), using the Forms collection.
    For i = 1 To Forms.Count - 1
        With Forms(i)

            ' If a given form displays an open file
            ' and if the current record has changed
            ' then the record needs to be written to
            ' disk before the program ends.
            If .tranFileOpen And .recordChanged Then _
                .SaveCurRec
        End With
    Next i

    ' Terminate the program performance only
    ' after making sure all records have been
    ' saved.
    End

End Sub   ' SaveAllFiles


Private Sub cmdNew_Click()

    ' The cmdNew_Click procedure responds to a
    ' click of the New button on the program's
    ' toolbar. The procedure makes a call to
    ' NewTranChild to create a new instance of
    ' the frmTranPlan form. Note that the
    ' cmdNew button is removed from the toolbar
    ' once the maximum number of forms has been
    ' created.

    NewTranChild

End Sub   ' cmdNew_Click


Private Sub cmdNext_Click()

    ' The cmdNext_Click procedure responds to a
    ' click of the Next button on the program's
    ' toolbar. The program uses the ActiveForm
    ' property to identify the current form, and
    ' makes a call to the form's mnuNext_Click
    ' procedure if the menu command is currently
    ' available.
```

```
    If ActiveForm.mnuNext.Enabled Then _
      ActiveForm.mnuNext_Click

End Sub   ' cmdNext_Click

Private Sub cmdOpen_Click()

    ' The cmdOpen_Click procedure makes a call to
    ' the mnuOpen_Click procedure on the active
    ' form, allowing the user to open a new
    ' travel file.

    ActiveForm.mnuOpen_Click

End Sub   ' cmdOpen_Click


Private Sub cmdPrevious_Click()

    ' The cmdPrevious_Click procedure responds to a
    ' click of the Previous button on the program's
    ' toolbar. The program uses the ActiveForm
    ' property to identify the current form, and
    ' makes a call to the form's mnuPrevious_Click
    ' procedure if the menu command is currently
    ' available.

    If ActiveForm.mnuPrevious.Enabled Then _
      ActiveForm.mnuPrevious_Click

End Sub   ' cmdPrevious_Click

Private Sub cmdSaveAs_Click()

    ' The cmdSaveAs_Click procedure makes a call to
    ' the mnuSaveAs_Click procedure on the active
    ' form, allowing the user to save the current
    ' travel file under a new name.

    ActiveForm.mnuSaveAs_Click

End Sub   ' cmdSaveAs_Click

Private Sub MDIForm_Load()

    ' The MDIForm_Load procedure initializes the
    ' tripNum variable to 1 (the first travel file
    ' to be created), and then makes a call to the
    ' NewTranChild procedure to open the first
    ' travel form.

    tripNum = 1
    NewTranChild

End Sub   ' MDIForm_Load
```

(continued)

(continued)

```vb
Sub NewTranChild()
  ' The NewTranChild procedure creates a new instance of
  ' the frmTranPlan form and displays it in the parent form.
  Dim i

  If tripNum <= MaxTrips Then
    Dim newTranPlan As New frmTranPlan

    ' Display a title and record it in the Tag property.
    newTranPlan.Caption = "Trip" & tripNum
    newTranPlan.Tag = newTranPlan.Caption

    ' Assign a unique file number to the new form.
    newTranPlan.fileNumber = tripNum

    ' Display the form and increment the tripNum counter.
    newTranPlan.Show
    tripNum = tripNum + 1
    Me.Arrange 0

    ' Disable the New command if MaxTrips has been reached.
    If tripNum > MaxTrips Then
      For i = 1 To Forms.Count - 1
        Forms(i).mnuNew.Enabled = False
      Next i
      cmdNew.Enabled = False
    End If
  End If
End Sub   ' NewTranChild

Private Sub MDIForm_QueryUnload(Cancel As Integer, _
  UnloadMode As Integer)

  ' The MDIForm_QueryUnload procedure ensures
  ' that all unsaved records are written to
  ' their respective disk files before the program
  ' run is terminated. This event procedure is
  ' triggered if the user ends the program by
  ' clicking the close button at the upper-right
  ' corner of the MDI form.

  SaveAllFiles

End Sub   ' MDIForm_QueryUnload


Private Sub picToolbar_Click()

  ' The picToolbar_Click procedure returns the
  ' focus to the active child form if the user
  ' clicks a background area of the toolbar.

  ActiveForm.SetFocus

End Sub   ' picToolbar_Click
```

The Transportation Planner, MDI — TranMDIc.Frm

```
' The Transportation Planner, MDI version.
'
' Project File:      TranMDI.VBP
' MDI Parent Form:   TranMDIp.FRM
' MDI Child Form:    TranMDIc.FRM (this file)
'
' This menu-driven program allows the user to manage travel
' files. Each random-access file contains records for the
' transportation plans of an upcoming business trip. Files
' are stored on disk with TRV extension names. The user
' can open a file, brows through records, and revise or
' add information.
Option Explicit
Const CopyFileNum = 6 ' Temporary file number for Save As.

' The structure of transportation records.
Private Type TranRecType
  TranMode As Integer
  RentalCar As Boolean
  Carrier As String * 30
  TripNumber As String * 30
  ReservedStatus As Boolean
  PaidStatus As Boolean
  TripDate As String * 30
  TripTime As String * 30
  TripFrom As String * 30
  TripTo As String * 30
  Comments As String * 200
End Type

' The file number for this instance of the form.
Public fileNumber As Integer

' Variables for this form.
Dim TranRecord As TranRecType ' A single record.
Dim curTranRecord As Integer  ' Current record number.

' Public variables for this form.
' (The parent form needs access to these.)
Public tranFileOpen As Boolean    ' Is a file open?
Public tranFileName As String     ' Name of open file.
Public recordChanged As Boolean   ' Has record changed?
'
' End of general declarations, frmTranPlan.


Private Sub BlankEOFRecord()

   ' This procedure moves the record pointer
   ' one position past the end of the current
   ' file, in preparation for a new record entry.
```

(continued)

(continued)

```
    curTranRecord = FindRecordCount + 1
    mnuClear_Click
    recordChanged = False

    ' Disable the Next command until the
    ' user makes an entry into this new record.
    mnuNext.Enabled = False

End Sub   ' BlankEOFRecord

Private Sub ChangedStatus()

    ' The ChangedStatus procedure sets the
    ' recordChanged variable and, if appropriate,
    ' enables the Next command, in response to
    ' a change in the contents of one of the
    ' program's text boxes.

    recordChanged = True
    If tranFileOpen Then mnuNext.Enabled = True

End Sub   ' ChangedStatus

Private Sub CopyDatabase _
    (toFile As String, fromFile As String)

    ' The CopyDatabase procedure copies the records
    ' of the current transportation file to a new
    ' file, in response to the user's instructions
    ' in the Save As command.

    Dim i As Long

    ' If the destination file already exists,
    ' delete it from disk. (Note that the Save As
    ' dialog box provides a warning if the user
    ' chooses an existing file; the Save As
    ' operation continues only if the user confirms.)
    On Error Resume Next
      Kill toFile
    On Error GoTo 0

    ' Open the two files, using the assigned
    ' file number for the current instance of the
    ' child form (fileNumber) and the temporary
    ' file number defined for this operation
    ' (CopyFileNum).
    Open toFile For Random As #fileNumber _
      Len = Len(TranRecord)
    Open fromFile For Random As #CopyFileNum _
      Len = Len(TranRecord)

    ' Copy all the records from the source file
    ' to the destination file.
```

```vb
      For i = 1 To LOF(CopyFileNum) / Len(TranRecord)
        Get #CopyFileNum, i, TranRecord
        Put #fileNumber, i, TranRecord
      Next i

      ' Close the source file. The destination
      ' file becomes the current tranporation
      ' database.
      Close #CopyFileNum
      tranFileName = toFile

End Sub   ' CopyDatabase

Private Sub PrintComments(noteStr As String)

      ' The PrintComments procedure arranges to
      ' print the Comments field of any record
      ' in a sequence of approximately 40-character
      ' lines, without breaking any words in the text.

      Const lineLen = 40    ' Line length.
      Const t1 = 5          ' Tab stop.

      Dim curPos As Integer
      Dim curLine As String
      Dim curChar As String

      ' Divide the text into 40-character lines.
      Do While Len(noteStr) > lineLen
        curPos = lineLen

        ' Break each line after a word.
        Do
          curChar = Mid(noteStr, curPos, 1)
          curPos = curPos - 1
        Loop Until curChar = " "

        ' Print the current line.
        Printer.Print Tab(t1); _
          Left(noteStr, curPos)

        ' Reduce the string by the line
        ' that has just been printed.
        noteStr = Mid(noteStr, curPos + 2)
      Loop

      ' Print the final line of the text.
      Printer.Print Tab(t1); noteStr

End Sub   ' PrintComments

Public Sub SaveCurRec()
```

(continued)

(continued)

```vb
    ' The SaveCurRec procedure writes the current
    ' transportation record to its correct position
    ' in the open file of the active child form.

    ' Copy the user's input to the
    ' TranRecord structure.
    MakeTranRecord

    ' Write the record to the file. The variable
    ' curTranRecord keeps track of the current
    ' record position. The variable fileNumber
    ' represents the open file for the active
    ' child form.
    Put #fileNumber, curTranRecord, TranRecord
    recordChanged = False

End Sub   ' SaveCurRec


Private Function YesNo(which As Boolean) As String

    ' The YesNo function converts a Boolean value
    ' into a string value of "Yes" or "No." This
    ' conversion is used in the process of printing
    ' transportation records.

    If which Then
      YesNo = "Yes"
    Else
      YesNo = "No"
    End If

End Function   ' YesNo


Private Sub chkPaid_Click()

    ' The chkPaid_Click procedure changes the
    ' Boolean value of the recordChanged variable
    ' if the user changes the status of the Paid
    ' check box.

    recordChanged = True

End Sub   ' chkPaid_Click


Private Sub mnuClose_Click()

    ' The mnuClose_Click procedure closes the travel file in
    ' the current child form when the user chooses Close.

    ' If a file is open, save its current record if
    ' necessary. Then close the file.
```

```
            If tranFileOpen And recordChanged Then SaveCurRec
            If tranFileOpen Then Close #fileNumber

            ' Clear entries from the form and initialize variables.
            tranFileName = ""
            tranFileOpen = False
            mnuClear_Click
            recordChanged = False
            curTranRecord = 1

            ' Disable the Previous and Next commands.
            mnuPrevious.Enabled = False
            mnuNext.Enabled = False

            ' Display a new caption in the title bar.
            ' (Note that the parent form stores the
            ' generic title for the form in the
            ' Tag property at the time the child form
            ' is first created.)
            Caption = Tag

End Sub   ' mnuClose_Click

Private Sub mnuCascade_Click()

      ' The mnuCascade_Click procedure rearranges
      ' the open child forms on the MDI form when
      ' the user chooses the Cascade command in
      ' the Window menu.

      frmTranParent.Arrange 0

End Sub   ' mnuCascade_Click

Private Sub mnuNew_Click()

      ' The mnuNew_Click procedure makes a call
      ' to the NewTranChild procedure in the parent
      ' form when the user chooses the New command
      ' from the File menu.

      frmTranParent.NewTranChild

End Sub   ' mnuNew_Click

Private Sub mnuPrint_Click()

      ' The mnuPrint_Click procedure prints one or
      ' more transportation records when the user
      ' chooses the Print command.

      Dim i As Long

      ' If a file is open, print all the records
      ' in the file, from beginning to end.
      If tranFileOpen Then
```

(continued)

(continued)

```
      ' Begin by saving the current record to
      ' the file if necessary.
      If recordChanged Then SaveCurRec
      recordChanged = False

      ' Print each record in turn. The variable
      ' fileNumber identifies the open file
      ' in the active child form.
      For i = 1 To FindRecordCount
        Get #fileNumber, i, TranRecord
        PrintRecord
      Next i

    ' If no file is open, just print the
    ' current contents of the form.
    Else
      MakeTranRecord
      PrintRecord
    End If

    ' Complete the output process.
    Printer.EndDoc

End Sub    ' mnuPrint_Click

Private Sub Form_KeyDown(KeyCode As Integer, _
  Shift As Integer)

    ' The Form_KeyDown procedure allows the user
    ' to press PgDn or PgUp to scroll through the
    ' records of an open transportation file.

    ' *** Note that the child form's KeyPreview
    '       property is set to True to make this
    '       event possible.

    ' Code numbers for the
    ' PgDn and PgUp keys.
    Const PgDn = 34
    Const PgUp = 33

    ' If the user presses PgDn and the Next
    ' command is currently enabled, force a call
    ' to the mnuNext_Click event procedure.
    If KeyCode = PgDn _
      And mnuNext.Enabled = True _
        Then mnuNext_Click

    ' If the user presses PgUp and the Previous
    ' command is currently enabled, force a call
    ' to the mnuPrevious_Click event procedure.
    If KeyCode = PgUp _
      And mnuPrevious.Enabled = True _
        Then mnuPrevious_Click
```

```
End Sub   ' Form_KeyDown
Private Sub chkRental_Click()

   ' The chkRental_Click procedure adjusts
   ' the Enabled properties of several controls,
   ' depending on the value of the chkRental
   ' check box. (If the car option is selected,
   ' the Rental box indicates whether the
   ' car is a rental or a private vehicle.)

   ' If chkRental is checked, enable the
   ' text boxes for the rental agency (txtCarrier)
   ' and the reservation number (txtTripNumber).
   ' Also enable the chkReserved check box, which
   ' indicates whether a reservation has been made.

   If optMode(3).Value Then
     If chkRental.Value = 1 Then
       txtCarrier.Enabled = True
       lblCarrier.Enabled = True
       txtTripNumber.Enabled = True
       lblTripNumber.Enabled = True
       chkReserved.Enabled = True
       chkReserved_Click

     ' If chkRental is unchecked, disable
     ' all these controls.
     Else
       txtCarrier.Enabled = False
       lblCarrier.Enabled = False
       txtTripNumber.Enabled = False
       lblTripNumber.Enabled = False
       chkReserved.Value = 0
       chkReserved.Enabled = False
     End If

     recordChanged = True
   End If

End Sub   ' chkRental_Click


Private Sub chkReserved_Click()

   ' The chkReserved_Click procedure enables or
   ' disables the "Reservation #" text box
   ' (txtTripNumber), depending on the value of
   ' the chkReserved check box. This action
   ' occurs only if the current transporation
   ' selection is "Car."

   If optMode(3).Value Then
     If chkReserved.Value = 0 Then
       txtTripNumber.Enabled = False
       lblTripNumber.Enabled = False
     Else
```

(continued)

(continued)

```
        txtTripNumber.Enabled = True
        lblTripNumber.Enabled = True
    End If
  End If

  recordChanged = True

End Sub   ' chkReserved_Click


Private Sub mnuClear_Click()

  ' The mnuClear_Click procedure clears the
  ' entries from all the controls in the
  ' Transportation Planner form, preparing
  ' for a new record entry.

  optMode(0).Value = True
  txtCarrier.Text = ""
  txtTripNumber.Text = ""
  chkReserved.Value = 0
  chkPaid.Value = 0
  txtDate.Text = ""
  txtTime.Text = ""
  txtFrom.Text = ""
  txtTo.Text = ""
  txtNotes.Text = ""

  txtCarrier.SetFocus

End Sub   ' mnuClear_Click

Private Sub mnuExit_Click()

  ' The mnuExit_Click procedure makes a call
  ' to the SaveAllFiles procedure in the parent
  ' form when the user chooses the Exit command
  ' from the File menu. SaveAllFiles ensures
  ' that all unsaved records are written to
  ' their respective files before the program
  ' run is terminated.

  frmTranParent.SaveAllFiles

End Sub   ' mnuExit_Click


Public Sub mnuNext_Click()

  ' The mnuNext_Click procedure scrolls to the
  ' next transportation record in the current file.
  ' (The Next command is disabled if no file is open;
```

```
' it is also unavailable if the record pointer is
' past the end of the file.)

' First save the current record
' if necessary.
If recordChanged Then SaveCurRec

' If the current record is the end of
' the file, prepare to accept a new
' record from the user.
If curTranRecord = FindRecordCount Then
  BlankEOFRecord

' Otherwise, read and display the
' next record in the file. The variable
' fileNumber represents the open file
' on the current child form.
Else
  curTranRecord = curTranRecord + 1
  Get #fileNumber, curTranRecord, TranRecord
  ShowRecord
  recordChanged = False
End If

  ' Display the file name and the record
  ' number in the child form's title bar.
Caption = tranFileName & ", #" _
    & curTranRecord

  ' Enable the Previous command, so the user
  ' can now scroll backward through the file.
mnuPrevious.Enabled = True

End Sub   ' mnuNext_Click


Public Sub mnuOpen_Click()

  ' The mnuOpen_Click procedure allows the user
  ' to open an existing TRV file from disk. Once
  ' the file is open, the user can browse through
  ' its records, revise any record, or add new
  ' records in the active child form.

  ' If a file is already open in the active form,
  ' begin by saving the current record to disk
  ' if necessary.
If tranFileOpen And recordChanged Then SaveCurRec
recordChanged = False

  ' Set the Flags property of the Open dialog box.
cdlFileManager.Flags = cdlOFNFileMustExist Or _
                       cdlOFNHideReadOnly Or _
                       cdlOFNNoChangeDir Or _
                       cdlOFNPathMustExist
```

(continued)

(continued)

```
' Use the ShowOpen method to display the Open
' dialog box. An error trap allows for the
' possibility that the user will click the
' Cancel button. In this case, terminate the
' procedure by jumping to the userCancel label.
On Error GoTo userCancel
   cdlFileManager.ShowOpen
On Error GoTo 0

' Check to see if the requested file is already open in
' another child form. (The IsAlreadyOpen function on the
' parent form returns a value of True if this is the
' case.) If so, ignore the user's request and exit.
If frmTranParent.IsAlreadyOpen _
 (cdlFileManager.filename) Then Exit Sub

' If a file is currently open in this child form, close
' it. Then record the requested file name as tranFileName.
If tranFileOpen Then Close #fileNumber
tranFileName = cdlFileManager.filename

' Open the file and switch tranFileOpen to true.
Open tranFileName For Random As #fileNumber _
   Len = Len(TranRecord)
tranFileOpen = True

' Prepare to append a new record to the end of the file.
BlankEOFRecord

' Enable the Previous command for multiple records.
If curTranRecord > 1 Then mnuPrevious.Enabled = True

' Display the new caption in the title bar.
Caption = tranFileName & ", #" & curTranRecord

' Terminate the procedure if the user clicks Cancel.
userCancel:
End Sub   ' mnuOpen_Click


Public Sub mnuPrevious_Click()

' The mnuPrevious_Click procedure scrolls one
' record back in the current file. Note that
' the Previous command is disabled until a file
' is open and the program determines that the
' file contains more than one record.

' First save the current record if necessary.
If recordChanged Then SaveCurRec

' Decrease the value of the record pointer
' (curTranRecord) by 1, and read the
```

```
' corresponding record from the file. Then
' display the record in the form. The variable
' fileNumber represents the open file in the
' active child form.
curTranRecord = curTranRecord - 1
Get #fileNumber, curTranRecord, TranRecord
ShowRecord
recordChanged = False

' Display the file name and the record number
' in the form's title bar.
Caption = tranFileName & _
  ", #" & curTranRecord

' Enable the Next command. If the user has
' scrolled back to the first record in the
' file, disable the Previous command.
mnuNext.Enabled = True
If curTranRecord = 1 Then _
  mnuPrevious.Enabled = False

End Sub   ' mnuPrevious_Click


Public Sub mnuSaveAs_Click()

' The mnuSave_Click procedure takes control when
' the user clicks the Save As command, and gives
' the user the opportunity to create a new file.

Dim newFileName As String

' Set the Flags property of the Save As
' dialog box.
cdlFileManager.Flags = cdlOFNOverwritePrompt Or _
                       cdlOFNHideReadOnly Or _
                       cdlOFNNoChangeDir Or _
                       cdlOFNPathMustExist

' If the user clicks Cancel on the Save
' dialog box, the ShowSave method generates
' an error. In this case, exit from this
' procedure.
On Error GoTo userCancel
  cdlFileManager.ShowSave
On Error GoTo 0

' Check to see if the requested file is already
' open in another child form. (The IsAlreadyOpen
' function on the parent form returns a value of
' True if this is the case.) If so, ignore the
' user's request and exit from this procedure.
If frmTranParent.IsAlreadyOpen _
  (cdlFileManager.filename) Then Exit Sub
```

(continued)

(continued)

```vb
' Record the file name
' that the user has entered.
newFileName = cdlFileManager.filename

' If a file is currently open, save its
' final record and then copy its records
' to the new "save as" file. The variable
' fileNumber represents the open file in
' the active child form.
If tranFileOpen Then
  If recordChanged Then SaveCurRec
  Close #fileNumber
  CopyDatabase newFileName, tranFileName
Else
' Otherwise, if no file is open, check
' to see if the "save as" file currently
' exists on disk; if it does, delete it.
  tranFileName = newFileName
  On Error Resume Next
    Kill tranFileName
  On Error GoTo 0

  ' Open the new file and save the current
  ' entry as its first record.
  Open tranFileName For Random As #fileNumber _
    Len = Len(TranRecord)
  If recordChanged Then
    SaveCurRec
    mnuNext.Enabled = True
  End If
End If

tranFileOpen = True
recordChanged = False

' Display the file name and record number
' on the form's title bar.
Caption = tranFileName & _
  ", #" & curTranRecord

' Terminate the procedure if the user
' has clicked the Cancel button.
userCancel:

End Sub    ' mnuSaveAs_Click


Private Sub Form_Load()

  ' The Form_Load procedure initializes a few
  ' of the program's variables and control
  ' properties.
```

```
    ' No file is open yet.
    tranFileOpen = False
    recordChanged = False

    ' Set the record pointer to 1.
    curTranRecord = 1

    ' Disable the Next and Previous
    ' commands.
    mnuNext.Enabled = False
    mnuPrevious.Enabled = False

End Sub  ' Form_Load

Private Sub mnuTile_Click()

    ' The mnuTile_Click procedure rearranges the
    ' child forms in the MDI form when the user
    ' chooses the Tile command from the Window menu.

    frmTranParent.Arrange 1

End Sub  ' mnuTile_Click


Private Sub optMode_Click(Index As Integer)

    ' The optMode_Click procedure sets the properties
    ' of relevant controls whenever the user changes
    ' the selection in the optMode control array.

    ' Set the default property values for the
    ' program's three check box controls.
    chkRental.Enabled = False
    chkRental.Value = 0
    chkReserved.Enabled = True
    chkPaid.Enabled = True

    ' Enable the txtCarrier and txtTripNumber
    ' controls and their associated labels.
    lblTripNumber.Enabled = True
    txtTripNumber.Enabled = True
    txtCarrier.Enabled = True
    lblCarrier.Enabled = True

    ' Adjust the label captions according
    ' to the selected mode of transportion.
    Select Case Index
      Case 0
        lblCarrier.Caption = "Air&line"
        lblTripNumber.Caption = "Flight &#"

      Case 1
        lblCarrier.Caption = "Rail &line"
        lblTripNumber.Caption = "Train &#"
```

(continued)

(continued)

```
      Case 2
        lblCarrier.Caption = "Bus &line"
        lblTripNumber.Caption = "Route &#"

      ' If the user chooses the Car option,
      ' adjust the appropriate check boxes.
      Case 3
        lblCarrier.Caption = "Renta&l agency"
        lblTripNumber.Caption = "Reservation &#"
        chkRental.Enabled = True
        chkRental.Value = 1
        chkReserved_Click
        chkPaid.Enabled = False
    End Select

    ' Give the focus to the txtCarrier
    ' text box control.
    txtCarrier.SetFocus

End Sub    ' optMode_Click


Private Sub MakeTranRecord()

    ' The MakeTranRecord procedure copies the
    ' user's entries for the current transportation
    ' record to the TranRecord structure.
    ' Note that the TranRecType and the TranRecord
    ' variable are declared in the general
    ' declarations section of this form.

    Dim i

    With TranRecord

      ' Determine which of the four optMode
      ' buttons is currently selected.
      For i = 0 To 3
        If optMode(i).Value Then
          .TranMode = i
        End If
      Next i

      ' If the selection is Car, read the
      ' value of the chkRental check box.
      If .TranMode = 3 Then
        If chkRental.Value = 0 Then
          .RentalCar = False
        Else
          .RentalCar = True
        End If
      End If
```

```
    ' Read the first two text boxes.
    .Carrier = txtCarrier.Text
    .TripNumber = txtTripNumber.Text

    ' Read the values of the Reserved
    ' and Paid check boxes.
    If chkReserved.Value = 0 Then
      .ReservedStatus = False
    Else
      .ReservedStatus = True
    End If

    If chkPaid.Value = 0 Then
      .PaidStatus = False
    Else
      .PaidStatus = True
    End If

    ' Read the remaining text boxes.
    .TripDate = txtDate.Text
    .TripTime = txtTime.Text
    .TripFrom = txtFrom.Text
    .TripTo = txtTo.Text

    .Comments = txtNotes.Text

  End With

End Sub   ' MakeTranRecord

Private Function FindRecordCount()

  ' The FindRecordCount function determines
  ' the number of records in the current
  ' transportation file. Note that this
  ' function is called only if a file is open.

  ' The variable fileNumber represents the
  ' open file in the active child form.
  FindRecordCount = LOF(fileNumber) / _
    Len(TranRecord)

End Function   ' FindRecordCount


Private Sub ShowRecord()

  ' The ShowRecord procedure displays the fields
  ' of the current record in an open file. Before
  ' calling this procedure, the program always
  ' reads a record from the open file into the
  ' TranRecord structure.
```

(continued)

(continued)

```
    With TranRecord

      ' Set the transportation selection.
      optMode(.TranMode).Value = True

      ' If the Car option is selected,
      ' set the value of the Rental check box.
      If .TranMode = 3 Then
        If .RentalCar Then
          chkRental.Value = 1
        Else
          chkRental.Value = 0
        End If
      End If

      ' Read the remaining fields and
      ' set the corresponding controls
      ' appropriately.
      txtCarrier.Text = Trim(.Carrier)
      txtTripNumber.Text = Trim(.TripNumber)

      If .ReservedStatus Then
        chkReserved.Value = 1
      Else
        chkReserved.Value = 0
      End If

      If .PaidStatus Then
        chkPaid.Value = 1
      Else
        chkPaid.Value = 0
      End If

      txtDate.Text = Trim(.TripDate)
      txtTime.Text = Trim(.TripTime)
      txtFrom.Text = Trim(.TripFrom)
      txtTo.Text = Trim(.TripTo)

      txtNotes.Text = Trim(.Comments)

    End With

  End Sub   ' ShowRecord


  Private Sub txtCarrier_Change()

    ' The txtCarrier_Change procedure sets
    ' recordChanged to True if the user enters
    ' new text into this text box control.

    ChangedStatus

  End Sub   ' txtCarrier_Change
```

```
Private Sub txtDate_Change()

    ' The txtDate_Change procedure sets
    ' recordChanged to True if the user enters
    ' new text into this text box control.

    ChangedStatus

End Sub   ' txtDate_Change


Private Sub txtFrom_Change()

    ' The txtFrom_Change procedure sets
    ' recordChanged to True if the user enters
    ' new text into this text box control.

    ChangedStatus

End Sub   ' txtFrom_Change


Private Sub txtNotes_Change()

    ' The txtNotes_Change procedure sets
    ' recordChanged to True if the user enters
    ' new text into this text box control.

    ChangedStatus

End Sub   ' txtNotes_Change


Private Sub txtTime_Change()

    ' The txtTime_Change procedure sets
    ' recordChanged to True if the user enters
    ' new text into this text box control.

    ChangedStatus

End Sub   ' txtTime_Change


Private Sub txtTo_Change()

    ' The txtTo_Change procedure sets
    ' recordChanged to True if the user enters
    ' new text into this text box control.

    ChangedStatus

End Sub   ' txtTo_Change
```

(continued)

(continued)

```
Private Sub txtTripNumber_Change()

   ' The txtCarrier_Change procedure sets
   ' recordChanged to True if the user enters
   ' new text into this text box control.

   ChangedStatus

End Sub   ' txtTripNumber_Change


Private Sub PrintRecord()

   ' The PrintRecord procedure uses the
   ' Printer.Print method to send the fields of
   ' the current record to the printer. The current
   ' record is stored in the TranRecord structure.

   Const t1 = 5   ' First tab stop.
   Const t2 = 15  ' Second tab stop.

   With TranRecord

      ' Print the transportation mode.
      Select Case .TranMode
        Case 0
          Printer.Print "Airline — ";
        Case 1
          Printer.Print "Train Line — ";

        Case 2
          Printer.Print "Bus Line — ";

        Case 3
          If .RentalCar Then
            Printer.Print "Car Rental Agency — ";
          Else
            Printer.Print "Private Car"
          End If
      End Select

      ' Print the Carrier and TripNumber fields.
      If .TranMode < 3 Then
        Printer.Print .Carrier
        Printer.Print Tab(t1); " #"; .TripNumber
      Else
        If .RentalCar Then
          Printer.Print .Carrier;
          If .ReservedStatus Then
            Printer.Print Tab(t1); " #"; .TripNumber
          Else
            Printer.Print
          End If
        End If
      End If
```

```
' Print the date, time, starting point,
' and destination.
Printer.Print
Printer.Print Tab(t1); "Date:";
Printer.Print Tab(t2); .TripDate
Printer.Print Tab(t1); "Time:";
Printer.Print Tab(t2); .TripTime
Printer.Print Tab(t1); "From:";
Printer.Print Tab(t2); .TripFrom
Printer.Print Tab(t1); "To:";
Printer.Print Tab(t2); .TripTo
Printer.Print

' Print the reservation and paid status.
' Note the use of the YesNo function to
' supply a printable value of "Yes" or "No."
If .TranMode < 3 Then
  Printer.Print Tab(t1); "Reserved:";
  Printer.Print Tab(t2); YesNo(.ReservedStatus)
  Printer.Print Tab(t1); "Paid:";
  Printer.Print Tab(t2); YesNo(.PaidStatus)
End If

' Print the comments.
Printer.Print
Printer.Print Tab(t1); "Comments:"
PrintComments (RTrim(.Comments))

Printer.Print
Printer.Print

End With

End Sub  ' PrintRecord
```

The International Sales Program, Excel Version

Chapter 15

The Excel version of the International Sales program (SalesExl.Vbp) illustrates ActiveX programming techniques. Specifically, it shows how you can include a Windows application as an ActiveX component in a Visual Basic project. Like the original version (Chapter 11), this program provides a grid of cells in which you can enter a table of sales figures. As you complete the table, the program calculates totals and displays a column chart or pie chart to depict the data, as shown in Figure A-29. (To simplify testing and experimentation, this version's Edit menu contains a Random Data command; when you choose this command, the program instantly fills the input grid with random four-digit sales figures, and produces the corresponding chart. You can use this command as a quick way to generate data so you can try out the program's main feature — the transfer of data to Excel.)

Once you've created a sales table, you can proceed by pulling down the File menu and choosing Transfer to Excel. Assuming Microsoft Excel is available on your system, the program creates a fully functional worksheet containing your sales data and chart, as in Figure A-30. In this process, the program illustrates the techniques for manipulating ActiveX component objects in a Visual Basic project.

As shown in Figure A-31, the program has one form, frmIntSales, which contains all the code.

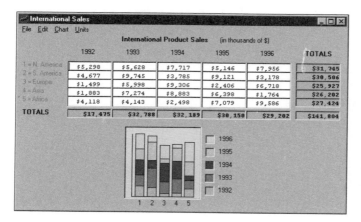

Figure A-29: Like its original, the Excel version of the International Sales program presents a grid of cells in which you can enter the figures of a sales table. In response, the program calculates totals and draws a chart.

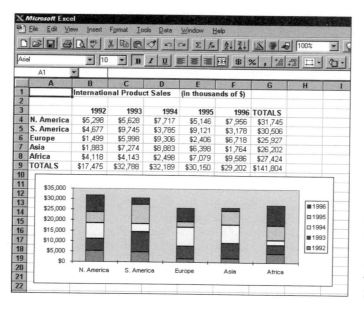

Figure A-30: When you choose the Transfer to Excel command, the program starts the Excel application and creates a worksheet version of the current sales data and chart. If you wish, you can save the resulting worksheet on disk as an Excel file before you continue your work with the International Sales program.

Figure A-31: The project includes a single form, which contains all the code.

International Sales, Excel Version — SalesExl.Frm

```
' The International Sales Program, Excel Version
'
' Project File:   SalesExl.VBP
' Form File:      SalesExl.FRM
'
' In this version of the International Sales program, the
' File menu contains a command that allows the user to
' transfer the current data set to an Excel worksheet
' (assuming Excel is installed).
Option Explicit
Const AmtFormat = "$#,####0"    ' Dollar-and-cents format.
Const colorOffset = 7           ' Color selection for charts.

' Variables to represent Excel objects.
Dim ExcelApp As Excel.Application
Dim ExcelWorkbook As Excel.Workbook
Dim ExcelSheet As Excel.Worksheet

' Arrays and variables to represent sales data.
Dim amounts(24)
Dim amountStr(24) As String
Dim periodTots(4)
Dim periodLabels(4) As String
Dim regionTots(4)
Dim regionLabels(4) As String
Dim IDPrefixes(4) As String
Dim grandTot
'
' End of general declarations, SalesExl.Frm.


Private Sub CopyToExcel()

   ' The CopyToExcel procedure is called by mnuExcel_Click
   ' when the user chooses the Transfer to Excel command.
   ' It copies the sales data, titles, and formulas to
   ' the sheet. It also formats specific worksheet cells
   ' as appropriate.

   Dim i, x, y

   ' Apply the boldface style to titles and labels.
   ExcelSheet.Range("$A$1:$G$3,$A$3:$A$9").Font.Bold = True
```

(continued)

(continued)

```
' Adjust the width of column A.
ExcelSheet.Columns("A").ColumnWidth = 10.29

' Copy the chart title and the units to the sheet.
ExcelSheet.Cells(1, 2).Value = txtTitle.Text
ExcelSheet.Cells(1, 5).Value = lblUnits.Caption

' Copy the entire table of numeric data.
For i = 0 To 24
  y = i Mod 5 + 2
  x = i \ 5 + 4
  ExcelSheet.Cells(x, y).Value = txtAmount(i).Text
Next i

' Copy the labels.
For i = 0 To 4
  With ExcelSheet
    .Cells(3, i + 2).Value = periodLabels(i)
    .Cells(i + 4, 1).Value = regionLabels(i)

    ' Enter the summation formulas.
    .Cells(9, i + 2).Formula = "=Sum(R[-5]C:R[-1]C)"
    .Cells(i + 4, 7).Formula = "=Sum(RC[-5]:RC[-1])"
  End With
Next i

' Enter the "TOTALS" labels and
' a formula for the grand total
' of all the sales data.
With ExcelSheet
  .Cells(9, 1).Value = "TOTALS"
  .Cells(3, 7).Value = "TOTALS"
  .Cells(9, 7).Formula = "=Sum(RC[-5]:RC[-1])"
End With

End Sub   ' CopyToExcel


Private Sub DrawExcelChart()

  ' The DrawExcelChart procedure is called by
  ' mnuExcel_Click. The procedure reads the settings of the
  ' mnuChartBy and mnuChartType menu options and uses
  ' Excel's ChartWizard method to create an equivalent
  ' chart. A ChartObject is a member of the ChartObjects
  ' collection, and is a container for a chart. The Chart
  ' object represents the actual drawn chart.

  ' Declare variables for a ChartObject and a Chart.
  Dim newChartObj As ChartObject
  Dim newChart As Chart
```

```
' Add a new ChartObject to the ChartObjects collection.
Set newChartObj = _
  ExcelSheet.ChartObjects.Add(10, 120, 400, 150)

' The newChart variable represents the Chart object.
Set newChart = newChartObj.Chart

' Read the settings of mnuChartBy and mnuChartType to
' determine what kind of chart to draw.
Select Case True
  ' A column chart. The legend shows time labels.
  Case mnuChartBy(0).Checked And mnuChartType(0).Checked
    newChart.ChartWizard ExcelSheet.Range("$A$3:$F$8"), _
    xlColumn, 3, xlColumns, 1, 1, True

    ' A column chart. The legend shows region labels.
  Case mnuChartBy(1).Checked And mnuChartType(0).Checked
    newChart.ChartWizard ExcelSheet.Range("$A$3:$F$8"), _
      xlColumn, 3, xlRows, 1, 1, True

    ' A pie chart. The legend shows time labels.
  Case mnuChartBy(0).Checked And mnuChartType(1).Checked
    newChart.ChartWizard _
      ExcelSheet.Range("$A$3:$F$3,$A$9:$F$9"), _
      xlPie, 1, xlRows, 1, 1, True

    ' A pie chart. The legend shows region labels.
  Case mnuChartBy(1).Checked And mnuChartType(1).Checked
    newChart.ChartWizard _
      ExcelSheet.Range("$A$3:$A$8,$G$3:$G$8"), _
      xlPie, 1, xlColumns, 1, 1, True

  End Select

End Sub   ' DrawExcelChart

Private Sub SaveReport()

  ' The SaveReport procedure creates a
  ' text file (named \IntSales.Txt) on disk and
  ' stores the numeric data currently displayed in
  ' the program's form.

  Dim i, j
  Dim f As String, b As String

  f = "$#,###0"
  b = "              "

  ' Create the file. (If the file already
  ' exists, overwrite the previous version.)
  Open "\IntSales.Txt" For Output As #1

    ' Write the title and the column labels
    ' to the file.
```

(continued)

(continued)

```
      Print #1, b; b; txtTitle
      Print #1, b; b; "    "; lblUnits
      Print #1,

      Print #1, b;
      For i = 0 To 4
        RSet b = txtYear(i)
        Print #1, b;
      Next i
      Print #1, "       Totals"
      Print #1,

      ' Write the table of sales data to the file.
      For i = 0 To 4
        LSet b = txtPlace(i).Text
        Print #1, b;
        For j = i * 5 To i * 5 + 4
          RSet b = txtAmount(j).Text
          Print #1, b;
        Next j
        RSet b = lblRegionTotal(i).Caption
        Print #1, b
      Next i

      ' Write the totals to the file.
      Print #1,
      Print #1, "Totals        ";
      For i = 0 To 4
        RSet b = lblPeriodTotal(i).Caption
        Print #1, b;
      Next i
      RSet b = lblGrandTotal
      Print #1, b

   Close #1

End Sub   ' SaveReport


Private Sub Form_Load()

   ' The Form_Load procedure performs a variety
   ' of initializations at the beginning of the
   ' program's performance.

   Dim i
   Dim tempYear As String

   ' Display the initial column labels and
   ' initialize the arrays that record the
   ' current labels.
   For i = 0 To 4
     tempYear = Year(Date) - (5 - i)
     txtYear(i).Text = tempYear
```

```
      periodLabels(i) = txtYear(i).Text
      regionLabels(i) = txtPlace(i).Text
      IDPrefixes(i) = Format((i + 1), "# = ")
   Next i

   ' Display the current dollar unit selection.
   ' (The user can change this display by making
   ' a new selection from the Units menu.)
   ShowUnits

End Sub   ' Form_Load

Private Sub mnuChartBy_Click(Index As Integer)

   ' The mnuChartBy_Click procedure responds to
   ' the user's choice of an option in the Chart
   ' menu. The user can choose to chart the data
   ' by region or by time period.

   Dim i

   ' Adjust the selection within the menu itself.
   If Index = 0 Then
      mnuChartBy(0).Checked = True
      mnuChartBy(1).Checked = False
   Else
      mnuChartBy(0).Checked = False
      mnuChartBy(1).Checked = True
   End If

   ' Restore the original column and row
   ' labels, in preparation for displaying
   ' new keys for a column chart.
   For i = 0 To 4
      txtYear(i).Text = periodLabels(i)
      txtYear(i).Enabled = True
      txtPlace(i).Text = regionLabels(i)
      txtPlace(i).Enabled = True
   Next i

   ' If any sales information has been entered
   ' into the table, redraw the chart at this point.
   If grandTot <> 0 Then DrawGraph

End Sub   ' mnuChartBy_Click


Private Sub mnuChartType_Click(Index As Integer)

   ' The mnuChartType_Click procedure responds to
   ' the user's choice of an option in the Chart
   ' menu. The user can choose to create a column
   ' chart or a pie chart.
```

(continued)

(continued)

```
      ' Adjust the current selection in the menu.
      If Index = 0 Then
        mnuChartType(0).Checked = True
        mnuChartType(1).Checked = False
      Else
        mnuChartType(0).Checked = False
        mnuChartType(1).Checked = True
      End If

      ' If any sales information has been entered
      ' into the table, redraw the chart at this point.
      If grandTot <> 0 Then DrawGraph

  End Sub   ' mnuChartType_Click


  Private Sub mnuClear_Click()

      ' The mnuClear_Click procedure takes control when
      ' the user chooses the Clear command from the
      ' Edit menu. The procedure clears all data from
      ' the sales table, and temporarily hides the
      ' objects in the chart area of the form.

      Dim i

      ' Reinitialize the text boxes in the sales
      ' table and the values in the amounts and
      ' amountStr arrays.
      For i = 0 To 24
        txtAmount(i).Text = ""
        amounts(i) = 0
        amountStr(i) = ""
      Next i

      ' Erase the totals and reinitialize the totals
      ' arrays. Also restore the original row and
      ' column labels.
      For i = 0 To 4
        lblPeriodTotal(i).Caption = ""
        lblRegionTotal(i).Caption = ""
        periodTots(i) = 0
        regionTots(i) = 0
        txtPlace(i).Text = regionLabels(i)
        txtYear(i).Text = periodLabels(i)
      Next i

      ' Erase the grand total and reinitialize
      ' the grandTot variable.
      lblGrandTotal.Caption = ""
      grandTot = 0

      ' Hide the graph objects.
      HideGraph
```

```
    ' Move the focus to the first text box in the
    ' table, in preparation for new data entries.
    txtAmount(0).SetFocus

End Sub    ' mnuClear_Click


Private Sub mnuCopy_Click()

    ' The mnuCopy_Click procedure takes control
    ' when the user chooses the Copy command from
    ' the Edit menu. The purpose of the procedure
    ' is to place a copy of the current sales table
    ' on the Windows Clipboard. From there, the
    ' user can paste the data to another software
    ' environment, such as a word processing
    ' program or a spreadsheet.

    Dim temp As String, inTemp As String

    ' Begin by creating a text file on disk for
    ' the current data set.
    SaveReport

    ' Then open the file and read each line it
    ' contains.
    temp = ""
    Open "\IntSales.Txt" For Input As #1
       Do While Not EOF(1)
          Line Input #1, inTemp

          ' Concatenate each line of text to
          ' the string variable temp.
          temp = temp + inTemp + Chr(13) + Chr(10)
       Loop
    Close #1

    ' Finally, place the temp string on
    ' the Clipboard.
    Clipboard.SetText temp

End Sub    ' mnuCopy_Click

Private Sub mnuExcel_Click()

    ' The mnuExcel_Click procedure takes control when the
    ' user chooses the Transfer to Excel command.
    Dim i, x, y

    ' If an error occurs, skip to the end of the procedure.
    On Error GoTo ActiveXProblem

    ' Create the objects, copy the data, and draw the chart.
    Set ExcelApp = CreateObject("Excel.Application")
    Set ExcelWorkbook = ExcelApp.Workbooks.Add
```

(continued)

(continued)

```
    Set ExcelSheet = ExcelWorkbook.Worksheets(1)
    ExcelApp.Visible = True
    CopyToExcel
    DrawExcelChart

    ' Pause to let the user examine and save the sheet.
    MsgBox "Save the Excel document if you wish. Then " & _
           "click OK to quit Excel.", , "International Sales"
    ExcelSheet.Application.Quit

ActiveXProblem:
    ' Release object references from memory.
    Set ExcelApp = Nothing
    Set ExcelWorkbook = Nothing
    Set ExcelSheet = Nothing

End Sub    ' mnuExcel_Click

Private Sub mnuExit_Click()

    ' The mnuExit_Click procedure takes control when
    ' the user chooses the Exit command from the
    ' File menu. The procedure simply terminates the
    ' program performance.

    End

End Sub    ' mnuExit_Click


Private Sub mnuRandomData_Click()

    ' The mnuRandomData_Click procedure creates
    ' a sales table of randomly-generated data
    ' items; this procedure allows the user to
    ' experiment with the ActiveX features of this
    ' program without having to enter a real
    ' data set.

    Dim i
    Randomize

    ' Enter random values, and call the
    ' LostFocus event procedure to process
    ' each data entry.
    For i = 0 To 24
      txtAmount(i).Text = Int(Rnd * 9000) + 1000
      txtAmount_LostFocus (i)
    Next i

End Sub    ' mnuRandomData_Click
```

```vb
Private Sub mnuUnitType_Click(Index As Integer)

  ' The mnuUnitType_Click procedure takes control
  ' when the user chooses a new option from the
  ' Units menu. (Note that the three options in
  ' this menu form a control array with Index
  ' values from 0 to 2.) The procedure changes
  ' the selection in the menu and then displays
  ' the appropriate caption in the lblUnits control.

  Dim i

  ' Determine which option should be checked.
  For i = 0 To 2
    If i = Index Then
      mnuUnitType(i).Checked = True
    Else
      mnuUnitType(i).Checked = False
    End If
  Next i

  ' Display the selected units caption.
  ShowUnits

End Sub   ' mnuUnitType_Click


Private Sub ShowUnits()

  ' The ShowUnits procedure reads the current
  ' selection in the Units menu and displays
  ' the corresponding units caption in the form.

  Select Case True
    Case mnuUnitType(0).Checked
      lblUnits.Caption = "(in dollars)"
    Case mnuUnitType(1).Checked
      lblUnits.Caption = "(in thousands of $)"
    Case mnuUnitType(2).Checked
      lblUnits.Caption = "(in millions of $)"
  End Select

End Sub    ' ShowUnits


Private Sub txtAmount_GotFocus(Index As Integer)

  ' The txtAmount_GotFocus procedure arranges to
  ' highlight the contents of a given txtAmount
  ' box when the control receives the focus. This
  ' effect is achieved through use of the SelStart
  ' and SelLength properties.
```

(continued)

(continued)

```
    txtAmount(Index).SelStart = 0
    txtAmount(Index).SelLength = _
      Len(txtAmount(Index).Text)

End Sub   ' txtAmount_GotFocus

Private Sub txtAmount_KeyDown(Index As Integer, _
  KeyCode As Integer, Shift As Integer)

  ' The txtAmount_KeyDown procedure allows the
  ' txtAmount text boxes to respond to the four
  ' arrow keys (left, up, right, and down) and to
  ' the Enter key as techniques for moving the
  ' focus from one box to the next. (Note that
  ' the 25 txtAmount boxes form a control array,
  ' with Index values from 0 to 24.)

  ' Define names to represent the code numbers of
  ' the relevant keys.
  Const leftKey = 37
  Const upKey = 38
  Const rightKey = 39
  Const downKey = 40
  Const enter = 13

  Select Case KeyCode

    ' Move the focus down to the next row,
    ' or from the bottom row to the top.
    Case downKey
      If Index < 20 Then
        txtAmount(Index + 5).SetFocus
      Else
        txtAmount(Index Mod 5).SetFocus
      End If

    ' Move the focus up to the previous row,
    ' or from the top row to the bottom.
    Case upKey
      If Index > 4 Then
        txtAmount(Index - 5).SetFocus
      Else
        txtAmount(Index + 20).SetFocus
      End If

    ' Move the focus to the previous text
    ' box, or from the upper-left corner to
    ' the lower-right corner of the table.
    Case leftKey
      If Index <> 0 Then
        txtAmount(Index - 1).SetFocus
      Else
        txtAmount(24).SetFocus
      End If
```

```
' Move the focus to the next text box,
' or from the lower-right corner to the
' upper-left corner of the table. (Note
' that the right-arrow key and the Enter
' key are both available for this action.)
Case rightKey, enter
  If Index <> 24 Then
    txtAmount(Index + 1).SetFocus
  Else
    txtAmount(0).SetFocus
  End If

End Select

End Sub   ' txtAmount_KeyDown


Private Sub CalculateTotals(amtIndex As Integer)

' The CalculateTotals procedure updates the
' row and column of sales totals each time the
' user enters a new value into the sales table.
' Note that the totals are displayed in two
' arrays of labels, named lblPeriodTotal and
' lblRegionTotal. Each array has Index values
' from 0 to 4.

Dim i As Integer
Dim periodIndex As Integer
Dim regionIndex As Integer
Dim firstRowIndex As Integer
Dim firstColIndex As Integer
Dim totTemp

' Create indexes to identify the
' totals that need to be recalculated.
periodIndex = amtIndex Mod 5
regionIndex = amtIndex \ 5
firstRowIndex = regionIndex * 5
firstColIndex = periodIndex

' Find the total sales for the current region.
totTemp = 0
For i = firstRowIndex To firstRowIndex + 4
  totTemp = totTemp + amounts(i)
Next i

' Record this numeric value in the
' regionTots array.
regionTots(regionIndex) = totTemp

' Display the formatted value in the
' appropriate lblRegionTotal control.
```

(continued)

(continued)

```
    If totTemp <> 0 Then
      lblRegionTotal(regionIndex).Caption = _
        Format(totTemp, AmtFormat)
    Else
      lblRegionTotal(regionIndex).Caption = ""
    End If

    ' Calculate the total sales for the
    ' current period.
    totTemp = 0
    For i = firstColIndex To firstColIndex + 20 Step 5
      totTemp = totTemp + amounts(i)
    Next i

    ' Record this numeric value in the
    ' periodTots array.
    periodTots(periodIndex) = totTemp

    ' Display the formatted value in the
    ' appropriate lblPeriodTotal control.
    If totTemp <> 0 Then
      lblPeriodTotal(periodIndex).Caption = _
        Format(totTemp, AmtFormat)
    Else
      lblPeriodTotal(periodIndex).Caption = ""
    End If

    ' Calculate the new grand total.
    totTemp = 0
    For i = 0 To 24
      totTemp = totTemp + amounts(i)
    Next i

    ' Record the numeric value in the
    ' grandTot variable.
    grandTot = totTemp

    ' Display the formatted value in the
    ' lblGrandTotal control.
    If totTemp <> 0 Then
      lblGrandTotal.Caption = _
        Format(totTemp, AmtFormat)
    Else
      lblGrandTotal.Caption = ""
    End If

End Sub    ' CalculateTotals


Private Sub txtAmount_LostFocus(Index As Integer)

    ' The txtAmount_LostFocus procedure performs
    ' a variety of important tasks after each new
    ' data item has been entered into the sales
```

```
' table. (Note that txtAmount is a control
' array, with Index values from 0 to 24.) The
' procedure validates the data entry, reformats
' it for display, recalculates the appropriate
' totals, and redraws the current chart.

' The entryWidth variable defines the width
' within which the program right-justifies
' entries into the sales table.
Dim entryWidth As String
entryWidth = Space(8)

' Compare the entry with the corresponding
' value in the amountStr array, to determine
' whether the value has changed.
If amountStr(Index) <> txtAmount(Index).Text Then

   ' If so, record the new numeric value in the
   ' amounts array. Use the Val function to
   ' eliminate any nonnumeric characters in the
   ' entry. (Note that an entry beginning with
   ' a nonnumeric character becomes zero.)
   amounts(Index) = Val(txtAmount(Index).Text)

   ' Do not allow negative entries or entries
   ' that are longer than six digits in the
   ' sales table.
   If amounts(Index) < 0 Or _
      amounts(Index) > 999999 _
      Then amounts(Index) = 0

   ' If the entry is not zero, display the value
   ' in a right-justified dollar-and-cent format.
   If amounts(Index) <> 0 Then
     RSet entryWidth = _
       Format(amounts(Index), AmtFormat)
     txtAmount(Index).Text = entryWidth
   Else
     ' Otherwise, if the entry is zero,
     ' display it as a blank entry.
     txtAmount(Index).Text = ""
   End If

   ' Record the formatted value in the
   ' string array named amountStr.
   amountStr(Index) = txtAmount(Index).Text

   ' Recaculate the totals for the row and
   ' column where this new entry is located.
   CalculateTotals Index

   ' If the current grand total is not zero,
   ' redraw the current chart. Otherwise,
   ' hide the chart controls.
```

(continued)

(continued)

```vb
      If grandTot <> 0 Then
        DrawGraph
      Else
        HideGraph
      End If

   End If

End Sub   ' txtAmount_LostFocus


Private Sub DrawGraph()

   ' The DrawGraph procedure redraws the chart,
   ' based on the current selections in the
   ' Chart menu.

   ' Display and picture box control and
   ' clear its contents.
   picSalesChart.Visible = True
   picSalesChart.Cls

   ' Determine which chart to draw, according
   ' to the current Checked values in the
   ' mnuChartBy and mnuChartType arrays.
   Select Case True

      Case mnuChartBy(0).Checked And _
           mnuChartType(0).Checked

         ' For a column chart, draw the
         ' vertical and horizontal axes first,
         ' then draw the columns of the chart.
         DrawAxes
         ColumnByYears

      Case mnuChartBy(0).Checked And _
           mnuChartType(1).Checked

         ' For a pie chart, no axes are needed.
         PieByYears

      Case mnuChartBy(1).Checked And _
           mnuChartType(0).Checked

         DrawAxes
         ColumnByRegion

      Case mnuChartBy(1).Checked And _
           mnuChartType(1).Checked

         PieByRegion

   End Select
```

```
      ' Display the legend for the chart.
      ShowLegend

End Sub   ' DrawGraph

Private Sub DrawAxes()

    ' The DrawAxes procedure draws the vertical
    ' and horizontal axes for a column chart.

    Dim i

    ' Begin by creating a convenient coordinate
    ' system for the chart. (The "origin" of the
    ' chart is located just above and to the right
    ' of the lower-left corner of the picture box.)
    picSalesChart.Scale (-1, 11)-(11, -0.25)

    ' Then draw the two axes, each starting
    ' at the "origin" defined by the coordinate
    ' scale.
    picSalesChart.Line (0, 0)-Step(10, 0)
    picSalesChart.Line (0, 0)-Step(0, 10)

End Sub   ' DrawAxes

Private Sub ShowLegend()

    ' The ShowLegend procedure displays the labels
    ' and colors of the legend for a pie chart or a
    ' column chart. In addition, the procedure adds
    ' numeric prefixes to labels above or to the left
    ' of the sales table, to identify the individual
    ' columns of a column chart.

    Dim i

    For i = 0 To 4

        ' If the "By Years" option has been selected
        ' in the Chart menu, display the years as the
        ' legend labels.
        If mnuChartBy(0).Checked Then
          If periodTots(i) <> 0 Then
            lblLegendColor(i).Visible = True
            lblLegendColor(i).BackColor = _
              QBColor(i + colorOffset)
            lblLegendText(i).Caption = periodLabels(i)

          ' But don't display a box or label for
          ' a sales table column that has a
          ' total value of zero.
          Else
            lblLegendColor(i).Visible = False
```

(continued)

(continued)

```
            lblLegendText(i).Caption = ""
        End If

        ' For a column chart, add a numeric
        ' prefix to the region labels to identify
        ' each column of the chart.
        If mnuChartType(0).Checked And _
            regionTots(i) <> 0 Then
          lblxAxis(i).Caption = i + 1
          txtPlace(i).Text = IDPrefixes(i) + _
            regionLabels(i)
          txtPlace(i).Enabled = False
        Else
          lblxAxis(i).Caption = ""
          txtPlace(i).Text = regionLabels(i)
          txtPlace(i).Enabled = True
        End If

    Else

        ' If the "By Region" option has been
        ' selected in the Chart menu, display
        ' the regions a the legend labels.
        If regionTots(i) <> 0 Then
          lblLegendColor(i).Visible = True
          lblLegendColor(i).BackColor = _
            QBColor(i + colorOffset)
          lblLegendText(i).Caption = regionLabels(i)
        Else
          lblLegendColor(i).Visible = False
          lblLegendText(i).Caption = ""
        End If

        ' For a column chart, add numeric prefixes
        ' to the year labels to identify each
        ' column of the chart.
        If mnuChartType(0).Checked And _
            periodTots(i) <> 0 Then
          lblxAxis(i).Caption = i + 1
          txtYear(i).Text = IDPrefixes(i) + _
            periodLabels(i)
          txtYear(i).Enabled = False
        Else
          lblxAxis(i).Caption = ""
          txtYear(i).Text = periodLabels(i)
          txtYear(i).Enabled = True
        End If

    End If
    Next i

End Sub    ' ShowLegend
```

```
Private Sub HideGraph()

  ' The HideGraph procedure hides the picture box
  ' and other controls related to the chart and
  ' its legend. The program calls this routine
  ' whenever the grand total value is zero.

  Dim i

  ' Hide the picture box.
  picSalesChart.Visible = False

  For i = 0 To 4

    ' Hide all of the legend labels.
    lblLegendColor(i).Visible = False
    lblLegendText(i).Caption = ""

    ' Erase the labels arranged beneath
    ' the horizontal axis of a column chart.
    lblxAxis(i).Caption = ""

    ' Restore the original year and region
    ' labels above and to the left of the
    ' sales table.
    txtYear(i).Text = periodLabels(i)
    txtYear(i).Enabled = True
    txtPlace(i).Text = regionLabels(i)
    txtPlace(i).Enabled = True
  Next i

End Sub   ' HideGraph


Private Sub txtPlace_LostFocus(Index As Integer)

  ' The txtPlace_LostFocus procedure is called when
  ' the user completes a change in any one of the
  ' region labels displayed to the left of the
  ' sales chart. The procedure records this change
  ' in the regionLabels array.

  regionLabels(Index) = txtPlace(Index).Text
  If grandTot <> 0 Then ShowLegend

End Sub   ' txtPlace_LostFocus


Private Sub ColumnByYears()

  ' The ColumnByYears procedure draws a column
  ' chart if the user has selected the "By Years"
  ' option in the Chart menu.
```

(continued)

(continued)

```
Dim i
Dim x, y, y2
Dim maxRegion
Dim scaleFactor

' Determine the largest region total.
maxRegion = 0
For i = 0 To 4
  If regionTots(i) > maxRegion Then _
    maxRegion = regionTots(i)
Next i

' The scale factor for the chart is based
' on the largest region total. (This value
' will have a height of 10 in the chart.)
scaleFactor = 10 / maxRegion

' Depict each nonzero value in the sales
' table as a "stack" in one of the charts.
For i = 0 To 24

  ' At the beginning of each row of data,
  ' reinitialize the x and y values for a
  ' new column in the chart.
  If i Mod 5 = 0 Then
    x = 0.5 + 2 * (i / 5)
    y = 0
  End If

  ' If an amount is not zero, calculate
  ' the height of the corresponding "stack."
  If amounts(i) <> 0 Then
    y2 = scaleFactor * amounts(i)

    ' Select a color and a fill style.
    picSalesChart.FillColor = _
      QBColor(i Mod 5 + colorOffset)
    picSalesChart.FillStyle = 0

    ' Draw the "stack."
    picSalesChart.Line (x, y)-Step(1.5, y2), _
      0, B

    ' Increment the value of y by the
    ' height of the previous "stack."
    y = y + y2
  End If
Next i

End Sub  ' ColumnByYears

Private Sub ColumnByRegion()
```

```
' The ColumnByRegion procedure draws a column
' chart if the user has selected the "By Region"
' option in the Chart menu.

Dim i, j
Dim x, y, y2
Dim maxPeriod
Dim scaleFactor

' Determine the largest year total
' in the sales table.
maxPeriod = 0
For i = 0 To 4
  If periodTots(i) > maxPeriod Then _
    maxPeriod = periodTots(i)
Next i

' The scale factor for the chart is based on
' the largest year total. (This value has a
' height of 10 in the chart.)
scaleFactor = 10 / maxPeriod


For i = 0 To 4

  ' Reinitialize the x and y values for the
  ' beginning of each new column in the chart.
  x = 0.5 + 2 * i
  y = 0

  ' Draw a "stack" for each numeric entry in
  ' a given year of the sales table.
  For j = i To i + 20 Step 5

    ' If the value is not zero, calculate
    ' the "stack" height that will represent
    ' this value in the column chart.
    If amounts(j) <> 0 Then
      y2 = scaleFactor * amounts(j)

      ' Select a color and a fill style.
      picSalesChart.FillColor = _
        QBColor(j \ 5 + colorOffset)
      picSalesChart.FillStyle = 0

      ' Draw the "stack."
      picSalesChart.Line (x, y)-Step(1.5, y2), _
        0, B

      ' Add the height of the previous
      ' "stack" to the current value of y.
      y = y + y2
    End If
```

(continued)

(continued)

```vb
      Next j
   Next i

End Sub   ' ColumnByRegion

Private Sub txtYear_LostFocus(Index As Integer)

   ' The txtYear_LostFocus procedure is called when
   ' the user completes a change in any one of the
   ' year labels displayed above the sales chart.
   ' The procedure records this change in the
   ' periodLabels array.

   periodLabels(Index) = txtYear(Index).Text
   If grandTot <> 0 Then ShowLegend

End Sub   ' txtYear_LostFocus


Private Sub PieByYears()

   ' The PieByYears procedure draws a pie chart
   ' if the user has selected the "By Years"
   ' option in the Chart menu.

   Dim i, pi, a1, a2

   ' Calculate the value of pi.
   pi = 4 * Atn(1)

   ' Set the scale for the picture box. The
   ' "origin" is located in the center of the
   ' box in this case.
   picSalesChart.Scale (-1, 1)-(1, -1)

   ' Because of a quirk in the Circle method, the
   ' starting angle for the first wedge in the chart
   ' must be a very small nonzero value.
   a1 = 0.00001

   ' Draw a wedge to represent the total sales
   ' for each year in the sales table.
   For i = 0 To 4
      If periodTots(i) <> 0 Then

         ' Calculate the ending angle of the
         ' current wedge.
         a2 = a1 + (2 * pi) * _
           (periodTots(i) / grandTot)

         ' Select a color and a fill style.
         picSalesChart.FillColor = _
           QBColor(i + colorOffset)
         picSalesChart.FillStyle = 0
```

```
      ' Draw the wedge.
      If periodTots(i) < grandTot Then
        picSalesChart.Circle (0, 0), 0.9, _
          0, -a1, -a2 + 0.00001

      ' But if this sales total is currently
      ' the only annual total availble in the
      ' table, draw a full circle instead.
      Else
        picSalesChart.Circle (0, 0), 0.9, 0
      End If

      ' The starting angle for the next wedge
      ' is the ending angle of the current wedge.
      a1 = a2
    End If
  Next i

End Sub   ' PieByYears

Private Sub PieByRegion()

  ' The PieByRegion procedure draws a pie chart
  ' if the user has selected the "By Region"
  ' option in the Chart menu.

  Dim i, pi, a1, a2

  ' Calculate the value of pi.
  pi = 4 * Atn(1)

  ' Set the scale of the picture box. The "origin"
  ' is at the center of the box in this case.
  picSalesChart.Scale (-1, 1)-(1, -1)

  ' Because of a quirk in the Circle method, the
  ' starting angle of the first wedge must be a
  ' very small nonzero value.
  a1 = 0.00001

  ' Draw a wedge to represent each regional
  ' sales total.
  For i = 0 To 4

    ' If the current sales total is not zero,
    ' calculate the ending angle of the wedge.
    If regionTots(i) <> 0 Then
      a2 = a1 + (2 * pi) * _
        (regionTots(i) / grandTot)

      ' Select a color and a fill style.
      picSalesChart.FillColor = _
        QBColor(i + colorOffset)
      picSalesChart.FillStyle = 0
```

(continued)

(continued)

```
      ' Draw the wedge.
      If regionTots(i) < grandTot Then
        picSalesChart.Circle (0, 0), 0.9, _
          0, -a1, -a2 + 0.00001

      ' But if this total value is currently
      ' the only regional total available in the
      ' sales table, draw a full circle instead.
      Else
        picSalesChart.Circle (0, 0), 0.9, 0
      End If

      ' The starting angle for the next wedge
      ' is the ending angle of the current wedge.
      a1 = a2
    End If
  Next i

End Sub   ' PieByRegion
```

The Currency Exchange Program, Database Version

Chapter 16

The database version of the International Currency Exchange program reads currency exchange data from an Access database file named Currency.Mdb. (You can develop this file directly in Microsoft Access, or you use the Visual Data Manager add-in to create the database file. Follow the instructions outlined in Chapter 16.) The application illustrates the use of Visual Basic's data control for establishing connections to external databases. Like the original, this version presents a list of countries for which currency exchange information is available. Once you've chosen a country, you can use the program to perform any number of exchange calculations, from dollars to the country's currency, or from the currency to dollars. Figure A-32 shows an example.

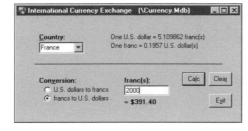

Figure A-32: When you start the program, it attempts to read currency exchange information from an Access database named Currency.Mdb. If the database connection is successful (that is, if the program finds the database on disk in the expected format), you can choose an entry from the Country list and begin performing exchange calculations.

As you can see in Figure A-33, the application has one form, named frmCurrExch. This form contains all of the program's Visual Basic code.

Figure A-33: The program contains one form, which contains all the code.

Currency Exchange, Database Version — CurrExDB.Frm

```
' Currency Exchange Program, Database version
'
'
' Files:
'
' Project File:  CurrExDB.VBP
' Form File:     CurrExDB.FRM  (this file)
'
' This program converts between dollars and
' the currencies of other countries.
' The daily exchange rates are stored in
' an Access database file named Currency.MDB.
' Within the database, the table that contains
' the currency data is called Exchange. This
' program illustrates the use of the Data control
' (and its associated methods and properties) in
' working successfully with an Access database in
' a Visual Basic program.
'
' Note that this program contains a Data control
' named dbCurrency. Here are some of the key
' design-time property settings of this control:
'
' Property        Setting          Explanation
'
' Connect         Access           MS Access database.
' DatabaseName    C:\Currency.MDB  The file name.
' RecordSource    Exchange         The table name.
' Visible         False            Not displayed.
'
' To work properly, the program needs to find
' the Currency.MDB file in the root directory
' of the current hard disk. The MDB file must
' contain a table named Exchange, which in turn
' has three fields:
'
' Country   — The name of a country.
' Currency  — The name of the country's currency.
' InDollars — The dollar-to-currency exchange rate.
```

(continued)

(continued)

```
Option Explicit
'
' End of general declarations, CurrExDB.FRM.

Private Sub cboCountry_Click()

    ' The cboCountry_Click procedure responds to the user's
    ' new selection in the cboCountry control. The
    ' corresponding record in the database table becomes the
    ' current record. The procedure reads the fields from
    ' the record and displays their information in the
    ' application window.

    Dim countryField As String
    Dim currencyField As String
    Dim inDollarsField As Single

    ' Use the FindFirst method to locate the
    ' record corresponding to the user's country
    ' choice. This becomes the current record.
    dbCurrency.Recordset.FindFirst "Country='" & _
        cboCountry.Text & "'"

    ' Read the country name, the currency name
    ' and the exchange rate from the fields of
    ' the current record.
    With dbCurrency.Recordset
        countryField = .Fields("Country").Value
        currencyField = .Fields("Currency").Value
        inDollarsField = .Fields("InDollars").Value
    End With

    ' Display the dollar-to-currency exchange rate.
    lblDollar.Caption = "One U.S. dollar = " & _
        1 / inDollarsField & " " & _
        currencyField & "(s)"

    ' Display the currency-to-dollar exchange rate.
    lblCurrency.Caption = "One " & _
        currencyField & " = " & _
        inDollarsField & " U.S. dollar(s)"

    ' Display the captions for the two currency
    ' exchange option buttons.
    optDollarsTo.Caption = "U.S. dollars to " _
        & currencyField & "s"
    optCurrTo.Caption = _
        currencyField & "s to U.S. dollars"

    ' Display the caption for the currency
    ' calculation box.
    lblConvCurr.Caption = "U.S. dollar(s):"
```

```
   optDollarsTo.Value = True
   cmdClear_Click

End Sub   ' cboCountry_Click


Private Sub cmdCalc_Click()
   ' Perform a currency exchange calculation.
   Dim currencyField As String, inDollarsField As Single

   ' First make sure that the user has entered a number
   ' (greater than zero) in the txtConvAmount text box.
   txtConvAmount.Text = Val(txtConvAmount.Text)
   If txtConvAmount.Text = 0 _
     Or dbCurrency.Recordset.EOF Then
       cmdClear_Click
   Else
   ' If the entry is valid, read fields from the record
   ' and display the results of the requested calculation.
     With dbCurrency.Recordset
       currencyField = .Fields("Currency").Value
       inDollarsField = .Fields("InDollars").Value
     End With
     If optDollarsTo.Value Then
       lblConvText.Caption = "= " & _
       Format(txtConvAmount.Text / _
       inDollarsField, "###,###.00") & " " & _
       currencyField & "(s)"
     Else
       lblConvText.Caption = "= " & _
         Format(txtConvAmount.Text * _
         inDollarsField, "$###,###.00")
     End If
   End If
End Sub   ' cmdCalc_Click

Private Sub cmdClear_Click()

   ' The cmdClear_Click procedure clears
   ' the previous conversion calculation.

   txtConvAmount.Text = ""
   lblConvText.Caption = ""

   ' Return the focus to the
   ' txtConvAmount text box.
   txtConvAmount.SetFocus

End Sub   ' cmdClear_Click

Private Sub cmdExit_Click()

   ' The cmdExit_Click procedure terminates
   ' the program when the user clicks the
```

(continued)

(continued)

```
        ' Exit button.

        End

    End Sub   ' cmdExit_Click


    Private Sub Form_Load()

        ' The Form_Load procedure reads the country
        ' list from the database table and adds each
        ' country name to the cboCountry combo box list.

        Dim temp1 As String
        Dim temp2 As Single

        ' Begin by adding the database file name to
        ' the title bar of the application window.
        frmCurrExch.Caption = frmCurrExch.Caption & _
            "  (" & dbCurrency.DatabaseName & ")"

        ' Set up an error trap. If the program
        ' can't find the database, or if the Exchange
        ' table is not organized as expected, the
        ' program displays an error message, and
        ' the performance ends.
        On Error GoTo databaseProblem

        ' Use the Refresh method to rebuild the
        ' RecordSet object and prepare the database
        ' table for reading.
        dbCurrency.Refresh

        With dbCurrency.Recordset

            ' Step through all the records of the database.
            Do While Not .EOF

                ' Read the country field from the
                ' current record and add the country
                ' name to the combo box list.
                cboCountry.AddItem .Fields("Country").Value

                ' Read the other two fields, just to
                ' confirm that the Exchange table is
                ' organized as expected.
                temp1 = .Fields("Currency").Value
                temp2 = .Fields("InDollars").Value

                ' Move down to the next record in the database.
                .MoveNext
            Loop
```

```
      End With
      Exit Sub

databaseProblem:
   ' Display an error message if the program
   ' has had a problem using the database. Then
   ' terminate the program performance.
   MsgBox "Problem opening or using the " & _
      dbCurrency.DatabaseName & " database.", , _
      "International Currency Exchange"
   End
End Sub   ' Form_Load

Private Sub optCurrTo_Click()

   ' The optCurrTo_Click procedure changes the conversion
   ' option: foreign currency to U.S. dollars.

   ' Read the currency name from the Currency field of the
   ' current record in the database table.
   With dbCurrency.Recordset
      If Not .EOF Then _
         lblConvCurr = .Fields("Currency").Value & "(s):"
   End With

   ' Clear the calculation text box.
   cmdClear_Click

End Sub   ' optCurrTo_Click

Private Sub optDollarsTo_Click()

   ' The optDollarsTo_Click procedure changes the currency
   ' option: U.S. dollars to foreign currency.

   If Not dbCurrency.Recordset.EOF Then _
      lblConvCurr = "U.S. dollar(s):"

   ' Clear the calculation text box.
   cmdClear_Click

End Sub   ' optDollarsTo_Click
```

The CheckLists Component and the List Maker

Chapter 17

The List Maker application is a demonstration program for an ActiveX DLL component named CheckLists. Both projects appear in the Lists.Vbg group. The CheckLists component contains a class module named CheckList. Objects created from this class are displayed on the desktop as check lists that the user develops interactively. The ListMaker project contains two forms and a module. The frmListData form is designed to elicit the specifications for a new set of lists, as shown in Figure A-34. The frmListOpen form allows the user to display of list objects on the screen, as in Figure A-35. The modListName module contains a Sub Main procedure, which is the startup code for the application.

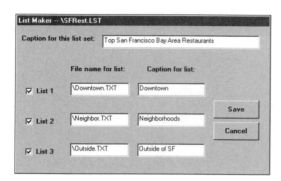

Figure A-34: The frmListData form gives the user the opportunity to define a new set of lists. When the user clicks Save, the program saves the list set definition in a text file on disk.

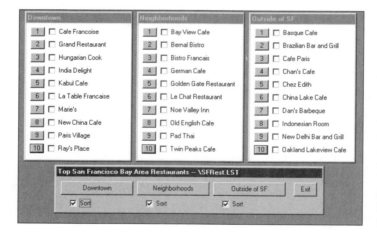

Figure A-35: The frmListOpen form allows the user to display list objects on the desktop. By clicking command buttons, the user can display or hide lists. The Sort check boxes determine the order of items in each list window.

The Project Explorer window for the Lists group shows all of the modules contained in the two projects. The CheckLists component has one form and one class module. The ListMaker project has two forms and one code module. All five modules contain code.

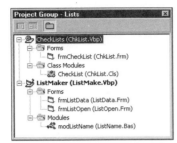

Figure A-36: The project group named Lists.Vbg contains both the CheckLists ActiveX DLL component and the ListMaker project. By opening both of these projects at the same time, you can test and debug the CheckLists component before compiling it. A reference to the CheckLists component has been established for the ListMaker project.

The CheckLists Component — ChkList.CLS

```
' The CheckList ActiveX DLL Component
'
' Form Module:    ChkList.Frm
' Class Module:   ChkList.Cls  (this file)
'
' The CheckList module defines the properties and
' methods of the class.
Option Explicit
Const ListLength = 9

' Create an instance of the frmCheckList form.
Private newList As New frmCheckList
Private newListActive As Boolean

Public TitleBar As String      ' The list caption.
Public ListFileName As String  ' The list's file name.
Public XPos As Integer         ' The position
Public YPos As Integer         '    coordinates.

Private Type curItemType    ' Fields to represent the
   itemText As String       ' characteristics of each
   itemStatus As Byte       ' list item.
   originalOrder As Byte
End Type

' The curList array represents all the items in the list.
Private curList(ListLength) As curItemType
'
' End of general declarations

Private Sub DisplayNewOrder()

   ' The DisplayNewOrder procedure redisplays the items of
   ' the list after a sort has been performed.

   Dim i
```

(continued)

(continued)

```vb
      For i = 0 To ListLength
        With newList.chkListItem(i)

          ' Display the caption and the check box status.
          .Caption = curList(i).itemText
          .Value = curList(i).itemStatus
        End With
      Next i

    End Sub   ' DisplayNewOrder

    Private Sub ReadData(inFile As String)
      ' The ReadData procedure attempts to read the target
      ' list file. If the file doesn't exist, the procedure
      ' simply displays number captions on the command buttons.
      Dim i, listItemTxt As String, checkStatus As Byte

      ' Open and read the file if it exists.
      On Error GoTo fileProblem
        Open inFile For Input As #1

        ' Read the file line by line.
        For i = 0 To ListLength
          Input #1, listItemTxt, checkStatus
          With newList.chkListItem(i)
            .Caption = listItemTxt
            .Value = checkStatus
          End With
        Next i
      On Error GoTo 0

    ' In the event of a file error, control arrives here.
    fileProblem:
      Close #1
      For i = 0 To ListLength
        ' Display an integer value on each cmdChange button.
        newList.cmdChange(i).Caption = i + 1
      Next i
    End Sub   ' ReadData


    Private Sub RecordCurOrder(saveOrderField)
      ' The ReadCurOrder reads through the list and records
      ' its items in their current order. A value of True in
      ' the saveOrderField argument indicates that the list
      ' is currently in its original unsorted order. In this
      ' case, the originalOrder field of the curList record
      ' receives an integer recording the order.
      Dim i

      For i = 0 To ListLength
        With newList.chkListItem(i)
          curList(i).itemText = .Caption
          curList(i).itemStatus = .Value
        End With
```

```vba
      If saveOrderField Then _
         curList(i).originalOrder = i
   Next i

End Sub   ' RecordCurOrder

Private Sub SaveCheckList()
   ' The SaveCheckList procedure writes the current list
   ' to its text file on disk. This occurs just before
   ' the list object is released from memory.

   Dim i

   On Error GoTo fileProblem
   With newList

      Open ListFileName For Output As #1
         For i = 0 To ListLength

            ' Write the text of the list item, and the
            ' current check box status.
            Write #1, _
               .chkListItem(i).Caption; _
               .chkListItem(i).Value
         Next i
      Close #1
   End With

' If a file problem occurs, terminate the procedure.
fileProblem:

End Sub   ' SaveCheckList

Public Sub ShowCheckList()

   ' The ShowCheckList procedure defines the method that
   ' a client application uses for the initial display of
   ' a list object. The procedure reads the list items
   ' from the specified text file on disk, sets the
   ' properties of the newList object, and displays the
   ' list.
   ReadData ListFileName

   newList.Caption = TitleBar

   newList.Top = YPos
   newList.Left = XPos

   newList.Show

   ' The module-level newListActive variable indicates
   ' that the list has been activated — that is, the
   ' program has read the list file and displayed the
```

(continued)

(continued)

```
    ' list box on the desktop.
    newListActive = True

End Sub   ' ShowCheckList

Public Sub SortCheckList(alphabetic As Boolean)

    ' The SortCheckList procedure defines the method that
    ' a client application uses to change the order of the
    ' list. Sending a True argument results in an alphabetic
    ' sort; a False argument results in a return to the
    ' list's original order.

    ' This method results in no action if the list has
    ' not yet been activated. (Note: A call to the
    ' ShowCheckList method activates and displays a
    ' list object. At the end of this procedure, the value
    ' of newListActive is set to True.)
    If newListActive Then
      RecordCurOrder alphabetic
      SortList alphabetic

      ' Display the list's new order.
      DisplayNewOrder
    End If

End Sub   ' SortCheckList

Private Sub SortList(byListItems As Boolean)
    ' The SortList procedure changes the order of the list.
    Dim i, j, tempItem As curItemType

    For i = 0 To ListLength - 1
      For j = i + 1 To ListLength

        ' Sort the list alphabetically.
        If byListItems Then
          If curList(i).itemText > _
            curList(j).itemText And _
            Trim(curList(j).itemText) <> "" Then
              tempItem = curList(i)
              curList(i) = curList(j)
              curList(j) = tempItem
          End If
        Else

          ' Return the list to its original order.
          If curList(i).originalOrder > _
            curList(j).originalOrder Then
              tempItem = curList(i)
              curList(i) = curList(j)
              curList(j) = tempItem
          End If
        End If
```

```
     Next j
   Next i
End Sub   ' SortList

Private Sub Class_Initialize()

   ' The Class_Initialize procedure is called when a
   ' new object is first created. The procedure sets the
   ' newListActive variable to False, indicating that the
   ' list object has not yet been displayed.

   newListActive = False

End Sub   ' Class_Initialize

Private Sub Class_Terminate()

   ' A call to the Class_Terminate procedure occurs when
   ' the object is released from memory by the client
   ' application. In this case, the procedure returns the
   ' list to its original order and saves the items of the
   ' list back the original test file on disk.

   ' The sort and save operations occur only if the
   ' newListActive status is true.
   If newListActive Then
     SortCheckList False
     SaveCheckList
   End If

   ' Release the newList form from memory.
   Set newList = Nothing

End Sub   ' Class_Terminate

Public Sub HideCheckList()

   ' The HideCheckList procedure defines the method that a
   ' client application can use to remove the list
   ' temporarily from the desktop.

   ' Change the form's Visible property to False. But
   ' if the newListActive status is False, no action
   ' takes place as a result of a call to this method.
   If newListActive Then newList.Visible = False

End Sub   ' HideCheckList

Public Sub UnHideCheckList()

   ' The UnHideCheckList procedure defines the method that a
   ' client application can use to redisplay the list
   ' on the desktop.
```

(continued)

(continued)

```
' Change the form's Visible property to True. But
' if the newListActive status is False, no action
' takes place as a result of a call to this method.
If newListActive Then newList.Visible = True

End Sub   ' UnHideCheckList
```

The CheckLists Component — ChkList.FRM

```
' The CheckList ActiveX DLL Component
'
' Form Module:    ChkList.Frm (this file)
' Class Module:   ChkList.Cls
'
' The CheckList ActiveX DLL component provides a class
' named clsCheckList. Instances of this class appear on
' the screen as check list windows. The class defines
' four methods that perform operations on list objects:
'
' — ShowCheckList displays a list object on the desktop.
' — SortCheckList changes the order of items in the list.
' — HideCheckList temporarily hides the list window.
' — UnHideCheckList redisplays the list on the desktop.
'
' Each instance of the clsCheckList class has the following
' four properties:
'
' — ListFileName is the file containing list items.
' — TitleBar is the caption for the list.
' — XPos is the horizontal position coordinate.
' — YPos is the vertical position coordinate.
'
' This form module, frmCheckList, is the displayable
' interface associated with each instance of the
' clsCheckList class. Whenever a client creates an instance
' of the class, the code in the clsCheckList module creates
' an associated instance of this form.

Private Sub cmdChange_Click(Index As Integer)

    ' The cmdChange_Click procedure prompts the user to enter
    ' the text of a new list item. This occurs in response
    ' to a click on the corresponding numbered command
    ' button. When the user completes the entry, the text
    ' is displayed as the caption of the adjacent check box.

    Dim newStr As String

    newStr = InputBox("Enter a new check list item", _
            Me.Caption)

    ' If the user clicks the Cancel button on the input
    ' box, the InputBox function returns an empty string.
```

```
    ' In this case, leave the current caption unchanged.
    If newStr <> "" Then _
        chkListItem(Index).Caption = newStr

End Sub   ' cmdChange_Click
```

The ListMaker Project — ListName.BAS

```
' The List Maker Program
'
' Project File:   ListMake.Vbp
' Form Files:     ListData.Frm
'                 ListOpen.Frm
' Module File:    ListName.Bas (this file)
'
' This program helps you develop sets of check lists,
' useful as reminders or task organizers. To create each
' check list window, the program uses the CheckList
' class from an ActiveX DLL component named CheckLists
' (ChkList.DLL). The program's startup code is Sub Main.

Option Explicit

' The listSetFileName variable represent the name of a
' list set file, a text file created by the code in the
' frmListData form.
Public listSetFileName As String
'
' End of General Declarations, ListName.Frm


Sub Main()
    ' The Sub Main procedure elicits the name of a list
    ' set file. If the file exists, the program opens the
    ' frmListOpen form; if not, the frmListData form.
    Dim inputPrompt As String

    inputPrompt = "This program helps you organize sets " & _
    "of checklists for activities, places, events, or " & _
    "other important items. A set contains up to three " & _
    "list windows, each with a corresponding text file " & _
    "recording the items in the list. A separate file " & _
    "stores information about the entire list set. Begin " & _
    "by entering the path and file name of the list set " & _
    "that you want to open or create."
    listSetFileName = InputBox(inputPrompt, "List Maker")
    If Trim(listSetFileName) = "" Then End   ' Cancel button.

    On Error GoTo noSuchFile

        ' Try to open the file. If no error, show frmListOpen.
        Open listSetFileName For Input As #1
        Close #1
```

(continued)

(continued)

```
        frmListOpen.Show
        Exit Sub

noSuchFile:
    ' If an error has taken place, display frmListData.
    frmListData.Show
End Sub   ' Sub Main
```

The ListMaker Project — ListData.FRM

```
' The List Maker Program
'
' Project File:   ListMake.Vbp
' Form Files:     ListData.Frm  (this file)
'                 ListOpen.Frm
' Module File:    ListName.Bas

' Code in the frmListData form creates a list set data file
' in response to the properties that the user enters into
' the form's text boxes.

Option Explicit

' The listLastIndex variable contains a value of 0, 1, or 2,
' depending on the number of lists the user chooses to
' create — one, two, or three.
Dim lastListIndex As Integer
'
' End of general declarations, frmListData form.


Private Sub chkListNum_Click(Index As Integer)
    ' The chkListNum_Click procedure enables or disables the
    ' appropriate controls in response to a List selection.
    Dim i

    ' If the list is checked, enable other controls.
    If chkListNum(Index).Value Then
      txtListFileName(Index).Enabled = True
      txtListCaption(Index).Enabled = True
      lastListIndex = Index
      If Index < 2 Then chkListNum(Index + 1).Enabled = True
    Else

      ' If unchecked, disable other controls as appropriate.
      For i = 2 To Index Step -1
        txtListFileName(i).Text = ""
        txtListFileName(i).Enabled = False
        txtListCaption(i).Text = ""
        txtListCaption(i).Enabled = False
        chkListNum(i).Value = False
        If i <> Index Then chkListNum(i).Enabled = False
      Next i
```

```
    ' Keep track of the final list index.
    lastListIndex = Index - 1
  End If

  ' Enable the Save button if one or more lists are chosen.
  cmdSave.Enabled = (lastListIndex >= 0)
End Sub   ' chkListNum_Click

Private Sub cmdCancel_Click()
  ' The cmdCancel_Click procedure ends the program run if
  ' the user clicks the Cancel button.

  End

End Sub   ' cmdCancel_Click

Private Sub cmdSave_Click()
  ' The cmdSave_Click procedure creates the list set file
  ' and saves all the relevant information from the form.
  Dim i

  On Error GoTo outFileProblem

  ' The listSetFileName variable is global for the project.
  Open listSetFileName For Output As #1

  Write #1, lastListIndex      ' Index of the final list.
  Write #1, txtListSetCaption.Text ' List set caption.
  For i = 0 To lastListIndex
    Write #1, txtListCaption(i).Text ' Caption for the list.
    Write #1, txtListFileName(i).Text ' File name for list.
  Next i
  Close #1

  ' Hide the current form and open frmListOpen.
  Me.Hide
  frmListOpen.Show
Exit Sub

' If a file error has occurred, terminate the run.
outFileProblem:
  End

End Sub   ' cmdSave_Click

Private Sub Form_Load()
  ' The Form_Load procedure displays an appropriate
  ' caption on this form's title bar, enables the first
  ' list check box, and initializes the list counter
  ' variable, lastlistIndex.

  Me.Caption = "List Maker — " & listSetFileName
  chkListNum(0).Enabled = True
  lastListIndex = -1

End Sub   ' Form_Load
```

The ListMaker Project — ListOpen.FRM

```
' The List Maker Program
'
' Project File:    ListMake.Vbp
' Form Files:      ListData.Frm
'                  ListOpen.Frm  (this file)
' Module File:     ListName.Bas

' Code in the frmListOpen form creates CheckList objects
' and displays them when the user clicks the corresponding
' command buttons. Check boxes offer the sort option for
' each list.
Option Explicit

' As many as three lists (indexed 0 to 2) may be created.
Const MaxListIndex = 2

' These constants represent the status of each list.
Enum DisplayStatus
  Unopened
  Hidden
  Displayed
End Enum

Dim lastListIndex As Byte

' The List array represents the checklist objects.
Dim List(MaxListIndex) As CheckList
'
' End of general declarations, frmListOpen form.

Private Sub chkListSort_Click(Index As Integer)

  ' The chkListSort_Click procedure makes a call to the
  ' SortCheckList method for the appropriate List object
  ' when the user changes the status of the corresponding
  ' sort check box. When the SortCheckList method receives
  ' a value of True, the list is sorted in alphabetical
  ' order. When False, the list is returned to its
  ' original order.

  List(Index).SortCheckList chkListSort(Index).Value

End Sub  ' chkListSort_Click

Private Sub cmdExit_Click()

  ' The cmdExit_Click procedure is performed when the
  ' user clicks the Exit button to end the program. The
  ' procedure releases all the List objects from memory.

  Dim Index As Byte
```

```
       For Index = 0 To lastListIndex
         Set List(Index) = Nothing
       Next Index

       End

End Sub   ' cmdExit_Click

Private Sub cmdList_Click(Index As Integer)

     ' The cmdList_Click procedure activates, displays, or
     ' hides a selected List object, depending on the object's
     ' current status. The Tag property of the corresponding
     ' command button indicates the status.

     Select Case cmdList(Index).Tag

     ' If the List object hasn't been opened yet, call the
     ' ShowCheckList method to create it.
     Case Unopened
       List(Index).ShowCheckList
       chkListSort(Index).Enabled = True
       cmdList(Index).Tag = Displayed

     ' If the List is hidden, call the UnHideCheckList method.
     ' If it is displayed, call the HideCheckList method.
     Case Hidden
       List(Index).UnHideCheckList
       cmdList(Index).Tag = Displayed
     Case Displayed
       List(Index).HideCheckList
       cmdList(Index).Tag = Hidden

     End Select

End Sub   ' cmdList_Click

Private Sub Form_Load()

     ' The Form_Load procedure creates the requested number
     ' of List objects and reads their properties from the
     ' listSetFileName text file.

     Dim Index As Byte
     Dim listSetTitle As String
     Dim inTitle As String, inFileName As String

     ' If a problem occurs with the file, jump down to
     ' FileProblem and terminate the program.
     On Error GoTo FileProblem

     ' Open the file and read the first two data items.
     Open listSetFileName For Input As #1
     Input #1, lastListIndex ' The index of the final list.
```

(continued)

(continued)

```
    Input #1, listSetTitle   ' The caption for the list.
    Me.Caption = listSetTitle & " — " & listSetFileName

    ' Read the title and file name for each List object.
    For Index = 0 To lastListIndex
      Input #1, inTitle
      Input #1, inFileName

      ' Create a new List object and set its properties.
      Set List(Index) = New CheckList
      With List(Index)
        .TitleBar = inTitle
        .ListFileName = inFileName
        .XPos = 300 + Index * 3000
        .YPos = 800
      End With

      ' Set the properties of the corresponding button.
      With cmdList(Index)
        .Enabled = True
        .Caption = inTitle
        .Tag = Unopened
      End With

    Next Index
    Close #1
    On Error GoTo 0
Exit Sub

' End the program run if a file problem has occurred.
FileProblem:
    End
End Sub   ' Form_Load
```

The France Program and the FranceGo Document

Chapter 18

The France.Vbp project is an ActiveX Document DLL component. It contains one UserDocument module named FranceGo. When compiled, the project generates a document file named FranceGo.Vbd. This document can be opened in the Microsoft Internet Explorer, as in Figure A-37. It provides links to a number of commercial Web sites related to travel and tourism in France. Notice that the document also contains a Currency Converter.

The Project Explorer window in Figure A-38 shows that the project contains only one module, the UserDocument object named FranceGo.Dob. This module contains all the code for the program.

Figure A-37: In the Internet Explorer window, the FranceGo document looks like any other Web page with links to other sites. But the program also provides characteristic Visual Basic functionality.

Figure A-38: The France project contains one module, the FranceGo UserDocument object.

The France Project — FranceGo.DOB

```
' The France Project and the FranceGo Document
' _____


' The France project is an ActiveX Document component
' that generates an Internet Explorer document named
' FranceGo.VBD. This document provides links to a variety
' of commercial Web sites that may be of interest to
' people who are planning trips to France.

Option Explicit
Private Sub cmdToDollars_Click()
```

(continued)

(continued)

```vb
' The cmdToDollars_Click procedure is part of the
' Currency Converter. Given valid input values, it
' converts from francs to dollars.
' Make sure the conversion rate entry is valid.
If Val(txtConversion.Text) <= 0 Then
  txtConversion.Text = ""
  Exit Sub
End If

' If the Francs entry is valid, perform the calculation.
If Val(txtFrancs.Text) > 0 Then
  txtDollars.Text = txtFrancs.Text / txtConversion.Text
Else
  txtFrancs.Text = ""
  txtDollars.Text = ""
End If

End Sub   ' cmdToDollars_Click

Private Sub cmdToFrancs_Click()

' The cmdToFrancs_Click procedure is part of the
' Currency Converter. Given valid input values, it
' converts from dollars to francs.

' Make sure the conversion rate entry is valid.
If Val(txtConversion.Text) <= 0 Then
  txtConversion.Text = ""
  Exit Sub
End If

' If the dollars entry is valid, perform the calculation.
If Val(txtDollars.Text) > 0 Then
  txtFrancs.Text = txtDollars.Text * txtConversion.Text
Else
  txtFrancs.Text = ""
  txtDollars.Text = ""
End If

End Sub   ' cmdToFrancs_Click

Private Sub cmdWebLink_Click(Index As Integer)

' The cmdWebLink_Click procedure uses the Hyperlink
' object to link to a France-related commercial
' web site.

Dim URL As String

Select Case Index
  Case 0                            ' France.COM
    URL = "WWW.France.COM"
  Case 1                            ' Paris Match
    URL = "WWW.ParisMatch.COM"
```

```
      Case 2                          ' Herald Tribune
        URL = "WWW.IHT.COM"
      Case 3                          ' At Home in France
        URL = "WWW.AtHomeInFrance.COM"
      Case 4                          ' Wine Collection
        URL = "WWW.WineCollection.COM"
    End Select

    On Error GoTo LinkProblem
      UserDocument.Hyperlink.NavigateTo URL
    On Error GoTo 0

LinkProblem:
End Sub   ' cmdWebLink_Click


Private Sub txtDollars_GotFocus()

    ' The txtDollars_Gotfocus procedure is part of the
    ' Currency Converter. When the user selects the Dollars
    ' box, this procedure highlights the current contents
    ' and switches the Default setting to true for the
    ' corresponding command button. As a result, the user
    ' can simply type a dollar amount and press Enter to
    ' perform a conversion.

    txtDollars.SelStart = 0
    txtDollars.SelLength = Len(txtDollars.Text)
    cmdToFrancs.Default = True

End Sub   ' txtDollars_GotFocus

Private Sub txtDollars_LostFocus()

    ' The txtDollars_LostFocus procedure is part of the
    ' Currency Converter. It switches off the Default status
    ' of the Francs commnd button.

    cmdToFrancs.Default = False

End Sub   ' txtDollars_LostFocus

Private Sub txtFrancs_GotFocus()

    ' The txtFrancs_Gotfocus procedure is part of the
    ' Currency Converter. When the user selects the Francs
    ' box, this procedure highlights the current contents
    ' and switches the Default setting to true for the
    ' corresponding command button. As a result, the user
    ' can simply type an amount in francs and press Enter to
    ' perform a conversion.

    txtFrancs.SelStart = 0
    txtFrancs.SelLength = Len(txtFrancs.Text)
    cmdToDollars.Default = True
```

(continued)

```
End Sub   ' txtFrancs_GotFocus

Private Sub txtFrancs_LostFocus()

    ' The txtFrancs_LostFocus procedure is part of the
    ' Currency Converter. It switches off the Default status
    ' of the Dollars commnd button.

    cmdToDollars.Default = False

End Sub   ' txtFrancs_LostFocus
```

Index

Symbols

Until keyword, 241
uppercase letters, 168
user-defined data type, 215, 254–261, 465
UserDocument, 523, 527, 530–536

V

Val function, 319, 491
ValidNumInput procedure, 156–158
Value box, 127
Value property, 461, 488
variable(s). *See also* variables
        (listed by name)
  assigning values to, 172–173
  basic description of, 92, 133–178
  data structures and, 98–99
  declaring, 168–171, 392–393, 455–456
  generic object, 396
  indexed, arrays as, 98–99
  initializing, 173–174
  local, 151
  module-level, 172
  names, 133, 168–171, 250
  record, 211, 215, 255
  scope, 134, 171–172, 249
  using, in a program, 167–178
variables (listed by name). *See also*
        variables
  After variable, 389, 391, 393–394
  amtIndex variable, 327
  Before variable, 389, 393–394, 397
  city$ variable, 133
  cityName variable, 168
  counter variable, 246
  countryName variable, 154–155,
        165, 168
  countryNdx variable, 99
  country variable, 168
  currCity variable, 190, 207, 208
  currCountry variable, 99, 113, 172
  curRec variable, 226–228
  curTranRecord variable, 358

During variable, 389, 390, 393–394
entryWidth variable, 320
ExcelApp variable, 456
ExcelSheet variable, 455, 456, 458, 462
ExcelWorkbook variable, 456, 458
exchRate variable, 168
fieldsComplete variable, 230
fileNumber variable, 423, 425, 429
firstOK variable, 230–231
grandTot variable, 324, 337
isSorted variable, 401
largeRate variable, 167, 177
lastListIndex variable, 513
lastOK variable, 230–231
listLength variable, 223
listSetFileName variable, 511
logFileName variable, 134, 168, 172, 173
maxPeriod variable, 333
MaxTrips variable, 430–432
Meeting variable, 221, 257–258
newListActive variable, 507, 508, 509,
        510–511
newList variable, 507
newPage variable, 398, 404
numInList variable, 259
numPhones variable, 278
public variable, 252, 378, 507
recordChanged variable, 358, 424, 437
recordNum variable, 276–278, 280
recordVariable variable, 276, 278
RestRecord variable, 190
smallRate variable, 167, 177
stackHeight variable, 120, 121, 122,
        123, 124
stackVert variable, 120, 121, 122, 123
temp variable, 340, 342
titleBarText variable, 358
totAmount variable, 175
TranRecord variable, 356–357
tripNum variable, 427–430
whichRecord variable, 285–286
Variant data type, 135, 160–161, 170, 171

IDG BOOKS WORLDWIDE, INC.
END-USER LICENSE AGREEMENT

Read This. You should carefully read these terms and conditions before open-ing the software packet(s) included with this book ("Book"). This is a license agreement ("Agreement") between you and IDG Books Worldwide, Inc. ("IDGB"). By opening the accompanying software packet(s), you acknowledge that you have read and accept the following terms and conditions. If you do not agree and do not want to be bound by such terms and conditions, promptly return the Book and the unopened software packet(s) to the place you obtained them for a full refund.

1. **License Grant**. IDGB grants to you (either an individual or entity) a nonexclusive license to use one copy of the enclosed software program(s) (collectively, the "Software") solely for your own personal or business purposes on a single computer (whether a standard computer or a workstation component of a multiuser network). The Software is in use on a computer when it is loaded into temporary memory (i.e., RAM) or installed into permanent memory (e.g., hard disk, CD-ROM, or other storage device). IDGB reserves all rights not expressly granted herein.

2. **Ownership**. IDGB is the owner of all right, title, and interest, including copyright, in and to the compilation of the Software recorded on the disk(s)/CD-ROM. Copyright to the individual programs on the disk(s)/CD-ROM is owned by the author or other authorized copyright owner of each program. Ownership of the Software and all proprietary rights relating thereto remain with IDGB and its licensors.

3. **Restrictions on Use and Transfer**.

   (a) You may only (i) make one copy of the Software for backup or archival purposes, or (ii) transfer the Software to a single hard disk, provided that you keep the original for backup or archival purposes. You may not (i) rent or lease the Software, (ii) copy or reproduce the Software through a LAN or other network system or through any computer subscriber system or bulletin-board system, or (iii) modify, adapt, or create derivative works based on the Software.

   (b) You may not reverse engineer, decompile, or disassemble the Software. You may transfer the Software and user documentation on a permanent basis, provided that the transferee agrees to accept the terms and conditions of this Agreement and you retain no copies. If the Software is an update or has been updated, any transfer must include the most recent update and all prior versions.

4. **Restrictions on Use of Individual Programs.** You must follow the individual requirements and restrictions detailed for running the source code that is described in the Installation Instructions and the Appendix at the back of the book. These limitations are contained in the individual license agreements recorded on the disk(s)/CD-ROM. These restrictions may include a requirement that after using the program for the period of time specified in its text, the user must pay a registration fee or discontinue use. By opening the Software packet(s), you will be agreeing to abide by the licenses and restrictions for these individual programs. None of the material on this disk(s) or listed in this Book may ever be distributed, in original or modified form, for commercial purposes.

5. **Limited Warranty.**

   (a) IDGB warrants that the Software and disk(s)/CD-ROM are free from defects in materials and workmanship under normal use for a period of sixty (60) days from the date of purchase of this Book. If IDGB receives notification within the warranty period of defects in materials or workmanship, IDGB will replace the defective disk(s)/CD-ROM.

   (b) **IDGB AND THE AUTHOR OF THE BOOK DISCLAIM ALL OTHER WARRAN-TIES, EXPRESS OR IMPLIED, INCLUDING WITHOUT LIMITATION IMPLIED WARRANTIES OF MERCHANTABILITY AND FITNESS FOR A PARTICULAR PURPOSE, WITH RESPECT TO THE SOFTWARE, THE PROGRAMS, THE SOURCE CODE CONTAINED THEREIN, AND/OR THE TECHNIQUES DE-SCRIBED IN THIS BOOK. IDGB DOES NOT WARRANT THAT THE FUNC-TIONS CONTAINED IN THE SOFTWARE WILL MEET YOUR REQUIRE-MENTS OR THAT THE OPERATION OF THE SOFTWARE WILL BE ERROR FREE.**

   (c) This limited warranty gives you specific legal rights, and you may have other rights which vary from jurisdiction to jurisdiction.

6. **Remedies.**

   (a) IDGB's entire liability and your exclusive remedy for defects in materials and workmanship shall be limited to replacement of the Software, which may be returned to IDGB with a copy of your receipt at the following address: Disk Fulfillment Department, Attn: Visual Basic 5 Bible, IDG Books Worldwide, Inc., 7260 Shadeland Station, Ste. 100, Indianapolis, IN 46256, or call 1-800-762-2974. Please allow 3-4 weeks for delivery. This Limited Warranty is void if failure of the Software has resulted from accident, abuse, or misapplica-tion. Any replacement Software will be warranted for the remainder of the original warranty period or thirty (30) days, whichever is longer.

   (b) In no event shall IDGB or the author be liable for any damages whatsoever (including without limitation damages for loss of business profits, business interruption, loss of business information, or any other pecuniary loss) arising from the use of or inability to use the Book or the Software, even if IDGB has been advised of the possibility of such damages.

(c) Because some jurisdictions do not allow the exclusion or limitation of liability for consequential or incidental damages, the above limitation or exclusion may not apply to you.

7. **U.S. Government Restricted Rights.** Use, duplication, or disclosure of the Software by the U.S. Government is subject to restrictions stated in paragraph (c) (1) (ii) of the Rights in Technical Data and Computer Software clause of DFARS 252.227-7013, and in subparagraphs (a) through (d) of the Commercial Computer—Restricted Rights clause at FAR 52.227-19, and in similar clauses in the NASA FAR supplement, when applicable.

8. **General.** This Agreement constitutes the entire understanding of the parties and revokes and supersedes all prior agreements, oral or written, between them and may not be modified or amended except in a writing signed by both parties hereto which specifically refers to this Agreement. This Agreement shall take precedence over any other documents that may be in conflict herewith. If any one or more provisions contained in this Agreement are held by any court or tribunal to be invalid, illegal, or otherwise unenforceable, each and every other provision shall remain in full force and effect.

Installing the Programs on the CD-ROM

The CD-ROM enclosed with this book contains a collection of working program examples, contained in a folder called **BookApps**. In addition, this CD-ROM includes Microsoft Internet Explorer 3.0.

To install Internet Explorer, insert the CD-ROM into the CD-ROM drive and click the Install Internet Explorer button on the opening screen.

To install the program files, copy all of the files to the main Visual Basic folder on your hard disk or to some other folder that you create for this purpose. You can copy the files by one of these methods:

+ Use the Windows Explorer utility to copy the files.

+ If you prefer to perform file operations in DOS, click the Start menu, choose Programs, and click the MS-DOS Prompt command. Then use the DOS Copy command to transfer all the programs from the **BookApps** folder on the CD-ROM to the appropriate folder on your hard disk.

Each chapter gives you instructions for loading and running the corresponding program, and shows code listings for specific procedures as they are discussed.